Virtual Politics

Virtual Politics

Faking Democracy in the Post-Soviet World

Andrew Wilson

Yale University Press

New Haven and London

For information about this and other Yale University Press publications,
please contact:
U.S. Office: sales.press@yale.edu   yalebooks.com
Europe Office: sales@yaleup.co.uk   www.yalebooks.co.uk

Set in Bembo by MATS, Southend-on-Sea, Essex
Printed in Great Britain by
St Edmundsbury Press, Bury St Edmunds, Suffolk

Library of Congress Cataloging-in-Publication Data

Wilson, Andrew, 1961–
    Virtual politics: faking democracy in the post-Soviet world/Andrew Wilson.—1st ed.
    p.   cm.
Includes bibliographical references and index.
    ISBN 0–300–09545–7 (cl.: alk. paper)
 1. Politics, Practical—Former Soviet republics. 2. Legitimacy of governments—
Former Soviet republics. 3. Mass media—Political aspects—Former Soviet republics.
4. Former Soviet republics—Politics and government. I. Title.
    JN6581.W47 2005
    320.947—dc22
                                                                        2004029345

A catalogue record for this book is available from the British Library.

10 9 8 7 6 5 4 3 2 1

To Yurii

Contents

Figures

Common Acronyms

BPF	Belarusian Popular Front
BSDP (PH)	Belarusian Social-Democratic Party (Popular Hramada)
BYuT	Block of Yuliia Tymoshenko
CPB	Communist Party of Belarus
CPK	Communist Party of Kazakhstan
CPRM	Communist Party of the Republic of Moldova
CPRF	Communist Party of the Russian Federation
CPSU	Communist Party of the Soviet Union
CPU	Communist Party of Ukraine
CPU(r)	Communist Party of Ukraine (renewed)
FAR	Fatherland-All Russia
KOP	Winter Crop Generation Team
KPRS	Communist Party of Workers and Peasants (Ukraine)
KRO	Congress of Russian Communities
LDPB	Liberal-Democratic Party of Belarus
LDPR	Liberal-Democratic Party of Russia
NDP	National-Democratic Party (of Ukraine)
NRU(e)	Rukh for Unity (Ukraine)
NSF	National Salvation Front
OGP	United Civic Party (of Belarus)
OHR	Our Home Is Russia
OUN	Organisation of Ukrainian Nationalists
PCB	Party of Communists of Belarus
PNS	Party of Popular Accord (of Belarus)
POUM	Workers' Party of Marxist Unification (Spain)
PSPU	Progressive Socialist Party of Ukraine
RNU	Russian National Unity
SBU	Security Service of Ukraine
SDPU(o)	Social-Democratic Party of Ukraine (united)
SPU	Socialist Party of Ukraine

UCP-CPSU	Union of Communist Parties – Communist Party of the Soviet Union
UNA-UNSO	Ukrainian National Assembly – Ukrainian National Self-Defence
URF	Union of Right Forces
URP	Ukrainian Republican Party

Introduction

> It should be remembered that the word 'democracy', which is used so frequently in the modern mass media, is by no means the same word 'democracy' as was so widespread in the nineteenth and early twentieth centuries. The two words are merely homonyms. The old word 'democracy' was derived from the Greek 'demos', while the new word is derived from the expression 'demo-version'.
>
> Viktor Pelevin, *Generation 'P'* (1999)[1]

If this book were intended mainly for a post-Soviet audience, it might easily have taken its subtitle from any number of peculiar local neologisms – perhaps 'Political Technology in . . .' or 'Electoral Technology in the Post-Soviet States'.[2] A Western reader might initially be mystified, however. Why 'technology'? The Bolsheviks fetishised technology. Their successors claim to have perfected the art of 'organising victory' in politics as 'technology', whatever the 'project' – apparently competitive elections, changing governments or launching some policy U-turn. As technology, their new political black arts are supposedly more sophisticated than the traditional formula for authoritarian states: cowing the population, imprisoning the opposition and stuffing the ballot box. Welcome therefore to the strange post-Soviet world of 'clones' and 'doubles'; of 'administrative resources', 'active measures' and '*kompromat*'; of parties that stand in elections but have no staff or membership or office; of bankers that stand as Communists; of well-paid insiders that stand as the regime's most vociferous opponents; and of scarecrow nationalists and fake coups. Welcome to a paradise for the most brazen liars and guileful con artists, where the most staid and respectable political technology agency in Moscow calls itself Nikkolo-M, after Machiavelli, and uses his face on its business cards.

It is easy to get lost inside this looking-glass world, to get too used to its virtual reality and start thinking in its own terms, forgetting that 'faking democracy' is the purpose of all this technology. The central theme of this book is that the results of democratisation in many post-Communist states have been, to say the least, disappointing – and not just in Central Asia, where the effort has never really been made (though the various forms of local window-dressing are discussed). Russia marked the new millennium not with Yeltsin's quiet retirement, but with a staggeringly cynical transfer of power involving a diversionary war, an instant decree of absolution for the past sons of the Yeltsin 'Family' (both literal and metaphorical), and allegations that the regime had blown up its own citizens' apartments. In Ukraine President Leonid Kuchma was accused of complicity in the murder of opposition journalist Hryhorii Gondazde in 2000. Moreover, secret recordings made in Kuchma's office seemed to indicate that this was only the tip of the iceberg. Aliaksandr Lukashenka, the president of Belarus (also with a string of 'disappearances' to his name), hardly needed to fix his 're-election' in 2001 – as he faced no truly dangerous opponent – but did so anyway. In Moldova the 'unreconstructed' Communist Party returned to power in 2001, and has since successfully reconstructed the local economy to serve its own interests. The Caucasian states have recently lost one president who gained a reputation for indolent corruption, Eduard Shevardnadze, but others seem well entrenched – in Azerbaijan well enough so to stage a dynastic transfer in 2003.

Of the former USSR, only the three Baltic States are not discussed here. Their peculiar history (their incorporation into the Soviet Union in 1940 was never legally recognised by Western countries, with the exception of France, and then only briefly) and the very different trajectory they have followed since 1991 means that post-Bolshevik political culture, although it has a foothold in all three, does not predominate as it does in the other 'newly independent' states. The counter-argument – that shadowy Russian business interests work through proxy parties rather than disenfranchised Russian-speaking populations – is not considered.

Something of a 'Who lost Russia?' debate has begun, usually extended to cover the region as a whole. Some have emphasised over-mighty presidents,[3] or blamed the transition from the anarchic democracy of the Yeltsin years to the Chekist authoritarianism of Putin. Others cite the Faustian bargain of 'market Bolshevism' – the sacrifice of real democracy to the imperative of enforced economic reform.[4] Others have argued that age-old cultural predispositions,[5] and historical, socio-economic and cultural indicators (limited previous experience of democracy, small native middle classes, the lack of well-distributed prosperity or a social capital of 'trust'), were never promising.[6] Fareed Zakaria has claimed both that the former USSR was not rich enough to make the transition to democracy and that the transition has had illiberal consequences.[7] Others blame institutional continuities with the Soviet era and key structural aspects of post-Communism (a shackled media, the near-absence of civil society) that were always likely to make democratic consolidation difficult after the initial breakthrough.[8] Stephen Holmes's essay 'Potemkin Democracy' is particularly insightful. He argues that 'the state that Yeltsin inherited from Soviet times, was, paradoxically, *too weak* to be democratized'. Political parties, legislatures, etc are so much 'surface froth', while 'the granular makeup of society disempowers the electoral majority, making it politically impotent', and forces the 'hovercraft elite' to find support in the only place it can, among 'intensely "networked"' predatory-redistributive elites. If its economic interests are secure, the elite is 'relatively uninterested in governing'. 'This system [therefore] requires neither tyranny . . . nor the exploitation of the vast majority of Russian citizens.' 'Postcommunist elites are neither patrons with a mass following nor cruel oppressors. They are simply opportunistic scavengers. Elites have little or no need for their fellow citizens'.[9] A façade will do, and the elite is happy to subcontract the necessary tasks of political manipulation to political technologists, while it gets on with its own task of asset-stripping the nation's resources.

Some other useful insights come from a discussion in the April 2002 issue of the *Journal of Democracy* on the subject of 'Elections without Democracy?',[10] especially Steven Levitsky and Lucan A. Way's distinction between 'façade electoral regimes', such as that in contemporary Uzbekistan, and 'competitive authoritarian' systems, such as those in Ukraine and Russia. The latter are characterised by 'the coexistence of democratic rules and autocratic methods'. 'Formal democratic institutions are widely viewed as the primary means of obtaining and exercising political authority', but 'violations of [democratic] criteria are both frequent enough and serious enough to create an uneven playing field between government and opposition. Although elections are regularly held and are generally free of massive fraud, incumbents routinely abuse state resources, deny the opposition adequate media coverage, harass opposition candidates and their supporters, and in some cases manipulate electoral results.'[11] Elections, in other words, are held in order to legitimate power, but not to provide any real threat to it.[12]

All of these factors are important, and form part of the story. My main emphasis, however, is on a particular aspect of political culture, namely the black arts of political manipulation and double-speak inherited from the Bolshevik era. I use the term 'political culture' with caution. I do not seek to make any deterministic argument. Political culture, is of course, both malleable and heterogeneous, as is demonstrated by the many versions of twentieth-century Germany: Wilhelmite, Weimar, Nazi, Communist and Federal. Choices are important. My argument is only about the elite, which has *found it useful* to maintain post-Bolshevik methods in order to disguise its venality. There is plenty of evidence, on the other hand, that popular attitudes towards democracy are not that different in East and West.[13] The elite gets away with it in current conditions; its methods are described in detail in Chapter 3.

In the 1980s many Sovietologists, as they were then called, preferred a broad definition of political culture that encompassed political behaviour, since at the time beliefs and attitudes were hard to examine. Now they are not, and the narrower, 'subjective' definition can be used, to avoid loading too much on one variable and diminishing its explanatory power. For our purposes here, then, political culture is 'the subjective perception of history and politics, the fundamental beliefs and values, the foci of identification and loyalty, and the political knowledge and expectations which are the product of the specific historical experiences of nations and groups'.[14] This book, it is hoped, provides sufficient evidence that elite political culture in the former Soviet world is still only partly post-Bolshevik: politics is still perceived as a form of warfare, 'beliefs and values' are either absent or amoral, 'political knowledge and expectations' are still shaped by the life experiences and inter-party politics of the Soviet period.

Using Levitsky and Way's definition, it is unclear whether countries such as Russia or Ukraine are 'semi-democratic' or 'semi-authoritarian'. The issue can be sidestepped.

In a democratic state, authority derives from some type of election process, however imperfect. In an authoritarian state, authority is asserted rather than earned (though it may still be accepted by many). The key to 'virtual politics', however, is that authority is invented; political technologists stage the basic mythology of the state. Inventing the opposition is as important as controlling it, and the governing 'core' of the system is not a traditional 'hegemonic party' like the Mexican PRI, but itself a series of virtual 'projects'. It may not come as too big a surprise to readers to be told that the Russian Communists are paper tigers, or that 'Mad Vlad', the nationalist firebrand Vladimir Zhirinovskii, was initially a KGB stooge. There has been little comment, however, on how such apparent misfits function as integral parts of post-Soviet politics, and virtually no analysis of how the culture of political manipulation operates as a system. Other apparently dysfunctional elements also have a purpose. Casual observers are also probably aware that there are hundreds of political parties in Russia, Ukraine and similar states. Politics seems diffuse, fragmented and unworkable. The proliferation of 'mosquito' parties, also known as 'taxi' or 'sofa' parties (i.e., parties providing sufficient metaphorical space for all of their members), however, is due to much more than the vanity of individual politicians too egocentric to compromise sufficiently to stay in the same organisation with even the closest of soulmates. Outgoing Ukrainian president Leonid Kuchma launched a diatribe against local political parties in 2004: 'the current party system is immature and weak, with parties reflecting the interests of business groups and parts of the administrative apparatus rather than those of the electorate.'[15] The hypocrisy of this statement is breathtaking. Bankivska Street, the local equivalent of the Kremlin, has itself covertly created many of the parties and brokered the takeover of many others by business groups. Once the scores of parties are reclassified according to the local terminology to identify the purposes they actually serve – 'satellites', 'scarecrows', 'cuckoos' and 'clones' – local politics becomes much more comprehensible, and the number of key players in any given country emerges as surprisingly low.

That said, plenty of democratic fragments exist, although several states (Belarus, Central Asia) are better considered as imperfect, but often still virtual, autocracies. I do not argue either that everything is 'lost' or that everything is 'virtual'. Post-Soviet states such as Russia and Ukraine have travelled a long way from their common totalitarian past. Virtual politics is the way that elites seek to manage, manipulate and contain democracy – but there are limits both to their ambitions and their capacities, and they are not always successful. Each new state is, of course, different, but they have sufficient in common to justify a comparative study.

The plan of the book is as follows. Chapter 1 provides a historical introduction, including an account of the development of early forms of manipulation in the late Soviet period. Chapter 2 describes what is meant by virtual politics, and Chapter 3 describes the work of the so-called political technologists in constructing and staging it. Chapter 4 addresses another dangerous local euphemism, the so-called administrative resources that are also used to make 'competitive authoritarianism' slightly less competitive. Chapter 5 discusses political technologists' basic task – disguising the true nature of their clients. Chapter 6 analyses the so-called 'many-layered pie': any sensible regime now adopts a multiplicity of disguises in case its main one is simply too transparent. Chapter 7 discusses political technologists' techniques for dealing with real and potential oppositions; Chapter 8 demonstrates how they often set up fake ones instead. Chapter 9 concentrates on the new Communist parties, which, given their genesis under the old regime, embody many of its pathologies in the clearest form. The Conclusions attempt to show the conditions in which virtual politics might survive and those in which it will not, or in which it will at least mutate into something else.

Methodologically I have not included every conspiracy theory I came across in the course of researching this study. I have quoted political technologists themselves and the analyses of respected commentators such as Andrei Riabov in Russia and Volodymyr Polokhalo in Ukraine. I have omitted much material with only a single source, but have followed up stories that seemed plausible or that fitted a general pattern. On the other hand, stories about 'agents' and 'infiltrators' are ten-a-penny in the former USSR. I have therefore tried to avoid being too *ad hominem*. I hope that I have established a comparative pattern and typology that makes the overall picture coherent. In a study of this size, however, examples and case studies have to be illustrative rather than comprehensive. I have not used examples from elsewhere in the former Communist world, although on occasion this might arguably have been appropriate.

The names of people and places have been rendered in local form. Therefore the biggest town in west Ukraine is Lviv (Ukrainian spelling), not Lvov (Russian spelling) or Lwów (Polish); the Belarusian president elected in 1994 and 2001 is Lukashenka not Lukashenko, and so on. East Slavic surnames are rendered in three different forms: as Pavlovskii (Russian), Khoroshkovskyi (Ukrainian) and Sharetski (Belarusian, where Yurii is also Yury). The unique Belarusian letter ў is rendered as a 'w' (pronounced as in 'how'). To make things easier for the reader, I have not transliterated soft signs: so Yeltsin not Yel'tsin (or El'tsin) in Russia, and Lviv not L'viv and Khmelnytskyi not Khmel'nyts'kyi in Ukraine. The spelling Glazev may surprise some readers; in other transliteration systems this would be given as Glaz'ev, Glazyev or Glaziev. On the other hand, original forms and complete transliterations are used in the footnotes. I have kept certain Anglicisms that remain standard forms, such as Kiev (not Kyyiv or Kyïv) and Trotsky (not Trotskii). I have rendered most acronyms by English equivalents. For example, in English the Komunistychna Partiia Ukraïny (onovelenna) is the Communist Party of Ukraine (renewed), so I have rendered it as CPU(r) rather than KPU(o). But some acronyms make more sense in the original – especially if there is a joke about their name. So the Komanda ozymoho pokolinnia is still referred to as KOP. Exceptions are also made for well-known acronyms such as KGB, or those whose translation would be tortuous, such as UNA-UNSO. At the time of writing, the *Ukraïns'ka pravda* website was reorganising its archive; so some references to it need updating.

Thanks are due to Jonathan Aves, Nina Djidjoeva, Andrei Riabov and Valerii Solovei in Moscow; in Minsk to Valer Bulhakaw and Vital Silitski; in Kiev to Oleh Protsyk, the Petrus family, Rostyslav Pavlenko, Oleksii Haran, Hryhorii Kasianov, Hryhorii Nemeriia, Valerii Khmelko, Ihor Kohut and Hryhorii Pocheptsov. In the UK thanks are due to Elena Korosteleva, Clelia Rontoyanni, Bhavna Dave, Luke March, Kate Peevor, and Liliana Vitu; at Yale University Press to Robert Baldock, Candida Brazil, Ewan Thompson and Steve Kent; and in the world at large to Oxana Shevel, Zaal Anjaparidze and Vladimir Tismaneanu. Biggest thanks are due to the British Academy, not just for providing generous research funds, but also for accommodating various requests for extensions. As always, warmest thanks go to family and friends. The book is dedicated to Yurii Petrus, a good man who died incomprehensibly young.

1 'Active Measures': A Russian Tradition

Some would claim that the tradition of black politics is universal. By using the image of Machiavelli as its business logo (see page 41), the Moscow political consultancy Nikkolo-M is not only laying claim to the intellectual authority of the Renaissance, but also seeking to advertise the historical legitimacy of its art. In a self-serving attempt to 'rehabilitate *kompromat*' (the use of compromising materials against opponents), one of its leading practitioners, Marat Gelman, has claimed that:

> as a genre it is as old as the world itself. . . . Roman senators, favourites of the
> Egyptian pharaohs, collected *kompromat* on one another (by the way, the wife
> of one of these ruined for a time the career of Joseph), as did the free citizens
> of Athens (someone did for Socrates), bureaucrats behind the doors of Chinese
> emperors and – for sure! – even 'generals' in the army of Genghis Khan. . . .
> we can find a primer for the model of the 'literary discrediting of opponents'
> in Dante's *Divine Comedy* . . . in Borges' masterful concoctions of falsification
> . . . and Umberto Eco's sensational *Foucault's Pendulum*.[1]

Nevertheless, the most important antecedents of today's post-Soviet culture of manipulation are decidedly local.[2] Some local 'technologies' are recognisable copies of universal archetypes, but many are not, and the complexity of their methods are also unique. It is therefore worth beginning with a little Russian history: many parallels with today's political black arts can be found in tsarist times. But it was the Soviet era, when a culture was formed without parallel elsewhere in the world, that played the key role in spawning the virtual politics of today.

Okhrana Operations
In the nascent European democracies of the nineteenth century an element of political manipulation and control was expected. Metternich's Austria and Bismarck's Germany were in part police states – or at least heavily policed – with huge armies of official and unofficial agents on their books. In west Ukraine, the Austrian secret police set up 'front' parties such as the Social Democratic Ukrainian Labour Party

and the Ukrainian Union of Revolutionary Socialists in 1914–15. Christy Campell's book *Fenian Fire* describes how British officials infiltrated radical Irish circles in the last third of the nineteenth century and encouraged them to discredit themselves in the 1887 Jubilee Plot to kill Queen Victoria.[3] The United Kingdom, however, had no formal secret service until 1909; whereas in tsarist Russia active manipulation of politics had long been a part of everyday life.

During the reign of Ivan the Terrible (1530–84) the fearsome *oprichniki* (from *oprich* 'separate', so a 'band apart') roamed the land receiving denunciations and dispensing arbitrary justice; they dressed in monastic black, rode equally black steeds and each carried a dog's head and long broom (not unlike the Nazgül in *The Lord of the Rings*). The symbolism was stark. 'This meant that first of all they bite like dogs, and then they sweep everything superfluous out of the land.'[4] As a result their activities weren't particularly secret. Peter the Great (1672–1725) established Russia's first true secret police, but in typically no-nonsense fashion gave the job to the army – the power to try all political offences being awarded to the Preobrazhenskii regiment near Moscow in 1696. He also set up the parallel Secret Chancellery in St Petersburg after deciding on the trial and torture of his son the tsarevich Aleksei in 1718. Under Empress Elizabeth (1741–61) the Chancellery came to be abhorred by the nobility, none of whom could ever feel safe in its twilight world of retrospective denunciation and arbitrary loss of favour. It was abolished by Peter II in 1762, but most of its inquisitors were shunted aside into a more 'Secret Expedition' under the Senate. A 'Third Section' Gendarme Corps was set up in 1826, and a Security Bureau established in St Petersburg in 1866. The Gendarme Corps operated like a league of gentlemen spies, acting largely within their own limited world and social mores. Its methods were therefore rather less effective once the lower orders began to take up arms against the state in the 1870s.

The Interior Ministry had long functioned almost as a state within a state. However, after the main revolutionary group, the People's Will, assassinated the 'Tsar Liberator' Aleksandr II in 1881, counter-revolutionary methodology acquired a domestic institutional base with the establishment of the Department for the Defence of Public Security and Order, or Okhrana for short.[5] A counterpart Foreign Agentura was set up in Paris in 1883 to monitor Russia's main colony of revolutionary émigrés.[6] The Okhrana's effectiveness depended less on numbers (one modern estimate is that it employed only 1,500–2,000 agents in the whole of Russia, two hundred in St Petersburg)[7] than on tactics. The Okhrana developed the tradition of using not just informers (*osvedomiteli*), but also active agents (*predateli* or 'traitors') within opposition groups. Georgii Sudeikin, the head of the Special Section of the Police Department in the 1880s (himself assassinated in 1883), defined the role of Russian agents extremely broadly. As well as collecting information, they should 'generate suspicion and demoralization, thereby greatly retarding possible revolutionary activity', attempt the 'cultivation of quarrels and clashes amongst the revolutionary groups, the spreading of false rumours to intimidate the revolutionaries and instil a fear of betrayal and espionage: and [just to make things even more complex] the discrediting of revolutionary leaflets and organs by attributing them to police provocation'.[8]

In his book on the double agent Sergei Degaev (1857–1921), Richard Pipes describes how Sudeikin claimed credit for breaking up the People's Will in the 1880s, and the methods he developed to prevent the formation of any other similar groups. Significantly, Pipes's key chapter is entitled 'The Police Run the Revolution'. Sudeikin's masterplan was 'to replace the genuine People's Will with a police-sponsored organization under the same name', supplying it with anti-regime pamphlets and two issues of an ersatz party paper *Listok Narodnoi Voli* ('Letters of the People's Will'), and even setting up a rival 'executive committee' to allow Degaev to command the underground: Sudeikin's apparent purpose being 'to redirect [a tamed] People's Will organization from terrorism to nationalism'.[9] According to the chief ideologue of the People's Will, who later became a tsarist stalwart, Lev Tikhomirov, the result was that by 1883 'the entire revolutionary organization was wholly in the hands of the police, which directed its top management and censored the revolutionary press'.[10]

Under Sergei Zubatov, chief of the Moscow bureau from 1896 to 1903, the Okhrana went still further. Zubatov's theory of 'police socialism' took the idea of controlling the opposition from within to new heights, with the shadow state now sponsoring its own political parties, student organisations and trade unions. One such venture employed Fr Georgii Gapon, the priest who was head of the Assembly of Russian Workers and leader of the fateful Bloody Sunday demonstration in January 1905. Gapon was murdered by the Socialist Revolutionary Party in 1906 after being exposed as a police informer. Zubatov was both policing the underground and putting into practice his belief that autocracy was better able to satisfy legitimate social demands than revolutionary violence. In a way, therefore, the Zubatov organisations were not fake: they were what they claimed to be – secular repre-sentatives of the will of a paternalistic tsar, an alternative to ideologues allegedly substituting themselves for the workers' true interests. Zubatov's critics, however, saw a monster that could easily escape Frankenstein's control – although in the Russian context a better analogy would be Petrushka, the doll in the traditional folk tale and Stravinsky ballet (1911), who escapes his strings and pokes fun at authority. Zubatov's rivals engineered his dismissal when his 'official' unions played rather too enthusiastic a role in the Odessa strike wave of 1903.

Nevertheless, Zubatov's tactics found fertile ground. Many historians, Bolshevik and other, refer to the times as the 'Zubatov era' (*Zubatovshchina*). All the major parties were thoroughly infiltrated. In the Socialist Revolutionary Party (the SRs) the corrosive tensions of the double life helped ideological and personal enmities morph into a constant war of accusation that severely disabled the party. No less a figure than the head of the SRs' 'Combat Organisation', the 'general of the revolution', Evno Azef, was a long-term agent. According to Anna Geifman, 'the shock of Azef's exposure [was] so tremendous that the SRs never fully recovered from the terrible moral wound that had been inflicted'.[11] In the 1900s the SRs, not the Bolsheviks, were the main threat to the regime. Arguably, Azef prevented the party from changing the course of history by stopping it from assassinating Nicholas II and other leading figures in the ruling regime in 1905–7.

The Okhrana had less desire to infiltrate the centre parties, the Liberals and Kadets, and its tactics on the right – manipulating anti-Semitism and financing the Black Hundreds – had mixed success. Pogroms were tolerated, and their perpetrators benefited from secret sympathy; but the threat to order dismayed many. The Russian People's Union and Vladimir Purishkevich's League of the Archangel Michael, which contained some real extremists and had links to yet others, were funded to the tune of 45,000 roubles between 1906 and 1916.[12] The flamboyant Purishkevich, who combined blood-curdling nationalist rhetoric with theatrical denunciations of the regime's opponents and helped murder Rasputin in 1916, performed a similar role to Vladimir Zhirinovskii in the present day (see pages 23–5 and 203–9).[13] Covert state sponsorship was designed to keep such individuals and organisations within manageable limits, but the Okhrana also created many monsters it could not control. Although its publishing history remains sketchy, the Okhrana almost certainly played the key role in the ongoing reworking of the various editions of the era's most notorious forgery, *The Protocols of the Elders of Zion* (1903 and after). Piotr Rachkovskii, the head of the Foreign Agentura and a compulsive forger (one of his earlier efforts was a letter supposedly from the veteran Russian leftist Plekhanov denouncing the People's Will in 1892, followed by an equally robust and equally fake reply), most probably organised the plundering of previous works by Maurice Joly, Elie de Cyon and Hermann Goedsche to cobble together *The Protocols*. The most likely author was another agent, Sergei Nilus.

Rachkovskii also acted as a channel of influence to the nascent Russian right, trying to set up his own front organisation, the Russian Patriotic League, in 1902. Intriguingly, recent research in Nicholas II's archives indicates that in September 1905 interior minister Dmitrii Trepov proposed that the authorities extend their reach to the centre and right by setting up 'a sure rallying point [around] a conservative party of order', in others words what modern Russians would call a 'party of power' that would enlist all local governors and coopt the press – but these now 'traditional' tactics never bore fruit, perhaps to the regime's ultimate cost.[14] The Fatherland-Patriotic Union set up by the Interior Ministry in 1915 was a half-hearted effort in comparison.

Cut free from the ties of political conviction, agents often forgot which side of the game they were supposed to be on – or got too caught up in the game itself. To borrow a phrase from the American spy-catcher James Angleton describing his own Cold War world of double and triple agents, what passed for political life in the tsarist era was often a 'wilderness of mirrors'. Both sides found it difficult to distinguish between image and reflection, original and copy, first and subsequent masks, which produced a poisonous double-dealing atmosphere best described by Dostoevsky in his novel *The Devils* (1871–72). Once agents were loosed into the outside world, 'it was assumed by the police that the informer's interests coincided with those of the

Okhrana. But in practice they often contradicted one another.'[15] Agents were not supposed to break the law, but they often found themselves nurturing the very world they were supposed to be trying to destroy. It was not uncommon, in other words, for tsarist agents to end up throwing the bombs themselves. The most famous double agent of all, Evno Azef, was forced to preserve his credibility by helping to murder his original boss, the hardline interior minister Viacheslav Plevhe, with a bomb that used his carriage as kindling. Azef was not exposed until four years later, when his uncertain role in a failed plot to kill the tsar on a visit to Kronstadt naval base in 1908 suggests that he had taken his autonomous role beyond any reasonable limits.

Just as most revolutionary organisations contained their nests of spies, Okhrana handlers or agents often sympathised with their charges and on occasion would defect to or inform the revolutionaries. The most famous such double agent was Aleksei Lopukhin, director of the Department of Police in 1902–05, another of Azef's handlers and also his ultimate exposer. Lopukhin's motivation in publicising Azef's past remains mysterious. It is not clear whether he was seeking to help the SRs or the government; nor is it clear whether he acted out of disquiet at his own agents breaking the law or because his daughter was being held hostage in London. Either way, his revelations led to his own arrest and internal exile in 1909.

As such, many agents had split personalities and played dual roles (for the idea of 'intertextuality', see page 46). It has often been argued that Azef 'went native', or was at least a classic double-dealer, and that his activities were encouraged by the authorities to justify their repressions. Also famously confused and apparently out of control (even somewhat deranged) was the agent Dmitrii Bogrov, who shot prime minister Piotr Stolypin in the Kiev opera house in 1911, probably in order to impress his 'fellow' revolutionaries. It therefore made perfect sense for earlier critics to suspect that Zubatov, himself something of a poacher turned gamekeeper, was in fact working to bring down the state from within – whether he was or not. Zubatov may even have encouraged such suspicions: confusing the issue was after all his original aim. Many were double or triple agents, but were equally fanatical, or fanatically self-interested, in all their roles. The 'other side' of their complicated lives was simply a means of dishing their rivals or settling private scores.

Sudeikin played a particularly complicated role. According to Richard Pipes, his empathetic interviewing technique with revolutionaries such as Degaev was the result of his own resentments against the authorities, largely over his lack of promotion. In 1883 Sudeikin proposed to Degaev that they 'work in tandem';[16] the usual indistinct line was soon crossed. Sudeikin apparently suggested an extraordinary plot to Degaev, involving the assassination of interior minister Count Dmitrii Tolstoi and the tsar's arch-conservative confidant Konstantin Pobedonostsov, procurator of the Holy Synod, as a means of provoking real reform. The final twist in the tale came when Degaev was persuaded by his (soon to be former) colleagues to assist in the minister's own bloody assassination in December 1883. Degaev lured Sudeikin to his apartment and shot him in the back, but it was left to a member of the People's Will to finish him off with an iron bar in the apartment's toilet.

It was in the wonderland world of the Bolshevik Party that the constant interplay between *agents provocateurs* and the Leninists' own methods had the most lasting consequences. One government agent, Roman Malinovskii, rose to the exalted position of the leading Bolshevik in Russia while Lenin was in enforced exile, also serving as chair of the party's Duma faction in 1912–14. Even when he was exposed, an incredulous Lenin initially kept him in place, not fully facing the facts until 1917. According to Robert Service, moreover, Malinovskii's 'main task was to remove any obstacles to the schismatic measures [within the revolutionary left] proposed by Lenin'. 'The Okhrana saw Lenin . . . the single greatest obstacle to unity amongst Russian Marxists . . . as a brilliant executor of the task demanded by the Emperor: the disintegration of the Russian Social-Democratic Labour Party. The enhancement of Lenin's career was [indirectly] the Okhrana's confidential priority.'[17] Their interests certainly coincided. 'The Okhrana wished to splinter the resurgent workers' movement and Lenin wished to bring it under his control.'[18] The secret police were happy to concentrate on arresting Lenin's opponents on the party's Central Committee, the 'Conciliators', to make any reconciliation between Bolsheviks and Mensheviks unlikely (the RSDLP split into the two factions in 1903; reconciliation proved impossible after 1912). Another agent, Miron Chernomazov, was editor of the party paper *Pravda* in 1913–14. His role was to set a radical line that made it easier for the Okhrana periodically to suppress the publication.

The exposure of both men made it difficult for the Bolsheviks properly to exploit the labour unrest on the eve of World War One. The Okhrana could not prevent the 1917 revolution, though some would argue that the revolutionaries were severely demoralised in 1912–14 before the outbreak of war changed everybody's expectations and plans; even that the Provisional Government could have kept the Bolsheviks at bay if its revolutionary liberalism had not persuaded it to abolish the Okhrana in March 1917.[19] At the very least, the constant struggle with the left had a decisive effect in shaping post-revolutionary political culture. Roman Brackman and others have argued that the Bolsheviks' double life before 1917 explains the show-trial mentality to which they succumbed once in power. Party committees had special commissions to deal with political provocation, and the national party had the Central Control Commission, which oversaw members' public and private lives in intrusive detail between 1920 and 1934. Both mirrored the tactics of the enemy. As Lenin said of 'Iron' Feliks Dzerzhinskii when recommending him as head of the Cheka, the Bolsheviks' own secret police in 1917: 'of all of us, it's Feliks who spent the most time behind bars of the Tsarist prisons [twelve years], and who had the most contact with the Okhrana. He knows what he's doing!'[20] Brackman also revisits the long-standing rumour that Stalin himself, born Josef Dzhugashvili, whose original Bolshevik codename was 'Koba' and sometimes 'Ivanovich', was also a one-time informer known to the Okhrana as 'Ivanov'.[21]

The Bolsheviks' Hall of Mirrors

> Any money-bag can always 'hire', buy or enlist any
> number of lawyers, writers and even parliamentary
> deputies, professors, parsons and the like to defend any
> views. . . . In politics it is not so important *who* directly
> advocates particular views. What is important is *who
> stands to gain* from these views, proposals, measures.
>
> Lenin, 'Who Stands to Gain?' 1913.[22]

Superficially, there was less need to manipulate political opposition in the Soviet
period. The possibilities for formal resistance were severely restricted, with even inter-
party factions banned after 1921. However, the party was locked into its old mode of
struggle with the Okhrana and was always shadow-boxing with its self-defined
enemies. For practical and ideological reasons (so-called 'vanguardism'), Leninist party
culture had become increasingly proactive, dedicated to the art of 'organising victories'
rather than simply hoping for them to turn up. Conspiracies, parties, tendencies and
'isms' – some phantom, some real – were constantly paraded as the justification, the
dramaturgiia (dramatic art, the moving spirit of a drama), for moving events.

During the Civil War the Bolsheviks took on most of their opponents head-on,
although electoral fraud was routinely used to prevent the Mensheviks *et al.* from
winning control of key Soviets. A now notorious secret telegram from Lenin to
Penza Communists in 1918 reads: '1. Hang (by all means hang, *so people will see*) no
fewer than 100 kulaks, fat cats, bloodsuckers. 2. Publish their names. 3. Take *all* their
grain. 4. Select hostages in accordance with yesterday's telegram. Do it so that for
hundreds of miles around people will see and tremble . . . . Yours, Lenin. P.S. Find
tougher people.'[23] The last instruction seems superfluous. On home ground,
however, cruder methods were unacceptable. Manipulation therefore came back
into its own. At the SR trial in 1922 ordinary workers were prodded into the streets
to demand 'revolutionary justice'. The 'real' defendants were also mixed with SR
defectors, who, with 'their defending counsel, vied throughout the trial with the
prosecution to incriminate both themselves, or their clients, and the members of the
first group'.[24] In 1920–22 trade unions and civic organisations were often replaced
with Bolshevik replicas – the railway workers' Vikzhel by the Vikzhedor, the union
of workers in the chemical industry by the Congress of Red Chemical Workers, and
so on. The original organisation was then repressed, with the replica settling into a
life of quiet control.[25]

It is true that the regime was beset by many enemies, but organisations such as the
Industrial Party or the Union for the Liberation of Ukraine (both 'uncovered' at
prototype show trials in 1930) were entirely fictitious. The so-called 'Mensheviks'
Trial' of 1931 contained relatively few Mensheviks. The marginal Trotskyist threat
was inflated to serve as public enemy number one, even in 1939–40 absorbing more
of Stalin's energies than the looming confrontation with Nazi Germany. The

organisation set up by Trotsky's son, Lev Sedov, in Paris was thoroughly infiltrated, as was the Fourth International. Sedov was probably assassinated by Soviet agents; his colleague, Rudolf Klement, founder of the Fourth International, certainly was. The spy mania of the 1930s produced a bewildering array of 'isms'. Some were virtual, some not; but the public was deprived of the chance to tell the difference. The Communist takeover of Eastern Europe expanded the repertoire: Laszlo Rajk was tried in Hungary as a CIA and 'Titoist' agent, Rudolf Slánský in Czechoslovakia as the unlikely front for a 'Zionist' plot.

Absurdistan

The denial of truth in the Soviet Union throughout most of the twentieth century created many of the preconditions for virtuality in the twenty-first. In this respect, the USSR was unique. As Solzhenitsyn had it, 'this universal force-feeding with lies is the most agonising aspect of existence in Russia, worse than all our material miseries, worse than any lack of civil liberties'.[26] Martin Amis takes a shot at defining the system's particularity in *Koba the Dread*:

> Hypocrisy didn't know what had hit it in October 1917. Until then, hypocrisy had had its moments, in politics, in religion, in commerce, it had played its part in innumerable social interactions; and it had starred in many Victorian novels, and so on; but it had never been asked to saturate one sixth of the planet; looking back, hypocrisy might have smiled at its earlier reticence, for it soon grew accustomed to the commanding heights.
>
> This vice flourishes when words and deeds abandon all contiguity . . . . In the USSR, that gap covered 11 time zones. The enemy of the people was the regime. The dictatorship of the proletariat was a lie [the dictatorship of a proletarian]; Union was a lie, and Soviet was a lie, and Socialist was a lie, and Republics was a lie. The Revolution was a lie.[27]

But Amis fails to explain how ordinary Soviets were drawn in and disoriented by the Big Lie. As Jeffrey Brooks sensibly puts it, the 'Soviet people could not take the public culture as a fairy tale because it infiltrated every aspect of their lives'.[28] The Soviet era was characterised by what Brooks has called 'performative culture',[29] which produced a profound distortion of any sense of time, agency or cause and effect. Performance substituted for reality; performance *was* reality. Moreover, it was impossible to predict the performance's direction. It was only *after* Stalin had decided on the existence of a Doctors' Plot (1952–53) or the Kirov Murder (1934) that foregoing events could be scripted, and previous phenomena defined as part of an unfolding pattern (hence the tragic difficulty for so many victims of the security state in making the right confession until it was provided for them). Policy shifts were not initiated by public debates or even leadership pronouncements, but rather by the latest 'affair' signalling a new type of drama and a new class of enemies.[30] According to Brooks again: 'In accord with the official culture's theatricality, party leaders stopped explaining publicly what they were doing and made the reason why something was done less important than the orders to do it.'[31] The general culture of messianic achievement and (apparent) plan fulfilment added another layer to the culture of public performance, as did the Bolsheviks' enthusiastic manipulation of new media technologies, defined by one writer as 'theatre therapy'. The film director Nikolai Evreinov's staging of 'the storming of the Winter Palace' in 1920, especially once canonised in Eisenstein's faux-documentary *October* (1927), became the official version of events – even though the actual historical occurrence was on a much smaller scale and was neither the spontaneous outburst of popular anger nor the decisive event presented.[32]

Sheila Fitzpatrick has written eloquently on the manner in which everyday folk got used to changing their own identities ('Soviet urban society in the 1920s and 1930s had some resemblance to a company of impersonators still learning their roles')[33] and to 'wearing the mask'.[34] Stephen Kotkin's study of everyday life in Magnitogorsk emphasises how people grew used to the 'dual reality' of 'speaking Bolshevik' and playing 'The Identification Game'.[35] Class roles obviously had to be relearned, as, for different reasons, did bureaucratically assigned alternatives such as 'nationality'. Hence the Soviet obsession with *razoblacheno* ('unmasking') and the constant reidentifying of individuals, or even whole social groups, as other than what they were previously presented as being. Catherine Wanner has shown how the Soviet culture of deceit extended to other republics such as Ukraine, and how it has survived and even prospered in the post-Soviet era.[36]

The key link between the elite and the popular versions of the 'culture of deceit' was, of course, the mass media, although ritualised performance in the workplace and other institutions was also important. The Soviet era was characterised by media 'saturation', which in the words of Jeffrey Brooks created 'a stylized, ritualistic, and internally consistent public culture that became its own reality and supplanted other forms of public reality and expression'.[37] This had to be a consistent voice: 'Whereas the Greek chorus often queried public values, the Soviet chorus certified them.'[38] The shifting nature of the Bolsheviks' totalitarian ambitions also meant that that voice had to reach almost everyone. Early Soviet double-speak was part of a mobilisational society, in which millions had to be inspired to play their allotted parts; afterwards it became a means of shifting from goal A to goal B, especially given the otherwise immense difficulty of properly explaining abrupt about-turns such as the Nazi-Soviet Pact. After the death of Stalin, Soviet society gradually settled into more predictable rhythms. By the 1970s public rhetoric had changed from a tool of persuasion to a mere means of social management. Brooks provides an apt summary of the effect on the Soviet peoples of living through the two contrasting periods: 'Decades of constrained formulaic commentaries about politics, nationality, ethnicity, human rights, and the economy shaped the consciousness and memory of people in postcommunist societies and now limit current attempts to understand these and other vital issues.'[39]

Significantly, however, the original Fordist model of hierarchical mass media, mass producing a standardised propaganda message, has survived its previous changes of function and been remodelled in the post-Soviet era by political or 'communication' technologists such as Marat Gelman. An alternative culture of samizdat emerged from the shadows in the late 1980s, but could never become a truly mass media. 'The second society's multiple centres worked well when they opposed the dominant system, but after the collapse of Communism, they did not take over the dominant system that was based on centralised, state-controlled communications technology.'[40] Centralised, state-controlled communications technology has therefore survived early hints of redundancy. The post-Soviet states that are really autocracies still rely on their secret police. In the post-Soviet states that are virtual democracies, it is the control of information and manipulation of image that is all-important. The consequent 'information inequality' has created at least the illusion of the malleability of the mass public and fed the elite's sense of its power of manipulation.

The KGB Tool Kit

A second aspect of Bolshevik methodology was mainly developed abroad: the 'active measures' and 'special tasks' that were designed for 'organising victory' beyond the USSR.[41] Here, the KGB's expertise went far beyond that of the Okhrana's agents. Originally known as the Cheka, the Soviet secret police went through various reorganisations and name changes, being called the OGPU from 1923 to 1934, before its reorganisation under the NKVD and final emergence as the KGB in 1954. The nature of its work was indicated by its many subsections, including an Administration for Special Tasks, a Department for Struggle with Ideological Diversions, the A-Service (Active Disinformation Service), as well as the hard-nosed Third Directorate (military counter-intelligence). Special Bureaus for 'diversionary work abroad' and 'special assignments inside the Soviet Union' involving disinformation and *kompromat* were set up in 1950.[42] The latter function would later become the basis of the most notorious subsection of all: the Fifth Chief Directorate, whose relations with domestic 'subversion' were extremely intimate, mere surveillance being supplemented with a variety of techniques of active manipulation.

A typical minimum programme would involve simple intelligence gathering or 'protective measures'. The KGB was particularly fond, however, of so-called 'active measures' (*aktivinye meropriiatiia*) involving 'aggressiveness' (*nastupatelnost*). According to the official KGB handbook, 'active measures' were that 'style of counter-intelligence (intelligence) activity which is proactive and full of initiative'. 'The side which takes the offensive,' the manual helpfully pointed out, 'will, all things being equal, achieve the best results.'[43] Under the heading of active measures, the KGB recommended various types of 'initiative', including the use of networks of *seksoti* (those engaged in 'secret collaboration', from *sekretnoe sotrudnichestvo*), agents of influence, agent *proniknovenie* ('penetration', either by infiltration or the turning of insiders), and the deployment of *agents provocateurs*. Agents should collect and deploy compromising information (*kompromat*) on both friends and enemies, and use disinformation (*dezinformatsiia* or just *deza*). Their tracks should be covered with local versions of capitalist 'ideological diversion', the creation of 'false flags', *maskirovka* or *legenda* (a mask or cover story for a particular operation) and black propaganda. *Profilaktika* ('prophylactic' or 'preventive action', also slang for a contraceptive) involved working actively with specific groups or individuals to prevent their opposition sympathies from being manifested in hostile action.

As with Sudeikin's instructions (see pages 2–3), active measures further involved 'misleading the adversary, undermining and weakening his positions, the disruption of his hostile plans', 'steps to create agent positions within the enemy camp and around the enemy, playing operational games with the enemy, spreading disinformation, compromising and breaking up the enemy's forces'.[44] One specific type was *presechenie* ('cutting short') or *razlozhenie* ('disruption'), defined as 'operationally cutting short the enemy's subversive activity . . . by introducing or exacerbating ideological disputes between members of the organisation (or group), discrediting the aims of the organisation in the eyes of rank and file members, intensifying conflicts between the leadership and rank and file members, arousing mutual mistrust amongst the leadership, intensifying their rivalries, etc' and 'intensifying the hostility between opposition groups' if more than one exists.[45]

One of the most notorious of these active measures was the destruction of the 'dissident Communist party', the POUM (the Workers' Party of Marxist Unification), rival to the Communist PCE during the Spanish Civil War. In *Homage to Catalonia* (1938), George Orwell recorded his revulsion against left-wing infighting and the Communists' warped priorities in the face of the Fascist advance. Soviet spymaster Pavel Sudoplatov later proudly described the OGPU-NKVD's victory in what he casually dubbed the 'the Civil War within the Civil War': 'the Spanish Republicans lost, but Stalin's men and women won. When the Spanish Civil war ended, there was no room left in the world for Trotsky.'[46] The campaign 'to totally discredit the POUM as a German-Francoist organisation' was organised by the OGPU station chief Aleksandr Orlov (real name Feldbin),[47] who also managed to spirit away all of Spain's gold reserves to Moscow while setting new standards for the provision of 'disinformation' and directing 'kidnapping and terrorism against Trotskyists and people whom the special service wanted to neutralise'. Orlov organised a fake denunciation of Trotsky by the POUM leader Andrés Nin (a confidant of Trotsky who was later tortured and killed, almost certainly by the OGPU), and the fake 'N Document', supposedly a compromising letter from Nin (N) to Franco.[48] Communist smear tactics sought simultaneously to claim that 'the POUM was a "Trotskyist" organisation and "Franco's Fifth Column"'. Orwell described one 'malignant [Communist] cartoon which was circulated, first in Madrid and then in Barcelona, representing the POUM as slipping off a mask marked with the hammer and sickle and revealing a face marked with the swastika'.[49] Local and international Communist propaganda depicted it as 'no more than a gang of disguised Fascists in the pay of Franco and Hitler, who were pressing a pseudo-revolutionary policy as a way of aiding the Fascist cause' – posing as ultra-leftist being a well-known tactic of the Bolsheviks. But as Orwell wrote, 'The accusation against the POUM amounted to this: that a body of some scores of thousands of people, almost entirely working class, besides numerous foreign helpers and sympathisers, mostly refugees from Fascist countries, and thousands of militia, were simply a vast spying organisation in Fascist pay.'

The OGPU campaign also accused the POUM of secretly passing on military secrets via radio and messages written in invisible ink, in order to persuade the government to take 'a range of administrative measures against the Spanish Trotskyists'. The final act came when the Communist press managed to depict the fighting around the Barcelona telephone exchange in May 1937 as a 'POUM "uprising" under Fascist orders'; the ploy successfully persuaded the new Negrín government to suppress the party in June.[50] At the time, it was in fact the Communists who were plotting to undermine the Republican cabinet and preparing their own move on power.[51]

The Comintern used similar tactics against other rivals, such as the German SAP or French Left Socialists. In 1926 a secret Comintern decision backed 'creating a whole solar system of organisations and smaller committees around the Communist Party ... actually working under the influence of the party, but not under its mechanical control'.[52] Dmitrii Manuilskii, secretary of the Comintern from 1931 to 1943, invented a fake conspiracy within the PCF (French Communist Party) in 1931 to 'increase its dependence on Moscow' once the party had exhausted itself in a fruitless internal witch-hunt.[53] The German Communist and media mogul Willi Münzenberg was a master at setting up fake front organisations, particularly the bogus aid agencies that channelled well-meaning donations intended for suffering Soviet citizens to Communist sources instead.[54]

A new type of political theatre of fake appeals and plebiscites was invented for the Soviet Union's interventions in Eastern Europe in the 1940s. After the invasion of the three Baltic States in the summer of 1940, Stalin's plenipotentiaries staged an elaborate six-week 'play' rather than simply announcing annexation. The first act was to establish the fiction that events were being guided by native Communist parties: an impressive feat given that the Estonian Communist Party, for example, had only 133 members at the time.[55] These parties were then used as the basis for setting up three imaginary Leagues of the Working People, which received impressive majorities ranging from a mere 92.8 per cent (Estonia) to as much as 99.2 per cent (Lithuania) in rigged elections held in July. The final act was the new People's Diets' unanimous votes to join the Soviet Union. Given the concurrent invasion, the internal drama was not very convincing, but the charade was nevertheless deemed important and set a precedent for the tactics used to install new Communist regimes in Eastern Europe in 1945–9.

The Soviet takeover of west Ukraine and west Belorussia in autumn 1939 also involved fake turnouts, fake majorities and fake political actors in the lead-up to the new puppet assemblies' unanimous clamour for 'union'. In both cases, the pretence was made harder to sustain than it might otherwise have been by the forcible dissolution of what had been relatively strong local Communist parties only a few years before. The Communist Party of West Ukraine, long suspected of national 'deviationism' (in other words sticking up for Ukrainian rights), had been wound up in 1938: most of the leading members of the (still enthusiastically pro-Soviet) Communist Party of West Belorussia were rounded up and shot after an NKVD raid on their training camp in 1935. Politicians from the respective Soviet hinterlands therefore had to be more directly involved.

A similarly fake Initiative Group of the Greek Catholic Church for Reunion with the Orthodox Church was set up by the NKGB in west Ukraine in 1945. According to the account by Bohdan Bociurkiw, the group's leader, Havryil Kostelnyk, had 'only four [real] supporters in the city of Lviv'. He claimed eight hundred priests had become members by October, but privately admitted that of these 'fewer than fifty had joined the group out of conviction'.[56] The rest had been coerced using the threat of deportation for themselves and their families. As no bishops had joined the group, however, it remained uncanonical. The fake Sobor that announced the 'reunion' in 1946 (the original creation of the Church in 1596 now being reinvented as 'schism') had to make do with two bishops who were already secretly Orthodox. The Initiative Group was therefore not even 'of the Greek Catholic Church'.

In the post-war interregnum before the advent of full-blown Stalinism (1945–48), Communist parties in East-Central Europe again used a combination of simply fraudulent and more carefully designed virtual tactics. As the East German Communist leader Walter Ulbricht put it in 1945: 'It's got to look democratic, but we must have everything under our control.'[57] Potential opponents were disenfranchised (former aristocrats, the wrong type of ethnic group) or prevented from standing (the Agrarian Party in Czechoslovakia); ballot boxes were stuffed; the pivotal power of the Interior Ministry was regularly abused. But the Communists also sought to disorient or outflank their opponents by setting up or 'encouraging' fake parties.

In Hungary, the right-wing Independent Smallholders' Party won 60 per cent of the seats in the 1945 elections, easily defeating the Communists, who won 17 per cent. The Communists won only 22.3 per cent at their second attempt in very different circumstances in 1947, but were able to displace the Smallholders, who slumped to 15.4 per cent, by 'encouraging the establishment of other right-wing parties . . . (the Christian Democratic People's Party [which won 16.4 per cent], Party of Hungarian Independence [13.4 per cent], Independent Hungarian Democrats [5.2 per cent], and Christian Women's League [1.4 per cent]), hoping [correctly] that these parties would gain votes among the Smallholders' supporters'. These so-called 'salami tactics' levered the Communists into power, despite their still minority position.

In Poland's 1947 elections, the Communists ran two 'satellites', the Labour Party (4.1 per cent) and a fake Peasant Party dubbed New Liberation (3.5 per cent), to take votes away from their main opponent, the real Peasant Party led by Stanisław Mikołajczyk, which was therefore kept down to a manageable 10.3 per cent – making it easier to force Mikołajczyk to flee the country. In Slovakia, 'the

Communists tried to split the opposition by encouraging the birth of new parties (Labour Party, Freedom Party)', although the latter two won only 6.8 per cent to add to the Communists' 30.4 per cent. The anti-Communist Democratic Party won 60 per cent, in the event making a coup necessary.[58]

In Hungary in 1956 and Czechoslovakia in 1968 the situation was never allowed to progress as far as elections. Nevertheless, KGB agents served as *agents provocateurs*, acting out the radical demands, such as Czechoslovakia's withdrawal from the Warsaw Pact in 1968, that would then be used to justify intervention.[59] Czechoslovakia was flooded with KGB 'illegals' who fabricated evidence of Western intelligence support for and 'penetration' of the dissident groups KAN and K-231, even of a 'secret cache' of American weapons (in Soviet packaging) to be used in an imminent 'rightist' coup.[60] In Czechoslovakia at least, however, the orchestrated calls for 'assistance' didn't work as planned. As Kieran Williams writes, the 'failed *coup d'état*' was replaced by a 'relatively successful *coup de main*'.[61]

Émigré movements were infiltrated by double agents and confused by active measures. Stalin's secretary, Boris Bazhanov, later confessed: 'I often heard Politburo members and major OGPU functionaries say that the émigré organisations were so saturated with [OGPU] agents that at times it was difficult to make out where émigré activities began and [INO, the International Department's] provocational work ended.'[62] The main 'White' émigré organisation, the Russian General Military Union (in Russian, ROVS), the exiles' would-be army of liberation, had its energies dissipated and its leading generals, Aleksandr Kutepov and Yevgenii Miller, abducted and killed. The OGPU also invented a Union for the Return to the Motherland to entrap returning men and materials, and a Monarchist Union of Central Russia (fake lifespan 1922–29) to trick the émigrés into believing they had partners within the USSR; a fake Trust was established to act as contact group (and cover name) between the two. Practically the whole émigré community and most of its intelligence contacts in the West were therefore tricked into believing what they wanted to believe: that the old order was still strong, that the Soviet project might falter, that Lenin's New Economic Policy (NEP) was worth supporting, and that they had their own ready-made 'service organisation' in Russia. (In Il'f and Petrov's 1928 novel *The Twelve Chairs*, tricksters invent a similar 'Alliance of the Sword and Ploughshare' to con money out of nostalgic merchants.) The émigrés promised not to take any action against the fledgling USSR without first consulting the Trust, thereby buying the Communists almost a decade of breathing space. The Trust even helped to finance the OGPU by selling disinformation to the intelligence services of the West. Britain's most famous 'Ace of Spies', Sidney Reilly, whom the Bolsheviks believed had come close to assassinating Lenin during the Civil War, was enticed to Moscow by the 'dangle'. His mysterious disappearance was confirmed in the 1990s as murder by his Lubianka gaolers.[63] A parallel (overlapping) operation dubbed Sindikat-2 helped ensnare the former SR Boris Savinkov of the Popular Union for the Defence of the Motherland and Freedom in 1924. The Bolsheviks feared Savinkov as a militant anti-Communist and anti-monarchist. He was therefore lured into making contact with a fake group of 'Liberal Democrats'. Badly burnt, Western intelligence agencies now cut the Whites loose. As a result of the Purges of the 1930s, most had no real intelligence operations inside the USSR until after 1941.

The Trust may well have been the (un)real-life inspiration for 'The Brotherhood' in George Orwell's *1984*, which, like the novel's faux-Trotsky opposition leader, Emmanuel Goldstein, serves to flush out real hostile elements rash enough to declare their support. The Trust project was so successful that it was relaunched at least twice. In the late 1940s a fake Polish underground movement, WiN ('Freedom and Independence'), duped the CIA into giving it funds and accepting disinformation. In 1969–82 yet another émigré group, the NTS ('National Alliance of Russian Solidarists'), was tricked into pouring money and effort into its fake 'contacts' back home in Russia.

The main émigré Ukrainian party, also then active among Ukrainian populations not under Soviet rule, the Organisation of Ukrainian Nationalists (OUN, 1929 to the present), was also thoroughly infiltrated. M. Matviieiko, one-time head of the OUN's internal security service, was an *agent provocateur*. NKVD 'active measures' included the deployment of rogue bands of fake OUN-UPA members to foster the nationalists' extremist image, and the setting of rival partisan groups against each other in occupied west Ukraine in 1944–47. The K3 operation to smuggle nationalist agents back into Ukraine was thoroughly infiltrated and betrayed (as were most OUN channels back home until 1988). More fundamentally, the OGPU-NKVD claimed the credit for generating the near-fatal split that developed in the OUN between the supporters of Andrii Melnyk, the OUN(M), and Stepan Bandera, the OUN(B), in 1939–41.[64] The split was probably coming anyway, but the OGPU-NKVD helped bring it about sooner by successfully assassinating the movement's charismatic leader Yevhen Konovalets with an exploding chocolate box in a Rotterdam café in 1938. Another KGB agent, Vasyl Lebed (Khomiak), had been in place in the OUN leadership since Viacheslav Menzhinskii, the head of the OGPU, had drawn up a plan 'to neutralise the terrorist actions of the Ukrainian nationalists' in 1933.[65] In the 1950s the KGB sought to exploit the new split between the supporters of Lev Rebet and Bandera that resulted in the former setting up the OUN (abroad) in 1956. The assassination of Rebet in 1957 failed to widen the split, however, and the same agent, fellow Ukrainian Bohdan Stashinskyi, killed Bandera by the same method (a gas gun) in 1959.[66]

Of course, Western secret services and their Third World clients used many of the same 'black bag' operations, and also employed specialists in 'psychological warfare'. A prime example was the fake Communist 'coup' in Indonesia in 1965 that prepared the way for the replacement of the 'nationalist' Sukharno regime by the 'anti-Communist' Suharto and the consequent bloodbath. The CIA also backed or created various 'third-force' anti-Communist politicians or fronts such as Mobutu in the Congo and the Committee for the Defence of National Interests in Laos, as the French had done before them. Bolshevik methods were copied by the CIA in the

Cold War to fund numerous cultural 'fronts'.[67] But both were clearly more habitual activities for the Soviet foreign services.[68] As no less a source than Yurii Andropov once candidly put it: 'The USSR's political role abroad must be supported by means of the dissemination of false stories and provocatory information.'[69] Soviet habits of manipulation were so ingrained that it has been alleged that several of the Gulag rebellions after the death of Stalin were stage-managed by camp bosses seeking to prove their continuing indispensability.[70]

The continued use of the same terminology and tactics speaks volumes about the nature of post-Soviet politics. Local political culture owes more to Dzerzhinskii than to de Tocqueville, more to the Cheka than Chekhov. More directly, the same people are often involved. Many political 'projects' are the work of the security services. The services also hire themselves out to political masters, and many a former agent is in their direct employ,[71] as with former deputy KGB head Filipp Bobkov working for the oligarch Vladimir Gusinskii, or Gennadii Petelin heading prime minister Viktor Chernomyrdin's Secretariat, where he was accused of amassing tens of millions of dollars of rake-offs in foreign bank accounts.[72]

Dissident Divide and Rule

Equally cynical but subtly different tactics were used at home, largely as a substitute for terror from the Khrushchev era onwards. Soviet dissidents, many of whom were the future politicians of the 1980s and 1990s (for reasons explained below, it was often difficult to make the transition), were trapped in a fetid environment of mutual mistrust – the KGB knew that it was much more demoralising to set their critics at each other's throats. The fact that so many former dissidents accused each other of working for the KGB does not necessarily mean that that they were all right. What it does undoubtedly mean is that the KGB succeeded in its manipulations to such an extent that mutual suspicion made effective collective action very difficult. Moreover, Andropov's final use of active measures to break up and marginalise dissident groups on the eve of the Moscow Olympics in 1979–80 meant that the resource base (human, structural and psychological) for a new and genuine civil-society politics was much less than it might otherwise have been when opportunities began to open up in 1987–88, by which time 'the dissident movement in the USSR was more of a Western myth than a Russian reality'.[73] Significantly, the future high priest of political technology, Gleb Pavlovskii, may also have informed on his fellow dissidents in the 1970s and 1980s.

By the 1960s the KGB's priority was to demoralise rather than simply to destroy dissident groups. As dissidents tried to develop new tactics of struggle within the law, they would be framed with arms 'finds', possession of pornography or incriminating bundles of US dollars, charged with hooliganism, or subjected to psychiatric incarceration, all of which was supposed to make it easier to isolate them from the rest of society.[74] Such 'special operations' were often backed up with fake 'civic condemnations', that is, carefully scripted attacks published in the official press from the ordinary citizens the dissidents sought to represent.[75] The KGB also set up clone organisations to supply disinformation to the West. For example, in the 1970s the real group working to expose the abuse of Soviet psychiatry (the Working Commission to Investigate the Use of Psychiatry for Political Purposes [Moscow], 1977–81, that is, the incarceration of dissidents in mental hospitals) suddenly found itself flanked by fake rivals who found no evidence of such abuse.

Similar tactics were used in the other republics. In Ukraine the historian Heorhii Kasianov has described 'a game without rules that the system constantly practised against opponents. [Because] moral content had a very high importance in the struggle of dissidents with the system, the *idée fixe* of the authorities was the demolarisation of its opponents, not just their physical removal from the sphere of social-political life.'[76] Where support networks were stronger, they had to be broken up with psychological active measures. Emblematic was operation 'Bloc' launched by the local KGB boss Vitalii Fedorchuk against dissident circles in the west Ukrainian heartland in 1976,[77] when the KGB used the 'differentiated approach' (divide and rule, differential punishment, rewards for cooperative agents) to 'break up the nationalist group and discredit its participants' – in this case those responsible for the main local samizdat journal *Ukrainian Herald*. The bad blood created by such tactics was still poisoning politics in Lviv as late as 2002, with the victims, now national deputies, trading accusations about just who exactly had worked for the KGB.[78]

In Ukraine there was also the extra element of relations with the diaspora, which the party and KGB took increasing care to misrepresent in both directions. Dissidents at home would be stereotyped as 'agents of the OUN'. In the 1970s foreign tourists and students were framed as 'emissaries of foreign centres' (one was Belgian – not a major centre for the Ukrainian diaspora) to justify a crackdown on dissent at home. The KGB also set up its own émigré organisations and publishing activities to disseminate false stories about the homeland, while at the same time masking its direct involvement behind front organisations such as the Society for Cultural Ties with Ukrainians Abroad.[79]

The enforced 'public repentance' of the dissident hero Ivan Dziuba in 1973 brought together most of these themes. The archives show that the KGB hoped the affair would 'seriously compromise him [Dziuba] in front of foreign centres of the OUN and the nationalist element in the republic, isolate and discredit him among nationalist elements, which will help his final ideological disarmament, re-education and tearing away from nationalist surroundings'. It would also 'help many of his former colleagues re-examine their positions, renounce hostile action and serve as a prophylactic influence on individuals who have accidentally fallen under the influence of Ukrainian bourgeois nationalism'.[80]

The Depth of the Rot

The Gorbachev era (1985–91) declared a new dawn, but much of the 'new politics' was still steeped in Bolshevik political culture. Gorbachev's ideological mentor, Aleksandr Yakovlev, retrospectively argued that the *perestroika* project might have had more success if it had been able to draw on the idealism that still existed before 1968.

> One thing is clear: perestroika was many years too late. If all of this had occurred much earlier, the wave of democratic enthusiasm would [have] be[en] far more powerful; what is more important, it would [have] be[en] morally pure. The persecution of dissent and the years of social stagnation almost killed social idealism and trust, sowing apathy, cynicism, disbelief and moral lassitude. That is why the current tide of democracy is like the surf which carries both clean water and trash. There is a subjective factor as well. Like any revolution 'from above,' it was difficult for perestroika to take the decisive step towards democratisation by itself.[81]

In other words, the sheer unadulterated cynicism and moral decay of the ruling party in the late Soviet era were factors in themselves.[82] Stephen Kotkin makes a persuasive case for arguing that the period 1970–2000 should be considered as a coherent whole, in that the same themes of 'the privatisation of public office and the neglect of the public interest' stretch across the three decades.[83] Time and again, the cynicism of political behaviour in most of the post-Soviet states can only be understood in terms of its deep roots in the late Soviet era. Moreover, a key reason why the Soviet Union collapsed with such apparent ease was that those who noisily defended the system in public were all too often the very same people who were laundering its assets in private. On the other hand, the KGB was the one institution that was not fatally weakened in the late Soviet period: hence the survival of its personnel and methodology.[84]

Revolution from Above, Again

Both the tactics used against enemies abroad and those deployed against dissidents at home in the 1960s and 1970s were revived in the late 1980s. Ironically, Aleksandr Yakovlev himself was in many ways the prototypical modern political manipulator.[85] As he admitted in a 1992 lecture on, of all things, 'Ethics and Reformation', delivered in, of all places, the Vatican, at the launch of *perestroika* 'there was no organized political opposition to the regime or serious and mass–scale resistance to the CPSU's unlimited power'. 'Everything in my country always happens differently than in others. In Poland, the instrument of change was the opposition – Wałeşa, Kuron and Michnik. In my country it was the "apparatchiks". We created an opposition to ourselves.'[86] In their book on 'market Bolshevism', Reddaway and Glinski have also emphasised 'the contrived origin of the Gorbachev-era opposition'. 'While Yakovlev's ideological department of the Central Committee was busy designing and anticipating various "informal" activities on the liberal, pro-Western flank, [Gorbachev's main conservative opponent] Yegor Ligachev and his apparatchiks laboured to complement and counterbalance that initiative by manufacturing conservative clubs and public events.'[87] Ultimately, according to one source, 'after Ligachev and his supporters inspired the creation of the RCP [Russian Communist Party, in late 1989 and early 1990], a group of workers at the CPSU [Central Committee], supporters of Yakovlev, began operatively to create in the eyes of the West the illusion of multi-partyism',[88] including, ironically, Vladimir Zhirinovskii's Liberal-Democratic Party (see pages 23–7). Ligachev's ally, Valerii Legostaiev, served as 'the Central Committee *apparat*'s envoy to extremist Communist groups that produced the hardline RSFSR CP, including the [bogus] USSR United Front of Workers (*OFT*), the Russian Communist Initiative Congress (*DKI*), and Nina Andreieva's "Yedinstvo", or "Unity for Leninism and Communist Ideals"'.[89] Another link man was Sergei Kurginian, who set up the state-supported Experimental Creative Centre, which helped establish the various United Workers' Fronts, Intermovements, etc., and in 1991 published prescient plans for reinventing Communism 'post-*perestroika*'.[90] Moscow Gorkom's first secretary Yurii Prokofiev was also a key coordinator. The Central Committee *apparat* even created the Coordinating Council of National-Patriotic Forces in February, which then issued an appeal to the CPSU, i.e., to itself![91] The notorious nationalist 'black colonels', Viktor Alksnis and Nikolai Petrushenko, who called loudest for 'order' to be imposed, also played a part dictated by the Central Committee, as did Vasilii Starodubtsev's Peasants' Union (to keep control of party finance from collective farms) and Aleksandr Tiziakov's USSR Association of State Enterprises, a rival to Arkadii Volskii's pro-Gorbachev NPS (Scientific-Industrial Union).

Gorbachev and Yakovlev might have courted the dissident hero Andrei Sakharov had he lived longer. They gave some support to nationalists such as Sergei Zalygin and Dmitrii Likhachev,[92] and secretly backed the United Council of Russia before the March 1990 elections, to steal their opponents' thunder – without noticeable electoral success. A final irony is that it made perfect sense for the Gorbachev–Yakovlev team to support their apparent nemesis in the conservative camp under Yegor Ligachev or, more exactly, the image of the Ligachev camp. The representation of late Soviet politics as a struggle between reformers and die-hards, democrats and authoritarians, good guys and bad, was the greatest illusion of all. It was also an unfortunate alternative to one of Gorbachev's greatest missed opportunities: even in 1990 it was still possible that the Communist Party monolith could be divided in two, creating both a 'conservative' and 'social-democratic' party and striking a radical blow against the myth of unitary 'power'. This path towards real rather than virtual pluralism was never taken: Gorbachev preferred artificial attempts to create a rigged contest between a 'party of the future' and the 'party of the past'. However, dividing the party's assets and stake holdings in the state proved more difficult than dividing the party.

Bogeymen and Bogeywomen
The Kremlin preferred *dramaturgiia* instead. One early project that served as a pointer to later developments was the right-wing 'scarecrow' party Pamiat ('Memory'). Its black-shirt activists with their skinhead haircuts, anti-Semitic ravings and conspiracy

theories began to fill column inches in the Western press in 1987–88. However, according to the Russian analyst Valerii Solovei:

> There is every reason to think that gradually the various Pamiat groups not only fell under the control of state structures, but also became, to a definite degree, directed by them. In using Pamiat they [the authorities] tried to shoot two hares: a) to discredit Russian nationalism as a whole, b) to attract additional allies on to the side of political reform. It can't be excluded that at the same time Pamiat can also be seen as [a then potentially] unique opponent to the all-democratic movement[93]

– and perhaps also as a warning to it not to head too far in a pro-Western, neo-liberal direction. Some saw Pamiat as a project designed to discredit liberalism as a whole, supported by sympathetic journalism in the Writers' Union paper *Nash sovremennik* ('Our Contemporary') and the Komsomol's *Molodaia gvardiia* ('Young Guard'). The latter aims were obviously in potential conflict with the first, but would account for the interest of the KGB, which had been secretly supporting or attempting to control right-wing groups for at least twenty years (see pages 209–100).[94] Some genuinely sympathised with Pamiat, others thought 'a vent was needed to relieve the pent-up steam of dissidence' and divert popular anger towards a faceless but all-culpable 'Zionism'. According to Yakovlev, writing in 1998, 'Pamiat was at the beginning an organisation with very noble goals. It consisted of restorers and history enthusiasts who were engaged in preserving monuments of antiquity. Then the KGB inserted its man there – the photographer Dmitrii Vasiliev, together with his comrades . . . in this way the KGB organisationally gave birth to Russian fascism.'[95]

Filipp Bobkov, first deputy chairman of the KGB until February 1991, head of the Fifth Chief Directorate responsible for all domestic 'counter-intelligence' and supposedly also the KGB's general link man with Russian nationalist groups, helped to set up Pamiat.[96] (In 1991 he left to join nomenclatura businessman Vladimir Gusinskii's Most ['Bridge', an unconscious metaphor] group, taking his information and his contacts with him.) Some versions of the story have it that Boris Yeltsin's early contacts with, and claimed revulsion at, the group during his time as Moscow city party boss may have masked secret support to bolster his populist anti-nomenclatura campaign.[97] According to the account by Anatolii Chernaiev, Gorbachev's senior foreign policy adviser, Yakovlev complained about one of many personal slanders at the time: 'all that scum has the direct support of Ligachev and [Vitalii] Vorotnikov [chair of the RSFSR Council of Ministers]. And I'm sure that this leaflet came out with [the KGB chair Viktor] Chebrikov's help.'[98] Gorbachev and Yakovlev were also happy to exploit the threat 'Support us, or you'll get Pamiat',[99] although there is no direct evidence that they themselves played any direct role in setting up or funding the group. By the end of the decade, with Pamiat taking part in anti-liberal 'pogroms' and distributing leaflets warning of further 'actions' throughout the USSR, it seemed that Chebrikov's successor, Vladimir Kriuchkov, was the main sponsor of the group, which was designed to scare flakier opposition elements back towards the authorities.

Early in its life clandestine official favour helped Pamiat demonstrate (in May 1987, actually in Red Square) and circulate its material. As well as the more 'extreme' Vasiliev group, the 'more reliable' Pamiat faction led by the then unknown artist Yurii Sychev and the poet Tamara Ponomareva was also backed by the KGB. Pamiat also embodied a classic active measures formula: it was big enough to seem a frightening alternative if Gorbachev's reforms went awry, but was kept small enough by conflicts engineered in its ranks to prevent it from growing too strong. Later (1988) debilitating splits in both the Moscow and Leningrad branches – when reform politics began to broaden out its agenda and transcend the potency of a threat still rooted in the limited political space of the dissident era – were not accidental.[100]

After Pamiat came the Nina Andreieva affair – when it seemed possible that a bitter attack on Gorbachev's policies by an unknown teacher from Leningrad might stop *perestroika* in its tracks. As the 'new politics' struggled to get off the ground in 1988, both sides in the seemingly all encompassing Gorbachev–Ligachev feud exploited the row, showing how deeply ingrained were Bolshevik habits of political manipulation and acting through proxies. Ligachev initiated it. Although Andreieva '*did* write something, a primitive letter in defence of Stalinist values that she sent to the Central Committee', the final version was drafted by Ligachev's contacts in the CPSU's Central Committee *OrgOtdel* (organisation department), and modelled on the work of Aleksandr Prokhanov.[101] It was edited with Andreieva in Leningrad by Vladimir Denisov, the science and *de facto* ideology correspondent of the conservative daily *Sovetskaia Rossiia* – and an old colleague of Ligachev's from Tomsk.[102] Of course, the 'letter' was designed to read like a manifesto, defining the new party line, not like the work of a mere chemistry teacher. The title of Andreieva's letter may have been 'I cannot forget my principles', but those principles were written for her.

At the same time, the Gorbachev–Yakovlev side used the affair to caricature conservative Communists such as Ligachev as part of a prototypical 'Red threat'. As Anatolii Chernaiev later remarked:

> If there had been no Nina Andreieva, we would have had to invent her. For such an avalanche of anti-Stalinism now ensued, such freedom in newspapers and magazines as never would have been tolerated even for a day by Ligachev and his team before the incident. Ligachev no longer acted with his old assurance in the Politburo meetings. Now he mostly kept quiet.[103]

'Democrat' Divide and Rule

The Soviet regime had no intention of imploding like its east European COMECOM counterparts. In 1989 KGB chairman Vladimir Kriuchkov signed a secret decree stating: 'The chief task of the KGB at the present time is not to permit the creation of a political opposition in the USSR. Toward that end, the organs of the KGB must take all measures to discredit the leaders of the democratic movement, to disrupt their plans and designs, and not to permit the holding of demonstrations and meetings of any kind.'[104] In the same year the KGB Collegium set out instructions for agents to establish close relations with newly elected deputies – many even ran for election themselves.[105]

The Communist Party and the KGB, working separately or in tandem, set themselves several tasks in the new climate. Most important was the job of disabling groups capable of challenging their hold on power. The rapid succession of ephemeral rivals demonstrated that such tactics were relatively successful. First there was the Democratic Party of Russia, which for a brief period after its foundation in May 1990 was the largest non-Communist party in Russia and potentially *the* party of the urban Russian intelligentsia. It was soon hijacked by Nikolai Travkin, leading to the departure of more principled anti-Communists such as Lev Ponomarev, and two formal schisms in April and December 1991. The party struggled on to a last hurrah with 5.5 per cent of the vote in the 1993 elections, but split into a pro- (Travkin) and anti-Kremlin faction soon after. (The peripatetic Travkin ended up in Our Home Is Russia, then Yabloko, then the Union of Right Forces.) The intelligentsia's second attempt at establishing a broad umbrella opposition in October 1990, Democratic Russia, posed a more formidable threat, but it too was thoroughly infiltrated and split from within (see page 152).[106] Other parties, such as Viktor Aksiuchits' Russian Christian Democratic Movement, were easily diverted into a nationalist ghetto.

Anointing an Opposition

The other side of the coin was the various attempts to create a tame opposition. In December 1989 Gorbachev had publicly rebuked the veteran dissident Andrei Sakharov for daring to suggest that the Communist Party abandon Article 6, the constitutional guarantee of its monopoly on power. Three months later, Gorbachev bowed to the inevitable, reluctantly accepting an official commitment to pluralism. Nevertheless, the former mayor of St Petersburg Anatolii Sobchak and others alleged in 1994 that the Politburo decided on the eve of the change: 'a multiparty system is lurking on the horizon: we have to overtake events. We have to create the first alternative party ourselves, but a party that can be managed.'[107] Gorbachev denied the allegation and suggested that Sobchak was himself the recipient of dis-information. Dmitrii Volkogonov, the 'house historian' of post-Communist Russia, with his privileged access to Politburo files, has commented only that:

> even when the infamous Article 6 had been removed from the constitution, Gorbachev did all he could to maintain the influence of the party in society, and several sessions of the Politburo were devoted to finding ways of doing this in the changed circumstances. A special resolution was adopted 'on certain measures for the lawful guarantee of the Party's viability'.[108]

This meant the transfer of state property to party control, laundering state funds[109] and developing various political insurance projects.

The most notorious such project in 1990–91 was the Liberal-Democratic Party of the Soviet Union, led by the not-yet notorious Vladimir Zhirinovskii.[110] Zhirinovskii had graduated from Moscow State University's Institute of Asian and African Countries and worked for the Soviet Peace Committee – both KGB stomping grounds – and may have been even more susceptible to 'influence' after several scrapes, such as being expelled from Turkey in 1969 for allegedly working for the KGB (significantly, he was not a member of nationalist circles at the time). In 1988 the neophyte rent-an-orator briefly worked for the Jewish organisation Shalom (another KGB 'anti-Zionist' front), although he also flirted with Sychev's branch of Pamiat in 1989. Zhirinovskii made a bizarre cameo appearance at the first 'congress' (i.e., a crowded meeting in a private flat) of the opposition Democratic Union in May 1988. As the organiser, Viktor Kuzin, later reminisced: 'Vladimir Zhirinovskii also showed up at the congress and made a most unintelligible speech, after which we realised that his mission was to create obstacles to the formation of our party.' He was 'asked to leave'.[111] (Two other co-founders of the Liberal-Democratic Party were also veterans of the Democratic Union, Vladimir Bogachev and Lev Ubozhko, who first set up the Democratic Party of the Soviet Union in August 1989.) The party's ambitions and political style were indicated by its initial claim that leading democrats Yurii Afanasiev and Gleb Yakunin were already members – which came as news to them.

Nevertheless, once he had been reincarnated as a party leader, Zhirinovskii's first appearance on the public stage did not involve the extremes of behaviour, such as throwing water, pulling women's hair or brawling with opponents, that would later characterise his performances. In any case, as two of Zhirinovskii's biographers point out, 'to claim Zhirinovskii is insane is like accusing the actor who plays Othello of murder'.[112] His Liberal-Democratic Party of the Soviet Union (LDP) was not yet the crazy gang it later became. There is now a well-established tradition of mocking the party's name as a multiple misnomer. In fact, for the circumstances of the time it was entirely appropriate. The party was designed to steal some of the opposition's clothes, and the main opposition to the CPSU at the time was the 'democrats'. So why not call it both 'Liberal' and 'Democratic'? Labels were more important than programmes. Zhirinovskii's original party platform was actually a fairly standard reform wish-list; radically Westernising, if anything. At the time Zhirinovskii himself glibly remarked: 'My programme? It's like everybody else's: perestroika, a free market, and democracy.'[113] It is, in other words, worth emphasising that Zhirinovskii's first role was as a fake liberal, not a fake nationalist. It is also tempting to speculate that the KGB drew on its institutional memory of the Liberal Democrat group, which the OGPU had invented to lure Boris Savinkov back to the USSR in 1924 (see pages 14–15).

Most explanations of Zhirinovskii's 'freak' success in the 1991 (and 1993) elections have focused on his sudden unanticipated advantage when Communist and right-wing alternatives temporarily found themselves discredited or disabled.

However, the Liberal-Democrats' unique credentials as a virtual party offer a better explanation. Zhirinovskii's initial sponsors knew they needed a populist force – but one that would connect only with issues that suited them. He therefore served as both a safety valve and part of a virtual chorus for their own policies (see the section below). Zhirinovskii's claim to speak for the whole of the Soviet Union was doubly important. His backers encouraged and coached his attempts to tap into the same vein of anti-nomenclatura populism as Yeltsin before him.[114] But his would be the only non-Communist party designed to function on the all-Union stage, as an adjunct or pseudo-opposition alongside the CPSU. Secondly, alongside his anodyne domestic wish-list and promise of cheap vodka for all, the rest of Zhirinovskii's programme was actually Soviet nationalist (maintaining the Union, even abolishing nationality and the republics, protecting their 'neglected' Russians and minor nationalities), which obviously suited the political aims of Kriuchkov and Supreme Soviet chair Anatolii Lukianov.

Administrative resources supporting Zhirinovskii lurked in the wings. Laundered CPSU monies undoubtedly reached the coffers of the party, as well as those of several other soon-to-be-forgotten groups such as the former KGB general Aleksandr Sterligov's Russian Council and the Russian National-Patriotic Workers' Party.[115] The Liberal-Democrats' founding congress in Moscow's Rusakov House of Culture received favourable publicity on *Vremia*, the flagship news programme on national TV, and in the heavyweight press (the conference on 31 March 1990 was reported the next day, when it was dubbed by some 'an April Fool's joke by the KGB'). The Liberal-Democrats' first press conference was in Moscow's best CPSU hotel, The October; the party platform was printed by Red Proletarian, one of the state publishing houses; fifty thousand copies of a party brochure were run off by another, Politizdat.[116] Within weeks of the party's formation, Zhirinovskii was enjoying apparently unlikely friendly handshakes with the likes of interior minister Boris Pugo, defence minister Dmitrii Yazov, Supreme Soviet chair Anatolii Lukianov and KGB boss Vladimir Kriuchkov,[117] if not with Gorbachev himself.[118] It was also likely that Zhirinovskii was used as a sounding board by elements in the GRU (Soviet Military Intelligence) – hence the prominence of foreign-policy agression in his rhetorical arsenal.

Zhirinovskii's links to Lukianov ensured the party was registered with indecent haste – it was only the second legal party in the Soviet Union after the CPSU. In August 1992 the newly 'democratic' authorities not surprisingly annulled the decision, as most of the party's declared membership consisted of the population of a single village in Abkhazia that Zhirinovskii had once visited. Most 'delegates' to the party's founding conference were handed their membership cards in the lobby. Zhirinovskii's running mate in the 1991 Russian presidential election, when he came third with 6.2 million votes, was the millionaire 'businessman' Andrei Zavidiia, who received three million roubles for the campaign in interest-free loans from the administrative bureau of the CPSU Central Committee. Zavidiia fronted the company Galand, a CPSU spin-off with some 180,000 employees.[119] 'Many of the LDP's political documents were drafted by two staff members at the Central Committee's Institute for Social Studies.'[120] Others were ghosted by Andrei Zagorodnikov, a Moscow lecturer in Marxism-Leninism.[121] In October 1990, a section of Zhirinovskii's rank and file (the members who actually existed) finally rebelled against 'political cooperation with the CPSU and pseudo-centrist puppet groups', and tried to expel him, citing his KGB past and 'pro-Communist activity'.[122] This internal opposition, led by Vladimir Bogachev, was soon quashed with outside help.

Zhirinovskii's usefulness to the authorities was also demonstrated by his role in Russia's groundbreaking presidential election in June 1991. Yeltsin's main opponent was former Soviet prime minister Nikolai Ryzhkov.

> Yeltsin's campaign team believed that all [the other] candidates were being supported by the Soviet regime in order to appeal to different parts of Yeltsin's electorate. Zhirinovskii was chosen to pull populist voters away from Yeltsin. [Aman-Geldy] Tuleiev [Party boss in Kemerovo oblast, Siberia, half-Kazakh and half-Tatar] was to deliver the ethnic vote, [General] Makashov the military vote, and [Vadim] Bakatin the 'reformist' vote within the CPSU,[123]

hopefully forcing Yeltsin into a second round. (Albert Makashov would later lead some of the White House 'insurgents' in 1993.) Arguably, this part of the plan was successful. It was certainly of a kind with other 'active measures' used against Yeltsin after his dramatic fall from grace in 1987, when he was sacked from the Politburo, and the KGB fed the press stories of his drunken and loutish behaviour in America.[124] In the final election Zhirinovskii won 7.8 per cent, Tuleiev 6.8 per cent, Makashov 3.7 per cent and Bakatin 3.4 per cent. It was Ryzhkov who did poorly. As the main establishment candidate, he needed to poll significantly more than 16.9 per cent if Yeltsin was to be kept below 50 per cent. In the event Yeltsin triumphed with 57.3 per cent.[125]

Staging Salvation

Once a fake opposition had been established, party conservatives toyed with the idea of actually inviting it to govern with the CPSU. The plans were stillborn, but, in the words of Michael Urban, the scheme closely resembled the 'standard Soviet scenario' for 'low-intensity' East European coups.[126] The debate about whether the ill-fated coup by Communist hard-liners of August 1991 was 'real' or not should be seen in this context. There were signs that, had the 'Emergency Committee' that sought to replace Gorbachev lasted longer than three days, its leaders were already hoping to manipulate and coopt the opposition in a similar fashion. In order to sell themselves to Western governments, they would have to have presented some kind of media-friendly story about opposition elements coming on board.

The main vehicle for the earlier 'virtual coalition' project was the so-called Centrist Bloc set up in June 1990, a compendium of the various types of virtual opposition in which Zhirinovskii also played his part. According to John Dunlop,

'A close examination of the activities of the Bloc suggest that it is not an alliance of authentic political parties and social organizations but a carefully conceived and orchestrated operation enjoying the support of conservative elements in the CPSU, the KGB and the armed forces.'[127] Early 'confidential gatherings behind closed doors [took place] at one of the Central Committee's residences in the Moscow suburban village of Arkhangelskoie'.[128] The Centrist Bloc's existence was announced by the Soviet Peace Committee. It claimed to be negotiating a way forward between left and right, but its political roots and members were all obscure. Many of its leaders had KGB connections, and it was soon promoted over real opposition groups such as the Inter-Regional Group and Democratic Russia as the authorities' main interlocutor, primed to advocate a Soviet nationalist programme (authoritarian rule, the abolition of the Union Republics) covertly authored by conservatives in the CPSU. Large parts of the December 1990 'manifesto' of the Centrist Bloc overlapped with that of the August 1991 putschists. In September–October 1990 Lukianov openly invited the Bloc to help form a 'government of national unity', and openly indulged the fantasy of a 'coalition government of national accord' between it and the CPSU.[129] Zhirinovskii's seemingly impartial suggestion that 'the confrontation between [Yeltsin's] Russia and the Centre [in other words the Kremlin] will end in civil war in the USSR'[130] actually concealed a solution that was decidedly to the Kremlin's benefit. The bloc's contribution to the debate on the proposed privatisation programme came in a form already prepared for it by the CPSU *apparat*: suspension of party politics during the 'economic transition', suspension of troublesome parliaments in the republics, even the creation of a Committee of National Salvation. In other words, the Centrist Bloc was a classic 'cut-out'. 'It floated proposals that the CPSU wished to put forward, so that the CPSU could then respond positively, as scripted, to these supposedly "democratic initiatives".'[131] Unfortunately, this charade substituted itself for real 'round-table' negotiations that might have launched a more stable transition, and distorted the possibilities for later 'normal' politics.

Zhirinovskii's Liberal Democrats were one part of the cocktail. Then there were blatant appropriations – parties designed to sound like others and steal their thunder: the Democratic Party, the Russian Democratic Party (neither of which had anything to do with Travkin's Democratic Party of Russia), the mysterious Blue Movement, the Andrei Sakharov Union of Democratic Forces led by Vladimir Voronin (who had spent three years in prison in 1976 to 1979 for 'currency violations'), which had nothing to do with the late dissident and which was roundly denounced by his widow, Elena Bonner. Then there was the All-Russian Popular Front led by Valerii Skurlatov, a radical nationalist in the 1960s (who wrote the nationalist, neo-pagan *Book of Vlas* and the *Code of Morals* – a call for 'moral purification' – prepared for the Moscow Komsomol) rumoured to have turned *agent provocateur*, [132] who played another classic role as opposition scarecrow. His *Action Programme-90* was rumoured to have been authored by the KGB – they certainly used it as evidence to argue that 'legitimate' political opposition was going off the rails.

Soon there was also the Union group in the Soviet parliament (which controlled almost a quarter of the seats in December 1990), and its equivalent faction Rossiia in the Russian Soviet – which would, of course, have had nothing to do with the radical opposition if the Centrist bloc had been a real alliance of like-minded people (leading members such as Sergei Baburin enjoyed chequered subsequent careers, but always as Kremlin loyalists).[133] Yakovlev would later admit that the Union was largely 'a creature of the Central Committee'[134] and of the Supreme Soviet chair, Lukianov, who ran his own virtual empire, backing groups such as the leftist CPSU faction Unity, the Interfronts in the Baltic republics, Moldova and Ukraine and Intersoiuz in Uzbekistan, and discreetly supporting Zhirinovskii's Liberal-Democrats.[135]

The Centrist bloc disappeared as quickly as it had arrived when Gorbachev changed tactics again in spring 1991. Nevertheless, there were reports that Zhirinovskii planned to reprise his role as a so-called 'third force' 'against' Gorbachev and (with rather more force) the democratic opposition in the presidential election planned for 1992.

The two tactics – the use of divide-and-rule ploys against potentially serious oppositions and the promotion of virtual ones – overlapped whenever splinter groups seemed capable of developing a life of their own. According to Julia Wishnevsky, this created an ideal middle way for 'the Gorbachev leadership [which] prefers to promote groups that lose elections rather than those that win them', giving airtime to fringe groups and promoting various false competitors.[136] And not without success. None of the parties founded in the early 1990s developed any real staying power – apart from Zhirinovskii's Liberal-Democrats, that is.

A Virtual Coup?

Two other types of 'salvation project' were tried out in the last days of the USSR. The violence that flared in Lithuania and Latvia in January 1991 was preceded by the appearance of so-called National Salvation Committees in the three Baltic republics and, in Lithuania, the previously unknown Lithuanian Congress of Democratic Forces. Their purpose was allegedly to obscure the planned crackdown by allowing Gorbachev to appear as the imposer of just order by banning the committees, the congress and the local parliaments,[137] instead of Moscow acting more 'unilaterally' against the three genuine representative assemblies. Lithuanian premier Kazimira Prunskiene first resigned in a seeming attempt to gift the Salvation Committee a political vacuum, before making a rash bid to return to power – she was later widely pilloried as a KGB agent. With Kriuchkov and Lukianov's all-Union Centrist bloc unsurprisingly backing its Baltic counterparts, Gorbachev may have flirted with one of several active measures, but failed to back any to the hilt. Or the scenario may have been prepared behind his back by hardliners such as Bolokov. Gorbachev's chief of staff, Valerii Boldin, supplied the standard fake literature of 'appeals' to 'restore order' that crowded the desks of both Gorbachev and Lukianov.[138] In any case, the idea that such an obvious reprise of the tactics used to undermine Baltic independence in 1940 would not prove politically fatal was astonishingly naïve.

The attempted Moscow coup in August 1991 had many of the same undertones.[139] The mythology retrospectively established of an illegitimate junta locking horns with a brave and intransigent public opposition certainly does not cover the range of scenarios being considered by the key actors. One possibility that fits with patterns already described is a scarecrow project. After his disastrous rebuff at the London G7 summit in July 1991, Gorbachev may have been privately complicit in fanning the possibility of acquiescing in or even himself launching a controllable mini-coup. In appearance this would be threatening enough to revivify his career as national saviour and to force relieved Western governments to reconsider financial assistance.[140] Hence his misguided assumption that he could return to the helm of the Communist Party afterwards – or relaunch the project to split it in two. Certainly, there remain many implausibilities in Gorbachev's account of his incarceration in Crimea. The frequency and duration of his meetings with the coup plotters in Foros (on the 18th and 21st) and beforehand gave him more than enough time to deliver a simple 'no' to any overtures they made. One respected account states that 'preparations for introducing a state of emergency had been going on since March 1991, with the sanction of the general secretary' (Gorbachev).[141] Another claims that Gorbachev was in regular contact with the authors (Gennadii Ziuganov and Aleksandr Prokhanov) of the notorious conservative call to arms, the manifesto 'A Word to the People', published in *Sovetskaia Rossiia* in July 1991, as a way of testing the waters.[142]

A second possible explanation, that it was a cooptation project, would instead ask some difficult questions of Yeltsin. There is no direct evidence for such a theory, save the mystery of at least three occasions when Yeltsin could easily have been arrested before making his way to the Moscow White House on the first day of the coup, and the ease with which he kept his lines of communication open thereafter. KGB head Kriuchkov had helped plan the Polish coup in 1981 with much greater efficiency. It is often overlooked that the coup's main initiators, Kriuchkov, Central Committee Secretariat head Oleg Shenin and Oleg Baklanov as the representative of the military-industrial complex, were relatively mainstream figures. Others such as vice-president Gennadii Yanaev (whose shaking hands at the Monday press conference became one of the coup's key images) and interior minister Boris Pugo were brought on board relatively late in the planning process. The reactionary right was not as prominent in support of the coup as it might have been. Its street-fighting wing was never unleashed. Kriuchkov and Lukianov seem to have gambled that their project would quickly acquire legitimacy and not require the use of excessive force. In which case, who better to coopt than Yeltsin, who had been under Kriuchkov's surveillance ('*pod kolpakom*') since at least 1989?[143] What better empire-saving strategy could there have been? Yeltsin had already changed tactics in spring 1991, building bridges with conservatives rather than attempting to assault the regime head-on – and for rather different reasons he also did not want the Union Treaty to be signed. And Yeltsin surprised many of his supporters, both old and new, after August by using his power base in the Russian Federation as a battering ram to destroy Union institutions rather than seeking to replace Gorbachev as Soviet president.[144] Both sides had therefore been dancing round each other for some months, although neither properly knew the other's mind. According to Roy Medvedev, 'the leaders of the GKChP [the junta] planned to organise some kind of meeting with Yeltsin in the course of 19 August to try and find some mutually acceptable compromise',[145] but events overwhelmed them. Yeltsin may well have been forewarned, and then discovered a more dramatic role for himself – or, of course, made promises he had no intention of keeping.

Speculation remains problematic, however. The junta's fundamental difficulty was that neither its motives nor intentions were ever clear, its *casi belli* too numerous – and its uncertainty was fatally conveyed to those supposed to execute its orders. The plotters no doubt sounded out many possibilities with different players, but whatever their original private intentions, things obviously did not turn out as expected. August 1991 was hardly a triumph of the political manipulator's art.

Politics beyond Moscow: Ukraine

In the republics, the tardy advent of even limited media freedom makes it difficult to uncover many of the machinations of the late Soviet period. In Ukraine, moreover, the republic's KGB documents began to head north around 1990. Mykola Holushko, local KGB chief from 1987 to 1991, took many files with him when he moved back to Moscow as first deputy head of the new Russian Security Service. (Yeltsin would later award him a medal for his role in the events of October 1993.) Then there was a veritable orgy of destruction immediately after the August 1991 coup, when parliament failed to pass a measure forbidding the shredding of documents. Nevertheless, Holushko's secret letter to the CPU (Communist Party of Ukraine) Central Committee setting out his plans for 'different variations of demol-ition work in democratic organisations' and different ways to foment hostility between the leading opposition figure Viacheslav Chornovil and other former dissidents gives a fairly good idea of what was going on.[146] In his memoirs, Leonid Kravchuk, the future Ukrainian president and then chair of parliament, rather implausibly claims that in 1990 he rejected Holushko's offer of *kompromat* on the new opposition and 'former informers'. He does accept, however, that the offer was made, and expresses no surprise that there was so much material on 'individuals who conducted themselves, to put it mildly, not very politely during plenary sessions'.[147]

In Ukraine, however, the 'era of stagnation' lasted until the resignation of local party boss and Brezhnev crony Volodymyr Shcherbytskyi in September 1989. There was therefore very little lead-in before the country was catapulted into the new politics in 1990–91. As was traditional in the 1970s, the tactics adopted by the local KGB and Party Central Committee were open and crude to a degree that would have been unacceptable in Moscow. Divide-and-rule tactics and active measures to discredit the opposition scored some successes, while attempts to set up fake oppositions and support groups often fell at the first hurdle.

The Ukrainian Communists' main opponent was the 'national-democratic' popular front, popularly known as Rukh ('Movement'), set up in the same month as Shcherbytskyi's resignation in September 1989. A string of fake Rukhs, and clones of other organisations such as Memorial, were established, especially in east and south Ukraine (Kharkiv, Odessa).[148] There was an abortive attempt to set up a rival, national Rukh of the Peoples of Ukraine for Perestroika in March 1990, but the most likely candidate for leader, the writer and former Gorbachev aide, Borys Oliinyk, backed away. Twice in 1989 more radical measures were prepared. Had Gorbachev given them the green light, in February fake workers' appeals would have led to a ban on the 'unconstitutional' movement (Ideology Secretary Yurii Yelchenko and his then deputy Leonid Kravchuk even listed the factories they had in mind), while in September 1989 Rukh's first congress would have been fatally disrupted by planted 'worker' and 'enterprise' delegates. This last idea was abandoned, but the party did go ahead with faking a rival assembly in Kiev's main sports stadium. Ukrainian Politburo minutes record that 'every city district' was required to supply a quota of '7,000 to 12,000' activists on a 'forced-voluntary basis'.[149] Kravchuk provided material assistance with the aim of setting up a 'good' Rukh under the control of the party and 'his men', who included many of the organisers of the first congress.[150] Many loyal Communists were kept out of Rukh, on the other hand.

The CPU's strategy was to create its own version of reality and then promote it as the only truth in the official media. Rukh was, however, well aware of many of the more obvious traps that were laid, and often out-manoeuvred the Party Central Committee. The attempt to foist an extremist image on Rukh involved the printing of hundreds of thousands of fake leaflets, including some calling for 'pogroms', which were distributed through the official Siouzpechat kiosk network. Yelchenko and others attempted to enlist leaders of national minorities against Rukh by setting up a series of leftist and/or 'regional' projects in Crimea and the Russian-speaking areas of south-east Ukraine, none of which ever really took off.[151] Rukh leader Ivan Drach could sarcastically afford to compliment the 'excellently rehearsed and executed demonstration' of 'protestors' from south Ukraine bused in to Kiev in November 1990.[152] Motivating Ukraine's Russophone or 'Soviet' population was difficult. The local working class saw no particular need to mobilise in support of the Union of Workers of Ukraine for Socialist Perestroika, which was launched with an official fanfare in party newspapers in December 1990 – after all, this was what the Communist Party was already supposed to stand for. Furthermore, unlike titular nationalist movements in the Baltic republics or Moldova, Rukh never seemed likely to win power on its own and its advance apparently stalled in the winter of 1990–91.

Despite its 'two million' claimed members, when the Union of Workers' founding documents were reported in the press there was no mention of where and when they had been adopted.[153] The Union announced itself with a fake appeal from 'simple workers' from the Ukrainian Potato Factory. 'The character, style and argumentation of the document clearly indicated that this was an *apparat* attempt to create an organisation on the model of the [anti-nationalist] 'Interfronts' or OFT (United Workers' Front).'[154] Attempts by conservative Communists to support the spring 1991 miners' strikes in the hope they would oust Gorbachev and the fake groups set up to call for 'order' in west Ukraine in the winter of 1990–91 were similarly ineffectual. Nevertheless, much of the Communists' counter-propaganda was passively accepted in south and east Ukraine, where Rukh's attempts to expand its appeal largely floundered in 1991.

Trouble was organised within other political parties, too. Dissension was sown in the Democratic Party (the main party of the intelligentsia), and between the Democratic Party and Rukh.[155] The Ukrainian Republican Party (URP), set up by former political prisoners as the formal successor of the Ukrainian Helsinki Group/Union of the 1970s (UHU), was the CPU's longest-standing rival and therefore developed more problems than most. Internal URP rows in 1991 revealed that the leadership felt they were being attacked from within. The former dissident Oles Shevchenko accused a radical named Roman Koval: 'This is a simple KGB provocation aimed at splitting the core of the UHU. My supposition is that you, Mr Koval, are carrying out the tasks of the KGB.'[156] Another veteran, Oles Serhiienko, complained that internal splits 'are KGB work'; Shevchenko was accused in turn of 'collaborationism' and demanded 'apologies for slander'.[157] In other meetings, the leadership traded insults ('insignificant (*vypadkova*) person', 'a hooligan – in the presence of women it is indecent to talk about him') and argued over whether they should address each other in the second person singular.[158] The party therefore copied the Bolshevik practice of imposing a preliminary 'candidate stage' for membership, 'with the aim of not allowing Chekist agents into the ranks of the URP'. Although party leader Levko Lukianenko later called for a relaxation of this procedure – 'any agent will expose himself sooner or later and will be easy to get rid of' – he was always complaining about the faux-radicals in the party and attempting to curbs their links with the far right.[159]

The Khmara affair was a classic example of active measures. At the height of the conservative reaction in November 1990, the former dissident and leading URP politician Stepan Khmara was approached by a woman in Kiev's main underpass who claimed to have been attacked. Khmara was then shown on state TV 'assaulting' the suspect, who turned out to be a police colonel. Parliament made a great show of stripping the radical deputy of his immunity, leading to his arrest on the premises. This *dramaturgiia* undoubtedly had its intended effect of diverting and dividing the opposition. Khmara was unpopular with many, including members of his own party who were not particularly enthusiastic about campaigning for his release. Trouble in the URP was kept bubbling under the surface throughout 1991. Khmara was let out just in time to make mischief at the party's second congress in June. Although a formal split was delayed until the summer of 1992, the URP already contained 'two parties' and the authorities' strategy was to play up the Khmara rather than the Lukianenko line, and then demonise it. According to the writer Volodymyr Ruban:

'The real victor can be considered the Communist Party of Ukraine. The second congress of the URP [1992] demonstrated that a party capable of reaching a level with the CPU wouldn't be appearing in the republic any time soon.'[160] The Republican Party of Ukraine, which had been set up to rival the URP, could therefore safely be left to wither on the vine.

The local KGB was also extremely active among the parties of the far right, where it encountered the nationalists' émigré sponsors. In particular it targeted the young ultra-radicals of the Ukrainian Nationalist Union, who in 1991 would set up the paramilitary UNA-UNSO (see pages 215–17). The once-powerful student movement was split from within after it organised hunger strikes against the authorities in October 1990.[161] Many in Ukraine's downright weird 'neo-pagan' movement, such as the Ukrainian Spiritual Republic, were also accused of acting to discredit the opposition as a whole.

Conclusions

It is not the purpose of this book to argue that all apparent public politics in the late Soviet period served simply to mask the manipulations of the omnipotent 'authorities'. Many commentators, such as Archie Brown, have seen the brief period between 1988 and 1991 as a relative golden age of pluralism. There may be some truth in this view. Nevertheless, many elements in the ruling regime fought long and hard to keep the role of real politics to a minimum. They faced a formidable task. At its peak, Democratic Russia could put a hundred thousand people on the streets of Moscow, as in the case of the demonstration of 28 March 1991 that temporarily thwarted the hardliners. Mark Beissinger has documented the thousands of cases of 'nationalist mobilisation' throughout the USSR in 1987–91.[162] Nevertheless, the authorities were able to prevent themselves being drowned in a real popular revolution, and the story of politics since the late 1980s can plausibly be told in terms of the attempt to reassert 'control'.

Neither is the history of political manipulation the entire history of Russian politics. It undoubtedly has a long pedigree, however. Some might trace it as far back as Boris Godunov's well-orchestrated manipulation of popular support for his summons to the throne in 1606, including the thousands bribed and intimidated to demonstrate in his name outside the Novodevichii monastery.[163] Examples of genuine public pluralism have been few and far between. Nevertheless, a political counterpoint has nearly always existed. Countries are not trapped by their history: Russia's tragedy since 1991 has been that alternative native or imported models have failed to take hold.

2 Politics as Virtuality in the Post–Soviet World

> By his very nature every politician is just a television broadcast . . . Names of goods and politicians do not indicate actual commercial products; they refer only to projections of elements of the politico-commercial informational field that have been forcibly induced as perceptual objects of the individual mind.
>
> Viktor Pelevin, *Generation 'P'* (1999)[1]

> On the screen of our cathode ray tube we could contemplate a Canada Dry reality: It was like reality, it was the same colour as reality, but it wasn't reality. The Greek *logos* had been replaced by logos projected on to the damp walls of our grotto.
>
> Frédéric Beigbeder, *99 francs* (2000)[2]

Why 'virtual politics'? Many of the active measures developed in the Soviet and even tsarist eras have been redesigned for contemporary use, with the main new design imperative being the post-Soviet media environment so elegantly satirised in Pelevin's novel (Generation 'P' is the last Soviet generation, the generation that chose Pepsi). More obvious dirty tricks can now be combined with the manipulation possibilities of modern media technology. Many of the latter were already apparent in the late Soviet era, most obviously with the launch of the Zhirinovskii project. Pelevin, however, depicts a world where all the main political actors (Yeltsin, Ziuganov, Chernomyrdin) are literally the creation of back-room design consultants and digital experts, only 'a cloud of points in space'. A special service, 'The People's Will', made up of ex-KGB members, therefore has only one function: 'to go around telling people they've just seen our leaders'.[3] Sometimes, post-Soviet politics does indeed exist only on TV: not in the modern American sense of personality-driven life-drama politics or the endless campaigning on TV for funds to support the next round of campaigning on TV, though. Post-Soviet politics forms a different kind of solipsistic universe. 'Parties' and 'politicians' are launched as TV 'projects', which have no other, more real reality. Some are totally fake. Even parties and politicians who have to return to the real world from the TV studio have a double life as virtual objects that have little or no relation to their real selves. 'Virtual politics' therefore seems an appropriate metaphor for the politics of the post-Soviet era.

Media Reality

In the modern – supposedly postmodern West – 'virtuality' has a double meaning. Players of computer games or purchasers of expensive virtual-reality equipment are said to be experiencing neither reality nor unreality but virtuality. The virtual world, the computer world, the world of the invented sign or image, the semiotics of capitalism (i.e., advertising), is deemed sufficient unto itself, and does not have to be tested against any other 'reality'. At the same time, on a more popular level, 'virtual' has become a synonym for the ersatz, the unreal real, the not really real. Virtual reality in this sense (the dictionary definition of the other meanings of 'virtual') is almost reality, not quite reality, something short of reality.

Philosophers stick to the first interpretation. In the solipsistic West, mediated reality (virtuality) is held to be its own reality. Once the subject is within this world, it is the only reality. It does not need to be, and indeed cannot be, measured against anything else. According to Umberto Eco, 'the copy substitutes itself for the real, becomes more real than the real itself'.[4] It does not relate to reality, it becomes it. The apostles of postmodernism have therefore competed with Nietzsche's announcement of the death of God with an expanded obituary list: the death of the subject (Jean Baudrillard), the death of the author (Roland Barthes), the death of intention and identity, the end of representation (the signifier absorbs its referent, 'the sign aims to be the thing'),[5] even the death of man as the logical subject of life's dramas, the necessary protagonist (Foucault). To Jacques Derrida, there is 'nothing beyond the text'; we live in an Age of Simulation, in mediated or electronic reality, in hyperreality, surrounded by 'the ecstasy of communication' (Baudrillard) in a world of simulacra. Virtuality – or postmodernism in general – is also allegedly responsible for the de-differentiation of realities and spheres, so that the cultural invades the economic, 'low' culture invades 'high' and vice versa; and for the radical 'eclecticisation' of spheres. Everything becomes possible: all manner of styles can be combined and recombined in history, culture, music, fashion and art. 'Reference' and 'citation' become the dominant cultural forms.

Baudrillard famously claimed that the 1991 Gulf War didn't happen. A charitable interpretation of his pronouncement would be that he meant that to most observers there was nothing beyond the TV version of the war. To some rather closer observers and participants, there obviously was, but Western TV consumers were unlikely to be confronted with their reality. Eco's novel *Baudolino* (2000) explores a related idea and goes a stage further: forgery can create its own reality. The eponymous hero is a medieval 'Prince of Falsehood' on a journey to a lost kingdom using a fake travelogue he has written himself. As Baudolino says, 'imagining other worlds, you end up changing this one'. 'All the time that you were inventing, you invented things that were not true, but then became true.'[6] Or, as the Argentinian writer Jorge Luis Borges once wrote: 'The greatest of all sorcerers would be the one who could cast a spell on himself to the degree of taking his own phantasmagoria for autonomous apparitions.'[7]

The key medium is, of course, no longer an individual storyteller or a concocted manuscript. Virtuality is above all life as lived through TV. 'The most important medium of communication is no longer Oldspeak or Newspeak – it is Viewspeak, the telescreen.'[8] Here virtual reality takes on more specific forms. According to Manuel Castells, a 'cool medium' such as TV 'represents an historical rupture with the typographic mind'. If typographic culture 'favours systemic exposition' and the 'ability to think conceptually, deductively and sequentially', TV is 'characterised by its seductiveness, its sensorial simulation of reality, and its easy communicability along the lines of least psychological effort'. On the other hand, TV also draws on earlier forms of oral or theatrical culture. It 'appeals to the associative/lyrical mind'; viewers become more emotionally involved, seeking out and identifying themselves with the forces of goodness (usually the protagonist).[9] Opposition plays its role in the public spectacle, but only unrepresentative radicals appear as a demiurge. The creators of the TV version of virtual reality aim at the subconscious.

Finally, the postmodern era is also the Information Age, in which communication trumps all other forms of technology. Consequently, 'political communication and information are essentially captured in the space of the media. Outside of the media sphere there is only political marginality. What happens in the media-dominated political space is not determined by the media: it is an open social and political process. But the logic, and organisation, of electronic media frame and structure politics.'[10] Castells sensibly warns against

> two simplistic, erroneous versions of the thesis according to which electronic media dominate politics. On the one hand, it is sometimes argued that the media impose their political choices on public opinion. This is not so, because . . . the media are extremely diverse [and] their linkages to politics and ideology are highly complex. . . . On the other hand, public opinion is often considered to be a passive recipient of messages, easily open to manipulation. Again, this is belied by the empirical record. . . . there is a two-way process of interaction between the media and their audience concerning the actual impact of messages, which are twisted, appropriated, and occasionally subverted by the audience.[11]

Both qualifications are true for the former USSR, but less so than elsewhere. The former USSR is where the forgers run wild.

Cultural Preconditions

It can be argued, although I would not seek to press the case too strongly, that beyond the critical legacy of the Soviet era, certain aspects of all-Russian culture have helped to create a unique background for virtual politics. Russians are used to venerating the state, but also to placing it a distance, on a pedestal. They are therefore also used to an indistinct image of power, and to coping with the plasticity or viscosity of power. To adapt the words of the nineteenth-century historian Vasilii Kliuchevskii, 'the state grew fat, the people grew lean' and strange things happened in the space in between. Medieval Russia abounded in tales of false authority and of authority unmasked. Peter the Great created a bizarre parallel world to his own authority, with a mock court, a 'Prince-Pope' and an 'All-Drunken, All-Jesting Assembly'. As the Old Believers (those who rejected the Church reforms of the 1650s) thought of the state as the Antichrist and withdrew from all contact with it, they kept alive popular myths of a purer, more real, Russia in some parallel world: such as the city of Kitezh under the lake of Svetloiar, or the ideal Christian community of Belovode, located somewhere on a Pacific island between Russia and Japan. Medieval Russia also had a peculiar tradition of 'truth-tellers' (*pravedniki*) and 'Holy fools' (*yurodivy*, literally 'Foolish in Christ'), jesters who were more than fools, who were licensed to tell awkward truths – implying that all others around authority could not be trusted to do the same. Russia has therefore often veered between the tyranny of the tsar and the imposture of the *samozvanets* ('self-styled'), with the 'real' ruler depicting his adversaries as emissaries of the devil's kingdom, but with the two swapping places surprisingly often, as, to varying degrees, with Boris Godunov and the False Dmitrii, Nicholas and Rasputin, Gorbachev and Yeltsin and, at least in the initial phase, Putin and Khodorkovskii.[12]

It is no coincidence that Russian literature has always celebrated the bizarre and the alienated, the outsiders and the in-betweens, the outlaws and the conmen. This is in many ways the other side of the coin to the arbitrary and distant nature of the state – and also a good means of dealing with its capricious practices. The nineteenth century saw many versions of the story of the puppet Petrushka as both hero and buffoon. Even amid the revolutionary fervour of the 1920s and early 1930s there were Soviet satirists who preferred to develop this literature of displacement, earning the wrath of the early Soviet censors by depicting the distance of the ordinary citizen from the state (e.g., Mikhail Zoshchenko's 'ventriloquism', Andrei Platonov's somnolent depressives). Il'f and Petrov's picaresque satires celebrated the Russian popular tradition of *samozvantsvo* ('self-promotion'). Their hero, Ostap Bender, was a *velikii kombinator* ('smooth operator'), *plut* ('trickster') or *aferist* ('confidence man'), making his way through the social dislocations of the post-revolutionary era by his ability to 'speak Bolshevik'.[13] In Il'f and Petrov's novel *The Little Golden Calf* (1931), Bender tracks down a post-NEP millionaire, Aleksandr Koreiko, who is quietly running an underground empire codenamed 'Hercules', almost a private state-within-a-state. In real life, the practice of setting up fake government departments, such as the Central Directorate for Extending Technical Aid to the Field of Construction Industry and the All-Union Trust for the Exploitation of Meteoric Metals, was already part of a venerable tradition.[14] Sheila Fitzpatrick and Golfo Alexopoulos have argued that such stories represented the 'flip-side' of Soviet propagandism, based as they were on real-life swindlers such as Nikolai Savin (in the late tsarist era) and Vladimir Gromov (in the 1930s).[15] It is no accident that Bender also poses as a journalist.[16] The popularity of such tales and life stories also reflected the fact that many of those in power behaved like crooks. After the mid-1930s, of course, writers were increasingly forced to leave such dangerously satirical opinions 'in the drawer'.

In Ukrainian culture, imperial authority could be presented as doubly alien. Remote power in St Petersburg was literally *samoderzhavie* – a law only unto itself; to some it was also perceived as nationally 'other'. Ukrainians grew used to thinking of power as something exercised by other people. In Gogol's story 'The Night before Christmas' (1832), external tsarist authority is represented in peculiar, magical, even diabolical form. Imperial Kiev also had more than its fair share of conmen. The city authorities have put up quite a few monuments since 1991, but the two genuinely popular new statues are both of local *aferisty*. One of Il'f and Petrov's conmen, Panikovskii, stands just up from the central department store on the main shopping street Khreshchatyk; he is depicted in the same blind beggar's pose that he uses to fleece passers-by in *The Little Golden Calf*. The second statue is to 'Fillip Petrovich Golokhvastov, man of property" (*sobstvennyi persona*), as he would always introduce himself, the anti-hero of the hugely popular film *Chasing Two Hares* (1961) based on the nineteenth-century drama by Mykhailo Starytskyi (1875). This stature stands opposite a new restaurant of the same name on Kiev's main tourist street, Andriivskii uzviz. Golokhvastov is actually a barber, but presents himself as a dandy in order to win the hand of the daughter whose family, unbeknown to him, are busy making similar efforts to lever themselves up the social scale.

Many modern-day political manipulators see themselves as contemporary versions of Ostap Bender and other celebrated fictional rogues. It gives themselves a more positive self-image, and a greater degree of licence in the public eye. Vladimir Zhirinovskii has endured for so long because many Russians love to see someone putting one over on the elite – as they see it. Significantly, in the late 1990s several of Kiev's 'political technologists' grouped together to call themselves the 'Golokhvastov Club'.

Post-Soviet Postmodernism

Put together Western theories of the postmodern virtual world and local post-Soviet culture, stir in KGB methodology, French philosophy and modern marketing psycho-babble, and you have a heady mix. Some have argued paradoxically that the 'Soviet postmodern' began in the 1930s, after the post-revolutionary love affair with the Modern,[17] the era of Malevich's *Black Square against a White Background* and Konstantin Melnikov's plans for a 537-metre-high concrete Constructivist Palace of the Soviets, capped with a 100-metre-high stature of Lenin. Others have claimed that the Soviet Union was 'anti-modern', at least in its clientelistic political culture. It might also be argued that if the former USSR was guilty of jumbling up so many '-isms', then nothing could be more characteristic of postmodernism.

Local literature at least has embraced postmodernism since 1991, with writers such as Viktor Pelevin, Sergei Gandlevskii and Dmitrii Prigov in Russia,[18] and Yurii Andrukhovych in Ukraine.[19] The theme of political postmodernism has also caught on. According to the Ukrainian commentator Dmytro Vydrin:

The contemporary political style, which I call postmodernism, surprisingly combines signs of classicism and the legacy of the Socialist past. We have a parliament, a president, governors of a sort, local self-rule of a sort, but they are not assembled in their real, democratic environment, but as soviet modern. Our postmodern is a veritable sewer. Parliament is used as a collective manager, as a collective plaintiff and petitioner, but not as a collective legislature. One can say the same about local self-government and about any democratic institution in Ukraine.[20]

Most importantly, so-called political technologists think of themselves as operating in this environment, where, in the famous line from Dostoevsky's *The Brothers Karamazov* (1879–80), if God does not exist, 'everything is permitted'. Post-Bolshevik political operators tend to have few scruples, anyway.

Designer Parties and Avatars

What then is meant by the idea of virtual politics in the post-Soviet world? Russia under Putin increasingly describes itself as a 'managed democracy'. The Russian phrase is actually *upravliaemaia demokratiia*, which is better translated as 'steered' or 'directed democracy'. *Upravlenie* was the term often used for Soviet state agencies, whose 'management' style was not exactly laidback. In Russian a 'manager' is actually more akin to a doorkeeper. 'Directed democracy' involves radical process management, rather than specific management tasks such as damage limitation, limit-setting, or prompting and pointing. Victories, whether in elections, politics in general or in business, are 'organised', as the old Bolshevik phrase had it, rather than simply won. Presidents such as Russia's Vladimir Putin and Ukraine's Leonid Kuchma have an aversion to *any* independent political activity. Almost every significant political force, and some insignificant ones, are subject to political manipulation. 'Outputs' (election results, the composition of the legislature) are, of course, 'managed', but, more fundamentally, so are 'inputs' (the cast of politicians and parties, the main themes of political *dramaturgiia*). The overall 'aim is not only to establish a monopoly of power but also to monopolise competition for it'.[21] The people may elect parties and politicians, but the Kremlin and its equivalents select the winners. In the words of Ukrainian analyst Volodymyr Polokhalo:

> Only the task of primitive falsification remains on election day. Western observers are looking for attributes of, or departures from, normal democratic procedure. But our elections are different. The big falsification is the falsification of the whole electoral process, the falsification of almost all the participants in that process. There are no real political subjects, no real independent political actors. To voters who lack sufficient information, they are not false, they are real; but most parties are only the creation of various donors looking for a suitable façade.[22]

The mid-1990s was the key turning point. The late Gorbachev era had elements of real drama, but many of the most famous players in the drama – 'Mad Vlad'

Zhirinovskii, the black-shirt hooligans of Pamiat – were already not what they seemed. Later, with elites realising the power of post-Soviet TV floating above an amorphous and atomised 'society', politics became more radically virtual in the true postmodern sense. According to Ivan Zassourskii, 'After the last street fights of October 1993, when the Russian parliament was disbanded and a new Constitution ensured the dominance of executive power, the political process moved to the symbolic space of the broadcast media.' States such as Russia are still incapable of reasserting total control. At the 1995 elections, 'the political elite [realised] they could no longer persuade. But, as it turned out, they could still manipulate.'[23] In the words of Gleb Pavlovskii, Russia's most notorious political manipulator, in the early 1990s 'the authorities still had control over all the main instruments of rule – a near-monopoly in fact – but, on the other hand, they couldn't do anything with them. This was the great paradox.' Political technologists understood how to manipulate the media. 'So they would go to Boris Nikolaevich [Yeltsin] and say, "You can't do this, but we can."'[24] And in this vacuum they flourished. The Putin era has brought further radical changes. The recentralisation of state control over TV has made the work of (approved) political technologists easier. But the Kremlin remains the most effective manipulator of democracy itself, and the scope of its ambitions has greatly increased. The crude use of administrative resources (i.e., the more traditional abuses of the electoral process) has become much more obvious (see Chapter 4). However, as this book argues, whatever the radical changes in other areas, the Putin era has only perfected techniques that were already common under Yeltsin, and already common elsewhere in the former USSR. The administrative vertical (the old Soviet term for centralised authority) has been re-created to an extent. Things that the Kremlin 'couldn't do' in 1993 had become possible in 2003. The Kremlin may therefore have since taken back certain functions from the technologists. According to Pavlovskii again (speaking in 2002), 'the market for political technology is now more dispersed'.[25]

To the makers of virtual democracy, of whatever type, politics should only exist as a series of designer projects, rather than as a real pattern of representation and account-ability. Parties and politicians are only avatars, as with the graphical icons that repre-sent users in cyberspace (an avatar was originally a Hindu deity in human form). When one party presented its programme 'Russian Breakthrough' with great fanfare at the 1995 elections, it was subsequently revealed to be nothing more than two sheets of paper containing the new Moscow telephone directory.[26] Local political tech-nologists are particularly skilled at creating media simulacra, but they are also building on a long Russian tradition of puppet politics and active measures to adapt to a new postmodern world of image manipulation and media projection. As Avtandil Tsuladze writes in his book *The Great Manipulative Game*, 'the peculiarity of the Game is that it models a certain conditional reality'; the public 'follow false orientations, which are formed in the course of the Game. These "indicators" direct the captive player towards the values selected by the manipulator.'[27] The manipulators, of course, 'work not with real objects, but with their virtual substitutes'.[28] Their overall aim is the 'Virtualisation of the [political] struggle [which] forces it into the information sphere, where the main role is played by information-communication technology'. Political technologists create virtual parties, which 'exist [on] TV and [in] radio broadcasting, in newspapers, on street billboards and in other outlets of the mass media. In other words, they exist in the public consciousness, manipulate the latter and greatly resemble the "information viruses" that shatter the "operational programmes" of society and block the dialogue mechanisms of the "public intellect".'[29] But they are not real. To quote the computer whiz kids who write the 'legendas' for Russian politicians in Pelevin's novel, post-Soviet politics is like the film *Starship Troopers*, 'where the starship troopers fight the bugs':

> It's the same thing. Only instead of the troopers we have farmers or small businessmen, instead of the automatics we have bread and salt, and instead of the bug we have [Communist leader] Ziuganov or [General] Lebed [Russia's 'Saviour' in 1996]. Then we match them up, paste in the Cathedral of Christ the Saviour or the Baikonur launch-pad in the background, copy it to Betacam and put it out on air.[30]

Many politicians in the post-Soviet world act as 'Vietnamese cosmonauts', who, as the old, racist Soviet joke had it, were not allowed to touch the controls, which were safely manipulated by the controllers on the ground. Potential democracy is therefore radically disorganised. 'Because political parties exist only as projects, society is deprived of a real chance of bringing politicians to account. Every election brings new figures, new faces. How can they possibly judge?'[31] In one Western view:

> The party system emerging in Russia is not based on an Anglo-American model of party accountability. Instead, it resembles the late nineteenth century Italian system of *trasformismo*, in which patronage-led political coalitions are formed without regard to accountability to the electorate. The labels that politicians use to describe themselves are taken up or discarded as opportunities arise for enrichment and access to power.[32]

Another has put it rather more bluntly: Russian political parties are defined not by a common ideology, but by a 'common source of income'.[33] Ukraine's 2001 law on political parties included a quaint clause to the effect that parties were required to 'have a programme'.

Richard Anderson has argued that transitions to democracy become possible when 'contestants for power, whether insiders or external challengers, begin to perceive the population as a political resource and move discourse further towards ordinary language'.[34] In the Soviet case, this would have meant abandoning the 'wooden language' of Central Committee-speak and adopting the ordinary vernacular, encouraging subjects to think of themselves and their rulers as citizens engaged in a common project. If ever there was a brief moment when this seemed to be the case, it is now long gone. It goes without saying that the post-Soviet world of deceit has moved back into obfuscation. The new virtual politics may ape common language, but it is a language dedicated to deception.

Maintaining Virtuality

How is such an edifice kept standing? There are four key conditions for the practice of virtual politics in the post-Soviet space: a powerful but amoral elite; a passive electorate; a culture of information control; and the lack of an external counterpoint, i.e., foreign intervention.[35] Each on its own is only part of the picture; together they are mutually reinforcing. Just as Borges regarded it as disturbing but logical 'that the man who ordered the erection of the almost infinite wall of China was that first Emperor, Shih Huang Ti, who also decreed that all books prior to him be burned', and 'that these two vast operations – the five to six hundred leagues of stone opposing the barbarians, the rigorous abolition of history, that is, of the past – should originate in one person'.[36]

Elites Are the Only Key Players

Nikkolo-M may use the image of Machiavelli on its business cards, but Machiavelli dispensed his advice directly to would-be princes. Political technologists have added an extra layer. They see themselves as puppet-masters, scene-setters, political programmers. The elite that employs them, on the other hand, is seemingly inert; or, more exactly, totally de-ideologised, 'relatively uninterested in governing', preferring to concentrate on the 'exchange of unaccountable power for untaxable wealth' and therefore keen to pass on the manipulators' role.[37] Post-Soviet elites have a strong aversion to political initiative, let alone self-sacrifice, and are used to politics as cue-and-clue – they will nearly always wait to act until they get the right signal from the top. Bureaucratic culture survives and even thrives in the new culture of virtual signalling. Moreover, writing specifically about Slovakia, Shari Cohen has put forward the idea of the post-Communist victory of a 'mass-elite', a 'historyless elite' with no ties to its own past except its traditional disdain for the masses from which it may itself have sprung. The notion can easily be applied to many of the states of the former USSR, including Russia in part.[38] Even many politicians are no longer interested in politics – and certainly not in history. So they buy in political, electoral and even humanitarian 'technology'. Russian political technologists like to talk of the *deputat-stabil*; not, of course, stable in the sense of maintaining ideological convictions, but stable in his or her demand for their PR services, requiring reinvention at every election.

Post-Soviet societies suffer from the legacy of both the super-ideologised Stalinist period and its almost complete opposite under Brezhnev. The standard tactics of post-Soviet elites – never set up a real regime party, coopt or neutralise the opposition – have further lessened the importance of real ideology, but the instrumental Soviet view of ideology as a top-down mobilisation instrument *and* as a public *dramaturgiia* survives. As does Bolshevik political culture. Elites are used to fighting dirty: as the Ukrainian phrase has it, *Abo pan, abo propav* ('Either lord and master, or lost'). There are no partners in politics, only opponents. Concessions are a means of demobilising an opponent until outright victory becomes possible. Opponents who compromise are only showing their weakness. Never trust anyone you can't control. There is therefore a permanent war for spheres of influence, leading to a constant turnover of new projects. In this sense, the instinct for political manipulation has much deeper roots than the short-term requirement of 'market Bolshevism' to emasculate democracy.[39]

The elite is also small and not that popular. 'New Capital', the socio-economic basis of most post-Soviet regimes, directly commands less than 10 per cent of the vote. Elites would lose if they didn't cheat. The original market zealots thought that political economy would dictate all in ten years, and that they could create a world safe for property if their reforms succeeded in growing their support base quickly enough. Instead political technologists have created a post-Soviet Hydra that now seems so strong that periodic sallies against it − elections, reform governments such as Viktor Yushchenko's in Ukraine (1999–2001) − may do relatively little to change the system.

There is also the elite belief that the concept of *dvoevlastie* (dual power) is oxymoronic. There can be only one *vlast* (power). When applied to the events of 1917, for example, *dvoevlastie* describes the allegedly unstable and irreconcilable competition between the Provisional Government and the Soviets. For many Russians, therefore − certainly not all, but for statist elites and their conservative constituency − 'multipartyism is often interpreted basically as a synonym for *smuta* ' (chaos), the term for the war between the *boyar* (noble) factions that took Russia to the brink of state collapse during the 'Time of Troubles' in 1604–13.[40] There are only 'superparties'. *Vlast* stands above the (always partial) parties.

Selling to the Swamp

Virtual politics is created by supply rather than demand, although the highly amorphous nature of most types of post-Soviet 'society' gives elites the freedom to 'graze' on designated support groups where necessary as autonomous actors. Obvious factors to emphasise are widespread and deep-rooted popular cynicism and ideophobia, and the extreme weakness of civil society or any other counterpoint to elite rule, indeed any real stable social constituencies at all. Economic 'reform' led to the impoverishment and near-complete disappearance of the old Soviet middle class; the limited growth in GDP achieved since 1998 has yet to create a new propertied consumerist class in its stead. National as well as social identities are often amorphous. In Ukraine there is a 'conscious Ukrainian' minority and an even smaller minority of 'conscious Russians', and a large mixed-identity 'swamp' in between. The current elite has a vested interest in maintaining this situation, minimising the basis for any challenge to its rule and playing the extremes against one another.[41] Russia's sense of itself (Russian or Soviet? State, empire or nation?) has been turned upside down several times over the last two decades. In Belarus almost the entire population shares an embryonic and vague 'Slavic-Soviet' version of Belarusian identity. Such populations lack clear identity markers or the confidence of a stable traditional cognitive environment, and are supposedly easy prey for the manipulative tactics of the political technologists.

On various estimates, the so-called *boloto* ('swamp') makes up between a fifth and a half of the electorate. It may also be growing. Disillusioned voters sell their support lightly and cheaply, without too much thought, and are easily attracted to PR ephemera. That said, it has been argued that 'the *boloto* also has a complicated structure . . . the biggest part are the most intelligent people. They understand that a candidate seeks power to set up his own life, not out of concern for the people.'[42] Cynical individual electors, however, face a classic collective-action dilemma: either settling for whatever selective benefits they can obtain at election time or combining to campaign for the public good of a fairer system. Weak collective identities make the latter course difficult. As such, it may be individually rational in this limited sense to welcome a particular party or oligarch's largesse, but few benefit ultimately from bidding wars that provide little more than baubles, such as free beer on election day or sports goods for a local school.

Ignorance Is Strength
Control of the mass media is, of course, key to control of the virtual world. Far from abandoning the idea of mass media as propaganda, the states of the former USSR have merely reshaped it to serve the new structure of interests.[43] In retrospect, it is the era of relative media freedom between around 1989 and 1996 that now seems the exception, a golden age of sorts – although it hardly seemed like it at the time. According to Gleb Pavlovskii, 'Russia's first privatisation had nothing to do with [Anatolii] Chubais [the architect of 'shock therapy']. It was the press and TV. Journalists freed themselves from state control but still enjoyed state subsidy.'[44] Journalists were harder to manipulate – though the task was far from impossible.

But the golden age could not last. First the oligarchs and then the state moved in. By the late 1990s the main element of pluralism left in the system was that each 'holding' in the media-political system pushed a slightly different virtual reality as 'branding' cover for the pursuit of its own interests: Vladimir Gusinskii residual liberalism, Yurii Luzhkov Slavic Orthodoxy. Under Putin a more unified message of Kremlin nationalism has been established. Significantly, the biggest challenges to the established order have involved a challenge to this media monopoly. It was no surprise that the first oligarchs to go when Putin came to power were the critical media moguls Gusinskii and Berezovskii. Former prime ministers Pavlo Lazarenko (Ukraine) and Akezhan Kazhegeldin (Kazakhstan) were both powerful challengers to the established order, but it was clear they had failed when they lost in their attempts to set up rival media empires; in Lazarenko's case *Pravda Ukrainy* ('Truth of Ukraine'),[45] Kiev News and All-Ukrainian News, in Kazhegeldin's KTK ('Commercial Television Channel').

According to Marat Gelman, 'Some say there was freedom of speech under

Yeltsin, but not under Putin. But Yeltsin wanted to put the press more under his control than it was. He just didn't have a mandate from the population . . . now [2004] they have. They can do anything.'[46] The golden age was already ending before Yeltsin left the stage, and media recentralisation was already beginning. In July 1999 Russia set up a super-ministry (the 'ministry of truth') of press, TV, radio and other means of mass communication under Mikhail Lesin. Putin's top priority was to expand the Kremlin's control of the media, TV in particular. RTR or Russia (the second channel) was already state-controlled; Berezovskii was forced out of the 'first channel' ORT (then 49 per cent private), and his channel TV6 simply closed in 2002; Gazprom was used to squeeze Gusinskii out of NTV. TVTs was loyal to Moscow mayor, Luzhkov.

The only real national channel in Belarus, BT, has always been state-owned. Until 2002, when the authorities began to replace them with hybrid entities broadcasting news produced in Minsk, its only serious competitors were ORT and RTR. The Ukrainian authorities tightened their grip after the re-election of Kuchma in 1999. After losing control briefly with the eruption of the Gongadze scandal in 2000, they sought to reimpose it with the appointment of Serhii Vasyliev as head of the president's Department of Information Policy in 2002. Control over the main channels was exercised through two interlocking empires. Viktor Medvedchuk, the head of the presidential administration, and his Social-Democratic Party (the Kiev business elite) ran the three biggest channels: UT-1, Inter and 1+1. The rival Dnipropetrovsk group, headed by leading oligarch Viktor Pinchuk, controlled the next three largest, STV, New Channel and ICTV, plus his colleague Andrii Derkach's Era channel. Only one, Channel 5, which was run by businessman Petro Poroshenko, was in any sense independent. But Ukrainian TV is notoriously dull – or at least its news and information programmes are. Marat Gelman of ORT, an adviser to Ukrainian TV, has expressed the information technologists' biggest fear: that too few Ukrainians are reached by the local media, and its propaganda passes unnoticed.[47]

Voters themselves are aware of the manipulation and of how it is achieved. After the 1999 elections, a huge majority (97 per cent) of Russian voters claimed to have experienced no direct pressure on their vote. On the other hand, 40 per cent said that the coverage of politics in the mass media was unfair, and 29 per cent thought the administration and/or counting of votes was unfair.[48] In a December 2003 survey by the Foundation for Social Opinion (FOM) about Putin, 45 per cent 'approved of his activity'. He scored 31 per cent for 'belief', and a promising 52 per cent rated him 'electorally'. In the 'informational' sphere, on the other hand, he scored only 7 per cent.[49]

The Attitude of the West

As Reddaway and Glinski aptly put it, 'while the West could tolerate the creeping unspoken victory of market bolshevism over democracy, it would probably not go along with a clear-cut, *explicit* victory by the anti-democratic forces. . . . This meant the Kremlin still had to win elections.'[50] It also had to pay at least lip service to the formal requirements of international observers. Election observers, however, pay most attention to faults in procedure – hence the abuse of 'administrative resources' described in Chapter 4. They pay less attention – and to be fair these are difficult to quantify – to abuses of the political *process*.

Western governments, on the other hand, have always combined democracy promotion with realpolitik. Putin's key balancing act is to try and see how close a relationship he can develop with the West while entrenching a 'directed democracy' at home – and using the techniques of virtual politics to give the West a blinkered view of that balance. The electoral cycle in 2003 to 2004 showed a clear preference for the domestic priority, on the assumption that Russia had been given greater leeway by the West since September 11, 2001. Oil-rich Azerbaijan benefited from the blindest of blind eyes being turned during controversial elections in 2003. Ukraine is larger, but the West can call its 'geopolitical bluff'.[51] According to the critic Mykola Riabchuk:

> For the Ukrainian powers-that-be every election turns into a personal journey across a minefield, where every step could be the last. A step to the left, in the direction of excessive repressions, could cause severe international sanctions; a step to the right, in the direction of insufficient repression, could lead to the loss of power and, it cannot be excluded, [eventual] juridicial sanctions in the country itself. . . . any election is turned into a unique form of 'Russian roulette' for quasi-democratic strong men (*vozhdiv*). None of them ever knows the minimal amount of violations necessary: whether they should close tens of opposition publications, or hundreds, kill a few journalists or more than ten, limit car accidents to [just] one leader of the opposition or . . . allow a little provocation with a hand-grenade. It's undesirable to carry this to extremes, but under-performing is also bad. The uncertainty forces oligarchic power to be nervous and make mistakes.[52]

And forces it to make sufficient pretence. In essence, virtual politics in the post-Soviet world can be defined as the bridging of this gap, the attempt to make the world that more certain, for the benefit of the elites.

Variations in Virtuality

Not everything is virtual. This book concentrates on a particular theme – the authorities' ambitions to achieve overall control – but does not argue that they always manage it. The post-Soviet states are not totalitarian. Other versions of reality creep in at the margins. The main priority of the powers-that-be is that their version of reality should predominate – they know that it can never exclusively dominate. They want the majority to believe something like their version of events; where necessary, they want key Western actors to buy the same story too. But more crudely, they are happy simply to get away with it; not every loose end needs to be tied up.

Post-Soviet politics is also multi-dimensional. Virtuality is not the only dimension. Nor are there only two versions of events – the false and the true. To borrow a term from poststructuralist literary theory, post-Soviet politics is characterised by 'intertextuality'.[53] In literary theory, this notion seeks to challenge the orthodoxy of 'authorial intention' by situating any given text at a crossroads of multiple axes – between reader and author, text and other texts, between one system of codes and another. In this view of the world, so-called 'authors' lose control of their works once they are launched into a sea of possible interpretations. This way of understanding communication is good news for post-Soviet politics. Political technologists are not omnipotent; they cannot reshape the whole world in their own image. The virtual reality of their designer projects interacts with other forms of meaning. A given party, person or event can be read totally differently in different circumstances. To put this in plainer English: in some contexts politics is perfectly normal. The Communist Party of the Russian Federation has real policies and a programme, and an electorate to represent. On the other hand, its habit of shadow-boxing with the authorities that it demonises in public is a form of theatre, and the leaders of the 'inner party' are just as corrupt as those they denounce.

'Post-Soviet politics' is a very general label. There are significant variations between states. Georgia periodically wants to impress its credentials on the West. Azerbaijan, with its oil wealth, doesn't really need to, but the big Western oil companies operating there have to bear public opinion at home in mind. On the whole, however, the states of the south Caucasus are too small and too poor to launch grandiose media projects. A case in point would be the campaign for the Union of Georgian Citizens in 1999, run by the Russian political technology company Image-Kontakt, which was euphemistically described as concentrating on 'improving the party's local infrastructure': that is, making better use of adminis-trative resources.[54] Central Asia may need to clean up its act, to the smallest degree possible, as a result of the long-term US commitment to the area after the 2001/2 Afghanistan campaign. In Kazakhstan President Nazarbaev's 'Eurasianism' means he periodically has to ape aspects of 'European' political practice.[55] After 2004, on the other hand, the Baltic States officially became part of institutional Europe. As a result of these variations, most of the examples cited here come from the core states of Ukraine and Russia. The Russian elite thinks it has created a world 'safe for property for a generation or two'.[56] Its priority is now the avoidance of real politics. In Ukraine, change was still possible at the key presidential election due in the autumn of 2004; but political technologists were being paid large sums to prevent that change. Belarus, despite President Lukashenka's sharp shift towards authoritarianism after 1996, shares much of the same culture, and many of the same patterns can be found. Moldova is an almost entirely virtual state, with a narrow range of interests operating behind a shifting pattern of party labels.

There are also many variations within states and over time. Elements of civil society and independent media are more likely to be found in national capitals. Myth has it that the former Habsburg territories of west Ukraine have a more vibrant political culture than the rest of 'Soviet Ukraine', almost like that of the Baltic States; in truth, this difference may be more apparent than real. Elections tended to be freer and fairer in the early 1990s; unfortunately, the main trend in recent years has been towards the distortion of democracy. Nevertheless, the clash of political civilisations not the reported internal regional 'clash of civilisations', brought real drama to the 2004 Ukrainian election, and a cleaning of the stables was at least promised in Georgia after Mikhail Saakashvili came to power in 2003.

Conclusions

There is a significant literature on the 'virtualisation' of politics in the West. With the decline of traditional class politics, mass activism and party systems (*parteien-verdrossenheit* or 'party fatigue'), and the consequent electoral volatility and 'partisan dealignment',[57] it is often argued that a new era of manipulative politics is beginning here, too. Commentators have bemoaned the all-consuming 'cool' mediation of TV,[58] the prevalence of simulation over information, and politicians' increasingly distant or ascriptive linkage with the electorate. A golden age of direct voter contact has supposedly given way to an increasingly intimate obsession with politics as script and spin, politics by focus group, and the manipulation of 'mass' opinion by politicians and their hirelings rather than real accountability to sovereign and active electorates. It has also been argued that more or less the opposite is true: that politicians are now enslaved to the *vox populi*, or at least to the interpretations of it made by the oracles of the political marketing profession. Many of these trends have gone furthest in America, where, it is said, the presidency's newly ephemeral power is no longer dependent on party or institutional channels, or on diminishing post-Cold War capital as commander-in-chief (at least before September 11), but on the incumbent's success or failure in a daily media plebiscite.[59]

America has also seen the growth of 'narrative politics', with Arnold Schwarzenegger's successful 'Total Recall' campaign for the governorship of California in 2003 being merely an extreme version of Bill Clinton's image projection in 1992, or George W. Bush's in 2000 and 2004.[60] In the media age, the candidate with the most media-friendly (virtual) personality or most compelling life story is likely to triumph, regardless of policy or programme. (The term 'politics of the personality' was actually first used to describe the gubernatorial race between Richard Nixon and Edmund Brown in 1962.)[61] Supposedly, the majority of the TV electorate is so used to absorbing manipulative emotional messages, it can now only be sold politics in such a form.

Politics in the heartlands of the former USSR is, however, 'virtual' in a much more radical sense and 'is becoming ever more intensely ritualised than in the West'.[62] There is much more (and much less) to post-Communist virtual politics than the triumph of the sign over substance. Politics is 'virtual' or 'theatrical' in the sense that so many aspects of public performance are purely epiphenomenal or instrumental, existing only for effect or to disguise the real substance of 'inner politics'. French postmodernist Jean Baudrillard's musings about political PR in the

West actually seem more relevant to the former USSR. 'Rather than creating communication,' he writes, political PR *'exhausts itself in the art of staging communication*. Rather than producing meaning, it exhausts itself in the staging of meaning. . . . A circular arrangement [exists] through which one stages the desire of the audience', and then moves on. Politics 'operates outside the logic of representation'.[63] In other words, politics is more radically solipsistic than in the West. The public face of politics exists as, and often only as, virtuality, most often in the form of 'broadcast parties' or politicians that are almost entirely media phenomena.

Post-Soviet virtuality is also a radically top-down phenomenon, unlike in the West, where politicians are now often overwhelmed by a plethora of new media and messages over which they have no control. Given the Soviet legacy of highly formalised, ritualised political participation, a true political society, 'those core institutions of a democratic political society – political parties, elections, electoral rules, political leadership, interparty alliances, and legislatures – by which society constitutes itself politically to select and monitor democratic government',[64] has yet to emerge, resulting in a 'demobilisation of the social' that is more radical than anything yet seen in the West.[65] Elites, moreover, want the masses to remain demobilised. 'The authorities cannot (or do not want) to engage in honest and open dialogue with the population.'[66] Using popular appeals as leverage into power is left to peripheral politicians. Even the safety valve of 'anti-politics' is itself subject to manipulation (see Chapter 8). At the same time, virtual politics continually evokes the *narod* – the masses, the people. Constitutions are enacted in their name; politicians claim to be in touch with their deepest feelings; but the popular presence is only virtual.

On the other hand, the tendency to ascribe an omnipotent behind-the-scenes influence to the 'inner party', or to its modern equivalent, a cabal of oligarchs, is typically post-Soviet. Truly omnipotent rulers can abandon the virtual, cease indeed to be politicians at all. The next chapter therefore seeks to provide a practical look at the industry of 'virtual politics'.

3   The 'Political Technologist': Machiavelli as Corporate Adviser

> People vote for the spectacle, not for the routine. All elections are *dramaturgiia*.
>
> Jacques Séguéla (2000)[1]

There have been a handful of interesting studies unmasking political conjuring tricks in the post-Communist world, such as Boris Yeltsin's Houdini re-election in 1996,[2] and Russia's apparent regime caesura in 1999–2000.[3] The West also has an ignominious history of 'dirty tricks', from rigged papal elections to the Zinoviev letter, Watergate and the 'vast right-wing conspiracy' Hillary Clinton claimed against her husband.[4] Indeed, the atmosphere in twenty-first-century Moscow, Kiev, Minsk or Chişinău is often most reminiscent of James Ellroy's vision of post-war America, with its ghoulish cast of mafiosi, molls, muckrakers, conmen and contract killers, and politicians on the make manipulating them all.[5] Britain has 'spin doctors' such as Peter Mandelson, the US political 'attack dogs' such as Lee Atwater and Karl Rove, 'Bush's Brain', the Machiavellian 'permanent consultant' to the presidency's now 'permanent campaign'.[6] Their partial equivalents can also be found in the former USSR, but the post-Soviet world has its own unique breed of 'political technologists', who bestride an entire culture of politics-as-performance, with common patterns and repeat performances, even a common vocabulary.

The job of the political technologist is completely different from that of the spin doctor, although the former USSR has press secretaries who perform a similar role, such as Sergei Yastrzhembskii, who became notorious for the euphemism he used when journalists asked after Yeltsin's health: 'The president is working on documents.' Yastrzhembskii's skills earned him an expanded role as propaganda chief under Putin, when he again attracted notice for his stonewalling over Chechnia. The art of the spin doctor is particular. If the term is taken literally, he or she is not responsible for originating a given story, but intercepts it and 'spins' it on its way into the public domain. By definition, although many spin doctors clearly plant stories of their own, their work is narrowly situated at the point where politics and media intersect. The political technologists, on the other hand, apply whatever 'technology' they can to the construction of politics as a whole. The manipulation of the media is central to their work, but by definition it extends beyond this – to the construction of parties, the destruction of others, the framing of general campaign dynamics and the manipulation of results. If Russia and other post-Soviet states are 'directed democracies', the job of the political technologist is to direct that version of democracy on their employers' behalf – though, of course, they take the initiative themselves often enough.

As no systematic analysis of this phenomenon yet exists, it is the purpose of this book to try and provide it, and to demonstrate just how radically post-Soviet politics is being corrupted by the political technologists' 'art'. In the words of its most famous practitioner, Gleb Pavlovskii:

> Politicians and political technologists – as two political subjects independent of one another – only exist in such a radically separate form in Russia, where political technologists play the crucial role, set the agenda, *change* the agenda. . . . They see themselves as more than mediators, helpers. . . . A commercial market exists – it is of course pleasant to receive money and contracts – but for many that is not enough. . . . There is a group of people, more like a corporation, who decide politics regardless of which party they belong to.[7]

Or, to quote the title of a book by one Kremlin insider, Sergei Markov, head of the Kremlin-backed Institute for Political Studies, 'PR in Russia is more than PR.'[8]

Some *Dramatis Personae*

In 2002 Hollywood released *Spinning Boris* (in the Russian version 'Project Yeltsin'). This strange film made hyperbolic claims that a handful of highly paid US PR men (Republican Party 'consultants' George Gorton, Richard Dresner and Joe Shumate, who engineered Pete Wilson's dramatic comeback win in the 1994 California race and later worked for Arnold Schwarzenegger in 2003) ran Boris Yeltsin's 1996 campaign. Particularly laughable was the idea that the Russians needed tutoring in the arts of dirty campaigning and black PR. By 1996, political technology in Russia was already well developed, although its 'success' in that year's campaign un-doubtedly did much to promote the image of the 'industry'. There are now a huge number of political manipulators in the former USSR.[9] Some claimed to detect a decline in the market after the excitements of the first post-Soviet decade; but as of 2002 there were almost two hundred firms operating in Russia alone, with an average of thirty employees each.[10] According to one leading practitioner, Igor Mintusov of Nikkolo-M, the industry turned over between $150 million and $200 million during the 1999 elections.[11] He should know: it has been said that 'lunch with Mr Mintusov costs 2,000 Deutschmarks'.[12] One contest alone, that between Aleksandr Khloponin and Aleksandr Uss to succeed Aleksandr Lebed as governor of Krasnoiarsk in 2002 (also featuring Sergei Glazev [see pages 260–2] and Artiom Tarasov as a mere also-ran), produced a new peak in honoraria – 'several million on both sides'.[13] Different sources predicted a dramatic escalation in the market to between $650 million and $1.8 billion for the Duma elections in 2003.[14]

There are several overlapping types of political technologist. First is the agencies in the election campaigning business, with the market dominated by five to ten big companies such as Nikkolo-M, Aleksei Sitnikov's Image-Kontakt and Piotr Shchedrovitskii's School of Cultural Policy. Second is the small number of agencies that provide classical political consulting, genuine analysis and strategic recommendations to key players, such as Igor Bunin's Centre of Political Technologies. Then there are the political PR agencies like Gleb Pavlovskii's Foundation for Effective Politics, which concentrate on media campaigns, most typically for elections, but also for specific 'scenarios' such as provoking a crisis in the Duma. For example, the furore over the introduction of a 7 per cent electoral barrier for the 2007 elections was a classic Pavlovskii project designed to shape political behaviour in 2003. Fourth is the *kompromat* agencies that exist mainly on the internet, such as www.stringer-news.ru, the site of the group led by Aleksandr Korzhakov, Yeltsin's notorious drinking buddy and Mr Fix-It. Some are anti-everybody, others anti-everybody except their sponsors. In 2002 Stringer-news was taken over by the energy company Yukos. The www.polit.ru site was launched by *Izvestiia* and the *Komsomolskaia pravda* group, and was safely loyal to the Kremlin. The Agency for Federal Research, www.flb.ru, originally relied on materials from Vladimir Gusinskii's security services and therefore indirectly from Filipp Bobkov after his time at the KGB. The purest example is www.kompromat.ru, as it allegedly sells the contents of each edition to the highest bidder.

A rough Ukrainian equivalent would be 'Criminal Ukraine' at www.cripo.com.ua, although its editor, Oleh Yeltsov, has a fairly independent reputation and the site faced severe censorship pressure in 2003/4. As such sites do not exactly publicise their ownership or agenda, they must be considered first and foremost as propaganda tools rather than information sources.

Political technologists, moreover, exist in many institutional settings. The private 'consulting' business is but one part of the overall industry. All large corporations have their own 'analytical centres', preparing active measures rather than mere passive analysis. Political centres such as the Kremlin and its Ukrainian equivalent, the presidential administration in Bankivska Street, also have their own schemers and fixers. Georgii Satarov and Mark Urnov served Yeltsin in the early years, alongside Aleksandr Korzhakov. Aleksandr Voloshin served two presidents as chief of staff; Vladislav Surkov rose to the position of his able assistant under Putin. Voloshin made his name with the project to oust Yevgenii Primakov as prime minister, and then (with Igor Shabduraslov, seconded from ORT) as the main political sponsor of the successful Unity project in 1999. He also directed the project to destroy the empire of leading oligarch Boris Berezovskii. Surkov, the 'supreme PR man', is a failed theatre director and former political technologist whose first big success was swinging the Duma vote to endorse Sergei Stepashin as prime minister in May 1999. Significantly, his informal title had him in charge of 'party-building',[15] and, most importantly, with his organisation of the shotgun merger of Unity and Fatherland-All Russia (FAR) in 2001 to create United Russia.

Ukraine's most effective political fixers have been President Kuchma's first and last heads of administration: Dmytro Tabachnyk in 1994 to 1996; and, rather more openly and controversially, Viktor Medvedchuk in 2002 to 2004. President Lukashenka in Belarus has used a series of shadowy manipulators, most of whom were previously employed in KGB counter-intelligence rather than as simple 'men of force': these include Siarhei Posakhow, Uladzimir Zamiatalin, Mikhail Sazonaw, architect of the controversial referenda in 1995 and 1996, and Ural Latypaw, who ran Lukashenka's 2001 re-election campaign. Ramiz Mekhtiev served as chief of staff to two Azerbaijani presidents after 1993, honing the arts he learnt as secretary for ideology in the local Communist Party in the late 1980s.

Active measures are also planned and executed from within the security services themselves. When Lukashenka was consolidating his power in 1995–96, for example, he relied on the local KGB (still proudly bearing its old name) because there was as yet no well-developed industry alternative in the relative backwater of Minsk (see pages 164–9). On other occasions, it is more the nature of the job that might push former security agents to the fore, as with professional surveillance in Ukraine's 'Gongadze affair' (the murder of an opposition journalist in 2000, followed by the 'Melnychenko tapes', secret recordings made in the president's office indicating his involvement);[16] or, allegedly, the apartment bombings in Russia in 1999 (see page 185). Also, incontrovertibly, part of the story of the Yeltsin succession in 1999–2000 was the security services' ability to direct events to ensure their own return to pre-eminence. Where such activities are obvious and provable, they are referred to here. On the other hand, it is not the argument of this book that every covert action can be traced to the successors of the KGB. The real growth industry in the former USSR is political technology, which overlaps in considerable part with Chekist methodology but is also a substitute for it.

Finally the so-called oligarchs themselves sometimes play the technologist's role, in so far as they initiate a project or finance it.[17] Most will, of course, employ 'regular' political technologists to do the detailed work; many have stable relationships with particular client groups. Nevertheless, it often makes sense to describe a certain project in shorthand that refers to the oligarch who devised or ordered it: the KOP in Ukraine was therefore a 'Pinchuk project', the Union of Right Forces in Russia in 1999 a 'Chubais project' and so on (see pages 192–5 and 99–100); although the 'Yukos affair' in 2003 (see pages 108–9) was deliberately designed to encourage them to stay out of politics.

To a limited extent, the recentralisation of power in the new millennium in Russia, Ukraine and elsewhere meant that Kremlin fixers like Surkov were taking over the private political technologist's role. In Boris Kagarlitskii's words:

> The new Kremlin machine has no need for outside political consultants. They are tolerated out of gratitude and as holdovers from the previous regime, but their services are no longer required. The real *éminence grises* work inside the administration using ordinary bureaucratic methods, while the oligarchs are trying to corner the political market without the help of middlemen by buying off political parties and installing loyal company men in key jobs.[18]

There is much truth in this, particularly the desire to save money, but there is also exaggeration, since 'ordinary bureaucratic methods' alone are not enough. Moreover, there are many functions that even shadowy insiders cannot be seen to perform. The boundary has never been clear. In Pavlovskii's words, 'traditionally separate roles – businessman and politician, lobbyist and politician – don't really apply in Russia'.[19] Project 'sponsors' may therefore be government officials, powerful oligarchs or the technologists themselves. All also have a vested interest in making sure that all other parties and would-be oppositions drink from the same poisoned well, so that all are drawn into the same web of *kompromat* and mutually assured destruction. This includes local Communist parties (see Chapter 9); in fact it concerns them especially.

A decade after the fall of Communism, the most famous of all Russian technologists was Gleb Pavlovskii, who ran the Foundation for Effective Politics (FEP) – note the stress on 'effective'. Some of his colleagues and rivals have claimed that Pavlovskii is not really a political technologist as such. 'He works in a different genre – political intrigue, where he is indeed a virtuoso.'[20] Others have called him 'a major expert in contaminating the political environment', 'nothing but a charlatan [who has] mastered the black art of self-mystification rather than showing the character of a contemporary Machiavelli'. 'He knows that more rumour means more respect, fear, and, ultimately, more money.' Pavlovskii has expressed himself with characteristic bluntness: 'Frankly, I'm not interested in clients. What excites me is political technology – pure and simple.'[21]

Pavlovskii was born in Odessa. Although a 'dissident', he is alleged to have made his compromises with the old regime, the KGB in particular. In 1974 he may have informed on his colleague Viacheslav Igrunov for printing samizdat. In 1979–80 Pavlovskii helped edit the journal *Poiski* ('Quests'), which was significantly subtitled 'Quests for Mutual Understanding [with the Authorities]'. In 1980–81 he reportedly testified against the son of the famous dissident Sergei Kovalev. Unlike others who were imprisoned in 1982, Pavlovskii got only three years' exile in Komi after returning to print in 1981 to propose a pact between 'state and society'.[22] On his return, 'tired of refuting these [KGB] accusations, he developed a new image built on "swaggering cynicism and intellectual epatage". He also decided to become an insider.'[23] The nature of his true loyalties and extent of his actual or potential 'mutual understanding' with the Soviet authorities can be gauged from his own words eulogising 'power'. 'Russian [*rossiiskaia*] power never was and never will be national power': that is, something exercised with the people. 'We' Russians, he continued, 'are mediocre "Slavs" and "Scythians". Our identity is defined by our communication, and our communication – is power, within power, about power, intimate power, spiteful power.' Pavlovskii is also fond of quoting the Russian philosopher Mikhail Gefler's (1918–95) paean to realpolitik: 'This [Russia] is not just a society of power. We are also an ethnos of power.'[24]

Pavlovskii's first project was for Yabloko in 1993, then the Congress of Russian Communities (KRO) in 1995 and Yeltsin in 1996.[25] In 1994 he premiered the 'virtual coup' project, when he penned a piece entitled 'Theory Number One', claiming that Luzhkov and other oligarchs were plotting to seize power.[26] Equally typical was the black PR organised by Pavlovskii against Fatherland-All Russia in 1999 (or, as the wags rearranged it, 'All Russia in the Struggle against Fatherland').[27] Characteristic of Pavlovskii's style were the pastiche websites www.lujkov.ru (parallel and remarkably similar to the 'real' www.luzhkov.ru) and www.primakov.ru, savaging its subject for his age, health and degenerative 'Brezhnevophilia', accusing him of being pro-Chechen and helping organise one of many attempts on Shevardnadze's life.[28] Pavlovskii also worked for Sergei Kirienko against Luzhkov in the 1999 Moscow mayoral race, using Kremlin media, especially ORT. Luzhkov still won easily – though his vote was down from 89 per cent in 1996 to a mere 71 per cent in 1999 – but enough mud stuck to encourage his early departure from the presidential race in 2000. Pavlovskii organised the Civic Forum that aimed to bring all Russian non-governmental organisations (NGOs) under Kremlin control in November 2001, and helped with the second attempt in June 2004, by which time even the mildest of dissident voices had been weeded out.

Pavlovskii's rise to prominence was owing to two factors. The first was his appropriation of the credit for Yeltsin's re-election in 1996 and the double-headed Unity/Putin project in 1999–2000.[29] He was also linked to the notorious Storms in Moscow 'plan' leaked to *Moskovskaia pravda* in July 1999 (see page 185). With such successes to their names, the likes of Pavlovskii now found themselves pushing at an open door. Putin, reflecting on his patron Sobchak's defeat in the 1996 St Petersburg elections, declared that 'after four years, it was understood that professionals, technologies for use in the election campaign were what [we] needed for victory, not [just] negotiations with deputies. These are absolutely different things.'[30] Once his methods had shown themselves apparently triumphant, Pavlovskii celebrated the demise of liberal, *in*effective Russia with an unashamed 'we are the masters now' article for *Nezavisimaia gazeta* in December 2000. Here he boasted about reconquering for Putin all the main centres of power from 'Belovezhskaia Russia' (in other words the anti-Soviet, anti-Communist Russia that Yeltsin created after the secret meeting at Belovezhskaia Pushcha, Belarus, in December 1991): 'The Kremlin is taken. Okhotnyi Riad, the Lubianka and Staraia Ploshchad are taken [respectively, the home of the Duma and former homes of the KGB and Central Committee]. Most, Ostankino and the banks are under the control of Russia. What are you waiting for? For the victor to leave and hand you the keys of the above-listed premises?'[31]

The second factor was the rise of the internet in Russia. Pavlovskii's media-feeding tactics worked because he initially controlled such a large portion of Russian internet space. Moreover, these were precisely the sites journalists would visit to source stories, such as www.strana.ru ('The Country Russia'), www.vesti.ru ('Russian News'), www.smi.ru ('Russian Mass Media') and, reportedly, www.russ.ru ('The Russian Journal'). Strana.ru, for example, was originally set up with Siberian oligarch Roman Abramovich's money to support the Kremlin. In November 2001 several of the sites were 'renationalised' by the authorities and their finances reduced, as Pavlovskii had oversold their potential for manipulating public opinion. Moreover, the target audience was relatively sophisticated, and preferred apparently more objective analysis from sites such as www.politcom.ru and www.grani.ru. It may also have been true that Kremlin manipulators such as Voloshin and Surkov preferred dissident thought to be out in the open, where it could be more easily monitored. There were also reports that Pavlovskii's methods were deemed to be 'too open' (sic) by the new Kremlin, and that the rising St Petersburg faction preferred the more straightforwardly dirty methods of their hometown technologist Aleksii Koshmarov (see overleaf).[32] Nevertheless, Pavlovskii bounced back with a new site, www.kreml.org, in October 2002.

Pavlovskii's sidekick and sometime FEP partner, Marat Gelman, has been described as a 'master of provocation', using his other profession as an art dealer as an alternative outlet for his 'postmodernism'. Gelman organised a semi-serious exhibition entitled *Kompromat* at his Moscow gallery in 1996, complete with a fake Israeli passport for Communist Party leader Gennadii Ziuganov and a mock photograph of nationalist general Aleksandr Lebed chatting on intimate terms with the Chechen leader Dzhokhar Dudaev.[33] In the 1996 election he led fellow artists in the Yakimanka group in mock support of the Communists. Gelman's reputation for 'intellectual provocations' and for bowdlerising politics into eclectic kitsch is therefore justified.[34] His first proper campaign was for Sergei Kirienko in 1999, followed by work in Ukraine in 2002, for Rodina in 2003 and in Ukraine again in 2004. Gelman also served as deputy director of ORT.

Also close to the Kremlin was Piotr Shchedrovitskii, founder of the School of Cultural Policy. Shchedrovitskii's father was a philosopher, so he likes to philosophise, too, as, even more so, does his business partner, Efim Ostrovskii, founder of GOST ('Group of Ostrovskii'), a linguist by profession. Ostrovskii's first jobs were for Aman Tuleiev, head of the Duma budget committee Nikolai Gonchar and the mayor of Sevastopol Viktor Semenov. Shchedrovitskii tends to work for Russia's dwindling band of liberals and claims not to go in for black PR. The Shchedrovitskii group's key contracts were with the Union of Right Forces in 1999 and the 'liberal' project KOP in Ukraine in 2002 (and therefore with oligarch Viktor Pinchuk via Volodymyr Hranovskyi's Agency of Humanitarian Technologies; see page 194). Nevertheless, the group worked for the fraudster Sergei Mavrodii in the mid-1990s, and reportedly Ukraine's President Kuchma in 1999.

Another 'pragmatic liberal' is Aleksei Golovkov, who was close to Gaidar and Chubais and ran Russia's Choice's 'analytical centre' in 1993. He was also one of its Duma candidates, switching to Our Home Is Russia in 1995 – hence the secrecy when he was handed responsibility for 'project Lebed' in 1996 (see pages 123–4). Golovkov's greatest gift to the deeply unpopular post-Soviet political class was his invention of the 'anti-political' campaign. Lebed's PR used actors masquerading as ordinary voters to muse out loud on the need for a firm hand. Lebed himself was sparingly used as a talking head and only appeared at the end of 'his' ads after the slogan matching the previous rhetorical demands had been flashed up: 'There is such a person. You know him.' The success of these ads helped bolster the similarly designed Yeltsin campaign. Golovkov then perfected the tactic as campaign manager for Unity in 1999 working alongside Pavlovskii for Putin in 2000. In 1999 he concentrated on creating now often wordless imagery for Unity's leaders, dubbed the 'Three Bogatyrs' (see pages 96–7); in 2000 Putin was again portrayed as a man of action, surrounded by fawning admirers from representative social groups. Politics in the usual Western sense was as such beneath him.[35] Golovkov also sensed that the incumbents' unpopularity in 1993 and 1995 had made it difficult for them to attack their opponents directly. He therefore advocated contracting out the job: just as Lebed was encouraged to take on the Communists in 1996 (in one particularly effective instance, he was interviewed by Yevgenii Kiselev on NTV about the 1962 massacres of striking workers in his home town of Novocherkassk), so Zhirinovskii was used against Fatherland-All Russia in 1999. By the late 1990s, Golovkov had been rewarded with the top job at Rosgosstrakh, Russia's biggest insurance company, and was also serving as deputy chair of the Duma's Budget Committee.

The 'St Petersburg School', centred around Aleksii Koshmarov's company Novokom, has a reputation for employing dirtier tactics, pioneering both the 'double' technique and many of the cruder 'organisational technologies' (see pages 66–7).[36] Koshmarov organised a string of victories for the local 'Yakovlev clan', which soon brushed aside the idealistic democrats who thought they had won power in 1990. He rose to prominence with the notorious victory for Yakovlev over Sobchak in 1996 (which cost an estimated $15 million, and led to Sobchak's flight to Paris), Yakovlev's re-election in 2000 and the city legislative elections in 1998. The latter saw the rout of the local democrats, thanks to the sudden appearance of several 'doubles' or 'clones': such as a fake 'Yabloko-St Petersburg', of which the Yabloko leader Grigorii Yavlinskii in Moscow was strangely ignorant.[37] Koshmarov also specialised in local gubernatorial elections where his organisational technologies (late-night phone calls from opponents' fake supporters, fake leaflets from opponents stuck to cars with superglue) could be deployed without attracting too much attention or generating too much fuss. Such tactics helped apparent lost causes such as Vladimir Yegorov win in Kaliningrad in 2000 and Vasilii Starodubtsev in Tula in 2001, though they could not help Krasnoiarsk governor Valerii Zubov against Lebed in 1998. (Novokom also ran a presidential 'election' in a virtual state, the so-called 'Dnistr Republic' in Moldova.) Novokom therefore also ran a lot of single-mandate Duma campaigns where its methods could escape the scrutiny of the national press, with eleven winners in 1999. Through Yakovlev, the Novokom group had links to conservatives in Moscow, first with Korzhakov, Luzhkov and Berezovskii, and then with Surkov, with whom Koshmarov had worked during his stint at Menatep Bank in the mid-1990s. (Koshmarov was once deputy head of the Committee of Youth Organisations of the USSR, then briefly a 'democrat'.)

Nikkolo-M, a partnership between Ekaterina Egorova and Igor Mintusov established in 1992, is perhaps the most mainstream PR organisation. In 1995 it worked on Our Home Is Russia alongside Sitnikov's Image-Kontakt, and claimed to have run 20 per cent of successful single-mandate constituency campaigns, with a similarly successful fifty-one out of 225 in 1999. It advised on Yeltsin's 'absent' campaign in 1996,[38] and worked on Putin's image in 2000 when he had no real political campaign as such, preferring to offer voters a king-sized 'Chancellor's bonus' instead.[39] Nikkolo-M has long-standing links with Gazprom, and according to Timothy Colton and Michael McFaul helped the company to create a covert lobby of fifty deputies in 1999.[40] In 2003 it worked mainly for the Party of Life. One anonymous insider described this as a perfect contract: 'They [the Party of Life] have lots of money. . . . And they aren't expected to win.'[41] Image-Kontakt, which also did the adverts for Our Home Is Russia in 1995, is also often to be found behind other people's work. Its boss, Aleksei Sitnikov, owns the political technologists' club in Moscow, named Petrovich after the hero of a cartoon series.

Smaller agencies include PRopaganda (its Nataliia Mandrova was Fatherland-All Russia's press spokeswoman in 1999), Publicity PR, Ya ('I') and Yelena Soirokina's Obratnaia Sviaz ('Reverse Connection', named after a hit film of the 1970s). Video International dominates the market for making actual adverts. The company was founded in 1992 by Mikhail Lesin, who linked its fortune to Gazprom. Despite holding government office under Putin, Lesin is still assumed to exercise a guiding influence, pushing contracts in the company's direction.

The Russians Are Coming

Russia doesn't have many export industries. Back in 1941 the Ukrainian nationalist Yurii Lypa dismissively predicted that Russia's main sources of foreign revenue in future years would be the 'export . . . of wood and oil'.[42] Now Russia has political technology. Russia's near-permanent election campaigning – with so many gubernatorial campaigns filling the gaps between national elections – has generated a high-capacity industry. Russian political technologists are also much better acquainted with local political culture than any of their Western equivalents who have dared to dip a toe in post-Soviet waters. Moreover, non-Russian (but post-Soviet) clients may be guided towards particular firms by their Russian business partners. Also, in the relatively fallow years at home between big national elections, Russian over-supply tends to find an outlet abroad, as with the Ukrainian elections in 2002 and 2004.

Moscow manipulators are also prestigious. Some of their clients have undoubtedly hoped that the announcement (or mere rumour) of a contract will be enough to give their ratings a boost. The Ukrainian commentator Viacheslav Pikhhovshek gives a rather simpler explanation: inferiority complex or cultural cringe. 'It's typical of the Ukrainian oligarchs. They want their own fleet of cars, their own island. They think Russian image-makers must be the best, because they're the most expensive.'[43] Ukraine does have political technologists of its own, but the local market clearly lagged behind the Russian one in development. Mykhailo Pohrebinskyi's Centre for

Conflict and Political Studies (www.analitik.org.ua) is analogous to the FEP, with which it is closely linked, but it is also narrowly associated locally with the local Social-Democratic Party or SDPU(o). Pohrebinskyi's group is also covertly linked to the Centre for Effective Politics, which had a central role in preparing so-called *temnyky*, daily attempts to set the media agenda (see page 65). It also helped revamp the president's website (www.president.gov.ua) and set up a linked site to promote the authorities' attempts to change the constitution in 2004 (www.reforma.org.ua), a textbook example of total virtuality, full of fake supporters' learned treatises. Volodymyr Hranovskyi's Agency for Humanitarian Technologies (www.aht.org) was linked to the Labour Ukraine clan and the liberal project KOP, while Mykola Bahraiev's Tavria Games Co was at one time associated with the Greens. Other 'think tanks' such as the Razumkov Centre (www.uceps.org) and Mykola Tomenko's Institute of Politics (www.tomenko.kiev.ua) have a better reputation for independent analysis. On the other hand, Ukraine has a well-developed market for 'sociological technology', in other words, running fake opinion polls. On the back of the Gongadze scandal Ukraine also began to develop a host of *kompromat* websites in 2001 to 1904: the supposedly independent 'Criminal Ukraine' (www.cripo. com.ua), but also www.provokator.com.ua, a newer equivalent to kompromat.ru,[44] www.bayki.com (*bayka* means 'fable'), www.temnik.com.ua, supported by Mikhail Pohrebinskyi and the SDPU(o) and designed to blacken their opponents, and www.aznews.narod.ru, devoted to a single politician, Yuliia Tymoshenko. Belarus under Lukashenka controls the internet much more tightly, but there are still sites such as the anti-Lukashenka www.batke.net.

However, Russian political technologists were not just in Ukraine and elsewhere to make money, although there was plenty of that around. According to Volodymyr Polokhalo, 'they aren't just making money, but serving as Russian agents of influence, "distributors" of Russian interests'. Those who arrived in Ukraine for the 2002 elections were 'particularly close to people like Sergei Karaganov', chair of the Russian Council for Foreign and Defence Policy, 'and German Gref', then minister for trade and head of the Centre for Strategic Planning.[45] According to Marat Gelman, who in 2002 was working for the SDPU(o):

> People are always looking for enemies. In America it's lawyers . . . life would be wonderful without them. You want something, but your opponent finds a good lawyer and wins the case against you! In Ukraine the enemy has also already been found – its political technologists. The unknown is always demonised . . . which means that people don't fully understand what the modern art [of PR] is today.[46]

Aleksei Sitnikov's Image-Kontakt has worked for Nazarbaev in Kazakhstan, and for Eduard Shevardnadze in Georgia in 1999 and 2000. Nikkolo-M was rumoured to have worked for Belarusia's President Lukashenka in 2001. However, it is in Ukraine that its activities are best documented, although even there much remains shrouded in a history of covert actions and commercial secrets. The Yuliia Rusova group worked for Hromada in 1998 (as part of Information Technology XXI), but Russian involvement really took off a year later. In 1999 three separate 'campaign teams' were set up under President Kuchma – not counting the front office under Dmytro Tabachnyk. The team under Volkov and Bakai was responsible for the application of administrative resources and the use of the so-called 'Social Protection Fund'; a second group, under Surkis and Medvedchuk, handled cash and the mass media. It was therefore the third 'creative' team, under Viktor Pinchuk and Andrii Derkach, that employed the Russian technologists (see pages 103–4 and 157–9).

In 2002 FEP worked for the SDPU(o), though the Social Democrats were surprisingly coy about it. Gleb Pavlovskii returned to Moscow, leaving Gelman in charge (raising fears about his close links to Kremlin chief of staff Voloshin). Trademark internet tactics built up a sizeable virtual holding for the SDPU(o) in 2001/2: www.ukraine.ru and a 'Ukraine' division at the Russian media portal www.smi.ru; plus domestically www.forum.ua, www.podrobnosti.com.ua ('Details'), and www.obozrevatel.com.ua ('The Observer'). One sign of their links was that all three recycled material from the Inter TV channel controlled by the SDPU(o). FEP people were already making their way into Inter, despite Medvedchuk's denials that he and Pavlovskii were cooperating. In November 2001 a Russo-Ukrainian Media Institute was established for direct TV propaganda. FEP was probably also behind the *kompromat* site www.yushchenko.com, which was similar to those used against Fatherland-All Russia in 1999. The young editor of www.strana.ru, Marina Litvinovych, admitted as much: 'I would advise the enemies of Yushchenko to create an unofficial site for the ex-premier.'[47] FEP also organised the 'Cassette Scandal 2' in January 2002 (see page 141) – in fact, its work was almost entirely negative.

Nikkolo-M was initially reported to be working for For a United Ukraine (FUU), if only as a 'team of undertakers' organising a 'place of exile' for the older generation,[48] although the FUU was also directly linked to advisers from the Kremlin. Nikkolo-M was also rumoured to be working for Yabluko and the Party of Regions, but the Yabluko project was taken over by Oleg Medvedev, formerly of FEP and *Moskovskii komsomolets* and, from 1999, editor of *Kievskie vedomosti* ('Kiev News'). Andrei Okar and Kazbek Bektursunov did some work for Yuliia Tymoshenko, who had turned down Nikkolo-M for being 'too expensive'.[49] Shchedrovitskii and Ostrovskii helped to run the New Liberal Union (NLO) project, later known as the Winter Crop Generation Team (Komanda ozymoho pokolinnia, or KOP), paid for by leading oligarch Viktor Pinchuk to target and mythologise Ukraine's new (pro-Russian) business elite. Even the Communists weighed in: Leonid Grach, the ambitious leader of the Crimean Communists, paid $0.5 million – 'obviously not from party coffers' – to Aleksii Koshmarov, although Pavlovskii was also rumoured to have been involved at the consultation stage (see also pages 247–8).

The relative failure of the Russians' efforts in 2002, however, stimulated the domestic market. Agencies such as Dmytro Vydrin's company PRovider in Dnipropetrovsk were now able to sell themselves as better attuned to local conditions.[50] As of 2004, the Donbas had the biggest market, with at least four local political-technology groups: Mykola Levchenko's Social Dialogue (KOD); Andrii Bondarenko's Korund/Parabellum; Vladislav Lukianov's FinFort PR, which has also worked in Russia as far away as Vladivostok, and the Donetsk Information-Analytical Centre. The Russian firm PR System Consulting Group is also very active in east Ukraine.[51]

Don't Believe the Hype: The Political Culture of Post-Soviet PR

So what do political technologists (other names include image-makers, humanitarian technologists, political programmers, *piarchiki*) actually do for their money? Some are ultra-cynical, happy to do almost anything and happy to argue that the public is almost infinitely malleable. Others are more restrained. According to Ekaterina Egorova of Nikkolo–M, 'the politician and the target electorate have to have *some* overlap, or there's nothing we can do for them. We work with that space in the middle.'[52] She may have lost some clients demanding the impossible as a result. Others have claimed an almost Nietzschean freedom. According to Efim Ostrovskii, this freedom arose because all the 'ultra-structures' of Soviet society ('the semantic and semiotic connections of society – the structure of belief, sublingual structures of an ideological type, providing for intercourse between people'),[53] as well, of course, as its infrastructure (material resources), were destroyed in the 1990s, creating a post-Soviet version of Year Zero in Germany in 1945. 'In any country,' Ostrovskii continues, 'any political technologist works with these ultra-structures, but we had to rebuild them . . . we were *fogelfrei* [free as a bird] . . . so much – the political system, the state – in modern Russia was built by political technologists.'[54] According to Marat Gelman, 'when you work with power, you don't just move the objects on the table, you can shift the table'.[55] After a century of trauma, on the other hand, post-Soviet society suffers from ideophobia and what Sergei Kurginian has called 'self-narcoticisation', 'the desire to drift for a while in virtual reality'.[56] According to Pavlovskii, image is therefore all. As all other institutions had collapsed, he claims that 'TV kept the country together in the early 1990s'.[57] TV is, however, a 'soft' cultural form (Arjun Appadurai), and its apparent pliability has encouraged the political technologists to believe that Russia, like the other post-Soviet states, has become a 'society of the spectacle',[58] or, perhaps more exactly, a society of spectators, ripe for their Situationist games. In any case, people 'don't believe political information any more'; so they have to be fed mythology instead.[59]

Most political technologists are deeply cynical, defined by their *prodazhnost* (willingness to sell themselves to anybody) and by moral relativism – or just amorality. In Gelman's words, 'technologists serve politicians, as gallerists [Gelman's other profession] serve artists. You must keep your distance. You must look at it as a game.'[60] Most come from backgrounds that encouraged their cynicism. According to the analyst Aleksei Mukhin, 'the basic corpus of PR men, as a rule, are former analysts of the First and Second Main Directorates and the Fifth Chief Directorate of the USSR KGB, former ideologues of the Central Committee of the CPSU and Komsomol, former *rezidenty* [KGB station chiefs abroad] and intelligence men a rank lower down'.[61] Also common at the lower end of the market is the *deklassirovannaia profesura*, former 'political scientists' or teachers of Marxism-Leninism. However, there are also many former dissidents and members of the late Soviet counter-culture who see themselves as ideas men (and occasionally women), working in what they like to call *fabriki mysli* ('factories of thought'). Pavlovskii is a former dissident; Aleksei Sitnikov studied psychotherapy and neurolinguistics. The linguist Ostrovskii is the most self-consciously intellectual, as demonstrated by the quotation above and by his sophistry in defending his work for Sergei Mavrodii in 1995. The notorious swindler was, Ostrovskii admitted, 'a scandalous person' – 'I wouldn't work in his commercial activities'. But in his political role, Ostrovskii claimed to see Mavrodii as the little guy 'working against the state machine', which 'wanted to get rid of him' and his MMM pyramid scheme 'in order to begin selling its own GKOs' (government bonds).[62] In other words, the younger technologists still see themselves as iconoclasts, struggling to create an 'old-fashioned' (i.e., actually democratic) political system.

In the relationship between the political technologist and the project financier, it is the former who provides the ideas, but it is not always clear who is responsible for creating virtuality. Clients tend just to want victory, by fair means or foul. They can also be led by the nose, as arguably with Aleksandr Lebed in 1996 and certainly with the cut-out 'independents' sponsored by Sitnikov to run for the Duma in 1999 (see page 126). On the other hand, Ostrovskii claims it was a 'romantic decision' on his part to try and create a liberal party in Ukraine in 2002 (see pages 192–5),[63] and that the sponsor-clients (Valerii Khoroshkovskii and, behind him, the oligarch Viktor Pinchuk) were more cynical than he. Several of those who worked on the Ukrainian side, such as the economist Vasyl Yurchyshyn, seemed committed to a truly liberal project,[64] but there wasn't enough money and Khoroshkovskyi used the project as a vehicle for his own ambitions.

Buy Me!

The relationship between political technologists and the market, on the other hand, is definitely one of supply creating demand – despite the maxim that propaganda works best when it meets latent demand, telling people what they were already prepared to hear. Some projects may be merely ahead of the market and might in time have happened spontaneously anyway, but even those which seem to meet an existing or latent demand are designed to 'graze' on it rather than give it proper expression. Most political technologists do not view themselves as creating a market, just ephemera – although some, such as Borges's sorcerer, are determined to convince others of the reality of their creations.

Sometimes projects emerge even further back in the chain of supply. An extreme example is the ready-made shell parties or 'pre-parties' pre-prepared by enterprising individuals, rather like the 'squatters' who sought to beat famous companies to registering their names in the early days of the internet boom. These political entrepreneurs will provide official registration along with the dead souls claiming to have attended a founding conference, necessary signatures of support, etc (100,000 to stand in the 1998 Ukrainian elections, 200,000 to gain free airtime on Russian TV), all for an off-the-shelf price – reported to be $100,000 in Russia as of 1999.[65] Many post-Soviet parties are long dormant, but they rarely disappear completely. It is usually worth maintaining the investment. Registration deadlines set twelve months before the actual poll also encourage the creation of 'sleeper' parties. Political entrepreneurs buy them up and rebrand them, deliberately seeking to make a splash, perhaps in the hope that a more established player will then buy into their project, as with the New Generation project in Ukraine in 2002 (see page 195). Alternatively someone may simply steal your idea, of course.

A similar phenomenon involves dummy candidates who intend to sell themselves all along. A good early example is Oleksandr Tkachenko, the leading figure in Ukraine's collective farm squirearchy (he set up a 'Village Party' in 1992) and supposedly the sole left-wing challenger to Leonid Kravchuk in the 1991 presidential election. His challenge fizzled out surprisingly quickly (though polls had him in respectable single figures) in favour of Kravchuk, who wanted to be free of enemies on his left in order to run a united front against his nationalist opponents and needed the captive rural electorate to ensure victory in the first round. Tkachenko's initial planned reward was to become ambassador to Poland,[66] but in the end he chose a more profitable dividend, using state funds to set up an agricultural firm, Land and People, and state contacts to set up an agreement in February 1993 for this front organisation to channel US loans designed to support the nascent independent farmers' movement to the old collective farm nomenclatura instead. Seventy million dollars that was supposed to be spent on seed, pesticides and agricultural produce was instead spent on thirty-two luxury cars and a large amount of leather office furniture (and one lawnmower). Only 197,000 tons of produce emerged; corn was used as animal feed or left to freeze. Nevertheless, the debt was conveniently written off by the Ukrainian ExImBank and Agriculture Ministry.[67] Tkachenko, meanwhile, prospered first as deputy chair (1994–98) and then chair (1998–2000) of parliament, before rejoining the Communist Party in 2001. He also entered the presidential race in 1999 – when he withdrew in favour of the Communist candidate Petro Symonenko.

The Local Medium of the Message
Every country has a different virtual reality. Terhi Rantanen has surveyed how Russia (and other successor states) have adopted globalised icons and images, at the same time as successfully reassessing – or raiding – their own cultures.[68] The result is 'creolisation', a mishmash of the global and the native. Political advertisers have been particularly eclectic. Ukrainian ads have adopted specifically Soviet symbols, such as the Kremlin clock tower used by the Communist Party of Ukraine (renewed) in 2002. The 1999 elections featured a puppet show on the 1+1 channel *Velyki*

perehony ('Great Races') which used Soviet, but also Ukrainian history to depict Ukraine's modern left-wing leaders (Moroz, Symonenko, Tkachenko and Vitrenko) as bickering Red Guards camped outside Kiev. Various versions of national Ukrainian symbolism are, of course, popular, ranging in 2002 from Our Ukraine's rebranding of the national colours to produce an azure and gold sunrise ('Morning in Ukraine', close in spirit to Ronald Reagan's sunny campaigns of the 1980s) to New Force's purloining of the wolverine imagery associated with the west Ukrainian neo-fascist Dmytro Dontsov (1883–1973).

Just as political technologists can't just import Western techniques or Western ads, 'full of American teeth',[69] there are also cultural barriers within the former Soviet space. Russian 'exports' don't necessarily sell unadapted, as with the failure of many of the projects designed by Russian firms for the Ukrainian elections in 2002. That said, local political technologists understand post-Soviet specifics much better than the occasional foreigners who venture into the market. The renowned London firm Saatchi & Saatchi worked with the Green Party of Ukraine in the 2002 elections. Their slogan 'Choose life', backed pictorially with a vaguely hippy-looking woman with an astrology chart and the party symbol in the background would probably have struggled in the West; it certainly didn't suit a Ukrainian party struggling to disguise the reality that it was run by bankers and energy traders. An interesting exception is François Mitterrand's campaign guru Jacques Séguéla, who has won several contracts in the former Soviet Union and whose written work has been translated into Russian.[70] The Mitterrand and Séguéla brand of Machiavellian 'realism' obviously transfers well.

A telling example of successful local styling was the runaway victory for the *arriviste* businessman Valerii Khoroshkovskyi in the Crimean constituency of Krasnoperekopsk in the 1998 Ukrainian elections. According to Efim Ostrovskii, the Russian designer of Khoroshkovskyi's 'New Generation' campaign, the secret of its success was that it was not just aimed at the here-and-now of actual youth. 'It was a teleological campaign. Soviet culture was so used to teleology.' This is where the modern Communist Party goes wrong, by 'offering the past in the present, not, as it used to, the future in the present'. Ostrovskii offered the voters a new version of the Soviet telos. 'The Soviet people got used to thinking "our life is hard – but our children's will be better".' So the campaign was designed to offer them the idea of 'a New Generation in their family as well. An old person cannot sympathise with Pinchuk [a middle-aged oligarch], but can sympathise with those just making their way.' Moreover, Ostrovskii approached them using a language they could under-stand, 'by reframing old Communist slogans' to present the candidate 'as a "young general of production" [a popular slogan from the Civil War period], thereby keeping the innovative content of the Red project, taking out the "Red" and keeping the "innovative", so that our message to them [the elderly] helped to validate their sense of their own heroic past.'[71] Khoroshkovskyi overcame a vener-able local Communist tradition to triumph with 53.6 per cent of the vote.

A rather cruder, but equally effective use of local symbolism, was the defamation campaign launched against the Belarusian opposition during the 2000 elections. The Belarusian TV film *An Autumn Fairytale* (voiced by Yury Azarenak) mocked first Gorbachev, Yeltsin ('Syrupy') and then Belarusian politicians as 'Know-Alls' in the pay of the rich and avaricious *Sprutsies* (Americans) from across the water to 'the Sunny Country' (the USSR), which was full of 'hard-working, hospitable and happy people [who] worked harmoniously, built space ships [and] blocked off inconvenient rivers', using well-known characters from Soviet animation. One day (i.e., in December 1991), 'together in a dark forest', the Know-Alls, 'drunk on syrup, decided that [the] Sunny Country shouldn't exist at all'. 'The distant Sprutsies were very happy about this,' the narrator continued, but in order to sell the locals their 'customs-free rubber fruit and vegetables . . . [the] Sunny Country had to be turned into an Island of Idiots.' The Sprutsies then switched their attention to 'the wonderful southern Flowery Country', i.e., Yugoslavia. 'The Sprutsies unleashed the evil Khashim Tachi on them, who lived in the neighbouring Dolbania, and gave him lots of money and weapons. But the inhabitants of the Flowery Country proved brave, beating Khashim and his rebels.' So 'the evil wizardess [Madeleine] Albright began to threaten them'. 'She ordered that their towns and villages be destroyed' – here there was a shot of a B-52 – while the Sprutsies 'tried to find another Know-All or Syrupy in the Flowery Country [shot of Vojislav Kostunica].' The moral was clear. 'Let us look around, and without difficulty we will see in our political arena our candidates for Know-All and Syrupy' (shots of opposition politicians and a prolonged close-up of an angry nationalist demonstrator). Azarenak finished by saying: 'The fairytale is make-believe, but in it lies a hint for the good guys.'[72]

After two campaigns in 1993 and 1995 in which the main establishment party was made to look out of touch, Russian political technologists soon grasped the importance of populist packaging well attuned to the local culture, in which the message is subliminal (or from which it is even absent). Vladimir Zhirinovskii was a pioneer of this type of campaigning; in his footsteps followed the Union of Right Forces in 1999 and, ironically since they were conservative parties, Rodina and the People's Party in 2003. Even after ten years' experience, however, money can still be misspent and certainly does not guarantee victory. In the 2001 Vladivostok campaign, one side spent the usual millions on concerts with free beer and food to promote its candidate's image; but victory went to the Image-Kontakt candidate (Sergei Darkin) after it organised groups of students in yellow T-shirts with the slogan *Nam tut zhyt* ('We have to live here') to clear up the mess afterwards. Sitnikov also claims to have subverted another big-money campaign (Lukoil) in the far north in 1999. Instead of spending money on concerts and billboards, Image-Kontakt provided local 'opinion-forming' grandmothers with good tea and honey, sufficient to make them sing the virtues of its candidate during the long polar nights.[73]

Media Technologies

Political technologists have many means of influencing the media agenda. Many are familiar in the West, but there is an overall cultural and structural difference. The larger groups*see themselves as more than mere service-providers for the media. Pavlovskii's aim is 'to create [his own virtual] media vertical to go alongside the administrative vertical of presidential power'.[74] FEP likes to organise 'experts meetings' on Tuesdays, which are designed to shape the news agenda for the next day. It has private links to the Foundation of Public Opinion (FPO), run by Aleksandr Oslon. FEP writes the questions, the FPO does the research. 'They then present the administration with a scenario on how to deal with their opponents in media space. Voloshin calls in the leading editors and tells them what is black, what is white, who to interview and who to not. The result is then [ideally] one big media information chain.'[75] In 2002 Marat Gelman was working on a similar project, trying to set up a 'brain' or 'analytical centre', 'the best in the country', to serve as 'a factory of ideas' within the main state channel, ORT.[76] As of 2004, the Ukrainian version of this system was the so-called *temnyky*, 'themes of the week', detailed instructions to the media on how to cover events, issued by Serhii Vasyliev, Kuchma's 'information tsar', which themselves served as a form of virtual reality.

Another type of direct influence is the covert employment of TV anchors, the dramatically labelled 'media-killers' (the widely used Anglicism being a pseudo-glamorised substitute for the traditional Russian term *ubiitsa*), who often deliver the crudest of attacks on their paymasters' enemies.[77] The close relationship between TV stars and their backers is indicated by the private terminology that classifies them as but one of any campaign's 'strike forces' (*udarnye sily*). Celebrity 'killers' include Sergei Dorenko at ORT, famous for his assault on Fatherland-All Russia in 1999, especially his lurid descriptions of Primakov's supposed health problems featuring gory operation footage (not, of course, showing Primakov himself); the liberal turned warmonger Mikhail Leontiev; Aleksandr Nevzorov, one of the original heroes of the *glasnost* press, also at ORT and originally close to Berezovskii; and Aleksandr Minkin at *Novaia gazeta,* Chubais' tormentor in 1997.[78] Other countries have their own 'killers', such as Yury Azarenak in Belarus, and Dmitrii Kiselev (ICTV) and Viacheslav Pikhovshek in Ukraine.

More indirectly, there is the practice of *zakazukha, dzhinsa* ('jeans', a term supposedly derived from the casual attire worn by most of the media's 'New Russian' sponsors in the early 1990s). This might involve placing stories. According to one price list for potential candidates published in 2001, 'a press conference would cost you about $500, an article in a solid paper at a regional level $1,500 to $2,000, placed in a central paper at the level of *Izvestiia* $10,000, a minute of air time on regional TV $250 to $300, and on central TV as much as $40,000'.[79] Alternatively, journalists might be paid to distort objectivity in news coverage. The variety of terms used to describe such practices shows the depth of 'professionalisation' involved. Russian euphemisms include 'partiality', 'reading [someone else's] thoughts', 'information filter' (interviewing experts, but only to back up one side of an argument), *konveier* ('conveyor belt' or 'assembly line'; i.e., hiding a particular scheme of falsehood in a general parade of truth), 'poisoned sandwich' (a negative stereotype buried in the middle of positive coverage) and 'sweet sandwich' (the reverse).[80]

Finally, there is the *kachka* ('toss'), the throwing out of 'news' stories which the mainstream media then quotes (now often via the internet). Lazy journalists may fail to check the original version of events, and the virtual version (or virtual invention) becomes validated by repetition as the original source is forgotten. This is not too dissimilar from American Republicans trying to influence the media agenda via *The Drudge Report*, but the post-Soviet way of doing things involves a much greater proportion of outright disinformation and embodies entire *dramaturgiia* rather than simple smears. A telling example is the story about the Communist Party's 'secret memo' outlining its supposed plans for a violent seizure of power, planted by the Kremlin's technologists in *Nezavismaia gazeta* on 8 June 1996 and then quoted as gospel truth by numerous reporters and even Yeltsin himself in a TV interview. The Kremlin's Plan B, if it looked as though the election could not be won, involved using the *kachka* as the excuse for their own unconstitutional prolongation of power.

Finally, the practice of publishing whole fake newspapers, usually in your opponent's name, is now common. Their purpose, moreover, is two fold: first to serve as anti-propaganda, to make your opponents look like anti-Semites, illiterates, etc.; second, to serve as a *kachka*, a series of virtual stories for tame media to pick up and exploit, such as the supposed 'Communist' paper *Ne dai bog* ('God Forbid') in 1996.

At election time, or at any major event such as the 2002 Dubrovka theatre hostage crisis, or after the mishandling of the sinking of the submarine Kursk in 2000, media blitzes or 'information shocks' (*informatsionnaia kontuziia*) are launched to obscure awkward details and drown out marginal voices. Russia's new media manipulators are great believers in Goebbels' principle that it takes a big lie or promise to swing a big vote. Hence the importance of *dramaturgiia*, which in Russian is not just 'drama' in the sense of excitement, but a whole scenario, like the work of a playwright (*dramaturg*). Advertising and fair reporting restrictions are only introduced with the formal opening of an election campaign, but by then the required 'scenario' may already be in place.

Organisational Technologies

A second area of work involves micro-technologies designed to grub for votes in the interstices of day-to-day campaigning, usually by blackening opponents. When 'elections don't incline to mass propaganda for or against a concrete candidate',[81] then the more technical micro-schemes of political technologists come into their own. Awkward individuals or covert 'partisan squads' (or 'purge groups', *gruppy zachistki*) are hired to disrupt rival candidates' public meetings, accusing them of promising the earth or not knowing what they are talking about or launching an unanswerable 'idiot question' (*duratstkii vopros*) such as 'Do you drink cognac in the morning, or just vodka, like before?'[82] Political technologists like Koshmarov have organised evening canvassing by company employees claiming to work for opponents, issued invitations to opponents' rallies in bad weather or to rallies that simply fail to happen, handed out free but shoddy goods from opponents (*imitatsiia podkupa*), superglued opponents' posters to car windscreens and freshly painted fences, organised fake support from sexual minorities and given out free condoms to conservative voters (there were many such gifts to elderly voters 'from Mr Symonenko', leader of the Ukrainian Communists, in 1999). This last tactic comes straight out of the Watergate history books. In 1972 Nixon aide Pat Buchanan smeared Pete McCloskey, Nixon's more moderate rival for the Republican nomination, by sending him donations from fake Gay Liberation and Black Panther organisations and then tipping off the press on the eve of the New Hampshire primary. In this tradition prostitutes have demonstrated in unsolicited support of the (supposedly too) liberal Moscow mayoral candidate Sergei Kirienko, and gays for macho man Lebed as governor of Krasnoiarsk.[83] Mere heterosexual activity does not seem to work as black PR in the post-Soviet states, however; it often has a positive effect instead. Zhirinovskii's technologists went so far as to organise his own sexual braggadocio in 1999, arranging for pictures of their boss to appear in *Playboy* and setting up a fake tryst with Italian porn star (and politician) Cicciolina.[84]

The organised abuse of sociology is another favourite campaign technology. The USSR bequeathed a relatively large 'industry' of academic sociology. However, apart from a brief period in the 1960s, Soviet sociology was subject to strict party control in the hope that it would help make the 'science' of planning more exact. (The KGB also had its own secret research department that examined some surprisingly sensitive questions, such as Estonians' attitude to foreign – Finnish – TV.)[85] The industry was large in scale, but its methodology was often imperfect, and, especially after tighter party control was introduced in the 1970s, the various agencies were too often used as means of winning inter-bureaucratic struggles by 'proving' that the people were on a particular faction's side.

Although many improvements were made after the onset of *glasnost* (the 'academic' legacy), post-Soviet sociology was therefore well practiced in manipulation (the 'party' legacy). According to the Ukrainian 'Progressive Socialist' Nataliia Vitrenko, herself something of an expert in fakery, 'some believe in witches, some in horoscopes, some in sociological surveys'.[86] The main tactic developed since 1991 is *risovat reiting* (literally 'ratings design'), particularly the use of false opinion polls to encourage public opinion to 'bandwagon [join in with] with the orchestra' (*efekt furgona z orkestrom*), a tactic also known as *reitingovyi pressing* (using ratings to pressure your opponents). Ukraine's 1999 presidential campaign showed the crucial importance of ratings manipulation in ensuring that candidates finished in the order planned by the technologists. The Pinchuk campaign team working for President Kuchma had its

> own sociological service ... making 'official' ratings with the aim of influencing public opinion (not just concerning the appropriate points for Kuchma – it was also possible here to 'help' the candidate who was considered the convenient opponent for Kuchma in the second round), and also for internal use (the real breakdown of forces in the electoral races and even the ratings of different television projects).[87]

Communist leader Petro Symonenko's ratings were therefore regularly over-reported to make sure he made it into the second round;[88] the opposite was true for the regime's main opponent, the Socialist Party leader Oleksandr Moroz.

For the elections to the Ukrainian parliament in 2002, the struggle was of a lower order – so-called 'barrier jumping' by smaller parties keen to convince voters they could hurdle the 4 per cent threshold to gain representation (5 per cent in Russia). For example, the Democratic Union implausibly claimed in autumn 2001 (albeit in its own party paper) to be running at an impressive 19.1 per cent, considerably better than the 0.9 per cent it eventually won.[89] On the other hand, massaged polls for the paper *Vecherni visti* ('Evening News'), which was close to the opposition Tymoshenko Bloc, helped to persuade voters to stick with the bloc, which eventually won 7.3 per cent of the vote. Most seriously, the main establishment coalition, For a United Ukraine, was claiming 18, even 20 per cent, instead of the then-consensus forecast of 4–5 per cent, which worried observers took as a portent of large-scale fraud. (It eventually settled for a claimed 11.8 per cent.) Opinion bandwagoning was rife in Russia in 2003, with United Russia, Rodina and the LDPR all pushed up, and the Communists and Yabloko pushed down.

False opinion polls are also used to try and demoralise opponents, as with Russia's Grigorii Yavlinskii in 1996, and even to persuade them to back out of the race. In a later case, also involving Yabloko and its leader in 1999, more or less the complete opposite happened: polls were fixed to persuade its supporters that the party was *already* guaranteed to get 5 per cent and that therefore they could safely defect to the rival 'liberal' party, the Union of Right Forces. Of course, such tactics require widespread media exposure to generate the desired effect. It is easy to suspect that some sociology may be completely virtual: i.e., that some surveys have never been carried out at all. The tactic can also backfire. Fatherland-All Russia's over-optimistic claims in 1999 may have persuaded many voters to back Unity instead. In 2003 the Kremlin threatened to institutionalise the abuse of sociology when it took over the main independent polling institute, Yurii Levada's VTsIOM, creating yet another type of 'strike force' for the more cynical technologists. Most political 'holdings' now include a tame survey firm, such as the Union of Right Forces and Leonid Sedov's All-Russian Centre for the Study of Public Opinion. Even the Communists were linked to the Centre for Researching Russian Political Culture.

Then there are tactics to undermine opponents' potential assets and advantages. The campaign organised by FEP for the SDPU(o) and indirectly for the other main regime group, For a United Ukraine, in 2002 was particularly rich in these owing to the lead in the opinion polls then enjoyed by the main opposition coalition, Our Ukraine. There are six such tactics. The first is *dovedenie do absurda*, mimicking your opponents' best features or most promising actions to 'reduce them to the absurd',[90] or, alternatively, the use of the 'double object', the cloning of such features to provide your own client with the same advantages. Or the opposite – attempting to depict your opponent as having the same deficiencies as yourself (hence in Ukraine the attempt to replay the 'cassette scandal' that beset the president in 2000). The second is providing a surplus of other positive information to drown out your opponent's advantages. The third is encouraging rivals to peak early; a trap or snare (*lovushka*) that caught out Our Ukraine in 2002. The fourth is *zamuchivannia*, the tiring out, worrying to death and general playing on the nerves of your opponents. The fifth is *zhab"iache oko* ('toad's eye', as toads can only see moving objects), creating a big *shou* (show), obscuring some original story with virtual alternatives, giving virtual candidates artificial highs and lows so that the public's attention is distracted from steadier, and more serious, rivals. The sixth is inoculation (*privivka*). As with more aggressive styles of media management in the West, it is sometimes better to go public with your opponent's attack strategy (your client's potential negatives) yourself, so that your version of events gets first airing and shapes subsequent discussion. But not always; it is rather easier to suppress such stories in the former USSR.

Virtual Labels

Media manipulation and 'organisational' chicanery are not unknown in the West. What makes post-Soviet political technologists truly different is that much of the time they 'do not work with real objects [at all], but with their virtual replacements'. Their job is to shift the political struggle from the real to the virtual plane, where it can be more decisively shaped by 'information-communication technology'.[91] The virtual object can be their client (in local jargon, the 'sponsor of communication') and associated image, the client's opponent and image, or a more general political 'scenario', an entire virtual *dramaturgiia* with its own cast of sub-objects and mythogems. Indeed, the most successful virtual objects tend to be those incorporated into a more general virtual drama.

If the client is the intended virtual object, he, she or it seeks either an improved image or a more radical disguise. There are various types of 'information strategy' for beautifying the client.[92] The first concerns the names of parties, their pro-grammes and advertising slogans, all chosen as marques (in the original meaning) designed for maximum marketing effectiveness. Often names seem to have been chosen with deliberate irony. They have not; advisers simply cluster around the best brand name or marque available. Vladimir Zhirinovskii's Liberal-Democratic Party is the most commonly mocked multiple misnomer, but other examples abound. A personal favourite of mine came from Estonia in 2000, when a crisis erupted in the governing coalition in Tallinn owing to the departure of the Coalition Party – the only party that refused to stay in the coalition (leading members had been accused of corruption). The short-lived Christian-Liberal Party of Crimea scores three out of four on the absurdity index. A straightforward mafia front, only the words 'of Crimea' bore any relation to reality, although many of the party's mobster leaders, who were not particularly liberal and who lacked most Christian virtues, had strong links to neighbouring gangs from Russia and the Caucasus. The party collapsed after several spectacular months of internecine warfare in 1994, which left many of its leaders dead on the streets. In one sense, the party's name was a pure irrelevance. In another, the decision to hyphenate was highly indicative. After all, on what possible grounds could such a party choose between the two rival masks, the two rival catch-all labels? Long, hyphenated, over-determined titles are therefore common. Why is the Popular-Democratic Party of Ukraine both 'Popular' and 'Democratic'? Why is Zhirinovskii's party both 'Liberal' and 'Democratic'? Party marques are also 'stick-on labels' (see below).

Black PR

Alternatively, the political technologist may be asked to virtualise the client's opponent, to substitute in informational space a virtual version of the opponent's image that then becomes its accepted reality – if only for the key captive mass audience. It is in this particular sphere that better-known genre terms such as *kompromat* and 'black PR' properly belong. The entire range of operations carried out by political technologists in the former USSR is often referred to as black PR. This is a misnomer. Not everything that they do is strictly negative or 'black'. Much of their work reflects practices elsewhere (most national leaders, for example, abuse incumbency for TV advantage); much is even positive. Neither is everything that is negative necessarily 'black' – as with most political advertising in the USA. Nor is all of their work 'PR' as such. 'Black PR', in other words, is a subcategory of political technology. Aleksii Koshmarov has claimed that there is no distinction between 'black' and 'white' PR, only between that which is legal and that which is not.[93] A better definition is that black PR is PR that breaks existing legislation or current social norms,[94] or that the difference between white and black PR is that the latter's intent or true message is hidden, possibly even contrary to the superficial message.[95]

Kompromat is mudslinging – the use of compromising material, real or imagined (financial details, lurid videos, simple slander), against opponents. If successful, it is termed a *gvozd* (hit). *Kompromat* may be large-scale. In a 'blackmail state',[96] every-body is encouraged to play according to the existing rules, everybody is exposable, and the rules go unchallenged. In 2000 Yavlinskii was smeared in three programmes on ORT for taking money from abroad, from Jews and homosexuals, and from Sergei Mavrodii, whose collapsed pyramid scheme MMM had left many Russians with burnt fingers. Yavlinskii was also accused of having had cosmetic surgery. Micro-*kompromat* can involve planting stories about rival candidates' children studying abroad, expensive apartment redecoration, etc. Other terminology used by the makers of *kompromat* includes *podtasovka kart*, the unfair shuffling of the cards (facts) before presenting 'information', and *nakleivanie yarlykov*, the use of 'stick-on labels' to caricature opponents.[97] *Kompromat* proper uses real, but manipulated, evidence. 'Media-killers', however, often go in for more blatant slander. At the height of the Gongadze scandal in 2001, Mykhailo Pohrebinskyi's Centre for Political Research and Conflict Studies (with its reputed links to Pavlovskii in Moscow) released a 'psychological profile' of Gongadze – this was in effect a character assassination of a murder victim with a widow and two young children.[98]

Some virtual objects are invented or exploited purely as stereotypes to provoke antipathy. In Ukraine's 1999 election, the image of the main would-be opposition alliance, the so-called Kaniv-4, was manipulated so that the appearance of disunity, opportunism and petty squabbling would encourage an eventual pro-Kuchma vote. Many other opposition 'round-tables', originally set up to find a common candidate, have been sabotaged to create the image of a few bald men struggling over a comb, as with the Belarusian opposition in 2001 (see pages 184 and 197).

Virtual Subjects

Finally, when all of the above are assembled together, political technologists can hope to create virtual subjects, even a whole system of them. Virtualising the image of a client party or opposition is one thing; the grandest creations, however, are the political parties or candidates that are constructed by the technologists but begin to act causally on other elements of the political system, becoming a motive force in that system, sometimes seemingly taking over the system itself. Vladimir Zhirinovskii, Aleksandr Lebed, the Rodina Party in 2003, the Green Party of Ukraine and the Communist Party of Belarus are all designer products, but all have acted as political subjects in their own right. Real politicians and parties adjust their behaviour to compete with them, and are even forced to ape certain of their qualities.

Conclusions

As George Orwell argued in *Politics and the English Language* (1946), manipulation of meaning is the first step towards manipulation of politics as a whole. Nowadays, the 'language' of politics extends to advertisements, TV and the internet, and so is a lot broader than in Orwell's day.

One political technologist, Efim Ostrovskii, has sought to define the difference between two separate types of technology. The first type is the 'rough technologies' used by one part of the Russian elite, basically post-KGB active measures and the abuse of the administrative resources of the state. The second type includes the 'soft technologies' preferred by Ostrovskii himself. Destroying your opponent is too easy and possibly even a bit too vulgar for the likes of Ostrovskii, who has to compete in the market with some genuine vulgarians; manipulating the virtual space is a more elegant activity.[99] Both exercises are part of the virtual politics that is now systemic rather than merely occasional in the post-Soviet world.

Manuel Castells sounded an important warning: 'What is characteristic of scandal politics is that all political actors practising it become trapped by the system, often reversing roles: today's hunter is tomorrow's game.'[100] The rest of this book seeks to describe the system in more detail. After detailing some of the vulgarians' methods in Chapter 4, the manner in which political technologists have sought to disguise the main 'party of power' is discussed in Chapter 5, and the launching of various satellite projects in Chapter 6. The creation of the virtual impression of a disunited, self-interested or petty-minded opposition is discussed in Chapter 7; the invention of fake oppositions is dealt with in Chapter 8; and the whole *dramaturgiia* surrounding post-Communist Communist parties and the supposed 'Red threat' in Chapter 9.

4 'Administrative Resources'

> Adviser to President: 'Mr President, I have good news
> and bad news. The good news is that you have been re-
> elected. The bad news is that nobody voted for you.'
>
> A joke common to many post-Soviet states

The virtualisation of the electoral process is not the only way for the post-Soviet powers-that-be to ensure that they are the powers-that-remain. There is also the abuse of the state's 'administrative resources' to defraud the electoral process. The growing tendency to resort to more 'traditional' forms of election-fixing is reflected in this particular euphemism receiving the ultimate accolade of its own abbreviation in post-Soviet Newspeak – *adminresurs*. Any observer of the post-Communist world is soon struck by the frequency of references to these administrative resources. Opposition groups catalogue their abuse. Journalists sympathetic to the government debate in a coldly technical fashion how effectively they are being displayed. Apart from 'ethnic cleansing', however, there is no more widespread or dangerous euphemism in the post-Communist world. To speak of the powers-that-be drawing on 'resources' confers an undeserved legitimacy on their activities, and most of the abuses in question have little to do with neutral Weberian 'administration'. Fraud is fraud. Cheating is cheating.

On the other hand, the types of resource in question constantly adapt to the changing circumstances. Post-Soviet 'administrative technologists' are constantly seeking to refine their art beyond the mere stuffing of ballot boxes. In the words of one Ukrainian commentator: 'The history of administrative resources' influence on the course of election campaigns in Ukraine has developed with every passing hour – together with the appearance of each new version of Microsoft Windows.'[1] Another commentator – no less an authority than a former adviser to the Ukrainian president, Dmytro Vydrin – has identified at least three types of resource. 'Direct administrative resources are the customary vulgar command-order methods, when local bureaucrats under central command order how to vote and whom to vote for, and whom to obstruct at elections.' The second type are 'concealed administrative resources [which] are, once again, vulgar manipulations of the results of elections (that is, with ballots, counting and so on)'. In Ukraine, according to Vydrin, the first type accounts for maybe 10 per cent of cases, the second only 5 per cent. Most instances are of the third, 'indirect' type which means 'budget financing for electoral projects supported by the powers-that-be' and 'one or another information project' linked to the former or for a more general purpose.[2] Another commentator adds a fourth category: 'so-called soft administrative currency', which includes 'lights in flats, heating', etc. – and the ability of the authorities to turn them on or off at will.[3] Money helps, but is not essential. 'If you have the power, you can do these things for free.'[4] Administrative resources can usually generate their own funds anyway. Even in the information sphere, 'administration' matters more than money; 'the influence of power on the mass media is always greater (and more open) than the influence of their owners themselves'.[5]

In the period before the official opening of the Ukrainian 2002 campaign, the Committee of Voters of Ukraine calculated that 34 per cent of abuses involved 'free or reduced-price hand-outs of goods and services', 29 per cent 'the use of official positions in the support of certain political forces' (including the redrawing of electoral boundaries to allow the most efficient application of administrative resources), 10 per cent 'enforced membership of a political party', just under 10 per cent 'opaque financing of preparations for election agitation' (advertisements supporting a particular candidate paid for out of a factory budget, etc), 7 per cent 'pressure on opposition political forces and mass media', 5 per cent 'the dissemination of anonymous and slanderous information', and 3 per cent 'compulsory meetings to raise election funds'. The rather baffling exactness of the proportions resulted from the committee's own classification of cases that were brought to its attention.[6]

Administrative resources alone do not guarantee electoral victory in the former USSR, although in a close race they obviously give incumbents a huge advantage. But just how much? Oleksandr Bulavin, the director of Ukraine's European Institute of Political Culture, once estimated that the overall effect of administrative resources gave the powers-that-be a 20–30 per cent head start in any election, not to mention the indirect effect in demoralising their opponents.[7] In practice, however, the effect is not fixed. It depends on the extent of the authorities' ambitions, the nature of the threats they wish to neutralise, the technical possibilities open to them and the strength of the countervailing pressure exerted by the international community and by domestic NGOs. It depends also on how 'virtual' the general environment is – and on whether administrative resources are used in alliance with virtual trickery, or as its substitute. It is a safe assumption, however, that the authorities' intentions do not vary much. In Belarus Lukashenka allegedly padded his victory by 20 per cent in 2001; in Azerbaijan in 2003 Ilham Aliyev by over 40 per cent. In Ukraine in 2002 administrative resources may have delivered 5–10 per cent of the overall vote.[8] The authorities wished to demonstrate that they had clean hands after the Gongadze affair, but were also well aware of their own unpopularity. They allowed in relatively large numbers of international observers – fraud was undoubtedly at lower levels than originally planned – but they could not allow the main pro-government parties to fail as they deserved. Pressure from abroad can therefore certainly reduce, if not eliminate, the use of administrative resources. In 2003 there was almost no such pressure on Azerbaijan, although there was some on Georgia.

Electoral Fraud

It is not argued here that electoral fraud is the primary means of securing power, but that such practices are overdetermined. The Kremlin resorted to administrative resources in the 2000 presidential election both to secure a first-round victory and as a matter of habit, and in 2004 to create as big a win as possible (as did Lukashenka in 2001 and Shevardnadze in 2000). On both occasions Putin would have won anyway. Crying foul is also part of local political ritual – to appease or mobilise supporters. The true extent of fraud is therefore often difficult to judge. Outright fraud is usually limited, relatively concealed and targeted. 'Falsification is a norm of politics in the post-Soviet space. Total violation of electoral law is not necessarily overt, brutal, but refined, well hidden – that has also become the norm.'[9] It is therefore in one sense also part of the virtual model, in so far as proclaimed results are not as they appear and the authorities' aim is to deceive rather than simply to overpower. The Central Asian states that still claim 99 per cent votes and turnouts are not really playing the credibility game.

The referendum on Russia's new constitution in 1993 was also in some ways an exception. The Yeltsin regime was playing for high stakes, and many of the methods used were relatively crude.[10] Turnout was claimed to be 54.8 per cent (50 was needed), but in reality was possibly as low as 46.1 per cent. Of these, fewer than half may have voted in favour of the constitution, rather than the reported 58.4 per cent.[11] Even the published figures told a strange story. The total number of votes in favour was recorded at 33 million, with 23.4 million against. This makes 56.4 million votes in total (58.2 million voters took a ballot paper, of which 0.5 million were not used and 1.3 million ruled invalid). In the simultaneous Duma elections there were supposedly 53.8 million effective votes (a turnout of 50.6 per cent). In adding dead souls[12] to the turnout in the final (normally quiet) hours, the Central Electoral Commission had failed to cover its tracks.[13] A second problem was that three votes were held on the same day, and the Kremlin gave the green light to local elites to fix their own election to the new upper house, the Council of the Federation. After padding the referendum *and* the vote for the upper house, the authorities then had to invent how the dead souls had voted in the Duma elections (at least seven million or an eighth of all votes, the difference between the claimed turnout of 56.4 million in the referendum vote and the probable actual 49 million). 'With the party lists it was easier and safer to attribute the surplus votes not to the forces that had been main opponents, and had sharp-sightedly shadowed one another [throughout the campaign, the main pro-government party], Russia's Choice and the Communists, but to the "dark horse" – the LDPR' (Zhirinovskii's Liberal-Democratic Party, now 'of Russia').[14] Furthermore, local elites (and the unsupervised summation of local voting protocols by regional 'working groups' provided the main possibility for fraud) had noticed the signals of covert official approval for the LDPR. Significantly, therefore, according to the commission under Aleksandr Sobianin set up by Yeltsin himself, the main beneficiary of vote fraud on the Duma side of elections was not Russia's Choice, Yegor Gaidar's supposed official Kremlin party (as Yeltsin was already backtracking towards more traditional allies in the 'force' ministries), but Zhirinovskii's party, which received an extra six million votes (that is, they perhaps really polled only 13, not 23 per cent). Zhirinovskii's party was awarded an extra twenty-three list seats, giving them fifty-nine rather than thirty-six. The other main beneficiaries were the Communists, with an extra 1.8 million votes and four seats, giving them thirty-two rather than twenty-eight; the Agrarians, an extra 1.7 million and a generous seven seats, giving them twenty-one rather than fourteen; and Women of Russia, an extra one million votes.[15] This only adds up if the extraordinary parallel claim that two million votes were taken *off* Russia's Choice (which it is worth restating was supposedly the establishment party) is also true – in which case the Kremlin's real priorities are revealed as hardly those of a liberal crusade.

There was parallel chicanery in the single-member districts. Zhirinovskii's victory in the safely hick region of Shchelkovo was initially queried by the local city court, which was quickly overruled by the higher Moscow oblast court in March 1994 (as was the victory of another regime 'scarecrow', Nataliia Vitrenko, in Ukraine's 1998 elections). Many other localities and ethnic republics were already gaining a reputation for being 'controlled regions':Tatarstan, for instance.[16]

After 1993 the authorities learnt the art of covering their tracks – but never with complete effectiveness, given the constant temptation to push for bigger fraud. In December 1995 the level of falsification was again extremely high. This time there was much less observation, and local authorities had recovered local power, particularly in 'controlled regions'. (The Chechens, who boycotted the 1993 elections, must have been particularly flattered by their 48 per cent vote for the new 'party of power', Our Home Is Russia, as with their 70 per cent vote for Yeltsin in 1996.) The possibilities for fraud were therefore to an extent more pluralistic. According to Sobianin, 'the lion's share of falsifications was once again received by the Communists and the national-patriots. However, around two million votes (about a sixth of all falsification) were received this time by Our Home Is Russia and the Rybkin Bloc, and around half a million by Women of Russia.' In 1995, therefore, Sobianin's calculation is that a total of 12 million votes were falsified.[17]

According to Aleksei Sitnikov, later president of the largest Russian PR group, Image-Kontakt, in the 1996 presidential election 'the Communists won, but didn't want to win. In the second round we miscounted ten million votes.'[18] Yeltsin's advisers later admitted to large-scale violations of electoral law, but claimed that as the Communists were just as bad, neither side could really accuse the other.[19] National turnout was adjusted at the last minute from 64 to 69 per cent; many votes 'against all' (4.8 per cent nationally) seem to have gone astray (only 0.9 per cent were found in Dagestan). Micro-fraud was relatively easy in most localities. Rather implausibly, between the rounds the Communist leader Gennadii Ziuganov's vote actually *went down* in areas such as Tatarstan, Dagestan and Kalmykia. However, in the twelve out of eighty-nine regions then controlled by Communist or neo-Communist governors (which contained some 25 per cent of the population), local power had to be bypassed – especially as the 'Red governors' had not been informed by the top Communist leadership of their willingness to be complicit in defeat. Sitnikov claimed to have set up 'secret projects' in these regions ('secret from everybody – local governors, media, even the FSB', Russia's successor organisation to the KGB). 'We were working like partisans,' he joked. The active measures favoured by these covert *gruppy zachistki* included disrupting Communist meetings, spreading false rumours and leaflets, and the 'interception' of rank-and-file Communists campaigning to get their vote out. The 'partisans' also forced shops in Krasnodar to stock the same range of goods as in 1991 (i.e., almost nothing – 'matches and vinegar' – though matches were a valuable item for some), and delivered Soviet-era ration cards (*talony*) direct to people's mailboxes – 'to remind them what Communism was really like'. 'This won us many more votes than media advertising. We got what we needed, at least an extra 15 per cent for Yeltsin.' Surprisingly, Sitnikov also considered the fake propaganda paper *Ne dai bog* potentially dangerous. 'It was printed on paper that was far too nice; its stories were too intellectual; it wouldn't work in the Red Belt. . . . So we stopped trains to prevent its distribution. We needed lorries to get the magazines off and dump them in the forest.'[20]

A pattern was established. The Communists' complaints were muted, not least because in the previous parliamentary elections it had been in the authorities' interest to distort their vote *upwards*. In the first round of voting in 1996 there was relatively little fraud, 'with the Communists' agreement',[21] as it suited the second-round scenario for Ziuganov to run Yeltsin fairly close in round one (he only trailed by 32.5 to 35.8 per cent), to help ensure that the gap would widen in the second round (40.7 to 54.4 per cent). Not that it would have suited the authorities to have Ziuganov leading Yeltsin in the first round, as many have claimed was actually the case.

In the 1999 Duma elections there was little need for fraud, as there were no particular targets to meet. Unity did relatively well anyway, but the Kremlin didn't try and push it into first place, as the 2000 presidential election was looming and the Communists would once again be required to function as bogeymen. The Luzhkov-Primakov Bloc, Fatherland–All Russia, on the other hand, had already been effectively dealt with by the black PR campaign against it (see page 54). This uncharacteristic self-restraint would be partly made up for in 2003, when the main aggrieved parties were Yabloko, which claimed 6 rather than 4.3 per cent and the Union of Right Forces, with 5.1 rather than 4 per cent.[22] This was almost certainly the result of late padding of the turnout (55.8 per cent was claimed, though Yabloko's partial parallel count put it nearer 46 per cent),[23] which diluted the vote for the outsider parties after Putin had phoned Yavlinskii at two o'clock in the morning to congratulate him on Yabloko's success.[24]

In the presidential election of 2000, however, Putin needed an extra cushion of votes to be elected outright in the first round, for which he required over 50 per cent. The electoral commission awarded him 52.9 per cent, but the truer figure was somewhere in the high 40s. Putin had a comfortable lead, but the election should have gone to a second round. In a country with a rapidly falling population, the electoral roll grew by an amazing 1.3 million between December 1999 and March 2000 (see Fig. 4.1). An extra 480,000 voters was perhaps plausible because of the addition of Chechnia, where voting was hardly possible in 1999, though the claim that 51 per cent of the newly re-enfranchised locals had voted for Putin was not. Again, the authorities were happy to promote the Communists in the early stages; but with Ziuganov's second place assured and a first-round majority for Putin within reach, the Communists now claimed some seven million votes had been taken from them, especially in controlled regions such as Dagestan (where this time Ziuganov supposedly won only 16.4 per cent) and Ingushetiia (4.6 per cent),[25] compared to Ziuganov's official national tally of 29.5 per cent (21.9 million votes). The *Moscow Times* estimated that 551,000 votes were added to Putin's total in Dagestan alone – where in the space of two hours, from 6 to 8 p.m., turnout soared from 59.2 to 83.6 per cent.[26] Once again the Communists made no serious challenge to the result.

First-round victories such as Putin's in 2000 are important for prestige reasons. In 2001 Lukashenka simply wanted to do better than Putin – hence his order to add 20 per cent to his winning total (75.7 rather than 57–58 per cent, see page 199).[27] This extra 20 per cent came from the government payroll vote, which, given the lack of privatisation, is still relatively large in Belarus, and from the so-called 'caterpillar', the progressive upward massaging of electoral returns by successive layers of bureaucracy as they travel towards the centre. In Armenia in 2003, on the other hand, the authorities seem to have been overcome by last-minute nerves. Sitting president Robert Kocharian was awarded only 49.5 per cent. Given widespread fraud,[28] the authorities could easily have pushed him over the 50 per cent threshold. Such faux-modesty was, of course, unconvincing; 49.5 per cent was just as implausibly precise as 50.5 per cent would have been. Kocharian, of course, won the second round.

In the elections to the Belarusian pocket parliament held in the same year as Putin's first victory (2000), *fewer* voters were necessary. As hardly any real opponents of the regime were allowed to stand, the fraudsters' main task was not to exaggerate the leads of regime supporters, but to claim a high-enough turnout (50 per cent plus) for the vote to be valid – mainly by cutting the electoral roll *after* the vote had taken place. A turnout of 61.08 per cent was finally claimed.[29] When turnout was most important in Russia, as with the December 1993 referendum on the new Yeltsin constitution, in which 50 per cent of voters were also required to vote, the same trick was pulled: that is, the opposite trick to inventing an expanded electorate in 2000. The registered electorate in December 1993 was a lowly 106.2 million, compared to 107.3 million only eight months earlier. (The turnout percentage automatically rises if fewer people are deemed to be eligible to vote.) Russia's yo-yo virtual voting population was apparently back up to 109.4 million in 2000 (see Fig. 4.1), then down again to 108.9 million in 2003. In 2004 it slumped dramatically to 106.97 million, when the turnout once again had to be raised (see page 113). Nevertheless, the alleged electorate was still larger than it was in 1991. Russia's total recorded census population, on the other hand, fell steadily over the period: from 148.5 million in 1991 to 145.2 million in 2002.

Fig. 4.1 The Russian Electorate and Russian Population, 1991–2004

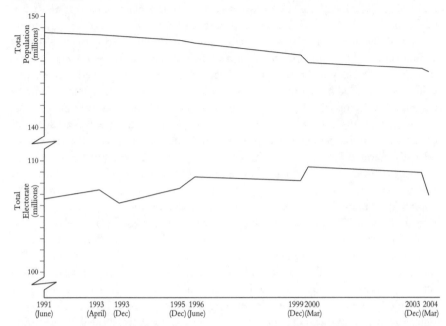

Sources for elections: www.cikrf.ru and www.essex.ac.uk/elections. Sources for population: for 1991 *Rossiia v tsifrakh, 1995* (Moscow: State Committee of the Russian Federation for Statistics, 1995), p. 24; for all other years to 2003, *Rossiia v tsifrakh, 2003* (Moscow: State Committee of the Russian Federation for Statistics, 2003), p. 67. Population figures usually refer to January of a given year (thus no second figure for December 1993), except in 2003, where the figure refers to the census taken in October 2002: hence the steep drop to 2004, where the estimate, for July, is from www.cia.gov. See also Goskomstat's site at www.info.gks.ru. Other estimates put the population as low as 142 million, given over-counting of up to five million in the 2002 census.[30]

A final, and rather more obvious, variant is to reduce the number of votes *cast*, rather than fiddling with the turnout or the claimed number of potential voters. In the 2002 Ukrainian elections the authorities faced a potentially powerful opposition (Our Ukraine). Hence the artificial obstacles, such as late opening and early closure of polling stations, placed in the way of Our Ukraine's relatively enthusiastic supporters in west and central Ukraine. Our Ukraine campaign chief Roman Bezsmertnyi claimed that his organisation's winning 23 per cent should really have been 27 per cent, which would have earned it an extra sixteen seats and made it much more difficult for the authorities' subsequent leapfrogging tactics to succeed (see pages 172–4).

'Election Technology' in Ukraine

Ukraine has its own history of electoral fraud. After a relatively clean first set of elections in 1994 (more exactly, limited fraud on behalf of the incumbent president Leonid Kravchuk in the west-centre was cancelled out by similar efforts for Kuchma in the east-centre), the 1998 parliamentary elections demonstrated both the possibilities for and limits of fraud. The Central Electoral Commission allowed mistrust to fester by taking almost four weeks to declare detailed results (massaging the figures required a certain amount of time, trying to get them to add up a little bit more). Election-night TV was therefore a bit dull. In the interim, the presidential administration's pressure on the commission managed to temper some results, though not all. Many of the key 'projects' backed by the authorities had been relative failures and needed a 'helping hand'. Delay also ensued because of the president's frustration at being unable to keep the opposition Socialists and feuding former prime minister Pavlo Lazarenko's Hromada party out of parliament. The Socialists (in alliance with the Village Party) comfortably cleared the 4 per cent barrier with its officially credited 8.6 per cent – though the party claimed another 4 per cent had been stolen from it.[31] Hromada was safe because its national rating of 4.7 per cent was heavily concentrated in the one (relatively populous) region safely controlled by Lazarenko, Dnipropetrovsk, where he also controlled the local electoral commission (Hromada won 37.4 per cent of the local vote). Hence Kuchma's preference for local administrations to be in charge of the count at the next elections in 1999.

The authorities therefore used two fall-back strategies: dead souls, of course, but also a tactic developed from Russia's 1993 and 1995 elections: 'donors'. Three official projects were struggling and required 'donations'. The Social-Democratic Party of Ukraine (united) of the Kiev elite, or SDPU(o), was rumoured to have won only 3.8 per cent of the vote. The National-Democratic Party, headed by the sitting prime minister, Valerii Pustovoitenko, could not be allowed to fail and fall anywhere near 4 per cent, and the administration also wanted to ensure the Progressive Socialist Party a place in parliament in order to weaken the official left. Fortunately, there was actually a surplus of other official projects in trouble, and two more, the Agrarian Party and Labour Ukraine, were designated as the main donors (the Agrarians would be officially tallied at 3.7 per cent, Labour Ukraine at 3.1 per cent). Moreover, the Agrarian Party's main function – drawing votes away from the Socialist-Village Party alliance – was now finished.

The Agrarians' official vote in its west Ukrainian strongholds such as Volyn (15 per cent) and Lviv (7 per cent) suddenly plummeted in neighbouring but equally rural Transcarpathia to allow the SDPU(o)'s national count to scrape over 4 per cent – it was awarded exactly 4.012 per cent. In the key constituencies, numbers seventy-one (where party leader Hryhorii Surkis was elected) and seventy-three (Viktor Medvedchuk), the Agrarian vote was tallied at a mere 1.9 and 1.4 per cent, the SDPU(o) at a massive 44.6 and 65.9 per cent.[32] On the other hand, the Progressive Socialist Party's strongholds were mainly in rural north and east Ukraine, so votes could be sliced off all parties' totals without them complaining too much. The biggest share of the party's overall vote, however, came from Sumy oblast (20.9 per cent), home to party leader Nataliia Vitrenko's constituency, but also to that of the main covert party sponsor, soon-to-be governor Volodymyr Shcherban. Nationally, Vitrenko's party was eventually awarded a similarly precise 4.046 per cent.

In 1999 rather cruder methods were used. Pressure was put on local governors and other vote-gatherers to pad President Kuchma's tally in the first round. On the Melnychenko tapes (secret recordings smuggled out of the country in 2000) Kuchma apparently says to Mykola Azarov, the head of the tax inspectorate:

> You should get together all your fucking tax inspectors . . . and warn them: those who lose the elections in the district will not work after the elections. . . . You should sit down with every [collective-farm] head and fucking tell them: either you sit in fucking jail – as I have more [*kompromat*] on you than anybody else – or you produce votes. Right or wrong?

Then Kuchma calls interior minister Yurii Kravchenko to encourage the police to work together with tax officials to reinforce the message:

> tell them: guys, if you don't fucking give as much as necessary, then tomorrow you will be where you should be – yes . . . those fucking central oblasts [where the challenge of Oleksandr Moroz, leader of the opposition Socialist Party, was strongest] they should be clear, we are not gonna play fucking games with them anymore . . . we must win with a formidable margin . . . when they say two or three per cent, it is not a victory . . . not a fucking place can say that it's protesting [that is, voting against the authorities].

Azarov concludes rather sheepishly with: 'Well right. Although not all of them are for Moroz.' The president, however, seems to prefer over-insurance.[33]

In 2002, with an influx of international observers after the Gongadze affair, the authorities were unable to prevent the most radical opposition parties – the Socialists (again) and Yuliia Tymoshenko's eponymous BYuT alliance (Bloc of Yuliia Tymoshenko) – from getting into parliament. A reversion to more indirect methods was necessary. Our Ukraine claimed that up to 1.5 million dead souls were available. Official data stretched all credibility by initially claiming an electorate of 38.27 million, compared to 37.5 million in 1998 and 38.2 million in 1994, before finally settling at 37.4 million (still a much higher percentage of the population than in Russia, 78 rather than 74 per cent);[34] although the December 2001 census recorded a three-million fall in the general population since 1989 (51.1 million in 1994, 49.5 million in 1998, 48.2 million in 2002). The company responsible for analysing the data was sacked after it began to point out the discrepancies. Moreover, up to 2.5 million Ukrainians were said to be working abroad – a larger proportion than in any other major European state. Third, the abolition of the *propiska* (residential permit) system in 2001 made it easier to manipulate the number of registered voters against the number of permanent residents (either way, but usually by increasing the former compared to the latter). Site workers and military personnel could easily be encouraged to move their place of registration *en masse*.

Opinion polls were predicting only 5–6 per cent for the authorities' main electoral vehicle, For a United Ukraine (FUU), but it eventually claimed 11.8 per cent. When the bloc's tame sociologist Mykola Mykhalchenko predicted 18 per cent, he was providing a cover story for the authorities maximum goal.[35] Late advertising is part of the explanation (see page 105), but clearly not all. Administrative resources were also used – though the scale of their deployment was diminished by the oversight operation. One analysis attributes up to 2 per cent of the FUU's total to crude manipulation of local voting protocols ('1' vote altered to '19' and so on) and about 3–4 per cent to dead souls (28,000–30,000 of the undead were brought back to life in Luhansk alone – whole invented buildings with more than average voter density were another favourite technique). The same analysis highlights the suspicious rejection of a huge number of 'faulty' or 'damaged' ballots: 963,462 or 3.7 per cent.[36] In the Donbas region (Donetsk and Luhansk), the 'technology' used was no more sophisticated than the 'directed voting' of entire workforces, the flagrant public distribution of fake ballot papers and thugs patrolling polling stations intimidating voters.[37]

The 2004 presidential election in Ukraine marked the development of yet another 'technology': this time the proliferation of covertly financed technical candidates. These might serve other purposes as 'flies' (to nibble at opponents' support, see pages 179–80), but were also designed to exploit the provision in the electoral law for each candidate to nominate 'trusted persons' to local election committees. In this way the official candidate Viktor Yanukovych was backed by thirteen out of twenty-three technical candidates, who were all polling less than 1 per cent but who had similar numbers (over 400) on the committees, so that overall Yanukovych could count on an estimated 60 to 65 per cent of the total numbers to do his bidding.[38] Another innovation, given the success of the exit poll sponsored by Western organisations for election night in 2002 in limiting the scope for plausible fraud, was the use of fake exit polls, which were more likely to tally with the fake results.[39]

Judicial Resources

The legal system is both an administrative and a propaganda resource. One 'laziness effect' has been an increasing trend towards crude judicial intervention in elections. Awkward candidates are simply pulled at the last minute by local courts or electoral commissions, as, in Russia, with the gubernatorial elections in Ingushetia in July 2000, Kursk in October 2000 (former vice-president Aleksandr Rutskoi) and Primorskii krai in June 2001. In 2003 former prosecutor general Yurii Skuratov – who had exposed corruption in the Yeltsin Family in 1999 before 'a man resembling the state prosecutor' featured in a black PR video with two prostitutes – was twice refused registration, both in a local constituency in Buriatia and on the Communist Party list. His bizarre 'offence' was to have concealed his qualifications as a professor. In the same year Rutskoi was again taken out of the race in Kursk. In Nizhnii-Novgorod Andrei Klimentiev was disqualified for the third time. People's Party leader Gennadii Raikov was granted an easy ride in Tiumen when both his

Communist and Union of Right Forces opponents were struck out on the same technicality – as state officials, their aides were allegedly illegitimately involved in their campaign. It goes without saying that this rule is never applied to establishment candidates who abuse their incumbency.[40] The call for 'reregistration' of political parties has become a regular occurrence in post-Soviet space. Not surprisingly, the new rules are never *easier*, and they sometimes fit the profiles of government parties (number of members, length of residence, etc) with uncanny accuracy.

The judicial harassment of opponents has received the nickname *Busmannizatsiia*, after the Moscow district where most of the pro-regime judgments have been made. In Ukraine, on the other hand, the Pechersk district in central Kiev, where the Rada (parliament) and many government offices are located, became notorious for the independence of the local judge Mykola Zamkovenko. He was therefore fired in 2001, and given a two-year suspended prison sentence in 2004. As a result of this activity, specialist lawyers can increasingly be found in campaign teams alongside 'political' and 'administrative' technologists: they are wanted not necessarily for their knowledge of the law, but rather for their good contacts with judges. Not-guilty verdicts are extremely rare and few legal judgements are overturned, so it is important to get your candidate's blow in first.

The General PRosecutor

The legal system is also used to label enemies as 'corrupt' – usually without actually getting round to prosecuting them. As in the Bolshevik era, opponents are often only 'warned', with a 'prophylactic' legal case initiated but not continued; alternatively, their associates are targeted first. The apex of the legal system in countries such as Russia and Ukraine has therefore been satirically dubbed 'the General PRosecutor'.[41] The PRosecutor is frequently used during election campaigns to air allegations that ought to remain sub judice – the primacy of the PR function being ably demonstrated by the timing, partiality and ephemerality of most allegations. Pre-election *ad hominem* attacks always masquerade as general 'wars on corruption'. However, as Volodymyr Polokhalo aptly commented on the eve of the 2002 Ukrainian elections, 'The struggle with shadow capital, with corruption, must begin more than two and a half months before elections. . . . Activating these issues just before the elections is evidence of the bias, opportunism and single-mindedness of exactly such actions we observe today.'[42]

The politicisation of the legal system is ably demonstrated on the Melnychenko tapes, when the Ukrainian state security chief Leonid Derkach is heard to say to Kuchma about Tymoshenko:

I have a plan laid out for dealing with Yuliia, and if, tomorrow, it suddenly becomes necessary, it will be set in motion. I have materials on contraband, criminal activities . . . [a criminal investigation that] is not over and was never closed, just set aside. [Based on the context, the reference appears to be to the occasion when Tymoshenko was caught flying out of the country with

$26,000 in cash, a criminal offence.] The material is just lying there. That is, we could open it up tomorrow and bring her in.[43]

Which is precisely what happened in February 2001. During the Gongadze affair, on the other hand, the Ukrainian PRosecutor Mykhailo Potebenko acted 'as if he were a defence lawyer for Kuchma', who was accused of ordering the disappearance of Gongadze, an outspoken opposition internet journalist,[44] stymieing any possibility of a substantive investigation. Potebenko stubbornly refused to accept that the mutilated body found just outside Kiev was Gongadze's, that the scars were Gongadze's, that the jewellery his wife recognised was Gongadze's, even initially that the DNA was Gongadze's. His reward was a free seat in parliament in 2002 – initially on the Communist list, though he left their ranks within a month.

Impunity and immunity, on the other hand, are defining characteristics of membership of the elite. PRosecutors' actions signal who is 'in' and who is 'out'. To this end, the legal system remains deliberately capricious. The Kremlin and its equivalents have sought to maintain the general difficulty of acting strictly within the law, so that anybody ultimately can be prosecuted if necessary. Nevertheless, the legal system is one of the areas where market principles have made an impact. Many PRosecutors at lower levels are simply for sale to the highest bidder.

The Inspectorate

Other state agencies are used in a similar fashion. Aggressive tax, fire and health-and-safety inspections are deployed to harass opposition groups and their financial supporters, even close them down; smaller-scale versions or merely the threat of such tactics help to keep the ruling circle united. Mykola Riabchuk eloquently describes how this fits with overall virtuality:

> The tax police and fire inspectors . . . numerous bodies established to license and supervise the *economic* activity of companies and individuals are widely used for *political* repression. Misrepresenting political reprisals as merely 'economic problems' not only circumvents international criticism and sanctions that the post-Soviet regimes deserve, but also effectively conceals the problem of the lack of political freedoms from the eyes of the public at home by subsuming this under the more general and, for most people, the more tangible problem of economic decline. An extremely corrupted economy and a highly intricate legal system provide the post-Soviet regimes with a perfect minefield on which any prospective opponent can be easily trapped and destroyed.[45]

In many post-Soviet states, the tax administration is regarded as almost as powerful as the security services. As with the legal system, moreover, the authorities have a vested interest in *not* cleaning the system up. So long as all are guilty to an extent, the state decides who is punished, as with Yukos's tax bill in 2003 or the extreme pressure on first Our Ukraine and then Socialist Party businessmen in 2002 to 2004.

Budgetary Resources

Money helps to an extent. The powers-that-be will always outspend their rivals, even if they use only their own considerable resources. The sums involved are enormous, even by Western standards. Yeltsin's victory in 1996 required somewhere between $1 and $2 billion; the authorities' likely spending for the 2004 presidential election in Ukraine was forecast to be $300 million. By comparison, even with the constant escalation of expenditure in American elections, the total official amount raised in 2000 was only $529 million ($193 million for George Bush, $133 million for Al Gore, plus others).[46]

'Organising victory' and cowing the opposition are only two reasons for spending money. The variety of covert uses explains why so much is raised, even when victory is assured. This can be seen most clearly when the favourite is not actually campaigning, as with Putin in 2000 and especially 2004; hundreds of millions of dollars still had to be raised. His virtual image had to be maintained, active measures against the opposition needed funding, and, most paradoxically and expensively, those who contributed to the campaign had to be allowed to take something back. (This important principle is described in detail in the next chapter.) Superficially, it seems that establishment candidates simply outspend the opposition by abusing the resources of the state. In fact, there is a deliberately complex nexus of 'private' and 'public' money, which can be dipped into from all sides. In 2002 one Russian, a certain Nikolai Chemodanov, a driver at the Constitutional Court, showed an excellent understanding of how the system works for others by forging Putin's signature to set up an entire fake ministry.[47] The planned budget of his Transport and Sports Maritime Service was $15 million. Chemodanov (in Russian 'Mr Suitcase') had no inside help and was arrested. Had he been better connected, few doubt he could have filled his suitcase with cash.

Covert monies constantly oil the system, not just at election time. One analysis puts the Kremlin's off-budget 'presidential fund' at an estimated $200 million per four-year electoral cycle, plus $50 million for PR services.[48] Regular irregular expenditures are also required to maintain loyal legislatures, prosecutors and judges. As of 2002, for example, Russian Duma deputies were paid a nominal salary of $400 a month, but for many of the most loyal or pivotal members this was topped up to $2,000 or even $5,000. According to Andrei Riabov, modern deputies are 'living the dream of the Brezhnev era. On the one hand, they belong to the ruling elite with all its privileges, but at the same time they are free to make their own money on the side – to vote for the authorities when required and work for big companies where necessary.'[49]

'Administrative Technology': Surkovism

Put all the above together and you have what might be called 'Surkovism', after Vladislav Surkov, deputy head of the Kremlin administration from May 1999. Surkov's preference was not for 'political technology' as such, but for 'the technology of strong political administration'. This meant the much more direct application of the key resources listed above (administrative, judicial *et al.*), and more direct pressure on key political actors: 'the Duma deputies, the eighty-eight governors, five to six TV bosses and the editors of twelve to fifteen leading newspapers'.[50] This got much quicker results and was, overall, much cheaper than launching expensive designer projects.

Indeed, by 2003 a new breed of service-provider was emerging, claiming that 'political' or 'election technology' was old hat. Instead, so-called 'administrative technologists' offered to arrange direct and privileged access to the kind of levers of power controlled by Surkov and his local equivalents. Not surprisingly, this only encouraged an increasingly passive understanding of the Kremlin's power. According to Ekaterina Egorova of Nikkolo-M, who was admittedly concerned to defend her traditional business, 'Nobody is working out proper strategies', instead they are just relying on the Kremlin to deliver the goods. 'You can have eight candidates in a constituency, and they are all after [what] the Kremlin [can give them].'[51] It is untrue that the 'administrative vertical' can operate in a vacuum without any other form of support, however. Surkov was only able to operate as he did because of other factors favouring a recentralisation of power: public opinion, the popularity of Putin at the system's apex, and economic growth oiling the system and easing grievances elsewhere. Moreover, naked power always needs a cover story: either democratic accountability or, as in this case, the virtual legitimacy created by political technology. The latter was not old hat after all.

Conclusions

Nevertheless, it was undoubtedly true that by the time of the 2003/4 electoral cycle, many Russian bureaucrats and politicians were developing a preference for administrative rather than electoral technology. By 2004 the likes of Gelman were complaining that they might soon be out of a job: 'Politics finished on 8 December [2003, the date of the Duma elections] . . . a technology of power has appeared [instead] in the form of the "tax inspection–procurator–court" triangle. And this political technology is far more effective than any that people like me can propose.'[52]

On the other hand, administrative resources alone do not guarantee victory in semi-democratic conditions (though they do where there is little pretence at democracy). Elections that rely on administrative manipulation alone can be problematic for the powers-that-be. Virtual trickery helps to disorient electorates and international observers, while simple fraud will provoke protest if oppositions have the power to react. Viewed solely from the authorities' selfish point of view, therefore, the 2003 presidential election in Azerbaijan was not virtual enough. The steal was too blatant, with 79.5 per cent claimed for Ilham Aliyev and 12.1 per cent for Isa Gambar of the Musavat party, when one respectable poll had Gambar on 36.3 per cent and Aliyev on 27.4 per cent.[53] (Azerbaijan's favourite fraud technique was simply to switch Gambar and Aliyev's regional totals.) Not enough was made of possible virtual tactics such as promoting Hafiz Hadjiev of the clone party Modern Musavat (at least he was awarded only 0.3 per cent) against Gambar, leader of the real Musavat ('Equality') party. The consequent protests had to be brutally suppressed.

Much publicity was given to Shevardnadze's last-gasp fraud in the 2003 Georgian elections a month later. In fact, Shevardnadze had pinned his survival hopes on a broad range of tactics. If anything, his coterie had assembled a more ambitious cover story for the elections than in Azerbaijan, running at least one fake opposition and trying to manipulate others (see page 189). Shevardnadze's failure demonstrated the importance of other factors: above all, a split in the regime and its consequently uncertain repressive capacities, and the fact that the new 'opposition' was able effectively to leverage international pressure.

The supposed 'constitutional settlement' announced by the Kremlin in Chechnia in 2003 was also implausibly crude – blatant stage-management that could only win credibility from the credulous (despite the neo-Bolshevik argument that such tactics make diplomatic protest impossible, unless you are prepared to call the Kremlin an outright liar). The script could have been lifted wholesale from a 1940 NKVD manual. In the fake constitutional referendum held in March 2003 turnout was claimed to be 85 per cent, but was probably nearer 30 per cent. The 'Yes' vote was supposedly 96 per cent.[54] At the fake presidential vote in October Moscow's candidate, Akhmed-hadji Kadyrov, was elected with 80.8 per cent on another massive turnout of 87.8 per cent. His nearest 'rivals', Abdula Bagaev and Shamil Buraiev, won 5.8 and 4 per cent, respectively; his real opponents, Aslanbek Aslakhanov and the businessman Malik Saidullaiev, had been forced out of the race entirely. By the time of the December 2003 Duma elections, officials were happy to announce a supposed 79.8 per cent vote (307,869 eager voters) for United Russia, followed by 92.3 per cent for Putin in 2004. In short, once votes begin to approach 90 per cent, all credibility is lost. The Kremlin's manoeuvring could not prevent Kadyrov's bloody assassination the following May.

Administrative technology is unlikely simply to take over, therefore. An element of pretence is still paramount. The balance may change, but virtual politics will survive. Significantly, in both Ukraine and Russia the powers-that-be seem to prefer mixed electoral systems. The proportional-representation element (national party lists) is a necessary vehicle for virtual parties. On the other hand, the constituency system has been retained, as it is in the constituencies that the cruder types of administrative resources can be more directly applied. In the 2002 Ukrainian elections, the three main opposition parties plus the Communists won the list vote with 57.8 per cent (and, given statistical overrepresentation, 170 out of 225 seats), but lost the districts, winning only 22.7 per cent (fifty-one out of 225 seats). In Belarus, where broadcast parties are less important, elections are still held using the constituency system. In Kazakhstan, proportional representation is used only for an experimental minority of seats. Volodymyr Polokhalo has therefore proposed that an 'index of administrative resources' can be calculated by comparing the number elected in the constituencies with the number elected on the party list. The higher the ratio, the more the party is dependent on its success in the constituencies. In 2002 For a United Ukraine won sixty-eight local districts and thirty-six list seats (a ratio of 1.9), Our Ukraine forty-two and seventy (0.6), the Communists six and fifty-nine (0.1). Significantly, of the thirty-seven incumbents standing for For a United Ukraine, twenty-two sought the true safety of the districts rather than the apparent safety of a guaranteed slot high on the party list,[55] despite the higher cost of the former. In the 2003 Duma elections, however, United Russia was successful both as a broadcast party, with 37.6 per cent in the list vote (120 out of 225 seats), and as a formidable user of administrative resources with 45.3 per cent of the constituencies (102 out of 225 seats). The Ukrainian authorities' concession of a pure proportional representation system for the next (parliamentary) elections due in 2006, made as a tactical manoeuvre during the 2004 (presidential) campaign, was therefore a significant setback for administrative technology – but possibly a boon for projects that relied on national TV exposure. Putin's announcement in 2004 that Russia would also move to pure proportional representation for the 2007 elections also heralded a likely shift back from 'Surkovist' to virtual technology.

5 Politics as Theatre: Disguising the State Holding Company

> Everything may be labelled – but everybody is not.
>
> Edith Wharton, *The Age of Innocence* (1920)[1]

Despite the revival of Bolshevik traditions of manipulation in the Gorbachev period, post-Soviet elites were often unsure how to conduct themselves in the immediate aftermath of 1991. The fine art of modern political technology only really came into its own with the Russian electoral cycle of 1995/6, since when it has been further refined in Russia and exported elsewhere. Many parties and politicians in 1991 to 1996 were of a 'transitional' type: not in the sense that some in the West might imagine of evolving towards the norms of liberal democracy, but in the sense that they were susceptible to manipulation without being originally designed as part of an entire (or core) system of manipulation. However, the reluctance of governing elites to submit themselves to free and open elections was already obvious. As incumbents they were usually unpopular, and as beneficiaries of the new economic order they had some very nefarious practices to cover up.[2]

Informatsionnaia Dramaturgiia

Political technologists' primary task is to reinvent their clients for the world of virtual democracy. There are two basic strategies. The first is simple image improvement, known locally as 'make me beautiful' (*sdelaite mne krasivo*), which seems superficially to be of the same type of 'image-making' as that familiar in the West. Politicians the world over require beautification, but in the post-Soviet world rather more is demanded of political technologists for their money. Their schemes must disguise the preservation of the old structures of power and their fusion with 'new' business opportunities, creating a giant state holding company, a permanent revolving door for melding political and economic power. Corruption and asset plunder are unlikely to figure prominently in anyone's election manifesto.[3] The bitter nature of inter-elite struggle also needs to be masked. As one observer has put it, 'the struggle among clans is more severe and immoral than among the political parties . . . the fighting is to the last man, until either of the warring sides emerges triumphant. And the end justifies the means: Politically discrediting the enemy and economically strangling the rival.'[4] Soviet elites were brought up in a ruthless political culture; many were of peasant origin and grew used to fighting hard and dirty on their way up. Putin chased rats in his stairwell as a child, the infamous Ukrainian prime minister Pavlo Lazarenko's first job was as a car driver on a collective farm. Given the criminalisation of the state, the opportunity cost of holding or not holding power is relatively high. Inside the magic circle, the rewards are stupendous; outside they disappear. It is, moreover, at the pre-election stage that the stakes are highest and the political struggle is often most bitter – there is more chance of losing out in a contest between elites than in being exposed to the electorate. The final act of voting itself can remain relatively 'free and fair', at least for the benefit of Western observers, as the real struggle has already been won.

Political technologists therefore employ virtual strategies of 'information make-up' (*informatsionnyi grim*) to reshape the raw political materials or push their clients into the background. A second, more radical, possibility is veiling the client behind an entire virtual drama (*informatsionnaia dramaturgiia*). According to Borges, there are only four basic devices in fantastic literature: 'the work within the work, the contamination of reality by dream, the voyage in time and the double';[5] this list can serve as a useful typology of virtual dramas in the post-Soviet world. In the first ('the work within the work'), public politics is increasingly difficult to read, being soaked in many complex layers of meaning, while the hinterland of subplots and private scripts is much less likely to be accessible to the reader or voter. Public politics is also 'intertextual', a kaleidoscope of different faces in different views. In the second ('the contamination of reality by dream'), the invented world can easily become the real. Borges invented the world of Tlön, whose history, language and philosophy were deemed so fabulous that they were adopted by the credulous real world in place of its own. In the post-Soviet world puppet politicians such as Zhirinovskii or Nataliia Vitrenko often end up playing a real political role. The great mass of voters stumbles around in an information haze, unsure of which are 'dream' and which are 'real' elements. In the third ('the voyage in time'), events are restaged at a time when their original meaning is lost, such as the 'Communist threat' to Russia in 1996, or, conversely, before they become more frighteningly real, like the 'terrorist threat' in 1999. And finally, in the fourth ('doubling' or the obfuscation of identity), the deliberate cloning of opponents or ideal-type assets is all-important in disconnecting political subjects, confusing observers and maintaining the theatricality of the system as a whole.

Many post-Soviet strategies combine various elements of the above. A favourite subtype of *dramaturgiia* is *perevod strelki* ('switching the points') to confuse both time and agency: shifting responsibility to blame the old regime, the IMF, the West or 'extremists' for society's current woes, or imposing a new drama over an old one, as with the Ukrainian authorities' attempts to redefine the issue at the 2004 election as being west versus east within Ukraine rather than being anything to do with moral issues of good governance after losing out at the dress rehearsal in 2002. Another favourite local strategy is *zelenye vorota* ('green gates'), the artificial polarisation of choice, usually involving the threat of *après moi, le deluge*, democracy in danger, or scarecrow extremists taking power.[6]

This Year's Model: The Primary Process
Post-Soviet elites did not grasp the need for disguise immediately after 1991. They first had to realise the inherently limited resource base for pure parties of the state: maybe a guaranteed minimum of 4 to 5 per cent from state bureaucrats and the same again from certain types of state employees and captive electorates (the prison population is usually reliable), and a variable amount of fraud. Our Home Is Russia won 10.1 per cent in the 1995 Duma elections, For a United Ukraine 11.8 per cent in the 2002 race for the Ukrainian Rada. More overtly successful state vehicles are either 'mass patriotic parties' in states with more direct use of administrative resources (Kazakhstan's Otan won a claimed 30.5 per cent in 1999, the New Azerbaijan Party 62.3 per cent in 2000, a no doubt disappointing drop on the 62.7 per cent it had first claimed in 1995), or are better disguised (Russia's Unity with 23.3 per cent in 1999).

The elite has therefore realised the need for candidates or parties without an obvious 'nomenclatura aura', though this does not mean giving up on the nomenclatura party. Certain types of administrative resource can only be dedicated to parties or politicians of the latter type. In other words, if there is to be more or less open encouragement to vote for the official party, people have to know which one it is. There is now often a common pattern of at least one project of each type (one overt, one or more covert: for example, United Russia and Rodina in 2003) – at least in Russia and Ukraine, as smaller states can sustain fewer projects.

A third stage is the development of what might be called a 'primary' process. Post-Soviet elites have few ideological commitments to constrain their choice of project beyond a vaguely defined 'centrism'. In a typical pre-election period, a variety of projects compete informally to win eventual baptism as the best vehicle or vehicles – most obviously for parties with the best disguise, possibly also even for the best nomenclatura vehicle. Alternatively, different varieties of the same project may be tried out to see which runs best – for the political analyst, it is therefore often worth revisiting the history of projects that never got off the ground to see why they were launched in the first place. If more than one of the various types seem to have legs, then several projects are combined in what is known as a 'many-layered pie' (see Chapter 6, especially page 119).[7] That is, the main 'official' party plus its satellites.

Sdelaite mne krasivo: **Early Official Projects in Russia**
A learning process was obviously under way in the early 1990s, affected by a variety of short-term factors in the first round of post-Soviet elections. In Russia in 1993 the Kremlin was divided between reformers and statists; both camps were further subdivided. The reformers' overestimation of their base electorate encouraged them to overproduce their party projects. There was no electoral incentive to unite their own ranks or divide the opposition's – as there would be in 1995, in advance of the presidential election due a year later. The campaign was also too short for serious plans to be laid. The outcome was therefore uncontrolled and unexpected to an extent, although not to the extent it appeared.

In 1993 the Kremlin also fumbled its first attempt to create a loyal two-party system by backing both Russia's Choice and the Party of Russian Unity and Accord – and making sure that eight out of twenty-one parties or blocs that sought to take part were kept off the ballot. These initial attempts at what Michael Urban dubbed 'democracy by design' were not as successful as later 'directed democracy'.[8] There is plenty of evidence for the Kremlin's underhand and illegal funding of Russia's Choice in 1992/3.[9] Former deputy prime minister Gennadii Burbulis and information minister Mikhail Poltoranin provided administrative resources. Viacheslav Bragin delivered state TV, but not especially effectively, as he was sacked four days after the elections. State and private structures were already blurred, with the State Property Fund (the custodian of the state's assets, pre-privatisation) working through the Association of Private and Privatised Enterprises, headed by Gaidar, Chubais and Filippov, to channel resources towards the main official 'projects'. Russia's Choice was never backed wholeheartedly, however, as its failings were already apparent by the autumn of 1993. Its TV adverts, prepared by Premier SV and RIM, were a disaster, lecturing voters on the need to back 'intellectuals' such as Gaidar, and depicting an unobtainable yuppie way of life 'in the style of Western product adverts'.[10] One famous image of a father's hand guiding a child, supposedly the symbol of Russia's chosen future, led most viewers to focus more immediately on the beautifully lacquered wood floor on which the youngster safely played. Other ads, which showed first the bloody confrontations between Yeltsin's forces and the Russian parliament that October (see pages 202–3) and then the hapless figure of the chubby Gaidar, only fanned the indifference of the large number of voters seeking to escape the polarised choice they presented; many ended up backing Zhirinovskii instead. Women of Russia (8.1 per cent) was also a surprise success, supposedly because of the large number of women recoiling from both sides of the bloody Moscow conflict. Gaidar's party won only 15.5 per cent, and only 3.9 per cent in 1995.

A useful second bet was the Party of Russian Unity and Accord (basically a proxy party for Prime Minister Chernomyrdin), which won 6.7 per cent. Although posing as a 'party of the regions', its real nature was demonstrated, and its political capital soon depleted, by its ultra-loyal voting record in 1993–95.[11] Hence it was an almost totally spent force in 1995, winning only 0.4 per cent. The Russian Movement for Democratic Reform won another 4.1 per cent and Yabloko 7.9 per cent (after the Kremlin had nudged financiers in its direction), so in fact the total, albeit badly divided, Kremlin vote was 34 per cent.

For the next Duma elections, in 1995, the much more ambitious plan launched by Yeltsin's chief of staff Sergei Filatov, and drawn up by the Kremlin technologists Georgii Satarov and Mark Urnov, initially aimed at completely 'reshuffl[ing] the political deck'.[12] Their original idea was to branch out right across the political spectrum – the strategy that would later be known as the many-layered pie. As well as helping to win seats by the back door, Satarov and Urnov argued that it would be better to accommodate rival clans within the Kremlin and so avoid the mistake made in 1993 of setting up a party too closely associated with the authorities to take all the potential public opprobrium on itself. A leaked document mentioned three Kremlin 'columns', although the idea of a third, nationalist bloc seems to have been quietly dropped.[13] So the Kremlin again ran a two-shot strategy by default, this time Our Home Is Russia (OHR) in the centre and the bloc led by Duma chair Ivan Rybkin on the left. However, the barrier had clearly been raised. Another leaked Kremlin memo baldly stated the authorities' other main goals: 'to straddle the wave of leftist sentiment, weaken the opposition's camp, and ensure that the ruling elite becomes fertile ground for a loyal mini-opposition', thereby providing 'a higher degree of insurance for the authorities'. The proposed two-bloc strategy, the authors warned, wouldn't capture the real nationalists, so some moderate rightists should be sponsored to 'ensure [their] relative loyalty . . . in the event they are successful in the elections'.[14]

The public parts of the strategy did not go too well. Georgii Yavlinskii attacked these fumbling early efforts at political control as 'puppet theatre' with a bad scriptwriter.[15] All the Kremlin projects were simply too public. The parties created were artificially designed to slot into particular spaces in the political spectrum, rather than being properly launched as PR projects. The most obvious satellite projects (first Civic Union, then the Congress of Russian Communities, known as KRO) were also too obvious. An OHR-Rybkin majority never seemed likely. Rybkin was given the task, but not the necessary resources to carry it out (though some money came from Gazprom's Imperial Bank via Sergei Rodinov), of drawing voters away from the real left. Rybkin's 'conversion' as Duma chair was a typical Yeltsin tactic, but his personal prominence made it impossible for the bloc to pose as a real opposition. The project's PR was also fairly unimaginative (the campaign was run by Yurii Petrov): first floating the name 'Accord', then 'Socialist Party', 'Russia's Regions', then the 'Union (*Souiz*) of Social Justice of Russia' (the acronym of which in Russian would have been 'SSSR', i.e., 'USSR'), before settling on a name that advertised to everybody both the artificial nature of the project and its incredibly narrow base. The bloc also suffered from Rybkin's loss of all his original suggested allies. First he quarrelled with the Agrarians, then lost General Gromov, the former Soviet commander in Afghanistan, and finally Mikhail Shmakov's trade-union bloc. All would more or less outscore Rybkin on their own. The Agrarian Party won 3.8 per cent; the Trade Union and Industrialists bloc 1.6 per cent; even Gromov won 0.7 per cent. (This at least was one big difference from the later era of 'directed democracy' under Putin – many political actors still possessed enough independence to operate awkwardly on their own.) The Rybkin Bloc, on the other hand, was left to achieve too much by itself, without the Kremlin organising substantial machinations elsewhere on the left, as it wanted to keep the Communist 'Red threat' intact for 1996. Rybkin was forced to concentrate on broadcast resources – it was the third-biggest spender on TV advertising – but only won 1.1 per cent,[16] which, allowing for some official 'help' on polling day, meant that almost no one actually voted for it. The project's adverts, produced by 'Russia's most talented admen', made the mistake of selling the bloc like chocolate, without any *dramaturgiia*.[17] Significantly, the Rybkin Bloc was only the first in a long series of failed projects on the centre-left (including earlier partial Kremlin support for Aleksandr Yakovlev's Russian Party of Social Democracy), demonstrating that the left brand was too closely associated with anti-systemic opposition for the voters to back 'loyal' reds. It was better, the Kremlin would soon conclude, to ensure that the existing opposition was neutered instead.

Our Home Is Russia (OHR) was awash with money at least. A complex offset scheme between Gazprom and the National Reserve Bank funded the OHR, and Yeltsin's later re-election campaign, to the tune of $20–$200 million.[18] Aleksandr Lebedev, head of the bank, was later accused of embezzling some $200 million and speculating with the funds of Vneshekonombank.[19] There is general agreement that Berezovskii was the 'main financial manager for Our Home Is Russia' and for Yeltsin's 1996 campaign – although whether he ended up as a net contributor after receiving certain 'pay-offs' is another question.[20] The OHR was, however, hampered by the two-stage election cycle. 'The aborted Soskovets strategy', drawn up by Yeltsin's hardline first deputy prime minister for 1996, would have involved the president leaning to the right.[21] Rival courtiers, Yeltsin's chief adviser Viktor Iliushin and privatisation guru Anatolii Chubais developed a three-stage polarisation plan instead: first, rehabilitate Yeltsin as a plausible reformer; second, mythologise him as the lesser of two evils; third, persuade voters to steer clear of any would-be 'third force'. Yeltsin therefore had an interest in encouraging disunion among his own apparent reformist supporters in the 1995 elections, so that he could then pose as the one man capable of uniting his 'pole', and also in preventing any other significant anti-Communist forces emerging. As Michael McFaul has it, 'according to some Kremlin officials, Yeltsin pressured Chernomyrdin to form a new block and to run in the parliamentary elections as an act of self-destruction'. Pointedly, the president never publicly endorsed Our Home Is Russia. 'Officials in the Congress of Russian Communities (KRO) tell a similar story about presidential manipulation of General Lebed', who was forced to play second fiddle to the Kremlin cuckoo Yurii Skokov.[22]

Our Home Is Russia's actual campaign, run by Nikkolo-M (Mintusov), Image-Kontakt (Sitnikov) and Yuliia Rusova, made many beginner's mistakes. The party's notorious 'roof' adverts prompted too many *krisha* jokes (referring to the mafia term for roof); and the party's name was too easily flipped into *Nash dom – gazprom*, a neat rhyme in Russian ('Our Home Is Gazprom') or *Nomenklaturnyi dom Rossii* ('The *Apparat*'s Home Is Russia'). The TV campaign (prepared once again by Premier SV, RIM and Aurora) attempted to convey the impression of Chernomydrin's 'personal responsibility for Russia', but instead created the reverse image of Russia as his personal property. By more clearly identifying the party of power, it also gave the opposition something to attack. The campaign also tried to free-ride on the 'synergetic' images of ORT's simultaneously broadcast series *The Russian Project* – which showed famous actors in various versions of Russian 'ideal reality' – though according to some this also boosted the Communist nostalgia vote.[23] The printing of the party's standard poster of Chernomyrdin on high-quality glossy paper was also distinctly unwise. The OHR ran too many 'foreign' ads featuring the likes of super-model Claudia Schiffer, attractive to some but too remote an image for most.[24] Finally, public perceptions were entirely correct. There was too much money in the OHR campaign. Too many of its leaders concentrated on spending it rather than leading the party to victory.[25] However, if the 1995 race once again showed the dangers of running too obviously pro-government a campaign, the conclusion drawn was not that the authorities would have to make themselves more popular, but that more subterfuge would be needed in the future.

Boris Yeltsin's re-election in 1996 is the archetype of the postmodern, post-Communist campaign. His startling comeback victory involved some standard political manoeuvring, particularly budgetary largesse and the promised end to the first Chechen War. But it also established the reputation of political technology, decisively breaking the previous pattern throughout the post-Communist world, whereby incumbents had found it very difficult to survive the traumas of 'transition' to secure re-election. Indeed, it is the campaign by which all others are now measured.

Two lessons were particularly clear: the importance of keeping politics 'within the family'; and the monopoly power of the state's residual resources if properly committed. It was, moreover, despite the hyperbolic claims made in the film *Spinning Boris*, almost entirely a domestic achievement. The campaign's main political technologists were Mintusov, Golovkov and Pavlovskii; the advertising campaign was run by Sergei Lisovskii and Mikhail Lesin.[26] From March onwards one group under Pavlovskii 'worked out scenarios in which Yeltsin would be re-elected and scenarios in which he would not',[27] while Image-Kontakt and others did the work on the ground. The project involved five main covert elements, which are all of sufficient importance to merit detailed discussion elsewhere here: the accumulation of huge financial resources to fund Yeltsin's campaign (see pages 114–15); an unprecedented use of administrative resources to distort the vote in 'controlled areas'; large-scale active measures to manipulate the voters in the so-called 'Red belt', where Communist governors could block the crudest methods (see pages 76–7); vigorous 'measures to destroy [each] opponent's resources' and ensure the 'separation of opponents from their funding sources and media access';[28] and, finally, the 'Lebed project' (see pages 123–5). The West bought the argument that the machinations it was aware of (the tip of a very large iceberg) were, in Strobe Talbott's words, the 'lesser of two evils – a deal that would help Russia avoid the real damnation of a return to power by the Communists'.[29] As did most Russians – although 4.8 per cent still voted 'against all' in the second round.

Yeltsin had little direct contact with the political technologists (apart from one meeting with Igor Mintusov), although his daughter Tatiana had more contact with Nikkolo-M, who devised a Russian version of Mitterrand's 1988 'Father of the Nation' strategy: 'Yeltsin – the President of All the Russians'. Most of Yeltsin's ads did not mention his name or attempt to defend his record (anti-politics always plays well in the former USSR). Slogans such as 'I believe, I love, I hope' and 'Vote with the heart' played on the myth that *Umon Rossiia ne poniat* ('Russia does not understand with the mind'). When the carefully orchestrated PR campaign did refer to Yeltsin, it emphasised all the qualities the president did not possess, such as public visibility, vigour and hard work.[30] The key to the whole campaign, however, was inverted *dramaturgiia* (*perevod strelki*).[31] A president who could not stand on his past stood on the Communists' past instead, except that Yeltsin's technologists coopted the Soviet habit of thinking teleologically so that Russia could look to the future without thinking too much about the present. Under the slogan 'Save Russia' a denim jacket (freedom for youth) was contrasted with a prisoner's coat, a globe (free travel) with barbed wire.[32] Ordinary folk (played by actors), natural Communist supporters, endorsed the president instead of the 'New Russians' who had played so badly in 1993. In the words of Alexei Levinson: 'You look at a person talking about the hardship of life, not necessarily linked to Communist rule, and all of a sudden he says "Let's vote for Yeltsin". It made a mishmash of their brains'.[33] The actual (virtual) Communist Party provided the perfect virtual object. One key poster expertly played with the fear that it was the Communists who were doing the inventing, showing the party's rose symbols as barbed wire below the ground: 'The Communist Party has not changed its name. It will not change its methods'. The 'Red threat', of course, had little to do with the real Communist Party, most of whose leaders had been safely – if privately – accommodated in the new political system (see pages 235–6 and 242–6).

The Three Bogatyrs

In 1999–2000 the two-shot strategy was finally successful – doubly so. In the Duma elections Kremlin-linked political technologists launched both Unity and the newly youthful and 'centrist' Union of Right Forces (URF). Moreover, the parliamentary (Unity–URF) and presidential projects (Putin) were designed to complement one another, playing on many of the same themes. All three owed their success to careful crafting of their virtual images on TV.

Unity was a party without an ideology and 'without a regional structure or even a real membership'; it nevertheless came from nowhere to win nearly a quarter of the vote (23.3 per cent) in the 1999 elections. Colton and McFaul quote Sergei Popov's observation that this election was 'an air war' directed from Moscow, not a hardslog 'ground war' in the provinces (significantly for a virtual TV party and a latecomer, Unity won only nine local constituencies, compared to thirty-one for its main rival Fatherland-All Russia [FAR]; it was created too late in the day to enjoy administrative resources).[34] This was not a victory for a particular programme – Unity didn't have one. Igor Shabduraslov, then first deputy head of the Russian presidential administration, candidly admitted in 2000:

Last Autumn [1999] ideology wasn't necessary from a tactical point of view, and couldn't be developed under the pressure of time [i.e., before the election]; but now, of course [a year later], if we are serious about the task of turning a movement into a party, an ideological platform is necessary. On the other hand, it's extremely difficult to think up anything original. If it [the missing ingredient X] does occur to someone, then that person deserves every praise.[35]

Instead, Unity combined a couple of images being tried out for the presidential race due in 2000 (i.e., not even for the election in hand): unity, of course; and a regional, even anti-metropolitan dynamic – invented by image-makers sitting in their Kremlin offices.[36] Two of the party's leaders were Siberians, who claimed they represented the *glubinka* ('regional depths'). Our Home Is Russia was deliberately kept out of the coalition and publicly humiliated to emphasise the 'new start'. Earlier projects from the political 'primary' season were quietly dropped, including Voice of Russia and the original idea that Unity should be a coalition of regional barons to rival FAR. The broader succession project required a new *dramaturgiia*, not just beating FAR at its own game.

At the same time, therefore, the project was part of the broader plan to re-mythologise power in Russia. Sergei Markov cites the popular Soviet film *A Station for Two* (1982) to back his claim that 'the Russian electorate is used to those who wear the right form [*kto nosit formu*], persons of authority'. As the film's hero says, 'A man came up in uniform [*v forme*] and asked for my passport. How could I not give it to him?'[37] One side of this project involved Putin the Chekist; the Unity side was designed (specifically by Gleb Pavlovskii) to evoke the image of the 'Three Bogatyrs' in Russian folklore; most famously depicted in Viktor Vasnetsov's painting *The Bogatyrs* (1898). The modern equivalents of the three (the legendary defenders of Rus: Ilia of Murom, Dobrinia Nikitich and Aliosha Popovich) were the three 'men of action' who topped the Unity list, none of whom was a proper politician – another Pavlovskii innovation. The one quasi-politician was Russia's minister for Emergency Situations Sergei Shoigu (who would ultimately decline to take up the post he won in the elections); the others were Aleksandr Gurov, one of the USSR's original virtual crime-fighters, and the wrestler and multiple Olympic medallist Aleksandr Karelin. Each had his allotted function in the election 'videodrome': 'Shoigu saves, Karelin fights and Gurov gives interviews.'[38] Hence also the logic in raiding Russian folktales to provide the party with its bear symbol. The party appeared on the ballot as 'Medved' ('Bear', a nickname from the party's full Russian name of *Mezhregionalnoe dvizhenie Edinstvo*, Me–dv–ed, 'Interregional Movement of Unity') – 'the tsar of the forest, not always good, but just'. The rival FAR bloc was depicted as a beaver, industrious and efficient, but Russians do not see careful husbandry as the function of politicians, certainly not, as was implied, of a state president.[39] Unity's main TV ad was actually a cartoon, showing a dilapidated house in the forest (the Russian state). Various animals symbolised other parties: a frog with a red shirt and hammer and sickle (the CPRF) swallows a fly with a cap (Luzhkov's trademark); a rabbit throws apples at the house (Yabloko); a ravenous wolf prowls (the oligarchs); but finally the bear stirs himself, kicks out the other animals and fixes up the house. For any viewer particularly slow on the uptake, the bear is dressed like a wrestler (Karelin). Unity's campaign posters showed the bear attacking a snarling wolf wearing a purple jacket and gold chain – an archetypal 'New Russian'.

As such, Unity pulled off another difficult double – winning votes through association with a popular incumbent prime minister (Putin), while disguising the true extent of its nomenclatura origins. Leading oligarch Boris Berezovskii therefore had to be discreetly pushed aside – much to his chagrin. Other Unity ads depicted fat-cat officials driving expensive cars, without the least sense of irony. By the end of the campaign, voters were actually *less* able to identify the 'party of power', and were just as likely to name FAR or the Communists as Unity.[40] Unity was, however, a quintessential Kremlin project. Aleksei Sitnikov claims credit for spotting as early as February 1999 'the niche for a new conservative party'.[41] Voloshin and his deputies Surkov and Shabduraslov were the main project 'administrators'. The biggest share of the credit for the project's overall design went to Pavlovskii and FEP, along with Golovkov, Yuliia Rusova and Sitnikov; its main initial financial sponsors were Berezovskii and Nikolai Aksenenko, the Family's nominee as first deputy prime minister (who also creamed off revenues from his old fiefdom in charge of the railways),[42] although Golovkov's Rosgosstrakh, Sibneft, Lukoil, despite being the main sponsor of FAR, and finally Gazprom (OHR) all eventually chipped in. In the end, though, money was less important than image. Launched as virtual projects, both Unity and Putin proved self-sustaining. Aksenenko would lose his job within months and Berezovskii ended up in exile. The relative failure of FAR, on the other hand, was blamed on its misguided preference for real instead of virtual politics – for 'building a party structure with local representatives and real membership' rather than 'cultivating its own image'. 'Neither Luzhkov nor Primakov, nor their consultants, believed in political adverts, and didn't understand the importance of their image and want to work on it.'[43] Their political consultants were from the second rank.[44] Even the Communist Party appeared on the ballot as a slogan – 'Victory' – inappropriately, as they didn't win or even want to. As a 'party of bureaucrats, they [FAR] considered that elections are managed administratively, and therefore in the main it's necessary to talk with [other] bureaucrats',[45] mainly other governors such as Luzhkov (Moscow), Yakovlev (St Petersburg) and Magomedali Magomadov (Dagestan). Finally, although the media environment was still relatively pluralistic in 1999, FAR failed to use 'its' channels (especially NTV) as effectively as Unity and the URF used 'theirs' (ORT, RTR to a lesser degree).

Unity also benefited by hiving off the 'liberal' brand to the Union of Right Forces (URF), making it easier for the former to pose as a party of (patriotic) power and displace FAR. As this time, the Kremlin still felt that it needed a liberal faction in the Duma, both to act as a ginger group and for display purposes in the West, but its political technologists knew that the discredited old brand would have to be reinvented. Originally this was to be achieved via a 'virtual Bulgarian scenario'. In Bulgaria the right had just returned to power after the left made a mess of governing in 1994–97; in the Russian version Prime Minister Primakov, who never enjoyed real power but provided a steady hand on the tiller after the economic crisis of 1998, was removed in favour of Sergei Stepashin, who wasn't around long enough to exercise power either. Nevertheless, 'new blood' was supposedly transfused.

The second trick was to run the URF as a 'New Generation' project, in parallel with the image-making for the Yeltsin–Putin succession, the first successful mass use of the principle *chem kruche, chem luche* ('the cooler, the better'). According to campaign strategist Piotr Shchedrovitskii (other key project designers included Leonid Gozman and Eldar Yanbukhtin of Kontakt PR, plus Gelman working for Kirienko), the ultimate secret of success for the URF was 'to combine two images', 'to keep hold of the 2–3 per cent who survived from the old electorate of Democratic Russia' and 'add the 5–6 per cent who backed the [carefully constructed] image of youth, energy and competence' built around Boris Nemtsov (Young Russia), Sergei Kirienko (New Force; both movements were set up in December 1998) and Irina Khakamada.[46] This 'New Generation' project, largely the work of Efim Ostrovskii, clearly benefited from its earlier trial runs, most recently for the young Ukrainian businessman, Valerii Khoroshkovskyi, in Crimea in 1998 (see page 193). The URF was also the first Russian party really to make good use of the internet, which had been developing in Russia since 1996/7 but in the 1999 elections went mainstream for the first time. The School of Cultural Policy supplied the URF with the pioneering websites 'Alternative Moscow' and 'Unofficial Moscow', Nemtsov's www.rosmol.ru and the 'virtual election' at www.elections.ru, reportedly the work of Marina Litvinovich of FEP. Ostrovskii and others aimed the project directly at youth, employing the flattering slogan *Ty prav* ('You're right', which has the same double meaning in Russian). The party also made a big splash on state TV, with a highly successful game show on which contestants could win places on the party's list (the so-called *kadrovyi konkurs*). This provided a double dose of newness: not just in the use of new technology, but also in promoting the image of youth and opportunity fighting against the cabalist nomenclatura of old (Kirienko's posters unfortunately also used the crass slogan 'Love women with new force').

Unpopular sponsors such as Chubais were kept in the background. Nevertheless, despite the technologists' makeover, the URF was still a party of big and usually elderly business, especially Chubais' United Energy Systems and the Guberniia group linked to Kirienko in Nizhnii-Novgorod, plus Alfa Bank, Transneft and, most importantly, Russian Aluminium. (The URF would later lose several deputies to the new Liberal Russia party who cited disillusionment with the party's business links as their reason for leaving, although their new party was backed by the exile Berezovskii.) The young and groovy URF also benefited from the old system's administrative resources. Via its connections with Mikhail Lesin and Video International, the URF received huge exposure on the second state channel, RTR. The final success for its technologists came in pulling off the difficult trick of combining ostensibly liberal ideas with a strong, even bellicose, line on Chechnia, which helped the URF to differentiate its brand from Georgii Yavlinskii's Yabloko and to free-ride on Putin's popularity at the same time.

Almost all of these lessons were forgotten in 2003 (after both Yanbukhtin and Litvinovich had left the campaign). Shchedrovitskii's percentage analysis was proved right. The URF's success in 1999 was not due to a sudden surge in support for Russian liberalism: the URF won because it had successfully posed as something else. This time it failed to do so. Kirienko drifted away and Chubais returned to prominence (he was described by one source as being 'like an elephant sitting on a horse').[47] Putin no longer provided direct endorsement, the party's tough line on Chechnia was now widespread, and the URF fell between two stools over the Khodorkovskii affair (the imprisonment of the Yukos oil tycoon, see pages 108–9) – angering the Kremlin by providing Khodorkovskii with some moral support, alienating other financial backers by not giving more. The URF failed to broaden its base by reaching out to the class of small- and medium-sized businesses which had expanded since 1999.[48] Many of these voted for Rodina or United Russia instead. The right parties' 'language was too ideological, and ideology is not the language of the new Russian middle class'.[49] The URF's campaign ads also repeated the mistakes made by Gaidar in 1993, depicting Nemtsov, Chubais and Khakamada aboard a private plane (supposedly symbolising economic take-off for Russia and its gilded elite), huddled over laptops and wielding expensive-looking pens.[50] The party's slogan, 'Vote for your future', was hopelessly bland, and failed to link voters to a future with the URF. Having been puffed up to 8.3 per cent in 1999, the URF collapsed back to 4 per cent four years later.

Colonel Ivan

An even more striking example of virtual campaigning is Vladimir Putin's extra-ordinary rise from obscurity. Many aspects of Putin's story are well known, but not the breadth of manipulation involved, or the difficulties he faced in his first term in tran-scending the many machinations involved in securing his election. Boris Kagarlitskii has asserted simply that 'Putin was thought up by political technology'; others that 'Putin is a political myth, created by specialists in PR campaigns', and his political strategy 'a snare of PR actions'.[51] Many of the same political technologists from the 1996 campaign and from Unity's more recent success, including Surkov, Pavlovskii, Nikkolo-M, Sergei Popov and Mikhail Margelov, formerly of Video International, helped prepare the 2000 campaign. Putin, however, was guaranteed victory from the moment Yelstin resigned in his favour. The real credit for 'Project Putin' goes to those who arranged the succession: Valentin Yumashev, Voloshin and Pavlovskii.

Despite some plotting for a Yeltsin 'third term' (none other than Putin, the future 'guarantor of the constitution', assured journalist Elena Tregubova privately 'that the Constitutional Court will take the decision that is necessary'),[52] it was clear after Yeltsin's many hospitalisations in 1996/7 that it would be difficult for him to repeat the success of 1996, although, as in 1996, cancelling the elections was also an option. The most striking success of what others dubbed the 'Manhattan Project' was therefore the superficially paradoxical creation of both a 'clone' and an 'anti-Yeltsin' as a means of securing regime continuity.[53] The symbolism of the transfer of power at New Year deliberately sought to play on Russian popular celebration of rites of death and renewal. Putin was invented as a man with the qualities the electorate had once seen in Yeltsin (his 'virtual deputy') and many of those they now saw in Primakov, as well as those which either man lacked.[54] Putin was therefore both an anti-Yeltsin (young, vigorous, comparatively erudite, sober – teetotal according to some of his propagandists) and an anti-Primakov (young, fresh, close to the more vigorous parts of the ancien régime rather than the CPRF). The 1999 apartment bombings also usefully discredited Primakov's partner, Yurii Luzhkov, as being unable to defend the capital. The genius of Project Putin was that it was also compatible with reviving the 'Red threat' tactic of 1996; not to threaten a Red victory – Putin's expected triumph was too obvious for that – but to keep turnout high and to contrast Putin further against the tired nostalgia of Ziuganov.

Sitnikov again claims credit for conducting voluminous research and creating the necessary profile – a politician 'who had to be young (forty to fifty), military, unknown to political life and, the main thing, different from other candidates (whatever they were), maybe even a nowhere man' – and then for getting his old ally Valentin Yumashev (Yeltsin's ghost writer, head of the presidential administration from 1997 and, after October 2001, his son-in-law) 'to convince Yeltsin that Putin would fit the bill'.[55] The question 'Who is Mr Putin?' keeps recurring, because the answer does not exist. As a virtual object, Putin was not a politician, not even a human life history as such, just a template. He had the main qualities required of him: malleability, saleability and loyalty to the ancien régime. Significantly, the first version of the project – *Preemnik-odin* ('Successor-1') – failed because Putin's predecessor as prime minister, Sergei Stepashin was too narrowly associated with Berezovskii and the Family, and because Stepashin was condemned in private as 'not a premier, but a milksop. A weakling',[56] who wouldn't act with sufficient force, both in Chechnia and against the regime's opponents. Loyalty was all-important. As a former Chekist who had already served some undistinguished masters (such as Sobchak in St Petersburg) quietly and efficiently, this came naturally to Putin. It can also be assumed that certain episodes in the past guaranteed his loyalty[57] – not because all post-Soviet politicians are necessarily corrupt, but because it can safely be assumed that Yeltsin's first question was: 'What do we have on him?' In one sense, therefore, Putin was like Dave in the eponymous 1993 Hollywood film: the president's body double who inherits the job when the real politician is incapacitated, but who is then warned by the White House staff that he is not really in charge. Yeltsin' daughter Tatiana said simply: 'He won't let us down.'[58] On the other hand, Putin was head of the FSB, the successor to the KGB, which wanted to bring the Yeltsin era to a close, and, as with Andropov in the late Brezhnev era, was already moving against key Family members. It is possible, even likely, that a balance of *kompromat* produced a Mexican stand-off of sorts,[59] given the uneasy balance of forces that survived until Putin's second election in 2004.

There were many layers to the transition deal. First was the notorious immunity decree issued by Putin on the day of his succession; second, the reported twelve-month 'stability of cadres' pact; third, the equally notorious deal with the oligarchs to keep out of their businesses if they kept out of politics. More generally, it was assumed that Voloshin would remain in charge of the Family's politics and Prime Minister Mikhail Kasianov would run the economy with an ear to the oligarchs' concerns. Both men's longevity was due to their adapting with their new master; it was only in 2003/4 that Putin finally outpaced them and emerged as his 'own man', sacking them both. In the end, of course, virtual objects turn into politicians too.

Project Putin also bridged other contradictions. On the one hand, Unity was used to help 'create a more attractive and understandable image for the Russian authorities and directly for President Putin in the eyes of Western public opinion . . . as [his] propagandists consider[ed], the Russian leader must cease to be "ex-KGB" and be seen as a conservative in the Western sense'[60] – although a big part of Unity's success came from attracting apolitical and/or apathetic voters with a low commitment to reform. On the other hand, Putin was also launched via the *dramaturgiia* of the second Chechen War. At best, this was, in Strobe Talbott's words, 'a gruesome bit of luck'.[61] Others have been more suspicious. Did elements in the FSB or one or other oligarch's 'special teams' help organise the invasion of Dagestan that provided the *casus belli* for renewing the war and/or the 1999 apartment bombings that ensured popular support? It would be rash to say yes – both for lack of direct evidence and because it might be dangerous to probe too far.[62] But it can certainly be said that events thereafter unfolded according to the priorities set by Kremlin political technologists earlier in the year. Aleksei Volin of the RIA allegedly told Tregubova privately (in response to a leading question) that the only way to raise Putin's rating from the 2 per cent he had recorded on his installation as prime minister in August was 'a small successful war'.[63] According to many versions of events, it was in any case Putin who persuaded Yeltsin to back all-out war rather than create some kind of 'sanitary cordon' around Chechnia. On the other hand, luck and timing were also crucial. The very same Volin and Mikhail Margelov, then the Kremlin's 'sharpest' technologists, had asked Tregubova a year earlier: 'How can we possibly market [*piarit*] something, when the client himself can't give us answers to fundamental questions?'[64] Tregubova's account depicts many parts of the Kremlin as in total chaos in Yeltsin's final years.

The idea of the anonymous national saviour has a pedigree in Russian literature, notably in Sergei Sharapov's novel *The Dictator* (1909), in which an everyman officer, 'Colonel Ivan', takes a commission from the tsar to rule with an iron hand. After he insists on 'complete, united and absolute' power, his rivals mass against him; but he asserts that there are a thousand like him to take his place.[65] There could, in other words, have been many Putins, many 'Ivans': he represented the revenge of the ordinary voter and his image was what others saw in him. Putin's key asset was his reliability in his allotted role and his fortunate timing. After more than a decade of turmoil, most Russians hankered after a period of order and stability, and Putin was ideally placed to sell such a promise.

Ukraine: *Vlada* Is Not *Vlast*

The first Ukrainian president, Leonid Kravchuk, was both unwilling and unable to organise anything like a 'party of power' for Ukraine's first post-Soviet elections in 1994. Four years later, in 1998, the main government vehicle was the National-Democratic Party (NDP). Its ponderous TV ads showed ministers and factory bosses in hard hats in the attempt to emphasise the party's 'experience'. Which, as with Chernomydrin's adverts for Our Home Is Russia in 1995, backfired badly. Set alongside images of Ukraine's industrial might, the adverts only served to underline who was really in charge of the country and what they had stolen or planned to steal. Party strategists promised 20 per cent or more of the vote, but delivered only 5 per cent. The popular joke dismissed the NDP as standing for *Nash dakh – prezydent* ('Our roof is the president' – using the Ukrainian version of the Russian mafia term *krisha* or roof), also a play on the neologism *Nash dom – Gazprom* in Russia in 1995. The other main regime party, the Social-Democratic Party of Ukraine (united), or SDPU(o), also found that its expensive PR operation backfired somewhat. Although credited by some neutral observers with running the most sophisticated campaign, the party did itself no favours with the slogan *Nasha komanda – nasha partiia* ('Our team – our party'), with the Dynamo Kiev football club and party logos placed side by side. It was far from clear what was 'social-democratic' about owning a football team. Even the citizens of Kiev were not impressed by such blatant free-riding, giving the party only 8.5 per cent of the vote, not much more than its national average of 4 per cent. (Significantly at these elections Rukh also made some early, partially successful, attempts to humanise its image, with more relaxed and personal adverts and the slogan 'Power to the people, bandits to prison!', prepared by Yaroslav Lesiuk and Roman Zvarych.)

Electoral technology really made its debut in Ukraine with the presidential election in 1999. Aleksei Sitnikov claims to have been brought in as 'a crisis manager' a month before the end of the campaign,[66] but the main group of technologists was from Dmitrii Alekseev's School for Election Techniques (bizarrely and implausibly disguised as the Fund for Interregional Ties between Moscow and Dnipropetrovsk). Working at a safe distance from Kiev in Dnipropetrovsk, it was they who were responsible for the black PR that disfigured the campaign.[67] On the other hand, according to an insider account by Viacheslav Yakubenko of the campaign team in Kiev:

> There weren't many true specialists here with broader Russian experience. . . . In truth they had worked only on local elections. Sergei Kotelnikov sorted out a candidate in one of the districts of Moscow, Petro Miloserdov worked in the faction of Vladimir Zhirinovskii, Iskander Valitov claimed never to have lost an election campaign – in Vladivostok and Usuriisk. Although Leonid Danylovych [Kuchma] didn't know about this. The majority of the other candidates also didn't know, although they hid in fright at the mention of 'Russian image-makers'. Therefore their biggest effect was psychological. They played the role of secret weapon.

Most of the Russian analytical team spent most of their time chasing local women and rewriting long strategy papers, although there was absolutely no doubt that 'to them this was just the latest contract, therefore moral principles and even the law didn't interest them much'.[68] The more hands-on creative team behind Kuchma's TV campaign – the fashionable Moscow clip-maker Andrei Semenov and Viktor Gelman, executive director of Russian MTV – had rather more impact. They created a carefully humanised mythology for Kuchma (who was about to emerge as a foul-mouthed thug on the Melnychenko tapes) in the programmes *Three Evenings with the President of Ukraine*, and faux-populist but carefully scripted chats with ordinary folk on the programme *Direct Broadcast* – though the staged 'conversation' between Kuchma on a giant TV screen and the 'average folk' on the street was anything but direct. The stilted, spliced dialogue wasn't even properly synchronised. The Russian 'creative team' also made sure the president's opponents were cast as quarrelling pygmies on the satirical puppet show *Great Races*, broadcast on the SDPU(o)-controlled channel 1+1. Other, more 'presidential', ads showed the newly rebuilt St Michael's Monastery, claiming credit for Kuchma for what was supposed to have been the result of a civic partnership between Kiev city council and Metropolitan Filaret's Ukrainian Orthodox Church.

Surprisingly the NDP was still around for the next Ukrainian parliamentary elections in 2002, although now serving as little more than a vehicle for the Kharkiv clan. Here it joined with four other parties to set up the bloc For a United Ukraine. Conceivably they might have won more votes separately, but they felt they had to unite to compete with former prime minister Viktor Yushchenko's Our Ukraine bloc. The government's advisers first proposed that their rival coalition run under the acronym TUNDRA, from Trudova Ukraïna (TU), or Labour Ukraine, actually the Dnipropetrovsk clan; the National-Democratic Party (ND) from Kharkiv; the Party of the Regions (R) in the Donbas, and the Agrarians (A) in the countryside. Such a name could hardly have been worse PR. In the words of Kiev mayor Oleksandr Omelchenko, 'I think anyone who knows at least some of this country's history, whose fate was to be born here and live through the great tragedies of this nation, is scared of the word "tundra"', with its obvious associations with Stalinist exile and its barren imagery – frozen and foreign – in a country that had suffered at least three famines in the twentieth century.'[69] Nor was its replacement acronym much better. In Ukrainian, For a United Ukraine (FUU) is Za edinu Ukraïnu, 'ZaedU' for short, which sounds too much like 'let's eat' – again, rather a risky image for a party with so many snouts in the trough. It was also too easily changed to 'ZaeBU' (with the alternative B standing for *bohatu*), creating 'For a United Rich Ukraine' – or 'I will fuck you' in Ukrainian. Also, the bloc's key 'sunflower' logo looked rather sinister – more like a jellyfish or medusa (the same word in many languages).

After the name change, the FUU's general PR improved. But it could not be sold in the same way as Unity in 1999 or United Russia in 2003 (see page 108). The Russian campaigns, with their stress on reasserting the mythology of the state, didn't transfer so well to Ukraine. *Vlada* (the Ukrainian for 'power') is not the same as *vlast* (the Russian). Ukrainians are used to thinking of power as something exercised elsewhere, by other people. The early adverts for the FUU therefore played safe, offering a ninety-second touchy-feely potted history of Ukraine modelled on Jacques Séguéla's montage *France 1789–1988* for François Mitterrand's successful re-election campaign in 1988.[70] Second, the FUU aired many of its adverts and infomercials during the Winter Olympics to make sure people saw them.

Significantly, however, unlike in Russia, the main campaign message had to be negative. As in Russia, the FUU copied Séguéla's 1988 slogan '*La France unie*' (For a 'united France'), but not 'A strong Russia is a united Russia' (see pages 108). Instead of playing on post-imperial psychology, the marketing of United Ukraine sought simply to exploit the popular yearning for stability and social accord. The FUU's final ads concentrated on the *threats* to Ukrainian 'unity', showing stark images of conflict (Chechnia, Palestine, the attack on the Twin Towers) with the slogan 'Somewhere there is war, but [there is] peace with us'. Ukraine's darker historical moments were invoked, followed by images of conscripts experiencing a tearful farewell as they get on to a call-up bus, off to defend a 'united Ukraine', but unlikely to be called to a real fight – unlike in Russia. This theme would be reprised in 2004, when the authorities' ads showed an idealistic cottage, enjoying the kind of prosperity not seen in the Ukrainian countryside for many a year. With threatening music offstage, the buxom collective farmer says 'I am for a *stable* Ukraine – What about you?'

FUU's central message in 2002 was therefore actually too Soviet, too paternalistic, too 'yesterday'; it consolidated the support of its target sub-electorate (elderly conservative voters), but no more. Respectable opinion polls had scored the alliance at a perilous 3.9 per cent in mid-February, recovering to 10 per cent precisely in the main exit poll, and an official 11.8 per cent.[71] The last, negative ads were the most effective. The FUU also went strongly negative against its opponents. These tactics, drawn up by Pavlovskii and Gelman, spoke volumes about the Ukrainian authorities' proclaimed 'Western' orientation, based as they were on the fanciful idea that the Gongadze scandal was actually a 'US conspiracy' designed to undermine Kuchma. Nevertheless, the message was pumped out on state TV and supported by the 'virtual chorus' of state-supported minor candidates (see pages 191–6), including Bohdan Boiko for a fake Rukh party on the right and Nataliia Vitrenko for the fake Progressive Socialists on the left. They were joined by a Western journalist, Charles Clover, formerly of the *Financial Times*, whose ill-judged and opaquely financed film *PR* was shown three times on the ICTV and 1+1 channels in the two weeks before the elections, spraying accusations against a standard list of supposed conspirators, including George Soros, the US ambassador, and Viktor Yushchenko's wife, apparently a CIA agent.

A final problem for the FUU derived from what Kimitaka Matsuzato has aptly termed the development of 'centralised *caciquismo*' (boss politics) in Ukraine.[72] The local machines that made up the FUU were a necessary part of the authorities' 'administrative' effort in the constituencies, but they made it much harder to reinvent the bloc for the list vote. (Unity, by contrast, did not really run in the constituencies in 1999.) The FUU's lopsided success in the elections (thirty-five seats on the party list but sixty-six in the constituencies, almost the exact inverse of Our Ukraine's ratio of seventy to forty-two), was dependent on its effort in the 225 territorial constituencies, particularly in the industrial heartlands of east Ukraine, where the local *caciquistas* now ruthlessly demolished the old 'Red belt'. This time around, the Communist Party won only six seats, compared to thirty-eight in 1998, only two of which were in its traditional stronghold in the Donbas. The very visibility of these political machines on the ground, however, made the FUU's national TV advertising less effective, and made it difficult to sell the bloc as something other than what it was. Finally, Russia's Unity continued to grow after the 1999 elections, but For a United Ukraine was not in the least bit united. By October 2002, not only had the bloc split into its original four constituent parts again, but it had also managed to create another four in the process.[73]

Kazakhstan

Politics in independent Kazakhstan has gone through at least two distinct phases. From 1991 to 1998 the regime made several clumsy and ultimately unsuccessful attempts to set up a powerful pro-presidential party. Thereafter it copied the 'many-layered pie' model used widely elsewhere. President Nazarbaev's first attempt was the Socialist Party, 'created in August 1991 to inherit the property and membership of the Kazakhstan Communist Party': that is, to make sure the powers-that-be would be the inheritors rather than a real opposition.[74] After ensuring that succession, Nazarbaev and his advisers briefly toyed with the idea that the Socialists could serve as the prescribed representatives of the Slavic half of Kazakhstan's ethnically divided society. The Kazakh half was to be represented by the Union of People's Unity (SNEK) set up in October 1992, later the People's Unity Party (PNEK). Kazakhstan's third party was the People's Congress Party (NKK), founded in October 1991, which became a 'soft opposition party' for one of President Nazarbaev's few real potential opponents, the poet Olzhas Suleimenov (his roots being in the 'quasi-governmental' Nevada-Semipalatinsk movement).[75]

This approach proved too 'divisive'. When the NKK briefly toyed with the idea of moving into real opposition, Suleimenov was quickly bought off with an ambassador's post in Italy. In the 1994 elections the PNEK won thirty-nine seats in the 177-member assembly and the Socialists fourteen, the by-then unreliable NKK thirteen. The Communist Party of Kazakhstan was prevented from taking part, but its leftist proxies (the Trade Union Federation and Peasants' Party) won sixteen seats.[76] The parliament was therefore dissolved within a year and the field thinned out for the 1995 elections, while another pro-presidential phantom, the Democratic Party (twelve seats), was set up to run alongside the PNEK (twenty-four seats). The Peasants' Union and the Trade Union Federation won five seats each; the Communists were allowed to win two.

Thereafter, party politics became more properly virtual, particularly after the regime faced what was potentially a serious challenge on the eve of the 1999 elections. Former prime minister Akezhan Kazhegeldin (served 1994–97) used his wealth and connections with Russian business to set up first the Republican People's Party of Kazakhstan, and then in 1998 the People's Front of Kazakhstan, along with the Communists and the would-be democratic party Azamat. The troika was pulled apart by classic divide-and-rule tactics (see pages 159–60) and the regime was forced to create a proper 'mass patriotic party', Otan (Fatherland), through the merger of the PNEK and the Democratic Party with some smaller groups such as the Liberal Movement of Kazakhstan and For Kazakhstan-2030.[77] The regime strong-armed state bureaucrats into joining, and Otan quickly claimed a membership of 126,500. It was also flanked by a variety of 'pie' parties (see pages 147–8).

Second Time Around

More than a decade into supposedly competitive politics in most successor states, the question of repeat performance has inevitably occurred. Sometimes the mask on a project has yet to be lifted, so it can be rerun. More likely, a new disguise has to be found, especially if a party or politician's 'nomenclatura aura' has been detected so that 'the process of changing political decorations' has to begin again. Fatally damaged projects have to be dumped and a 'single-use' rule maintained, as with the Ukrainian Green Party's inability to repeat its 1998 success in 2002. Sometimes projects can be reinvented, as, in part, with the Ukrainian SDPU(o) between 1998 and 2002 (see pages 140–2). More generally, *dramaturgiias* have to adapt if they are to remain effective. Russia successfully replaced the 'clash of ideology' drama in 1996 with the idea of the renewal of power in 1999/2000. But in 2003 the technologists had to begin again. According to Andrei Riabov of the Moscow Carnegie Centre in 2002, 'few people can be scared now by frightening stories about the CPRF'. On the other hand, 'there is no attractive [positive] project . . . United Fatherland or United Russia', what's the difference? (Unity and Fatherland – All Russia having cynically merged in 2001, and chosen the latter name): 'a virtual party and we already have a perfect idea of what that is: a party which is actually "mothballed" up to the election campaign, it offers few manifestations of its political activity and then the advanced media technologies are resorted to to swell the party to the size of a giant and it gets through the election campaign with a success.'[78] A negative consensus had emerged since 1999/2000: both market liberalism and opposition Communism seemed exhausted, but nothing positive had taken their places. According to one lament, 'many political technologists say that big political PR has lost the drama, the game, the poetry'.[79]

In 2003, moreover, United Russia could no longer pose as a neophyte, as by then it was the obvious 'party of power' – only more popular than some of its predecessors, given Putin's enduring appeal. It was also little more than a coalition of rival clans: one representing the former Our Home Is Russia and Yeltsin 'Family'; another, led by Aleksandr Bespalov, the Petersburg *chekisti*; and a third, led by Boris Gryzlov, the protégés of Vladislav Surkov – the man most interested in crafting a new image.[80] *Moskovskii komsomolets* reported that the competition between the groups was inflating the price of a seat on the party's election list to $1 million (the twenty-nine sitting governors on the list also fuelling the bidding war).[81] Nevertheless, all the leading companies (Interros, Lukoil, more of a FAR backer in 1999, even Yukos) had signed up by autumn 2003.[82] All had their share of seats, such as Lukoil's Valerii Prozorovskii. Voloshin and Surkov reportedly sold many positions on the list several times over.[83] Estimates of United Russia's total war chest range from $400 to $500 million and even $1 billion.[84]

One option for United Russia was therefore simply to outspend its opponents and rely on administrative technologies, such as the FAR in 1999. The easy PR option was to sell itself as the newly reinvigorated party of power. Its campaign posters in the summer of 2003 therefore featured the likes of Pushkin and Stolypin under the slogan 'A strong Russia is a united Russia'. The campaign of celebrity endorsements from beyond the grave really took off in the autumn when the party ran the notorious '145 faces' poster (one for each million of the Russian population – see illustration on p. 118). Superimposed on a map of Russia were Tolstoy, Pushkin and Stolypin (again), Dzherzhinskii, Stalin, Khrushchev, Josef Brodskii, et al. Surviving relatives complained about the use of Sakharov (then still alive), Solzhenitsyn and, a particularly cynical piece of exploitation, Artiom Borovik, a crusading anti-corruption journalist who wrote an exposé of the Soviet Union's 'hidden war' in Afghanistan[85] and died in a plane crash in 2000.[86]

Unity's 1999 campaign had skilfully presented the party as both a new virtual power and a virtual opposition. The secret of United Russia's success in 2003 was to rework this combination (Surkov had deputised Eldar Yanbukhtin for this particular job). United Russia was relaunched in spring 2003 as a 'popular people's party', and often seemed to be campaigning against its own government. The party's election-year programme marked a shift to the centre-left, where strategists could remember that the FAR had at one time threatened to outflank them in 1999. In the absence of any real leaders or emotive appeal, however, the necessary *dramaturgiia* was found in operation 'anti-oligarch' – the year's new big idea.[87] But which oligarch? In a sense any might serve as a sacrificial lamb – especially as it was always going to be one and never all. A seemingly arbitrary choice would in fact better serve to tar all with the same brush in the eyes of the public, and to 'shock and awe' the others, reminding them who's boss and how power and the protection of the law, in the Russian tradition, can never be routinised. There were many reasons for picking Mikhail Khodorkovskii, however. His company, Yukos, was the biggest, soon to get even bigger after its merger with Sibneft. More importantly, if the rumoured $24 billion sale of up to 40 per cent of its stock to ExxonMobil or Shevron-Texaco were to go through, the company would be almost untouchable. Khodorkovskii was also a real and symbolic representative of the old Yeltsin Family, busily promoting 'liberal' business and open accounting standards (more exactly, promoting a PR myth about such standards) that were anathema to the *siloviki* ('men of force' – the security services, defence, and the like). He was also funding the 'opposition'. How big a crime this was is not clear, as the opposition wasn't really in opposition. The Kremlin normally allocated such funding tasks anyway, and Yukos was also funding United Russia.[88] Khodorkovskii was breaking the normal rules, however, by concentrating on Yabloko (three positions on Yabloko's 2003 list, numbers eleven to thirteen, went to Yukos insiders)[89] and refusing to back the Seleznev project (see pages 257–8), while Yukos security supremo Aleksei Kondaurov was funding the Communists so generously as to imply company not Kremlin control (see pages 234–5). Khodorkovskii was also rash to assume that, if Putin's re-election in 2004 was to be a coronation of sorts, then the oligarchs had freedom to manoeuvre for 2008 – even talking of his own candidacy. Khodorkovskii was one of those who saw himself as kingmaker in 1999 and allegedly gave Putin 'insufficient respect'.[90]

On the other hand, Khodorkovskii's eventual arrest in October 2003 was prepared in a classic virtual fashion, via the May 2003 report by the National Strategy Council on the 'plot' by a cabal of oligarchs led by Khodorkovskii to take power in a new, more parliamentary republic (the threat of a Yukos-dominated Duma was semi-plausible). The council's director was one of the Kremlin *siloviki*'s new favourite technologists, Stanislav Belkovskii (he was rumoured to have a KGB past), but his scare story entitled 'The State and Oligarchs', alleging that 'Russia is on the verge of a creeping oligarchic coup', was very much of the *kachka* type premiered by Pavlovskii with his 'Theory Number One' about a Luzhkov plot back in 1994. (Although this time around Pavlovskii strongly opposed upsetting the traditional arithmetic with such a strategy.)[91] Just in case anybody missed it the first time, Belkovskii also penned an article on 'Putin's Loneliness', repeating his predictions of a coup.[92] As always, the *kachka* was itself designed to be the story, the virtual text to become the real news; and it was indeed used as the initial excuse for what at first were depicted as the 'prophylactic' arrests of Yukos executives. Belkovskii, however, advocated a general policy of 'national revanche', continuing the post-Yeltsin process of 'recapturing' state power and taking back the ill-gotten gains of the 1990s.

Many oligarchs close to the government were less keen on the campaign. First because they were themselves oligarchs and feared for the security of their own persons and property. Voloshin at least preferred a negative, anti-Communist campaign, and argued that the populist strategy favoured by the St Petersburg/*siloviki* faction would play into the hands of the CPRF. A bigger problem with the Belkovskii plan was that United Russia, or something like it, was likely still to be around at the next elections. The 'State and Oligarchs' campaign was conceived as PR, but carried its own momentum. Others in and around the Kremlin still favoured contracting out such campaigns to smaller parties, which could then be safely scuppered after any election. In so far as United Russia was now expected to deliver its promises or slogans, a politics of accountability risked entering the system by the back door.

However, in the short term at least, the anti-oligarch *dramaturgiia* proved to be the perfect virtual object, an enormously powerful lodestone realigning all parts of the political system – helped by the virtual chorus of 'satellite parties', such as the People's Party, Zhirinovskii and Rus (see pages 213–15), all harping on the same Belkovskii-inspired theme of 'national revanche'. United Russia and the Communists were still within competitive distance in September 2003. The year's 'October surprise', was the dramatic arrest of Khodorkovskii, with special forces storming his private plane. After this everything fell into place. United Russia, whose association with Putin grew more direct with every 'success' for the anti-Yukos campaign, won a resounding 37.6 per cent. The Communist Party's electorate was divided on two fronts. Traditional 'Brezhnevite' conservatives were tempted away to vote for United Russia, radicals for the Kremlin invention Rodina (9.1 per cent, see pages 260–4). The PR onslaught against the Communist Party leadership for its links with the oligarchs also caused many traditional voters to stay at home, so that its final vote plunged from 24.3 per cent in 1999 to 12.6 per cent. The Union of Right Forces was similarly split (4 per cent), with the 'law and order' voters it had won in 1999 now deserting for United Russia. The ground for Rodina's success and Zhirinovskii's revival (11.5 per cent, see pages 208–9) was prepared by the new virtual consensus of, in the words of Zhirinovskii's double-headed campaign slogan, 'We are for the Poor!', 'We are for the Russians!' Even Yabloko fell victim, with only 4.3 per cent. The ferocious black PR depicting the liberals as a tool of Yukos forced Yavlinskii on to the defensive, suggesting that he too shared many of Putin's values. As a result, too many of Yabloko's traditional anti-Kremlin voters may have stayed at home.[93] The overall results were spectacular. With greater use of administrative resources in the constituencies, the Kremlin now controlled more than 90 per cent of the Duma.

2004: The Search for Putin's Virtual Rival

Even before the 2003 Duma elections, Putin was reportedly 'fed up of competing with Ziuganov'.[94] A simple rerun of 2000 in 2004 would do nothing to launch his second term and would not play as well in the West. Moreover, Putin's opaque image was best defined by the nature of his opponents. There were many difficulties, however, with choosing the best 'certain loser',[95] particularly as the Kremlin's political technologists now faced the problem of their, if anything, having been too successful in the December Duma elections. All the other standard candidates, such as Yavlinskii after Yabloko's failure to win 5 per cent in 2003 or Zhirinovskii despite his success (or indeed because of it), faced credibility issues, but allowing a newer politician to emerge would create uncomfortable management problems for the next election cycle in 2007–08. It was also difficult to pluck candidates from nowhere as they needed two million signatures (if not backed by a specific party) to stand.

Moreover, Putin was more concerned with overcoming the original sin of his selection/election in 1999–2000. He felt like an 'accidental president', whose popular support was broad-based, but who was given insufficient respect by the men who considered they had put him in office. Having been elected as a virtual personality in 2000, Putin therefore sought an intensely personal victory in 2004.

One of the many benefits of the Yukos affair was that it distanced him from the oligarchs and from the Family; if only in virtual space. The Berezovskii-backed candidate Ivan Rybkin was forced to flee to London after calling Putin the 'number one oligarch in the country'.[96] Using the 'shock and awe' of Khodorkovskii's arrest and Voloshin's final ouster in October, he was able at last to stamp his authority on the elite. The Kremlin's steamroller strategy in 2004 was therefore to crush all opponents: originally in fact it hoped the 'against all' vote would come second, to demonstrate that Putin was the only 'serious politician' in the country; cynically ignoring the dangers of courting a protest vote.[97]

Putin himself projected a type of anti-politics. In February he used his main media set-piece to declare: 'To hold meetings, to compose all those beautiful [political] fairytales is [indeed] beautiful, but far from our real life. Instead I consider that I am simply obliged [*obiazan*] to give an account before my electors and the whole country of what has been done in the last four years.'[98] 'Giving an account' is not the same thing as being accountable, however. The Kremlin neither saw the public vote as a real election, capable of conferring a mandate for his second term, nor even as a plebiscite, given Putin's passive reference to his record ('what has been done'). The 'old Kremlin professional PR men (Vladislav Surkov, Gleb Pavlovskii)' were actually more concerned with manipulative scenarios to 'secure the "quality" of Putin's victory';[99] while to the increasingly dominant St Petersburg camp led by Dmitrii Kozak (after Voloshin's departure, the first deputy chief of the presidential staff), the point of the election was purely and simply the accumulation of votes for their own sake. Although the ground for Putin's second victory was prepared via the anti-oligarch *dramaturgiia* in the 2003 Duma campaign, politics as such was left behind when it ended. Instead, 'coronation' was an apt metaphor: not because there was a lot of pomp and circumstance, but because no one was allowed to question Putin's right to rule. While the privatisation of the economy may not have worked particularly well in modern Russia, basic aspects of politics have been effectively contracted out.

All 'opponents' were therefore to be controlled within extremely narrow limits. A token liberal should win a limited vote. Yavlinskii wisely turned down Surkov's private and unreliable offer of the premiership, even though he was told that he would be allowed to criticise the regime in public. Irina Khakamada from the Union of Right Forces, the so-called 'Samurai in a blouse' (kamikaze might have been more apt), was thinking of running anyway, but allegedly received private encouragement from the Kremlin.[100] One theory has it that she turned Petrushka with her bitingly critical comments on the 2002 theatre siege; another that she had a green light from Surkov, who had agreed $2.5 million to fund her signature collection, to 'liven up' the campaign.[101] The possibility of support from 'foreign oligarchs' (Berezovskii) was also rumoured. Much of Khakamada's other finance came from Leonid Nevzlin of Yukos, now resident in Israel. The Kremlin immediately issued an international arrest warrant against him in a crude black PR move – though in the looking-glass world of Russian politics this was not at all incompatible with private Kremlin support. Independent deputy Vladimir Ryzhkov was also briefly touted for the job of assembling a few remaining liberals in some kind of 'Union of Democratic Forces'. Other parties failed to put forward their biggest hitters. The Communists nominated Nikolai Kharitonov of the associated Agrarian-Industrial group rather than Ziuganov. His campaign had no momentum initially, forcing the Kremlin to give him covert support in the regions to keep him in the race. Zhirinovskii's nomination of his brawling bodyguard, Oleg Malyshkin, seemed designed to reduce all other candidates – bar Putin – to the same level. The final candidate, Sergei Mironov of the Party of Life, had a strange view of political competition, stating of Putin that 'when a leader goes into battle, he cannot be left without support'.[102]

The Western media devoted most of its attention to the problems faced by the token liberal, Khakamada. The Kremlin's biggest problem, though, was with Putin's alter ego, Sergei Glazev, who offered the only significant challenge on Putin's own electoral territory, as it was he who in many ways had first developed the populist politics of 'national revanche'.[103] Indeed, the nationalist party Glazev co-headed, Rodina ('Motherland'), was originally a Kremlin project to split the Communist vote in December 2003. Its 9.1 per cent share of the vote was the biggest surprise of the elections (see pages 260–4). So far, but no further. Although the Kremlin (Surkov) had backed the project, it did not want it to take on a life of its own. After December Rodina's Duma faction was not allowed to expand – although it was not allowed to contract, either. The Kremlin also considered Glazev's job done. As one commentator aptly put it, 'Glazev was useful to the Kremlin as a "spoiler" for the CPRF, but not as a politician who tried to "privatise" the anti-oligarch theme with pretensions to the presidential post in 2008.'[104] Moreover, Glazev broke a specific promise to his Kremlin managers not to stand in 2004. The Kremlin therefore sought to slow his bandwagon, first with covert finance – $3 million – and then in February by offering him the same post it had offered to Aleksandr Lebed in 1996, head of the National Security Council.[105] When Glazev refused, his more reliable colleagues Dmitrii Rogozin and Sergei Baburin were used to cut him off from Rodina's resources (a second wave of Kremlin money was released to make sure of their loyalty). Rodina therefore proposed the former Central Bank governor Viktor Gerashchenko as its candidate; but Gerashchenko ran a particularly lazy campaign that petered out when he failed to raise enough signatures. The parties in the Rodina bloc were then persuaded to desert Glazev one by one. In early March the Rodina Duma faction dropped him as its leader, forcing him to rely henceforth on his own image and resources. Other potential financiers such as Suleiman Kerimov (Nafta-Moskva), Oleg Deripaska (Russian Aluminium), Gennadii Kulik (Yeltsin's former chief of security) and Potanin's Interros were warned off.[106] On the ground, Glazev's 'campaign' was harassed at every turn. The deployment of a mixture of both carrot and stick was by now entirely to be expected. Predictably Glazev's response was to attack his tormentors, but this was also part of their plan. The Rodina electorate of December 2003 was largely pro-Putin; Glazev's otherwise understandable criticisms of the Kremlin were not what it wanted to hear.

Conversely, the Kremlin now backed the Communist candidate Kharitonov to leapfrog over Glazev into second place. In February it dished talk of a Communist boycott of the vote by promising Kharitonov free exposure on state TV, and made doubly sure by threatening the party's leading financier, Viktor Vidmanov (see pages 229–30), with prosecution.[107] Local authorities were told to help the Communists' campaign.[108] Once again, the vote was easily manipulated. Until the middle of February, when his troubles at home really began, Glazev still led Kharitonov in the polls.[109] But as his former allies deserted him, support began to ebb away. The final result gave Putin his desired triumph with 71.2 per cent of the vote. Kharitonov came second with 13.7 per cent (largely the CPRF's 'core' electorate, which did not particularly worry the Kremlin); while Glazev trailed in third with 4.1 per cent. Khakamada won 3.9, Malyshkin 2 and Mironov 0.8 per cent. The 'against alls' accounted for only 3.5 per cent. It is worth stressing that the Kremlin and its technologists had therefore done the exact opposite to 2003, when they had pushed the Communists down and Glazev up. Only three months later, they devoted all their efforts to pushing Glazev down and the Communists back up.

The other potential problem the Kremlin faced was low turnout. The 'race' for second place provided some interest for political junkies, but Putin's serene progress created little excitement around the main event. The order therefore went out for '70 on 70': Putin should win about 70 per cent of the vote and turnout should also be 70 per cent.[110] The simplest way to raise turnout was to remove those who didn't vote last time from the list. The official electorate in December 2003 was 108.9 million. By March 2004 the figure had fallen dramatically, and most implausibly, by almost two million to 106.97 million.[111] This time, however, administrative resources played a more important role than fraud. Their effective use by local governors became a test of their ability and willingness to give good service to the Kremlin: 'turnout became a striking indicator of the level of [local] authoritarianism and the enslavement of society.' In the 'controlled regions' run by the *otlichniki* (Kremlin favourites), turnout also correlated strongly with the vote for Putin: Kabardino-Balkariia came first with a 95.9 per cent turnout and 96.5 per cent for Putin, Ingushetia recorded a 91.1 per cent turnout and 98.2 per cent for Putin, Chechnia as ever an insulting 89.7 per cent turnout and 92.3 per cent for Putin.[112] The new, improved 'administrative vertical' demonstrated that it could get the vote out when it was really needed (turnout not having been so crucial in 2003). But it did not quite reach 70 per cent. An overall turnout of 64.3 per cent was claimed, up on 55.8 per cent in 2003.

The Honey Pot

State support for a particular party, formal or informal, can be a mixed blessing. A single drop of blood in the water will attract the piranhas. In so far as Russia at least has consolidated its party of power after the 2003–04 election cycle, this problem is only likely to grow. Russia's Party of Life, for example, launched with something of a media splash in 2002, was little more than a vehicle for laundering money via concerts, receptions and TV shows. Russian politicians have, after all, been taught the profit motive.[113] According to one Kremlin worker, Leonid Ivlev, 'party-building has turned into a form of business'.[114] The close link between business and campaign finance can work in either direction. With ongoing privatisation programmes, business supporters may either be persuaded to pay excessive prices or campaign contributions or be allowed to underpay as a reward for political service. In 2003 it was rumoured that Rosneft's payment of $600 million for Severnaia Neft was some $100-$200 million over the odds, with the excess funding official campaign coffers.[115] In Ukraine in 2004, the giant Kryvorizhstal steelworks were sold to a consortium headed by Rinat Akhmetov and Viktor Pinchuk for $800 million (4.26 billion hrivnias), despite US Steel and India's LNM Group offering $1.5 billion, in the hope that in return both the Donetsk (Akhmetov) and Dnipropetrovsk (Pinchuk) clans would work their hardest for the authorities in the election. To narrow the field, the authorities insisted that bidders had to have produced 1 million tons of coke and 2 million tons of rolled steel in Ukraine for the last three years, with at least two of the years being in profit. Electoral politics also provides an excellent lever for property redistribution. For 2004 the St Petersburg clan was seeking to expand its influence in Gazprom, Rosspirtprom, Rosneft and Rosoboroneksport – and, of course, benefit from the potential fire sale of Khodorkhovskii's Yukos empire (on the Yukos affair, see pages 108–9). That so much money is made at election time provides at least one good reason for expecting them to continue to be held.

Particularly in presidential campaigns, with hundreds of millions of dollars in soft money being bundled together from so many sources, the temptations can be considerable. Stage one is the collection of the money. According to Sitnikov, 'Berezovskii was the [financial] hero of the 1996 campaign', in that 'it was he who persuaded the other oligarchs that only Yeltsin could win' and then helped unlock the necessary resources for the campaign. On Sitnikov's perhaps fanciful account, an initial meeting with oligarchs was held in the Kremlin Oval Room, hosted by Yeltsin's director for administration, Pavel Borodin, who had previously helped enrich many of their number and would later play a nefarious role in the notorious Presidential Property Agency and the Mabetex scandal. The twelve main oligarchs were asked for $100 million each to fund the campaign. As several demurred, Yeltsin's head of security 'Korzhakov and Barsukov joined the party' and presented each of them with their KGB files, resulting in the rapid collection of $1.2 billion (the official limit was just under $3 million).[116] (Mikhail Barsukov, who had helped plan the assault on the Moscow White House in 1993, was then head of Yeltsin's Main Protective Administration.) Korzhakov himself remembers ten contributions of $50 million and a meeting in Yeltsin's daughter Tatiana's apartments – and says he wasn't there.[117] Other reports had it that the down payment was 280 million roubles, as paid by both Gazprom and the Smolenskii group.[118] The money assembled was then augmented by speculation on the Russian stock market in advance of Chubais' press conferences – with Chubais deliberately switching between optimism and pessimism to manipulate market activity. According to Sitnikov, this added 'more than $100 million' to the kitty.[119] Nevertheless, the money soon ran out or was diverted to other uses (see below).[120] According to Sitnikov, therefore: 'We needed more and created a special company, Montesori, controlled by Chubais and his accountant Arkadii Yevstafiev, to arrange all legal and illegal money flows.' Yevstafiev was one of those caught at the height of the campaign carrying $538,000 in cash (in reality just the tip of the iceberg) out of the White House in a Xerox box, accompanied by the mafia-connected Sergei Lisovskii, a powerful figure in TV advertising. 'Chubais was the brains behind the project, Yurii Yarov the hands, the executive director of the project.' Yarov's reward was to become first deputy head of the presidential administration and ultimately secretary of the Commonwealth of Independent States. 'Money flows were controlled by two men, Georgii Rogozin', a former KGB general who was then deputy director of personal security for Boris Yeltsin (i.e., Korzhakov's deputy), 'and Viktor Gaft', later general director of Image-Kontakt with Sitnikov.[121]

Stage two is spending the money. The united front presented by the oligarchs was obviously politically necessary. It was also economically essential, allowing the oligarchs to drain as much state money as possible. The money, in short, often wasn't even theirs. It simply represented the sum, though not the total, of the covert rents (subsidies, cheap loans, state spending channelled through the oligarchs' banks, etc) paid to them. Chernomyrdin complained in private about the campaign team: 'they're such an unreliable lot . . . whatever happens, they'll steal; the question is: how much?' If the official campaign limit was $3 million, and between $1 and $2 billion was raised, at least $200–$300 million was embezzled – not to mention the promises that were made of future privatisation 'dividends' further down the line.[122] Reddaway and Glinski record that 'at a minimum' $115 million was sent abroad, and that $137 million out of $169 million handed to Berezovskii to finance his TV company ORT may have disappeared.[123] Government bonds were also sold cheaply to the oligarchs.[124] Of the 67 trillion roubles (pre-revaluation) of state debt funded by Menatep, Oneksimbank, Alfa-Bank, the Moscow National Bank and National Reserve Bank in 1995–97, 36 trillion were estimated to be 'underfinanced'. At the April 1997 exchange rate, this was equivalent to a staggering $6.3 billion.[125] Other pay-offs included Sibneft going to Berezovskii, and Gusinskii gaining $120 million from the sale of 30 per cent of NTV to Gazprom.

Putin's 2000 campaign was financed in a similar manner.[126] The oligarchs were again tapped to repay some $1.5–$2 billion of outstanding debt to the state, but were allowed to pay in securities for which 'plenipotentiary' banks then paid hard cash at way over the market price. Moreover, after the 1998 rouble crash foreign bond investors had been offered the scant compensation of (non-equivalent) roubles frozen at the Central Bank. The oligarchs, especially Lukoil and TNK, now bought these up at a 30 per cent discount and sold them back to the Central Bank. Arms exporters received credit for goods already sold, while state bodies such as the customs office and Minatom were required to place their incomes in 'accessible' banks. Gazprom and others offset their debt to the state against monies owed by

Ukraine and the vague promise of equity in future privatisations. Once again, it was the state coffers that lost out. The amounts skimmed off were variously spent on the elections (25 to 33 per cent), and given to the oligarchs (the rest). The key asset 'redistribution' was of the Russian Aluminium Company to the Family.

Significantly, therefore, money flows in all directions and enmeshes all parties, patron and client.[127] By 2003 the oligarchs seemed more worried that they were being asked for unreasonable funds for United Russia (an estimated $300–$500 million) which might then be siphoned off by the Kremlin or the party leadership.[128] Voloshin and Surkov, and no doubt many others, were also allegedly lining their own pockets (see page 108). The 'tribute' nexus can also cross state boundaries. Russian oligarchs were intimately involved in Ukraine's 1999 election, with Berezovskii allegedly pledging $150 million (for a reported interest in the Inter TV channel and the Zaporizhzhia Aluminium Combine).[129] And vice versa: in 2000, Kuchma supposedly financed Putin to the slightly less generous tune of $50 million.[130] Belarus under Lukashenka wove an even more intimate web of intrigue with Russia's nexus of politics and business. Companies such as Torgexpo, the Mahmed Esambaiev Cultural Foundation and even the local Orthodox Church have made millions from 'transit income' and tax-free importing (the first two an estimated $320 million, 11 per cent of national income in 1995 to 1996).[131] Together with off-budget arms sales, Lukashenka's circle netted a supposed $4.5 billion, with the 'unofficial' budget rivalling the 'official' budget in size.[132] Lukashenka also provided privileges to the Yeltsin Family, especially Berezovskii again, through the tax-free passage into Russia of oil, cars, alcohol and tobacco – plus an interest in BMZ, the Belarusian Metallurgical Factory. Pavel Borodin, the Russian Communists and Duma chair Gennadii Seleznev have all used Belarus as their 'reserve aerodrome' (Seleznev having supposedly been a neutral arbiter sent to smooth the 1996 referendum crisis).[133] However, Russian funding for Lukashenka's 2001 campaign (and the arguably more important delivery of the Russian media to his side of the campaign) was conditional on his opening doors for Russian capital – which he then conspicuously failed to do. This, plus his past association with Berezovskii, was a key reason for the frosty relations that developed under Putin.

Ukraine's 1999 presidential election showed the same principles at work domestically, with similar 'contributions' expected from all the leading oligarchs and no fewer than three separate 'teams' channelling huge sums of money. The original sources of the money were many: campaign 'contributions', budget leaching, the Ukraïna bank (which collapsed under the strain in July 2001), and the network of companies controlled by those closest to Kuchma. Many, however, took out more than they put in. The point of such operations is not necessarily to make a net profit for the state; rather, it is to draw all the key players into the same corrupt game. Even the president complained about the feeding frenzy. On the Melnychenko tapes, he grumbles that 'after Lazarenko fell [in early 1999], an epic, so to speak, began, that Ukraine should help everybody'.[134] The prosecutor, general Mykhailo Potebenko, was allegedly bribed $100,000 to look the other way.[135] Kuchma is also heard on the tapes complaining to Ihor Bakai, head of the state energy monopoly Oil and Gas of Ukraine: 'I was looking in your eyes and you told me, "I will provide 250 million dollars for your election campaign."' According to the report to the president by the chief tax-sneak Mykola Azarov, however:

> roughly half of it . . . was not accounted for. . . . And I literally told him 'Well, Ihor, you have put at least 100 million in your pocket, at least. I understand that, of course, I will not set you up. I give you two weeks, a month at the most. (Then I showed him all the schemes.) Destroy them, these, so to say, your papers, which prove directly or indirectly all of your – you did it foolishly and stupidly' . . . he did it so that any stupid inspector could see his false schemes. Even a stupid one.[136]

Bakai lost his position soon after the election. In 2002–03, however, complicated refinancing deals between Oil and Gas of Ukraine and Russia's Gazprom were once again used to cream off funds for the authorities to spend in the 2004 election.[137] In 2004 the opposition accused the government of deliberately underrepresenting economic growth, so as to keep 15 billion hrivnias ($3.3 billion – not a credible amount) to spend on the campaign.[138]

Opposition parties are not immune from such temptations. Many are fronts run as businesses; even those with the best of intentions can be corrupted by an excess of funds. The Belarusian opposition was accused of diverting American aid in 2001 (see pages 199–200). Russia's Union of Right Forces lost two-thirds of its campaign funds in 2003.[139] Potential oppositions have often been neutered after receiving more funds than they needed, such as the CPRF in 2003.

Conclusions

> In the world of nature you can trust: but in the world of artifice – beware
>
> Saul Bellow, *The Adventures of Augie March* (1953)

A key weakness of all pro-government parties in the former USSR, however well they are disguised, is that they are not really parties of power. They are parties that *support* power. A good example is Unity, relabelled United Russia after its shotgun marriage with Fatherland-All Russia in 2001. It functioned well enough as a super-faction in the Duma, but Putin and Voloshin were reluctant to cede it any real power in running the country. Generous funding by the Kremlin and by businesspeople close to the Kremlin also created something of a feeding frenzy, as with misappropriations from presidential campaign budgets in Russia in 1996 and Ukraine in 1999. All the top leaders of United Russia – as well as Voloshin – were rumoured to be guilty of siphoning funds in 2003. Which is why the Kremlin's hopes of creating a 'dominant party' system akin to that of Mexico under the PRI or even Japan under the Liberal Democrats were misplaced. In Ukraine's 2002 elections, the For a United Ukraine coalition had no post-electoral life, lasting only long enough to prevail over the opposition and elect a parliamentary chair of its own choice before breaking up into its constituent parts (actually in this case further multiplying from four groups to nine). The cycle then begins again. Once the 'party of power' uses up the political capital originally won for it by its image-makers or starts to turn in on itself, a successor project has to be launched. Hence, making one of United Russia's leading sharks, Boris Gryzlov, Duma chair after the 2003 elections was a risky step.

United Russia's '145 faces' poster, 2003.
The Kremlin's version of Russian Who's Who.

6   How Many Towers in the Kremlin?
The 'Many-Layered Pie'

Normally in elections, the powers-that-be do not just run as beautified versions of themselves. To avoid placing too many eggs in one basket, post-Soviet political technologists have developed a tactic known as the 'many-layered pie' (*mnogosloinyi pirog*): that is, running a variety of ancillary projects to the main 'party of power' under various forms of disguise. The pie project gives the authorities more than one throw of the dice. It allows more controversial aspects of official politics to be contracted out, opprobrium to be shared or placed elsewhere, and plausible deniability preserved. Conversely, it also allows various opposition functions to be subcontracted to actors whose covert links to the authorities mean their 'opposition' will never be particularly vigorous. By definition, this second type of party and politician have more distant covert linkages; these will be discussed separately in Chapter 8. Finally, the pie principle provides the governing elite with a virtual chorus, a supposedly autonomous plurality of opinion that in fact echoes the main priorities of that elite. Hitting all of these targets at once is, of course, extremely difficult, as is the technologists' task of marketing the various layers of the pie as sufficiently different but still compatible.

Particularly in Russia, it is difficult overtly to market more than one party of power. The portion of the electorate that backs 'power', regardless of who holds it (the traditionalist subculture), believes by definition in 'one country, one tsar'. Moreover, the temptations of single-party rule are still strong. After the relative failure of the two-shot strategy in 1995 and the success of Unity in 1999, the Kremlin was more inclined to concentrate its efforts in 2003 (though it still hedged its bets with a variety of pie projects). On the other hand, there is also a strong incentive for elites to push their own particular projects, in the hope of being blessed with some share of electoral funds if they are added to the pie. Alternatively, the pie may be deliberately partitioned in order to draw rivals into the game – providing 'starter capital' and, it is hoped, buying future loyalty.[1] Parties run primarily as businesses are often launched with the intention of selling on their 'brand' once they have made their initial mark. Not surprisingly, therefore, there is often a problem with oversupply.

Sometimes, the pie can be assembled after the event (normally an election) from whatever ingredients have become available; sometimes it is planned well in advance – although some parts may not come out as intended. Various types of projects are used when there is pre-planning. One possibility is the 'Trojan Horse', designed to smuggle 'sponsors' into parliament under suitable disguises. The true nature of such a party can best be gleaned by examining its candidate list. A second type of project involves the creation of more remote 'satellite' parties (*sputniki*), which run more or less independently but then make a 'surprise' addition to sponsors' ranks after the elections. Here, the party's finances may be a better indicator of where its true loyalties lie. A third type is the 'proxy party', which maintains an independent existence but serves as an ally of the original sponsors in its parliamentary or general afterlife.

Pie politics has been important in both the Yeltsin and Putin eras. In the earlier period, creating successful parties of power was difficult, so the regime needed more options. Significantly, however, the Kremlin did not give up on pie politics once Unity and United Russia had triumphed in 1999 and 2003; it simply raised its ambitions and used the pie principle to win total control of public politics.

Early Experiments

In the early 1990s the pie principle was relatively undeveloped. In the 1993 Russian Duma elections a variety of parties with covert links to the Kremlin ran, but their efforts were largely uncoordinated and too often competitive. Kremlin 'satellites' performed poorly: the Civic Union won only 1.9 per cent, though the latter's 'youth' offshoot, New Names – its candidates' average age was thirty-four – won 1.25 per cent. The ecology front Cedar was already attracting some business sponsors, but not enough to back a serious 'project', and only won a lowly 0.8 per cent. Although the disappointing performance of Russia's Choice (15.5 per cent) was slightly offset by a handy 6.7 per cent for the Party of Russian Unity and Accord, the powers-that-be had few other irons in the fire.

There were, however, parties of a 'transitional' type: not in the sense of transition towards proper electoral vehicles conforming to the Western ideal, but in transition from acting as fairly independent launch pads to becoming (after the elections) full creatures of the Kremlin. The Agrarian Party, which won 8 per cent, was set up on the eve of the elections, launched in part by the Communists as a second bet or life-raft if the CPRF ban remained in place. To their way of thinking, it was natural to have two ostensibly 'class'-based parties, but it was also natural to second (then) Communists such as Ivan Rybkin on to its list. But a more remote satellite was always more susceptible to Kremlin influence, and the party was soon drawn into its orbit because the 'top of the Agrarian elite is engaged in business which is Kremlin-dependent' (for export or alcohol-production licences, etc).[2] In particular, from 1996 Aleksandr Smolenskii's Agroprombank became a key sponsor; ostensibly to help the party 'conquer the agrarian electorate',[3] but also to make sure of the Kremlin's conquest of the party. The Agrarians' main representative in government, deputy premier Aleksandr Zaveriukha, became close to Chernomyrdin and is now a big landowner on the Russian-Kazakh border. By January 2002 party leader Mikhail Lapshin was fully reliant on Kremlin resources to win a seat in Altai.

The other main transitional party was Women of Russia. Its leader, Ekaterina Lakhova, was a quintessential insider: the head of the Supreme Soviet women's committee from 1990, a presidential adviser in 1991, and chair of the presidential commission on women, family and demography from 1993. Lakhova's party was a surprise success in 1993, winning 8.1 per cent (see page 92), but contained too many Soviet stalwarts like herself who happily made their compromises with the Kremlin afterwards. The party proved both business-and Kremlin-friendly, backing the 1994 privatisation programme, the 1995 and 1996 budgets, abstaining in the 1995 no-confidence votes and taking a surprisingly muted line, given many soldiers' mothers' protests, on the first Chechen War. Hence its impressive list of sponsors seeking to exploit its 'brand' politics at the next elections in 1995 and providing a huge campaign budget of $25 million.[4] The party's flexible voting record cost it support, however, and it failed to win 5 per cent – much to its sponsors' annoyance.

Zhirinovskii's Liberal-Democratic Party also played a (multi-functional) transitional role in 1993. At this stage, it was a relatively independent project, but its alleged usefulness to the Kremlin included scaring voters into the Gaidar camp, taking votes away from the banned nationalists and winning votes for the constitution – which Zhirinovskii endorsed (see pages 203–5). It was also true that Yeltsin partially wanted to discredit the Duma. Hence the LDPR's stunning success with 22.9 per cent, which, if a shock to the West, was more of a surprise overshoot to Kremlin strategists, who backed the-eve-of poll *Hawk* TV documentary designed to clip his wings. Finally, Grigorii Yavlinskii's Yabloko party (7.9 per cent) was not as independent as it appeared, given that Gusinkii's Most Group financed both Russia's Choice and Yabloko, giving 200 million roubles to the latter.[5]

In other words, the 1993 elections, although hardly a triumph of either manipulation or management, were not the complete disaster for the authorities many claimed at the time. Taken together, the parties of the potential Kremlin pie won almost half the vote – or, more exactly, at least half the parties were susceptible to Kremlin influence after the event.[6] The shelling of the Russian White House in October 1993 was not the only reason for the often passive behaviour of it successor parliament in 1993–95.

1995: Formal Projects, Limited Success

In 1995 there were more trial projects. Moreover, a general proliferation of parties was encouraged to increase the Kremlin's room for manoeuvre. Registration procedures were made easier, so that forty-three parties and party blocs were on the list, resulting in almost half the electorate (49.5 per cent) voting for parties that failed to win the necessary 5 per cent, compared to only 13 per cent in 1993. Yeltsin seemed to be encouraging his courtiers to pitch in with their own projects, so there were more near-misses than in 1993. The Kremlin wasn't yet proficient at hitting its targets (on its general plans for 1995, see pages 92–3). Clearly, Yeltsin at least expected Our Home Is Russia (OHR) and the nationalist party KRO (see below) to take more votes from the Communists and Liberal Democrats. According to one insider account, when Mark Urnov met the president in his sanatorium to pass him the disappointing forecasts three days before the election, 'Yeltsin took out his pen and began sweepingly to strike out the figures on the report [the Communists were forecast to win forty single seats, the OHR only thirty-five] and insert his own. Naturally, he gave many more places to the OHR and fewer to the CPRF. Then he pushed the document back to his advisers and said, "That is how it will be! After the elections we'll see!"' Chernomyrdin quietly pocketed this 'unique document' and Yeltsin's intervention was quickly forgotten.[7]

The mainstream project in 1995 was Our Home Is Russia, with a disappointing 10.1 per cent. Its supposed partner, the Rybkin Bloc, fared even worse, with a mere 1.1 per cent (see pages 93–5). The big new Kremlin satellite project, meanwhile, was the Congress of Russian Communities (known by its Russian acronym of KRO), set up by Dmitrii Rogozin. According to one of its technologists, the then-relatively unknown Gleb Pavlovskii, the KRO aimed to be a party 'using the European variant of nationalism'.[8] It therefore expected to win more than its eventual 4.3 per cent. However, KRO was also 'a reserve variant of the "party of power"'.[9] Its secondary purpose was to draw votes away from nationalists not under Kremlin control. In 1993 the right had largely boycotted the poll, but now there were no fewer than twelve nationalist groups contesting the elections; these included the Derzhava ('Great Power') party led by former vice president Aleksandr Rutskoi, which won 2.6 per cent, and Duma deputy chair Sergei Baburin's Power to the People (1.6 per cent). The Kremlin had planted many agents in these and other nationalist parties – the Stanislav Govorukhin Bloc (1.0 per cent), Boris Gromov's My Fatherland (0.7 per cent), and Nikolai Lysenko's National-Republican Party (0.5 per cent) – but it controlled none of them outright. Hence KRO was in many ways a sacrificial lamb. It failed to get into the Duma, but it took enough votes from the other right parties to keep them out, too. (Baburin's group was also somewhat neutered by its sponsors in the metallurgy sector.)[10]

Women of Russia was still around, its image only partially tarnished, a near-miss with 4.6 per cent. The Kremlin was happy to place a second bet on the LDPR, which won 11.2 per cent. Other projects were less successful. The presidential administration, through Sergei Filatov, was this time much more heavily involved in the Agrarian Party (3.8 per cent), and, through the Federation Council chair Vladimir Shumeiko (empowered by Yeltsin to divide the opposition in the regions), Sverdlovsk governor Eduard Rossel's Transformation of the Fatherland (0.7 per cent). Trade Unions and Industrialists (1.6 per cent) also had Kremlin origins. Stable Russia was a big TV spender, forking out more than the Communists' entire budget, but was a total failure (0.12 per cent); as were Duma '96 (0.08 per cent), and the Korzhakov-inspired For the Motherland! (0.28 per cent) led by one of the traditional nationalist scarecrows, Vladimir Polevanov.

The Kremlin also attempted to draw the teeth of the radical left and to hold back the Communists' competitors to ensure that Ziuganov would be Yeltsin's unchallenged opponent in 1996, at the same time as ensuring that the far left provided useful pre-publicity for the 'Red radical' scaremongering tactics used in 1996: hence the Agrarians falling short with 3.8 per cent, but Viktor Anpilov ultra-radicals scored an impressive 4.5 per cent (see pages 251–2). The authorities also wished to simplify the arithmetic in the Duma. According to Andrei Riabov: 'There was an agreement between Our Home Is Russia and the Communists. Our Home Is Russia faced competition from the die-hard liberals in Democratic Choice of Russia; the Communists from the KRO and Anpilov. All were kept just below 5 per cent.'[11] Democratic Choice was officially awarded 3.9 per cent, the Anpilov Bloc 4.5 per cent and KRO 4.3 per cent. Ekaterina Lakhova, the leader of Women of Russia, which this time also just missed the barrier, pleaded with the Kremlin for the necessary extra votes from the 'presidential fund', but was told they were needed elsewhere.[12] Overall, the Kremlin could not yet 'multi-task' but developed the capacity to do at subsequent elections. Its covert projects mainly had a negative purpose, and did indeed curb the growth of the radical left and right. However, the 1995 elections showed again that the Kremlin was not yet capable of simultaneously advancing several of its columns into parliament.

Mini-Me

Yeltsin's 1996 campaign showed much greater skill in running a satellite project, in the person of General Aleksandr Lebed. The Lebed project was in some respects *sui generis*, but in others a trial run for a specific type of 'dummy candidate' project designed to replay Zhirinovskii's success in 1993 (in a safer form) and thereby take nationalist votes away from the Communist leader, Ziuganov. Lebed's eventual 'contribution' of 14.5 per cent of the vote was also the key to Gleb Pavlovskii's preferred 'patriotic-centre' strategy. That is, the FEP's sociological surveys showed that the potential centre-right electorate outnumbered the left, but also that Yeltsin was unlikely to draw it all on his own.[13] Lebed was therefore designed to start what the political technologists call a 'relay race' (*estafeta*), where a fake candidate more capable of posing as, in this case, an anti-establishment populist first stakes out the electorate and then passes the baton to a covert 'co-worker' (*napamik*),[14] in this case Yeltsin, the intended ultimate recipient of his votes. Interestingly, the Communists also tried out this tactic in 1996, but their half-hearted version, featuring the popular governor of Kemerovo, Aman-Geldy Tuleiev, who withdrew in favour of Ziuganov, was not managed nearly as well. The Communists didn't have the necessary information resources to make a big media splash. More importantly, Tuleiev was already a double agent, having asked Prime Minister Chernomyrdin for the post of minister for cooperation with CIS countries 'before the result of the second round'.[15] In 1999 Tuleiev would be run by the Kremlin *against* Ziuganov (see page 252).

Administrative resources for Lebed came through the use of NTV, money from banks such as Potanin's Oneksimbank and Inkombank, and the secondment of the

Gaidar-Chubais technologist Aleksei Golovkov (Gaidar's former chief of staff), Yuliia Rusova and an entire team of 'Yeltsin spies' at an alleged cost of $2 million.[16] One version of events, supported by Dmitrii Rogozin, has it that the key Kremlin link was Yeltsin strategist Gennadii Burbulis, from whom money had allegedly been flowing as early as January 1996.[17] Another is that the main channel of communication was established through Rogozin to Korzhakov from late March onwards.[18] Korzhakov claims he had arranged 'confidential meetings' for Lebed and Yeltsin back in 1991 (Korzhakov had also leant on certain papers to improve their coverage of Lebed), and that Lebed came to him asking for money for a project originally backed by Gusinskii, stressing loyally that ultimately 'we will go together with Boris Nikolaevich [Yeltsin]'.[19] Lebed also had private meetings with Berezovskii, who was another key source of finance – despite Lebed's public attacks on Berezovskii for his role in Chechnia.[20] Yet another oligarch, Vladimir Vinogradov, claimed to have funded Lebed to the tune of $10 million.[21] Gusinskii and Berezovskii's TV channels guaranteed Lebed his main exposure. In terms of the political technologists involved, Sitnikov claims to have come up with the research, Pavlovskii to have provided the strategic background and Golovkov to have worked on image creation.[22] As always, a successful project has many claimed authors. Whatever the truth of its authorship, a deal was done *before* the meeting with Yeltsin in the Kremlin in April 1996 that became semi-public.

Brazenly, this army of covert imagemakers chose to project Lebed as personally incorruptible, someone who would not 'bring his supporters to the marketplace' (see also pages 55–6 on Lebed's PR). He was even groomed to resemble General Ivolgin (Mikhalych), played by Aleksei Buldakov in the (then) recent hit film *Peculiarities of the National Hunt* (1995). The myth of the 'lone general' could not have been further from the truth. In any case, Lebed lacked real roots inside the Kremlin magic circle and was therefore for display only, whereas his supposed 'clone' in the 1999 Ukrainian campaign, Yevhen Marchuk, proved to have much greater staying power. Lebed's usefulness was soon at an end. He negotiated a peace in Chechnia that the *siloviki* bitterly opposed, and his 'third-way' economic programme was simply ignored. 'In so far as Lebed was absolutely unpredictable and had a pretty good chance of winning pre-term elections (if Yeltsin died in the course of an operation), then the whole of the political establishment – from liberals to communists – united against him.' Berezovskii came up with the idea 'to keep Lebed on the safe side, far from Moscow', by providing him with 'parachute' money to run as governor of Krasnoiarsk in 1998 (where Berezovskii and Abramovich also had interests in the aluminium industry).[23] Safely out of the way and eclipsed by the rise of Putin in 1999, Lebed died in a helicopter crash in April 2002. For once, nobody suspected foul play.

Dummy candidates or relay racers who suddenly declare their support for the incumbent are now a favourite tactic. The notion that their voters simply transfer their support en masse is questionable, but symptomatic of a general assumption of social passivity. Just as the former general Lebed eventually backed Yeltsin in 1996, ex-security chief and 'anti-corruption' campaigner Yevhen Marchuk endorsed Kuchma between the rounds in 1999, 'passing on' most of his 8.1 per cent vote in round one (see page 158). Lukashenka's supporters in 2001 briefly toyed with the candidacy of Nataliia Masherava, the daughter of his hero Piotr Masheraw, the 'incorruptible' leader of the Belarusian Communist Party from 1965 to 1980, but she was forced to withdraw unexpectedly early in Lukashenka's favour when she began to threaten his electorate (at least one poll had her at 17 per cent – see pages 197–8).[24]

1999: Inevitable Over-Production

Yeltsin's victory in 1996 convinced the presidential administration to play for higher stakes in the 1999 Duma elections. This time the dual-shot strategy was a big success, both for the Unity project and the highly successful relaunch of the liberal right as the Union of Right Forces (URF). Unity's apparent leadership had an excellent public image (despite the party being mainly financed by the likes of Berezovskii and Aksenenko); the URF used Irina Khakamada to front its campaign instead of the highly unpopular Chubais (whose United Energy Systems provided much of the real finance),[25] and the so-called 'Aluminium Party' oligarchs such as Oleg Deripaska of Siberian Aluminium whose representative on the party list, Konstantin Remchukov, became surprisingly protectionist for a liberal politician once he was ensconced in the Duma. Before the 1995 elections Yeltsin had privately declared that 'Chubais means minus 10 per cent for Our Home Is Russia'[26] now he and the others were kept safely in the background. Although not so closely linked to the Kremlin, Yabloko (6 per cent) was much more tightly integrated into the pie system than its public positions suggested. (Given its traditional prominence on economic policy committees, it was particularly targeted by Russian banks.) According to Aleksei Mukhin, Yavlinskii 'in fact sold his political image to at least two groups – to Gusinskii's [Most] Group and Khodorkovskii's [Yukos] Group – obviously. They appeared as sponsors of his election campaign in 1999 and, accordingly, later received the Yabloko faction in the capacity of a group lobbyist for their interests in the state Duma.'[27] Yabloko was also increasingly dependent on Sergei Zverev's PR development company for its campaigning technology, which was closely linked to the Most Group. As Gusinskii also backed Fatherland-All Russia and was soon out of favour with the Kremlin, Yabloko became increasingly close to Khodorkovskii. Indeed, in the Duma the powers-that-be sought to turn the URF and Yabloko into 'interchangeable twins', forcing them to compete for the Kremlin's favour. It was relatively easy to ignore the fact that the two had different electorates; that they had different sponsors, however, would create trouble in the years ahead.

This time, medium-size satellite projects were less important; but smaller 'mushroom' parties were if anything over-produced. Many were shells of previous projects, including Women of Russia, which won 2 per cent, Our Home Is Russia on 1.2 per cent plus seven or eight single-mandate seats, the KRO with 0.6 per cent plus one seat and, of course, out on its own, the Zhirinovskii Bloc with 6 per cent and seventeen seats. The most obvious satellite or 'fly' (see page 161) was the new

Party of Pensioners, nothing more than 'a Kremlin project to take votes away from the Communists'.[28] Behind the scenes the strings were being pulled by the flamboyantly youthful Pavel Borodin – hence the party's swanky downtown offices and lavish October 1999 congress in the nearby State Kremlin Palace (featuring Soviet tunes from the pensioners' favourite Georgii Sviridov),[29] the first such party assembly since the demise of the CPSU. The party's handlers toyed with plans to set up a bloc with Cedar or Women of Russia, or even the corpse of Our Home Is Russia, but eventually left it to run alone, winning a respectable 2 per cent. There were plenty of businesspeople and functionaries on the party list, 'among whom,' one commentator felt obliged to point out, 'there are people of far from pensionable age'.[30] The project was a blatant attempt to free-ride on 1999 as the UN Year of the Elderly; its brazenly false slogan was 'Our business is not politics, but the defence of pensioners'.

The bloc of General Andrei Nikolaev and Sviatoslav Federov, on the other hand, was designed to take votes away from the FAR,[31] although it only won 0.56 per cent. The ecological party Cedar (and Yurii Petrov's Movement for a New Socialism) was this time initially linked to Moscow's mayor Yurii Luzhkov. The Kremlin (through Lev Chernoi) played with the idea of sponsoring the largely moribund party – Berezovskii was rebuffed in his attempt to buy it – but in the end decided that it was not worthy of inclusion in the Unity coalition.[32]

Aleksei Sitnikov claims credit for a further scam in 1999. Using his agency's huge database (with polls in all 225 districts) and its 'expert' network, he says, 'We approached independents with no previous experience, men in the street who fitted our research template. We ran thirty-two such campaigns – and they all joined Unity later on! We even created Communist shadows for them if it was necessary [to help shape their profile].'[33]

A Different Dish for 2003: *Chilaquiles* ('Mexican Pie')

It has often been said of Putin's Russia that 'the Kremlin wants a Mexican-type party system',[34] This is a statement that can be interpreted in at least two ways. Some would love the Russian 'party of power' to be as dominant as Mexico's Institutional Revolutionary Party (PRI – half party, half simply the governing 'institutions') was between 1929 and 1988. On the other hand, there are many parallels between modern Russia and Mexico after 'democratisation'. The PRI prolonged its dominance by sharing the 'pie' in two senses. First, it exploited virtual satellite parties to take votes from the real opposition, such as the Authentic Party of the Mexican Revolution (PARM), first used to channel the leftist upsurge of the 1960s, Popular Socialist Party (PPS), Greens (PVEM) and, in part, the Labour Party (PT). Second, real opposition parties such as the National Action Party (PAN) and Party of Democratic Revolution (PRD) were drawn into the spoils system, with the PRI covertly providing money, personnel and fan-financing of their candidates. Such parties split the vote in areas where the PRI was weaker and allowed the authorities to claim wide support for PRI initiatives. Internal democracy was even staged within the PRI, with rigged 'primaries' for the party's presidential candidate in 2000.

In 2003 Kremlin planners hoped to combine the two ages of the PRI, without succumbing to the ultimate setback that befell the PRI when it opted to regenerate itself in opposition after losing the presidency to the PAN's Vicente Fox in 2000. In previous Russian elections a multi-layered pie had been a necessary form of spread-betting: if any project linked to the government was potentially unpopular, then the more layers in the pie, the greater the chances that one or more project would gain virtual credibility and the voters' attention. In 2003 the government wished to capitalise on the popularity of United Russia (really the popularity of Putin) *and* reach beyond that by using other projects to assemble a potential constitutional majority in the Duma.

As Regina Smyth pointed out in advance of the vote, United Russia 'does not need to win the election in order for the Kremlin to win'.[35] She looked mainly at the number of independents who were likely to join the Kremlin pie, but 'reserve' projects were again of crucial importance. The most obvious of these was the Party of Life, set up in June 2002. If United Russia represented Moscow, the Party of Life was its double in St Petersburg; where United Russia dominated the Duma, the Party of Life was led by the Federation Council chair Sergei Mironov and labour minister Aleksandr Pochinok. The party was also linked to Liudmilla Putin and Ivan Tyryshkin, president of the RTS Stock Exchange. Other than that, the basic reason for its existence remained unclear. Piotr Romanov, Communist deputy chair of the Duma, declared: 'this party will live only as long as a soap bubble, or, to put it more precisely, only as long as the presidential administration wants it to.'[36] The party seemed to be a dilettante project, whose fundamental message was ill-defined. After all, everybody backs 'life'.[37] Its campaign posters, designed by Nikkolo-M in the summer of 2003, featured different aspects of 'life': a woman in a field (under the slogan 'For labour') and two children kissing ('For childhood').[38] By the autumn it had settled on a strawberry (to suggest the party's bucolic authenticity), the meaningless slogan 'Make your choice to serve Russia', and ambient music accompanying children's laughter. The party's balloon advert subconsciously portrayed it as a will-o'-the-wisp. Like the People's Party, it copied traditional Communist demands for higher pensions, interest-free loans for young families, etc. Much of its pitch therefore seemed aimed at women, although the bizarre coupling of Valentina Tereshkova, veteran Soviet cosmonaut and first woman in space, and Oksana Fedorova, briefly Miss Universe in 2002 (she was removed for 'failing to fulfil her duties', a euphemism for reputedly being married and pregnant), at numbers two and three behind Mironov on its election list, was just further evidence of the party's aimless flashiness. As with the Pensioners' Party, the Party of Life also featured a popular singer, the Bolshoi's Nikolai Baskov, who would, so the project's designers thought, appeal to women of a certain age.

Other parties with more electoral life therefore began to appear on the reserve list. First was Gennadii Raikov's People's Party. Originally assembled from independents in the Duma, largely using its own finances, the party made a pitch for a Kremlin top-up, which drew a flood of money from Gazprom, Rosneft, Severstal and Sergei Pugachev's Mezhprombank, once Surkov and the *siloviki*, namely Viktor Ivanov, deputy head of the presidential administration, and Igor Sechin, his counterpart in the Secretariat, decided to back the project in 2003.[39] They also bought the services of Igor Bunin's Centre for Political Technologies, one of Russia's best operators, who positioned the party on the left-centre-cum-nationalist flank, pitching to non-Communist 'vagrant' voters and making much of its supposed moral conservatism and traditional Orthodoxy. Number two on the party list was Gennadii Troshev, a former commander of Russian forces in Chechnia; number three was Nikolai Derzhavin, a prominent aide to Patriarch Aleksii. In contrast with the other parties, whose advertisements featured squirrels and flowers, the People's Party ad men chose a tank (in general, ads were shorter in 2003, not just because ten-second clips 'are cheaper, but because [the parties] simply have nothing to say').[40] Other 'tough' ads featured Vasnetsov's painting of *The Three Bogatyrs*, accompanied by the slogan 'For truth and justice'; another suggested the party's firm hand in preventing Semitic-seeming oligarchs and spivs from 'pillaging the motherland' (*rastashchit rodinu*). The party also purloined the traditional Communist slogan 'For the people! For the motherland!' and called itself 'the only party of the people'.

Dormant projects that the Kremlin maintained as possible future vehicles included the Democratic Party, led since September 2001 by Mikhail Prusak, governor of Novgorod. Given competing sources of Kremlin finance this was basically the Interros (Potanin) party, whose 'handler' was Vladislav Surkov. This project also fell into the 'buy me' category. Prusak's main, indeed only, message was the need to replace the old Yeltsin elite with vigorous new faces from the regions – mainly himself, obviously – but his real aim was to sell the consequent 'media storm' to the St Petersburg clan to further their own self-promotion. The Kremlin toyed with the idea of reviving the Democratic Party as a rival to the Union of Right Forces when it was briefly prepared to give thought to who might serve as the best 'liberal showcase' for the West, as Yabloko was deemed too unreliable and Yavlinskii too capricious. In the end the party only won 0.2 per cent.[41] After the elections, there were reports of a planned fresh start, with the Kremlin musing about launching its own 'liberal' party in the one area of the political spectrum it could not fully control. Marat Gelman, fresh from his triumph with Rodina, and Aleksei Chadaev, a refugee from the URF, were reportedly plotting the launch of a party of 'New Rightists'.[42] Other 'sleeper parties' were the mafiosi singer and Russian Frank Sinatra Iosif Kobzon's Party of Peace, Ivan Grachev's Party of Business and Entrepreneurial Development and Elena Panina's United Industry Party.[43]

In 2003 there was the usual division of labour between the various elements of the pie, but the overlapping nationalist projects were also designed to provide a virtual chorus for United Russia. They were also gifted some foreign-policy posturing in the form of the 'Tuzla' incident staged against neighbouring Ukraine, which seems to have been entirely fake (it was certainly resolved immediately after the elections).[44] Circles close to the Ukrainian president seemed to have no qualms about cooperating in the mini-drama. On the other hand, the overall proliferation of projects was, as in 1999, linked to struggles within the Kremlin. The *siloviki* favoured giving the Life and People's parties more support. Pavlovskii and Surkov favoured placing most bets on United Russia. Ivanov wanted more of a many-layered pie (splitting the pro-presidential vote in order to expand it). Sechin backed a left-populist campaign that embraced both the People's Party and the Glazev project Rodina alongside the CPRF. One result of the infighting was the arbitrary yoking together of Rebirth and Life, Glazev and Rogozin, and the loss of potential assets such as Aleksandr Dugin (see pages 258 and 261). 'Directed democracy' was a partial victim of its own success. No one now dared launch a party without the Kremlin's approval, but the Kremlin was not always clear about its own intentions. Too many parties got in each other's way: the People's Party won only 1.2 per cent (although it collected nineteen single-mandate seats), Rebirth-Life 1.9 per cent; and the Democratic Party a mere 0.2 per cent. Among the smaller nationalist projects (see pages 213–15), Rus won 0.25 per cent, For Holy Rus 0.5 per cent and Edinenie 1.2 per cent. Overall, however, the Kremlin swept the board in 2003. Its virtual Communist project, Rodina (9.1 per cent) and the revived Liberal Democrats (11.5 per cent) were the only two parties to share the Duma with United Russia (37.6 per cent) and the chastened Communists (12.6 per cent). Belarusians were able to joke that there were more real independents in their own fake parliament.[45]

Ukraine's First Attempt: All the President's Men, and All of their Parties

In the 1998 Ukrainian elections, the main pro-government force, the National-Democratic Party (NDP), won a meagre 5 per cent of the vote, yet pro-government deputies ended up with almost half of seats. How? The original plan of the president's entourage (mainly that of prime minister Valerii Pustovoitenko) was to assemble a majority in parliament from at least four separate 'hares' – given the mistaken expectation that the new mixed voting system would benefit each and any project with tacit or semi-secret official support. Socialist Party leader Oleksandr Moroz publicised a secret letter from the presidential administration giving instructions to support the NDP, Agrarian, Democratic, SDPU(o), Christian-Democratic and Labour parties, all of which were now run by oligarchs. Leading members of the ruling elite could also be found in the NEP Party ('People's Power, Economy, Order', see page 133), the European Choice Party and the Party of National-Economic Development.[46]

The one open alliance would be with the NDP, as the core of a more or less official bloc, which was supposed to free-ride on the New Ukraine brand popular in the early 1990s. Pustovoitenko predicted it would win 25 per cent or more of the seats, but found it difficult to attract allies to create a proper coalition, although some covert support was given by the NDP to one liberal project, Forward Ukraine!, which won 1.7 per cent, against another, Reforms and Order, 3.1 per cent.[47] Pustovoitenko himself carried too obvious a nomenclatura aura (see also page 103).

The NDP, with the sitting prime minister heading its list, won a woeful 5.01 per cent; though this did not stop the authorities from dragooning ninety-three out of 450 deputies, 21 per cent of the total number, into its ranks by the summer, once parliament had actually assembled.

Second, a 'regional bloc' was supposed to run an action replay of Kuchma's 1994 presidential campaign by appealing to the non-leftist protest vote in south-east Ukraine. However, despite the establishment of a strong presence in the outgoing parliament (fourteen deputies were persuaded that their career prospects required them to join), both the Regional Revival (0.9 per cent) and Social-Liberal Union (0.9 per cent) parties were failures. The latter, known by its acronym SLOn (the Russian for elephant), bought the shell of the Kadet Party, first registered in May 1993, but then played the wrong game. Its glossy adverts featuring Russian Ukrainian cultural heroes pitched a narrow appeal to ethnic Russians rather than playing up to regional barons – such as Lazarenko in Dnipropetrovsk or Ruslan Bodelan in Odesa who were now harvesting the vote with considerably more success.

The two other parts of the would-be coalition were designed to draw votes away from right and left. 'Pro-presidential financial circles' supported two satellites: the Progressive Socialists against the Socialists and Communists, and the far-right UNA-UNSO (see pages 215–17) against Rukh.[48] Bankivska's more positive plans were less successful, however. The 'presidential left' ended up fragmented. Its strongest component, Labour Ukraine (1998 version), was a relative failure (3.1 per cent), except in the Donbas (460,000 votes, 17 per cent of the local total), where the project marked a successful debut for the local PR firm Korund, which skilfully combined traditional (strong exposure in local media) and modern (personalised 'phone calls and flier leaflets) campaigning techniques to sell a party that didn't exist.[49] Korund's success served as a trial run for the more aggressive demolition of the Communist vote in the Donbas in 2002. However, by switching tactics in 1998 and running a whole gamut of virtual left parties (the Progressive Socialists, Village Party, Party of Defenders of the Fatherland, the All-Ukrainian Workers' Party and so on), this side of the plan succeeded in taking 12 per cent of the vote away from the Socialists (who won 8.6 per cent) and Communists (24.7 per cent), though the satellite parties themselves won only a handful of seats in parliament. Only the Progressive Socialists, via some careful massaging of the results, hurdled the 4 per cent barrier with 4.05 per cent (see pages 218–20 for a case study of this peculiar party).

Nor was there much success in creating a 'nomenclatura right'. This would have to be done after the event by splitting the relatively successful Rukh party (second overall with 9.4 per cent in 1998) in 1999 (see pages 155–6). According to Rukh's leader, Viacheslav Chornovil, in west Ukraine 'where the Communists were weak and we had every chance for considerable success', the administration encouraged other 'opponents from the right parties' to stand against them.[50] Nevertheless, the main party to Rukh's right, the National Front, which contained many pro-presidential elements receiving covert support, won only 2.7 per cent. The UNA stood without the UNSO, and won only 0.4 per cent.

'Private Business Buying Small Parties with Interesting Names'[51]

Other satellite parties contracted out to individual oligarchs had greater success, although a lot of projects were stillborn or ill-conceived. Some extremely rich men ended up outside parliament, including Derkach father and son, the former soon to be made head of the Ukranian security services (chosen vehicle: Labour Ukraine), Ihor Bakai and Prominvestbank (the Party of National-Economic Development), his brother Oleh and Interhaz (the Republican-Christian Party, another splinter from the URP), and Oleksandr Volkov (the Democratic Party/NEP).

Most oligarchs simply bought existing parties. Ukraine has had an official Green Party since May 1991, but it made no electoral impact until 1998, when it won a surprise 5.4 per cent of the vote – thanks to covert sponsorship by some distinctly non-ecological businesses. The Greens' long-term leader, Vitalii Kononov, with his plausible ponytail, was retained as party frontman, but behind him stood four deputy leaders, all of whom were businessmen with rich and diverse interests that often led to internal squabbles. Oleh Shevchuk (metallurgy, telecoms, a possible future player in the privatisation of Ukrtelekom) paid for the PR campaign. Vasyl Khmelnytskyi, a former gas trader, was only thirty-one in 1998, and with his colleague Serhii Pavlenko of the Real Group used the party's lobby in the Rada to win a stake in the metals giant Zaporizhstal and a share in the Zaporozhian and several other oblast energy companies. Ihor Voronov, playboy investor in many of the capital's restaurants, had close links with Hryhorii Surkis of the SDPU(o) – ostensibly Khmelnytskyi's rival in the energy industry. Finally came Oleh Yatsenko, owner of the Narodnyi (People's) bank and the Kremenchuk oil company, and Serhii Rhys of the Shelton oil company. The Oriana chemical concern was privatised (at cut price) to Shelton in October 1998. Khmelnytskyi and Yatsenko (a former engineer at Pivdenmash, the missile factory formerly headed by Kuchma) had close links with the Kuchma family, especially his wife Liudmilla and daughter Yelena.[52]

Further in the background of the Green Party's finances stood the Ukrainian-Israeli businessman and media mogul Vadym Rabinovych. His TV channels Era and 1+1 and his media company Prioritet provided the main vehicles for the party's ads, while his business colleague Mykhailo Bahraiev, director of the Crimean Games music festival, lined up pop stars to support the party (see page 191).[53] Rabinovych had a more ambitious entrée into Ukrainian politics in mind, but arguments over arms sales led to his exclusion from the country in 1999. (Rabinovych was an Israeli citizen, another reason why he couldn't run for office himself.) In December 2001 a Russian Duma deputy accused him of trading arms (over two hundred tanks, two hundred armoured personnel carriers and thirty light aircraft) to the Taliban together with the notorious mafioso Semion Mogilevich.[54] He was also accused of organising cigarette smuggling with Leonid Derkach (head of the customs service, 1996–9)[55] and of helping to sell off Ukraine's merchant marine (Blasco).

The other new brand party was Hromada, a classic sleeper set up in 1993 by Oleksandr Turchynov, an adviser first to Leonid Kuchma when he was prime minister in 1992–93 and then to his successor, Yukhym Zviahilskyi. The party was therefore lying around, close to home, when another former prime minister, Pavlo Lazarenko, like Turchynov also from Dnipropetrovsk, was looking for a political home in late 1997. 'Hromada' was a particularly bizarre name for Lazarenko's version of the party, which was one of the first Ukrainian groups to employ Russian political technologists. The latter advised a message of East Slavic unity. (The historian Petro Tolochko was later embarrassed by the fact that his 1997 book, *From Rus to Ukraine* was published with the party's support.) The original nineteenth-century Hromadas were in fact home to the nascent Ukrainian national movement, but then history was definitely something Lazarenko contracted out to others. As with the government parties, Hromada was full of businessmen (Dnepr-Credit and 'Ukranian Gold') rather than intelligentsia.

Overall, only one of the eight parties/factions initially represented in the 1998-2002 parliament was openly pro-presidential: the NDP with twenty-nine seats. The pie, however, was much bigger, including the SDPU (o) with seventeen (see pages 133–4), the Progressive Socialists (sixteen) and Greens (nineteen), and numerous 'moles' in most of the other parties – though still well short of the 60–70 per cent that Prime Minister Pustovoitenko had promised the president. Hromada won 4.7 per cent and twenty-three seats, and its abundant finances soon helped expand its ranks to forty deputies. The administration therefore had to work harder to change elected members' loyalties after the elections, and pay more attention to the Communist Party in particular. An initial plan to dragoon as many deputies as possible into a swollen NDP – which reached ninety-three seats in June 1998 – was abandoned when Volkov and Kuchma agreed the Rada would be easier to manipulate with a kaleidoscope of ever-changing factions and no obvious centre of gravity. A centre-right alliance led by the NDP could undoubtedly have taken control of parliament in the summer of 1998, but Kuchma preferred to let the left take charge in order to bolster the 'Red threat' myth for his own campaigning purposes in the 1999 presidential election. (Several Greens and Social-Democrats were eventually ordered to back Oleksandr Tkachenko, ostensibly the 'left' candidate to chair the Rada, but with many commercial links to the regime.) Sure enough, immediately after Kuchma's re-election, a new centre-right leadership was installed in the 'velvet revolution' of January/February 2000,[56] and the very same parliament changed (albeit again temporarily) from 'left-dominated' to 'right-wing revolutionary'. By this time, the pie was made up of twelve factions, fully nine of which were artificial creations set up after the 1998 elections (Revival of the Regions, Regions of Ukraine, Fatherland, Reforms-Congress, Labour Ukraine, Solidarity, Yabluko and two Rukh factions).

Serial Failure

Oleksandr Volkov was for many years a leading confidant of President Kuchma. He had a distinctly murky past. His unofficial CV begins with an alleged career in the Kiev underworld in the 1980s, and trading in arms and precious metals with top

Interpol target Boris Birshtein and his Seabeco companies in the 1990s, before going semi-legitimate with the launch of Hravis TV, a key asset for Kuchma's election campaign in 1994. Volkov was the main financial manager of both Kuchma's 1994 and 1999 campaigns, as well as, according to Major Melnychenko, acting as the chief handler of the president's foreign accounts. Volkov himself was certainly active abroad, with an alleged thirty-two bank accounts in Belgium, property in Spain and a luxury jet registered in the Caribbean. Belgium started proceedings against Volkov for money laundering in 1997; he was refused a visa to enter the USA in 1999. Even Volkov himself has admitted: 'I'm not a supermodel, I can't please everybody.'[57]

The Democratic Party of Ukraine, on the other hand, was originally founded as the great white hope of nationalist intellectuals in 1990. The writers and historians who personified the party were, however, pretty hopeless at organising any serious effort in constituency elections (winning only two seats in 1994). Its anodyne name, however, seemed like a good brand for the half-proportional-representation elections due in 1998, so Volkov decided to barge in. Old hands were edged out in a leveraged buy-out organised by vodka baroness Hanna Antonieva, and replaced by the likes of Yukhym Zviahilskyi (acting prime minister in 1993-4, recently returned from three years in Israel dodging corruption charges) and leading figures from the Crimean underworld, including the notorious Seleim mafia. Volkov, however, had not bought good advice. The party's poll ratings were largely based on its name, but this advantage was disastrously squandered when an alliance was forged with the Party of Economic Revival controlled by Volkov's Crimean 'business' friends under the unfortunate acronym NEP (as with the New Economic Policy of the Soviet 1920s). The NEP won a mere 1.3 per cent of the vote.

Volkov flopped again in 2002. The awkward pairing of the Democratic Party with his own Democratic Union was a tired rerun. The bloc used Richard Strauss's *Also Sprach Zarathustra* for its ponderous TV ads, but the dramatic opening wasn't followed by any actual message. The overall campaign was flat and uninspiring, probably because of the sharp deterioration of Volkov's finances since the economic reforms introduced in 1999-2001. Together the parties won only 0.9 per cent of the vote. Financial largesse in local constituencies, where four seats were won, still paid off in a more traditional fashion.

'(o)' for 'oligarchs': The SDPU(o) Tries to Take Over Ukraine

It is not only presidents and state elements that run satellite empires: powerful oligarchs have used the pie principle in the same way. In Russia, it has been said in relation to Boris Berezovskii that 'the only thing better than your own personal political party is two personal political parties',[58] though Berezovskii had easily surpassed that number by the time of his exile. The Most Group managed to finance Russia's Choice, Yabloko and the Communists at the same time in the mid-1990s. Oleg Deripaska's Siberian Aluminium financed the Union of Right Forces, the Communists *and* their main rival, Rodina, in 2003. Yukos played the same game (for higher stakes) in 2003 – or at least different parts of the Yukos empire sought to further their individual empire-building ambitions by backing different parties (and the New Civilisation youth movement). Aleksei Kondaurov funded the People's Patriotic Union, and indirectly the Communists; Sergei Muravlenko supported Seleznev. Once Yabloko lost Gusinskii as its financier, it took money from Yukos and Legprombank. By 2003, however, the Kremlin was claiming a renewed monopoly on empire-building. It needed business to finance parties, but it also needed insecure property rights and a universal system of *kompromat* to force business to play and pay on the Kremlin's terms. Only Berezovskii and Yukos had enough money to pose as alternative independent sources: hence the destruction of both.

In Ukraine oligarchs continued to do much of the work, seeking to create an interlocking pie in the 2002 elections. There were four main 'holdings'. The first belonged to the Green Party's younger businessmen, who also adopted the 'Women' brand for this election (see pages 191–2). The second belonged to the Donetsk group. The third was controlled by Viktor Pinchuk, whose covert operations covered almost the whole of the fake political spectrum. These included his home project, Labour Ukraine, a shell party whose brand was hijacked and whose original ideologues such as Mykhailo Syrota were kicked out in 1999; the fake Communist party, the 'renewed' CPU(r) (see pages 255–6); and the faux-liberal KOP (see pages 192–5). Some Pinchuk money also found its way to the All-Ukrainian Union of Christians, which was mainly supported by the Moscow Patriarchate. The most bizarre project of all was New Force – yet another name that had once been proposed for the KOP, but that now ran as an ultra-nationalist project and won only 0.1 per cent. Rumours that this was yet another (semi-detached) Pinchuk project could not be substantiated, however. Nor was it clear who financed the fake left-wing firebrand Nataliia Vitrenko, but she was certainly prominent on TV channels controlled by Pinchuk. Together, the more obvious 'flies' won 4 per cent of the vote; Pinchuk's 'official' project, Labour Ukraine, part of the For a United Ukraine coalition on the proportional-representation list, expanded from an original thirty-eight seats to over sixty in 2003.

The most interesting virtual empire, however, belonged to the Social-Democratic Party of Ukraine (united). In Ukrainian 'united' is *obiednana* and the party acronym is SDPU(o) – hence the joke that 'o' stands for 'oligarchs'. According to the Ukrainian commentator, Dmytro Chobit, the SDPU(o) is 'a pseudo-party, which has no relation to the ideology it officially declares'. 'The SDPU(o) has the same relation to social democracy as a Mercedes has to a tractor.' The real 'mission of the SDPU(o) is the legalisation of the influence of [party leaders] Viktor Medvedchuk and Hryhorii Surkis and their business companions through the Ukrainian Verkhovna Rada, the organs of executive power and local government and, most importantly, creating a platform which would help them storm the highest echelon of power – the post of president of Ukraine'.[59] Socialist leader Oleksandr Moroz made the same point rather more bluntly: 'What have guinea pigs [in Ukrainian *morski svynki*, "sea pigs"] and the SDPU(o) got in common? The former have nothing to do with the sea or with pigs; the latter have nothing to do with Socialism or with democracy.'[60] According to

Fig. 6.1 Ukraine's 2002 'Pie'

	percentage of votes	seats
For a United Ukraine (FUU)	11.8	101
(i) Dnipropetrovsk clan		
Labour Ukraine	–	38
Vitrenko Bloc	3.2	
KOP	2.0	
CPU(r)	1.4	
Union of Christians	0.3	
New Force	0.1	
(ii) Kiev clan		
SDPU(o)	6.3	24
People's Power	–	17
Yabluko	1.2	
NRU(e)	0.15	
(iii) Donetsk clan		
Regions of Ukraine	–	35
European Choice	–	15
New Generation	0.8	
KPRS	0.4	
(iv) Khmelnytskyi clan		
Women for the Future	2.1	
Green Party	1.3	

Source: author's calculations from the Central Election Commission website at www.cvk.ukrpack.net and the Rada site at www.rada.kiev.ua/depkor.htm.

Stepan Khmara, the SDPU(o) 'is a party of criminal capital . . . based on a mafia system of values – money, criminal discipline, the irrefutable authority of elders. Intimidation and bribery are its main methods of activity.'[61]

The party has, however, been one of Ukraine's most successful, if not perhaps in terms of its own ambitions. It has survived two elections, winning 4 per cent and seventeen seats in 1998 and 6.3 per cent and twenty-four seats in 2002. More importantly, perhaps, it has proved adept at winning seats without winning votes – accumulating twenty-five deputies by the end of 1998 and forty by the end of 2002. After the 2002 election, Medvedchuk headed the presidential administration with two deputies from the SDPU(o); Oleksandr Zinchenko took his place as the deputy chair of parliament; the party had control of two ministries (education and labour) and three oblasts (Transcarpathia, Cherkassy and Chernihiv); and numerous 'informals' were in other positions of power, including (at one time) Yevhen Marchuk, head of the National Security Council, and Serhii Vasyliev, head of the president's notorious

Department of Information Policy (in other words, the country's chief censor).

However, the SDPU(o) was a perfect example of almost total virtuality. It claimed to be a social democratic party, but was really a cover for business interests. It claimed to be on the centre-left, but has swung wildly in all political directions. The United Social Democrats saw themselves as potential members of the Socialist International; but their prospective comrades would have been less than keen if they had known that the party was in fact run by the 'magnificent seven' – Kiev's business elite. Viktor Medvedchuk had once been a lawyer, but his 'defence' of leading dissidents, Yurii Lytvyn in 1979 and Vasyl Stus in 1980, was more like a prosecution. He was rumoured to have convictions for 'hooliganism'. Both Medvedchuk (codename: Sokolovskyi) and strong-arm business partner Hryhorii Surkis were alleged to have worked as long-term KGB agents. Surkis also had connections to the international gangster Semion Mogilevich, and was said to run rackets in Kiev markets, including the one in Troeshchyn linked to the notorious mobster Kysel (Mykhailo Kyseliev).[62] Surkis and Medvedchuk's initial fortunes – under the patronage of the city's last big boss of the Soviet era, Valerii Zhurskyi – were made variously through means legitimate if down-to-earth (importing toilet suites), semi-legitimate (the Ometa financial pyramid scheme that ended in the traditional tears in 1995, the purchase of Ukraine's most famous football team, Dynamo Kiev, for minimal actual payment in 1993,[63] indiscriminate logging in Transcarpathia earning $100 million a year and exacerbating flash floods), and downright dodgy (alleged corruption of the Kiev police). Political power was then parleyed to make real money – creating a media empire out of the three main TV channels (the first national channel UT-1, Inter and 1+1, also Kiev News and TET) and securing control of privatised *oblenergos* (local energy companies) at a knockdown price.[64] Seven, possibly eight, of the latter were secured in the mid-1990s; shares in nine more were secured in 2002 from the Grigorishin group (see page 174). On the Melnychenko tapes, interior minister Yurii Kravchenko claims the dimensions of this empire are 'more serious than before Lazarenko'. Kuchma complains bitterly that 'we can't give them all of Ukraine' and bridles at suggestions that the SDPU(o) will one day push him aside. 'Do I look like someone who would hand over power?!' he exclaims.[65]

After January 2000 most of the Social-Democrats' new interests were run through the consortium Metalurhiia. Its undeclared 'holdings' in other companies interconnected in various scams. For example, in 2000 Ukrainian Credit Bank lent 25 million hrivnias at 40 per cent to the state nuclear power utility Energoatom, then run by the Surkis-Medvedchuk protégé Volodymyr Bronnikov, receiving virtually free electricity as security. It also provided a bill of exchange to Oil and Gas of Ukraine to take responsibility for its debt at a 37.5 per cent discount ($44.3 million), which was then settled using extremely cheap energy from Dniproenergo, which was then consumed by thirsty metallurgy works such as Dniprospetsstal and Kharkiv's turbine factory Turboatom – completing a perfect circle of SDPU(o) shell businesses. Former president Leonid Kravchuk also brought on board his 'arts foundation', whose artistic activities involved importing alcohol and tobacco.

Zinchenko once declared a little too candidly: 'Funding has never been a problem for our party.'[66] However, the SDPU(o) is unlike other clans in Ukraine. Its regional powerbases are not particularly secure. It is far from dominant in Kiev, and Transcarpathia is too much of a backwater from which to dominate all of Ukraine. The party's economic interests are widely but thinly spread, which is both a strength and a weakness, and are nearly always anonymously held. The SDPU(o) has never parleyed its influence into real ownership. Hence, in many ways it was the most virtual Ukrainian party of all, forced to rely on its media resources and their virtual messages to an even greater extent than most.

The SDPU(o) adopted its current name in 1996, after taking over a group first established in 1990. On their own, the original Social-Democrats were going nowhere fast – and certainly not making the most of their potential brand. They first contrived a split at their founding congress in 1990, which was followed by two acrimonious changes of leader in 1991/2, a botched attempt at reunion in 1993, two more damaging splits and another 'reunification' farce in 1994/5. Only two Social-Democrats were elected in the 1994 elections. The party's original leader, the serious-minded Vasyl Onopenko, did not seem to have grasped the nature of the takeover deal, however, and was soon kicked out. He now heads one of at least three rival Social-Democratic parties (the Ukrainian Social-Democratic Party, alongside the Social-Democratic Party of Ukraine, one of Ukraine's few serious 'real' parties, 0.32 per cent in 1998, 0.3 per cent in 2002, and the Social-Democratic Party of Youth), none of which, without administrative resources, has ever been able to get off the ground. It wasn't that the SDPU(o) didn't like ideologues – it commissioned local intellectuals to write a suitable programme – it just didn't want them as leading members of the party. Medvedchuk, on the other hand, liked to pose as an intellectual manqué, producing two weighty tomes: *The Modern Ukrainian National Idea and Questions of State-Building* (1997), and *The Spirit and Principles of Social-Democracy: A Ukrainian Perspective* (2000). These were, of course, all his own work.[67]

The SDPU(o)'s Political Empire
The Social-Democrats first built up their own shell party and then tried to create a whole mini-universe of satellite parties from 1998 to 2002. The scale of their ambition was startling. Uniquely among Ukrainian parties, the SDPU(o) has put huge efforts into developing its grassroots structure and membership (mainly by paying people to join, rather than the other way around, the standard fee being $20),[68] but it would be classic investors' folly to risk so much capital on one venture. The party has therefore sought to extend its holdings throughout the political spectrum – in part compensating for the naked ambition that made it difficult to find normal political allies, its virtual partners acting as substitutes for its lack of partners in the real world. Some 230 national and local NGOs were in its sphere of influence. The party's membership peaked at 347,000 in 2001, by which time even Zinchenko admitted the SDPU(o) was a 'trendy party', with too many careerists and even 'double agents' of

its opponents from Our Ukraine (including himself) or the Donetsk group in its ranks – there being no small irony in the party finding its entryist tactics turned on itself. Some 25,000 members were 'purged' in 2002, with most being culled in Kiev.[69]

On the right the SDPU(o) infiltrated all the various branches of Rukh (on the splits in Rukh, see pages 154–7).[70] The main channels of influence were via Viacheslav Koval and his 'informal clique', the deputies Yevhen Sihal, who defected to the Social-Democrats in December 1999, and Oleksii Hudyma (then part of Yurii Kostenko's branch of Rukh), who served on the board of the Lviv *oblenergo* and sat on the Rada's privatisation committee. The SDPU(o) also provided regular covert support to the far right in west Ukraine in its ongoing rivalry with Viktor Yushchenko's Our Ukraine. Former far-right firebrand Dmytro Korchynskyi set up a quasi-paramilitary group, Brotherhood, which was privately funded by the SDPU(o), and was given regular airtime as a 'media-killer' on SDPU(o) TV, at first to attack the moderate right, then just about anybody who failed to support his sponsors. Medvedchuk's younger brother, Serhii, in Lviv acted as a link to the People's Rukh for Unity or NRU(e), members of whose rent-a-mob wing, Trident, were frequently used as *agents provocateurs*. In January 2002 Viacheslav Chornovil's former press secretary Dmytro Ponamarchuk, then working directly for the SDPU(o), played a key role in the black PR against Our Ukraine (see page 141).[71] Chornovil's younger son, Andrii, stood for the NRU(e) in Galicia and was also reportedly in receipt of SDPU(o) money.

The party's middle-aged leaders were also great believers in youth, exercising powerful behind-the-scenes influence over the Ukrainian National Committee of Youth Organisations (UNCYO), set up in 1992, ensuring that it enjoyed the monopoly right to distribute state funds allocated for youth projects (13 million hrivnias in 2001), until the Constitutional Court decided the money was being allocated with too much blatant partiality in December 2001. The parallel 'youth committee' under the president was run by Medvedchuk, then aged forty-nine.[72] UNCYO head Volodymyr Raibyka was at number four on the Social-Democrats' 2002 electoral list.

Yet another SDPU(o) project, this time posing on the centre-left, was Yabluko, first set up in parliament in 1999.[73] Yabluko (the Ukrainian for 'apple') was, of course, an absurd name, as its supposed Russia equivalent (Yabloko) was originally the collective acronym of its three leading politicians – Yavlinskii, Boldyrev and Lukin – none of whom happened to be members of the Ukrainian party. The Ukrainian 'Apple' was led by Mykhailo Brodskyi, who had once flirted with Rukh, but more importantly had known Surkis since childhood (hence their common mafia connections) and helped run the Dendi pyramid scheme in the mid-1990s. On the Melnychenko tapes (the conversation is dated 10 July 2000), then interior minister Kravchenko discusses with Kuchma the close links between Medvedchuk and Brodskyi, whom Melnychenko considers 'responsible for running PR campaigns against the SPDU(o)'s opponents'. Kravchenko comments: 'The worst thing is that they [Surkis and Medvedchuk] are in together with this Yabluko.'[74]

The faction's other members could hardly have been more diverse, including both a former Communist and another tainted businessman, Eduard Krech, with links to the NRU(e) (see pages 155–6). The political career of Oleksandr Charodieiev makes for interesting reading: first he was in the Democratic Platform of the CPSU, then in Rukh in Donetsk, next in the Progressive Socialist Party; once he had joined Yabluko, he was mocked as 'today an apple, tomorrow a pear'.[75] Yabluko was also designed to persuade rightists away from Yushchenko and hollow out his support (Brodskyi, Krech, Chaika and Valentyna Protsenko were all formerly of Rukh), and, of course, to act as a surrogate critic of the SDPU(o)'s opponents, occasionally the government, but more often Yushchenko. When Brodskyi and Viktor Chaika, another former Rukh businessmen, had control of the paper *Kievskie vedomosti*, it made the kind of harsh criticisms that the SDPU(o)'s leaders didn't want to utter themselves in public. Hence also the logic of buying in a former stalwart of the Socialist Party, Viktor Suslov, one of his more persistent harriers, to wear away at Yushchenko's nerves with a supply of *kompromat* relating to his time at the National Bank – which also served to please the president and maintain his often-strained links with the SDPU(o). Yabluko was also used in the struggle with Yushchenko over the privatisation of Mariupol 'Illich' metallurgical factory against Siberia Aluminium. Ultimately, thirteen of the 'liberal' faction's deputies, including Brodskyi and Krech, voted for the ousting of Yushchenko, the real liberal, in April 2001.[76] Not surprisingly, it proved difficult even for the best-paid political technologists to disguise Yabluko at the 2002 elections (see page 196). It won only 1.2 per cent. The party survived, however, now being used by Surkis to contract out criticism of Kuchma that he dared not make himself (Brodskyi had seen most of his business interests squeezed by the president's circle). Suddenly, Yabluko activists were ubiquitous at demonstrations over the Gongadze affair.[77]

Two other projects launched by former SDPU(o) men were kept on the backburner for potential future use: Solidarity, led by Petro Poroshenko, and the All-Ukrainian Union of Christians, led by Valerii Babich. On the left, with few real friends and its position in parliament always precarious, the SDPU(o) tried to cultivate a holding in the Communist Party via Medvedchuk's good contacts with Adam Martyniuk and the Crimean Communist leader Leonid Grach (see also pages 247–8).[78] Brodskyi allegedly financed the Socialist paper *Hrani*,[79] but relations between the virtual social democrats in the SDPU(o) and would-be social democrats in the Socialist Party (SPU) were usually competitive and hostile. The SDPU(o) helped encourage the various splits in the SPU when it was most hostile to the powers-that-be in 1999/2000, including via the rival Solidarity project. Surkis convinced Vadym Misiura to defect from the Socialists in order to head the Kiev branch of the SDPU(o) in March 2003. On the one hand, it therefore seemed scarcely credible that the SDPU(o) was seeking to build bridges with the SPU in 2004. On the other hand, this was now standard behaviour for the SDPU(o), which was interested in splitting the opposition and repairing its own tarnished image possibly by allying with the SPU for the parliamentary elections due in 2006 (see also pages 177–8).

Such a broad portfolio meant that the SDPU(o) was always clashing with its rivals and having to reinvent itself. Medvedchuk and Surkis helped to finance Leonid Kravchuk's election campaign in 1994, and therefore had to do some serious toadying to win their way back into favour with new President Kuchma in 1995/6. The party's *folie de grandeur* and aggressive business tactics led to another temporary backlash in 2001, with Medvedchuk losing his position as deputy chair of parliament. Rival groups began to copy their party-building techniques: after the 2002 elections, for example, the Donetsk group ran both its Regions of Ukraine and a satellite group, European Choice (a bizarre name choice for a group based in the Donbas). The elections thrust the SDPU(o) back into the limelight, however, both because the other clan groups could not dominate parliament without it and because Kuchma gambled that Medvedchuk's strong-arm tactics provided his own best chance of survival. Rumours persist, however, that Surkis and Medvedchuk (or Marchuk or Brodskyi) had backed Gongadze to set up his website in 2000. It has also been claimed that the SDPU(o) backed the 'Anti-Mafia' group in the Ukrainian parliament as a channel for *kompromat* against Kuchma and his entourage,[80] and finally that Medvedchuk overreached himself by privately proposing to take over from the troubled Kuchma in 2000.

Two Very Different Campaigns

In 1998 the SDPU(o) ran as a left-centre party with a west Ukrainian base and control of Dynamo Kiev, the 'patriotic' football team. Its main strongholds were in the rural fringes, especially the westernmost region of Transcarpathia, where votes could easily be bought. This geographical bias also reflected the importance of the SDPU(o)'s logging interests and the leadership's business ties with the Slovak president Rudolf Shuster. In 2002 the SDPU(o) then ran as a centre-left party with a base in south-east Ukraine and Crimea, where the party now had business links with Leonid Grach. Three out of four of the party's best results were in the south: Mykolaïv (12.1 per cent), Zaporizhzhia (10.7 per cent) and Crimea (12.5 per cent and two seats – Voiush and Yevdokimov), where most other parties left the field clear for 'local interests'. In June two more Crimean deputies, Valerii Horbatov and Ihor Franchuk, left For a United Ukraine for the SDPU(o). The party also won a useful three seats in the Crimean assembly. In 1998 it tried to free-ride on Dynamo Kiev's popularity with the faux-patriotic slogan 'Our team – our party' (see page 103). In 2002, with former president Leonid Kravchuk, who had tried to promote the Ukrainian language when in office, now a leading member, Medvedchuk spearheaded a campaign to upgrade the status of the Russian language. Two-thirds (65 per cent) of the party's 2002 adverts were in Russian (only the Progressive Socialist Party had more).[81] Hence the importance of the party's control of the Russophone Inter channel, the most popular in south-east Ukraine.

The SDPU(o) employed Gleb Pavlovskii's FEP to run its 2002 campaign, although Pavlovskii himself left Kiev in autumn 2001,[82] resulting in a certain ineffectiveness and confusion.[83] According to Oleksandr Zinchenko in a rare moment of subsequent candour, 'we gave preference to easier, less demanding methods of "office management" – TV, trendy technologists, showy PR events'.[84] The PR campaign did have an early impact, however, with the party polling at a high of 15.1 per cent in mid-February,[85] before declining funds and waning impetus led to it limping over the finishing line with a final official 6.3 per cent. The party's coyness about its links with Pavlovskii also reflected the fact that his main legacy was not so much the success of the SDPU(o) as the black PR used against Yushchenko and others. Certainly, the methodology of the internet *kachka* ('toss') – putting out false or anonymous stories which the mainstream media then quotes – was already well known from other FEP campaigns in Russia. The FEP claimed it had only been hired to help set up a party website, but even a cursory look at this (www.sdpuo.org.ua, also briefly www.nedovira.com.ua) and linked addresses (see page 59) demonstrates how news material was passed back and forth with AiN and 'Podrobnosti', the main news show and website of the Inter TV channel, then controlled by Zinchenko.

This network was the main source of the black PR launched against Yushchenko in a typical 'toad's eye' media storm.[86] The two main examples were 'Tapegate 2' and the attempt to blacken Yushchenko by associating him with the ultra-right. The first concerned an alleged recording of a conversation between Yushchenko and Kiev mayor Omelchenko about the removal of Medvedchuk as deputy chair of parliament in December 2001, and was designed to tarnish the former prime minister's reputation for relative honesty and diminish the 'Gongadze problem' by convincing voters that politicians were all the same. Except, of course, they weren't. 'Tapegate 2' had nothing like the magnitude of the original Kuchma scandal. Nothing illegal was discussed; Yushchenko's private personality was little different from his public face. Attempts to link Yushchenko's family with the plundering of the Ukraïna bank also enjoyed little obvious success. The second *kachka*, in the very last week of the campaign, sought to link Yushchenko to an alleged decision by Ivano-Frankivsk city council in west Ukraine to grant former combatants in the wartime SS-Galicia division the status of war veterans – with some success. The cumulative effect was to drag down Our Ukraine's support in the south and east *and* to lose the SDPU(o) votes in the west.

As a virtual party, the SDPU(o) relied mainly on its media empire for success. It was therefore the top spender on TV advertising, with a recorded $2.14 million as against an official budget limit of $480,000. As with For a United Ukraine, the party's slickly produced adverts contained no political programme or concrete promises. Instead, it depicted 2002 as the 'year of social democracy', showing the party's supposed equivalents in government elsewhere throughout Europe. The campaign was also designed to appeal to the elite who wanted to live *à la européenne*. In fact at the time many social democrats were losing power, in particular in Holland and (later) in France. Some SDPU (o) leaders rather misguidedly sought to double the bandwagon effect by congratulating the Portuguese Social Democratic Party on its victory just weeks before the Ukrainian poll. Unfortunately the Portuguese SDP is a right-wing party with a misleading name. In the event, many potential SDPU(o) supporters went off in search of real social democrats in the Socialist Party or in Our Ukraine. Worse, the party's leaders, Medvedchuk and Zinchenko, couldn't resist hijacking the campaign with personal bio-clips, safely diverting most viewers from abstract thoughts on the nature of modern social democracy. Medvedchuk's clips celebrated his role in seizing control of parliament from the left and passing the new (privatising) land code – neither of which acts was likely to bolster his image as a social democrat.

This inability to disguise the party's true nature took its toll. The SDPU(o)'s final score of 6.3 per cent represented little more than the sum total of the party's patronage networks. That gave the party only nineteen seats – which was rather awkward as two of its main financiers were at numbers twenty and twenty-one on the party list. In forty-five areas of Ukraine, the party had fewer recorded votes than nominal members.[87] Clearly, the party's image had become too negative, and in the post-election postmortem there was even a recognition that money (Surkis, Ihor Pluzhnikov) and influence (Medvedchuk, Zinchenko) could take the party only so far – and even that 'the odium of Medvedchuk and Surkis might limit the party's political manoeuvrability'. One party official even dared voice the fear that: 'We are good actors. Our major task now is for the party stage not to turn into a one-man theatre. With no audience to see the play.' Another ventured the idea that the SDPU(o) party should present itself as the 'party of success for the people' rather than the 'party of successful people'; but this was just another slogan.[88] Zinchenko, the main source of the criticisms, left the party in 2003, surprising even the most cynical of observers by becoming Yushchenko's campaign manager for the 2004 election.

Despite its lack of electoral success, the SDPU(o) continued to bully its way into power at a local level in Uzhhorod, Lviv and Rivne. Nationally, Medvedchuk concentrated on burying his supporters in the 'force ministries', especially the Ministry of the Interior and the tax inspectorate. As in the last parliament, the SDPU(o) was soon running two factions, its own (thirty-seven deputies as of October 2003) and a covert satellite, this time the 'People's Power' group under Bohdan Hubskyi (eighteen deputies), another member of Kiev's original 'magnificent seven', with the further possibility that Oleksandr Volkov might be spun out to organise a third group.

Armenia

In the small states of the south Caucasus, there is not much chance of running full-blooded virtual projects. Everyone knows who the local powers-that-be are. But they can still be dressed up – alternatively, relatively crude methods can be used. In Armenia's first parliamentary elections in 1995, an enormous 35 per cent of the votes cast for parties were declared invalid;[89] the election of Levon Ter-Petrosian as president in 1996 was a blatant steal. The Armenian National Movement (ANM) which had cruised to power in the late *perestroika* era, was increasingly corrupt and faction-ridden, so some basic chicanery was also deemed necessary in 1995. The

ANM-dominated Hanrapetutiun ('Republic') Bloc won 42.7 per cent of the vote, but hedged its bets with Shamiram, a sham women's party set up two months before the elections by interior minister Vano Siradeghian: its members included a suspiciously large member of the wives of the governing elite. Both the Armenian Revolutionary Federation and Ramgavar-Azatakan were sponsored by the authorities as rivals to the émigré ARF or Dashnak party (both splinters from historical parties). The 'real' ARF was banned, with polls indicating it would have won 24 per cent.[90] The pie received its final layer when thirty-one of the forty-five independents set up a Reform Bloc, actually organised by Ter-Petrosian's elder brother, Telman, using the resources of his Hrazdanmash factory. (The Ter-Petrosian family's power was based on the construction industry, which was big business in Armenia after the 1989 earthquake.)

Fig. 6.2 Armenian Parliamentary Elections, 1995 (150-seat assembly)

	percentage of votes	seats
Hanrapetutiun ('Republic', incl ANM)	42.7	119
Shamiram (Women)	16.9	8
Communists	12.1	7
National Democratic Union	7.5	5
Christian National Self-Determination Union	5.6	3
Ramgavar-Azatakan	2.5	1
Armenian Revolutionary Federation	2.0	1
Independents	n/a	45

Source: www.csce.gov/pdf/1995ArmeniaElectionsRport.pdf.

In the late 1990s, politics became even more corrupt, in essence little more than a struggle between the *karabakhtsis* (the militaristic faction from Nagorno-Karabakh) and the *hayastantsi* (homeland, or 'nomenclatura', Armenians). The former's Republican Party and the latter's People's Party entered into a shotgun marriage for the 1999 elections, with their Unity Alliance (Miusnutyun) triumphing with 41.7 per cent of the vote, but the fragile peace was shattered by the spectacular murders in parliament in October 1999 of prime minister Vazgen Sarkisian, parliamentary chair Karen Demirchian and six others; after which the *karabakhtsis* were able to entrench their power in the May 2003 elections. However, the new elite, well aware that its own Republican Party (HHK) was unable to win a majority on its own, encouraged its business friends to fan out among a variety of new parties (in Armenia's impoverished post-Soviet economy, most of these seemed to specialise in keeping the locals supplied with alcohol, petrol and tobacco). Up to half of the 131 deputies were estimated to be new businessmen.[91] Some remained in the HHK, such as the heads of the Kilikii brewery and the Ghukasian family clan from Nagorno-

Karabakh (one brother being the region's self-styled 'president', the other a manager of a large salt mine), which won thirty-five seats. Others were to be found in the neophyte parties Law–Based State (eighteen deputies) and the United Labour Party (six seats), funded with conspicuous abandon by the petrol and cigarette importer Gurgen Arsenian. The once-banned émigré Dashnak party had seemingly also made its peace with the powers-that-be, or at least with the Avshar liquor company and yet another tobacco tycoon, Hrant Vartanian; it won eleven seats. Altogether, the members of the pie controlled seventy out of 131 seats. Dignity, Democracy and Fatherland was the only part of the pie that failed to reach 5 per cent. The opposition Artarutiun ('Justice') Bloc won only three seats directly, and only 13.6 per cent of the list vote (see also pages 160–1).

Azerbaijan

Neighbouring Azerbaijan was ostensibly very different, dominated by the sultanistic Aliyev family, who created (after 1992) a more stable governing regime and governing party, the New Azerbaijan Party (Yeni Azerbaycan Party or YAP), a sort of holding company for the Nakhichevan clan, those displaced by the war with Armenia, and the national energy company SOCAR. The Aliyev regime also used political technology techniques to stage the appearance of pluralism, while the real opposition parties were kept well way from power, however. These included the (Party of the) Popular Front of Azerbaijan (PPFA), the original powerbase of Heydar Aliyev's predecessor, Abulfaz Elchibey, the Communists (absent in 1995, split into four factions by 2000, with the main faction leader, Firuddun Hasanov, reliably pro-Aliyev), and Yeni Musavat (Equality), led by Aliyev's *bête noire,* Isa Gambar.

At least five satellite parties were 'created [by Aliyev and his chief of staff Ramiz Mekhtiev] to give the illusion of multi-party support for the president'.[92] These included the Azerbaijan National Independence Party (AzNIP), an anti-Elchibey breakaway from the PPFA that supported Aliyev's coup against him (like Aliyev, most of its leaders were from Nakhichevan). AzNIP was safely enmeshed in the spoils system and its tame leader, Etibar Mammadov, put forward as the only real permitted opponent to Aliyev in the 1998 presidential election, winning just 11.6 per cent against Aliyev's claimed 76.1 per cent (though probably nearer 25–30 per cent). Having served its purpose, the party was reined in thereafter. The other regime satellites were Ana Vatan (Motherland), the Party of National Statehood (led by Neymat Panatov, a provocateur in the dramas of 1992–93, later a presidential adviser who was forced into opposition in 1997), the Alliance in the Name of Azerbaijan, the Party of Democratic Property Holders and the Party of Democratic Independence, another offshoot of AzNIP (led by three more Aliyev advisers), which itself split in 1997. The government lost credibility, however, by restaging pretty much the same elections, with the same participants and the same results, in 1995 and 2000.

Fig. 6.3 Parliamentary Elections in Azerbaijan

	percentage of votes 1995	seats 2000
New Azerbaijan Party	62.7	62.3
PPFA	9.7	11.0
AzNIP	9.3	3.9
Democratic Property Holders	4	–
Motherland/Ana Vatan	4	–*
Party of Democratic Independence	3	–
Party of National Statehood	1.2	–
Alliance for Azerbaijan	0.86	1.0
Musavat	–**	4.9

*Motherland won one seat
**Musavat won three seats

Source: www.electionworld.org/election/Azerbaijan.htm. See also
www.eurasianet.org/departments/election/azerbaijan/azparties.html#ana.

Moldova

The same problem of limited size makes virtual projects more difficult in Moldova. Party labels, however, are usually fronts for specific clans and their economic interests – the only real parties being the Pan-Romanianists and the Communists, although they too have been penetrated by economic interests (see pages 248–50). No single clan has ever consolidated its interests sufficiently to create a dominant party, with the possible exception of the Communists after they returned to power in 2001. Labels therefore change with bewildering frequency, at almost every election, in fact, making it easier to trace lineages than party histories.

A first line of descent involved the declining remnants of the old pan-Romanian Congress of Intelligentsia set up in 1992, which contested the 1994 elections as the Peasants and Intelligentsia Bloc, winning 9.2 per cent of the vote. In 1998 it converted itself into the Party of Democratic Forces (PDF) and won a roughly comparable 8.8 per cent and eleven seats. In 2001, now led by Valeriu Matei, despite having absorbed the groups led by Gheorghe Ghimpu and Anatol Dubrovschi (the Democratic-Christian Party), it miraculously kept the same name. A second line of descent goes through the Party of Rebirth and Conciliation (PRC), set up in 1995, which represented the 'team' of first president Mircea Snegur (at that time close to the notorious mobster Boris Birshtein) and the supposedly pro-Western deputy prime minister Nicolae Andronic, who later became embroiled in a secret deal to export Russian nuclear waste and a controversial land-swap deal with Ukraine. The PRC marketed itself as the Democratic Convention in the 1998 elections, when it came second with 19.4 per cent and twenty-six seats, then returned to its old name in 2001. A third group was controlled by Snegur's successor, Petru Lucinschi, who set up the party For a Democratic and Prosperous Moldova in 1997 (which won 18.2 per cent and twenty-four seats in 1998). However, parliamentary chair Dumitru Diacov broke with Lucinschi over the issue of privatising the wine and tobacco industries in 1999 and morphed the group into the Democratic Party (DP) in 2000. (The publicly stated reason for the split was Lucinschi's desire to establish a presidential regime.) Lucinschi responded by getting his crony Dumitru Braghiş to front the Braghiş Alliance, an ambitious amalgam that included several virtual left parties (the Socialist Party from the mid-1990s, the Labour Union and the Party of Social-Democracy 'Furnica', which won 3.3 per cent in 1998) to draw supporters away from the Communists and Russophone voters away from Diacov's DP. Braghiş benefited from saturation media backing, especially from ORT Moldova, and from free-riding on the brief economic growth resulting from the reforms of the Sturza government (see below), which allowed him some pensions largesse.

Lucinschi was also manoeuvring in 1998-2000 with the Communists and the Christian-Democratic People's Party (CDPP) under the cynical and authoritarian Iurie Roşca (formerly of the PRC), whom many suspected of being an *agent provocateur* employed to destroy unity on the right. Roşca was indeed instrumental in the downfall of the Ion Sturza government (Moldova's only real reformist government) in November 1999, a manoeuvre designed to smooth Braghiş's accession as prime minister (the Christian Democratic Group led by former deputy prime minister Valentin Dolganiuc quit the CDPP in 2000 in protest at Roşca's dealings with the Communists).[93] Lucinschi continued his covert backing for Roşca's CDPP in 2001, supplying it with *kompromat* to break Diacov and loaning it the popular anti-corruption campaigner General Nicolae Aleksei as an electoral 'strike force'. Lucinschi hoped thereby to create a pie, big enough either to keep the Communists from governing alone and force them to share power with Braghiş, or (as happened) to trim their victory and ensure that he and Braghiş survived to fight another day. The CDPP emerged as the dominant new force on the right after the elections (see Fig. 6.4, overleaf). The PRC, DP and PDF, on the other hand, destroyed each other in a war of *kompromat*, with (relatively) honest men such as Vasile Nedelciuc of the PDF and Vladimir Solonar of the DP being forced out.

After 2001 there was another flurry of reinventions and image relaunches. In 2002 Braghiş re-emerged as the head of Our Moldova, incorporating the old PRC that had become the Liberal Party in 2002, the Party of Social Democracy 'Furnica', which had become the Social-Democratic Alliance, and his key ally, the three-time mayor of Chişinaŭ Serafim Urecheanu, who invented the Independents' Alliance in 2001. Diacov, on the other hand, headed a new Social-Democratic umbrella movement with Communist support – having first leant on President Voronin to preserve his tobacco interests and help his son-in-law escape arms-trading charges. Despite the war in the early 1990s, Braghiş, Urecheanu and, behind them, Lucinschi were

Fig. 6.4 Parliamentary Elections in Moldova, February 2001 (Main Parties Only)

	percentage of votes	*seats*
Communists (PCRM)	50.1	71
Braghiş Alliance	13.4	19
Christian-Democratic People's Party (CDPP, Roşca)	8.2	11
Party of Rebirth and Conciliation (PRC)	5.8	0
Democratic Party (DP, Diacov)	5.0	0
Party of Democratic Forces (PDF, Matei)	1.2	0
Democratic Agrarian Party	1.2	0

Source: www.essex.ac.uk/elections.

also close to the rebels in the breakaway 'Dnistr Republic' in the east of Moldova and their lucrative arms and steel trade. (The 'rebel' republic's main economic asset is the steel works at Rybnitsa, the products of which are actually exported with Moldovan documentation.) Braghiş, Urecheanu and Diacov set up the bloc Democratic Moldova in May 2004.

Confused? You should be. If the reader's mind has become blurred by the constant Brownian motion, he or she has reached a good understanding of Moldovan politics.

Kazakhstan: Virtual Pluralism
Although President Nazarbaev's power seemed to face no significant challenges after the mid-1990s (see pages 159–61), the regime was wary of placing all of its bets on a single party, in this case Otan. In a classic many-layered pie,

> the presidential apparatus sought to overcome the lack of public support for a single presidential party by stage-managing the creation of a multiparty system, sponsoring the creation of a variety of pro-regime parties, each designed to appeal to its own group of voters. These include the Civic Party, formed in November 1998, and the Agrarian Party, formed in January 1999, to appeal to entrepreneurs in business and industry and to proponents of private property in agriculture, respectively.[94]

To this list could be added a third satellite, the Party of Revival of Kazakhstan, designed to appear to be pro-women, and led by the writer Altynshash Zhaganova, and a fourth, the Republican Political Labour Party, set up in 1995 on the back of the Union of Engineers of Kazakhstan to 'represent' the technical intelligentsia.

Helped along by considerably more fraud than was normal, either in Russia or

Ukraine, the formula was a success. In the 1999 elections Otan won a claimed twenty-four seats, the Civic Party eleven and the Agrarians three; fugitive former prime minister Akezhan Kazhegeldin's Republican People's Party (RNPK) withdrew from the vote but nonetheless won one seat; the Communists won three. The party list vote shows the preponderance of virtual satellite parties in more detail, although the designers of the election law ensured that only ten seats would be distributed by this potentially dangerous process, and doubled their insurance with a threshold for representation of 7 per cent. Otan won 30.9 per cent, the Agrarians 12.6 per cent and the Civic Party 11.2 per cent. Of the minor satellites, the Party of Revival won 2 per cent and the Republican Political Labour Party 1.4 per cent. The now-tame People's Congress Party (NKK) won 2.8 per cent and the semi-tame Azamat 4.6 per cent. The only gatecrasher was the Communist Party, with a supposed 17.8 per cent.

The new 'Law on Political Parties', passed in July 2002, forced existing parties to undergo re-registration, for which they now needed a minimum of 50,000 members. As a result the nineteen parties then active were whittled down to seven (specifically excluding the real opposition like Kazhegeldin's RNPK and Democratic Choice of Kazakhstan – see pages 159–60): the Agrarians, Ak Zhol (the virtual alternative to Democratic Choice), Auyl (the 'Village' Party), the Civic Party, Otan, Gani Kasymov's Party of Patriots and the Communists. Two more puppet parties were added later: Rukhaniyat ('Spirituality', now lead by Zhaganova) and Asar ('All Together'), a party of no doubt considerable promise as it was headed by Nazarbaev's daughter, Darigha, who also controlled the main state media holding company, Khabar. The 2004 elections were then staged as a 'contest' between father and daughter; between Otan (60.6 per cent and 42 seats) and Asar (11.4 per cent and four). The Agrarians ran with the Civic Party and won 7.1 per cent and eleven seats. Ak Zhol won one seat. Democratic Choice was allowed to cobble together an alliance with the Communists, but the two won only 3.4 per cent and no seats.

Uzbekistan

Uzbekistan is currently an autocracy, but with more window-dressing than some. In 1990 to 1992 it was necessary to manipulate rather than simply deny democracy. Uzbekistan's increased geopolitical importance after the US-led Afghan campaign beginning in 2001 has led the governing regime to pay more attention to the importance of window-dressing – a much better option than actually moving towards democracy. The old Communist Party of Uzbekistan (CPUz) survived 1991 more or less intact, renaming itself the Popular Democratic Party of Uzbekistan (PDPU), and has been all-powerful since 1992. Early opposition groups such as Birlik ('Unity') were banned, and even its tame leader, Muhammad Salih, marginalised, with Erk ('Freedom') being forcibly converted into a new Progress of the Homeland Party (Vatan Taraqqiyati), led by another Birlik defector, Usman Azim (see also page 200). Any remotely 'Islamic' party has been banned, with the authorities using the spectre of fundamentalism to tar every shade of more moderate opposition. Sarvar Azimov was prevented from reviving the CPUz.

As in Belarus in 1995/6, however (see pages 164–9), the regime ultimately decided on a 'displacement' operation. Only the PDPU and the Progress of the Homeland Party (PHP) (a 'business' party) were allowed to nominate candidates in the 1994/5 elections. 'Dissatisfied with the low number of party factions in parliament, which failed to give the appearance of a multi-party system, the state sponsored the creation of a new party, the Adolat (Justice) Social-Democratic Party of Uzbekistan, only five days before the opening session of the Oliy Majlis'[95] – but this was still *after* the elections. The authorities were clearly not trying very hard to con the electors or even the most superficial of Western observers. Adolat appropriated the name of a real opposition party set up by former vice-president (and for a time President Islam Karimov's only serious opponent) Shukrulla Mirsaidov. Its head, Anvar Jorabayev, was also editor of the government paper, *Khalq sozi* ('People's Word'). Adolat was soon followed in May 1995 by the Milliy Tiklanish, or National Revival Democratic Party (a faux-intelligentsia party), and a fake Birlik, in Uzbek Xalq Birligi ('People's Unity', made up of a handful of Uncle Tom leaders of minority ethnic groups), in a final act of appropriation.

Fig. 6.5 Parliamentary Elections in Uzbekistan
(250 seats; only 83 were directly elected, the other 167 were indirectly 'selected' by local councils)

The 1994–95 Elections	seats
PDPU	69
Vatan Taraqqiyati ('Homeland Progress Party')	14
Adolat ('Justice') Social Democratic Party	47

The 1999 Elections	
PDPU	48
Fidokorlar ('Self-Sacrificers' National Democratic Party')	34
Vatan Taraqqiyati ('Homeland Progress Party')	20
Adolat	11
Milliy Tiklanish ('National Revival Democratic Party')	10

Source: Resul Yalcin, *The Rebirth of Uzbekistan: Politics, Economy and Society in the Post-Soviet Era* (Reading: Ithaca Press, 2002), chapter three.

For his delayed re-election in January 2000, Karimov put up much less of a pretence, claiming a vote of 91.9 per cent against Abulchafiz Dzjalalov, who actually also came from the PDPU, with 4.1 per cent. Dzjalalov later admitted to having voted for Karimov. Uzbekistan also specialises in fake NGOs paralleling groups critical of the autocracy, such as the Human Rights Committee of Uzbekistan. Marat Zahidov ran a rival Committee for the Protection of the Rights of the

Individual, which regularly concluded that its work was barely necessary. Zahidov also emerged as the leader of a highly suspect Agrarian Party when the US Congress began to call for greater political pluralism in 2003. No opposition parties were allowed to contest the elections held in December 2004 and January 2005. The PDPU won 30 seats, the new 'Liberal-Democratic' Party 41, Fidokorlar 18, Milliy Tiklanish II and Adolat 10.

Conclusions

There are actually nineteen towers in the Kremlin's walls, and one outlier. By analogy, there is therefore plenty of scope for virtual pluralism. In a way, this is an old Russian tradition. In Il'f and Petrov's satirical novel, *The Twelve Chairs*, a group of friends in the Sword and Ploughshare secret society grant themselves imaginary titles in a game of imaginary politics: 'There was nobody present more Left Wing than the Octobrists, represented at the meeting by Kisliarskii. Charushnikov declared himself to be the "centre". The extreme Right Wing was the fire chief. He was so Right Wing that he did not know which party he belonged to.'[96] Pie politics is likely to remain a standard feature throughout the former USSR. If ruling elites fail in their ambition to create a truly dominant ruling party, they will have to keep resorting to the many-layered pie. If they succeed, the appearance of opposition also needs to be maintained. Even a successful 'party of power' cannot hope to represent all parts of the political spectrum.

'The main thing is that we pass the 5 per cent barrier...'.
The many layered pie depicted as a hydra.

7 Dishing the Opposition

'Active measures' (*aktivnye meropriiatia*) against any opposition or would-be opposition are a key part of the new governing formula. Over and above the use of black PR and *kompromat* (see pages 70–1), or the cruder types of administrative resource (legal deregistration, etc.), active measures proper involve the deployment of virtual objects or events created or staged by political technologists to weaken the opposition. This chapter defines the various types of project that have been developed in the former USSR, and in the course of so doing introduces the reader to some particularly strange local terminology.

Divide and rule is one obvious ploy, but it has many local variants – as is indicated by the sheer number of specialist terms used in the post Soviet states. Sometimes the divisions are large, sometimes small. Parties may be split down the middle, or plagued by tiny rivals, evocatively named 'flies' (*mukhi*). Rival parties may appear from within, as 'off-cuts' (*otkoly*), or from without, the most common being artificial 'spoiler parties' (*partii-spoiler*), or candidates deliberately created to poach the electorates of potentially threatening oppositions. A special type of artificial rival is the 'double' (*dvoinik, dubler* or *dubl-obekt*) or 'clone'. Potential splitters may lie dormant as 'cuckoos' (*kukushki*), 'moles' (*kroti*), or as a 'Trojan Horse' (*troianskii kon*). Splits may be generated before an election or after, if an actual opposition proves too successful. The most ambitious projects produce total displacement or substitution of unwanted oppositions (*pochkovanie*, the germination of an alternative, followed by *zameshchenie*, substitution for the original): the artificial party surpasses its original rival, which is then left to wither on the vine. Finally, political technologists can seek to alter the entire dynamic of the political system to work against the opposition, most often via artificial polarisation or so-called 'strategies of tension'.

It is no coincidence that many post-Communist states now work with electoral barriers (5 per cent in Russia, 7 per cent after 2007, 4 per cent in Ukraine) and other hurdles for smaller parties (minimum levels of membership, regular but difficult 'reregistration' demands). After a period in the early 1990s when smaller parties were scattered to the winds without thought for the consequences, the purpose of divide-and-rule strategies is now to narrow the range of representation to the parties of the governing elite – parties that could never hope to gain anything like a majority via free and open elections. In other words, the purpose of the barrier is at least in part to make the game of divide and rule easier.

Divide et impera: Dealing with the Popular Fronts

Marat Gelman is right to say that many political tactics characteristic of the post-Soviet states are as old as the hills. The most obvious active measure is the traditional game of divide and rule. Post-Communist politicians usually don't need too much encouragement to disagree with one another. Rampant egos have erupted in many a public clash. However, while it is tempting to ascribe the weakness of post-Communist party systems to a lack of *partiinost* (party discipline), many such splits have in fact been organised behind the scenes: that is, they are also virtual projects designed by the powers-that-be and their political technologists. Countries such as Russia and Ukraine are often mocked for having more than a hundred parties each, but that inflation in numbers is largely artificial; and it is, of course, artificial parties that are most likely to multiply or have a short lifespan. As with puppet parties (see Chapter 8, especially pages 187–8), it can be difficult to get the balance right – for instance, creating spoiler parties that serve as credible challengers, but at the same time preventing them from becoming forces in their own right. Another problem as old as the use of moles and *agents provocateurs* elsewhere in the world is therefore how much licence to give agents in penetrated organisations, and how much autonomy the 'insertion strategy' itself may take on. Britain's recent experience with the army's Force Research Unit's and attempts to manipulate politics in Northern Ireland is a telling example.

Significantly, divide and rule was the tactic of first choice in all the core states of the former USSR as the old elite sought to frustrate the initial challenge to its power that came with the launch of anti-Communist 'Popular Fronts' in 1990/1.[1] Similar methods over exactly the same time frame were used against the main potential oppositions, despite their very different character. In Russia, the main original anti-nomenclatura force was Democratic Russia. Its surprisingly rapid demise came after two splits in November 1991 and January 1992.[2] The first was largely self-inflicted and saw the departure of Nikolai Travkin and his drift to the right. The second saw an artificially expanded pro-Kremlin camp defeat the rank and file (led by intelligentsia stalwarts such as Yurii Afanasiev and Marina Sale), although the anti-establishment group represented the real majority. Awkwardly articulate critics such as Yurii Burtin were forced out. Voting was fixed to keep the radicals off the key 'coordinating committee'; Sale's alternative congress in July was sabotaged to ensure that it remained inquorate. The more loyal elements of the leadership (Lev Ponomarev, Ilia Zaslavskii, Gavriil Popov's Moscow administration) were first coopted and then sidelined in a series of new organisations which they were encouraged to believe would become the government's main prop (the short-lived Public Committees for Russian Reforms, the more nomenclatura-friendly Civic Union and Yegor Gaidar's Democratic Choice), but which were soon allowed to wither away.

In Belarus the nearest local equivalent to Democratic Russia was the Belarusian

Popular Front Adradzhenne ('Rebirth'), or BPF, set up in 1989. Given the limited local constituency for nationalism, it was never as strong as Democratic Russia or Ukraine's Rukh (see below) – it only controlled thirty-seven out of 345 seats in the 1990 parliament – and it didn't need too much assistance towards its spectacular demise in the mid-1990s; but assisted it certainly was, all the same. Active measures prevented it from winning a single seat in the 1995 elections, though its thinly spread 10 per cent of the national vote was also a handicap. This failure produced the first split in the BPF and the sidelining of Vintsuk Viachorka, who acted as gatekeeper to the NGOs linked to the BPF. After President Lukashenka's victory in the 1996 constitutional crisis (see page 164), however, the BPF's days were clearly numbered. Its leader, Zianon Pazniak, left the country to pre-empt an alleged assassination plot. His attempt to run in the 1999 'unofficial' presidential elections from abroad was challenged at every turn, most notably by 'Project Chyhir', named for the former Lukashenka associate who was now selected to block Pazniak's every move. (Pazniak claimed Mikhail Chyhir was a Russian tool; it seems unlikely he received covert support from Lukashenka, as he spent most of 1999 in prison.)[3] The election farce led to a second fatal split in the BPF, and the replacement of Pazniak by Viachorka and deputy chair Yury Khadyka. The suspicion that the presidential administration had supported the Viachorka group was fuelled by the attempt to gift it control of the old BPF infrastructure, especially Pazniak's offices in Minsk. Certainly, the Viachorka-Khadyka group was later accused of 'collaboration' with the authorities after agreeing to run in the 2000 elections to Lukashenka's pocket parliament. Pazniak and the minority called for a boycott and were left to set up the Conservative Christian Party-BPF.[4] Further splits followed in 2001 and 2003. As was characteristic of such developments in Russia too, the Viachorka–Khadyka group soon found itself discarded in turn.

In Ukraine the regime's tactics were more or less identical to those used in Russia, although the main opposition movement, Rukh, proved more resilient. Despite repeated splits, a solid minority in west Ukraine and among the Ukrainophone intelligentsia has continued to vote for its various successor parties, which were still serious contenders in the 2002 elections. The disabling of the movement has therefore been an ongoing task. The authorities have encouraged splits and defections on at least four occasions: most importantly in 1992, but also in 1993, 1999 and 2000. One commentator has therefore argued that since 1989 the 'regime has always used Rukh, even better than the [new, virtual opposition,] Communist party'.[5]

Ukraine became independent in 1991 as a result of a bargain between the old Communist Party and those Rukh members who valued independence above de-Communisation. The old Communist Party had been happy to dissolve itself in August 1991 because it believed it could exploit nascent divisions within Rukh, particularly because the most fervent nationalists were often also the ones on whom the party held most *kompromat* from the Soviet era.[6] Rukh's radical standard-bearer, Viacheslav Chornovil, therefore accused those whom he dubbed the 'strategic partners' in the 1991 presidential election (the new nomenclatura president Leonid Kravchuk, and Rukh's ultra-patriots) of organising an assault on him from the right at Rukh's third, and first post-independence, congress in February–March 1992. An attack by one of their number, Larysa Skoryk, smearing him for dismissing 'the OUN-UPA [the Organisation of Ukrainian Nationalists set up in 1929 and the People's Army it helped set up in 1943 – heroes to many nationalists, villains to others] as the tatters of history',[7] heralded a split when Chornovil seemed likely to be elected by rank-and-file members, denying him the fruits of victory when he (temporarily) settled for unity instead.[8] 'The "Heroes" of the third congress – Dmytro Pavlychko, Ivan Drach, Pavlo Movchan,' Chornovil later bitterly complained, then 'carried out a furious war against both me and Rukh for five years, supporting and creating various All-Ukrainian Rukhs and CNDFs.'[9] The latter was the Congress of National-Democratic Forces set up in August 1992, and supported behind the scenes by Bohdan Ternopilskyi in Kravchuk's presidential office, who was also accused of writing the CNDF's programmes.[10] Typically, however, the CNDF was dumped when it had outlived its usefulness. Many leading Rukhites were coopted on to a new presidential council, the 'State Duma', although it only existed from February to October 1992 (seven out of twelve members of the main Council of State, including Skoryk, were in some measure former oppositionists),[11] and its successor network of 'councils' and 'presidential commissions'. Some survived as ministers, or were appointed to head Ukraine's new embassies. Having drawn the opposition's teeth, the various bodies gradually lost importance, despite Kravchuk's obsession with *zlahoda* ('public accord'). Skoryk and Mykola Porovskyi staged a brief second coming of an All-Ukrainian Rukh in 1993/4, but it too disappeared without trace within a year.

Rukh proper survived, but once Chornovil had established it as a political party like any other (in December 1992), his attempts to play 'normal' politics among Ukraine's naked business interests and clan lobbies resulted in Rukh's ensnarement by the system it had originally sought to oppose. Chornovil sought business 'sponsors' (Mykhailo Brodskyi and Viktor Chaika, Eduard Krech, Oleh Ishchenko, Eduard Hurvits), but these either drifted away, or acted as Trojan Horses, splitting the movement from within.[12] By the late 1990s Rukh was the hunted rather than the hunter. Its small but guaranteed representation in parliament was now too tempting a target for the new oligarchs who were either too odious to win direct election as themselves, or too lazy or unwilling to pay for their own political project. Many of Rukh's remaining leaders were bought up by the presidential administration and the Social-Democratic Party, the SDPU(o).[13] Chornovil's son, Taras, 'claimed that Rukh's leadership was penetrated by over twenty incognito adherents of the SDPU(o) . . . the leader of this informal clique, Viacheslav Koval, was even, at one time, a candidate for the post of Rukh's chairman.'[14] Others sought finance from energy barons (see overleaf) and from the media mogul Vadym Rabinovych (who then controlled the channels Era and 1+1).[15] Rabinovych was also backing the Green Party.

In the 1998 elections Rukh was opposed on the right by the National Front, an alliance of émigrés and veterans from the CNDF, and in the centre by Reforms and Order, although it was not targeted with particular vigour as it was not expected to do well. After its relative success, with 9.4 per cent and an eventual forty-seven seats, Rukh was doubly unfortunate. The powers-that-be could not ignore such a large faction, and the carpetbagging businessmen on the Rukh list began an all-too-obvious attempt to muscle in on the country's lucrative oil and gas business, in particular via the attempted privatisation of Ukraine's leading energy monopoly, Oil and Gas of Ukraine. Most of the money (at least $1 million) spent to encourage the next big split in 1999 was supplied by the energy magnate Oleh Ishchenko, head of Olhaz and the Russo-Ukrainian Oil Society, who had bought his way on to the Rukh list in 1998 – although he soon defected to the SDPU(o).[16] Chornovil himself blamed Ishchenko, a surprising bedfellow for a nationalist party given his former membership of the Russophile Interregional Bloc and his links to 'Russian dirty money',[17] plus shadowy 'gas traders, especially Yaroslav Fedorych [head of the investment company Geopromresurs] and others'. Noticeably Chornovil didn't blame himself for accepting such potential Trojan Horses on to the list. 'The actions of the splitters,' he continued, 'were provoked by mercantile interests, with the aim of "privatising" Rukh, as a host of other parties had already been privatised in Ukraine.' Behind them stood political forces; his main rival, Yurii Kostenko, according to Chornovil, being financially backed by 'one of the vice-premiers' and ultimately by 'his patron', the president.[18] Chornovil later accused his rivals of being in the president's pay to the (implausible) tune of $40,000 a month.[19]

On the other hand, the newspapers *Den* and *Zerkalo nedeli* accused Chornovil of excessive closeness to Kuchma,[20] while others mentioned his links to certain oligarchs.[21] Former Rukh stalwarts Oleksandr Lavrynovych, Taras Stetskiv and Ihor Koliushko considered that Chornovil's support for the lacklustre former foreign minister Hennadii Udovenko in the 1999 presidential election was deliberately designed to set up a more 'withdrawable' candidate, for Kuchma's ultimate benefit.[22] Indeed, Udovenko, the leader of the supposedly more 'official' Rukh faction after Chornovil's death, can be heard on the Melnychenko tapes (dated 20 September 2000) paying homage to the president. He declares, 'I am your servant' (*ya Vasha liudyna*), and pleads for more money as he claims that his version of Rukh is 'on the verge of bankruptcy', needing '$200,000 to $300,000 a year, one and a half a million [dollars of] expenses'. Udovenko stresses that his faction has been the most stable and loyal in the Rada, but says that it needs more money to attract other supporters. 'Last time you promised something,' he pleads. Kuchma gives in: 'I will support [you], support [you] financially.'[23] As so often, it was entirely possible that the regime hedged its bets by playing on both sides.

In February 1999 Rukh split into two parts, one led by Udovenko, the other by Kostenko. Chornovil was killed in a car accident in March (see overleaf). In 2000 yet another split resulted in the formation of the comically misnamed Movement for a United Rukh, or NRU(e), under Bohdan Boiko, formerly of the Kostenko

Rukh.[24] Finance was again provided by a renegade Rukh businessman, Eduard Krech, who had spent a period of enforced exile in Austria after allegedly plundering the coffers of his chemical company. Krech also had alleged security-service (SBU) connections. The NRU(e) was also covertly linked to the SDPU(o) through Chornovil's former press secretary Dmtryo Ponamarchuk, and thence to the presidential administration. Major Melnychenko has claimed: 'I have on my recordings one of the main Rukhites, Bohdan Boiko, who in Kuchma's office [on 20 September 2000] comes to an agreement with him about the birth of the united Rukh and asks the president to finance the process of creating this renegade organisation.'[25] Boiko played the traditional Zhirinovskii role in the 2002 campaign on state TV, accusing independent opinion pollsters such as the Razumkov Centre of furthering American interests, and parties like the Socialists and Tymoshenko Bloc of plotting a *coup d'état* by trying to organise parallel vote counts (providing a virtual chorus with the Progressive Socialists; Boiko was thus mocked as 'Vitrenko in trousers').[26] A similar function was performed by Oleksandr Rzhavskyi, also reportedly funded by the SDPU(o), whose job was to 'shadow' Viktor Yushchenko (see page 164). 'The scheme is the same – Rzhavskyi and Boiko just settle on 1+1 and Inter, and then their every sneeze gets broadcast.'[27] Boiko headed a separate Bloc of the People's Movement of Ukraine, which unashamedly appropriated the image of the dead Chornovil in its TV ads – but still won only 0.15 per cent.

Rukh was once intensely proud of its claimed status as 'Slayer of the [Communist] Dragon'.[28] But its internal problems were well illustrated by its initially ambiguous behaviour during the Gongadze scandal, which erupted in November 2000. Hryhorii Gongadze was an opposition internet journalist, who disappeared on 16 September 2000. His headless corpse was found buried just outside Kiev on 2 November; on 28 November Oleksandr Moroz, leader of the Socialist Party, made the dramatic accusation in parliament that President Kuchma had ordered his disappearance, and backed up his story with the 'Melynchenko Tapes', hours of secret recordings supposedly made in the president's office by a former member of his security detail, on which Kuchma's apparent voice angrily calls Gongadze 'simply shit . . . son-of-a-bitch – he needs to be deported – the scum – to Georgia and thrown there on his ass! . . . The Chechens should kidnap him.'[29] Many Rukh members took to the streets, but the party's leaders did not, supporting parliamentary criticism of Moroz and helping to frustrate plans to organise a referendum calling for the president's removal.[30] Rukh's support for the December hunger strikes against the president was decidedly half-hearted. The role of opposition was temporarily gifted to Tymoshenko and the Socialists – and to *faux*-nationalist *agents provocateurs* from UNA-UNSO (see pages 215–17), NRU(e) and Trident, a linked group allegedly set up by the Ukrainian security services.[31] On 6 February 2001 student 'anarchists' (their disdain for regimented authority was easy to spot, as all 'wore identical arm and head bands with the word Anarchist printed on them'), and then Trident, were involved in provocations,[32] including attacks on left-wing demonstrators that provided a useful excuse to the Communist leader Symonenko to quit the protests. Trident activists also played a prominent role in the 9 March demonstration that brought the campaign for Kuchma's resignation to a close (he had long sought to paint the entire opposition as 'Fascist'). Fifty of those arrested (mostly members of Trident and UNA-UNSO) were eventually charged. On the other hand, Rukh remained an 'intertextual' party (or parties) and recovered from its leaders' mistakes to play a key part in Viktor Yushchenko's Our Ukraine coalition in 2002.

Ukraine's 1999 Compendium
In Ukraine's 1999 presidential election the incumbent was so unpopular that at least three major oppositions had to be disabled. First, there was the traditional opposition on the right. As well as financing the split between Rukh (Udovenko) and Rukh (Kostenko), the authorities were allegedly behind the car crash that killed Chornovil. In December 2000 the leader of the Anti-Mafia group in parliament, Hryhorii Omelchenko, accused the interior minister, Yurii Kravchenko, of organising the 'accident'. Although no longer the political force he had once been, Chornovil still posed a problem for the authorities' chosen strategy of self-selecting easy opponents – not so much for the danger posed by his own candidacy, but because he might encourage the still considerable 'national-democratic' electorate to support someone else. His death came just two weeks after he had said that he would not run, but that he would also not support Kuchma.[33]

Similar moves were made against other potential 'third forces' in the centre ground. Kuchma's eventual nemesis, the Central Bank governor, Viktor Yushchenko, ruled himself out of the race after the murder of his predecessor and patron, Vadym Hetman, in 1998. A confidential document addressed to the president also laid out plans for 'the political and economic neutralisation of Hromada and its leaders'. This was the party built up by former premier Pavlo Lazarenko and future Yushchenko ally Yuliia Tymoshenko, whose financial resources had already threatened to create 'an extraordinarily dangerous realignment of votes in the new Verkhovna Rada' (parliament). The 'main plan' and 'reserve schemes' included black PR, the preparation of criminal cases by the Procurator's Office, and 'using the forces of the State Tax Administration, Interior Ministry and Security Service to undertake operational control of the activities of the firms, funds and other structures . . . of the central and regional structures of Hromada'. The accumulated 'evidence', it was predicted, would persuade the Central Election Commission to cancel Hromada's registration for the elections.[34] It did not. But in December 1998, either via entrapment or fortuitous accident, Lazarenko was caught entering Switzerland on a Panamanian passport and arrested. He jumped bail of $3 million and returned to Ukraine, but fled again in early 1999 after parliament voted 337-0 to lift his immunity, this time to the USA via Greece (using a plane allegedly supplied by Boris Berezovskii).[35] Tymoshenko meanwhile had been temporarily gathered into the presidential embrace and used to split Hromada. Of the party's forty-two deputies when Lazarenko was arrested, only seventeen remained after Tymoshenko set up the breakaway Fatherland group, which attracted twenty-eight deputies into its ranks. On the other hand, Tymoshenko was warned against standing herself this time.

Then there was the left. Administrative resources were constantly used to disrupt the campaign of the Socialist leader Oleksandr Moroz, denying him premises for meetings, intimidating potential supporters and smearing him in official media. The more 'active' measures that were planned against him were numerous; many have already been, or will be, mentioned elsewhere in this book. The Village Party, the Socialists' allies in the 1998 elections, was 'detached'; party leader Serhii Dovhan was used as a cuckoo (see pages 169–70). The so-called Kaniv 4 – an alliance of Moroz, former security chief Yevhen Marchuk and Oleksandr Tkachenko, Moroz's successor as chair of parliament (the fourth member was an obscure local mayor) – was exploited as a virtual object, an object lesson in political failure. The *de facto* three were hardly the Three Bogatyrs, and were more like the Three Hetmen (Cossack leaders) in traditional jokes about Ukrainians who can start an argument in an empty room. Vitalii Shybko of the Socialist Party accused *both* Tkachenko and Marchuk of working for Bankivska 'to neutralise the more powerful figure of Moroz',[36] as did one of Marchuk's own campaign staff, former KGB General Oleksandr Nezdolia.[37]

As Moroz was challenging from a much stronger base than Russian third forces such as Yavlinskii or Fedorov, the authorities doubled their bets against him by backing Nataliia Vitrenko, leader of the so-called Progressive Socialist Party. 'To use football terminology, she was entrusted with the man-marking' (*opika*) of Moroz.[38] According to Major Melnychenko, Vitrenko was frequently taken to private meetings with the president 'through the kitchen garden', where they discussed and agreed strategy (see pages 218–20). Vitrenko's dogged harassment of Moroz prevented him from challenging Symonenko for second place. The *coup de grâce*, the grenade-throwing incident at a Vitrenko rally, which was blamed on local members of Moroz's party, was probably designed to push him down further, into fourth place (see page 183).

Extreme long-term pressure was exerted on the parliamentary Socialist group and its money men. Three of the party's key financiers were forced out: Anatolii Novyk of the Ukrainian Press Group, owner of the daily paper *Den*, close to Marchuk; Volodymyr Satsiuk of Ukrros and the Ukraïna bank; and Mykola Kushnirov, secretary of the party's political council, who also had media interests. Novyk, Oleksii Kostusiev of Iren and Oleksandr Shpak of Ukrnaftoprodukt joined the usual suspect Labour Ukraine – which made something of a speciality of organising such defections (see page 239). Seven more deputies from the original joint Socialist–Village Party faction went to the new Solidarity project, three to yet another rival virtual party dubbed Justice. Weakening the Socialists was the sole purpose of both groups; neither was run as a serious project at the 2002 elections. (Justice won a miniscule 0.08 per cent and Solidarity changed functions to serve as a potential cuckoo within Our Ukraine.)

As in Russia in 1996, the presidential administration covertly supported the more easily defeatable Communist leader, Petro Symonenko (see also pages 237–8).[39] On the Melnychenko tapes, Kuchma confirms that 'we never worked against the Communists' in 1999. When he meets Symonenko for a private chat shortly after the election in February 2000, 'they talk like the frankest of friends. Kuchma, for example, says to Symonenko, summing up the presidential elections: "We worked [*popratsiuvaly*] well with you [using the familiar second person singular *ty*]. Everything was done as we agreed." '[40] Money had a role in ensuring the Communists played ball (see pages 238–9). An equally important dividend for Symonenko was keeping his main rival in his place: Leonid Grach, the powerful boss of the Crimean Communists. Grach would have been a more vigorous and more Russophile leader, but his business interests in the Crimea left him more open to official pressure (see pages 246–8).

Given the sheer number of opponents targeted in the 1999 Ukrainian campaign, the most innovative political technology used was ratings manipulation to keep all the candidates in the desired order, especially to depress Moroz's support, demoralise his supporters, and to feed his rivals' ambitions. Finally, of course, administrative resources were used to ensure that they finished in the required positions. Melnychenko, without providing any evidence, claims that the Communist leader Symonenko was ahead in one or both rounds. The official result was Kuchma 36.5 per cent (second round 56.2 per cent), Symonenko 22.2 per cent (second round 37.8 per cent), Moroz 11.3 per cent, Vitrenko 11 per cent and Marchuk 8.1 per cent. The two Rukh candidates trailed far behind, with Kostenko winning a mere 2.2 per cent and Udovenko only 1.2 per cent.

Divide and Rule Elsewhere

In Kazakhstan a potentially dangerous challenge to the regime was averted by breaking up the powerful troika that created the People's Front of Kazakhstan in 1998. The most dangerous opponent, given his wealth and links to the Russian military-industrial complex (and Oleg Soksovets and the Trans-World Group), former prime minister Akezhan Kazhegeldin, who was now bankrolling the Republican People's Party, was arrested and then exiled. His attempts to take over the leading paper, *Karavan*, and the TV channel KTK were also thwarted. Other opponents, such as the Russian Petr Svoik and former mayor of Almaty, Zamanek Nurkadilov, were bought off. The second party in the People's Front was Azamat ('Citizen'), but its leading light, Murat Auezov, son of the famous writer Muhtar Auezov and therefore the favourite to win the support of the intelligentsia, also pulled out. Azamat made a surprise declaration backing Nazarbaev in December 1998 (Auezov would later join forces with Nazarbaev's daughter in the movement Asar ['Altogether']). Nazarbaev was therefore able to claim easy victory in the January 1999 presidential election, with 81 per cent of the vote, against his main remaining opponent, the Communist leader Serikbolsyn Abdildin, a former chairman of the Supreme Soviet who had also done time in Nazarbaev's Socialist Party and had been safely neutered after an audit of his finances, who was awarded

12 per cent. Former customs chief, Gani Kasymov, derided by Kazhegeldin as a 'decoy duck for the protest electorate' (he certainly copied Zhirinovskii's antics by throwing a vase at a presenter on KTK),[41] was awarded 4.7 per cent. (Turnout was claimed to be 88 per cent.)

Another serious challenge to the regime emerged in November 2001 when pro-reform Young Turks set up a new party, Democratic Choice of Kazakhstan. Nazarbaev's political technologists promptly created a clone, the Ak Zhol ('Bright Path') Democratic Party.[42] Both the US State Department and *The Economist* bought this particular good-news story as evidence of 'democratisation'.[43] Significantly, however, Ak Zhol supported the draconian new procedures for re-registering political parties, and was duly the first party to manage to complete them. Democratic Choice's leaders, on the other hand, former energy minister Mukhtar Ablyazov and regional boss Gaklimzhan Shakiyanov, received six- and seven-year prison terms. Nevertheless, posing as it did as the natural home for the Kazakh business elite, it was not clear that Ak Zhol would stay under Nazarbaev's control forever.

In Armenia's presidential election in February 2003 the allies of the incumbent president, Robert Kocharian adopted the now almost standard Russian methodology although crude fraud was also widespread. First, Kocharian and his campaign manager, the hard-line defence minister Serzh Sarkisian, discreetly supported the former mayor of Yerevan, Komsomol opportunist and left-wing populist Artashes Geghamian, against their main opponent Stepan Demirchian, son of Karen Demirchian, the former local Communist Party boss gunned down in parliament in 1999. (Demirchian also played dirty by claiming that Geghamian had pulled out of the race.)[44] Second, the Communist Party was split, as it might have been expected to back Demirchian. The official rump withdrew its own candidate, Vladimir Darbinian. One faction backed Kocharian; the other the more obvious choice of Geghamian, a populist advocate of Slavic/Orthodox Reunion. The rival 'Renewed' Communist Party of Armenia, which broke away in 2001 and then united with half-a-dozen other groupuscles in July 2003, was thought to have covert official support. Project three involved less important flies, who were supposed to take votes from the opposition; although the main suspects, Ruben Avagian and Aran Harutiunian, won only 0.4 per cent and 0.1 per cent, respectively.[45]

Geghamian, with an official 17.7 per cent in the first round, duly blunted Demirchian's (28.2 per cent) potential challenge to Kocharian (49.5 per cent), although the authorities baulked at carrying out their original plan to declare outright victory after the first round. Kocharian supposedly cruised to victory over Demirchian in the second round, by 67.5 per cent to 32.5 per cent.[46] In the parliamentary elections that followed in May 2003, the authorities played the same trick, with Geghamian's National Accord Party refusing to join Demirchian's broad opposition alliance Artarutiun ('Justice') against Kocharian's Republican Party (HHK). Geghamian's party was awarded 9.7 per cent of the vote, and Artarutiun pegged back to 14.3 per cent, allowing the HHK to claim victory with 26.4 per cent, given its many covert supporters elsewhere on the list (see pages 143–4). Artarutiun was also cloned, although the rival Justice Party won only 0.5 per cent compared to the Justice bloc's 14.3 per cent. Of the three rival Communist parties, only Vladimir Darbinian's Communist Party of Armenia (HKK) won a significant proportion of the vote, but only 2.1 per cent, compared to 12.1 per cent and second place in 1999. The 'Renewed' Communist Party (NKK) won only 0.5 per cent.

Flies (*Mukhi*) and Off-cuts (*Otkoly*)

Division does not have to be down the middle. Many projects are of more limited ambition. Often an actual or potential opponent faces a swarm of smaller candidates or parties: 'flies' (*mukhi*), whose purpose is only to nibble away at their support base or electorate. Individual fly projects may only win 1 per cent or 2 per cent of the vote, but may still be considered a success. Any bite out of the target party's share of the vote is worth taking; and flies may even be deliberately designed to miss the barrier for representation (5 per cent in Russia, 4 per cent in Ukraine), so as to add to what is known as the *moloko* ('milk'), the seats then available for redistribution to the winners.[47] Plus, in Russia at least, fly projects get free airtime if they win at least 2 per cent of the vote, and since 2001 state funding (23 kopecks a vote) if they win 3 per cent. It is also easier and cheaper to set up a party without having to worry about who its successful representatives in parliament might be, how they might behave and how they might be paid. Flies may also act like the peons who harry and tire the bull for the matadors, or the picadors who wound the target in preparation for the kill. The main opponent, such as the Russian Communists in 2003, and, as was originally planned, Yushchenko in 2004, then has no strength left for the fight.

Two-round presidential elections also increase the temptation to use flies against your most potent competitor to prevent him or her getting to the second stage. And, of course, to return to the original metaphor, flies can easily be swatted by their creators when they are no longer deemed useful. It is therefore a mistake to decry or ignore the tiny 'taxi' or 'divan' parties that proliferate in the former USSR; their negative cumulative effect is often considerable.

The same point applies to splits generated within opposition parties. An 'agent of influence' may take precious few followers with him or her (such as Bohdan Boiko in Ukraine), and have precious little political career thereafter, but political technologists are certain to be calculating the costs and benefits. A small split resulting from a minimal expenditure of resources (financial, spent *kompromat*) is fine: accumulated off-cuts can leave a much smaller carcass behind. Sometimes, the split itself is all that matters, the virtual object to be spun in official state media. A project is only a failure if it fails to take off as intended (such as Seleznev's Russian Rebirth Party in 2002). A given project may be promised resources that the political technologists fail to deliver (as in the case of the Justice Party in Ukraine). Sometimes, projects are just badly managed (for example, Ak Zhol in Kazakhstan). And sometimes the flies take bites out of unintended targets: in early 2003 Kremlin strategists worried that United Russia was losing ground in the polls to some of its own (other) creations.[48]

Body Doubles

The first type of double is the simple clone. Running candidates with the same name as your opponent is a pretty unsophisticated project, requiring very little effort, but it is a common one and often surprisingly successful. The tactic was developed by Aleksii Koshmarov's 'St Petersburg School', and was first used on a large scale for the local elections in 1998. After an inflation in use in the 1999 Duma elections, the tactic really took off in Ukraine in 2002. Out of 225 local constituencies, doubles were used in 119 – almost always hampering leading members of the opposition. In Uzhhorod there were six candidates called Ratushniak.[49] The Rukh leader Taras Stetskiv claimed his two namesakes were paid between $1,000 and $3,000 to stand against him.[50] Volodymyr Alekseiev, an ally of Yuliia Tymoshenko who had sat for Kharkiv since 1994, was defeated by the tactic. In this case, two rival Alekseievs were used, 'one unemployed and one a labourer'. They had no function other than to put forward their names; 'they did not meet voters, refused to participate in a TV debate, and did almost nothing in the campaign'. Nevertheless, the two clones took three thousand votes, enough to account for the original Alekseiev's losing margin of 1,774.[51] Ivan Popescu, the respected representative of the Romanian minority, who had also served since 1994, was unseated in a similar fashion in Chernivtsi by the pro-presidential candidate, Mykhailo Bauer, after another Popescu appeared from nowhere to win 4,500 votes. In this case the crude invalidation of 11,728 votes (10.5 per cent) also helped. In Stryi (Galicia), on the other hand, Ihor Ostash (56 per cent) comfortably held on to the constituency he had represented since 1994, despite facing an Ivan Ostash (7 per cent) who was backed by his For a United Ukraine opponent, Vitalii Antonov, of the local energy company Halnaftohaz and ultimately Yukos (22 per cent).[52] Despite some claims that the tactic was already outdated, at least forty-four doubles appeared in the 2003 Russian Duma elections,[53] including two candidates with the bizarre surname KPRF (the Russian for CPRF).

Sometimes a tiny element of sophistication is added. In one Russian election the candidate Volchenko ('Wolfy') found himself opposed by a Zaichenko ('Rabbity'); while a certain Tveriozyi ('Mr Sober') found himself opposed by 'two antipodes', a Pianii ('Drunk') and Pivovarova ('Brewer') – and lost.[54] Sometimes doubles can be used by both sides. In the Briansk gubernatorial election in 2000, both the sitting governor, Yurii Lodkin, and his main rival, Nikolai Denin, were plagued by doubles. The two camps' efforts largely cancelled each other out: 'the pseudo-governor won 7 per cent, the pseudo-opponent 6 per cent'.[55]

Such seemingly obvious tactics are likely to survive as long as they continue to have even a minimal effect, as are the less obvious doubles which copy an opponent's key demographic or programmatic strengths rather than his or her surname. 'If the main opponent is a woman – you sneak in a woman. If the main opponent can count on the support of those who believe in a "firm hand", you sneak in a candidate made in the mould of the very same "hand".'[56] In one Russian local election, in Samara in 2002, Nikkolo-M helped finance a policewoman to run against an opponent who made much of his crusading role as a deputy prosecutor.

Clone Parties: The Sons of Lieutenant Schmidt

A special type of double is not the duplicated individual but the copy or clone party. In Il'f and Petrov's novel, *The Little Golden Calf*, several conmen bump into each other and find that they are all making a living by bogusly claiming to be the son of Lieutenant Schmidt, a hero in the 1905 revolution. No fewer than thirty rival sons and four daughters eventually organise a convention to divide the USSR into thirty-four 'spheres of influence'. In addition to the sons of Lieutenant Schmidt, Il'f and Petrov write, 'grandsons of Karl Marx, non-existent nephews of Friedrich Engels, brothers of [Anatolii] Lunacharskii [the Bolshevik commissar for education], cousins of Clara Tsetkin [the founder of International Women's Day], or, in extremis, descendants of the famous anarchist Prince Kropotkin, were travelling across the whole country, extorting and begging'.[57] One Ukrainian commentator has depicted the post-Soviet states as being full of 'the sons of Lieutenant Schmidt', noisy rivals to the inheritance of particular popular parties or brands.[58] Early examples are the Democratic Party and the Andrei Sakharov Union of Democratic Forces set up in 1990 (see page 26), and the cloning of opposition parties in Uzbekistan (see page 200).

This mushroom effect is not simply a result of brand competition. Political technologists are paid to undermine oppositions with cloning tactics that leave voters unable to distinguish original from fake and that enable the regime to steal the opposition's clothes by stealing its name. This type of strategy is also called 'creating decoy ducks' (*podsadnye utki*), so that the naïve or ill-informed chase the plastic fake.[59] Such projects are also designed to exploit the sociotropic tendency of well-defined social groups to empathy, so that, for instance, workers or women are persuaded to back parties that appear to be 'their own', but are actually fake, such as the CPU(r) and Women for the Future in the 2002 Ukrainian elections. Another name for this ploy, if it leads to a successful displacement, is 'Bolivar can't carry double' – a reference to the short story by the American author O. Henry 'The Roads We Take', popular in the former USSR, in which two bandits plan to escape together on a horse named Bolivar. In the event one kills the other, claiming that the horse is too weak to carry them both. If opposition supporters are more difficult to distract, the tactic develops into what is called promoting a 'heavy athlete in a light division': in other words, pushing the image or pushing up the rating of a virtual party or candidate so that voters will back it as the more likely to progress beyond 'lighter' rivals.[60]

In Ukraine's 2002 elections the opposition Socialist Party led by Oleksandr Moroz faced a clone All-Ukrainian Party of Workers – also led by a certain Oleksandr Moroz. In this case the clone party was allegedly backed by Oleksandr Stoian,[61] head of the official trade union organisation and number two on Viktor Yushchenko's Our Ukraine list, supposedly allies of the Socialists – until Stoian's enforced defection to the government 'majority' in December 2002. As so often, it was far from clear who was pulling the strings. The real Moroz's Socialist Party won 6.9 per cent of the list vote, its fake rival only 0.3 per cent. Bohdan Boiko's fake

Rukh won only 0.15 per cent (see pages 155–6). Yushchenko was able to see off the fake For Yushchenko! Bloc set up by Oleksandr Rzhavskyi because he had had the foresight to copyright his own name. In the 2003 Russian elections, a Yabloko Without Yavlinskii movement enjoyed some brief publicity; it was headed by Igor Morozov, but covertly backed by the Union of Right Forces' in-house technologists, Leonid Gozman and Alfred Kokh. The latter also allegedly led a campaign to foist on to Yabloko 'the reputation of a marginal political force' led astray by the personal ambitions of its leader, whom they also sought to discredit in the eyes of the Kremlin.[62] Yabloko was further smeared via anonymous posters linking it to the CPRF.[63]

Cloning must not be too obvious, of course, especially if parties are to function as 'life rafts' or 'spare aerodromes' (*zapasnye aerodromy*) to help leaders of a discredited existing party regroup under a more popular label.[64] Moldovan politics has specialised in extreme volatility, with politicians constantly jumping ship. The Agrarian Democratic Party, which won 43.2 per cent of the vote in 1994, disappeared almost completely in 1998, winning only 3.6 per cent. Its leaders were now to be found in the Democratic Convention of Moldova, the Party of Democratic Forces and the Party for a Democratic and Prosperous Moldova (see pages 145–7). Many then joined the victorious Communists in 2001 (see page 249). However, the life raft has no existence of its own. It must also serve as a project of another type if electors are to be persuaded to vote for it.

Displacement: Authoritarianism in Belarus by Sleight of Hand

Cloning has been a particularly popular tactic in Belarus. As one domestic critic has aptly put it, Belarusian president 'Lukashenka doesn't need allies, he needs subjects'.[65] Nevertheless, Belarus is not like those central Asian states where even a pretence at democracy is rarely made. Lukashenka managed the crucial transition from the chaotic proto-democracy of the early 1990s to authoritarianism via two rigged referenda that extended his own term of office and disbanded the legitimate parliament. But he also had to get the politics right to maintain momentum to the key vote in November 1996 – and head off the very real threat of impeachment. The key to his strategy was the cloning of three virtual 'pocket parties': the Communist Party of Belarus, the Agrarian Party and the Social-Democratic Party of People's Accord, led by Leanid Sechka, to replace real equivalents that posed a real threat to his power before the referendum. Moreover, even after Lukashenka began another wave of repression of his opponents following his successful 're-election' in 2001, politics in Belarus has remained latent. The appearance of pluralism remains. Parties are usually harassed rather than banned. Moreover, the regime has periodically shown some signs of seeking a normalisation of relations with the West – but by a return to virtuality rather than democracy.

Lukashenka was elected president by a landslide 80.4 per cent vote in July 1994. Within a year, however, he was faced with a new parliament in which his supporters could only muster sixty out of 198 seats. He was correctly confident that he was unlikely to be troubled by the nationalist opposition (the Belarusian Popular Front), although he nevertheless fomented division in its ranks (see page 153). Nor was there much trouble at the other extreme of the political spectrum. The demagogic leaders of the Russophile nationalist Slavic Council – White Rus, set up in June 1992 like Yury Azarenak, were easily used by Lukashenka for black PR against the Popular Front. The two groups that posed the most significant challenge to his Russophilia were the local Communists and the centrists who wanted to take the Russian path to market reform.

In this most 'Soviet' of the successor states, Lukashenka's foremost concern was to prevent any serious Communist challenge to his rule from outflanking him on the left. When Belarus held its first parliamentary elections as an independent state in 1995, the original successor party, the Party of Communists of Belarus (PCB), led by Siarhei Kaliakin, won forty-two (eventually forty-five) out of 198 seats.[66] Moreover, although strongly in favour of Lukashenka's Russophile foreign policy, the party opposed his authoritarian bent and, more surprisingly, reached agreement with Belarusian liberals in opposition to his economic policy. Finally, many of Belarus's 'traditional' economic lobbies had backed the party in 1994/5, and now needed to be 'reoriented' towards the new regime.[67] In July 1996 the party, keen to defend 'Soviet power' (that is, its own powerbase in the local Soviets) and realising it would be a very junior partner in any new authoritarian regime, announced its formal opposition to the president. In the run-up to the November 1996 constitutional referendum, therefore, Lukashenka decided to clone the PCB with a rival Communist Party of Belarus (CPB).[68] Siarhei Posakhow, his adviser on political parties and non-government organisations (i.e., Lukashenka's in-house technologist), organised the split.[69] The one member of the PCB's leadership troika without a deputy's seat, Viktar Chikin, was persuaded to become leader of the virtual Communists (he later commented cynically: 'I calculated better').[70] Chikin confirmed his establishment status by becoming first deputy mayor of Minsk and then head of the state TV and radio company in July 2000. He left the now largely decorative CPB, and was replaced by another renegade, Valer Zakharchanka.

In 1996, however, Chikin was gifted administrative resources, resurrected frontmen from the Soviet era and media backing to consolidate the project. There was money to pay for the new party's founding conference. The PCB, on the other hand, had developed a variety of covert business links since its revival, which were now cut off. The party's leading financier, Anatol Lashkevich, ambitiously nicknamed the 'Belarusian Engels', was harassed and defamed, ultimately leaving for Russia in 1997, where he took up the post of head of Rubin TV. Anatol Malafeew, last leader of the old Communists in 1990–91, was promised the chair of the new Palace of Representatives if he helped set up the CPB. Aliaksei Kamai, former party boss in Homel and agriculture minister, was also brought on board, also acting as midwife to the 'New' Agrarian Party (see overleaf). The official mass media brazenly depicted the real Communists as fakes (agents of the West, usually America, ideological gadflies), and anointed the fake Communists as real Leninists. According to Kaliakhin, leader of the PCB: 'There was a huge PR campaign against us, we were accused of working with the nationalists, being agents of the West, of becoming social democrats' (the last being a term of abuse if applied to Communists).[71] The result was 'not virtual reality, but absurd reality'. Although the official media portrayed the new CPB as the 'real Communists', 'the party itself was not real'. It pretended to stick behind the old (1994) party programme because in that way it could avoid having to engage in real politics. Like all good Communists, in public they were against the private ownership of land, but 'they didn't even campaign against Lukashenka's 1997 law on land privatisation', although the supposedly social democratic PCB did.[72]

Before the constitutional coup the (old) Communists had the biggest single faction in parliament, with forty-five deputies. KGB pressure and presidential money ensured that only twenty-three stayed with the PCB, while twenty-two joined the CPB and went into the new unelected Palace of Representatives. Many Western commentators failed to notice the sleight of hand. The Economist Intelligence Unit, for example, seemed to think that the two different Communist parties that successively won most seats at the 1995 and 2000 elections were one and the same.[73] The new Communists had state support; but, not surprisingly, the 'old' Communists had significantly more flesh-and-blood members – fifteen thousand compared to seven thousand. [74] The contest between the two has continued, with the CPB supported by the official media and the PCB and its leader Kaliakhin regularly vilified: one TV broadcast described him as 'not a big player, but [one who] thirsts after power . . . a spy sent by the Cossacks', a natural dictator with 'good genetic memories of [the Bolsheviks'] struggle against the enemies of the people'.[75] In the 2003 local elections, the rival Communists were the only two parties to win a significant number of seats. The PCB won seventy-eight, the CPB 107. No other party won more than eleven.[76]

The Agrarian Party, the second largest in Belarus, was also neutered, although in this case without the need to set up a new party (as was also the case in Russia; in Ukraine the left-leaning Village Party set up in 1992 was displaced by the government-backed Agrarian Party, set up in 1996). The Agrarian Party of Belarus was originally established in 1992, when it was close to the then powers-that-be: party leader Siamion Sharetski served as an adviser to Prime Minister Kebich in 1993–94 on rural affairs. At the 1995 elections the Agrarians won thirty-three seats, and, swollen by extra independents, briefly grew into a faction with forty-seven seats. In alliance with the original Communists (forty-five) and 'Civic Action' (twenty-one, based on the United Civic Party, see overleaf) against the pro-Lukashenka Accord faction (sixty), they helped tip the balance and elect Sharetski as chair. The party was then dealt similar medicine to that administered to the PCB. First, in 1996 Lukashenka's men split the party. The original group was harassed and Sharetski forced into exile in 1999. Then the pro-presidential usurpers were declared to be the 'official' version of the party. This group, led by Mikalai Shymanski (editor of the pro-government paper *Narodnaia gazeta*), was the only version of the party allowed to sit in the new House of Representatives, although it had ceased to function as a party in any meaningful sense. By the time of the Agrarians' next congress in March 2000, inertia and self-interest ensured that the collective-farm elite signed up *en masse* to the new version of the party.

Lukashenka's final sleight of hand was against his other potential opponents: the four main parties of the liberal centre. The oldest, the United Democratic Party (ODP), set up in November 1990, was the main party of the Russophile intelligentsia, the would-be Belarusian equivalent of Democratic Russia or Yabloko; second was the revived Hramada, first established in 1903 and re-established in March 1991, third, the Party of Popular Accord (Partiia Narodnogo Soglasiia, hence PNS), set up in 1992; and fourth, the Civic Party, set up in late 1994. Hramada was left of centre; the other three were more or less ideologically indistinguishable. Nevertheless, the attempt to set up an ODP-PNS alliance for the first round of the 1995 elections was a failure. Before the second round, however, the ODP and Civic Party united to form the United Civic Party (OGP), which reached a seat-sharing agreement with the Popular Front that allowed it to win most seats in Minsk and set up the twenty-one-strong Civic Accord faction in parliament. The OGP, moreover, represented a double threat to Lukashenka, as it was basically the 'centrist party of the nomenclatura' with good links to Moscow (it tried to act as a go-between in the 1996 crisis).

Lukashenka's administration therefore arranged a reverse takeover of the other two centre parties, then puffed them up to substitute for the likes of the OGP.[77] Hennadii Karpenko, the original leader of the PNS, was forced out and replaced by Leanid Sechka, who 'was rewarded with a high post in the Committee of State Control'.[78] Another presidential centrist, Vasil Dalhalew, ended up as deputy prime minister. The anti-presidential forces were forced out of Hramada during the crisis in autumn 1996, with the new leader, former lieutenant-colonel Mikalai Statkevich, sometimes on one side and sometimes on the other. In January 1996 a shotgun marriage helped the PNS swallow Hramada in order to create a new Belarusian Social-Democratic Party (Popular Hramada). Just to complicate matters, the party split between Statkevich's and Sechka's wings, with the latter now calling themselves the Social-Democratic Party of Popular Accord. Furthermore, an oppositional Social-Democratic Party was revived in 1998. The electorate, many of whom had centre-left sympathies, were left totally confused.

The operation – involving three classic substitutions – proved highly successful. After 1996 there were no distinct voices against Lukashenka capable of mobilising a significant opposition. The three new parties now formed the core of Lukashenka's pie and were the only ones allowed representation in the remodelled parliament after the November 1996 coup. Chikin's new Communist Party had twenty-two seats, Shymanski's Agrarians fourteen and the Party of Popular Accord five, although none bothered setting up a formal party faction. In 2000, when Lukashenka staged rigged elections to a new version of the rigged parliament set up

Fig. 7.1 Elections to the Belarusian Parliament, 1995

	number elected
Party of Communists of Belarus (PCB, Kaliakin)	42
'Old' Agrarians (Sharetski)	33
United Civic Party (OGP)	9
Party of Popular Accord (PNS)	8
All-Belarusian Party of People's Unity and Accord	2
Belarusian Social-Democratic Assembly (Hramada)	2
Other	7
Independents	95
Total	198

Source: http://binghamton.edu/crc/elections/blr95par.html.

in 1996 to 1997 (Malafeew's Palace of Representatives), the pro-regime Communists emerged as the largest party, albeit with only six seats (eighty-one out of 110 were 'independents'). The new Agrarians had five, the new Hramada one; the old parties (PCB, etc.) had none.

Overall, however, parties just weren't that important any more. Lukashenka had set up a system more akin to the 'regime parties' of the old East Germany. The new Communists and Agrarians now functioned as tame regime satellites, flanked by pseudo-civic front organisations, so-called 'Lukamol' parties such as the Sporting Party aimed at youth, and the Party of Labour and Justice, a pseudo-leftist party aimed at pensioners. The local Liberal-Democratic Party, like Zhirinovskii's Russian equivalent, maintained its covert links with the regime (see page 197). In September 2002 Lukashenka's advisers set up a Belarusian National Youth Party, although ironically it soon fell victim to grant leechers.

Fig. 7.2 Elections to the Belarusian Palace of Representatives, October 2000

	number elected
Communist Party of Belarus (CPB, Chikin/Zakharchanka)	6
'New' Agrarians (Shymanski)	5
Republican Party of Labour and Justice	2
Liberal-Democratic Party of Belarus	1
Social-Democratic Party of Popular Accord	1
Belarusian Socialist-Sporting Party	1
Independents	81
Vacant/invalid	13

Source: www.electionworld.org/belarus.htm.

The motley opposition could only summon 15.6 per cent of the vote in the face of Lukashenka's triumphant 're-election' campaign in 2001. Lukashenka liked to keep his options open, however. Chikin's Communist Party of Belarus provided a useful bridge to the CPRF and the Kremlin when union with Russia was the president's priority. Kaliakin's Party of Communists of Belarus served as a usefully old-fashioned scarecrow opposition when his attention turned to building his authority at home (though Lukashenka has on several occasions toyed with the idea of the CPB swallowing the PCB).

Divide and rule has, of course, continued since 2001. The BPF split in 1999, 2001 and 2003; the BSDP (Narodna Hramada) in 2001 and 2005; the old OGP in 2002. The regime did not want to allow the potentially popular Women brand to be gifted to the opposition, so in August 2002 it split the Women's Party Nadzeia ('Hope') in the same way as it had the Party of Communists, on this occasion with the intention of pre-empting Nadzeia's discussions with the opposition Social Democrats about creating a possible United Social Democratic Party. Valiantsina Palevikova was replaced as leader by the more 'reliable' Valiantsina Matusevich. In the run-up to the 2004 elections the main opposition alliance, dubbed the Popular Coalition Five Plus (five of the older parties), immediately found itself opposed by the European Coalition of Free Belarus. Given the past form of some of the latter's members, including Statkevich's BSDP(NH), the 'new' Nadzeia and Charter 97, and their extremely unlikely cohabitation, it seemed certain that the regime would exploit the inevitable disagreements, even had it not – as was possibly the case – encouraged the formation of the European Coalition in the first place. Neither won any seats. The only parties allowed to win representation were the 'official' Communists (CPB) with eight, the official Agrarians with three, and one Liberal-Democrat, no less than the party leader Siarhei Haidukevich himself.

Cuckoos

Another project that may overlap with the game of divide and rule is the placing of cuckoos in the nests of opposition groups. Often the host party will be unaware of the placement. In the 1999 Ukrainian presidential election, Serhii Dovhan, then leader of the Village Party and head of Oleksandr Tkachenko's campaign team, was a Kuchma plant. The Socialist-Village Party alliance had won 8.6 per cent of the vote in the 1998 parliamentary elections (third place) and was therefore a potential rival to the Communists (24.6 per cent in 1998), whose leader was Kuchma's planned opponent in the second round in 1999. On the Melnychenko tapes, Dovhan boasts in the summer of 2000 (after the campaign, having now broken with Tkachenko): 'I already knew that everything would be as it turned out.' His job was to make sure that 'it seemed that we [the Kaniv 4] were organising a struggle against President Kuchma. In accordance with the agreement', and to 'control [the Socialist leader Oleksandr] Moroz', to make sure that the Village Party (i.e., the collective-farm nomenclatura) would not back the president's most dangerous rival as it had in 1998, and that Tkachenko would urge his supporters to back the Communist leader

Symonenko instead. Tkachenko was apparently easy to manipulate. Dovhan says: 'I wouldn't want to use the word "stupid" [of him] as he [Tkachenko] is older [than I am].' Kuchma even speculates amusedly that his endorsement may have 'worked against Symonenko'.[79]

In Russia, Yurii Skokov, a former Yeltsin aide and 'consummate insider', with links to the military-industrial complex and the RAU corporation (see page 225), performed a similar function within the leadership of the Congress of Russian Communities (KRO) in 1995. According to Michael McFaul, 'several original KRO officials were convinced that Skokov was sent by the Kremlin to deliberately sabotage Lebed and the bloc's electoral prospects.'[80] As a reward, Skokov was briefly touted as a possible prime minister, albeit mainly by himself.

In a slightly different scenario the cuckoo is invited into the nest, as in the Ukrainian fairytale 'Koza-dereza', in which a friendly hare gets stuck with a billy goat who squats in his house and helps himself to his food and drink. For example, the former writer and one-time Rukh stalwart Volodymyr Yavorivskyi soon found himself playing the hare to billy goats such as Yukhym Zviahilskyi and Hanna Antonieva when he tried to attract business sponsors into his Democratic Party of Ukraine in the late 1990s (see page 133). The Democratic Party, originally the party of the Ukrainian intelligentsia, ended up under the control of leading oligarch Oleksandr Volkov, who incidentally also provided a home for Volodymyr Satsiuk, one of the leading cuckoos on the Socialist-Village Party list in 1998. Nearly all of whom were gone within the year, taking their finance and their lucrative committee posts with them. Satsiuk ended up as deputy head of the Ukranian security services – a rather surprising home for a Socialist.

A much more serious situation faced Kuchma's main rivals in the 2002 election. Desperately short of money and keen to attract defectors from the ruling elite, the Our Ukraine coalition set up by former prime minister Viktor Yushchenko sought to attract Ukraine's new businesspeople into its ranks. Many, however, turned out to be cuckoos or presidential sleepers, such as the campaign chief and former deputy prime minister Yurii Yekhanurov, and Roman Bezsmertnyi, 'general manager of the project named Yushchenko',[81] former presidential representative in parliament and a recent refugee from the National-Democratic Party, and in 2002 prominent in the For a United Ukraine coalition. Both men were protégés of the then head of the presidential administration, Volodymyr Lytvyn. As with Unity and Fatherland-All Russia in Russia in 1999, business representatives hopped back and forth between the 'opposition' bloc Our Ukraine and the 'government' bloc For a United Ukraine (although the former had more bankers and heads of small-to-medium-sized businesses, and the latter more state bureaucrats, big factory bosses and energy barons, such as Heorhii Kirpa, head of the state railways).[82] Solidarity, the Agrarian Party, even the Donbas-based Party of the Regions, could happily have ended up in either bloc, just as the original All Russia, essentially a coalition of regional governors, could have lined up with the Kremlin in 1999 if the signals had been right. The 'chocolate king', businessman Petro Poroshenko, formerly of both the

Village Party and SDPU(o), headed the Solidarity group, which had been set up to draw votes away from the opposition during the parliamentary crisis of 2000. Solidarity's belated switch to Our Ukraine therefore led many to suspect that it would serve as a collective cuckoo, given that it included the likes of Volodymyr Pliutynskyi, who, though twice declared a Hero of Socialist Labour, was also one of the 'monsters' of agrarian business, and Volodymyr Makeienko, former head of Ukrhazprombank. Poroshenko, head of Ukrprominvest and effectively 'boss' of Vinnytsia oblast, also brought on board business 'protégés' such as Oleksandr Stoian, long-time head of the official trade unions, and Yurii Karmazin, head of Party of the Defenders of the Fatherland, one of the official clone parties run against the Socialist-Village alliance in 1998.

Yushchenko also accepted many surprising business outsiders on to his list (some others unsuccessfully offered 'up to' 'a record $5 million' for a place). The list of the supposedly 'nationalist' Our Ukraine Bloc included a formidable 'Russian lobby': Dmytro Sandler was included as a favour to Lukoil boss Agit Alekperov, who deputised him to gain a share of the Berdiansk lubricant plant; Oleksii Yaroslavskyi of Techproject Ltd and Ernest Haliev had links to Russian Aluminium (Yaroslavskyi's brother Oleksandr was one of the Green Party's 'new businessmen', with powerful agricultural interests and a place alongside Haliev at Ukrsibbank); Pavel Ihnatenko was linked to the Alfa Group; Oleksandr Tretiakov was co-chair of Lukoil Ukraine; Volodymyr Shandra was big in construction and had links to the son of the Kiev mayor Oleksandr Omelchenko. Further down the list came Davyd Zhvaniia of the energy company Brinkford; Oleksandr Morozov, who had tussled with Viktor Pinchuk over control of the insurance firm Oranta; and the notorious Donetsk clansman turned governor of Sumy oblast, Volodymyr Shcherban. The main financiers of the bloc were Poroshenko, Zhvaniia, Yaroslavskyi and Mykola Martynenko.

From Yushchenko's point of view the function of the cuckoos was to gain some share of administrative resources (or at least to provide some shelter from negative campaigning); from Kuchma's point of view their purpose was the opposite: to ensure that any supply was choked off at source. Yushchenko may have thought he could split the governing coalition; in the end the boot proved to be mainly on the other foot. (The same game was played in 2004, when Yushchenko appointed Oleksandr Zinchenko, ex-SDPU(o), as his campaign chief.) Some presidential technologists also hoped that Our Ukraine

> will be a pro-presidential coalition; even if they criticise Leonid Kuchma, their criticism will only be political-PR steps. Yushchenko [will therefore be] the manager of a presidential project, which can [also act as] an obstacle to Moroz, Fatherland [Tymoshenko's party] and the Communists. . . . The main aim is to subdue the support of that part of the electorate which would give its votes to opponents of the president.[83]

Some even hoped to create a Ukrainian version of United Russia, albeit through the assembly of three distinct parts: the FUU, the other pie parties (see pages 134–5) and the 'loyal' part of Our Ukraine. For businessmen seeking a flag of convenience, loyalties could be sold to the highest bidder after the election (see overleaf), although not in every case. A number of businessmen stayed put in the Razom subfaction, particularly Poroshenko, Zhvaniia, Yevhen Chervonenko and Oleh Rybachuk, founder of the Ukrainian *FT*, the paper *Business Ukraine*, although the likes of Poroshenko clearly had their own interests to pursue. In a sense, therefore, Yushchenko was vindicated; Our Ukraine retained just enough resources to fight another day.

After the Final Bell: 'Parliamentary Technology'

According to the ever-precise Marat Gelman, the winner in any given set of parliamentary elections is not simply the one who gets the most votes: 'The winner is the one that can make its configuration [in other words, manipulate its way to a majority] in parliament.'[84] In the 2002 elections, the two main pro-presidential parties, For a United Ukraine and the SDPU(o), together won only 18.1 per cent of the list vote, well behind the 37.8 per cent garnered by the three main opposition parties (Our Ukraine, the Tymoshenko Bloc and the Socialists). The Communists, who claimed to be in opposition, won another 20 per cent. After this first half of the elections, which rightly made all the initial headlines, the government forces initially had fifty-eight seats and the opposition troika (that is, not counting the Communists, who had fifty-nine) 174. Regardless, it was the former who were soon claiming a 'majority'.

The operation to reverse the parliamentary arithmetic was necessarily complex. First, it should be recalled that black PR in the last few days of the campaign (see pages 105 and 141) had in any case brought Our Ukraine down from a high of 33 per cent in the polls on 10 March to an official 23.6 per cent (24.5 per cent in the main independent exit poll) on the election day of 31 March, largely through votes lost in east Ukraine.[85] Second, although none of the clone parties run against Our Ukraine (see pages 190–6) was individually successful in terms of winning the 4 per cent necessary to enter parliament, as collective flies they won 10 per cent of the vote, much (if not all) of which would otherwise have gone to the opposition parties.[86] Third, administrative resources cost the bloc another possible 4 per cent (see pages 81–2). Fourth, the authorities ran several groups of sympathisers under neutral colours, such as the group led by Serhii Tihipko in Dnipropetrovsk. Fifth, the new presidential chief of staff, the SDPU(o)'s Viktor Medvedchuk, cajoled nearly all those elected as (real) independents into joining the FUU. The crude financial pressure applied by Medvedchuk's brother, Serhii, head of the local tax administration in Lviv, led to a revolt by the local council in October 2003 – and to the prompt dismissal of the protesting officials. Sixth were the cuckoos in the various opposition parties. The outgoing Rada had failed to press through an amendment to Article 81 of the Constitution, which since December 1998 has been interpreted as giving even deputies elected on the party list *carte blanche* to change allegiance. The early signs were that many political loyalties in the new parliament were again highly flexible. Fig. 7.3, below shows the changing balance of power in parliament. Factions are listed in order of their precedence in the original party list vote in order to show how the electorate's verdict was turned upside down.

Fig. 7.3 Early Dynamics of Faction Change in the Ukrainian Parliament after the 2002 Elections

		Faction changes			
	Original	*15 May*	*18 July*	*Nov.*	*2 Jan.*
Our Ukraine	70+41	119	110	110	102
Tymoshenko Bloc	22+0	23	23	20	18
Socialists	20+2	22	21	20	20
Communists	59+7	64	63	61	60
(For a) United Ukraine	35+66	175	187★	184	191
SDPU(o)	19+5	31	34	39	40
Other parties	0+9	–	–	–	–
Independents	92	14	17	14	19★★
Vacant or contested seats	3	3	3	0	0

Sources: *RFE/RL Daily Report*, 15 May 2002, and regular updates from the Rada website at www.rada.kiev.ua. See http://oracle2.rada.gov.ua/pls/radac/fr_list.

★ After July 2002, total for all successor groups to For a United Ukraine.
★★ Non-faction group formed January 2003.

Two weeks before the March poll a document was leaked from the campaign headquarters of For a United Ukraine to Our Ukraine. The latter claimed it showed plans 'to drain away (*po vidtoku*) deputies . . . from the Our Ukraine list . . . in order to separate off two to three independent deputy groups from the bloc'.[87] The new parliament assembled on 14 May, but For a United Ukraine, with 182 deputies, and the SDPU(o), with thirty, still fell short of the simple majority of 226 votes necessary to elect a parliamentary leadership to their liking (Our Ukraine had 119). That majority was only scraped together on 28 May, when seven of the cuckoos in Our Ukraine were persuaded to break ranks and support the election of Volodymyr Lytvyn as chair (an operation that cost an alleged $15 million);[88] they included many of Yushchenko's leading business sponsors whom the nationalist right had always distrusted, among them Sandler, Yaroslavskyi, Haliev and the ever-unreliable Shcherban. The seven were promptly expelled. A steady stream of defections followed throughout the rest of the year. Many came from Solidarity. Pliutynskyi left in July, joining the rival Agrarians' spin-off from the FUU; Makeienko jumped ship in December. Loyal Our Ukraine businessmen came under intense 'administrative' pressure: Chervonenko (trucking, soft drinks) and Shandra (roofing) claimed political measures cost their businesses millions.[89] Yurii Orobets said he was offered $500,000 to defect.[90] In December 2002 Oleksandr Stoian, leader of the official trade unions, changed sides to save his job from an opponent backed by the SDPU(o). In October the authorities in Kiev arrested and roughed up Konstantin Grigorishin, head of the Russo-Ukrainian venture Energy Standard Group, which then controlled eleven oblast energy companies coveted by the SDPU(o). At the time Grigorishin had $370 million invested in Ukraine. He immediately blamed Medvedchuk for the attack, claiming he had refused to finance the SDPU(o) instead of his rumoured support for Our Ukraine. Even more clumsily, the police manhandled Grigorishin's associate, Rada deputy Volodymyr Syvkovych (former head of the independent TV station STV that Kuchma had put under pressure in 1999 – supposedly for emitting harmful radiation). He and four others from the People's Power faction promptly resigned from the 'majority'. Other businessmen to experience 'pressure' included Vasyl Bartkiv, Taras Dovhyi, Volodymyr Maistryshyn and Petro Dyminskyi.

All the other opposition parties suffered defections. Former prosecutor general Mykhailo Potebenko, a surprise recruit to the Communists' election list at number twenty, broke ranks to vote for Lytvyn and was expelled. The Socialists also experienced the dangers of attracting sponsors, when Leonid Hadiatskyi, a former associate of exiled prime minister Pavlo Lazarenko and his Hromada party, showed his loyalty to the Dnipropetrovsk machine and defected to the Labour Ukraine wing of the FUU. Once Yuliia Tymoshenko restarted her campaign for Kuchma's resignation in the autumn of 2002, her bloc (BYuT) was also targeted. Under intense pressure, three deputies defected in October, including the historian Petro Tolochko and Vasyl Onopenko, head of the tiny Social Democratic Party, a rival to the SDPU(o); they were followed by two more in November, reducing BYuT's parliamentary strength to eighteen. The legal noose around Tymoshenko's neck was also tightened when Turkey extradited her father-in-law and three former business colleagues in October.

The 'Stop Yushchenko' Project

Round three in the protracted Ukrainian contest was the race for the presidency in 2004. This high-stakes campaign was a taxonomist's dream, as the authorities' strategists were forced to use their entire repertoire of dirty tricks. The involvement of Voloshin and Russian political technologists, mainly Marat Gelman, later Gleb Pavlovskii, Sergei Markov and Viacheslav Nikonov, was apparent from autumn 2002,[91] as was the use of their characteristic tactic of 'toad's eye'; in other words, the attempt to make the electorate forget its enthusiasm for Yushchenko by creating both diversions and mirror images (double objects) of his assets. The new prime minister, Viktor Yanukovych, and the new chair of the national bank, Serhii Tihipko, were installed and marketed as 'doubles'. The Donetsk clan which stood behind Yanukovych bought the website www.for-ua.com to reshape his image, hiring the Lviv journalist Kost Bondarenko (chosen because of his past credibility in the opposition camp) to create a series of artful templates. First he compared Yanukovych to Stolypin, both 'former provincial governors' who took office in a time of chaos and 'restored order [sic]'; then to Disraeli, the lesson this time being the latter's role in reinventing and reuniting the governing (British Conservative) party. Internationally, Yanukovych was presented as being as capable of opening doors as Yushchenko, stress being laid on his European travels and his ability to extract concessions from the WTO and TAFT. Domestically, Yanukovych was advised to devalue his predecessor's most famous achievement by massively increasing pensions, though this time sparking inflation and devaluing the currency. The final comparison was to the young 'model European', Helmut Kohl, although the closest resemblance between the two men was physical rather than ideological or philosophical (with two youthful convictions for theft and assault, Yanukovych was an altogether different type of 'heavy').[92] Much of this PR was relayed to the USA via the firm Creative Response Concepts, and by Viktor Pinchuk's efforts to court a string of American worthies, including George Bush Senior and Henry Kissinger, to spread the message that Yushchenko could claim no monopoly on democratic credentials.

On the other hand, Yanukovych's advisers embraced his tough guy image at home, marketing him as a 'Ukrainian Putin' for Russophone Ukraine. This side of the campaign was handed over to a new Donetsk-based company, Social Dialogue, headed by Mykola Levchenko, behind which stood Piotr Shchedrovitskii.[93] Unfortunately, Yanukovych's past cast too long a shadow, as did those of the people who lurked behind him, primarily Donbas's strongman Rinat Akhmetov (his personal wealth an estimated $1.7 billion).[94] Yanukovych's PR people also had to fight their way past Medvedchuk for exposure on national TV – hence Akhmetov and others trying to win more exposure for their own channels Ukraine and Kievan Rus (founded in 2003), both of which, along with the paper Today, had close contacts with Gleb Pavlovskii's FEP.[95] Social Dialogue also helped set up a rival to the main Kiev-based portals in the form of www.ostro.org.

The young and apparently pragmatic Tihipko was more of a tabula rasa. He was therefore levered into place at the National Bank in November 2003, ousting with some difficulty Yushchenko's protégé Volodymyr Stelmakh, to 'double' Yushchenko's other past career as a banker. Tihipko's PR, supposedly run from outside by Jacques Séguéla's Euro RSCG Worldwide (see overleaf),[96] was soon parading a list of virtual achievements, such as 'protecting' the exchange rate during the second Iraq War, introducing a 'new' currency (newer and shinier notes, palely cloning Yushchenko's real achievement in launching the Ukrainian hrivnia in 1996), and claiming sole credit for admittedly impressive GDP growth (over 8 per cent in 2003). Although most of this boom was due to the ongoing effects of the Yushchenko government's reforms in 1999 to 2001, the authorities' PR now brazenly depicted the opposition as the main threat to 'stability' and risk-free growth – their best hope for a new 'big idea' (the government programme for 2004 was entitled 'Steadfastness. Effectiveness. Responsibility'). Tihipko had a lot to lose if he ran, however, and eventually settled for the job of Yanukovych's campaign manager. Others backed Valerii Khoroshkovskyi, the former leader of KOP (see pages 193–6), as an alternative faux-liberal 'Kinder-Surprise'.[97]

The other side of the 'double-object' strategy were the efforts, akin to those to create a 'Cassette 2' scandal before the 2002 elections, to paint Yushchenko as 'just as bad' as the authorities. In this case the idea was to depict all oligarchs as alike: in the first case, ironically, by advertising the role of the 2002 cuckoos and trying to blame fiscal theft on the budget committee run by the Our Ukraine financier Petro Poroshenko. More carefully formulated black PR came in June 2003, with a legal verdict against Yushchenko's former deputy at the National Bank, Volodymyr Bondar, for alleged foreign-currency manipulations back in 1997. The SDPU(o) was also behind a crude book-length attack on Yushchenko entitled 'Yushchenko: A History of Illness', with its own website at http://kniga.temnik.com.ua, not so far from www.temnik.com.ua, rather more obviously linked to the SDPU(o). Dmytro Ponomarchuk, who was also behind the well-financed journal *Patriot*, was again involved. Both websites continued the 'doubler' technique, accusing Yushchenko of the financial improprieties and political double-dealing for which its backers were more famous. The rather cruder site at http://geocities.com/uysh_us was thought to be backed by the Donetsk clan.

The Rybkin affair (the disappearance of the Berezovskii-backed candidate in Russia's 2004 presidential election, and the tale he subsequently told of being drugged and filmed in 'perverted acts' in Kiev) was also exploited in spring 2004 to try and link Yushchenko, via Rybkin's supposed business partner in Our Ukraine, Davyd Zhvaniia, with Berezovskii and 'bad' oligarchs in general. However, this was not the equivalent of the silver bullet the Yukos affair had provided the Kremlin with in the 2003 elections. In Ukraine, most of the oligarchs were on the government's side. A similar plan to simulate 'clan conflict' over privatised assets, and 'to drag Symonenko into the conflict on the side of the workers, and Yushchenko in defence of the business interests of his partners',[98] came to naught, given the risk to actual investments in an election year when there was more money to be made.

Divide and rule was another obvious ploy, given the success of the three-headed opposition (Yushchenko, Tymoshenko and the Socialists) in 2002. Assuming that she was just another virtual object, available for manipulation or sale, some in the Russian political *beau monde* initially thought (particularly just after March 2002) that Yuliia Tymoshenko, 'a charismatic, responsible and not anti-Russian politician', was worth supporting 'in those regions of west Ukraine where she was capable of taking the maximum number of votes from the former prime minister'.[99] According to Mykola Tomenko, one of the early recommendations of the Russian technologists was to exploit 'Tymoshenko's participation in the presidential race . . . [and] let the ByuTy leader come fourth', which will 'help Yushchenko to be third'.[100] A more likely option for Gelman, *et al.* was to have Tymoshenko 'call on her supporters to vote against all in the second round'.[101]

However, in the end they settled for making trouble. In February 2003 two million copies of a fake 'open letter to my electors' circulated in west Ukraine', bearing Yushchenko's picture and the Our Ukraine logo. This detailed the kind of trouble Tymoshenko could bring to Yushchenko's campaign, 'whether or not [she] has stolen those hundreds of millions of dollars', and called for her to be returned to prison,[102] probably indicating one scenario the Russian advisers were themselves hoping to bring about – the other being, of course, to encourage her to break ranks with Yushchenko and run on her own. To help create the right 'objective conditions', Tymoshenko was constantly lambasted on the websites www.aznews.narod.ru and http://timoshenkogate.narod.ru – and the *kompromat* continued to flow. In May an alleged SBU (Ukrainian security service) agent in her party, Volodymyr Borovko, provided the authorities with a video tape on which Tymoshenko apparently discussed bribing a judge. Her immunity could not be lifted, however. Then in September Russian prosecutors sought to question her in Moscow over an alleged scam with Gazprom and the Russian Defence Ministry in the mid-1990s. Tymoshenko remained steadfast in her support of Yushchenko throughout, but guilt by association was all the technologists desired.

The technologists also played divide and rule on the left. They knew they could rely on the Communist Party. One technologist commented approvingly in private on the Communists' willingness 'to talk and to trade'.[103] Unlike in Russia in 2003/4 (see pages 257–65), it made sense to revive the Communists as a stumbling block for a more powerful (real) opposition. In private, the technologists planned to help Symonenko come third, assuming that his 'personal' interests (surviving as party leader until 2006) would then force him to back the authorities' candidate in the second round.[104] The Communists also served as part of the virtual chorus in the pre-election game, launching a simultaneous attack with Medvedchuk on 'inter-ference' by foreign NGOs in December 2003 and backing his plans to reform the constitution in 2004 (to deprive any incoming president of much of his or her power).

In March 2004 www.provokator.com.ua published details of yet another project, this time to exploit the ambitions of the Socialist Party (SPU).[105] The project's rumoured author was again Marat Gelman; its cynicism was, of course, absolute. To the political technologists, the fact that the SPU had been the main target of their manipulations in 1999 was irrelevant. It was just another virtual object to play with. Yesterday's enemy is today's ally, if there is enough money and unsatisfied ambition to fuel the process. It was no different from the Kremlin supporting Rodina in order to split the Communist vote in 2003, and then doing the exact opposite in 2004. Nevertheless, it seemed shocking that Moroz would be naïve enough to cooperate with Bankivska – although private channels existed through the Socialists' campaign chief, Iosyp Vinskyi, to Medvedchuk, who wished to rehabilitate the SDPU(o) via a future alliance with the SPU. The authorities, however, used both sticks and carrots. The Socialists' surviving business supporters were under severe pressure

(Mykola Rudkovskyi had interests in an oil well in Poltava), while the offer of a proportional representation system for the 2006 elections promised medium-term 'salvation' for the SPU.[106] Briefly, Moroz also received softer treatment on SDPU(o) TV. Again, it would be a sufficient dividend for the authorities if Moroz (the SPU won 6.9 per cent in 2002) failed to endorse Yushchenko (23.6 per cent, Tymoshenko's Bloc won 7.3 per cent) in the second round.

The authorities' Russian advisers also pushed a long-term project depicting 'the schism of Ukraine as a virtual reality', and inverting reality by caricaturing Yushchenko as the cause of that schism and presenting support for the powers-that-be as the only means of avoiding it. In Pavlovskii's key phrase: as Kuchma 'is the guarantor of the political state unity of Ukraine in the period up to the next presidential elections', so would Yanukovych be thereafter.[107] The SDPU(o) media therefore churned out propaganda against the *'Nashisty'* (from the equation of 'Our Ukraine', *Nasha Ukraïna*, with 'fascists', *fashisty*) in east Ukraine, where it could focus on a handful of genuine extremists such as Oleh Tiahnybok of the Social-National Party (whom Yushchenko eventually expelled), and on so-called Galician 'separatists'. At the same time, the Russian political technologists aimed to play the 'Russian card' in a way that would actually initiate such a split. First Medvedchuk and then Yanukovych sought to resuscitate the language and dual citizenships issues to replay Kuchma's original victory in 1994. The idea of a 'Unified Economic Space' covering Russia, Ukraine, Belarus and Kazakhstan, formally launched in September 2003, was similarly designed to revivify Ukraine's Russophiles, and to provide a campaign gift to the Communists to puff them up for 2004. A referendum on the three issues was at one time a serious possibility.

In June 2004 a detailed plan, reportedly drawn up by Gelman in November 2003, was leaked to www.pravda.com.ua. Although its more ambitious projects were sidelined, many of its detailed proposals had clearly been adopted. The 'main scenario for the campaign', declared the report, must be 'directed conflict'. 'Apocalyptic scenarios for the possible future must not be presented as utopian, but become reality.' 'Our task is to destabilise the situation in the regions (maybe involving political games, but not the everyday economy), and drag Yushchenko into this process.' 'The task of the media [in other places, "our media"] is to interpret this as an ontological "East-West" conflict, a political conflict between Our Ukraine and the Party of the Regions, and a personal conflict between Yushchenko and Yanukovych.'

The report suggested various ways in which this could be done. Governors from the east, 'not just the Donetsk clan, but representatives of the close circles of Yanukovych and Akhmetov', could be parachuted in to the west to stir up animosity; hostility between Poles and (west) Ukrainians could be revived by exploiting the Orliat cemetery affair (the burial of Polish war dead in Lviv); confessional conflict could be created by privatising the eleventh-century St Antonii Caves in Chernihiv to either the Moscow or Kievan patriarchate (probably the latter so as to force Yushchenko to support them); and 'Cossacks' from Russia or Ukraine

(Korchynskyi's skinhead group 'Brotherhood' was mentioned) might be encouraged to revive their historical role as frontiersmen in Crimea, building new settlements and provoking land disputes with the Crimean Tatars.[108] The point? 'Yushchenko must be represented as an enemy of Russians in Crimea,' the report argued. 'If Ukraine can't defend the interests of Slavs in Crimea, then nearby Russia is always prepared to offer support.' In a final ultra-cynical touch, the report recommended that 'volunteers' from the Kuban and the Don should offer their services in Crimea, though 'in fact it isn't necessary to set anything up, it's enough to show some Cossacks on TV in military gatherings, anywhere near Krasnodar or Rostov.'[109]

The report confidently declared that the proposed virtual conflict would escalate like 'the arms race between the USSR and USA', and ultimately force Yushchenko 'to the margins of Ukrainian politics [to] become a politician of the class of Vitrenko',[110] one of the technologists' earlier playthings. Would Russian political technologists be cynical enough to play such games in their own country? Probably, but the dangers of such a virtual conflict becoming real were obvious enough. The one time the authorities seemed seriously to be contemplating a 'strategy of conflict' was on 20 August, when a bomb in Kiev's Troieshchyna market killed one and injured eleven (followed by a smaller bomb two weeks later).[111] Although the bomb was blamed on Yushchenko's supporters with surprising speed, three of those arrested were later found to work for the fake nationalists sponsored by the government (see below): Bohdan Boiko, Trident and Eduard Kovalenko's UNA.[112]

In the actual election there were twenty-three candidates. Six were 'technical candidates', passive proxies with no other role than to stuff election committees with their, in other words, Yanukovych's, supporters (Mykola Hrabar, Ihor Dushyn, Vladislav Kryvobokov, Volodymyr Nechyporuk, Mykola Rohozhnyskyi and Hryhorii Chernysh). Seven others were more active proxies. Three of these were designed to 'activate' radical leftist and Russophile voters in east Ukraine. Opinion polls showed that this segment of the electorate was tempted to vote against Yushchenko in the second round, but was also disillusioned with the powers-that-be. Therefore the political technologists argued it was better to use proxies to stimulate them into action. The eventual vote 'dividend' for Yanukovych was worth the risk that the three would take votes away from him in round one.[113] Nataliia Vitrenko was now too old a trick to play this part (see pages 218–20), but was wheeled out anyway. Oleksandr Yakovenko of the faux-radical Communist Party of Workers and Peasants (see page 255) doubled up her role; while both he and Oleksandr Bazyliuk of the Slavic Party served as a virtual chorus for the black PR attacking Yushchenko as an 'ultra-nationalist' and 'American puppet' (see illustration on p. 273).

The other four technical candidates were 'nationalist projects' covertly supported by the SDPU(o) and Yanukovych's Regions of Ukraine party.[114] It was natural for the Donetsk clan to play the nationalist card in public; in private, however, they gave financial support to two of the four (particularly Roman Kozak, see overleaf). The SDPU(o) was interested in hurting Yushchenko and Kiev mayor Oleksandr Omelchenko (after he defeated their Hryhorii Surkis in the race to run the capital in

1999) and controlled the necessary TV channels to carry the message. It backed Korchynskyi and Chornovil (see below); Boiko had covert links to both groups. The Donetsk clan also helped set up organisations such as the Rukh-Statist Opposition, later Rukh for the Nation, the Society for the Rebirth of the Ukrainian Nation, and the UNA-UNSO branch under Yurii Tyma; the SDPU(o) also shared with Bankivska the funding of Kovalenko's UNA and the People's President Bloc, providing the same mock support for Yushchenko as in 2002 – Bazyliuk's Slavic Party was an otherwise inexplicable fellow member.

The division of labour between the various 'nationalist projects' was as follows. Roman Kozak of the previously obscure Organisation of Ukrainian Nationalists (OUN) in Ukraine, served to discredit Yushchenko by mock-association, demonstrating uninvited in his support and receiving plenty of air time on official TV as with the UNA. Kozak's TV adverts were even placed right before Yushchenko's, so that viewers could hear his call to 'Vote for Yushchenko. Together with Yushchenko, we will kick the Russians and Jews out of Ukraine!' After a particularly xenophobic broadcast on 26 September, the State Committee on Nationalities and Migration called on Kozak to be prosecuted,[115] – perhaps by previous agreement. In this fashion, the Russian technologists hoped to cost Yushchenko votes in the east and south. Boiko and Chornovil, on the other hand, because of their past association with Rukh, were programmed to attack Yushchenko's 'betrayal' of its legacy and take votes from him on the right, mainly in west Ukraine. Andrii Chornovil, the son of the veteran dissident, supposedly had his 'brand' appeal, but was actually a member of the SDPU(o) faction on Lviv council. Bohdan Boiko, the former deputy chair of Rukh and head of Ternopil council in the 1990s (when he had mainly distinguished himself by speculating in the local sugar crop), was now head of Rukh for Unity, reliable in his 'political dilettantism' and long in receipt of money from the SDPU(o). Boiko was also linked to the Trident paramilitary group led by Vasyl Evanyshyn, also based in Ternopil, but covertly financed by another oligarch, Oleksandr Volkov, and by his one-time colleague Volodymyr Satsiuk, since February 2004 a member of the SDPU(o) and deputy head, 'Kuchma's man', in the SBU. The final nationalist candidate was Dmytro Korchynskyi, media-killer on SDPU(o) TV, who functioned as an 'intellectual provocateur',[116] to divert the energies of the (small) nationalist intelligentsia and generally further to poison the atmosphere against Yushchenko.

Finally, there was a handful of 'moderate' avatars, designed to steal Yushchenko's centrist support. However, both Tihipko and Khoroshkovskyi backed away from possible exploitation as a faux-liberal 'third force'; and others seemed reluctant to risk their future careers by serving as 'Vietnamese cosmonauts'. Some suspected that Anatolii Kinakh, who served as prime minister in between Yushchenko and Yanukovych from May 2001 to November 2002, was a government 'reserve', but he, too, was too busy staking out his own survival prospects. His financial and organisational resources as head of the Ukrainian Union of Industrialists and Enterprise Bosses were considerable, though both the Union and its sister party were split between Kinakh and supporters of Yanukovych. His image-building resources, on the other hand, were meagre.[117] Vasyl Volha of the neophyte Social Control Party was supposedly an anti-corruption campaigner double, but his party was too much of a business project. Mykhailo Brodskyi, whose fake liberal Yabluko party had served the authorities in 2002, was too widely distrusted. Kiev major Oleksandr Omelchenko was popular in the capital, but had few resources to reach beyond it and was too close to the opposition camp.

A final 'technology' to debut in 2004 involved what might be termed competitive victimhood. Yushchenko's staff claimed that he was poisoned on the night of 5/6 September, necessitating two weeks of lost campaigning and a trip to a Vienna clinic – and even that the incident took place at a secret 'clear the air' meeting with the heads of the Ukrainian Security Service, Ihor Smeshko and Volodymyr Satsiuk.[118] A fake statement from the Vienna clinic, the Rudolfinerhaus, denying that poison was involved, was faxed to Reuters, who initially took it to be genuine, and it was given wide circulation in official state media. The same channels publicised Yushchenko's (less than perfect) health records that had been submitted to a parliamentary commission investigating the affair. According to one report, the fax was traced to Euro RSCG, behind which stood Viktor Pinchuk and the French *chef des scandales* Jacques Séguéla.[119]

The government camp replied with an 'attack' (*terakt*) on Yanukovych, after 'several large objects' were thrown at the prime minister in Ivano-Frankivsk on 24 September. Although immediately hospitalised, Yanukovych found time to blame the incident on extremist supporters of Yushchenko. A video shown on Petro Poroshenko's Channel 5 revealed the event to be rather farcical, and the 'several objects' to be one raw egg. Yanukovych, a big, even burly man, nevertheless collapsed as if poleaxed – after a peculiar pause.[120] As often, the double object was but a pale reflection of the real.

Administrative Overload: The Orange Revolution

As in 2002, the Russian political technologists working in Ukraine ultimately proved to be too Russian. Their mistakes this time were of a different order, however. First, they relied too heavily on *dramaturgiia*. On the one hand, their selling of Yanukovych, the black PR against Yushchenko and the various 'nationalist projects' succeeded in drawing out Ukraine's latent east–west differences. The electoral polarisation that had tripped them up in 2002 was not deconstructed, but it was recast. Ukraine now split regionally, not just for and against the authorities. However, Pavlovskii, Gelman, Markov, *et al.* fundamentally misunderstood the nature of the regional politics they had unleashed. As Russians, they assumed west Ukraine could be cast as the natural minority: but it was their client Yanukovych not the pragmatic Yushchenko who was too extreme a figure, politically, personally, and in terms of his regional origins (Donetsk). The key middle ground was also alienated by their own interference.

Second, the Russian aides-de-camp behaved like the newer breed of administrative technologists and over relied on crude fraud. Admittedly, their instincts in this case overlapped with those of the Donetsk clan and Viktor Medvedchuk, Kuchma's chief of staff, and their local equivalents like Yurii Levenets, responsible for many dirty tricks in 1999. But the Dnipropetrovsk group (Pinchuk, *et al.*) might have chosen subtler methods. As well as traditional 'technologies' like padding the turnout with dead souls and 'cookies' (extra ballot papers), the Yanukovych team this time added 'electoral tourism', transporting activists by bus and special trains from one polling station to another for repeat voting. Where polling stations were controlled thanks to Yanukovych-financed 'technical candidates' (see page 82), blatant intimidation was possible. If not, the *khustynka* ('kerchief') method was used instead. Yanukovych people would wear some distinguishing mark to guide their voters (both forced and voluntary) to their part of the polling booth. Most importantly, however, the Central Election Commission (CEC) was corrupted and its computer systems infiltrated. A secret team at work in the Zoriany ('Stars') cinema, linked by fibre optic to the CEC, was, however, caught in the act by telephone taps planted by the patriotic part of the SBU. This raised interesting questions about Yushchenko's secret discussions with the SBU in September, whether he was poisoned then or not.

The count for the first round was twice suspended as Yushchenko rapidly closed a fictitious gap. The final official result admitted his lead was 39.9 per cent to 39.3 per cent, compared to 44.4 per cent to 38 in the main exit poll. Moroz won 5.8 per cent, Symonenko only 5 per cent, Vitrenko 1.5, Kinakh 0.9, and Yakovenko 0.8 per cent. All others scored less than 0.5 per cent. The 'Toad's Eye' of minor candidates had done its work in solidifying the Yanukovych vote in eastern Ukraine, but they failed to score well enough to provide a cover story – the transfer of their votes – to explain the planned Yanukovych victory in the second round. On 21 November the Zoriany team could therefore be heard demanding 'We have a negative result [Yushchenko was winning] . . . we have agreed a 3 to 3.5 per cent difference in our favour.' Yanukovych was duly declared the winner by 49.4 per cent to 46.7, but it was immediately clear how – and where – the deed was done. Turnout was up by 6 per cent to 80.8 per cent, and in Donetsk reached 96.7 per cent, 96.2 per cent of whom backed Yanukovych (in three constituencies Yushchenko polled 0.6 per cent). Local turnout had always previously been lower than average; in 1999 it was 66 per cent. Yanukovych's team claimed to have found almost one million extra votes in Donetsk on top of the apparent maximum he had already reached in round one; 2.88 million in the first round rising to 3.71 million in the second – more or less his overall national margin of victory.

A storm of protest ensued. Political technology is an adjunct, but also an alternative, to the cruder types of electoral fraud. The technologists had failed in their main task: delivering a victory achievable by minimal, i.e. deniable, fraud. Significantly, when the second round was re-run in fairer conditions on 26 December, the result was not a big shift of votes to Yushchenko, and little different to the real result in the original second round. Yanukovych still won in the east; but his figures were now almost plausible. Turnout in Donetsk was now claimed at 'only' 86.9 per cent (77.3 per cent nationally). Overall, Yushchenko won by 52 per cent to Yanukovych's 44.2 per cent.

The technologists' third crucial error was to miss an obvious trick. Whereas Yanukovych simply had too many problems as a candidate (his criminal past, the Donetsk mafia behind him, his ability to speak both Ukrainian and Russian equally badly), a fake 'third force' might have won them the election. Serhii Tihipko's late attempt to usurp Yanukovych's place in the 'third' round came far too late, however. By then, popular revolution was the real story (see page 271). And revolutions sweep much away in their path. Some of the government side were openly regretting they hadn't used more – that is more subtle – political technology; but it was now far from clear what their options would be at the planned rematch at the Rada elections due in March 2006.

Frame-Ups

Not all active measures are sophisticated. The simple frame-up is popular, for instance. The Ukrainian whistleblower Mykola Melnychenko claims he was provoked to make his patriotic tape recording when he 'learned by accident about the order by Ukrainian President Leonid Danylovych Kuchma to organise a terrorist attack on the presidential candidate Nataliia Vitrenko with the purpose of the political destruction of Oleksandr Oleksandrovych Moroz'.[121] On 2 October 1999 grenades were thrown at an election rally for Vitrenko in the small town of Inhulets, near Dnipropetrovsk, lightly injuring Vitrenko and (allegedly – there were no TV cameras present) forty of her supporters. Within an hour, state media, particularly one of the more honey-toned media-killers, Oksana Marchenko (later married to Viktor Medvedchuk), were blaming the incident on Moroz's local election agent, a certain Serhii Ivanchenko, and his brother. UT-1 provided all sorts of information with implausible swiftness: who supplied the grenades, who drove the getaway car, etc. Moroz, it was more or less openly intimated, had ordered the crime (parliament told UT-1 to give Moroz a right of reply, but the station wheedled out of it). Vitrenko parroted the same story.

In 2001 Moroz released a portion of tape from the summer of 2000 in which the then SBU chief Leonid Derkach tells the president, 'On the Ivanchenko affair, everything is going according to plan. There are no hitches.'[122] In another fragment an unknown voice says, 'it's going beautifully with Ivanchenko. Going at full speed. . . . There's just one thing – the judge loves to talk about this with [Prosecutor] Potebenko.'[123] According to Melnychenko, Derkach himself planned the whole 'provocation'.[124] Ivanchenko, it was reported, had once belonged to the Democratic Rebirth Party now run in tandem with the Democratic Party by Oleksandr Volkov.[125] In June 2001 the two accused and their 'accomplice' all received fifteen-year jail sentences.

Hired Hatchets

A common project involves contracting out the task of discrediting the (real) opposition to a candidate or party with apparent (virtual) opposition credentials, but covert links to the ruling regime. This allows the powers-that-be to remain aloof from the grubby realities of 'politicking', while providing scripted weaknesses as 'stick-ons' for the opposition. Such apparently independent voices can be media-killers such as Dorenko or Azarenak, or politicians like Zhirinovskii, loyally turning his fire on first Primakov in 1999 and then the Communists in 2000. Hafiz Hadjiev and his opponent from the Popular Front threw glasses at each other on TV in the 2003 Azerbaijani election (see page 86), but Hadjiev also threw mud that stuck, accusing regime opponents of homosexuality and of being in league with the CIA. In a similar fashion Nataliia Vitrenko and Bohdan Boiko's so-called Rukh in Ukraine's 2002 elections, or Siarhei Haidukevich in Belarus in 2001, may have failed as electoral vehicles, but achieved their goals in so far as they damaged their allotted targets. Sometimes hatchets will say the things their sponsors do not want to say (publicly); sometimes they will help provide a virtual chorus by echoing the same themes as more public projects. Zhirinovskii's attacks on Communist corruption in 2003 chimed with those of United Russia; Haidukevich's assault on the 'destructive' Belarusian opposition in 2001 perfectly suited Lukashenka's interests (see page 197). The regular attacks on Viktor Yushchenko from the fake far right in 2002–04 caricaturing him as an American 'agent of influence', were merely extreme versions of the conspiracy theories being peddled by the authorities.

Round-Table Discord

Another type of organised disagreement involves setting up opposition 'round tables' for a fall. If a cuckoo, mole or hatchet man or woman can be smuggled into round-table discussions designed to produce a common candidate or prepare a joint strategy for the would-be opposition, the resulting failure and appearance of disunity will do the regime's opponents great damage in the virtual sphere, especially if, as is often the case in the post-Soviet world, the powers-that-be are relying on their own conservative counter-image of stability and 'leadership'. The powers-that-remain may even prefer to see (virtualised) superficially anti-regime manoeuvres take place, in order to see them fail.

In Russia Lebed was used to undermine the 'third-force' negotiations with Yavlinskii and Fedorov in 1996 (a considerable threat as Yavlinskii's party had won 6.9 and Fedorov's party 4 per cent of the vote in 1995), while the troika's backers, Luzhkov and Gusinskii's Most Group, were pressured to limit their financial support. Primakov was kept from joining forces with the Communists in 2000 by the deal between Unity and the Communists that dished the FAR in the Duma. The 'Kaniv 4' in Ukraine in 1999 (see page 158) came to a particularly bitter end, providing a perfect composite image of squabbling, selfish, Lilliputian ambition. During the Belarusian presidential election in 2001, 'at every meeting [of the opposition round table] Siarhei Haidukevich or his party comrade Aliaksandr Rabatai accused the rest of the delegation of being "non-constructive". The state-owned media regularly echoed those statements.'[126] One theory has it that Yavlinskii's Yabloko and the Union of Right Forces were deliberately set on each other by the FSB in

2003.[127] As always, the *legenda* of the democrats being unable to unite was but the mirror-image of the 'strong leadership' provided by Putin.

Strategies of Tension

The original 'strategy of tension' was pursued by elements in the Italian right wing and security services, including the notorious P2 Lodge and the 'Gladio' paramilitary group, in 1969-82 to justify the exclusion of the Communists from power and possibly even bring about a lurch to the extreme right. It allegedly involved sponsoring a series of bombings, from that in the Piazza Fontana in Milan in 1969 to the 1980 Bologna explosion that killed eighty-five people, which would then be blamed on their leftist opponents. A similar fake coup was used to justify a clamp-down on the opposition in Haiti in December 2001;[128] while the Algerian army backed radical elements in and around the GIA (Armed Islamic Group) to discredit 'Islamic extremism' during the 1993-97 'dirty war' and to justify its retention of power after denying the Islamists victory in the aborted elections of 1991.[129]

Such ploys have tended to be only temporary in the former Soviet Union, given the desire to maintain social apathy and keep society demobilised. On occasion, however, minor acts of destabilisation have been used to encourage conservative voters to stick with the devil they know, such as the 'attack' on Vitrenko in 1999, or to remind voters of previous dramas. The events in Italy and Algeria were real enough, but in the post-Soviet states there is a definite preference for staging such events on TV, with a minimal amount of real-time incident to justify the story. The attempt on Turkmenistan president Saparmurat Niyazov's life in November 2002 served as a pretext for suppressing the opposition and defining the regime as part of the global struggle against 'international terrorism' (in this case a motley collection of exiles and 'Georgian drug addicts').[130] Ukrainian prime minister Pavlo Lazarenko (1996) and Belarusian presidential candidate Aliaksandr Lukashenka (1994) were both accused of staging similar incidents.

It may have been the case that the 'Storms in Moscow' plan, developed in the presidential administration in 1999 (by the group close to Yeltsin's daughter), was originally intended to serve a similar purpose, by 'destabilising the social-psycho-logical situation in Moscow' with minor terrorist acts.[131] It certainly fitted the pattern familiar since 1996 of 'developing the impression that Yeltsin was still [reliving his heroic deeds of 1991 and] struggling bravely against his foes: such as the Communist threat, the generals' plots' (i.e. Pavel Grachev, Yeltsin's notoriously corrupt defence minister, sacked on the eve of the 1996 election).[132] Hence the repeated allegations concerning the links between Berezovskii and Chechen commander Shamil Basaev, with the former supposedly sponsoring the incursion into Dagestan that Moscow used as a *casus belli*.[133] Certainly, it has prompted the Moscow intelligentsia at least to suspect covert manoeuvrings behind every subsequent tragedy – although the final tragedy may also be that virtual terrorism can beget real terrorism, as in the October 2002 Moscow Dubrovka ('Nord-Ost') theatre siege. John Dunlop has called the latter a 'joint venture' to scupper the negotiations in Liechtenstein that had a real possibility of reaching compromise, discredit the relatively moderate Chechan leader Aslan Maskhadov, renew support for Russia's 'war on terrorism', and prepare for the planned endgame in Chechnia in time for the 2003-04 domestic election cycle. There were no real Arabs or members of al-Qaeda involved. Several of the kidnappers were later alleged to have been in recent custody, to have had contacts with the FSB, and even to have escaped unharmed.[134]

Conclusions

Making trouble for your political opponents is not particularly unusual. There is, however, a clear distinction between taking advantage of their misfortunes and projects that are actively designed to create such troubles in the first place. Moreover, in so far as these projects slip beneath the radar of public perception, they count as 'virtual'. The apparent weakness of political opposition in the former USSR is not entirely owing to a lack of *partiinost*, personal ambition or the weakness of civil society. In fact, one unfortunate paradox making democratisation *en profondeur* even more difficult is that it is precisely those opposition parties that display real longevity and vigour (the Russian Communists by 1999, Rukh in Ukraine by 1998) that become a target for divide-and-rule tactics, or free-riding by less popular government or oligarchic forces.

The extent of troublemaking is also derived from Bolshevik culture. One of the Russian expressions for 'divide' (and rule) is *razdrobliat*, that is, 'smash into pieces' rather than merely 'divide' – recalling Stalin's criticism of Eisenstein that in his film *Ivan the Terrible* he did not make Ivan terrible enough. 'One of the mistakes of [the historical] Ivan the Terrible was that he did not completely finish off the five big feudal families,' Stalin claimed. 'If he had destroyed these five families then there would . . . have been [no] Time of Troubles.'[135] Another Russian expression for the complete destruction of your opponents is *vtolkovyvat* ('hammering'), like the 'tolchoking' or 'bit of the old ultra-violent' that the 'droogs' dish out in the Russian-inspired argot of Anthony Burgess's 1962 novel *A Clockwork Orange*. Lenin's famous dictum *Khto kogo*? (roughly and inadequately, 'Who does whom in?') is still current. The niceties of liberal democracy stand little chance when pitted against such destructive urges. It has to be assumed that local elites will behave as badly as circumstances allow them to, if they are then to be subject to any kind of effective restraint.

8 Inventing the Opposition: Kremlin Parties

The other side of the coin to neutering real or potentially dangerous oppositions is promoting 'virtual oppositions' in their stead. There are several basic types of invented or virtual opposition. The first is virtual populists: politicians or parties who have been allotted the role of tribune of the people; as they are covertly supported by the regime, they have no intention of really challenging it, of course. A second, related type is virtual neophytes. Even apathy or anti-politics can be exploited by the invention of 'anti-political' parties, both to drain away such sentiment and exploit it as a political springboard. The third type is soft opponents, who can play the part of real challengers to convince domestic audiences or international observers that a contest is taking place, but who are either safely unelectable or have no intention of pushing the contest too hard. The fourth are bogey or scarecrow (*pugal*) individuals or parties. These have to seem a sufficiently bad alternative to the powers-that-be as to frighten domestic electorates or foreign governments and lenders into backing the incumbents. This may not necessarily involve a plausible electoral challenge – it may be enough for the dark forces to remain lurking offstage. Finally, if the desire for change is strong enough, such change can always be staged. These categories, of course, overlap, and may also overlap with those of the many-layered pie: that is, many of the elements that end up in such a pie will previously have posed as oppositions.

Parties that are secretly backed by the powers-that-be may therefore be found across the formal left–right political spectrum. The authorities may also try to manipulate the balance of forces within the opposition. They may play up the extremes, inflating radical fringe elements to discredit the mainstream opposition, or even to justify a crackdown against it. Or they may play a game of 'calm and control', seeking to manipulate mainstream opposition parties to keep their 'opposition' within manageable bounds, as again with the still-huge Communist parties in both Russia and Ukraine – to which the next chapter is therefore devoted. Sometimes the authorities may do both, which is most characteristic of the more developed Russian and Ukrainian systems. The authorities may play large against small, preferring to deal with the devil they know and have invested in before. Or they may play small against large, as when the authorities sponsor smaller radical groups on the far left or right in order to play divide and rule.

It can, of course, be objected that one or more elements in a virtual system would have existed anyway, and the fact that a given politician or party has covert links to the authorities or their technologist hirelings does not necessarily mean they are subject to total covert control. Nor, of course, are some of the cruder tactics involved unknown elsewhere. It is the scale of ambition, the sophisticated tactics and the use of 'new' technologies, plus the attempt by the Kremlin or Bankivska Street to control so many pieces on the political chessboard, that make the game being played in the former USSR so unique. The overall strategy is directed democracy, but to a much greater degree than is normally understood.

Virtual Populism

The first thing oppositions are invented to do is oppose. One element in the existing regime can be contracted out to oppose another, but with the drama kept safely virtual. A prime example is the People's Party of Russia in 2002–03, ostensibly led by Gennadii Raikov, but in reality a St Petersburg project. The main regime party, United Russia, was itself toying with the idea of running 'against' the regime (i.e., against itself), but its high profile made this difficult, although this was the main reason behind the summer campaign against the oligarchs, Yukos in particular (see pages 108–9). In the event it was easier to contract out that function to a new party – hence the launch of the People's Party with a barrage of populist initiatives on restoring the death penalty and recriminalising homosexuality. Party 'activists' demonstrated against the 'proselytising' Catholic Church, and noisily picketed the Danish embassy in protest against the Chechen Congress held in Copenhagen in October 2002. Given the simultaneous launch of the Party of Life, the wags therefore dubbed it the 'Party of Death'. This regime-backed party was also allotted the contracted-out function of opposing the energy reforms (sharply increasing household utility payments) proposed by other elements in the regime, namely United Energy Systems, although behind Duma doors the People's Party (as the People's Deputy faction) backed Chubais's bill to restructure the company. This type of ritualised opposition was, of course, better than real protest, and the powers-that-be also preferred to stage such symbolic actions on the TV news rather than on the streets. The party was also used to test out populist proposals for taxing 'natural rents' (in other words, 'windfall' profits in the energy sector) while the national security arguments in the party's draft bill on nationalisation drawn up in early 2003 (which was soon lost in the Duma) bore a strong resemblance to those used in the campaign against Yukos later in the year.

Although Raikov's party was set up in September 2001, it only really began to attract attention in the first half of 2003, in an attempt to 'soften up' voters for the autumn Duma campaign. Donations duly flooded in. Raikov himself was something of a buffoon; the party's real backers were Igor Sechin from the Kremlin, and Sergei Pugachev and Sergei Veremeenko from Mezhprombank, who also helped secure funds from Gazprom.[1] The money ensured that the party's ads were suddenly omnipresent in the summer of 2003. According to Video International, the 'populist' party's business backers made it the top spender in the 'pre-campaign' period, with $3.5 million on TV advertising – more even than United Russia's $2.7 million.[2] By 8 October it had 85 million roubles in the kitty (then $2.9 million), second only to United Russia's 141 million ($4.7 million).[3] Further evidence of the party's real nature came from its loyal voting record in the Duma in 2003, backing, for example, the Kremlin's version of the law on customs tariff that favoured primary energy exporters, despite the party's public policy of protectionist preference for manufacturing and processed products.[4] The fact that the party only won 1.2 per cent in the elections was not especially important. It had already succeeded in its primary substitution function of mimicking real protest and redefining it in a way that United Russia and Rodina could exploit in the Duma campaign. It also played a role in the Kremlin pie, picking up nineteen single-mandate seats.

Many other parties have fulfilled the dual function of soaking up the protest vote and stealing the opposition's clothes. In Georgia the Labour Party (a sleeper since 1995), led by Shalva Natelashvili, was used in the ultimately unsuccessful attempt to siphon off popular resentment in the late Shevardnadze era, taking first place in the June 2002 local elections. However, despite eye-catching campaign promises to nationalise all energy companies and provide free electricity for all, it was in fact a creature of the Interior Ministry.[5] In the 2003 parliamentary elections Shevardnadze hoped that, alongside another pocket party, the New Rightists, the virtual opposition would help blunt the attack of the real opposition, Mikhail Saakashvili's National Movement.[6] Hence, despite all the reports of rampant ballot stuffing, the elections were quite precisely fixed in advance: the pro-Shevardnadze party For a New Georgia claimed first place with 21.3 per cent, the Labour Party was awarded a supposed 12 per cent and the New Rightists 7.4 per cent. The parties of the potential pie therefore had 41 per cent and a potential majority in alliance with the Revival Party (18.8 per cent) led by Aslan Abashidze, the neo-feudal boss of the Ajaran Republic. The National Movement was allotted 18.1 per cent and its ally the Zhvania-Burdjanadze Democrats 7.4 per cent. The failure of Labour, the 'party of the people', to take part in the demonstrations against the rigging of the elections raised further suspicions – even more so when many over-eager rank and file broke ranks to join the protests. The plan failed because arithmetic isn't everything: Saakashvili had the all-important momentum and attracted more and more defectors from the tottering regime (see also pages 217–18). When the elections were replayed in March 2004, Saakashvili's National Movement swept the board with 67 per cent. The Labour Party collapsed to 5.8 per cent.

Perhaps the most striking example of virtual populism is the rise from obscurity of Belarusian president Aliaksandr Lukashenka. His anti-corruption platform won him a landslide victory in the 1994 election, with 80.4 per cent of the vote, but his triumph owed much to manoeuvring behind the scenes. At the time, at least three groups thought it was in their interests to promote his brand of virtual populism by appointing him chair of a temporary parliamentary commission 'to fight corruption' in June 1993. Some in the team of the prime minister, such as Viacheslaw Kebich, thought Lukashenka could be used to discredit their main rival, parliamentary speaker Stanislaw Shushkevich. Another group included many 'people who were, in fact, secretly working for the benefit of his rival [Lukashenka] and filled key posts in Kebich's team. This included [deputy prime minister] Mikhail Miasnikovich, Kebich's closest aide [and later head of Lukashenka's presidential administration], Siarehei Linh and people associated with them', other former nomenclatura stalwarts such as Ivan Tsitsiankow, chair of the Chernobyl committee, and deputies like Leanid Sinitsyn.[7] Finally, it is alleged that the Kremlin covertly backed the future president, 'their man' in Belarus, and that the project was codenamed 'Operation Zont' ('Umbrella');[8] the Kebich group having flirted rather too obviously with the White House opposition, then the main proponents of the monetary union project that Kremlin 'liberals' sought to sabotage. The Kebich 'traitors' therefore saw in Lukashenka a more Russia-friendly frontman who would launch mass privatisation and line their pockets. All agreed that, in a country where the limited appeal of the 'national idea' was already wearing thin by 1993–94, virtual populism was the way forward; and all thought a political novice such as Lukashenka could be manipulated to their own ends (167 deputies voted to appoint him in June 1993). Lukashenka was therefore not quite the penniless novice, the former chair of a collective pig farm, that he presented himself as being. His main financial backer was Mikhail Chyhir, whose Belahroprombank helped square some key companies behind Lukashenka by clearing their debts. (Chyhir would later be accused of financial irregularities in his dealings with the highly irregular North American firm that offered office space to serve as campaign headquarters.)[9] Lukashenka saved a lot of shoe leather on the campaign trail thanks to the sudden appearance of two new Mercedes. Two of his campaign stunts received suspiciously wide coverage on state TV. The first was the so-called 'Liozna sketch' (after the name of the town where the 'attack' took place), when shots were fired at his new car – possibly by one of his own men, Afghan veteran Viktar Sheiman, who would later organise 'counter-measures' against the opposition during the 1999 'unofficial' election; the second was a comic-opera attempt by the 'corrupt' police to bar the anti-corruption cam-paigner from his office.[10] Both events were classic performances in the 'society of the spectacle': neither had any dramatic credibility.

Ironically, of course, Lukashenka later proved surprisingly adept at picking off his would-be puppet masters. Moreover, having been gifted the populist brand, he used it to stay in office for a decade. Staging protest is therefore a dangerous strategy for the powers-that-be. It risks, as with Lukashenka, developing a momentum of its own. It also risks empowering real regime opponents, or at least playing to their cam-paigning strengths, or in countries such as Russia puffing up parties like the CPRF.

Virtual Neophytes

A special type of virtual populism, one of the most cynical of all schemes in post-Soviet politics, involves shamelessly exploiting public disillusion with politics.

'Apolitical' and even 'anti-political' are other useful political brands that technologists, well aware that their better-publicised activities have done much to foster disillusion with 'democratisation', have sought to exploit as short-term assets. Virgin, 'outsider' status can be a useful quality in a given party, or aspect in mainstream projects, as with Russia's Unity in 1999. The powers-that-be have also tried to exploit the quality when it is possessed by others. Many in the Ukrainian administration clearly thought they could free-ride on Viktor Yushchenko's 'clean' image in 2002, mistakenly assuming after the February 2001 'letter of the three' (when Yushchenko, still prime minister, was persuaded to condemn the campaign for Kuchma's resignation during the Gongadze affair) that he was no real threat to their interests.

An early prototype was Stanisław Tymiński in the first Polish presidential election in 1990. At such an early stage, Lech Wałęsa's opponents could not be confident in running a project under more discredited labels. In his memoirs Wałęsa's complains that Tymiński's 'campaign staff contained many former Communist Party and Secret Service members', who fed him *kompromat* and worked up Tymiński's image as 'a *hochstapler* [adventurer], a screwball', who 'managed to bamboozle nearly five million people by playing on their cynicism, their ignorance, and their weariness with poverty'.[11] Tymiński came a surprise second in the first round with 23.1 per cent, compared to Wałęsa's 40 per cent, but was smothered in the second round.

In Ukraine the early success of one virtual neophyte project in the 1998 elections, the Green Party, led to a flood of later imitations. The Greens won 5.4 per cent and twenty-nine deputies, who arrived in parliament on ecologically sound bicycles, but in truth the party was only 'green' in the sense that the US dollar is green. Most of the shadowy bankers and businessmen who had bought the party's good name were notorious polluters (see page 131). The secret of the Greens' surprise success was a slick TV campaign that exploited memories of the Chernobyl disaster and, more importantly, associated images of a fresh and clean environment with a fresh and clean (and young) party, capped with good anti-slogans: 'Not politics, but ecology' and 'Politicians busy themselves with demagoguery'. The Greens also staged a highly successful series of pop concerts in twenty-six towns and cities, headlined by the youthful band Skriabin (named after the Russian composer), under the banner 'Preserve nature for life!'

In 2002 several 'young representatives of the old Communo-Oligarchic power' rushed to repeat this success.[12] The field became overcrowded, with too many parties trying to pull off the same trick as the original Greens, including the Greens themselves. Pretending to be apolitical is actually quite difficult during elections. The number of voters who are sufficiently uncommitted but still likely to vote is not that large. In 1998 the Greens won 5.4 per cent. In 2002 the rival neophytes scored 7.5 per cent between them, but split the vote so that no single party passed the 4 per cent barrier.

The first obviously 'new' brand was women, Ukraine never having really tried the idea before as Russia had in 1993 and 1995, and Armenia in 1995. Hence the development of the Women for the Future project, with the 'blessing of two solid businessmen', including the Green Party's Vasyl Khmelnytskyi, who was clearly hedging his bets this time around. Real women were, of course, placed at the very top of the party list, with only number five, Khmelnytskyi's right-hand man Andrii Ivanov, head of the board at his steel company Zaporizhstal, indicating what lay beneath. After number ten, the party list suddenly became seriously crowded with male Khmelnytskyi protégés (if a party passes the 4 per cent threshold in a system like that of Ukraine, it can expect a minimum of fifteen seats). Number eleven was Shamsaddin Abdynov, head of the Zaporozhskaia confectionery firm, twelve was Mykhailo Pasichnyk, boss of the pharmaceutical company Falbi, thirteen was Volodymyr Linnyk, head of the rubber company Rosava. It is worth noting that most of their products were suitable to serve as free hand-outs at election rallies. The project was also closely linked to Kuchma's wife, Liudmilla, and through her to the personnel and resources of the old Union of Ukrainian Women from the Soviet era – most notably Valentyna Dovzhenko, party leader and former minister for family and youth affairs.

One did not have to look too closely, therefore, to find administrative resources working in the party's favour. Women for the Future was registered suspiciously late, on 30 March 2001, only one day before the deadline for the 2002 vote. Then in February 2002 the Central Election Commission annulled the registration of the rival Women of Ukraine party. Yet another rival, Women for the Future of Children (led by the serial party-splitter Larysa Skoryk, who had stood for Lazarenko's Hromada party in 1998), was forced to reinvent itself as the All-Ukrainian Party of Inter-Ethnic Understanding. Women for the Future claimed a suspiciously large membership of 320,000; it also turned out to be the campaign's second-highest spender on TV advertising ($1.25 million – the official limit was $480,000).[13] According to the Committee of Voters of Ukraine, its glossy campaign (pop stars, mini-buses providing free hand-outs) made it one of the worst abusers of 'soft' administrative resources. Ukraine's many impoverished and frustrated women seemed an easy target for the party's cynical backers.

The initial PR blitz had an impact, with the faux-party running at between 5 per cent and 8 per cent in respectable early opinion polls.[14] Women for the Future's final showing of 2.1 per cent was therefore a disappointment. Much of its largesse was handed out too early and too readily. Its carefully constructed image was also too soft and amorphous. The party's TV campaign only helped to expose it as an ideological nullity.[15] On ICTV in March 2002 Dovzhenko was asked about the party's ideology. 'We thought about it a long time,' she replied, 'and settled on conservatism.'[16] The party's TV slogans, 'For goodness and happiness', 'Vote for women, they will make politics more friendly and honest', failed to explain how a bloc of deputies from the party would actually campaign for women's interests. Unlike Rodina in the 2003 Russian election, Women for the Future had not been gifted any policy issues that seemed likely to be acted on after the elections.

The second new brand in 2002 was youth. In a typical first step, four older shell parties were bought: the Liberal-Democrats, the Ukrainian version of the Kadets (on sale for the second time; see page 130), along with the Party of Private Property and (presumably for no other reason than that it was available for purchase) the Peasant Democrats. None of the four was a party of 'youth'. One source said of the Kadets with a shrug: 'What do you do? Their leader was an *inteligent* (intellectual) – he needed the money.'[17] The project came before an actual name. While still on the drawing board, the project had been known as the Liberal-Democratic Union, later New Liberal Union or NLO – unfortunately also the Russian acronym for a UFO. The name eventually settled on, Winter Crop Generation Team (Komanda ozymoho pokolinnia), was supposed to evoke an image of hardy youth – an attempt to exploit disillusion with the older generation who had survived and enriched themselves after 1991 – but was adopted relatively late in the day, to general bemusement. The new acronym, KOP, also resulted in sniggering – Ukrainian youth was not particularly fond of the local police.

The KOP project was run by the Russian political technologists Piotr Shchedrovistkii and Efim Ostrovskii, following the blueprint of their successful campaign for the Union of Right Forces in 1999. In fact, KOP was a simple copy. It also had a similarly young and clean-cut leadership trio. Boris Nemtsov of the Union of Right Forces became Valerii Khoroshkovskyi, head of Ukrsotsbank, one of Ukraine's largest banks. Irina Khakamada was cloned by the glamorous lawyer Inna Bohoslovska. Kirienko's less exact equivalent was Mykola Veresen, one-time host of the 1+1 TV talk show *Taboo*. All were sold as self-made meritocrats. Khoroshkovskyi, however, owed his initial fortune to Merks International, a furniture company set up with Komsomol money that later supplied government offices and embassies, even the presidential administration. After his election to parliament in 1998, Khoroshkovskyi's links to former prime minister Valerii Pustovoitenko and the oligarchic National Democratic Party (NDP) helped him secure control of Ukrsotsbank in a rigged privatisation in 2001. The bank had capital of 340 million hrivnia (then about $63 million), but was bought for 20 million.[18] Khoroshkovskyi was also instrumental in setting up the notorious 'Sivash' free economic zone around the northern Crimean town of Krasnoperekopsk. His 1998 campaign in Crimea, run by Efim Ostrovskii (see page 99), cost an estimated $3 million, which was a big sum even for successful New Ukrainians – mainly because his agents were supplying free petrol to the agricultural parts of the constituency. Total expenditure on the 2002 KOP campaign was estimated at a scarcely credible $13–$16 million.[19] One small piece of confirmatory evidence was that the overstretched Khoroshkovskyi had to liquidate some of his business interests after the elections.

The KOP proudly displayed a number of young business backers, brave young 'Generation X' entrepreneurs such as Iryna Haryna in the dairy and laundry business; but these were not the party's real sponsors.[20] Most of the finance for the slim young people in leather jackets came from the middle-aged men in Labour Ukraine, whom Bohoslovska had formerly represented in parliament, along with the NDP and Greens. KOP was therefore in essence a Pinchuk project,[21] that is Labour Ukraine attempted to spread its influence to the 'apolitical' portion of the electorate some of its smaller business rivals had targeted so successfully in 1998 – and also to take votes off Our Ukraine by creating a rival Russophone liberal party. Significantly, Pinchuk's channels, ICTV and New Channel (also linked to Russia's Alfa Bank), backed both For a United Ukraine and KOP. In an acrimonious pre-election debate on International Women's Day, 8 March 2002, held on Pinchuk's ICTV after being switched from the higher-ratings channel of 1+1, Bohoslovska showed her true colours by siding with the faux-firebrand Vitrenko against Tymoshenko, focusing on the latter's past as oligarchic 'poacher' rather than her successes as liberal 'gamekeeper' in the 1999–2001 government. As too often with virtual objects, political technologists overloaded their creation with too many tasks. In this case, criticising a business opponent of Pinchuk's with reformist credentials only served to undermine KOP's would-be liberal image. Other indicators of the party's true nature included the fact that Shchedrovitskii, who was semi-openly working for KOP, was also working with Pinchuk.[22] An even bigger clue was Khoroshkovskyi's common business interests in the Luhansk energy company with Pinchuk. Bought for only 112 million hryvnia (about $21 million) with 217 million outstanding, this was cheap even by Ukrainian standards, as 700 million had initially been mooted as the purchase price, and over a billion in debt had been written off. Khoroshkovskyi was also involved with Pinchuk's Labour Ukraine partner, Andrii Derkach, in the radio stations Renaissance and Ukrainian News.[23] Both groups were based in the so-called Agency for Humanitarian Technologies (AHT) set up in 1998, whose director, Maksym Karyskyi, also headed KOP's press service. Money from parliament helped set up the AHT, which ran the website www.part.org.ua until January 2003, and its own www.aht.org. AHT's Volodymyr Hranovskyi introduced Khoroshkovskyi to Shchedrovistkii and Ostrovskii.

Many of those who worked on the project claimed they were only trying to force the pace. KOP's problems were also indicative of Ukraine's 'missing liberal' problem: the effective absence of a proper centre party. However, all pretence was dropped soon after the elections in August 2002 when Khoroshkovskyi accepted the post of deputy head of Kuchma's presidential administration. In December, he was made minister for the economy in the new Yanukovych government on the recommendation of Labour Ukraine. The faux-liberal Khoroshkovskyi was also revealed as having voted to bring down the real liberals of the Yushchenko government.[24]

Nevertheless, some of Shchedrovitskii and Ostrovskii's efforts initially seemed worth paying for. KOP had the best, certainly the grooviest, adverts, created on the principle *chem kruche, chem luche* ('the cooler, the better'). On an interactive reality show broadcast on the Pinchuk TV channels (STV, ICTV) members of the public competed to win a place on the party's list for the elections. The ploy was designed to play up the image of youth and opportunity in contrast to the old closed elite, but only served to confirm that the project was a copy of the Union of Right Forces in 1999. Just as the not especially popular Chubais had been hidden behind Khakamada and Pinchuk behind Bohoslovska, exactly the same kind of show (with the trademark *kadrovyi konkurs* or 'places competition') had been run by Shchedrovitskii in Russia. KOP also handed out well-packaged free pop videos by the band Skriabin, who had also sung for the Greens' backers in 1998. They dutifully produced an ode to *Ozumi liudy* ('Winter Crop People'), a truly dreadful song on a mediocre album. The project's Russian origins were also reflected in KOP's commitment to raising the status of the Russian language in Ukraine – a subject fatally uninteresting to the target audience.

On the day KOP won only 2 per cent. According to exit polls, they did little better with the under-thirties, who tend to be the most apolitical and most reliant on TV for political information, yet too few of them were likely to vote.[25] Clearly, a 'yuppie' image was not right for Ukraine, where urban 'lifestyle liberal' voters are even fewer in number than in Russia. The attempt to suggest that Ukraine was a land of meritocratic opportunity for the young and dynamic only led a cynical audience to reflect on the likely real sources of KOP leaders' riches. Like Women for the Future, moreover, the party's free goods were distributed too readily and, well, free. The video packages that were handed out in Kiev were eagerly accepted and the party stickers removed. Skriabin had a lot of teenage fans who were too young to vote. Only on Pinchuk's home turf in Dnipropetrovsk was KOP at all successful, winning its best vote of 5 per cent. Shchedrovitskii himself blamed *force majeure*. 'In different circumstances we would have had a promising liberal faction – the basis for a real liberal party in another four years. But the election's dynamic became who was for Kuchma and who was against – and we were squeezed in the middle.'[26] And like Women for the Future or the CPU(r), KOP's glossy TV blitz failed to get across concrete reasons for voting for the party. Nor did the party pay sufficient attention to organisation on the ground.[27]

KOP also had too many competitors for its USP. Although Yurii Miroshnychenko's New Generation party was actually set up first in 1998, it suffered from the perception that it was only a copy of a copy – a copy of KOP's copy of the Union of Right Forces. Its image was more aggressively youthful than KOP's, but its original sponsors were the SDPU(o) and Volodymyr Semynozhenko in the Party of the Regions with some interest from Volkov. At first it 'tried to sell itself [as a cuckoo] to Our Ukraine, but basically failed'.[28] Running next on its own, the project was designed to compete with Yushchenko, who made several unexplained appearances on the party's website. A final 0.8 per cent of the (potential youth) vote did not represent too big a bite out of the Our Ukraine electorate, however.

Then there were the Greens, who by 2002 had alienated their original early 1990s voters (i.e., real environmentalists) and faced too much competition for their new 'apolitical' supporters. They tried to revamp their 1998 image by sponsoring the popular TV show *The Last Hero*, a copy of the US *Survivor* series. The party's younger businessmen had split with Rabinovych, whose rival Rainbow coalition soon disappeared without trace. The 'environmentalists' had fewer businessmen on the list this time around, and many of these were in the optimistic twenty-something nether regions of the party's list. The party had also shifted under more direct presidential control. The remaining party magnates were personally loyal to Kuchma, after the possibility of corruption charges against four of the party's deputies was first raised and then quietly dropped in 2000.[29] This time the party won only 1.3 per cent of the vote, as others stole its act.

After the failure of two projects in 2002, the rootless Khmelnytskyi's next venture was to buy a seat in the Crimean parliament (using his good relations with Khoroshkovskyi, Medvedchuk and Grach) and to try to take over the Crimean government in partnership with notorious local 'businessman' Lev Myrymskyi, the president of the Imperiia Corporation. Khmelnytskyi returned to the national parliament in a December 2002 by-election in neighbouring Zaporizhzhia (ironically beating Nataliia Vitrenko), which the Committee of Voters of Ukraine condemned for outright 'criminalisation of the electoral process': thousands were struck off the electoral roll and there was brazen bribery of the remaining voters.[30] Clearly, post-Soviet businessmen need to keep playing the political game to survive. Once back in parliament, Khmelnytskyi teamed up with Bohdan Hubskyi's People's Power faction, effectively now throwing in his lot with the SDPU(o).

Finally, there was Yabluko, one of many satellite projects for the United Social Democrats (see pages 138–9), which again posed as a populist 'anti-party'. It had some of the most striking, if bizarre, ads (featuring dancing cartoon apples that promised to do what foreign fruit – pineapples – could not, that is, lower prices) and an optimistically anodyne image, but impaled itself on the pretence of being a liberal party whose main campaign promise was to abolish VAT. In reality it was only a 'liberal' party because the business circles that backed it already controlled a 'social democratic' one. Yabluko won only 1.2 per cent.

Preventing Polarisation: Belarus in 2001

In 2001 Belarusian president Aliaksandr Lukashenka's position was essentially the opposite of that of Boris Yeltsin in 1996 or Leonid Kuchma in 1999. The Russian and Ukrainian presidents were polling badly, and their political technologists' chosen strategy was to polarise the election, building up the Communist threat to convince reluctant voters to back their man as the 'lesser evil', while preventing potential (genuinely independent) 'third-force' alternatives such as Yavlinskii-Fedorov in Russia or Oleksandr Moroz in Ukraine from complicating the dichotomy. Lukashenka, by contrast, was still popular. According to the opposition's analysis, he was guaranteed 30-35 per cent of the vote, while its own hardcore support was estimated at only 15 per cent. That, however, left 40-50 per cent of voters undecided.[31] Lukashenka's strategy was therefore to prevent the consolidation of a negative pole, allowing a single candidate to accumulate all the potential anti-presidential votes; and, conversely, positively to encourage the formation of third forces (according to one source, the list was vetted by the National Security Council).[32] In the early election period there was therefore a whirlwind of candidates supported in various degrees by the administration to prevent anyone they disapproved of stealing an early march.

Lukashenka's most dangerous opponents disappeared or died. Henadz Karpenka of the United Civic Party died in an implausible accident when a brain haemorrhage was apparently provoked by coffee-drinking in April 1999. Former Central Bank head, Tamara Vinnikova, who held much alleged *kompromat* on Lukashenka's corruption, was forced into exile. Yury Zakharanka, former interior minister, went missing, presumed dead in May 1999; Viktar Hanchar, the organiser of the 'alternative' presidential election that year, followed him in September. The remaining mainstream opposition began 'round-table' negotiations, but was forced to settle on the relatively uncharismatic Uladzimir Hancharyk, then chair of the National Trade Union Federation, as its leader, as the Americans considered his main opponent, Siamion Domash, to be too close to the nationalist Popular Front. Several other 'buy me' projects competed for international favour: the rival union leader (head of the agricultural workers' union), Aliaksandr Yarashuk, was hoping for a share of US money; Leanid Sinitsyn got some money from Gazprom as a warning shot to the president. Nataliia Masherava's flirtation with possible Russian sponsors led to her early enforced withdrawal.

Mikhail Marynich played the role of a liberal pro-Western candidate (with the 'terminator of the former BSDP PH' [Belarusian Social-Democratic Party, see page 167], Leanid Sechka, in his team),[33] he was paired with Leanid Sinitsyn, a former presidential chief of staff and lobbyist for Belarusian-Russian integration, who took the part of the virtual Russophile. Leanid Kaluhin was designed to attract support from the military-industrial complex. Yawhen Kryzhanowski, a burlesque actor, performed one aspect of the Zhirinovskii role; the other was played by Siarhei Haidukevich, leader of the Liberal-Democratic Party of Belarus (LDPB), who made all the required faux-radical noises about immediate union with Russia and backing Saddam Hussein, but was in fact deeply involved in shadowy business ventures, such as providing security at the Zhdanovichi market on the western fringes of Minsk – and in Belarusia, nearly all shadowy business ventures were somehow connected to state elements (unlike Zhirinovskii's Liberal-Democrats, Haidukevich's party had no parliamentary faction to rent). Both parties were named as recipients of Saddam Hussein's covert oil payments in 2004, with Haidukevich's party allegedly receiving one million barrels.[34] Like Zhirinovskii, Haidukevich seemed more extreme than Lukashenka – and was even licensed to criticise him for 'primitive populism'.[35] But conveniently he constantly argued with the rest of the opposition and concentrated most of his fire on Lukashenka's opponents, most notably a scurrilous slander on Hancharyk published throughout the state media only ten days before the election.[36]

Nataliia Masherava's candidacy was more complicated. Originally a Lukashenka stooge, she was set up to run against another of the opposition 'round-table' leaders, Mikhail Chyhir, and (successfully) block his path to parliament in autumn 2000. At the time, Masherava was all over official TV,[37] sponsored by the militant Russophile and deputy head of the presidential administration, Uladzimir Zamiatalin.[38] She was able to use the 'soap opera' charisma of her dead father, Piotr Masheraw (the genuinely popular head of the local Communist Party from 1965 to 1980, when he died in a suspicious car accident), but 'consciously avoided . . . targeting any particular social group to avoid attracting any part of Lukashenka's electorate'.[39] Ultimately, however, although she may have been considered for the role of a Belarusian equivalent of Aleksandr Lebed in 1996 (consolidating the 'rightist', or in this case 'Soviet Orthodox', vote and then selling her support to the incumbent), Lukashenka wished to keep the 'myth of Masheraw' to himself, and worried about a Masherava bandwagon he could not control. Moreover, Masherava's alleged virtual 'charisma' proved too obviously manufactured, her real personality a little too flat, and she was lent on to withdraw before her campaign had even really begun.

Fig. 8.1 Poll Ratings of the Main Candidates for Belarusian President, 2001

	IISEPS* April	IISEPS June	ISPI† June
Lukashenka	39.8	43.8	40.7
Hancharyk‡	10.1	10.3	1.6
Domash	8.1	12.0	3.8
Masherava	n/a	17.0	3.2
Haidukevich	4.0	4.2	1.2
Sinitsyn	2.0	1.9	0.1
Kryzhanowski	4.3	4.1	0.4
Marynich	n/a	n/a	0.5
Yarashuk	2.6	2.3	0.2

Sources: www.iiseps.by and Evgenii Dmitriev and Mikhail Khurs, *Belarus': Itogi i uroki prezidentskikh vyborov 2001* (Minsk: ISPI, 2002), pp. 124–25. ISPI recorded percentages of those already decided; 35.1 per cent had still to make up their minds.

*Independent Institute of Socio-Economic and Political Research.

†Institute of Social-Political Research.

‡Excludes the other candidates of the opposition 'five' (Chyhir, Kaliakin of the PCB, and former defence minister Pavel Kazlowski of the OGP), who eventually withdrew to back Hancharyk, as agreed.

For the second stage of the elections, Lukashenka gave a direct, though obviously secret, order to reduce the field to four. Thirteen candidates claimed to have collected the necessary 100,000 signatures, but at Lukashenka's request the Central Election Commission now only validated those of the chosen four.[40] This simplified scenario pitted Lukashenka against Hancharyk or Domash as easily defeatable opponents (Domash withdrew in favour of Hancharyk in August),[41] but retained Haidukevich as the third force with most staying power. (Once the election was over, arguments over money and Haidukevich's domineering leadership ultimately led to a split in the LDPB in September 2003.)[42]

The remaining real opposition was now roundly abused, the campaign led by local media-killer Yury Azarenak bearing many of the hallmarks of Nikkolo-M, whose services had reportedly been retained by Lukashenka's team.[43] The PR onslaught ignored the choice of Hancharyk rather than Domash, and depicted the moderate opposition as a cover for the same old fanatical nationalists as in the early 1990s, and behind them the American 'Sprutsies' (see pages 63–4), who the authorities argued would soon be bombing Minsk just as they had recently bombed Belgrade. An opposition victory would mean the unleashing of their criminal associates, the end of all social benefits and massive price rises (the last at least duly happened anyway).

The final element in the campaign was the exaggeration of Lukashenka's admittedly assured victory. The independent pollsters IISEPS estimated that he won 57-58 per cent on voting day, compared to 28–29 per cent for Hancharyk, roughly in line with poll trends.[44] The NGO Independent Observation was unable to watch all polling stations, but reached similar conclusions. (Hancharyk claimed to have lost by only 41 per cent to 47 per cent).[45] Administrative resources – in Belarus, given the scarcity of election observers, mainly the manipulation of local protocols – added the extra 20 per cent necessary to produce the more impressive final official result of 75.7 per cent for Lukashenka, 15.7 per cent for Hancharyk and 2.5 per cent for Haidukevich. Turnout was supposedly enormous, at 84 per cent (IISEPS had predicted 76 per cent).[46] Lukashenka's extra million votes came mainly from Hancharyk (-780,000), but also from those who voted against all (-225,000) and from Haidukevych (-59,000).[47]

It should be pointed out that the opposition in Belarus has also run its fair share of questionable projects. Lukashenka should have faced re-election after his five-year term earned in 1994 ended in 1999, but a controversial 1996 referendum granted him an extra two years. The Belarusian Popular Front (BPF) first proposed the frankly bizarre idea of collecting signatures to replace him with a re-animation of the short-lived Belarusian People's Republic of 1918, before staging its own 'unofficial' presidential election in 1999. The authorities obviously made this extremely difficult and Popular Front leader Zianon Pazniak eventually pulled out, but the organiser, Viktar Hanchar (formerly head of the Central Election Commission), stretched all credibility by claiming that 53 per cent had voted using flimsy ballot boxes that were carried by hand from place to place. Surveys indicated as few as 5 per cent admitting to having voted,[48] and the affair proved a PR disaster.

Donor-seeking from the West blighted the 'official' presidential election in 2001. Up to a third of such aid, mainly from the USA (totalling $50 million over two years), may have gone missing, particularly to the nebulous NGO sector, but parties (the BPF) and opposition politicians were also accused (Hancharyk, Chyhir, Yarashuk). The Americans also funded Charter 97, a would-be copy of the Czechoslovak Charter-77, and the would-be student pranksters Zubr ('Bison'), modelled on Yugoslavia's Otpor ('Resistance'). All had expensive websites with few recorded hits. Charter 97 was almost entirely a video-and-CD-Rom experience. The opposition was also guilty of massaging polls to try and create a bandwagon effect.[49] Indeed, with both the regime and the opposition in Belarus often playing virtual politics, and with the 'virtualisation of institutions' denying any normal space for meaningful contest, to take place, public politics since 1996 has often been little more than shadow-boxing. Periodic 'consultations' between the two sides, such as the virtual dialogue during the 1996 crisis and before the 2000 election, have been particularly unenlightening and inconsequential.

Soft Opponents

Central Asian states have specialised in putting minimal effort into the promotion of fall-guy opponents. In the case of Uzbekistan, even such a small amount of energy has been expended only once, for the presidential election in December 1991. A real opposition party, Birlik ('Unity'), appeared in 1988. The authorities immediately created an ersatz alternative, persuading the popular but 'bought-off' poet and head of the Writers' Union, Muhammad Salih, to set up the pocket rival Erk ('Freedom') Democratic Party in February 1990 – which conveniently placed less emphasis on democratisation before independence.[50] Birlik had more members, but Erk got the Writers' Union building as its headquarters. Birlik was nonetheless allowed to register, though not to field a candidate, while the other serious regime opponent, the Islamic Renaissance Party, was banned outright. The local Communist Party leader, Islam Karimov, was left with no one to defeat but Salih. As Salih accepted that it would be disrespectful to campaign with enthusiasm, Karimov won a walk-over victory: 86 per cent to 12.3 per cent. Since 1991, the Communist Party, renamed the Popular Democratic Party, has been all-powerful. Birlik was banned in 1992, and even Salih was marginalised, with Erk being forcibly converted into a new Homeland Progress Party.

'False Aerodromes'

A different type of soft opponent involves the creation of politicians or parties specifically to fail or to be criticised by others: in other words, projects that are deliberately designed to draw opponents' fire away from more important targets. In Russian terminology, this is the *lozhnyi aerodrom* ('false aerodrome'), designed to waste enemy bombs. Our Home Is Russia in 1995 was arguably a sacrificial lamb for Yeltsin in 1996. Sometimes it has even proved worth investing hard cash in a project that fails – even if it was not originally supposed to fail – in order to concentrate opprobrium on to the likes of the Rybkin Bloc in 1995. Rodina ('Motherland') was initially suspected of being set up to draw liberal fire away from the Kremlin in 2003 (see pages 262–3).

In December 2003 President Kuchma twisted the arm of the Constitutional Court to grant him the theoretical right to run for a third term in 2004 (using the totally specious argument that he had first been elected in 1994, before the Constitution was passed in 1996, although the phrase stating that 'one and the same individual may serve no more than two consecutive terms' was identical to that in the 1991 law on the presidency). In this case, the consequent media storm was designed as cover for a varity of possible scenarios (see pages 177–9), ranging from cancelling the elections to encouraging support for his chosen successor, Viktor Yanukovych, as the 'lesser evil'.

Conversely, another theory had it that Yanukovych himself was the 'technical candidate', designed to frighten moderate deputies into backing a reform of the constitution that would deprive any incoming president of most of his or her power, and moderate voters into backing some possible 'third force'.

Lesser Evil, Greater Evil

Beware of newspaper headlines that urge support for the incumbent as a 'lesser evil'; the incumbent is more than likely to be delighted with such faint praise. The tactic has a long history. George Liber's book on the great Soviet Ukrainian film director Oleksandr Dovzhenko describes how Pavlo, one of the heroes of his film *Zvenyhora* (1928), develops a piece of 'performance art' in which he threatens to shoot himself before credulous Western audiences if they do not back his crusade against the Bolshevik threat – though he is really raising the money to finance his search for Cossack gold buried in the mountain at Zvenyhora.[51] Chapter 1 discussed how Gorbachev and Yakovlev used this ploy in the late 1980s, playing up the threat of Pamiat in 1987–88, Nina Andreieva in 1988 and of an impending coup in 1991. Countries must have sufficient geopolitical or economic importance for this ploy to work: 'Some are granted a waiver because of their dimension and power, like Russia and China; others due to their strategic importance and "honourable" status as "our sons of bitches".'[52] It is worth tabulating the various versions of this tactic to show just how common it is.

Fig. 8.2 Occasions When the West Has Bought the Myth of 'Lesser Evil', to date

(i) *Communist Bogey*
(Russia, 'Red-Brown') Boris Yeltsin v White House 1993
(Russia) Yeltsin v Gennadii Ziuganov, 1996
(Russia) Vladimir Putin v Ziuganov, 2000
also parliamentary 1995
(Ukraine) Leonid Kuchma v Petro Symonenko, 1999
Nataliia Vitrenko, 1998 and 1999
(Georgia) Eduard Shevardnadze v Dzhumber Patiashvili, 1995 and 2000
(Kazakhstan) Nursultan Nazarbaev v Serikbolsyn Abdildin, 1999
(Moldova) Petru Lucinschi v CPRM, 1998
(Armenia) Unity v Communists, 1999

(ii) *Nationalist Bogey*
Yeltsin v Zhirinovskii, 1993
Yeltsin v Russian National Unity, 1998–99

Manoeuvring the leaders of local successor Communist parties into position as the main opponent is a favourite tactic. In many states, such as Georgia, where memories of the 1989 Tbilisi massacre are still vivid, successor parties are still unelectable. Eduard Shevardnadze twice ran for president against the 'Communist scarecrow', Dzhumber Patiashvili, his local successor as Communist boss in 1985-89 (whom Shevardnadze himself had forced out, and into local business, after the killings). In 1995 Shevardnadze won 74.3 per cent against Patiashvili's 19.4 per cent; in 2000 a similar 78.8 per cent to Patiashvili's 16.7 per cent. According to one local analyst, on both occasions 'Shevardnadze and his team badly needed a serious and weighty figure with a Communist background as a ritual challenger to Shevardnadze'. 'The [other] main goal of the regime was to [depict] Eduard Shevardnadze in public eyes as the more progressive and pro-Western candidate [against] the background of the pro-Russian Patiashvili.' However, the Communist leader would not run too hard, as 'local sources say the regime possessed a package of serious *kompromat* on Patiashvili'.[53] Pointedly, the 2000 election was held on 9 April, the eleventh anniversary of the 1989 massacre. Other awkward candidates, such as Aslan Abashidze, boss of the Ajaran Republic and leader of the Batumi Alliance in 2000, withdrew at the last minute. Its usefulness at an end, the Communist Party of Georgia faded away rapidly after 2000.

Other Communist leaders are more serious threats – sufficiently serious to serve as scarecrows, both domestically and internationally. This tactic, used with decisive effect in Russia in 1996 and 2000, and Ukraine and Kazakhstan in 1999, is important enough to merit separate treatment in the following chapter. Scarecrow nationalist opponents are the second main type.

Scarecrows in the Russian White House

Having already been used with success in the late 1980s with Pamiat *et al.*, it was not surprising that the scarecrow project should re-emerge so quickly after 1991, as Yeltsin struggled with the Russian parliament. Kremlin propaganda orchestrated by Yeltsin's minister of information Mikhail Poltoranin depicted the parliament as a Soviet hangover, even antediluvian – although it had been Yeltsin's powerbase before the Russian presidential election in June 1991. In reality, much of his support had withered away there, as in Russia as a whole, with the pain of 'shock therapy'. As such, the Kremlin needed a cover-story, and the 'Red-Brown threat' (Communist-Nationalist) would play abroad, and among the urban intelligentsia, who at this stage could still be persuaded to renew their backing for the reform project. Bill Clinton for one bought the argument that 'the Duma was full of people who longed for the old order or an equally oppressive new one rooted in ultra-nationalism', and later that 'it was clear that Yeltsin's opponents had started the violence'. 'Yeltsin was up to his ears in alligators, and I wanted to help him.'[54] Deputy secretary of state and presidential adviser on Russia, Strobe Talbott, while encouraging Clinton to warn Yeltsin not to destroy democracy in order to save it, still argued that 'we had to be careful . . . not to let ourselves be pushed into accepting the verdict that Yeltsin was a dictator or an imperialist – especially when he was locked in combat with forces that were unambiguously anti-democratic and aggressively nationalistic'.[55]

There were already some real extremists around, but the Kremlin wanted more. According to Valerii Solovei, throughout the crisis months of 1993 'the authorities, judging by some indications, didn't stop themselves from using provocation in order to turn demonstrations into confrontations and destroy them'.[56] The final dénouement around the Moscow White House, when Yeltsin's opponents first sailed forth to stage an attempted 'coup', and were then cornered and bombarded into submission, producing an official death toll of 187, was clearly covertly stage-managed, at least in part.[57] The White House's 'militia' contained both right-wing (Aleksandr Barkashov's skinheads from Russian National Unity) and left-wing provocateurs (General Albert Makashov's rather more elderly followers), as well as Viktor Anpilov's Working Russia militants outside. All three men had KGB affiliations. The one to three hundred *Barkashovtsi*, with their swastika armbands, fitted Clinton's picture of 'ultra-nationalism' perfectly; but, according to one source, the 'intermediary' who made sure of their prominence was none other than the former KGB general, Filipp Bobkov.[58] On a smaller scale, individual provocateurs urged rasher action where necessary. Anpilov's men found little obstruction and much encouragement on their march to 'liberate' the White House on the Sunday afternoon, as did the subsequent 'break-out' by those holed up inside. Just to make sure, snipers from the nearby City Hall and Hotel Mir goaded them on.[59] One version has it that a column of pro-Yeltsin militia actually accompanied Makashov's men to Ostankino.[60] The PR side of events was much better managed than the junta's ham-fisted attempts in August 1991. State and foreign TV was on hand to publicise the White House break-out, and Rutskoi and Khasbulatov's calls to storm the Kremlin, but not the alleged 'storming' of Ostankino that evening, when the supposedly ill-defended TV station was in fact packed with soldiers from the aptly named Dzerzhinskii Division, who easily saw off their attackers. Approximately sixty were killed, including several old women, but in virtual space the regime still claimed it had been in mortal danger. The Ostankino boss Viacheslav Bragin made sure his station did not broadcast the events on his doorstep: in fact, the TV cameras had been turned off before Makashov supposedly committed the unforgivable sin of plunging the country into an information black-out and of interrupting the audience's normal viewing pleasures.[61] It was these night-time events that were used to justify the more famous scenes of the tanks shelling the White House the following morning – and Yeltsin's effective dictatorship until December 1993.

Zhirinovskii 2: 'Very Expensive, But Very Effective'

The events of October 1993 also brought to prominence Zhirinovskii 2, his 1993–99 persona – a rather different figure from Zhirinovskii 1, when he first came to more limited attention in 1990–91. Strictly speaking, his first function was as a second bet for the CPSU under nascent 'pluralism'. His success in the June 1991 Russian presidential election briefly encouraged him to act as a more independent figure, but Zhirinovskii backed the putsch in August, and its failure lost him both his covert official backers and his niche in all-Soviet politics. The annulment of his party's registration in August 1992 showed it had enemies, and that a new role would have to be found for it.

However, Zhirinovskii's remodelled party did not reappear from nowhere for its finest hours, the first Duma elections in 1993 and 1995. Rather, his reborn Liberal-Democratic Party of Russia (LDPR) first found itself of potential use to the regime again in spring 1993. The first reason, playing divide and rule in any new parliament after the traumas of the 'Red-Brown' opposition in 1992–93, overlapped with the second, keeping the protest electorate away from the newly revived Communist Party – a task made all the easier by the fact that the CPRF was too cautious really to attack the regime in 1993.[62] Third, at the same time 'the Russian powers in the Yeltsin epoch greatly feared the emergence of an influential nationalist force, capable of accumulating non-Communist protest, and attempted to neutralise it by bringing on to their side striking nationalist leaders'.[63] The Kremlin, of course, preferred a controllable maverick. In 1991–92, as he sought a new image, Zhirinovskii had flirted with the likes of Viktor Yakushev, a neo-pagan Hitler-worshipper whom even Barkashov thought a bit crazy. But Zhirinovskii's skilful populism marked him out from the esoteric obscurantism of the new right. Significantly, his party was the only real nationalist force allowed to run in the 1993 elections. The Kremlin banned real extremists such as the National Salvation Front (NSF), and campaigned hard to prevent moderate nationalist parties like Sergei Baburin's Russian All-People's Union (later Fatherland) and the Christian Democrats getting the 100,000 signatures they needed to stand in the elections. (In 1995 there would be twelve nationalist parties on the ballot.) Fourth, and only in partial contradiction, the old Communist bogeyman was yet to be reinvented and the 'threat from the right' was a vital argument in steadying the ship of state through the economic traumas of the early 1990s. Finally, if necessary, Zhirinovskii's antics could be used to discredit the Duma as a whole.

Cooption also worked on a local level. In 1993, the 'anti-establishment' LDPR was in fact a better bet for local elites than the already discredited Russia's Choice or the risky bet of the possibly stillborn Communist revival, especially after the grand bargain of autumn 1993 positively encouraged them to use it as a cover. According to the analysis by Sobianin and Liubarskii, far from Zhirinovskii's success in 1993 being a 'surprise', he benefited greatly from local bosses adjusting the tally, padding his vote as they were padding their own (see also pages 75–6).[64] To the Kremlin, the more important vote in December 1993 was the referendum on the constituion that would legitimise its *de facto* dictatorship, in place since October. Earlier in March 1993 at the Constitutional Convention Zhirinovskii had signalled his support for Yeltsin's plans to bolster his own power; he later bragged that his voters had swung the referendum – although it was really the other way around. Given the allegations that so many extra 'yes' votes had been added to ensure over 50 per cent backed the new constitution, it made sense to tally these with extra LDPR votes in the Duma elections. The LDPR's supposed final 22.9 per cent of the vote was undoubtedly an unintentional 'overshoot'. In 1995 the party would be trimmed back to 11.2 per cent.

Strobe Talbott certainly bought the argument that Zhirinovskii was liberalism's 'antipode (and our anathema)', although Primakov once told him that Zhirinovskii was 'like a cat – you stroke him once and he turns all sweet'. The US vice-president, Al Gore, was on 'Air Force Two headed toward Moscow' when he heard the 1993 election results. He 'told Leon Fuerth and me [Talbott] that he had decided to suspend the usual practice of not commenting on other countries' domestic politics and declare Zhirinovskii the personification of much that the US was sworn to oppose'.[65]

However, Zhirinovskii's populist bluster concealed a lack of *real* extremism. According to Gleb Pavlovskii, 'Zhirinovskii was our first political technologist.' His 1993 campaign was cleverly 'non-ideological': 'he ignored the debate for and against Communism' and concentrated on using the media for his own interests. Moreover, his style, 'both tough and technical', especially his direct and amusing monologues on TV, provided a template for others to follow.[66] As Soloviov and Klepikova argue in their book on the man who in 1995 threw orange juice at Boris Nemtsov on TV and fought with two female deputies, pulling their hair, 'Zhirinovskii's secret of success is not only in his slogans but in the genre he has selected, more stage performance than politics.' The performance was Zhirinovskii himself. So long as he could maintain it, he could keep selling his faction's votes. Soloviov and Klepikova credit him with having 'introduced the language of the street into politics'.[67] Access to TV was the key, with Zhirinovskii granted a massive eleven hours of commercial airtime (only Russia's Choice had more).[68] By the time he could afford proper TV ads, Zhirinovskii's repertoire included almost 'everything, from effectively playing on the mass [fear] of market prices, emotional monologues and vulgar political kitsch . . . including a clip with a woman, similar to the famous Ellochka-Liudoedka' – that is, 'Ellochka the Cannibal' Shukin, a character in Il'f and Petrov's *Twelve Chairs*, a social climber of few but generally ferocious words, and wearer of dyed Mexican jerboa fur, who shuts her naked husband out of the apartment – the point being to encourage every self-respecting male to defy the nag. 'The very same kitsch is shown in the "musical" clip where an unknown singer-poet hails Vladimir Volfovich [Zhirinovskii]: "This world was boring without you . . .". And the camera all this time is trying to creep under her skirt.'[69] Zhirinovskii, who has been aptly compared to a character out of the works of Zoshchenko or Raikin, has also used the popular Soviet adventure film *Na grafskikh razvalinakh* ('In the Count's Ruins', 1957) to portray himself as a lovable rogue, or one of the *yurodivy* ('holy fools') of popular tradition. Sergei Kibalnik, on the other hand, considers that Zhirinovskii is 'like Khlestakov in Gogol's *The Government Inspector*, [he] constantly displays what he really is [a rogue], and consequently nobody believes it'.[70] By 1999 Zhirinovskii's ads were being produced by the mainstream Kremlin favourite, Video International, which had worked for the Yeltsin campaign in 1996 and was also working for the Union of Right Forces this time around.

By the mid-1990s, Zhirinovskii's was also a rich party, since it was now able to diversify its operations by abusing its position in the Duma. Its earliest sponsors have proved hard to identify.

To this day the question as to who funded Zhirinovskii's campaign [in 1993] has not been answered. Was it Saddam Hussein? [German far-right leader] Gerhard Frey? [Frey financed the German translation of his book; Zhirinovskii also had links with Austrian businessman Edwin Meuwirth.] The International Bulgarian adventurers Dmitry Klinkov and Svetoslav Stoilov? The Dutch firm GMM? The Berlin firm Werner Girke? The KGB – directly and by proxy through cutouts? Russian businessmen . . . ? . . . Or perhaps the LDP itself was successfully pulling off financial deals through dummy corporations?[71]

Early sponsors who have been unearthed include the KGB 'financier' and neo-Fascist fantasist Aleksei Vedenkin, who has a long history of sponsoring nationalist scarecrows, including Russian National Unity after Zhirinovskii (see page 211). Vedenkin's murky past included allegations of money laundering for the CPSU in the early 1990s and a brief arrest after he threatened to kill human–rights activist (and 'meddler' in Chechnia) Sergei Kovalev on national TV. Zhirinovskii backed the notorious pyramid swindler Sergei Mavrodii in his 1994 by-election campaign despite the collapse of his MMM scheme. (Zhirinovskii's LDPR deputy, Aleksei Mitrofanov, tried to set up a People's Capital faction with Mavrodii in 1994; Mavrodii was finally arrested in 2003.)[72] In 1993 Aleksandr Smolenskii (SBS Agro, Stolichnyi, Agroprombank) sponsored both Russia's Choice and Zhirinovskii.[73] Eduard Limonov split with Zhirinovskii as early as 1992, denouncing him for selling his support to all-comers. Another colleague turned critic claimed Zhirinovskii sold ordinary seats on the party list for $1 million[74] and the top seats for $1.5 million – and by 1995 prices had gone up.[75] Prominent on the party's 1995 list was the Ingush businessman Mikhail Gutseriev, who served as deputy chair of the Duma before switching to the presidency of Slavneft in 1999. He was removed in 2002 for allegedly creaming off money to fund his brother Khamzat's unsuccessful campaign for the presidency of Ingushetia; another brother ended up on the United Russia list in 2003. Zhirinovskii dropped eleven candidates with alleged Mafia connections, but then quetly reinstated the most important, Mikhail Monastyrskii, whose criminal record extended to twenty years of penal sentence.

After his 1993 success, Zhirinovskii was politely reminded that he would never be president or prime minister, but that he was welcome to enrich himself in the Duma, where the LDPR sought out lucrative committees that had nothing to do with its own programme, such as those on natural resources, building, transport and energy. From the Kremlin's point of view, the LDPR's 'overshoot' meant that from 1993 to 1995 Zhirinovskii's party – and the Agrarians – were often the key to swinging votes in the Duma. In return, they were offered 'money and integration into the political system. By voting as the Kremlin needed, Zhirinovskii's party received considerable financial facilities in exchange. In the Kremlin they characterised Zhirinovskii in the following way: "Very expensive, but very effective."'[76] Between 1993 and 1995 Zhirinovskii's non-stop campaigning and impressive party-building in the regions again raised suspicions of covert official support.[77] More crudely, he was persuaded to back the 1995 budget by being given a personal stake in it. Central Bank funds were also used,[78] channelled on his behalf through the Chara and Progress banks.[79] For the 1996 budget, when the first Chechen War was at its height, Zhirinovskii lobbied for the interests of an offshore zone set up in Ingushetia that would soon become notorious as a black hole for the federal budget and an alleged conduit for Chechen finances. (Vedenkin was also a rumoured contact with the then Chechen leader Dzhokhar Dudaev.) Gutseriev later headed the operation and its related bank, BIN. Zhirinovskii's party fast became the most radical embodiment of a new paradigm – politics as pure business. The LDPR became a 'party to rent', its Duma offices a plush place to do business – or just to party.

Zhirinovskii's party also had close links with the military-industrial complex, especially Viktor Kobelev and Aleksandr Vengerovskii, a colleague of Vedenkin who became deputy head of the Duma in 1994–95; and with the former GRU, such as Sergei Abeltsev, his would-be security minister.[80] These links were in part financial: also on the 1995 list was Aleksandr Zhukovskii, head of Voenkombank (Military Commercial Bank); Vengerovskii became notorious as a hard-working lobbyist; Zhirinovskii brokered energy deals with Baghdad.[81] In January 2004, after the fall of Saddam Hussein, Zhirinovskii was named by the Iraqi paper *Al-Mada* as one of the main recipients of the Iraqi leader's oil-for-favours largesse, receiving 79.8 million barrels, $11.6 million over five years.[82] The links were also ideological. Zhirinovskii's book *Last Thrust to the South*, and his trips to Saddam were designed to present the image of a foreign policy threat if 'Mad Vlad' ever came to power,[83] but in truth his views, and those of his colleague Aleksei Mitrofanov, who headed the Duma 'geopolitics' committee, were not far removed from those of many in *siloviki* circles. Zhirinovskii effectively acted as a sounding board for ideas that would later become mainstream.

Zhirinovskii's subcontracted activities were often dangerous, however. The murder of LDPR deputy Sergei Skorochkin in 1995 was an early sign that the party was involved in some seriously risky enterprises. (The previous year Skorochkin had taken out his Kalashnikov on a busy street and killed both an alleged Georgian 'extortionist' and a passer-by.) Two LDPR deputies from the 'Tambov [mafia] group', Mikhail Glushchenko and Viacheslav Shevchenko, were rumoured to be behind the murder of prominent democrat Galina Starovoitova in 1998, possibly because she was about to go public on the LDPR's misdeeds. In February 1996 Vengerovskii was shot and wounded in the knee. Tensions were also fuelled by Zhirinovskii's attempts to monopolise the party by increasingly turning it into a family concern, with his half-sister Liubov acting as bursar and his son, Igor Lebedev, anointed as leader of the Duma faction in 1999 – even if he wasn't prepared to take the family name. Hence the conflict with Vengerovskii, Kobelev and others.

In 1996, therefore, 'Zhirinovskii's first new strategy . . . was to avoid participating in the election',[84] instead selling his support to anybody who would pay for it. After his inevitable low score (5.7 per cent), Zhirinovskii took second place to the much-stronger Communist faction in the 1995–99 Duma, but was again periodically useful to the Kremlin and the oligarchs. In April 1998 his deputies helped ensure the election of Sergei Kirienko as prime minister, as the Communists could not be relied on to support such a 'liberal'. In May 1999 the LDPR abstained along with Our Home Is Russia in the Yeltsin impeachment vote – at a rumoured $20–$30,000 a vote. Zhirinovskii also diversified, seeking to reinvent his party as a front for local 'interests' (basically mafias) in Novosibiirsk, Novgorod, Izmail and elsewhere. These reserve territories or 'spare aerodromes', however, often did not stay with the LDPR for long. Party wheeler-dealer Evgenii Mikhailov decamped to his native Pskov in 1996, but by 1999 was supporting first Fatherland-All Russia (FAR) and then Putin.

When the time came to assemble the party's 1999 list, Zhirinovskii had lost any sense of restraint and included known criminals such as Anatolii Bykov, former owner of the Krasnoiarsk aluminium factory; Sergei Mikhailov, assumed leader of Moscow's main mob, the Solntsevo mafia; and the notorious lawyer Dmitrii Yakubovskii ('General Dima'), a former Mr Fix-It who played a key role in the 'war of *kompromat*' between Yeltsin's administration and the Russian White House in 1993, but fell from grace following his conviction for stealing ancient manuscripts worth a reported $300 million from the Russian National Library in St Petersburg.[85] This time Zhirinovskii had gone too far. The party list was refused after a massive thirty-five candidates were struck off, and he was forced to cobble together a 'Zhirinovskii Bloc' instead. Ironically, although Bykov was excluded and eventually imprisoned in 2001, the other three members of his expensive 'quota', Vladimir Semenkov, Aleksei Guzanov and Vladislav Demin, remained on the list. Semenkov and Guzanov joined Unity; Semenkov died in a car accident in 2002; Demin beat up a police patrolman outside a Moscow night club in 2003. The authorities succumbed to Zhirinovskii's private appeals, however – in no small part because they believed his electorate overlapped with that of the Primakov-Luzhkov FAR bloc. A blitz of last-minute TV publicity, especially on RTR and ORT, allowed his party to hobble over the 5 per cent barrier – after Zhirinovskii spent most of his airtime attacking FAR. Gutseriev was the main party backer this time around, seconding his brother, Sait, to serve in the LDPR faction. Zhirinovskii also recruited two oil barons: Yurii Bespalov and Suleiman Kerimov of Nafta Moskva.

In the Putin era, it seemed initially that Zhirinovskii's usefulness might be coming to an end. With Yeltsin gone, Zhirinovskii looked to many 'like a tired old actor in some provincial play that has been running for five or six years'.[86] Moreover, the 'opportunistic' nature of his 'organisation, in which not even inert nationalism now remained',[87] had been laid bare. Surkov in particular wanted him out of mainstream politics, and Zhirinovskii's thoughts began to turn to a comfortable retirement. The 1999 'impeachment money' was used to fund Zhirinovskii's unsuccessful campaign for the governorship of Belgorod later that year, where he would have had access to lucrative border rackets. He came third, with 17 per cent. He also flirted with Ekaterinburg, but the powerful local mafia scared him off. Zhirinovskii had seemingly lost his traditional electorate, and was now more than ever dependent on Kremlin favour, although his party received no obvious 'dividend' in the new

Duma, in particular being denied any lucrative committee chairs. Zhirinovskii's faction dwindled accordingly; its seventeen deputies were down to twelve by May 2001. His supporters' ugly attempts to exploit the bomb in Pushkin Square in August 2000, parading banners that read 'The Only Good Chechen is a Dead Chechen' were a sign of desperation.

Nevertheless, Zhirinovskii survived. By keeping his nose clean(er) and holding up in the polls, he showed himself a useful port in a storm for second-or third-string oligarchs who had nowhere else to invest their money. In 2003 Zhirinovskii sold himself energetically, this time courting bankers rather than obvious mafiosi. In fact, there were so many bankers on his list (Ashot Egiazarian; Konstantin Vetrov, an old colleague of Surkov from Alfa-Bank; Leonid Slutskii of Prominvestbank and Investkredit; plus again Suleiman Kerimov, who tried to buy the Italian football club Roma in 2004) that Zhirinovskii risked ending up without much of a faction if his sponsors decided to 'migrate' to better homes.[88] Moreover, unlike in 1999 when the new tough guy on the block, Putin, stole part of his act, in 2003 the Kremlin's anti-oligarch campaign was so wide-ranging that it created a definite niche for Zhirinovskii, given his skill in distilling a populist message more effectively than most technologists. Zhirinovskii was also well placed to exploit the growing popular mood 'against all' (other) politicians. As one source aptly said of him: 'What's his message? "Down with the (insert favourite enemy here)!".'[89] The Kremlin's and the public's enemies were not always the same, but Zhirinovskii was better than anyone at bridging the gap between them. If in 1999 Zhirinovskii had lambasted FAR, this time he was happy to turn his fire on the Communists. (He also mocked the URF's chances on TV, claiming that most of their voters had already gone to live abroad.) Moreover, he could be relied on to back the Kremlin over the arrest of Khodorkovskii. The Communists equivocated, creating a useful 'wedge' issue to further depress the CPRF vote. The LDPR had been polling at a respectable 6–8 per cent, but its final tally was 11.6 per cent. Some suspected administrative assistance – as before, Zhirinovskii was preferable to a real nationalist. With Putin moving to the right, it was useful to have someone even further right, even if reviving Zhirinovskii as a fully fledged scarecrow would surely stretch all credibility.

Clinton's Alligators: The Fascist Threat

The saying, attributed to both Joseph De Maistre and Napoleon, 'Scratch a Russian and you'll find a Tatar', could easily be adapted into 'Scratch a Russian nationalist and you'll find a Chekist'. The Kremlin prefers to work with nationalist groups from the inside. Its desire to maintain monopoly control of public politics has always been much stronger than the temptation to play the nationalist card. As in the 1900s, a real street-level nationalist movement would not be to the Kremlin's liking at all. Yeltsin's 1995 'anti-Fascism' decree was therefore an unnecessarily blunt instrument against so many paper tigers.[90]

'Since the Gorbachev era,' therefore, 'the KGB has worked intensively [plotno] with Russian nationalists, trying to prevent the appearance of a [real] radical organisation in the nationalist camp.'[91] In fact, the Soviet authorities' long history of close observation and manipulation of various strands of Russian nationalism goes back to at least the 1960s. As Yitzhak Brudny has aptly observed, however, the 'politics of inclusion' periodically practised by the Party Central Committee in the late Soviet era was 'more of a golden straitjacket than a policy initiative designed to co-opt Russian nationalists'.[92] The decades of control have therefore left their mark. The extent of interpenetration has periodically raised hopes among many nationalists that the security state at least could be won over to their point of view, but it has fostered just as much disillusion. The Russian political scene is littered with burnt-out former nationalists. On the other hand, many 'nationalists themselves don't worry they are being manipulated. They need money, and hope that they can outwit the authorities [*vlast*].'[93] The would-be Russian *Führer*, Aleksandr Barkashov, persuaded himself that he would receive a call to glory in a 'Chilean variant' national-salvation government,[94] and belatedly admitted that he had naïvely sought to use Kremlin money 'to build a powerful structure' for himself.[95]

On the other hand, nationalist groups who don't play by the rules have been dealt with harshly, the best example being the National-Bolshevik Party led by the radical writer Eduard Limonov. Limonov's punk counter-culture aesthetic, with its 'fantasies of taking up arms against Power, of machine-gunning the Suits, of living forever outside of the world of the Normals' and the 'Cubicle Serfs', owed rather too much to his exile in France from 1974 to 1992.[96] It was not, therefore, the kind of politics the KGB or FSB was used to manipulating. Limonov's newspaper, *Limonka* (a pun on his name and the Russian for 'grenade'), was a little too exciting, and much too iconoclastic. Its masthead proudly proclaimed it was a 'paper of direct action'. Furthermore, by writing for the English-language *Exile* newspaper, Limonov stepped outside of the xenophobic ghetto where he could easily be controlled. The idea of Limonov fulfilling his ambition of inviting the former Sex Pistols singer John Lyndon to Moscow was not a scenario the FSB was likely to be comfortable with. When his party threatened to develop a skinhead following, based around nationalist punk bands such as the Forbidden Drummers (who had a Russian number one with 'Dead Negro'), Metal Corrosion and their singer Spider (real name Sergei Troitskii), Limonov was arrested. The implausible charge laid against him in April 2001 was possession of illegal arms in preparation for an invasion of northern Kazakhstan – Limonov was sentenced to four years in April 2003. *Limonka* was suspended but re-emerged. Others who have been subject to 'prophylactic' arrests include Nikolai Lysenko in 1996 (he had insulted Chernomyrdin in the Duma) and Konstantin Kasimovskii, leader of the Russian National Union, later Russian Action, who was much less of a problem after his two-year warning sentence in 1999.

Ever since Pamiat, therefore, the secret services have sought to control a succession of nationalist 'fronts'. An early example was the Russian National Council (Russkii Natsionalnii Sobor), set up in February 1992 as a lavishly funded rival to Viktor Aksiuchits's Russian National Assembly (Russkoe Natsionalnoe Sobranie), to keep nationalism mainstream and marginalise the real extremists, so that the Kremlin could properly manage the 'Red-Brown threat'. The Council's membership was a veritable Who's Who of former KGB personnel, including its leader, Aleksandr Sterligov, Stanislav Terentev, editor of the hate-sheet *Kolokol* ('The Bell'), and Igor Kuznetsov, plus Ziuganov and some former Yeltsin nomenclatura such as Ilia Konstantinov and Mikhail Astafaiev. The Council was financed by German Sterligov, nephew of Aleksandr and then partner of Artiom Tarasov (later leader of the Orthodox Party of Russia), and other shadowy industrialists. Konstantin Borovoi of the Moscow Commodity Exchange bankrolled Aksiuchits's rival Assembly.

The most prominent Russian nationalist group in the 1990s was Russian National Unity – known to its supporters simply as Unity – led by Aleksandr Barkashov. To most observers, the so-called *Barkashovtsi* fitted the bill perfectly: hundreds of angry young men with tattoos and neo-Nazi regalia, peddling anti-Semitic conspiracy theories and enjoying a justified reputation for casual violence. Further alarm was provoked by the highly visible sympathy and support for the organisation shown by many rank-and-file Russian police and militia. On closer inspection, however, Barkashov proved to have an obviously establishment past, with links to the KGB's Fifth Directorate after his army service. He joined Pamiat in 1985, but soon quarrelled with Vasiliev. Barkashov accused his leader of 'empty theatrical stunts'; Vasiliev accused his dauphin of working for the KGB.[97] Given Vasiliev's own earlier links (see pages 20–1), it was entirely possible that the KGB was playing one against the other.

After his stormy departure from Pamiat in August 1990, Barkashov reportedly maintained links with Viktor Barannikov, head of the FSB in 1991–93, and was regularly 'manipulated by the security services'.[98] Former KGB agent Aleksei Vedenkin, 'who apparently still had influential friends in the security services', organised the party's finances, and secured money from Gusinkii to fund Barkashov's performance in the role of 'a Fascist threat' to the new order, the 'alligators' threatening Yeltsin that Clinton found so alarming (the equivalent Russian phrase literally means 'devils in a sack').[99] Berezovskii supposedly paid the party 48 million roubles (less than $10,000) after Vedenkin's false claim that the RNU was investing in an Aeroflot computerisation project scared off IBM.[100] Having briefly provided Sterligov's 'security', Barkashov got his first real break when the Yeltsin group needed *agents provocateurs* in October 1993,[101] or at least people who would advertise their involvement in the White House's military defence and the Ostankino 'storming'. 'Testimony to the fact that Barkashov was enlisted by the militia comes from people close to Barkashov . . . control over his organisation was made all the easier by the fact that Barksahov suffered from "the Russian national disease" – alcoholism.'[102] Money from the security services had been arriving since the early 1990s.[103] Korzhakov flirted with the party in 1995, although its apparent refusal to take a relatively low place in the nationalist coalition he was trying to assemble led to a 'prophylactic' visit by armed men to its offices in April and the release of an embarrassing video in which Barkashov 'asked forgiveness of Jews, Negroes and Arabs'.[104]

As with Zhirinovskii's earlier rise, administrative resources were available on occasion.[105] The Interior Ministry often backed Russian National Unity in the provinces; the reliably rabid party paper *Russkii poriadok* ('Russian Order') was printed at a Ministry of Defence press, originally with a run of 400,000 copies; the pro-Yeltsin media often gave the organisation a friendly ride. His rivals therefore called Barkashov a 'grey TV star' and phoney nationalist.[106] An implicit deal seems to have been made, however, that Barkashov would not make too big a splash at election time. One reason that the authorities could indulge the RNU was that 'it didn't engage in politics in the generally understood sense' of the term.[107] In 1996 Barkashov toyed with running for president, but finally backed Yeltsin instead – making a considerable dent in nationalist support for the Communist leader Ziuganov, much to the latter's surprise.

The RNU's real moment in the sun, however, came in the autumn of 1998, after the economic collapse of the summer and before the rise of first Primakov and then Putin. Russia was seemingly leaderless and a populist backlash was bringing forth a flood of recruits, the 'active part of the population about whose participation in their nomenclatura parties all leaders dreamt'. The killing of radical general Lev Rokhlin in July further helped to stoke the heated atmosphere. The RNU now claimed to be attracting hundreds of former and current members of the police and ordinary militia. Initially, these 'white collars' (*belye vorotnichki*) seemed like a boon, an ideal 'vanguard', but they were more used to corruption than the party's earlier ideologues – and serious money was now beginning to flow in. For the first time, the RNU came to the attention of Kremlin dreamers who tried 'to use the organisation in their intrigues'.[108] Barkashov was eventually accused of selling the party membership list to businesses in need of security staff, etc, even helpfully pointing out which names represented 'the living and the healthy'.[109]

In 1999–2000 'Barkashov began, according to [his former] brothers-in-arms, to work completely for the Kremlin authorities'.[110] First, the 'RNU was successfully used against opponents of the Kremlin: when it was necessary to compromise Luzhkov [in January 1999, when he was linking up with Primakov], a march was organised through one of Moscow's suburbs, and given wide exposure in the mass media'.[111] Anti-Semitic RNU leaflets attacking Lukhzkov and Gusinskii were printed by the million. 'For this operation, according to well-attested rumours, the RNU leadership received $1.5 million.'[112] Luzhkov took his revenge by banning Barkashov's men from most of their Moscow parade grounds, but the damage, both in terms of tarnishing the mayor's image in his own backyard and upsetting his play for the nationalist vote, had been done.

The delicacy of this balancing act was well illustrated by the fate of the SPAS movement established for the 1999 Duma elections. (SPAS was short for *spasenie*, 'salvation'; any party that had such links with the Russian Orthodox Church was probably KGB-approved.) Its leading lights were all old lags with alleged KGB pasts: Barkashov joined up with Valerii Skurlatov's Vozrozhdenia ('Rebirth') and a former deputy from Zhirinovskii's LDPR, Vladimir Davidenko. The project was pulled at the last minute via a court ruling in November 1999. The SPAS would have distracted too much attention from Unity's mainstream 'dictatorship of the law' message. Some commentators also speculated that it was dismantled because it threatened to beat the 5 per cent barrier (though polls indicated 2 per cent was more likely),[113] maybe at the expense of Zhirinovskii. Either way, 'the authorities didn't want to risk it. Secondly, and more importantly, they were afraid of an unwanted precedent: the inevitable advertisement (at election time) for radical nationalism.'[114] The Kremlin did not want a proper nationalist movement developing beyond its control. The most likely explanation is that the flies run against the SPAS were unsuccessful, so the SPAS was pulled. Barkashov and his more pliable deputies, such as Aleksandr Kasin, received orders (via a secret meeting in the *bania* – Russian baths) to step down, and sufficient money to make sure they cooperated.

The RNU was basically drowned in money. 'Veterans [of the RNU] recall that in this period almost all the Moscow banks helped the RNU. . . . If earlier they had helped Yabloko, the CPRF, Our Home Is Russia, so in the same way the nationalists were now included on the list' as potential contenders for power. 'If they gave Ziuganov ten million, they gave the RNU three million.' Barkashov, who in the early 1990s was happy with a fifth-edition Zhiguli (the most workaday Soviet car), was now no longer 'interested in the strength of the organisation, in potential success, but simply in money'.[115] By late 2000 the RNU was primed for final implosion. 'Although the split in the RNU was in part inspired from outside, the ground for it had been prepared inside the organisation, which was unhappy with the political passivity of the party and its *Vozhd* ['charismatic leader']'[116] – and, of course, seriously disillusioned after 1999. None of the RNU's successor splinter groups had any real prospects, as the Kremlin has since concentrated its energies on creating its own safer substitutes for the RNU and SPAS, with Surkov backing Vasilii Yakemenko's quasi-paramilitary youth movement Walking Together and the Renaissance offshoot (Evgenii Ishenko and Konstantin Sevenard) from the RNU. But, of course, such carefully sanitised alternatives are not as exciting for real skinheads. In the Putin era, manipulation of the right has been much less common 'as the Russian powers don't feel the need'. 'President Putin succeeded in accumulating the vote of Russian nationalists without any help on the side.'[117] Even so, 'from time to time' the regime could still 'manipulate them to create the image of a Fascist threat with the aim of legitimising harsh measures [by those in] power and accentuating [their relatively] democratic character'.[118] The idea of an ultra-nationalist threat to Putin, hammer of the Chechens, was initially much less plausible than one to Yeltsin, destroyer of the USSR – although the scenario could conceivably be rewritten as 'forces unleashed beyond the Kremlin's control'.

National Revanche

As Putin consolidated his grip on power, however, the Kremlin increasingly turned its attention towards mainstream nationalism. In 2002 Pavlovskii backed the creation of yet another right-wing vehicle, the Eurasia Party, led by Aleksandr Dugin (a party that was initially unabashed about its loyalty to Putin as they understood him).[119] It was unclear whether Pavlovskii's purpose was electoral, or just to test out Dugin's neo-imperial Eurasianist version of the 'national idea' via Dugin's own virtual empire on the internet (which interconnected closely with Pavlovskii's own).[120] Dugin's party was well funded, in part by the FSB, and was full of former intelligence figures, such as the party number two, Petr Suslov, a colonel in the SVR (Foreign Intelligence Service) until 1995 and organiser of a notorious 2001 conference on the 'Islamic Threat',[121] and General Nikolai Klokotov, from 1988 to 1996 chair of strategy at the General Staff's Military Academy. Eurasia's ranks also included Talgat Taj-al-Din, Supreme Mufti of Russia (leader of all Russian Muslims), whose position was a longstanding KGB sinecure. Dugin himself was another alleged Pamiat 'plant' back in 1988, who flirted with Limonov's party before moving in CPRF 'Red-Brown' circles and becoming an adviser to Seleznev in the late 1990s. Initially, therefore, it seemed that Pavlovskii wanted Dugin to link up with Seleznev's Russia's Rebirth party, but Dugin was too much his own man and too committed to his own particular version of anti-American 'clash of civilisations' theory (he once set up a website named '*Delenda est carthago*', 'Carthage must fall') to stay too close to the Kremlin after September 11. After the loss of such an influential iconoclast, the main Red-Brown project for 2003, Rodina, became more predictably pro-Kremlin (see pages 260–2).

As a result of Dugin's unreliability (from the Kremlin's perspective), his party soon found itself cloned. The rival Great Russia–Eurasia Bloc was pitched more at the Muslim vote, but was basically the Family's version of the Dugin-Pavlovskii party. It was financed by Aleksei Golovkov and Igor Shabduraslov, formerly of both the presidential administration and ORT, and headed by Pavel Borodin, who had plenty of resources of his own. The bloc also included the Citizens' Party and Iosif Kobzon's Party of Peace. As this year's project for Borodin (who had backed the Pensioners' Party in 1999 and served as secretary of the Russia-Belarus Union since 2000, in which capacity he found himself briefly arrested at New York's Kennedy airport on the way to President George W. Bush's inauguration in 2001), this version of 'Eurasia' was potentially a solid investment vehicle, but it seems to have lost out in the primary process to Rodina.

The other main nationalist project for 2003 was the United Russian Party or Rus. Nominally an extreme-right party, two months before the elections it had the fifth-highest sponsorship, with 50.6 million roubles ($1.7 million) – more than the Union of Right Forces.[122] Total covert party finance was 'at least $2 million'.[123] The rumour that the Orthodox multi-millionaire, Sergei Pugachev of Mezhprombank, a fellow former student at Leningrad State University and close confidant of Putin (and of Sechin and Ivanov), was a key background sponsor, was plausible, as Rus was clearly part of the same ideological family of projects prepared for 2003. Like United Russia, Rodina and the People's Party, Rus played on the themes laid out in Belkovskii's 'State and Oligarchs' report, the new left-populist ideology of state-oriented, anti-oligarchical capitalism based on revitalised 'power' ministries and Orthodox culture. Rus's ads were indeed prominent on national TV and its billboards numerous.

The project was designed by Aleksii Koshmarov of Novokom and linked to his patron, Vladimir Yakovlev in St Petersburg. (Several party figures in fact worked in PR, including Igor Titov, head of the Centre for Electoral Technology attached to Our Home Is Russia from 1996.) Koshmarov had taken over an old shell party, the liberal Russian Stability Party, and infused it with the mystical ideology of Aleksandr Gorianin, another confidant of the presidential administration and a bestselling author who advocated the revival of 'the spirit of the nation' by challenging the myths of Russian backwardness.[124] Although Rus talked loudly of 'Russia for the Russians', its definition of 'Russianness' was actually much closer to the statist nationalism of the Kremlin *siloviki* than the ethnocentrism of the RNU or SPAS.[125] Whereas the RNU was always difficult to control, Rus proudly quoted from Putin's books in its election literature.

The political technologists were again guilty of overproduction – given the success of the main nationalist project, Rodina (see pages 260–5), where Dmitrii Rogozin, once also touted as leader of Rus, ended up. Rus's campaign technologists aimed to create a demotic image, parading a range of tie-less middle-ranking figures on TV, but such tactics only served to emphasise the project's lack of real leaders, such as Ukraine's CPU(r) in 2002. Rus in the end was 'a sociological project'. It had its potential audience right – given the rise in anti-Caucasian sentiment in particular – but it was 'too virtual' to persuade it to vote.[126] Rus won only 0.25 per cent, and the Great Russia–Eurasia Bloc only 0.3 per cent. Both were marginally outpolled by Sergei Popov's For Holy Rus (0.5 per cent); a project of obscure, if apparently well-funded, origins, whose anonymous adverts did little more than quote scripture on TV (the party slogan was *Ne voru!*, 'Thou shalt not steal'). Nevertheless, these various efforts served to keep the non-Kremlin right divided and out of parliament.

The Ukrainian Blackshirts

In Ukraine, the main scarecrow party has been the far-right Ukrainian National Assembly (UNA) and its paramilitary wing, the Ukrainian Self-Defence Force (Ukraïnska Natsionalna Samo-Oborona, or UNSO), normally known by the combined acronym UNA-UNSO. Like Russian National Unity, the UNA-UNSO has made easy copy for foreign journalists, unaware that extreme nationalism has only the tiniest of support bases in Ukraine. At its peak in 1994, the UNA-UNSO claimed thirteen thousand members and three deputies in parliament. However, its members were always the noisiest at nationalist demonstrations. Its testosterone-fuelled rallies often degenerated into violence, as did its more spectacular stunts, including various attempts to storm Russian Orthodox churches and the wanton mayhem at the funeral of Patriarch Volodymyr in Kiev in 1995. The UNA-UNSO's populist eye for slogans and its eclectic, even bizarre, ideology also generated many a headline. Its policy on Crimea was clear enough: the peninsula should be 'Ukrainian, or depopulated' (*bezliudnym*); in 1994 it promised its supporters that a vote for UNA-UNSO this time meant 'you won't have to bother next time'.

The UNA-UNSO therefore played the scarecrow function, not just abroad to bolster the new regime, but also for a domestic audience used to Soviet demonisation of wartime 'neo-Nazi' Ukrainian nationalism. Unlike in Russia, the threat of a nationalist takeover was one of the nomenclatura's best arguments for preserving its own power. However, traditional nationalist groups had roots in the Ukrainian emigration, so a home-gown alternative was needed. To block the émigrés' return, the UNA-UNSO was fed with arguments against them.[127] The UNA-UNSO's secret supporters in the post-Soviet nomenclatura also needed to develop a new type of ideology, more suitable to their purposes than the blood-and-soil ethno-nationalism developed in the 1930s by the west Ukrainian OUN (Organisation of Ukrainian Nationalists). As with Dugin or Zhirinovskii in Russia, the UNA-UNSO served as a proving ground for the private thoughts of the powers-that-be, in this case an incipient 'nativist' nationalism.[128] In fact, the UNA-UNSO's arguments in favour of supporting the current elite were often better than the elite's own, and seem to have been purpose-written. According to the group's leaders: 'The [only real] question [in Ukraine today] is who will bring order.' 'Reform is only possible within a framework of order, within the framework of a powerful state.' 'The building of a Ukrainian state is our first task, even if it is built by Communists.' As against the romantic illusions of Ukrainian nationalists, they accepted as of 1991 that a Ukrainian nation did not yet exist, and that only the 'powerful [post-Communist] state' apparatus 'can be an instrument for forming the nation'. Unlike the dilettante intelligentsia in Rukh, they argued, former Communists and KGB had the 'state-building' know-how.[129]

The seemingly obscurantist UNA-UNSO also served to mythologise a second version of power in Dnieper Ukraine for the *de facto* head of the new Ukrainian Orthodox Church (Kievan Patriarchate), Filaret – the traditional Ukrainian nationalist heartland in Galicia, west Ukraine being Greek Catholic in faith. As well as serving as his physical bodyguard, and attacking rival churches (both the Moscow Patriarchate and the Autocephalous Orthodox), the party also devoted much space in its publications to developing an ideology for the Church, and was particularly keen on martial images of the crusaders and knights templar.[130]

The mainstream Ukrainian right was therefore deeply suspicious of the UNA-UNSO from the very beginning. Its ultra-radical leaders such as Dmytro Korchynskyi were suspected of being KGB provocateurs.[131] Oleksandr Skipalskyi, a major-general in the local KGB turned SBU (later named in a black PR story about a 'plot' to assassinate Kuchma in 1994), claims that in 1992 his boss, Yevhen Marchuk, asked him to infiltrate the UNA-UNSO and contact Korchynskyi – only to find that Marchuk had got there first. Oleh Vitovych, another alleged agent in the nationalists' ranks, eventually followed Marchuk, and indirectly Korchynskyi, into, of all places, the oligarchic SDPU(o). Other versions have it that Skipalskyi himself set up the UNA-UNSO.[132] Either way, the UNA-UNSO's publications in the 1990s were far too numerous and of far too high a (technical) quality for a real opposition party. Another alleged early secret sponsor was Prominvestbank.[133]

Members of the UNA-UNSO were also notorious for their frequent use as *agents provocateurs*. Marchuk was alleged to have played a role in the violence at Patriarch Volodymyr's funeral in 1995 when Kuchma was out of the country. The Gongadze affair provoked a domestic protest campaign against the authorities during the winter of 2000-01. On 9 March 2001 a big set-piece rally degenerated into violence, providing the authorities with the excuse they needed for a crackdown.[134] Although several UNA-UNSO members were arrested, they were accused by the real opposition of provoking the trouble in order to discredit the peaceful protests. The campaign against the authorities never really recovered momentum, despite two attempted restarts. At the same time, the SBU was playing divide and rule inside the organisation – technically, there was now both an UNA-UNSO and a more pro-government UNA.[135] Most of those arrested in 2001 represented the former, most of the *provocateurs* the latter. In the 2004 elections, the UNA faction, led by Eduard Kovalenko,[136] frequently demonstrated uninvited in support of Yushchenko, receiving both money from the SDPU(o) and plenty of publicity on SDPU(o) TV.[137]

Staging Regime Change

In Peter Huber's 1994 version of *1984*, *Orwell's Revenge*, the author expressed scepticism that the regime could in fact survive as Orwell suggests, its 'boot forever in a human face'. In Huber's novel there is no revolutionary insurrection, however. The 'inner party' fakes a change of government by deposing Big Brother and claiming that Emmanuel Goldstein (under the name of 'Kenneth Blythe', one of Orwell's more obscure pseudonyms) is back in power. Ignorance, however, remains strength: nothing has really changed and the cycle begins again.[138]

By analogy, post-Soviet elites have often promoted a semi-detached member of the elite as a challenger for power, most notably Putin himself in 1999–2000. Most other post-Soviet states are not as far advanced as Russia in this cycle of staging change *within* virtual politics. The Putin succession was itself brought forward because of Yeltsin's ill health. In Ukraine in 2004 the authorities hoped to gift a similar 'transition' to a regime insider posing on the outside, though someone such as Serhii Tihipko could have posed as more 'independent' than Yanukovych (see pages 182–3).

The double-headed Georgian opposition claimed to be running 'against' the discredited Shevardnadze in 2003. Its eventual success in toppling him was, however, also an inside job, perpetrated by those who only split with the regime in 2001-02. One wing was represented by Zurab Zhvania and his United Democrats, the other by former justice minister Mikhail Saakashvili's National Movement. Zhvania reportedly received $1 million from the Russian deputy premier Nikolai Aksenenko to fund a dozen Russian political technologists working on the Union of Georgian Citizens' 1999 and 2000 campaigns. Zhvania admitted to employing 'two or three',[139] from Aleksei Sitnikov's Image-Kontakt.[140] Putin, however, detested Shevardnadze as a remnant of the Gorbachev era and Image-Kontakt switched sides in 2003 to advise the Zhvania-Burdjanadze bloc, including making recommendations on post-election 'destabillisation'.[141] (Badri Patarkatsishvili, exiled financier and media kingmaker, linked to Berezovskii, was also financing the United Democrats.) The virtual 'youth rallies' against Shevardnadze were a characteristic company ploy.

Za nashu i Vashu Natashu!: **The Progressive Socialist Party of Ukraine**

The Progressive Socialist Party of Ukraine (PSPU) fulfils so many of the virtual functions described above that it is worth considering on its own. As a spoiler party it divided the left-wing vote in both the 1998 and 1999 elections. Party leader Nataliia Vitrenko played a scarecrow role in 1999, as, in the words of one Ukrainian paper, 'Symonenko was regarded by Bankivska Street as not spectacular enough to act the bogey in the presidential campaign script, repeating Russia's scenario of reformer vs. Red peril.'[142] Vitrenko was also a useful prop for Kuchma in his negotiations with the IMF in 1999, intimating that there was a worse alternative even to his own highly partial compliance with its conditions. Vitrenko, 'the Konotop witch',[143] reserved most of her venom not for the domestic oligarchs reputed to be her backers but for the ogres of international capitalism, whose investment in Ukraine was minimal. In this allotted role, she featured heavily in Western media coverage of the 1999 election, particularly after her most important cameo performance in October of that year, when an alleged grenade attack on her at an election rally was blamed on supporters of Oleksandr Moroz, leader of the rival Socialist Party (see page 183).

Her party may have originally split from the Socialists as a result of perfectly normal rivalries. Thereafter, however, there is much evidence to indicate covert support from the powers-that-be:

i)   A close examination of the biographies of the fourteen deputies originally elected by the party in 1998 reveals some surprising anomalies for a party of 'pure proletarians'. Two were businessmen/bankers accused of buying their seats, Viacheslav Kviat and Serhii Tykhonov, whom even the Communists and Socialists had rejected.[144] Another was deputy head of the State Property (i.e., privatisation) Fund. Another government 'businessman', Volodymyr Yelchaninov, was loaned to the party from the faux-Greens when the PSPU faction was threatened with dissolution in 1999. The party faction was wound up in 2000 when it was no longer deemed useful: the 'ideological' core of six (including Vitrenko) became independents, but the remaining nine all found financially more comfortable homes in oligarchic factions, including four who joined Viktor Pinchuk's Labour Ukraine. None joined rival left parties (Yelchaninov went back to the Greens).[145]

ii) The state lent its administrative resources to the party. The barrier for representation in the 1998 elections was 4 per cent. The Progressive Socialists won a very precise 4.046 per cent, after some ill-concealed padding.[146] A local court in Konotop (Sumy oblast) initially quashed

Vitrenko's victory in constituency number 160, which would have left the party with only 3.85 per cent of the vote and kept it out of parliament, but the higher court in Kiev reversed the decision. In a similar fashion, the Central Election Commission accepted 1,012,000 signatures in support of Vitrenko's presidential bid in 1999 (the necessary minimum of one million was obtained because the Commission rejected the lowest percentage (9) of any would-be candidate after some private pressure from Oleksandr Volkov).[147] On the Melnychenko tapes Kuchma is heard to complain about regions where Moroz did well in the first round; he later fired the heads of Vinnytsia and Poltava oblasts. He has no such complaints about areas where Vitrenko's vote is high. Tellingly, unlike Moroz, but like Zhirinovskii in Russia, Vitrenko was omnipresent on state TV in 1999, then promptly disappeared after the election. On one 'protest march' in 1997, the party's not particularly weary marchers were provided with transport by the militia.[148]

iii) Financial support was extended to Vitrenko through people close to the president, allegedly including leading oligarch Viktor Pinchuk and another Dnipropetrovsk favourite, deputy head of the State Security Council, Oleksandr Razumkov. 'Mass channels of finance came through the head of Sumy oblast state administration, Volodymyr Shcherban', who helped fund the party's conferences.[149] Media mogul Vadym Rabinovych was also frequently mentioned as a sponsor.[150]

iv) Vitrenko's image was carefully sculpted. Radical in rhetoric but not in action, with a voracious appetite for image and none for content, she was surprisingly sophisticated in her use of imagery. On the one hand, Vitrenko, the 'image vampire',[151] tried to sell herself as a modern equivalent of the radical poet Lesiia Ukraïnka. On the other hand, like Zhirinovskii, she, or rather her advisers, carefully exploited (post-) Soviet populism. The illustration on page 221 shows her main election poster for 1999, in which she is depicted in the style of a famous Socialist Realist poster from 1941. In the original the 'Motherland-Mother' (*Rodina-mat*) holds out an enlistment oath;[152] Vitrenko is holding a copy of her book *Save Ukraine!* The slogan *Za rodinu! Za nashu i Vashu Natashu!* ('For the Motherland! For our and your Natasha!') also echoes wartime equivalents. Hence Vitrenko's success as a project designed to appeal to the *boloto*, Ukraine's amorphous middle-ground voters in between the Ukrainophile leftism of Moroz, strongest in central Ukraine, and the Soviet traditionalism of the Communists, strongest in the east.

v) The main purpose of her party in 1998–99 was to split the left vote, but it also proved useful in parliament. Like Zhirinvoskii's Liberal Democrats, Vitrenko's anti-government rhetoric often stood in sharp contrast to a surprisingly loyal voting record. The rest of the left cried foul when the Progressive Socialists failed to support a crucial no-confidence motion against the government in October 1998, resulting in the attempt falling twenty votes short. The PSPU had no legislative achievements to speak of.

vi)   According to Melnychenko, referring to a taped conversation at the height of the election campaign on 3 November 1999:

> In Kuchma's office she [Vitrenko] openly agrees with him how to act, and with ordinary folk talks about her implacable [opposition] to the criminal regime. They took her to Kuchma in his office 'through the kitchen garden' [*horodamy*] so that no one would see her [escorted by the then head of the security service of Ukraine, Leonid Derkach], and she conducted herself at these rendezvous like an obedient Pioneer [a reference to the Soviet Youth League]. I have many such moments which show Who is [really] Who in Ukraine.[153]

Kuchma is heard to demand on the tapes, 'Go fucking easy on her . . . because any leakage will hit her, badly'. Even rival oligarch Volkov is kept in the dark about the meetings, which were attended only by Kuchma, security chief Derkach and one unknown other.[154]

vii)   The grenade attack on Vitrenko in October 1999 (see page 183) was carefully timed. Vitrenko was not overtaking Moroz in the polls and it briefly seemed possible that Yevhen Marchuk might withdraw in favour of Moroz. A reserve scenario for a different 'October surprise' had earlier been rumoured: appointing Vitrenko head of some kind of People's Commissariat to establish economic 'order',[155] just as the virtual anti-corruption candidate Marchuk was appointed to head the National Security Council.

viii)   Despite her seeming eclipse after 1999 (the dissolution of the Progressive Socialist faction in parliament, the cutting loose of party rank and file), Vitrenko was revived for the 2002 campaign, appearing on the Pinchuk (and former Rabinovych) channels STV, ICTV, Era and even UT-1 to denounce the regime's enemies, depicting Moroz as an American stooge and Tymoshenko as corrupt. In early March her words were cited almost as often as those of Yushchenko, Tymoshenko and Moroz put together.[156] This time around her function was to compete with both for the relatively apolitical protest vote, and she did surprisingly well, gaining 3.2 per cent. She switched targets with consummate ease, barely revisiting the script of 1999, the IMF and international capitalism seemingly having forgotten their interest in Ukraine.

Conclusions

How big a problem is manufactured supply? Manufactured acts are ten-a-penny in pop music – even 'anti-industry' rebels. Politics, however, has to be about more than consumption if democracy is to be at all 'representative'. When Edmund Burke argued that the representatives of the people must never act as mere delegates, so as to keep the politics of demotic impulse at arm's length, he was assuming that his autonomous MPs operated within a world of real contesting forces and articulated interests. In the post-Soviet 'society of the spectacle', the people have the vote but are otherwise only spectators. Their ability to influence the action on the stage in front of them is minimal. The electorate is more radically disengaged from real politics than Burke can ever have imagined.

It might be argued that some types of opposition are better left invented: manipulating and 'turning' neo-Fascist (or far-left) groups from within, for instance, is much better than the emergence of a real neo-Fascist alternative, and Russia, with potentially one of the biggest far-right electorates, is rather adept at this task. But the practice of 'control' now extends right across the political spectrum. By 2003-04 in Russia it was clear that the Kremlin sought to control all significant political agents, both real and potential, rather than just those at the extremes. In this task it is not always successful, but its ambitions are clear.

'For the motherland! For our and your Natasha!'
Nataliia Vitrenko poses as Mother of the Nation, 1999.

9 Inventing the Opposition: Virtual Communists

The West has often fretted about the 'Red threat' in the former Communist world. However, many post-Communist leaders – Yeltsin in Russia, Kuchma in Ukraine, Shevardnadze in Georgia – have found it convenient to maintain such a threat as a justification for their hold on power. As one commentary cynically put it in 2001: 'Every four years the party of power (Yeltsin twice, Putin so far just once) wins presidential elections under the slogan "Communism shall not pass!".'[1] The new – but not too new – Communist parties have therefore served as necessary opponents for the powers-that-be; a radical, but not too radical threat, powerful enough to maintain the fear of a reversion to the worst of the old order, but (except in Moldova and Crimea) not actually to return to power. Most existing Communist parties, however, are not as radical as they seem. Most were allowed to reform with a degree of official connivance to prevent the emergence of more radical alternatives.

The convenience is mutual. Many Communist successor parties have basked in their status of 'official opposition' and become 'normalised', growing into stable parts of the political system. According to Luke March, the new Russian Communists' 'integration with the regime was logical, protecting the party from its own supporters and giving it improved access to resources that might prolong its short- and medium-term influence'.[2] The new Communist parties' role as protest bodies is now safely ritualised. The key marching dates in the Communist calendar – the October Revolution, May Day, the March anniversary of Gorbachev's 1991 referendum on preserving the USSR – are nicely spaced through the year periodically to remind voters of their existence. Arguably, however, successor Communist parties have also performed a more positive stabilising function by keeping a lid on protest, and helping to reconcile potentially large loser electorates, those who have suffered most from the 'transition', to the new regime.

Communist successor parties have also developed business interests in the new economy – often because they are the *only* party in many areas for local businesses to deal with – and have developed links with oligarchs in both business and government. According to Yeltsin's former Mr Fix-It, Aleksandr Korzhakov, 'The Communists now are not like they were. They drive Audis [at least], they live in

Snegiriakh [one of Moscow's well-to-do dacha districts]. The kind of people who got something out of power.'[3] In 1998 the Communist Party of Kazakhstan was briefly allied with former prime minister Akezhan Kazhegeldin (served 1994–97) before he was forced into exile in 1999, accused of embezzling several hundred million dollars from state coffers. In Moldova unofficial 'left businesses' include wine, tobacco and sweets; in Ukraine metallurgy; in Russia just about anything. Slovakia's Democratic Party of the Left makes money from its old links to the east. Hence the new Communist parties' fondness for the mythology of 'national' versus 'cosmopolitan' or '*comprador*' (agents of foreign business) capital.

It often seems at first glance that the new Communist parties were founded by second-echelon ideologues (the residual true believers), while the old elite went 'non-party'. But beneath the surface the same old cynics of the inner circle can usually be found, and to them the new Communist parties are just another project, needing plausible frontmen. Having kept their distance in 1992–93, men such as the coup leader Anatolii Lukianov and the former head of Gosplan, Yurii Masliukov, jumped aboard the bandwagon as soon as electoral success was achieved. As of 2000, for example, 'twenty-one of the CPRF's twenty-four top leaders were from the CPSU apparat'.[4] Significantly for parties trading on their former connections, it now tends to be older figures from the late Soviet era who predominate in new business spheres. In Russia it is the former Soviet premier (1985–90) Nikolai Ryzhkov, so often spokesman for the Red directors in the Gorbachev era, when allegations of his corruption were first aired (he helped set up the shell company, ANT, that was used to cut the Ministry of Foreign Trade out of lucrative commodity exporting), who lobbies for a variety of companies' interests in the Duma.[5] In 1993 Ryzhkov set up the Moscow Intellectual-Business Club as a forum for nascent left businesses, followed in 2001 by the more unashamedly lobbyist, Russian Union of Commodity Producers. Ryzkhov's new expertise involved easing the passage of pork-barrel laws 'on the distribution of production'. In Ukraine Stanislav Hurenko, last leader of the local Communists in 1990–91, enjoyed a new career as *de facto* head of the successful metals trading joint venture (metals dumping would be more exact) Navasko, and exploited his position as head of the parliamentary committee on economic policy to act as a formidable lobbyist.

Successor parties, however, still have to play to their rank and file and to their electorates. The new Communist parties are therefore especially 'intertextual' and multi-dimensional. Most ordinary party members are still convinced Communists, often of a radical hue. Electoral setbacks for the Ukrainian Communists in 2002 and the Russians in 2003 forced both parties (at least temporarily) to try to rebuild their image. However, most ordinary members joined up largely for psychological reasons, seeking to maintain whatever links they could to the old Soviet culture (now subculture). Their passive view of party work has left the field open for the party elders. New leaderships tend to maintain the essentially conservative Soviet elite culture of *apparat* intrigue, state dependency, lobbyism, aversion to social disorder, cult of unity and cynical suppression of dissent. Party programmes are dominated by nostalgic symbolism and ritualistic Sov-speak (*dubovii yazyk*, 'wooden language' or, more literally, 'oak/oaken language'), rather than actionable proposals, leaving leaders free in practice to develop their lobbying interests. For successor Communist parties, therefore, another aspect of virtuality is the gap between how they appear to their memberships and how they actually operate in private.

The key problem for the powers-that-be, on the other hand, is keeping the successor parties 'in the box' – that is, radical enough to keep the rank-and-file happy and any real opposition at bay, but still getting them to play by the existing rules of the game. This is not always possible, but the importance of the task can be seen by the sheer number of projects devised by the likes of Pavlovskii and Surkov to build and maintain the box. Although so often faux-radical, there is no doubt that former Communist parties could have returned to some kind of power in a more honest political system: in Russia in 1996, in Ukraine or in Kazakhstan in 1999. Stopping them so doing has involved a variety of 'special tasks'.

The 'New' Russian Communists: *Staraia ploshchad*'s [6] Diaspora

The Communist Party of the Russian Federation (CPRF) has never been as radical as it might have seemed. The first version of the party that appeared in 1990–91 was the spawn of quintessential Central Committee bureaucrats (*tsekovchiki*) such as Valerii Legostaiev and Sergei Kurginian (see page 19), the covert political entrepreneurs who had earlier helped to set up the leftist 'fronts' (United Workers' 'Intermovements') of the late Soviet era. (The nickname *tsekovchik*, is derived from the abbreviation 'TsK', which stands for *Tsentralnyi Komitet*). The party's *éminence grise*, Valentin Kuptsov, a Soviet Politburo member who headed the Central Committee department 'for liaison with socio-political organisations' before taking over as leader from Ivan Polozkov in early August 1991, gained an early reputation among more radical rank-and-file for collaborating with first Gorbachev and then Yeltsin.[7] Although soon overturned by events, the Kuptsov succession therefore marked a turn away from the 'Vendée' tactics of 1990 and early 1991, when the Russian Communists had represented the revolt of the regional secretaries against *perestroika*, and the recapture of the party by the *apparat*. Kuptsov's private channels of communication with the Yeltsin Kremlin later helped establish the CPRF as the favoured successor in the 'war for the left brand'.[8] Kuptsov was a serious contender for the leadership until a threatened rank-and-file revolt at the party's founding congress in 1993 made Gennadii Ziuganov a safer choice. Ziuganov, though, was yet another quintessential *tsekovchik*, whose boss as deputy head of the Ideology Department in 1989–90 was none other than Aleksandr Yakovlev. Indeed, Ziuganov has been accused of taking money from Gorbachev and Yakovlev to help undermine the conservatives in the 'old' CPSU – and much less plausibly of helping to prepare the proposal to ban the old party after the August coup, during which he conveniently absented himself at a sanatorium in Kislovodsk.[9]

Even during the apparent Communist nadir in 1991–92, it seemed that some of the 'revolutionaries' in the new Kremlin wished to keep a version of the old party alive for insurance purposes. Its embryonic leadership had an office in the Russian

Social-Political Centre, an organisation close to the presidential administration, whose president and director, Sergei Stankevich and Georgii Satarov, were both Yeltsin advisers. (The fact that Ziugnaov and Yeltsin had flats in the same old Central Committee building is probably of more than trivial importance – they must at least have had some interesting chats in the lift.) Old party newspapers were not closed, and they were 'gently recommended to orient themselves to the CPRF'. Administrative resources gave a few further nudges when necessary. *Leninskoe znamia* ('Leninist Star'), which flirted with the more radical leftists, found itself reregistered as *Narodnaia gazeta* ('The People's Paper').[10]

Another link came through Aleksei Podberezkin and Dmitrii Rogozin's RAU Corporation, where the new party ideology was developed, helped by the fact that the new Communist Party had no real codified programme until 1995. The RAU, the bizarrely named Russian-American University, was not a club for devotees of Americana, but more or less the opposite, given its close ties to the defence and intelligence services, and the early patronage of former Supreme Soviet chair Anatolii Lukianov.[11] Rogozin was responsible for organising a sequence of nationalist 'primaries' (see page 91) in the early 1990s, launching a whole series of projects with similar names: the Union for the Rebirth of Russia, the Congress of Civic and Patriotic Forces of Russia, the Union of the Peoples of Russia, Fatherland. Another of these was the Russian National Council, set up in February 1992 (see pages 210–11), whose essentially statist, anti-street ideology Rogozin shared with co-founders Ziuganov and Aleksandr Sterligov (whose KGB links and financial resources were well known).

Podberezkin, who was also ex-KGB, was one of Ziuganov's ghost writers and the prime mover behind the Spiritual Heritage Group in 1994–95 (financed by the colourful businessman Vladimir Semago; see page 228). According to *Nezavisimaia gazeta*:

> the extensive connections of . . . Podberezkin to the Ministry of Defence, the FSB and security organs were used by Ziuganov to establish contacts and effective relations with the leadership of the power ministries and departments. By all accounts, Gennadii Ziuganov was able to establish contacts with prominent commercial banks through Spiritual Heritage, using the principle of 'fan-financing' those candidates for president whose election they considered preferable.[12]

According to Luke March, Spiritual Heritage 'used its pre-existing connections with the state apparatus and security services to re-establish links between the patriots and CPRF, power ministries and banks'.[13] One Duma deputy said that Podberezkin, mocked as 'Mephistopheles seducing Faust' (i.e., Ziuganov),[14] was a straightforward Kremlin 'agent of influence'.[15] The departing ideology secretary, Aleksandr Kravets, accused the party of replacing 'Marxism with Machiavellianism' under Podberezkin's influence.[16] (The very same Kravets would later act as the party's link man to exiled oligarch Boris Berezovskii, visiting him in London, cap in hand in

October 2002.)[17] Podberezkin had indeed worked with Yeltsin's aide Aleksei Tsaregodtsev in 1990–91, and later co-authored the programme of Chernomyrdin's Our Home Is Russia.[18] In the mid-1990s, Viktor Zorkaltsev was also a key link to the Kremlin via Korzhakov, and was useful for cultivating links to rightists and the Russian Orthodox Church.[19] Many party members claimed that the 1993 party documents were 'doctored' by Kuptsov and the 'outsiders' to make the necessary compromises with the Kremlin.[20] Podberezkin was expelled in August 1999, but by then the party was safely enmeshed in more straightforwardly economic interests.

Ideologically, Ziuganovism was perfect for the Kremlin's shadow-boxing. Regime strategists appreciated its essentially conservative message, especially its anti-revolutionary stress on social stability. A serious Soviet restorationist or Russian ethnonationalist project capable of encouraging the defection of segments of the new ruling elite would have been much more of a threat to the state. Ziuganov's worldview, on the other hand, mixing pan-Slavic and East Slavic ('Great Russian') rhetoric with the myths of a 'single stream' of Russian history and the natural proclivity for Socialism shared by downtrodden serfs and the post-Soviet dispossessed, safely overlapped with elements of official rhetoric in the Yeltsin era – and provided a useful smokescreen for the party's economic accommodation with the Kremlin. As Luke March has put it, 'Arguably the biggest service the CPRF provided the regime was failing to provide a coherent alternative vision with which to replace it.'[21] Organisationally, Ziuganov's establishment of a left–right diarchy by pairing the CPRF with the People's Patriotic Union of Russia in 1996 provided a perfect institutional filter for two-thirds of the political spectrum. Significantly, the Kremlin has never allowed the CPRF to tap different electorates by running its two blocs as real independent forces and complementary projects, as was briefly contemplated in 1998–99.

The same, in opposite form, was true of the Communist Party of Ukraine (CPU). Its virulent opposition to the 'Ukrainian idea' was anathema to the right, but casually acceptable to the elite, who were also happy to use the threat of a Communist revanche to control the right. The CPU's particular cul-de-sac, however, was vague but impractical Soviet nostalgia – suitable for building an electoral base among the Russophone half of the population, but unlikely to encourage it on to the streets. The party had to be much more carefully policed after it increasingly began to ape the East Slavic nationalism of its Russian counterpart after the 1999 Kosovo War – hence the powers-that-be creating two virtual parties on either flank (see pages 254–6) in order to keep its options relatively circumscribed.

In the early 1990s, the CPRF was also a safe alternative to the White House opposition (the National Salvation Front [NSF], *et al.*) and the more radical neo-Communists within its ranks – just as the CPU was preferable to any real Russian nationalist movement in Ukraine. As with the original suspension of the party in 1991, the Kremlin's priority was to pre-empt real popular mobilisation. According to one source, 'already at the end of 1991, Ziuganov together with Rybkin (behind the back of Gorbachev) met for consultations with Gennadii Burbulis and Boris

Yeltsin and received an OK [*dobro*] from them for creating a non-extremist party of Socialist direction'. 'The decision to allow the CPRF to [take part in later] elections was taken at the very top.'[22] However, Ziuganov only really became a serious player in Russian politics after turning his back on the Communist radicals in the Moscow White House in October 1993. The CPRF's temporary suspension was designed to make sure that it would play by the new rules, while its potential street-fighting rivals such as Anpilov's Working Russia, the Russian Communist Workers' Party and in many ways the most logical successor party, the All-Soviet Union of Communist Parties-CPSU, were either banned or boycotted the elections. Dirty tactics were also used against most of the NSF's successors, such as Sergei Baburin's Russian All-People's Union, to prevent them from taking part (no fewer than eight out of twenty-one parties or blocs were kept off the ballot). Before the CPRF was 'anointed' in this way, it was just one party among others (on one count, fifteen parties had 'Communist' somewhere in their name); Ziuganov's personal rating was only 1 per cent above Anpilov's.[23] After 1993, the CPRF was the only serious left party, with 12.4 per cent of the vote.

Financial Origins

Aleksei Podberezkin once said money was one of the CPRF's 'most terrible secrets'.[24] With its tight internal discipline, the CPRF has managed to keep most of these secrets. Some things, however, eventually become too big to hide. In the words of one analyst, referring to another original sin in 1917: 'In a way it's traditional, like Lenin taking money from the Germans for the Revolution.'[25] Some of the proceeds from the orgy of money laundering in the late Soviet era found their way to the successor parties, as money placed in commercial structures or abroad was funnelled back through old contacts and companies such as the notorious Seabeco and Nordex. In August 1990 deputy party chair Volodymyr Ivashko wrote a secret memorandum on creating 'an invisible party economy',[26] leading to the establishment of a special 'First Directorate' working group within the Central Committee in October 1990 under Ivashko, KGB heads Kriuchkov and Bobkov, and Nikolai Kruchina, who was in charge of party property at the Central Committee. In another memorandum, written to Kruchina in 1990, KGB officer Leonid Veselovskii described this particular special operation: 'to create a stable source of revenue, irrespective of what may happen to the Party', via 'special rapid response groups' and 'trusted individuals', and building up a network of shadow banks and trading enterprises.[27] Ivashko was an emblematic figure. He had been installed by Gorbachev as Ukrainian Communist Party leader in September 1989 as a replacement for the aging Brezhnevite Volodymyr Shcherbytskyi. This was in many ways a shrewd move. The national-democratic opposition, Rukh, based in west and central Ukraine was challenging for power. Ivashko was from Kharkiv in east-central Ukraine and, unlike Shcherbytskyi, spoke Ukrainian and Russian equally well. As a typical Soviet Ukrainian, he was better placed to keep a united Ukraine in the Soviet camp than a Ukrainophobe from the far east, that is, the Donbas or Crimea.

Unfortunately, he was also typical of Soviet Ukrainians in his venality. He could have made a good career for himself, and lots of money, as head of the nascent independent Ukraine – as first president Leonid Kravchuk allegedly did in his stead.[28] It had to be a pretty good offer to trump that: it was to help organise the last years of the CPSU's leeching and bleaching of state funds.

An estimated $2.5 billion was spirited away in Gorbachev's last months (bizarrely, but credibly, so-called 'loyalty forms' were printed for an alleged fifty thousand 'trustees' for the money).[29] For comparison, the entire official Russian banking sector had barely this much capital in 2001. The fact that much bigger sums are now laundered on a regular basis hardly excuses such hypocrisy at such a key moment. Nikolai Kruchina threw himself out of a window after the failure of the coup, leaving a file of incriminating documents and a note that protested: 'I am not a conspirator, I am a coward!' Significantly, most of the other suicides or suspicious deaths at this time, including that of the Central Committee administrator, Georgii Pavlov, involved those caught up in the party's money trail.[30] That said, most of the larger sums involved in late-Soviet money laundering have probably not found their way into the coffers of the successor Communist parties. There were better opportunities elsewhere.

Still, some money found its way back as planned. According to one analysis made in 1996, 'the basic finance for the activity of the [Russian Communist Party's] federal leadership comes from funds already laid by in commercial structures (in part abroad) before August 1991 – that part of the notorious "CPSU money" which was not plundered by its "custodians" with the changing circumstances, and also was not talentlessly squandered like the money entrusted to [the likes of] Andrei Zavidiia.' Zavidiia was the businessman who served as Zhirinovskii's running mate in 1991 and was also the first sponsor of the Red-Brown newspapers *Den* and *Sovetskaia Rossiia*.

Part of these resources were recovered thanks to [the 'Red Banker'] Vladimir Semago [one of the richest cooperative kings of the Gorbachev era, owner of the Golden Palace casino chain and later a key figure in Mosbiznesbank],[31] by all accounts the intermediary between the leadership of the party and the party businessmen. According to rumour, the same Semago received fairly large sums from Artiom Tarasov [later a key player in the World Chess Federation] after the latter's return to Russia – not excluding that the aforementioned 'pioneer of Russian capitalism' [yet another founder of the cooperative movement, whose trading company, Istok, was used to cream off various raw-material surpluses] partly learnt to crawl through 'CPSU money'. . . . As is claimed, the sums returned by Tarasov were left to circulate '*na prokrutku*' [monies given over to a bank without interest for three months as a pay-off for previous or future services] in Mosbiznesbank (Vladimir Bukato) and Tver Universal Bank (at that time [under the influence of Nikolai] Ryzhkov) and deductions were then regularly placed 'in rotation' with the CPRF.[32]

Other key backers in the early 1990s included Grigorii Kuevda, another cooperative pioneer, Valerii Neverov, head of the Hermes trading group, and the Mikom concern run by the Zhivilo brothers.

A slightly different slant on events is provided by Robert Otto, who in 1999 wrote:

> Semago maintains that in the twilight of the Soviet era, a good deal of the CPSU's funds were invested in a variety of commercial structures. After the formation of the CPRF in 1993 [Valentin] Kuptsov negotiated for the return of some of this money. The pivotal moment came in 1995, when he agreed to drop these efforts. According to Semago (certainly not a disinterested source), abandoning the claims enabled Kuptsov to reach a 'series of extremely promising' agreements with the powers that be.[33]

Others, including Aleksandr Lebed in his time, have alleged that the CPRF was receiving a share of state funds as early as 1993–94.[34] Some was relatively small change. After the CPRF's success in the 1995 elections, official largesse from the state budget to political parties was 'said to provide up to 95 per cent of its funding by such means as funding the approximately eight hundred parliamentary aides who doubled as the party's unofficial *apparat*'.[35] Some budget money also came from local governors hedging their bets.[36] More serious by far, especially as the CPRF – included Yeltsin's responsibility for the first Chechen debacle in the impeachment charges it laid against him in 1999, is the suggestion that the party creamed off funds allocated for the reconstruction of Chechnia (most of the $3 billion approved being allegedly misappropriated).[37] Thanks to the Communists' lobbying efforts, much of this money was channelled through Viktor Vidmanov's Agropromstroibank set up with old party capital in 1992, later involved in the mobster-linked Chara bank that collapsed in 1994,[38] and Agropromservis. Vidmanov,[39] the former RSFSR minister for village construction and therefore well connected with others of his Brezhnev generation who helped him set up the Rosagropromstroi corporation, with numerous banking affiliates and a workforce of some 700,000, was the Communists' main early financier. Vidmanov's bank and its construction offshoots under Rosagropromstroi reportedly received 16 billion roubles from the state in 1995–96, of which 700 million roubles (then worth over $150 million) went missing. Vidmanov's firms were also accused of overcharging by 30 per cent for their services.[40] Vidmanov no doubt had many personal uses for the money, but he was rewarded with a place on the party presidium in 1997 after helping finance Ziuganov's 1996 campaign, as well as numerous foreign trips, party congresses and the party's head office on Moscow's Tsvetnoi Boulevard. He also provided capital for *Pravda* and other party publications.[41]

The fact that the party was given access to such huge sums at such a key stage in the political process was obviously intended to constrain its future behaviour as well as pre-empt any broader opposition 'front', such as the alliance then being mooted between the CPRF and Yabloko. The Communists' incorporation into the spoils system developed further under the Primakov government in 1998–9. Leading

Communist Yurii Masliukov served as first deputy prime minister, while the Communists' Agrarian allies provided the deputy prime minister, Gennadii Kulik, both of whom 'allegedly diverted state funds into party coffers'.[42] Much of the party's finance in this period came from Rosenergoatom, via Masliukov,[43] as well as, again, Agropromstroibank, Rosagropromstroi, Inter-Marketing and FM-Building.[44] Allegations also surfaced of Masliukov's links to another of the usual suspects, Mosbiznesbank, then controlled by the notorious Ashot Egiazarian (after 1999 a deputy for Zhirinovskii's Liberal-Democratic Party), and to Leonard Vid at Alfa-Bank; there were even rumours of his cosy relations with Anatolii Chubais, the Communists' main public *bête noire*. Businesses linked to the CPRF also received a large share of Saddam Hussein's oil-for-favours money: an alleged $23.3 million over five years, until May 2002.[45]

Money from Oligarchs

One of Ziuganov's many ghost-written books contains a succinct rationale for the Communists' accommodation with domestic capital: 'We defend a private apartment against burglars, and a street stall against racketeers. We defend a Russian commercial bank against the foreign Chase Manhattan or Bavaria Bank.'[46] In return, Russian oligarchs who liked to spread their bets (Gusinskii, Luzhkov, Potanin, who was close to Ziuganov through Yevgenii Kiselev of NTV) have long provided top-up financing for the party – like the businessmen in Weimar Germany who thought they could control all potential threats by paying all sides. In Russia, however, the down payment was fairly cheap, and the political threat not so real. Gusinskii provided most funds for the 1995 campaign, hence his NTV station being almost neutral towards the CPRF.[47] Companies close to Gusinskii, Smolenskii and Berezovskii (Most-bank, Menatep, SBS-Agro and Oneksim) funded Ziuganov's campaign in 1996.[48] According to Aleksii Sitnikov, the top CPRF leadership had to be bought off discreetly: 'The oligarchs paid the Communists themselves, in safe havens.'[49] The fact that the same men, both the oligarchs and the political technologists such as Sitnikov, also boasted of organising Yeltsin's victory, indicates the way they work.

According to Valentin Falin, former head of the Central Committee's International Department:

> As concerns links with oligarchs, I would remind you that the Bolsheviks received millions in subsidies from big businessmen, bankers, aristocrats. . . . Prince Obolenskii gave a million roubles, Rybakov – the banker – millions, [Savva] Morozov [the Moscow millionaire and arts patron] bequeathed 100,000 roubles and before that gave hundreds of thousands [not to mention the alleged 50 million gold Marks from Germany in 1917-18]. I share the view of those who consider that big-business corporations worked with [all sides]. And in so far as we have two forces – the centre-right and a powerful left – these boys for sure financed one and the other to be on the safe side. Why? The self-preservation principle.[50]

The CPRF Duma lobby was at its most attractive from 1995 to 1999, the CPU's from 1994 to 2002. In both countries almost every leading oligarch at this time had some link with the Communists, as the size of the two parties' parliamentary factions was just so tempting. Much of the CPRF's initial funding in the early 1990s came from the raw-material (oil and gas) and agrarian sectors. (Chernomyrdin and Ziuganov developed close personal links as early as 1994; the then prime minister also had links to Vidmanov's Agropromstroibank.) Gazprom was repeatedly alleged to be a key secret source of money.[51] Its boss, Rem Viakhirev, went public with an appeal to the party to help preserve its patriotic gas monopoly in April 1997. Gazprom also made use of *Pravda* in the 2000 'aluminium wars'. Kuptsov lobbied on behalf of the Perm businessman Dmitrii Rybolovlev.[52] Another Spiritual Heritage veteran (a former deputy head of the KGB's Fifth Directorate), Valerii Vorotnikov, number twelve on the party's 1995 list, provided a link to Gusinskii (Vorotnikov's security firm, Vzor, is a subsidiary of Most). Vorotnikov's former boss, Filipp Bobkov, led an exodus of former KGB to Most-bank in 1992, bringing with him many of his contacts on both left and right, Gusinskii having been set up to run the KGB's favourite bank on its behalf in 1989. However, the Communists' *prodazhnost* ('availability for sale') meant casually cynical relations with all their sponsors: their Duma lobby lined up with Berezovskii against Chernomyrdin over the sale of Rosneft in 1998; Ziuganov *et al.* did nothing to save Gusinskii when his empire came under attack in 2000.

According to Andrei Piontkovskii of the Moscow Centre for Strategic Studies, 'in the 1995 Duma elections, the Communists got hand-outs from big banks and corporations who were hedging their bets in case the left won', particularly Oneksimbank, with its useful links to the newspaper *Izvestiia*. 'This time round [1999] the Communists hardly got anything, because no one believes they'll ever come to power. So they had to resort to other revenue sources.'[53] The possibilities for drawing on the state budget were also much more limited after Primakov fell from power in May 1999. Since the late 1990s, therefore, 'the Communists have changed their political resources,' and sought ever-closer relationships with potential sponsors.[54]

If phase one involved new Russian businessmen seeking favour with likely election winners, then phase two found them seeking Duma sinecures for them-selves via suitable 'hosts' – to act as lobbyists and enjoy the blanket immunity from prosecution granted by the 1993 constitution (which, it should be noted, guarantees only that 'no deputy may be detained, arrested, or searched except when detained in the act of perpetrating a crime', although the last proviso has been waived often enough). In the first stage, Red businessmen such as the flamboyant and perma-tanned Semago, seemed like colourful exceptions (he quarrelled with Gennadii Seleznev (see pages 257–8) and left to form his own 'New Leftists' party' in 1998). By the 1999 elections, however, the Communists' durability had earned them a new respectability. Companies such as Vinogradov's Inkombank were now less abashed about open sponsorship, as were Gazprom, and even Chubais's United Energy Systems. Imperial Bank, without a trace of irony, began to sponsor *Pravda*.

The Communists' list this time included five company managers, most notably Rikrat Shakirov of the Vniist energy company, Sergei Zolotilin of Progress and Renewal, and Igor Annenskii, president of Alba-Alliance Bank. Others belonged to a new generation of 'apoliticals', such as Igor Igoshin of Real-Agro, then less than thirty years of age. Others 'converged' with the party after the elections, such as Kirill Minovalov of the Avangard Bank, who ended up an adviser to the man the Communists were able to help install as chair of the Duma, Gennadii Seleznev. Several places on the party list were allegedly sold by Kuptsov for 'up to $1.5 million',[55] the high price being justified by the prospect of Communist control of the budget and banking committees. To secure more places, the Communists seconded many of their sponsors to the Agrarian-Industrial deputies' group. The most notable newcomer among the party's sponsors was Gennadii Semigin, a would-be sophisticate mocked by many as the 'Kolkhoz Elvis'. He had nevertheless made serious money in arms 'deliveries for the Ministry of Defence',[56] and headed the Congress of Russian Business Circles as well as holding a useful position on the board of the Russian Union of Industrialists and Entrepreneurs and Enterprise Bosses. Semigin also ensured places for two key allies, Valerii Shutuev and Sergei Proshchin, and reaped a good return on his investment (a reported '$2 million') by ending up as deputy chair of the Duma.[57] Seleznev, meanwhile, displayed an impressive ability to manipulate the favour system.[58] The Communists tried to cover some of their financial tracks in the 1999 campaign with a fundraising drive targeting pensioners for donations of 25,000 roubles. The average pension was then 500 roubles.[59]

The party's four main money men in the Putin era were Vidmanov and Semigin, Yevgenii Marchenko, a former director (with Zhirinovskii's financier Mikhail Gutseriev) of the Ingush finance company BIN, and Piotr Romanov, formerly of Yenisei chemicals in Krasnoiarsk. Zhores Alferov, vice-president of the Academy of Sciences and winner of the Nobel Prize for physics, but also a leading electro-energy businessman, was also one of the party's leading business 'pragmatists', as was Leonid Ivanchenko, party co-chair and yet another Red director.

Lurking in the shadows, however, was none other than the *velikii kombinator* ('smooth operator') Boris Berezovskii.[60] Once in exile (from November 2000), Berezovskii was obviously more inclined to support the 'opposition', but his links with the CPRF leadership went back to the 1996 campaign – after which he had briefly flirted with the idea of funding a new left party based on the Rybkin Bloc.[61] In the 1997 'information war' Berezovskii's press secretary, Vladimir Ruga, fed *Pravda* anti-Chubais material. Kuptsov enlisted Berezovskii to see off the Greek businessman Yannis Yannikos, after his investment in *Pravda* from 1992 to 1996 began to produce an editorial line that was rather too truthful and critical of the compromises made by the party leadership. Berezovskii also backed Prokhanov's paper for Red intellectuals, *Zavtra* ('Tomorrow'), which combined national Communism with 'anti-globalism', and in 2002 funded Aleksandr Prokhanov's *roman-à-clef Mr Hexagon* (and an expensive advertising campaign) through the publisher Ad marginem, close to the oligarch's old car company, Logovaz. Prokhanov's prize-winning novel was a surrealist version of Berezovskii's allegations about the 1999 apartment bombings (the title being a reference to the explosive used in one of the blasts). Berezovskii's main business link to the Communists was through Vidmanov, who was now Ziuganov's key business asset. Much publicity was given by state media during the 2003 elections to the alleged visit to Berezovskii in London in October 2002 made by CPRF deputy Leonid Maevskii and former ideology secretary Aleksandr Kravets in search of 'finance . . . and political support'.[62] A 'first tranche' of '$3.2 million' was allegedly paid in 2003 through Vidmanov.[63]

It is in this light that the CPRF's troubles in 2002–03 can best be understood. The split between Ziuganov and Vidmanov and the Seleznev group was not ideological. Nor was it a simple opposition between 'true believers' and 'moles' (see pages 257–60). If one group was now deemed by the Kremlin to be too close to the exiled Berezovskii and his partial business successor, the other had closer links to businesses approved by the presidential administration and to the St Petersburg political faction. Hence the Kremlin backing the latter, in the hope of re-creating a left movement as docile as that of the best Yeltsin years. More generally, the powers-that-be did not want the Communists to develop too many independent resources. The Kremlin was determined 'that the [Communist] party be financed by business groups more loyal to power' (therefore ultimately not Yukos; see page 234), and thereby to make it clear that it was 'not the sponsor who should be loyal to Ziuganov, but Ziuganov to the sponsor'.[64] The CPRF, on the other hand, calculated that their voters wouldn't care or even notice. As one commentator put it: 'the electorate doesn't vote for a list, but for a brand',[65] and the Communists' was still one of the best known. In summer 2003, therefore, the Kremlin launched a PR campaign against Vidmanov, with Seleznev sanctioning a Duma investigation claiming that Rosagropromstroi had received a further 450 million budget roubles between 1998 and 2001 from the rural building programme 'Svoi dom', after energetic lobbying by the CPRF's Yurii Voronin, chair of the Duma budget committee – of which 200 million supposedly disappeared.[66]

By 2003 the CPRF had reached a third stage in its financial development. Prominent business sponsors from 1999 such as Semigin, Igoshin and Annenskii were happy to repeat their investment. Gutseriev's BIN bank was again represented, this time by Alikhan Amirkhanov. The party also had some new 'parachutists', such as Nikolai Lugovskii, whose joint Russian-Belize citizenship would doubtless have raised a few eyebrows among ordinary party rank and file had it been more widely known. However, to the biggest businesses, 'the sale of [individual] seats on lists as practised by the LDPR and CPRF [in 1999 had] become frankly archaic'. Putin's chief party technologist, Vladislav Surkov, and his business friends were more interested in larger investments capable of changing the party's 'general line' and promoting the business-friendly policies of 'Semigin, Kuptsov and [Sergei] Glazev',[67] as well as the likes of Gennadii Khodyrev, who captured the liberal 'model city' of Nizhnii-Novgorod in 2001 (not a good example, or perhaps a perfect one, as he left the party soon after), rather than simply parachuting one or two colleagues on to the party's list. The more ambitious oligarchs believed 'it was no longer necessary to fear the Communist Party – it was necessary to buy it'.[68] Other businessmen, relative outsiders, reluctantly accepted that supporting the CPRF was one way of keeping the Kremlin monster under control. Many rank-and-file Communists, on the other hand (now that such schemes were leaking out into wider circles than in the early 1990s), deluded themselves that they were simply 'getting back' the people's money, or that the oligarchs were seeking to ensure that 'they would not be shot first when [the CPRF] won power'.[69]

Oleg Deripaska of Russian Aluminium was the main new sponsor, via his channel of influence to Semigin and Kuptsov. As Deripaska's aim was to promote a two-party system with a newly moderate opposition, the Kremlin was broadly neutral to his venture.[70] Potanin and Interros (that is, vice-president Sergei Batchikov, a past supporter of Glazev) 'quickly joined the game' with a promise of $11.5 million.[71] The CPRF was also reportedly fishing for money from Gazprom, after a meeting with CEO Aleksei Miller in May. According to several reports, the energy giant Yukos, which was closer to Ziuganov, was initially prepared to invest $70 million in the Communists ($10 million a year for five years, with double that amount in the Duma election years of 2003 and 2007) if the new line were to prevail – but only for a sizeable 'packet' of seats (reportedly ten: five on the national list and five in the regions).[72] According to another version of events, Yukos was prepared to invest $12.5 million in return for five places on the list.[73] The leadership was pragmatic enough to adapt. Reportedly, according to a 'source within the CPRF' in 2003, 'when Ziuganov was offered financial assistance by one such businessman at a meeting, he asked point blank how many places on the party list he was expected to provide'.[74] Yukos also helped the Communists set up an 'information and technology centre' run by ex-Yukos manager Ilia Ponomarev and Yaroslav Grekov, the founder of the *kachka* websites www.ricn.ru and www.cremlin.ru; this was charged with developing counter-measures against all active measures to split the CPRF vote (see page 263). Their promise that 'modern campaigning techniques' could add 5–7 per cent to the party's vote was never really tested;[75] but herein lay the danger of a deal, even one that was initially prompted by the Kremlin. Yukos and Khodorkovskii may have hoped to use a 'modernised', 'social-democratic' CPRF as a springboard for their own ambitions during the next electoral cycle in 2007–08. Neutering the Communists was one thing, helping them was another. Nor did the Kremlin's managers want the independent businessmen they were trying to cut down to size to enter the Duma by the back door. As such, the deal crashed spectacularly. Moreover, in part, both Yukos and the Communists were simply set up to destroy one another (see pages 109–10). Nevertheless, according to one insider, overall the Communist leadership collected 'a total of $25 million in 2003' – a lot of money, even by Western parties' standards – 'but only $5 million was spent on their campaign'.[76] The party's disappointing performance meant that only ten out of forty businessmen on the list were elected, forcing a reluctant leadership to hand out some painful refunds.[77]

Ritual Opposition, Regular Support

> Thank God. We lost. The party is saved.
>
> Senior adviser to the CPRF Central Committee, 1996[78]

Passivity was normally what was required of the CPRF, although *in extremis* the party could be called on to take the kind of action that seriously risked its oppositional image: for instance, helping to frustrate a no-confidence vote in the Duma as early as October 1994. The CPRF has ignored at least four golden political opportunities. In October 1993 Ziuganov knew precisely what was expected of him if the CPRF were also not to be banned, appearing twice on state TV to call for calm (right after Gaidar) – specifically addressing the defenders of the White House, many of whom were members of his own party. In 1996 the Communists were not exactly charging at the barricades. Kuptsov blocked attempts to set up a party press centre, declaring loftily that it was a matter best left to the Duma.[79] Ziuganov's behaviour between the rounds was extremely passive for a man who claimed to have been robbed of a real lead in the first round (he was supposedly behind by 32.5 per cent to 35.8 per cent) – especially as he undoubtedly knew of Yeltsin's sudden illness. According to Podberezkin, the 'campaign was artificially wound up'.[80] After the second round, Ziuganov accepted defeat at 12.30, long before the count was complete. Korzhakov's memoir states that Podberezkin and Ziuganov would have acquiesced in the postponement of an election they were at one time strong favourites to win.[81]

In 1998 the CPRF failed to mobilise against the regime after the August economic crisis, bravely setting its first demonstration to take place on 19 October. In 1999 the Communists failed to join forces with the ousted hero of the left, Primakov – instead Ziuganov agreed with Berezovskii not to obstruct the appointment of the young and liberal Sergei Kirienko (the so-called *kinder-siurpriz*) as prime minister in return for the green light to begin the symbolic attempt to impeach Yeltsin.[82] At this time, Ziuganov and Berezovskii allegedly met frequently in diplomatic residences or private offices.[83] The party provided between twenty-five and forty votes for Kirienko in April 1998.[84] The affair provided the clearest possible demonstration of the Communist leadership's priorities: a revolutionary challenge to the regime was clearly off limits; an introspective sop to its rank-and-file members was worth much more in terms of prolonging its own tenure. Arguably, in fact, the impeachment tactic only undermined Primakov by raising the stakes for Yeltsin. And, of course, the Communists did nothing to hasten Yeltsin's departure, serving only as passive spectators of the succession drama.

All this time, the People's Patriotic Union under the *de facto* control of Kuptsov was being allowed to atrophy, regularly losing key members such as Rutskoi, Govorukhin and the polemicist Yurii Ivanov.[85] By 2004 the CPRF would abandon it altogether. Even after the Communists' humiliation at the polls in 2003 (see pages 263–4), the leadership was happy to do the Kremlin's bidding in 2004, scotching all talk of a boycott and appearing grateful for the meagre crumbs of second place. Passivity was now ingrained in the party culture.

Mention has already been made of the administrative resources the CPRF received in return. The Communists have also benefited from soft treatment at election time, especially for the Duma elections in 1993, 1995 and 1999. In addition, Ziuganov was given considerable media access, particularly in the 1999 elections, including long interviews on the state-controlled channels RTR and ORT. At the time the regime was more concerned about the threat from Fatherland-All Russia. According to one analysis, the media onslaught against FAR 'appears to have boosted the CPRF's final vote by up to 5 per cent'.[86] Presidential elections, of course, had a different logic. Ziuganov was treated with kid gloves initially to ensure he made the second round in 1996 and 2000 – then slaughtered to make sure he stayed in his place.

'His Majesty's Official Opposition': The Communist Party of Ukraine

According to Volodymyr Polokhalo, 'the new Communist Party of Ukraine [CPU] was the first virtual project in Ukraine'.[87] A party that had basically banned itself (the suspension decision on 30 August 1991 was taken by the presidium of parliament, whose membership overlapped by two-thirds with that of the CPU Politburo) was always likely to influence the terms of its eventual revival, albeit in the first case by free-riding on the plans of others. According to Polokhalo again, a 'first transitional project was the Socialist Party' of Oleksandr Moroz, established in October 1991.[88] This hastily assembled 'moderate opposition' project helped to soak up the energies of the old rank and file, while leaving the party's old guard free to pursue other opportunities. One insider, Adam Martyniuk, former Communist boss in Lviv, declared at a private meeting of the Veterans' Union in April 1992 that the purpose of the new party was 'to [re]form the Communist Party, but under a different name . . . 90 per cent of the existing members of the Socialist Party are Communists who temporarily find themselves' in a different home.[89] Private contacts determined the limits of permissible activity. Above all this meant no serious challenge to Ukrainian independence.

In autumn 1991 Leonid Kravchuk was well on the way to the presidency, but he was never senior enough in the CPU to challenge the old guard (Stanislav Hurenko, Martyniuk, Red directors such as Volodymyr Matvieiev) when they began moves to re-establish the CPU in early 1993. In January, 242 deputies called for a review of the 1991 banning decision sometime during the first half of the year. It was originally placed only ninety-fifth out of 135 parliamentary questions, but Kravchuk was soon forced to change his mind by the growing economic crisis, especially the strike wave that hit the Donbas in the summer of 1993.[90] Kravchuk wanted to head off the growth of a really powerful opposition, especially one that might reopen the property issue – an issue of paramount importance to all those former Communists who had inherited the party's goods. According to no less an authority than Volodymyr Lytvyn (see below), as with Yeltsin and the CPRF, Kravchuk 'met confidentially with the leaders of the movement for reviving the Communist Party and discussed with them ways of unblocking the indicated question', i.e., concerning the ban.[91] As in autumn 1991, there was much private conditionality on the national question: the party would be reborn as the CPU, not as a local branch of the old CPSU, and as the 'new' CPU, not the old; demands for the restitution of all Communist property were to be safely ritualised (members of the smaller Union of Communists of Ukraine, who backed a radical line on both issues, were eased out of leadership positions at the congress); and former leader Hurenko would stay in the background – even though he effectively organised and bankrolled the 1993 congress on home territory.[92] Petro Symonenko, former second secretary of the old party in Donetsk, was chosen instead. At the same time, Kravchuk also unsuccessfully proposed to the writer and former Gorbachev aide Borys Oliinyk that he 'create a properly national Communist Party'.[93] After 1993 the Socialist Party increasingly took on this role instead. Its 'neo-Communist' sleeper membership transferred to the new CPU; the two parties were in initial alliance, but the Socialists began to drift into opposition after 1998.

The new Communist Party's east Ukrainian financiers, on the other hand, really were playing with fire. In 1993–94 they backed both Kravchuk's former prime minister (and quintessential Red director) Leonid Kuchma and the Communists. Kuchma secretly contacted the Communists between March and June 1994, after the CPU polled much better than his own party, the Interregional Bloc for Reforms, at the parliamentary elections in the spring (the CPU won 28 per cent of the seats). According to Kravchuk again: 'I have information that at that moment there was already clear agreement between Petro Symonenko, Oleksandr Moroz and Leonid Kuchma concerning support for the latter. They met several times one on one and together.' Although the CPU plenum between the rounds of the summer presidential election decided on a position of formal neutrality, 'a second unofficial decision' had already been taken at the beginning of July to work where possible for Kuchma,[94] who duly defeated Kravchuk by 52.1 per cent to 45.1 per cent in the second round.

Hence, albeit for different reasons, the new Ukrainian Communists were just as tightly enmeshed in the local political system as their Russian kin. As a confident Russophile, Kuchma's forceful first chief of staff, Dmytro Tabachnyk, laid down the rules to the party faction in 1994–96.[95] Thereafter, the Communists' main link was with Volodymyr Lytvyn, head of the presidential administration from 1999 to 2002, but in his previous life an aide to Hurenko from 1989 until August 1991.[96] Lytvyn was extremely close to the Communists' party whip, Adam Martyniuk, who sometimes worked with Bankivska direct without informing Symonenko. According to Polokahlo, 'the personal link between Lytvyn and Martyniuk is one of the most important in all Ukrainian politics'.[97] In the main, the 'inner party' have always been 'latent supporters' of the powers-that-be.[98] Major Melnychenko has said of his taped treasure: 'I did not go to Symonenko, because I knew Symonenko and Kuchma are one and the same.'[99] On the tapes, Kuchma dismissively refers to Symonenko's 'constant nervousness', and the official leaders of the new Communist Party as 'remnants of the most unfortunate types'.[100]

After the 2002 elections the position of the inner party if anything grew stronger. In December 2001 the Constitutional Court declared the original 1991 ban illegal. At a special 'unity congress' in May 2002 the 'old' party was symbolically revived and merged with the 'new'. Hurenko did not revive his leadership ambitions, however, in return for a strengthening of his control of party finance and the *apparat*. The party was now effectively a duumvirate, with Symonenko only its public face. The threat of reviving property claims, or publicising money trails involving the party's new business partners, led to a temporary improvement in party finances. Certainly, morale seemed to be very high for a party that had just suffered a serious electoral reversal (down to 20 per cent from 24.6 per cent in 1998) – as, unlike its equivalent in Russia, the party felt it would still have its uses for the authorities in 2004 (see page 177).

Finally, in the Ukrainian case it is worth pointing out that there are two channels of covert influence, given the party's close contacts in the north. According to Marat Gelman, 'Kuptsov is curator of the Ukrainian party', and 'part of its finances, when necessary, come directly from the Kremlin'.[101]

Links with Oligarchs

In its revival year (1993), the CPU received support from east Ukrainian Red directors seeking to displace President Leonid Kravchuk from power, including the heads of Azovstal and the huge Zasiadka mine in the Donbas, as well as from Red director-politicians such as Oleksandr Bulianda and Zasiadka's Yukhym Zviahilskyi.[102] Kravchuk would, of course, have known of this: hence, for both sides, the choice of Symonenko, who was well known in such circles, and after 1991 had worked as deputy director of the huge local coke plant Ukrvuhlemash. At this early stage neither Hurenko nor Grach was prepared to risk their business interests in what then seemed a risky project.

In the mid-1990s the party's darkest secret was its links with Pavlo Lazarenko. His brief tenure as prime minister in 1996–97 served as a rough Ukrainian equivalent of the Primakov era in Russia (1998–99), in that the Communists were then at their closest to power (hence, again, the Ukrainian Communists were corrupted earlier). In 1998 many Communists were contemplating backing Lazarenko for the presidency. It was only after he became publicly caught up in the Panamanian passport scandal (see page 157) that they agreed to side with Kuchma to neutralise the greater danger (to their own dominance on the left) of Lazarenko backing the Socialist leader, Oleksandr Moroz.[103] Some of Oleksandr Volkov's Social Defence Fund money then went to the CPU to get it to play ball in 1999. Volkov allegedly 'ensured' that the easily defeatable Communist leader Symonenko stayed in the race against Kuchma in 1999, thereby blocking the challenge of his more electable Socialist rival,[104] despite many moderates urging Symonenko to withdraw in his favour.

After the 1999 election the tables temporarily turned. Attacking the left was now a popular task, with at least two oligarchic groups competing to put them in their place. Hence a certain initial confusion between rival projects presented at court (see pages 254–5). First was again Volkov. Moroz initially declared that the new Communist Party of Ukraine (renewed), or CPU(r), 'should be called the CPU(v), the Communist Party of Oleksandr Volkov'.[105] Ultimately, however, the project was controlled by the Labour Ukraine group. Given Labour Ukraine's eastern roots and links to the defence and security services, manipulation of the left was something of a speciality, particularly for Viktor Pinchuk and Ihor Sharov, another free-spending gas entrepreneur. Mykhailo Savenko, nominal leader of the CPU(r), was previously in Labour Ukraine. Most of the defectors enticed away from the CPU in 2000 found a comfortable home in Labour Ukraine (four – Druziuk, Kyrychenko, Kondratenko and Synenko – head of the committee on legal policy), no more than one went to any other faction. Labour Ukraine was also the main home for defectors from Nataliia Vitrenko's Progressive Socialist Party once the latter was no longer considered a useful force. Symonenko's son was married to the daughter of Kataryna Vashchuk of the Agrarian Party and worked for Pinchuk's Privatbank. Vashchuk, then the *de facto* head of her party, acted as a go-between.

Support from the third main oligarchic group, the SDPU(o), went mainly to Leonid Grach, leader of the Communists in Crimea (see pages 247–8). Whenever the Social Democrats' fortunes seemed to be on the slide (as in late 2001) and the hostility of other oligarchs grew, the party needed the insurance of some extra support in parliament. Just as a useful relationship had developed between Kuchma and Symonenko, the SDPU(o) hoped to count on informal lobby support from that part of the Communist Party close to Grach, even promoting him as a rival leader. Such links were also useful to the SDPU(o)'s reinvention of its image to target south-east Ukraine in the 2002 elections, having largely exposed its true nature in the far west since 1998.

The Communists were always close to the Donestsk clan. On one of Major Melnychenko's tapes dated August 2000, Viktor Yanukovych, then in charge of Donetsk oblast, complains to Kuchma that he has given them so much, but that 'they take the money and do everything the opposite'. He decides to set up his own, more reliable, faction (Regions of Ukraine) instead. Some Communists have already defected (see above) so 'we're clipping his [Symonenko's] wings a little.' But 'besides those we're pulling away, there's still plenty in his faction with whom we can maintain links, and, in principle, will go along with everything' being planned. Kuchma helpfully suggests shafting the Socialists and Yuliia Tymoshenko's Fatherland faction at the same time.[106]

The relationship was so close that the Communist leadership acquiesced in the destruction of their electoral base in the Donbas between the elections of 1998 and 2004 (see pages 130 and 243). In the 2004 presidential race, Symonenko ran an extraordinarily passive campaign as lapdog to Yanukovych, whose chances of victory depended on poaching almost all of the Communists' traditional electorate. According to one source, 'Almost 670,000 [votes] in Donetsk and Luhansk were added to Yanukovych with [the CPU leaders'] approval.' Certainly, it was hardly plausible that Symonenko won only 3.3 per cent in Donetsk, less than his national score of 5 per cent, or 5.8 per cent in Luhansk, compared to Yanukovych's 86.7 per cent and 80 per cent.

All the major oligarchic parties have paid the CPU for extra 'golden shares in parliament' (directly, not through the president), and the Communists have repaid their clients by 'lobbying for privileges for tractor lubricant suppliers at sowing and harvest times, for VAT recovery terms, customs problems, etc.' 'In some circles, conscientious lobbying is regarded almost as the Communists' calling card.'[107] The CPU's key direct business sponsors were in the agrarian sector (the bread and salt companies Krymkhlib and Ukrsil) and among the 'metal monsters', as the party faction often helped to secure licences for the big exporters (such as the Zaporizhzhia Illich metallurgy works). In January 2004 the CPU was named as the biggest Ukrainian recipient of Saddam Hussein's oil-for-favours payments, receiving an alleged six million barrels of oil.[108] A third source was industry in regional strongholds that tended to be Russophile or part of the military-industrial complex (the Donbas locomotive factory, Luhanskteplovoz, the Mykolaïv shipbuilding factory; Khartron, which makes high-tech electronic equipment for aviation and aerospace control systems). In more recent years the party has cooperated with energy baron Kostiantyn Hryhoryshyn, a former partner of both Lazarenko and Surkis, who is reportedly close to Rinat Akhmetov, 'boss' of the Donbas.[109] Hurenko has strong links with Oleksandr Borovyk, a leading figure in agribusiness and friend of the president, with strong influence in both the Peasant and Agrarian parties. Tsentrenergo and the capital's residential construction company Kyïvmiskbud also provided funds.

Party Businesses

The CPU is not a poor party. More exactly, in the words of one Ukrainian analyst, 'the Communist Party may not want the money, but certain Communists do'. However, like their Russian comrades, 'they are quite a close circle; they keep their secrets'.[110] The Communists' '"inner party" consists of Hurenko, Adam Martyniuk (the party Cerberus and the authorities' key "administrative partner"), Matvieiev, and at one time Yevhen Marmazov'. (In the late 1990s Marmazov was deputy head of the Rada fuel and energy committee, had interests in the power-supply market and served as a key link with Moscow business circles.)[111] The first three controlled the party *apparat*, not Symonenko; Hurenko has always controlled the purse strings. They kept the ambitious Grach at bay, and ensured that Symonenko, whom they looked down on as a former *komsomolite* (he was a lowly secretary in the youth movement for six years), acted as their front-man and contact with the president, if necessary, via Vashchuk. Significantly, the party's ideologues have gradually lost importance, like Heorhii Kriuchkov, who was only fourteenth on the 2002 party list.

Apart from the likes of Hurenko and Grach (for his business interests see pages 246–8), Communist businessmen tend to represent state behemoths – such as Matvieiev, deputy general director of Mykolaïv's main shipbuilding concern, and Alla Aleksandrovska of Khartron, and numerous mining officials – or smaller private businesses, such as Volodymyr Petrenko of the Kiev firm Viktoriia-RUS, rather than Ukraine's new corporate giants. Ukraine's new banking class was noticeably absent from the party's 1998 list. Andrii Snihach ran a US–Ukrainian joint agro-venture in Kherson. Most were small-scale operators compared to the 'Red millionaires' in the Communist parties of Russia and Moldova. The same was true of the party's 2002 list, with most sponsors tucked away in the lower reaches of the list. This time around, the party also had to try to accommodate 113 sitting deputies (in 1998 it was happy to cull many of those who had voted for the 1996 constitution, or taken bribes that were too obvious). On the other hand, two party businessmen had grown in stature: Agrarian boss Omelian Parubok was now at number two, and 'trade unionist' Vasyl Khara was at number sixteen, thanks to his good connections with the business elite in the Donbas (so good, in fact, that he joined its Regions of Ukraine faction after the elections, as did another local 'loyal Communist', Oleh Panasovskyi). The only candidate to provoke discussion at the party's 2002 congress (apart from former prosecutor Mykhailo Potebenko; see page 243) was the unknown Mykhailo Loboda, a surprise 'parachute' appearance at number thirty on the list. Symonenko's story was that Loboda was 'a doctor . . . a wonderful professional'.[112] If so, he was a hard-working public sector professional of a very special type, since he was also the head of Ukrprofozdorovnytsia, the main post-Soviet workers' holiday fund.

Like the Russian Communists, their Ukrainian comrades benefited from money recycling in the early and mid-1990s. According to one source:

> the main party cashier is Hurenko. There are also in the party, if it can be so expressed, direct custodians of the party treasury chest. It is said that as a rule these are little-known individuals, who often formally have no link to the party; but firms, real estate, cars in which party money has been placed are registered in their names. Especially trustworthy comrades have party accounts in their names . . . this kind of scheme for putting aside party funds allows [the leadership] to acquire any sum painlessly at any moment, without attracting needless attention.[113]

Many of those 'close to hand' were repaying previous favours or protecting themselves against disclosures as to how exactly they made their money in the late 1980s or early 1990s. Secret ideological sympathisers were rather less important. The main vehicle for such 'returns' of funds was Privatbank (close to Labour Ukraine), one of Ukraine's seven largest banks, in which the inner party held an 'informal share'. Smaller sums came from Prominvestbank. The CPU also itself controlled Brokbiznessbank (headed by its informal ally Serhii Buriak), another of Ukraine's largest financial institutions, which bought a handy 10 per cent of Ukrainian Telecom for $15.4 million in 2000.[114] Once again, the post-Soviet scene cannot be understood without an appreciation of the true extent of regime degradation in the 1970s and 1980s.

In a speech in July 2001 Symonenko was prepared to admit that 'we must pay [more] attention to business projects'. One such project was Hurenko's metals trading company, Navasko, a privatised work collective under the control of its directors – one reason why its finances tended to be a closely guarded secret. Another was the DCC mobile telephone company, set up with some party capital in the late 1990s in Donetsk, but quickly sold on to regional boss Akhmetov. A third was the family of businesses brought on board when former parliamentary chair Oleksandr Tkachenko joined the party in February 2001,[115] including the Ukraïna bank. Tkachenko's links with the inner party went back to at least 1991 (see page 62) and the Land and People affair of the early 1990s. They helped ensure that the investigation headed by the Communist-friendly Donetsk deputy Mykhailo Chechitov (briefly in Volodymyr Shcherban's chronically misnamed Liberal Party) produced a whitewash report in November 1994.

Covert Conformism

Also like their Russian counterparts, the Ukrainian Communists' private behaviour has often been at odds with their public stance, and they have frequently collaborated with a regime they profess to abhor. Ukraine was the last post-Soviet state to adopt a new constitution, in June 1996, and much of the delay was due to the Communists' vehement opposition to a 'bourgeois' document that, according to their public rhetoric,[116] threatened to institutionalise the conversion of the common wealth into private property and the Soviet 'friendship of peoples' into 'Ukraine for the Ukrainians'. Nevertheless, the Communists provided twenty of the 315 votes in favour (ten more abstained and twenty did not vote). Without them, the necessary two-thirds majority (three hundred out of 450 votes) would not have been achieved.

In the 1999 presidential election, a more united left could easily have triumphed if it could have collectively backed Moroz. Symonenko was the first candidate to declare, and shunned all overtures from the Kaniv 4 (see page 158) either to ally with them or withdraw. This was not the action of a brave independent, however. His passive acceptance of his eventual defeat spoke volumes. Despite ritual protests, no use was really made of the thousands of Communists who sat on election committees.[117] At Symonenko's (first and only) press conference after the election, one journalist remarked 'you are smiling so happily – as if the people chose you and not Leonid Kuchma'.[118]

The Communists backed down during the January–February 2000 'velvet revolution' against the left leadership in parliament, despite their die-hard public stand against the resulting symbolic changes (especially the abolition of the November 1917 anniversary holiday). The party agreed to register and vote on

17 February after a private meeting between Symonenko and Kuchma.[119] (Melnychenko dates the key meeting to 9 February.) Vitrenko's Progressive Socialist Party was left holding the baby again, as during the shadow play surrounding the April 2000 referendum, when the Communists initially announced plans for a counter-referendum but then failed to join in the signature campaign with their ideological comrades. Clearly, the authorities preferred ritualised protest to be carried out by a party they more closely controlled.

The remaining Communists in parliament were privately happy to support some surprising legislative projects. During the first reading of plans to privatise Ukrtelekom in June 2000 (the sale was eventually put off until 2004), not a single Communist was among the small number of eighteen deputies who voted for the plan put forward by the Progressive Socialist Olena Mazur and Anatolii Khmelovyi. As Khmelovyi was himself a Communist, the absence of his support was particularly striking. The leftist alternative envisaged consolidation with the international service Ukrainian Telecom (Utel), a full and proper audit and the sale of 40 per cent of stock via open tender, with 25 per cent going to a 'strategic investor'. The Communists instead allowed the passage of the 'oligarchic' draft version of the plans, drawn up by Oleksii Kostusiev (Labour Ukraine) and Iryna Bielousova (Greens), which was more of an impetuous bargain sale: no Utel, no audit, sale of 50 per cent of shares minus one. In the same month a plan to grant an amnesty for flight capital received a surprising sixty-six Communist votes out of a total of 252 in favour.

The party failed to join in the protests during the Gongadze affair. Instead, its criticism of the 'Ukraine without Kuchma' campaign and 'the ultra-nationalist threat' echoed the notorious 'letter of three' signed by Kuchma, then Rada chair, Ivan Pliushch and, most unfortunately, prime minister Viktor Yushchenko. In January 2001 Communist abstentions saved the embattled prosecutor Mykhailo Potebenko in the key censure vote. A year later he turned up at number twenty on the party's list for the 2002 elections – providing key information resources in return for his own immunity from possible prosecution (see pages 116–17 for Potebenko's alleged corruption). Despite a mini-rebellion at the party's selection congress by rank-and-file members disturbed by the electoral risk of such a move, his selection was approved by 217 votes to thirty-eight. In return the Communists gained 'the scalps of those [supposedly nationalist students] who attacked the party's office in autumn 2000', a clear run as the 'only opposition party' in Ukraine,[120] and the hope that administrative resources would be used to keep mutual enemies such as Tymoshenko and Moroz's Socialist Party out of parliament. They were, but with insufficient effect. The Communists expected to do better in the elections, as they thought they had an understanding that twenty to thirty first-grade candidates would be given a fair run in the constituencies, but Kuchma ratted on the deal. The Communist vote dropped to 20 per cent (fifty-nine seats) and only six other constituency seats were won.

At the height of the Gongadze affair in April 2001, it was Communist votes that helped to unseat Prime Minister Yushchenko, who had squeezed the oligarchs to repay all back pensions and salary arrears in his sixteen months in office, rather than President Kuchma, who was facing allegations of corruption and complicity in political murder. A reported 17 million hrivnias (then worth approximately $3 million) changed hands.[121] The December 2001 Constitutional Court decision ruling the 1991 ban on the party 'unconstitutional' was also a rumoured payback and a huge boost to morale.

After the elections the Communists, still posing as an opposition party, helped ensure the defeat of the opposition in the parliamentary coup that reversed the voters' verdict (see pages 172–4), and were secretly happy to see their old contact Volodymyr Lytvyn installed in the powerful post of chair of parliament. There was no exact equivalent of the cynical deal between Unity and the Russian Communists to divide up influence in the Russian Duma after the 1999 elections, but a similar pattern of behaviour and reward was clear. First, the CPU reneged on a deal with the other opposition parties to back a rival slate for the parliamentary leadership that included Roman Bezsmertnyi (former presidential representative to the Rada) as a sop to Kuchma, and their own Adam Martyniuk. Second, in the key vote in which Lytvyn scraped the bare minimum of 226 votes, the Communists abstained, although both Potebenko and Grach voted in favour. The Communists were, however, primed to vote if the authorities' (i.e., Medvedchuk's) preferred method, enticing 'cuckoos' away from the Yushchenko camp, had failed to produce enough votes. [122]

Symonenko attempted to explain the Communists' action by claiming that both Our Ukraine and For a United Ukraine were 'parties of big capital'. This was rather disingenuous. The authorities were offering control of some committees and help with 'material problems', whereas Yushchenko's socio-economic record and his (then) programme to reduce executive power had much in common with the CPU's formal manifesto. The Communists also helped their business friends in the Donbas in their attempted 'storming' of key parliamentary committees.[123] This was less successful – although Hennadii Vasyliev was made deputy chair of parliament, and the Donetsk clan seized control of the fuel and energy committee, a vital instrument in their struggle with the Social Democrats for control of the national energy market. The obvious pay-off was that the Communists, despite their much-reduced parliamentary strength, ended up controlling six committees (at the very same time that the CPRF was losing all of its strongholds in the Duma). Most useful in material terms was Hurenko again heading the economic policy committee, and Heorhii Kriuchkov the committee on national security and defence, a useful link to Russian interests. Kuchma and the government under Anatolii Kinakh, it should be pointed out, were at the time trumpeting a deepening of Ukraine's 'liberal' reforms. Their real priorities clearly lay elsewhere.

The return of Martyniuk as deputy chair of parliament in November 2003 heralded a renewal of even closer cooperation. If the Russian Communists were crashing to defeat in the Duma elections at this time, their Ukrainian counterparts were needed to try and head off Yushchenko's challenge in 2004. Over the winter of 2003–04 the Communists ran suspiciously parallel campaigns to two of the authorities' key initiatives: an anti-NGO campaign designed to prevent a 'Georgian scenario' of alleged Western interference developing in Ukraine (ie. a campaign against foreign NGOs) and the plans to amend the constitution to deny Yushchenko the fruits of his expected victory. In fact, the key reform project was popularly known as the 'Medvedchuk-Symonenko' plan.

Maintaining Credibility

The extent of possible complicity is always limited by the need to maintain credibility with electorates and rank-and-file party membership, and by leaderships' own capacity for double-speak. Left-wing electorates want both nostalgia symbolism and practical welfare gains. The CPU and CPRF have both therefore combined lobbying work for big business with control of the social defence and pensions committees. In their more sensible moments, the parties' handlers have accepted that the two functions can be simultaneously maintained. Many party members joined up for genuine ideological reasons, and were looking to create ideal-type parties free of the double-dealing of the late Soviet era. They were therefore harder to please than the phantom mass memberships of mainstream parties (often just a bunch of employees in party leaders' enterprises who signed up under duress). However, the CPRF's 547,000 members (as of 2000) or the CPU's 160,000 (2001) are not necessarily just the ideological residue left after the departure of the careerists (in Russian, *vremenshchiki*, 'those who live for today'). Both parties have an extremely elderly membership base, much of which was seeking to prove via nostalgia symbolism that they hadn't led wasted lives. They are therefore easier to placate. Indeed, arguably one aspect of their nostalgia culture involves replicating the sado-masochistic disciplines of democratic centralism.

Nevertheless, the CPRF rank and file staged a mini-revolt in 1996–97 after Ziuganov's quixotic challenge to Yeltsin in 1996; a radical Leninist-Stalinist platform enjoyed a brief existence within the party in 1998. Viktor Iliukhin was the most persistent leader of the party left, though even he was alleged to be sponsored by the big vodka companies Stolichnaia and Moskovskaia.[124] Party documents always came back more radical after discussion by party members. As Luke March has written, there is therefore a considerable difference between the CPRF's 'public' and 'party' ideologies: 'From 1995 onwards the party increasingly said totally different things to its core membership and wider electorate.'[125] Hence the periodic sops to the party membership to maintain public face, such as the attempts to impeach Yeltsin in 1999 and Kuchma in 1997.

Despite close covert links with both men, the Ukrainian Communists felt forced to back the removal of Pavlo Lazarenko's deputy's immunity in 1999, and to depose the odious Viktor Medvedchuk as deputy chair of parliament in 2001 – on both occasions on the eve of an election. In March 2002, however, the CPU still lost votes. Many of its pensioner supporters resented the leadership's role in the removal of Yushchenko, for the simple reason that he had cleared their pension backlog. The

CPU therefore temporarily joined the opposition after March, even campaigning for President Kuchma's impeachment in the autumn (the campaign being restarted on the second anniversary of Gongadze's disappearance). Bankivska allowed it to do so, confident that Kuchma faced no real threat, and because it wished to help the CPU rebuild its opposition image in advance of 2004. The real opposition, Our Ukraine, the Socialists and the Tymoshenko Bloc, campaigned on the assumption that the Communists would desert them – which they duly did at the end of 2003 (see page 177).

Communists Back in Power: Crimea

The cynical adaptation of the new Communist parties to post-Soviet realities can also be seen in the two places where they have actually returned to power. In Crimea they controlled the local assembly (but not the cabinet of ministers) from 1998 to 2002, and in Moldova they have held all the principal reins of power since winning an outright majority in the 2001 elections.

Crimea's Communists can claim to have been in the vanguard of the general post-Soviet Communist renaissance after 1991. Indeed, they were back almost before they went away. Their first vehicle, the Union of Communists of Crimea, was set up by the peninsula's last official CPSU boss, Leonid Grach, as early as May 1992, and was officially registered as the Communist Party of Crimea (CPC) by the local authorities in September 1993 (the first official party in Crimea). At the same time it was federating with the CPU, which led to a certain superiority complex concerning the broader party thereafter. Its finances are run separately, and the semi-autonomous Communist Party of Crimea often still uses its own name. The CPC was initially rumoured to be supported by the Crimean branch of the new Ukrainian security services (SBU) as an alternative to the greater danger of the more explicitly separatist Russia Bloc[126] – which was not incompatible with the SBU also backing the short-lived ultra-radical Communist Party of Workers of Crimea as a second bet in 1993. However, the CPC suffered from backing the White House opposition in autumn 1993, when both the CPRF and CPU remained largely silent.[127] In the 1994 Crimean elections it won only 11.6 per cent in the list vote (technically, the vote for the majority population; there were separate lists for the Crimean Tatars and four other minorities), coming second to the Russia Bloc and gaining only two seats overall. Grach, however, was busy recuperating. Communist Party funds laundered in the late Soviet era were used to set up the import-export business Impeks and its partner bank, plus a variety of fake funds and commercial fronts, including an all-union charitable newspaper, and, after channelling money via Bulgaria, the building of a lucrative aquapark for local tourists. Monies 'fanned out' through the Crimean version of *Pravda* were also controlled by Grach.[128]

By 1998 the CPC was better placed to take advantage of a double disarray: the implosion of the Russia Bloc and infighting in the local business parties. It also benefited from the abolition of the special representation quotas for minorities. This time the Communists won thirty-six seats out of a hundred, plus twenty-five allies in the People's Power faction; enough to win control of the local assembly, although they remained in intermittent conflict with the Council of Ministers, whose head now had to be approved by President Kuchma in Kiev. Since 1998 the party has established links with serious money in Crimea, mainly through the local branch of Labour Ukraine, a motley crew by any standards. Although in theory a scion of the national party, Crimean Labour was a flag of convenience for local powerbrokers: shady characters such as Volodymyr and Anatolii Tuterov, both linked to the Bashmaki and Sloni mafias, Mykola Kotliarevskyi, also known as Kolia the Killer, and old-guard criminals such as Oleksii Shatskykh and Vitalii Dychuk. (They were obviously old guard because Dychuk had three convictions from the bygone era when the local militia were actually brave enough to arrest him.)

Grach has been aptly described as 'a Chinese type of Communist';[129] not a fervent believer in Cultural Revolution, of course, but a 'pragmatic' new capitalist. Once back in office, to mix metaphors, he played the *padrone*: helping rebuild the main square in Simferopol, directing investments for his clan in the car company Krymavtogaz (whose commercial manager was another local Communist, Anatolii Lazariev) and talking grandiosely of building a bridge to Russia over the Kerch Straits. Most of the businesses under Grach's direct control, however, were small-to-medium in size: mainly petrol pump stations run by his sidekick Lentun Bezaziev, and alcohol sales. The party also hoped for a dividend from the privatisation of Krymtelekominvest, whose declaration of independence in 2001 from the national company, U-Tel, came as something of a surprise to leading lights in its own office in Kiev.[130] The tax administration gave Grach an easy ride over the finances of the Union Viktan vodka company, while the police turned a blind eye to his possible links with the Marimskii mafia. Viacheslav Zakharov, leader of the Communist faction in the local assembly, took part in the physical 'repossession' of the Foros sanatorium by its 'rightful owners' in July 2001.

A mutual interest in Crimean property led to a burgeoning but mainly private relationship with the SDPU(o), reportedly encouraged by Gleb Pavlovskii. Grach certainly received a huge amount of favourable coverage on SDPU(o) media (1+1, Inter, TET, UT-2, Kiev News) and on Pavlovskii's website www.ukraina.ru. Nevertheless, many observers were surprised that a Communist should hire one of the most notorious political technology companies, Aleksii Koshmarov's Novokom from St Petersburg, to run his next election campaign in 2002. Novokom had little difficulty in selling the vain leader the idea of creating a Crimean Bloc of Leonid Grach, which was supposed to represent a much broader coalition than his local Communist powerbase, promising Grach an outright majority in the local assembly and consequent control over all of the government. However, the northerners' Russian nationalist tendencies worked in the other direction. The company's Red–Brown campaign stirred up animosity against the Crimean Tatars.[131] They also steered into dangerous waters by depicting Grach beside both Kuchma and Putin on billboards, and crediting his bridge-building (metaphorical and actual) with stimulating record Russian 'investment', much higher than elsewhere in Ukraine.

Grach promised to settle accounts with his Russian financiers using key assets, especially in the holiday peninsula's sanatoria-thermal complex.[132] Much of the money reportedly came from Siberian Aluminium, which was interested in buying the car company Krymavtogaz (Grach was close to the Russian aluminium baron Oleg Deripaska, who was also funding the CPRF).

Grach was therefore undone by a simple dirty-tricks campaign. His *folie de grandeur* and the obvious threat to Ukrainian business interests aligned against him Crimean premier Serhii Kunitsyn, the Donetsk clan, which was seeking to expand its influence in neighbouring Crimea, and both Kuchma and Putin after they were made to take second place to Grach on his posters. Putin disliked him because he was too close to Luzhkov, another *bête noire*, and because he didn't like Communist ideologues as a type, even those who only appear to be such. Kunitsyn was entrusted with delivering votes in the national election on behalf of For a United Ukraine, and therefore with blunting the ambitions of Grach and the SDPU(o). Grach and Koshmarov were too weak on their own. An early warning shot came in the form of a double, 'Leonid Grach of the Crimean Republic Organisation of the Communist Party of Ukraine (Workers)', followed by a website peddling *kompromat*, www.gracha.net. Most of Grach's allies were therefore primed to desert him when a local court disqualified him for failing to declare all of his property interests in March. (Although Koshmarov was also famous for mock-scandals, inviting publicity by violating the letter of the law – one unlikely explanation floated for Grach's disqualification.) The Grach Bloc won a mere twenty-five seats, only fifteen of them actually Communists, compared to the Kunitsyn Bloc's thirty-nine. In the end, Grach's business interests (all in rather 'grey areas') provided too much easy *kompromat* for the authorities in Kiev – and led him to retire quietly to fight another day.

Communists Back in Power: Moldova

The Communist Party of the Republic of Moldova (CPRM) won 30 per cent of the vote and forty out of 101 seats in the 1998 elections, but was kept on the fringes of power. In 2001 it became the first former Soviet Communist Party to win an election outright, with a triumphant 50.1 per cent and seventy-one seats. Party leader Vladimir Voronin was elected as Moldova's third president by the new parliament. Like the Russian and Ukrainian Communists, however, the CPRM is dominated by 'new business' interests, although in the Moldovan case the range of relevant interest groups is relatively narrow. Energy imports were controlled by Moldova's first two presidents, Mircea Snegur and Petru Lucinschi. In the early 1990s the 'left' business elite dominated the production of wine (nearly all of which went to the Russian market), tobacco, and the big local sugar and confectionery industry. One half gravitated towards the Democratic Agrarian Party, the other to the Socialists/Unity alliance (joint winners of the 1994 elections, with 43.2 per cent and 22 per cent, respectively), largely according to ethnic group.

In the beginning, the CPRM was therefore initially only a fringe movement of unlucky or lower-rank nomenclatura. However, in Moldovan conditions, its 'brand' began to build mass support among nostalgic voters and those who maintained a Slavic-Moldovan, or Soviet, identity. Old nomenclatura businessmen such as Vasile Iovv and Constantin Tampiza, director general of Energo, were therefore tempted simply to switch labels. Despite his public rhetoric about the Communist 'threat', Lucinschi established good business links with Voronin, whom he hoped would siphon off radicals from his Democratic Agrarian Party and serve as a junior coalition partner. Lucinschi's interests (including a walnut business) were protected after 2001 – so long as he did not interfere in politics. Six ministers (initially) survived the changeover of power. Interior minister Vladimir Turcanu was accused of involvement in people and organ trafficking. Former 'centrists' (see pages 145–6) such as Dumitru Braghiş, Nicolae Andronic and Dumitru Diacov, even leading opposition radical Iurie Roşca (who had business interests, including publishing concerns, to protect) maintained covert links with the Communists. After 2001 Diacov and to an extent Braghiş, reinvented themselves as heads of Communist-approved satellite movements (see page 147). The CPRM has more problems with its rank and file, many of whom are genuinely radical, than with the self-styled opposition.

As elsewhere, the inner party set about enriching itself after 2001 thanks to leading businessmen who 'wanted to shrink from privatisation'.[133] Since there was only a handful of real business interests in Moldova, it was a huge temptation for the Communists just to reinvent them in their own image.[134] The key members of the inner party were Voronin's son, Oleg (although not strictly a party member); the new prime minister, Vasile Tarlev, director general of Bucuria, Moldova's biggest sweet company, Vladimir Turcanu, ambassador to Russia; Vadim Misin, deputy chair of parliament, and his ally, Petru Sosev, boss of the Moldovan south and its tobacco and wine industries; Nicolae Bondarciuc, deputy mayor of Chişinaŭ and head of the parliamentary committee on the economy; and Victor Stepaniuc, head of the CPRM faction in parliament and the self-proclaimed leader of the party left.

President Voronin's son was the party linchpin, controlling half-a-dozen linked business consortia in metals (Metal-Market), exports (Transline), construction, hotels, sugar and banking. His ownership of the large sugar factory, Soroca, in the north, privatised in the late 1990s, stood in remarkable contrast to the official CPRM line on this issue. Voronin's businesses, of course, benefited from his political links after 2001. His Finkombank, now Moldova's second largest bank, swelled its coffers with the compulsory channelling of all Moldtelekom transactions through it after 2002; his refurbishment company was granted a monopoly on servicing all the state hotels in Chişinaŭ, and even the Church of Moldova. Misin controlled the tobacco factory Tutun and the lucrative railway network – important work obviously mandated by his position in parliament. Sosev, who was also allegedly close to the mafia boss Boris Birshtein, was known to have survived several assassination attempts and was accused of kidnapping rival government officials in 2002. Tarlev helped Tatgazgrup (owned by Iurii Nikov) 'from behind the scenes' with importing liquid natural gas from Russia and Ukraine – at hugely subsidised prices – and with winning control of the Ungheni terminal. In return, Tarlev's close links to the then Lukoil vice-president Ralif Safin in Moscow helped the Russians obtain the sugar cane they needed for the linked Codapun enterprise, while his political contacts at home shielded him from the 'Bucuria affair'. (His former company had its assets put up as collateral for a state loan of $200,000 that mysteriously disappeared, and was consequently threatened with bankruptcy.) With deputy finance minister Elvira Lupan, Tarlev aimed at 'monopolisation of the energy market' by persuading Moldova-Gaz SA to buy from Lukoil at inflated prices.[135] Russian gas giant Itera was busy lobbying the Communists for a share in the privatisation of the northern sector of the local electricity grid.

The CPRM is not in the same scarecrow category as other post-Communist parties (a real threat to the status quo would have to come from the pan-Romanian right, though see page 254). Nor does it function as a toothless opposition, as it has actually won power. Its economic and social policy has been noticeably more populist than that of the Ion Sturza government in 1999, but its attitude to 'privatised' business has not: it has not threatened the Lucinschi Family's business interests. Significantly, with its economic profile increasingly indistinct, the CPRM has placed more emphasis on language, history and identity issues.

Red Divide and Rule: Keeping Communist Parties in the Box

There is no small irony in the fact that the roughhouse tactics developed by the Bolsheviks are now used against Communist successor parties themselves, although in so far as such methods are actually being used by one group of former Communists against another the irony is not that great. The mainstream Communist successor parties have also fought dirty against their leftist rivals. The hibernating CPRF used entryist tactics to prevent the rival Socialist Party of Workers stealing a march in 1991–92, and employed dirty tricks, first to sideline the Komsomol when setting up its own Union of Communist Youth and then to remove Oleg Shenin when the wandering UCP-CPSU threatened to find a home by transforming itself into the Communist Party of the Union of Belarus and Russia in 2000,[136] or, even worse, by setting up its own faction in the Duma. Communists in power have used the same new/old administrative resource methods, as with the Crimean Communists gerrymandering constituencies in the run-up to the 2002 elections in an unsuccessful attempt to hang on to local power. Their Moldovan counterparts did the same, with more success. Though much reduced in scale, all such parties have also tried to maintain a satellite universe typical of Soviet times.

The theory has been advanced, however, that active measures and black PR are mainly used against the left. Because the latter's elderly supporters vote out of habit and respect for authority, this type of political technology is mainly a tool of the centre and right parties – supposedly the good guys. Pure electoral technology, i.e, virtual image-making, is better at motivating younger voters, who allegedly pay more attention to adverts.[137]

Divide-and-rule tactics on behalf of the successor powers make sure that the commonest successor parties stay in the mainstream. This reversal of roles began back in the late Soviet period, when Rutskoi's Democratic Party of Communists of Russia (DPCR) was promoted by Gorbachev to displace the ultra-conservative Ivan Polozkov from his leadership of the Communist Party of the RSFSR,[138] and by Yeltsin to split the Communist faction in the Russian parliament that might otherwise have ousted him from his position as chair in spring 1991. Even more ambitiously, the presence of Gorbachev aide Georgii Arbatov at the DPCR's founding congress in August 1991 hinted at the plans Gorbachev had discussed with Yakovlev in July: for the DPCR to ally with Yakovlev and Shevardnadze's Movement for Democratic Reforms and the remaining reformist elements in the mainstream Communist Party to set up a 'new' meta-party that would marginalise the hardliners and inherit most of the assets of the old CPSU.[139]

There was little point in specifically targeting the new Communists in the early 1990s. In 1993 the CPRF was still finding its feet, as was the Kremlin. In 1995 the Kremlin wanted to build up the 'Red threat' and the myth of the dangerous extreme within Ziuganov's camp in advance of the all-important presidential election due in 1996. Significantly, whatever intrigues existed were mainly on the far left. John Dunlop, for example, cites two sources claiming that the streetfighting radical Viktor Anpilov was manipulated by the KGB (one of the sources being Yeltsin himself).[140] According to Andrei Riabov, Anpilov is 'a player who will be used by the Kremlin whenever he is needed'.[141] Often, the authorities and the Communists have had a mutual interest in swatting rivals on the far left. At other times, support for far-left groups has served to provide a safety valve for genuine extremists, while keeping the mainstream Communists mainstream. Not too mainstream, however: the main successor parties are denied the political space on the far left, but the competition effect serves as an anchor on any break to the centre.

However, with the CPRF aiming at the centre-left at the next Duma elections in 1999, and the Kremlin extremely nervous about reactions to the 1998 economic crisis, there was a sudden rash of far-left projects aimed at draining the votes of the 'lumpen' electorate. That said, most of these projects were of limited ambition, as the Kremlin still wanted the Communists to do well enough to reprise their 1996 role in the upcoming 2000 presidential election (the overall left vote went down in 1999, but the Communists won a larger share), and most of their PR efforts were concentrated on 'Project Putin'.[142] On the other hand, the election law was changed to benefit the smaller parties, by allowing them to qualify via a cash deposit rather than signatures, and various bankers were prompted to provide the necessary financial favours.[143] This time around, the left-wing 'flies', again mainly on the far left, included, with a startling amount of coverage in official mass media and Semago as its main financier, Podberezkin's breakaway Spiritual Heritage party (0.1 per cent), Baburin's Russian All-People's Union (0.4 per cent) and Peace, Labour, May (0.6 per cent). The Party of Pensioners (2 per cent; see also pages 125–6) was obviously targeted at the Communists' more elderly supporters. Aleksandr Prokhanov of the paper, *Zavtra*, accused the Communists, Workers of Russia for the Soviet Union bloc (an alliance of Aleksei Prigarin's Russian Communist

Party-CPSU and Anatolii Kriuchkov's Russian Party of Communists, which won 2.2 per cent) of 'provocation' and 'paid agent activity in the service of the party of power'.[144] The rival Stalinist Bloc – for the USSR (which included Anpilov, 0.6 per cent) put out a suspiciously large amount of party propaganda and paid advertising for a far-left group. According to the analyst Sergei Cherniakhivskii, the 'funds [came] from the oil company Yukos. Perhaps this was connected with the presidential administration trying to use the Stalinist Bloc to reduce the number of votes given to the CPRF . . . rumours about support for the Stalinist Bloc from the Kremlin circulated repeatedly before the elections.'[145] One other fly to benefit from Kremlin backing was Sergei Umalatov's Peace and Unity (0.4 per cent). Ivan Rybkin's Russian Socialist Party was thought 'unsound' on Chechnia and only won 0.1 per cent, despite money from Berezovskii.[146] Overall, according to Prokhanov, 'the "Red" leaders planted by the regime, the Lilliputian nationalists, the narcissistic haughties, the regime marionettes with certificates from the FSB by way of pension books stole 7 per cent of the votes from the CPRF'.[147]

Berezovskii money (supposedly $1.2 million in the first instance) was also used to try and neutralise General Lev Rokhlin's Movement in Support of the Army (MSA), set up in 1997. The rabble-rousing Rokhlin, hero of the first Chechen War, briefly rattled the Kremlin's windows by promising to bring down the government, impeach Yeltsin and send 'guilty men' to the Hague tribunal. This potential populist bandwagon was deeply disturbing to the establishment technologists, who were struggling to fake such an effect on their own. Rokhlin was therefore surrounded with moles of more questionable background, such as Aleksandr Morozov, a veteran of 'offshore business' in Cyprus with links to Zhirinovskii's LDPR. Berezovskii hoped simultaneously both to neutralise and exploit the threat. Rokhlin's refusal to cooperate was the alleged reason for his murder in July 1998.[148] Without him, the MSA won only 0.6 per cent in 1999.

In the 2000 presidential election, after the Kremlin had covertly encouraged Ziuganov to stand in the first place, it backed both Aman-Geldy Tuleiev (3.0 per cent and fourth place) and, rather less successfully, Podberezkin (0.1 per cent) to 'nibble at' Ziuganov's electorate,[149] to keep the Communist leader below 30 per cent in the first round and ensure that Putin's margin of victory was correspondingly large. With Podberezkin and Tuleiev both endorsing Putin themselves, it was clear how the CPRF was supposed to behave. Stanislav Govorukhin (0.44 per cent), Yurii Skuratov (0.43 per cent) and, of course, Zhirinovskii (2.7 per cent), who again hammered away loyally at Ziuganov, also received tacit Kremlin support.[150] Konstantin Titov (1.5 per cent) was allegedly used to split the right vote.

Between 1993 and 2000, periodic banning threats and general psychological pressure also served to keep the successor parties within 'the box' – in opposition (otherwise the role might be gifted to a real opposition), though not of too radical a hue. In Russia the CPRF was briefly 'suspended' in October 1993; the possibility of a proper ban was raised during Yeltsin's aborted coup in March 1996, and briefly revived in 1999. In Ukraine the threat was most real during the authorities' so-called 'velvet revolution' (the mini-coup that displaced the left from the parliamentary leadership) in early 2000, which successfully forced the CPU to acquiesce in the abolition of the October Revolution holiday and the removal of Soviet insignia from the parliament building.

The game of divide and rule is also played within parliaments. Communist parties might be built up at election time, but are then likely to be cut back over the lifetime of a parliament. In the face of large bribes to quit ranks, Communist discipline has usually been impressive, but a predictable cycle has nevertheless developed – Communist parties always end up with fewer deputies than when they start. For instance, the CPRF maintained its original strength in the first post-Soviet Duma (forty-two were originally elected in 1993, forty-five when the Duma then assembled), but thereafter it became a more tempting target. It had 158 deputies in 1995 (149 on the first day in the Duma, albeit mainly because sixteen were 'loaned' to the Agrarians and People's Power factions; six independents and one other also joined), but was down to 128 by September 1999. In the 1999 elections it won 113 seats, down to eighty-three in November 2003.[151] In a similar fashion CPU representation in the Ukrainian Rada fell from ninety-five in 1994 to eighty-six in 1997, and from 122 to 113 in the next cycle from 1998 to 2002.[152]

Anti-Communist Measures Elsewhere

Active measures against the new Communist parties are commonplace now that the boot is on the other foot. Given the ethnic make-up of Kazakh society and the lack of any real tradition of statehood or party politics – as in Belarus – the Communists were always the most likely potential opposition. Nazarbaev therefore jumped the gun by creating a Socialist Party 'in August 1991 to inherit the property and membership of the Kazakhstan Communist Party' of old,[153] and to serve as an alternative to the (actually Communist) Communist Party of Kazakhstan (CPK) founded in September 1991. The full range of tactics was used against the CPK. First, it was denied registration until March 1994, and not allowed to compete in that year's elections, forcing its supporters to vote for one of three tame substitutes: the Socialists (who won 15 per cent), the Trade Unions' Federation (12 per cent) and the Peasants' Union (4 per cent). The CPK was then forced to reconstitute itself for the next elections in 1995, when it won only two seats. The usual banning threat was again made in April 1996 to keep it in line. In 1998 the CPK's attempt to set up a broad opposition bloc, the People's Front of Kazakhstan, along with Azamat and the former prime minister Akezhan Kazhegeldin's Republican People's Party, some Communist fronts and Russophile parties, was met with classic divide-and-rule tactics. The bloc was broken up and the Communists' allies scattered (see pages 159–60). The CPK won only three seats in 1999, although it was awarded an official 17.8 per cent of the list vote, and in a fair election 'would have taken more seats on party-list balloting than any other group'.[154] Finally, on the eve of new elections in 2004, the CPK was split to create a new and reliably docile 'Communist People's Party of the Republic of Kazakhstan' led by Vladislav Kosarev.[155] The latter did its job with 1.2 per cent;

the CPK (in alliance with Democratic Choice see pages 156–60), therefore missed the barrier for representation (7 per cent) with only 3.4 per cent.

The Braghiş Alliance created for the 2001 Moldovan elections included several virtual left parties (the Socialists, Labour Union and the Party of Social Democracy 'Furnica') designed to draw votes away from the Communists (see page 146). Rather more dangerous was the Citizens' Union Patria-Rodina, this time alleged to be backed by Moscow, Pavlovskii *et al.* (and with links to the rebel 'Dnistr Republic'), set up in May 2004 after the official Communists refused to back Moscow's plan to federalise Moldova. Its slogan was a 'United Motherland with Great Russia', and its obvious inspiration Russia's own Rodina Party, which cut into the Russian Communists' vote in the 2003 Duma elections (see below). One theory foresaw Patria-Rodina linking up with Moscow's new favourites, opportunists such as Braghiş and Urecheanu, in advance of elections due in February 2005; another that it would be used to pressure the official Communists back into line. In Belarus the Communist Party was split by regime forces in 1996 (see pages 165–6). In Armenia 'the national tradition of reliance on Russia means the local Communist Party has neither a stigma to lose nor a distinct card to play'.[156] Karen Demirchian, first secretary of the Communist Party in Armenia (CPA) from 1974 until 1988, made a comeback in the late 1990s and denied the Communists the nostalgia card until his assassination in 1999, as did Lukashenka in Belarus. However, a split was deemed necessary before the 2003 elections, with the new president, Robert Kocharian, backing the creation of a Renewed Communist Party of Armenia to rival the old CPA.[157] In Azerbaijan there are four rival Communist parties. The pro-Aliyev party led by Firuddun Hasanov now predominates over the older version led by Ramiz Ahmedov, which is closer to the CPRF,[158] after splitting away from it in 1996. Hasanov's 'Reformist' Communists were allowed to win 6.3 per cent in the 2000 elections. None of the others were allowed to take part.

Squeezing the Box

More than a decade after the fall of Communism, the illusion of a Communist revanche was gradually losing credibility – although there were some in the West who would still buy it. The powers-that-be therefore had other uses for the quarter or so of the vote that the successor parties could still command (24.6 per cent in Ukraine in 1998, 24.3 per cent in Russia in 1999). In Ukraine in 2002 and in Russia in 2003 there were therefore serious attempts to cut the local Communists down to size.

In Ukraine the regime largely avoided playing any games with the CPU immediately after its re-foundation in 1993, as its behaviour was sufficiently docile and its ideology not a credible challenger for power. After Kuchma's re-election in 1999, however, at least three overlapping projects were launched. The CPU had served its purpose in helping Kuchma to a second term, but remained simply too large in light of the manoeuvres that the president's supporters now had in mind.

Its ideological evolution in the wake of the Kosovo War also worried some. The opening shot in the anti-Communist campaign (largely the work of circles close to Viktor Pinchuk, with some tasks also undertaken by Oleksandr Volkov's camp) was the creation of a 'New Majority' in parliament in January 2000 (the 'centre-right' elbowing aside the left, who had enjoyed control since the previous elections in 1998). Communist deputies were made straightforward cash offers to join the main oligarchic factions. The likes of Fedor Marmazin were paid an alleged $10,000 to quit (in his case, only temporarily);[159] others were offered between $30,000 and $50,000. According to one source, 'all efforts were hurled at all sides of the party. Deputies were offered *big* money to change factions, but there wasn't significant movement.'[160] Only half a dozen left immediately (eventually eight), four of whom went, as usual, to Pinchuk's Labour Ukraine. Simultaneously, several councils in west Ukraine attempted to ban the party outright, a warning signal that obviously required Kiev's official approval.

The next step was the creation of two rival parties: one for the Soviet ultra-patriots (to serve as a left buffer); and one that was more 'national' (the right buffer). The left buffer was the Communist Party of Workers and Peasants. Its acronym in Ukrainian (from Komunistychna partiia robotnykiv i Selian, therefore KPRS) was the same as the Ukrainian for CPSU; the party's banner a simple hammer and sickle. The party's leaders, Volodymyr Moiseienko (rumoured to have long-standing links to Russia and the former KGB) and Oleksandr Yakovenko, claimed to preside over a party of 'ordinary workers'. Eleven out of the first twenty on the party's election list were 'representatives of the working class', and the party made a special pitch at Donbas workers, miners in particular. The party's TV slots for the 2002 elections promised a 'vanguard' party, with plenty of martial images. The KPRS, Yakovenko stated, 'is discipline, organisation and strength', leading 'a mass movement of workers' to 'peaceful revolution'.[161] Party activists were usually prominent at leftist demonstrations (thereby at least helping to annoy the official Communists), but as *official* Communist Party policy was relatively radical, there was little real space to organise on the far left. Furthermore, the party's virtual class credentials were more convincing than its call to arms. Even among radical workers in the Donbas, the KPRS won little more than its national average of 0.4 per cent. The KPRS was therefore a useful fly, but was more successful in diverting activists (many of its members were genuine) and mimicking a blunted criticism of the leadership of the CPU.

The launch of a rival project that the Communists feared more – a revival of the Ukrainian Communist Party that had existed in 1920–25 (known as the UKP, its members were therefore the *Ukapisti*) – was first rumoured to be imminent in early 2000;[162] but ultimately emerged under a different name, as the Communist Party of Ukraine (renewed): in Ukrainian the KPU(o), in English the CPU(r).[163] The initial confusion was indicative. Like the *Ukapisti*, the 'renewed' Communists accepted state sovereignty as a given, and their economic programme was relatively moderate. Their real function, however, was to serve as the party of virtual Soviet patriotism. The virtual TV campaign of the CPU(r) was much better judged than the crude opportunism of the KPRS. The party's slickly produced dual-language (Ukrainian and Russian) adverts were a careful amalgam of images of Soviet success under the slogan 'We remember how it was'. These included a smiling Yurii Gagarin; a parade of 'labour achievements'; the Kremlin clock tower striking twelve (the party's number on the electoral list) to the strains of 'Moscow Nights' (the tune that marked time on Soviet radio); and an old film of the post-war reconstruction of Kiev, 'the shining joy in the life of the Soviet people, victoriously building Communism', designed to flatter the sedentary target electorate that their earlier, more activist, lives had not been spent in vain.

The voiceover for the CPU(r)'s adverts was particularly brazen, claiming:

> We aren't advertising anything
> They have taken everything from us
> Just as with you
> The only thing that we have preserved
> Is Memory
> Striving for the Truth
> And our Red Banner.

The party's posters read: 'We unite all genuine Communists', 'We cannot sit with idle hands', 'Only together will we win!' and, even more shamelessly, 'Don't let yourself be fooled, vote for number 12'. The party was entirely virtual, however. There wasn't a 'genuine' Communist in sight. Apart from a theoretical leader, Mykhailo Savenko, the party had no real talking heads; its TV ads all used voice-overs.[164] The party's listed address was a fiction, its official phone numbers silent. The CPU(r) was purely and simply an 'advertising project' aimed at the nostalgic TV electorate. Whereas putting KPRS *agents provocateurs* on the streets was a job for the presidential administration and security services, the CPU(r) project was therefore the work of a media magnate – namely Kuchma's close ally Viktor Pinchuk. The fact that the party could afford regular (sometimes hourly) TV ads – usually on TV channels controlled by Pinchuk – was an indication of the party's real backer.[165] According to one analysis, the ads cost $347,000, putting the party an impressive seventh in the overall spending league.[166]

The CPU(r) netted a useful 1.4 per cent of the poll (362,712 votes), but could have won more. It might have done better if the official Communists (CPU) hadn't lucked out by being placed first on the ballot paper, but more importantly the project was *too* virtual – a little bit lazy (Pinchuk's technologists didn't want to spend too much on a mere fly). The party hadn't bothered to secure any high-placed defectors for the virtual Communist leadership, and the ads for the 'campaign without candidates' failed to provide a reason to explain just why the CPU(r) was different from the CPU (or from Vitrenko, for that matter).[167] After the elections, even its virtual reality disintegrated.

The final Communist clone produced for the 2002 elections was an 'East Slavic nationalist' project, Bison. (The party's official name, For Ukraine, Belarus and Russia, or Za Ukraïnu, Belarus i Rossiiu produced the acronym ZUBR, which also means 'Bison': the animal was used as the party symbol.) 'Bison' won only 0.4 per cent of the vote, but its main purpose was to make a pre-emptive strike to discourage the mainstream CPU from straying into its nationalist territory.

It is worth pausing to reflect on how bizarre, and potentially risky, it was that all three of these projects were backed by those formally in charge of the Ukrainian state. Overall, the purpose of the Communist clones in 2002 was not to replace or even usurp the mainstream CPU, but just to keep it under control and channel its energies in the desired direction. Kuchma still needed the party to do reasonably well: to serve as a situational ally when called upon and, in the short term, to ensure that Symonenko survived as leader at least until 2004. The CPU's support in the list vote fell only from 25 per cent to 20 per cent. Administrative resources were used much more effectively against it in the constituencies, particularly in the Donbas, where Akhmetov's supporters swept the board. The CPU won thirty-eight constituencies in 1998, this time only six.

'Operation Mole'

The Russian Communists' relations with the powers-that-be also entered a new phase after the 1999–2000 electoral cycle. Unity (23.3 per cent) and the CPRF (24.3 per cent) were roughly level-pegging in the 1999 Duma elections. In 2000 Ziuganov played a useful reprise scarecrow role, with the Kremlin this time more worried about the threat of a low turnout in an otherwise easily won election. In 2001, however, Unity merged with FAR (13.3 per cent in 1999). The new United Russia party was supposed to sweep all before it on the way to creating a 'Mexican-style party system', and the Communists began losing contacts with big business as a result of Kremlin pressure. However, after an initial boost from the merger, the new behemoth was soon polling fewer votes than its original constituent parts, head to head with the CPRF (usually in the low 20s) in the ratings war.[168] None of the Kremlin's other projects seemed likely to make an impression and the electorate as a whole was thought to be drifting to the left. The authorities therefore turned their attention back to the Communists, who were also deemed to be guilty of paying too much attention to their rank-and-file members after 1999.

The Kremlin's first option was to create a big split within the party, via the kind of cynical manoeuvres that were common currency.[169] First, Duma chair Gennadii Seleznev was used to create a patriotic bloc, Rossiia (Russia), within the CPRF. Then, in April 2002 a palace coup in the Duma removed the Communists from the lucrative committee chairs that Unity had cynically agreed to share with them in 2000, and ousted the Communists' Nikolai Troshkin from the equally profitable position as chief of the Duma *apparat*. Business sponsors at lower levels and those who had been seconded to the agrarian-industrial Duma faction kept their posts, as, of course, did the splitters themselves. Seleznev left the CPRF, but remained as chair of the Duma. Svetlana Goriacheva, number two on the party's 1995 list and one-time deputy chair of the Duma, continued to head the committee on women, family and youth, and Nikolai Gubenko kept the culture committee.

As with the project that eventually became the CPU(r), the split was everything. The new Russia party initially had no agreed name; Seleznev toyed with the idea of setting up another Socialist Party of Russia or a Russian Social-Democratic Republican Party: The initials RSDRP were familiar to every Russian, since it was also that of the Russian Social-Democratic Labour Party, which had given birth to the Bolsheviks. Significantly, Putin seemed to endorse this cloning project in July 2001 when he advertised his hope that the Communists might survive as part of a reduced three-party system, but only by restoring the old name.[170]

The changes, especially the loss of all other committees, temporarily depressed the CPRF's poll rating, but party discipline worked to prevent a major split. Gubenko was welcomed back to the Communist fold in 2003. Seleznev's project was eventually launched as the Party of Russia's Rebirth in September 2002 (Putin sent a message of congratulations). His eventual alliance with Sergei Mironov's Party of Life was dubbed the 'Bloc of Two Speakers' (Mironov was then chair of the upper house); like the Rybkin Bloc in 1995, it was too obviously a 'reserve' party of power to be able to make any serious play for the centre-left vote. Moreover, its packaging (by Publicity PR) was neither particularly serious nor especially effective (see page 127). However, the Seleznev project had at least narrowed the CPRF leadership's freedom of manoeuvre, both by usurping its particular brand of state patriotism and by making any centre-left strategy more difficult, like that of the CPU(r) in Ukraine.

The authorities' more fundamental problem was that the CPRF seemed to have a stable electorate, and to represent an identifiable subculture, which knew a wasted vote when it saw one. According to Valerii Solovei, 'The left electorate just won't vote for other parties like Seleznev's or [Andrei] Brezhnev's [New Communist Party].'[171] By 2003 Seleznev had clearly 'failed to fulfil the task before him: to draw as many pawns away from the Communists [i.e., their side of the chess board] as possible'.[172] Significantly, Khodorkovskii's Yukos reportedly declined the invitation to finance the project, as it considered its prospects poor, earning itself another black mark for 2003. (Boris Shpigel's Biotek pharmaceutical company stepped in instead.)[173] Moreover, unlike Ukraine in 2002, the authorities' scope for squeezing the CPRF out of its local powerbases was limited, as many governors' loyalties to the Kremlin were only nominal – even if others' loyalties to the CPRF were equally nominal. The political niche for a powerful left-centre alternative did not yet seem to be there. It was in Ukraine – which is why Kuchma has traditionally harassed the Socialist Party. The Kremlin, however, continued to believe that, even if the Communist Party's radical core electorate couldn't be tempted away, its penumbra of largely conservative 'supporters of the values of the Brezhnev era' could.[174]

Another option was to work within the party. The Kremlin also had to consider the greater danger of a sudden lurch to the left and the possible emergence of a smaller but more radical party. There was some suggestion that the Kremlin would prefer such a strategy if it allowed it the space to build a proper 'left-centre' party *and* if its own man, possibly the faux-radical head of the Moscow city party, Aleksandr Kuvaiev, were in charge (a past beneficiary of Kuptsov and Semigin finance), but this would be an extremely difficult trick to pull off.[175] Nevertheless, the banker Igor Igoshin – of all people – floated the idea of a new radical Communist Party in late 2003. The All-Russian Communist Party of the Future with the initials of the old Bolshevik Party, VKPB, that emerged in 2004, was either backed by the authorities or likely to be hijacked by them.

Surkov initially seemed to give the green light to the Yukos-Communist project in 2003, if only because it would help wean the Communists away from the sponsorship of Berezovskii. Yukos was looking for a sizeable 'golden share' in the CPRF, parachuting in its own Aleksei Kondaurov (a former member of the KGB, who oversaw security at Yukos and had previously stood for the Communists in 1999) to head the umbrella organisation People's Patriotic Union, and seconding Anton Surikov's PR group which had helped Khodyrev win Nizhnii-Novgorod in 2001. Another channel was through Sergei Muravlenko, former president of the board at Yukos, who had also helped Seleznev and Podberezkin in the past.[176] However, after the moves against Yukos in summer 2003, the door was slammed shut and the 'Yukos five' were slimmed down to three. On the final Communist list, Kondaurov was at unlucky number thirteen, Muravlenko at fourteen and Yulii Kvitsinskii, former ambassador to Norway, at fifteen. With personal wealth reported at $47 million, including four flats, two Mercedes and a Porsche, Muravlenko was merely the richest of four dollar millionaires on the Communist list. The others were Semigin ($16 million), Glazev's ally Sergei Batchikov ($2.2 million) and Igor Annenskii ($1.8 million).[177] According to one analyst, 24 per cent of the CPRF's list were businessmen, compared to 7 per cent in 1999; more than the surmised average across the Duma of 20 per cent and hardly any different from United Russia's 27 per cent.[178] Much of this information was broadcast on the state media, so that the CPRF was overwhelmed by an anti-oligarch campaign that should have been its own.

Yukos's entryism may have been frustrated, but the Kremlin had already inserted another mole. The party rank and file knew Ziuganov couldn't win a third race. A new candidate offered the party the hope of progress – if not in this race then in the next. The Kremlin was still uncertain whether a move towards the centre-left would make a hardline breakaway more or less likely. But, if a new candidate were to achieve a good second place, he might get another run in four years, and Russia would then be safe for private property for five or six. In 2002 Gennadii Semigin, who had a powerful position as treasurer of the People's Patriotic Union, seemed to be taking over from his patron, the ailing Kuptsov, and began using his resources (and those of Sibneft and Deripaska, coyly referred to in one account only as a major 'aluminium oligarch')[179] to provide faxes, computers, etc, for local party branches, and to fund the impoverished regional press (the People's Patriotic Union now offered salaries, unlike the CPRF). According to one source, Semigin was funded by the Kremlin to the tune of $80,000 a month.[180] The Ziuganov-Vidmanov group considered the threat serious enough to begin publicising Semigin's links to the

Kremlin.[181] Valentin Chikin, the editor of *Sovetskaia Rossiia,* and Aleksandr Prokhanov of *Zavtra* attacked Semigin as a Surkov 'agent of influence' in an article condemning the creation 'of an opposition within the opposition' entitled 'Operation Mole'.[182] Nevertheless, Semigin, with Kuptsov's backing, was number eighteen on the party list, and remained a long-term threat to Ziuganov if he refused to play ball.

Rodina

The final option for the Kremlin's multi-dimensional onslaught was the creation of spoiler parties to steal the Communists' vote. At this early planning stage it was assumed that the CPRF would maintain most of its traditional electorate: 'small piranhas cannot eat a big elephant' – and not just because elephants don't live in South America.[183] But if the Kremlin were to back three or four mini-projects, each of which might take a percentage point or more, the CPRF could be pushed into a safe second place behind United Russia. An additional benefit, to mix metaphors, was that the *mukhi* (flies) would help thicken the *moloko* (milk) – the over-representation dividend for those parties who get more than the requisite 5 per cent.[184]

The Kremlin began with practice runs, sponsoring far-left candidates against mainstream Communists in gubernatorial races.[185] Surkov gave a green light to Andrei Brezhnev's New Communist Party (sponsored by Aleksandr Mamut, who was once married to Nora Brezhneva) and Oleg Shein's Labour Party (see overleaf). Several of these early projects were undermined by Berezovskii, who was happy to swat the smaller flies from his exile in London.[186] There was little irony in the fact that Berezovskii had earlier been rumoured to have funded Viktor Tiulkin's ultra-radical Russian Communist Workers' Party (denied registration in 2002). This, however, provided the Kremlin with good black PR. Podberezkin *et al.* accused the CPRF of 'being tempted by Berezovskii and his accomplices'.[187] In April 2003 Kremlin technologists set up a fake Communist rally 'in defence of Berezovskii'.

The key plan, however, was to turn the Communists' own long-standing (if unrealised) 'two-bloc' strategy against them, by expanding the Communists' traditional 'second column', the 'patriotic bloc', at the CPRF's expense – but, of course, under Kremlin influence. A decision was therefore taken to launch the project outside rather than within the CPRF. Berezovskii had harboured similar ambitions of creating an anti-Kremlin nationalist 'column', so the Kremlin's technologists took great pleasure in stealing some of his ideas, and allegedly even money, for their own project.[188] Seleznev's Party of Russian Rebirth, Leonid Ivashov of the Military Power Union, Podberezkin's Socialist Unity Party (formerly Spiritual Heritage) and Dugin's Eurasia Party were all at one time considered as elements in this strategy. Many in the CPRF therefore saw all, except perhaps Dugin, as agents of influence.[189] By late 2002 the political technologist Marat Gelman thought he had found a safe pair of hands – Sergei Glazev, who came an impressive third, with 21.4 per cent, in the race for Krasnoiarsk governor earlier in the same year.[190] (Glazev was allegedly covertly sponsored by the victorious Khloponin to take votes off his rival

Uss.)[191] Glazev was originally an economist close to Gaidar; he drew up Lebed's ill-fated alternative economic plan in 1996. He had therefore been a member of both the DPR and KRO before emerging at number three on the CPRF ticket in 1999, when he wrote the party's economic programme. In the new Duma Glazev served as co-head of Russia's Regions. He was perhaps not an ideal anti-Ziuganov, but his Kremlin backers, who had ignored all his policy suggestions when he chaired the Duma Committee on Economic Policy in the mid-1990s, now calculated that his social-statist approach was an excellent pitch to the left-centre electorate, and his economic theories about 'natural rent' (imposing windfall taxes on monopoly profits in the energy sector) a perfect fit for the general anti-oligarch campaign.

The original project would have been called '*Tovarishch*' ('Comrade' – Gelman actually set up a news agency with this name under Anna Gorbatova). In this first 'leftist' incarnation, the key role of bloc exemplar was to be have been played by Sergei Khramov of the Socialist Trade Union Association and Oleg Shein's Russian Party of Labour.[192] This 'new' Labour Party was a clone of a real opposition party that had briefly flourished in the early 1990s under old *inteligenty* such as Boris Kagarlitskii and Nikolai Gonchar; it was designed to tie the newer 'independent' unions (miners, dockers, air-traffic controllers) into the system of directed democracy – the official unions having been tamed a long time ago. The main sponsor of the party was reportedly Oleg Morozov, formerly of FAR and now allied with Glazev in Russian Regions. The ultra-radical RCWP-RPC was also supposed to join with Glazev.[193] The bloc's strategists made the usual pretence of coalition-building by assembling a large but lazy collection of shell and virtual parties: twenty-eight initially. One was Aleksandr Chuev's Russian Transnational Party, which under its previous name of the Russian Christian-Democratic Party had sold itself to Unity in a similar fashion in 1999. Other jigsaw pieces included the corpse of KRO, the Party of Russia's Regions, the Socialist Unity Party, the airborne troops commander, Georgii Shpak, the leading Orthodox fundamentalist, Aleksandr Krutov, and Aleksandr Bludyshev, a 'strategist' from the Union of Right Forces.

However, in August the project abruptly turned into the Rodina-National Patriotic Union, its rightward transformation becoming obvious after Glazev was roped in as co-leader to the young firebrand Dmitrii Rogozin, a serial Kremlin troublemaker (the sudden nature of the change being, of course, indicative of the virtual nature of the project).[194] Rodina's design now bore a striking resemblance to that of Unity in 1999: 'a virtual PR construction, formed on the eve of the elections on the basis of a "strike" troika',[195] consisting of Glazev, Rogozin and former putschist Valentin Varennikov. Rodina also received the services of Nataliia Narochnitskaia (number nine on the list), one of Russia's leading ideologues of the 'clash of civilisations' between the Orthodox world and the West worldview.[196] Glazev's most surprising ally, however, was Sergei Baburin's People's Will/Party of National Rebirth, full of former activists from Russian National Unity and SPAS, including Vladimir Davidenko and Barkashov's former 'political adviser', Mikhail Burlakov. Igor Rodionov's People's Patriotic Party also contained rather too many neo-Nazis (the 'professional economist' Glazev in fact had something of a right-wing bent himself, as evidenced by his book *Genocide*).[197] Many had been promised a new home after acquiescing in the destruction of SPAS, but the ensuing publicity marred the initial launch.

On the other hand, 'Project Glazev' also included Viacheslav Igrunov's SLON (the Union of People of Education and Science), a Yabloko breakaway. The idea that Glazev's 'third-way' economics would take votes off Yabloko seemed a serious overburdening of the project with too many divergent tasks. However, the Kremlin's technologists had successfully calculated that Yavlinskii was drifting away from the centre-left preferences of the patriotic new middle class.

Initially, the whole artificial package scared away first Khramov, then Dugin and SLON, and reportedly left even the cynical Gelman disillusioned.[198] Dugin was particularly scathing about the fake 'hurrah-patriots' and 'irresponsible populism' of so many former KGB and Kremlin insiders (the idea of 'Russia for the Russians' was also anathema to Dugin's Eurasianism). Dugin also complained that the bloc had been in preparation since April 2003, and that the extremists were only parachuted in in August.[199] Glazev's thinning ranks included only two sitting Communist deputies, plus former defence minister Igor Rodionov. Rodina's only real leftist catch was Varennikov – but only because he had quarrelled with Ziuganov. Glazev's financial backer, Sergei Batchikov, recently of Interros, stayed with the Communists. In fact, the Rodina project initially seemed such a mess that it aroused suspicions that Glazev was being set up to fail, a 'false aerodrome' for the liberal parties to waste their energies railing against. If this was true, the URF certainly fell into the trap.

At first, the Kremlin also seemed uncertain what line to take, unclear whether it could achieve its 'maximum programme' against the Communists or not. Pavlovskii had at one time thought that the CPRF could be broken up, at least after a 'last hurrah' in the 2003–04 electoral cycle.[200] Others thought it better 'to accept the leftward drift of the electorate as a given and try to take charge of the process'.[201] The most ambitious thought the two approaches could be combined, particularly as the 'Zhirinovskii electorate' of 1993 was as yet untapped, and the number of 'floating nationalist' voters had actually grown since then.[202] The Jeremiahs worried that a project such as Glazev's might be too successful, taking as many votes from United Russia or Raikov's People's Party as the CPRF,[203] or that Glazev might play Petrushka like Zhirinovskii in 1993 and slip Kremlin control (there were reports that press minister Lesin ordered state TV to cut back on Rodina's coverage in the last days of the campaign).[204] One camp in the Kremlin saw an all-out assault on the CPRF as the only way to win the coveted two-thirds majority in the Duma; another saw Rodina as merely a larger than average 'fly' that could be squashed after the election; another still wanted to slim the Communists' vote but argued that too much had been invested in taming their leadership to risk swapping it for a new virtual opposition on the right.[205] Unlike the CPU(r), Rodina contained a lot of real, ambitious politicians. In the past Ziuganov had consistently proven eager to play within the rules, if it was to his advantage and if the Kremlin let him. However, in

2003 he was clearly banking on backing from Yukos. The Kremlin's attack on the company therefore made him adopt a more radical line. Unlike in the previous campaign in 1999, the CPRF had few enemies on its left. Both Viktor Tiulkin's Russian Communist Workers' Party and the Movement in Support of the Army were this time on the CPRF list. After he became disillusioned with Rodina, the Communists also had Dugin's support and also that of a man resembling the former prosecutor Yurii Skuratov.

Given the seeming opportunity on the Communists' 'right', and Voloshin's declining influence, the Kremlin maximalists won out. The Communists later claimed no fewer than fifteen separate 'operations' against them. The list is worth quoting in full: 'Project Glazev'; the 'pigmy parties' (*partii-zhivopyrki*) who stole the CPRF's slogans (see below); the black PR linking the 'CPRF and the oligarchs' (more exactly, the two discredited oligarchs Berezovskii and Khodorkovskii), and 'exposing' [*sic*] the millionaires on the party list (according to one TV critic, 'Every Marx should have an Engels by his side, carrying a fat wallet');[206] next the 'big lies' about Ziuganov's private plane, 'accounts in Cyprus', etc; 'the CPRF's connections with Chechen terrorists'; the general discrediting of Ziuganov as leader; the use of fake opinion polls to depress the party's rating; fake 'anger of veterans' demos, when pensioners were paid to vent their 'disillusion' with the CPRF; black PR against the 'Red governors'; the use of doubles; 'psychological pressure on the opposition'; 'using the leader of the LDPR [Zhirinovskii] for frontal attacks and insults on the CPRF and Ziuganov'; and finally 'operation Semigin and the fifth column within the CPRF'.[207]

In contrast to the easy ride given to the Communists in 1999 – Sergei Dorenko actually joined the CPRF in 2003 – Andrei Karaulov now assumed his role of media-killer to savage them on state TV. All three main channels joined in what *Nezavisimaia gazeta* termed the 'gang rape' of the Communists and the CPRF itself called state TV a 'collective Goebbels'.[208] The Communists, who had grown used to Kremlin favour and assumed an 'inertia scenario', were totally unprepared.[209] As the leadership of the official Communist Party was now belatedly being depicted as corrupt, Rodina, the virtual Communist party, was gifted the brazen slogan 'Vote for the real Communists' (like the Ukrainian CPU(r) the year before). It was given life by the radical rhetoric of Rogozin and other Young Turks ('When will Chubais be in jail?!'), which stood in sharp contrast to the jaded quality of Ziuganov's performances. State TV, particularly Gelman's channel ORT, gave huge publicity to Glazev's 'big idea', the proposal for a $4-$5 billion annual tax on 'natural rents' in the energy sector to replenish the state welfare budget. His campaign slogans were 'Russians must take Russia back for themselves' and 'We shall return the country's natural wealth to the people'. One commentator called Glazev 'the Lionia Golubkov of Russian politics', referring to the fictional character in the briefly omnipresent TV adverts for Sergei Mavrodii's MMM pyramid scheme in 1994, which seduced investors with a snake-oil salesman's promises of enormous instant returns.[210] Moreover, other oligarchs lurked in the background as Rodina's financiers. The energy tycoon Aleksandr Babakov, who owned four Ukrainian *oblenergos* through a Slovak front company and a share of Moscow's Luzhnikii market, was at number eight on the party list. Aleksandr Lebedev, boss of the National Reserve Bank, which then had $1.5 billion in assets, was also initially involved, but pulled back. (Other rumoured 'investors' were Suleiman Kerimov of Nafta Moscow and Avtobank.) Even Oleg Deripaska, the Communists' sponsor, had reportedly chipped in at the Kremlin's behest.[211] Nevertheless, Glazev's demonology chimed well with Stanislav Belkovskii's campaign of 'national revanche' against the oligarchs run for the benefit of United Russia (see pages 109–10).

The redesigned Rodina project won a triumphant 9.1 per cent of the vote (the parallel count had it on 10.75 per cent).[212] Moreover, Rodina was flanked by several rejuvenated flies that were much more successful than in 1999. The Kremlin had rewritten the 2001 Law on Political Parties so that fly parties could now also be financial projects, designed to recoup state funding by passing the 3 if not the 5 per cent barrier. The Pensioners' Party, allied with businessman Vladimir Kishenin's Party of Social Justice, whose commitment to social justice involved servicing the cars of the Kremlin administration, won 3.1 per cent. (According to legend, a Russian sociology firm once included an imaginary Party of Social Justice in a poll, and it came a surprise third. Kishenin, spotting the opportunity, named his virtual party after the imaginary one.) The Pensioners' Party 'used its free airtime solely for the baiting [*travli*] of the CPRF', using state TV's new trick of employing faux-news clips with 'the voices of "disillusioned" pensioners and veterans', sadly explaining why they were abandoning the CPRF.[213] The same ploy reappeared on the Pensioners' Party's paid TV adverts, which showed a 'real' old man refusing to get up for a canvasser at his door – a presumed CPRF foot soldier – and growling 'we can look after ourselves'. Lapshin's Agrarians were brought back under the Kremlin wing and, with financial support channelled through Mikhail Fridman's Alfa Bank, won a similarly impressive 3.7 per cent.[214] After spending 'millions', all pretence was dropped in 2004, and Vladimir Plotinkov parachuted in from United Russia to replace Lapshin. Seleznev's lacklustre project secured 1.9 per cent, and the CPRF also lost votes to 'other mythical organisations of the type of Rus [which won 0.25 per cent] or Great Russia–Eurasia Union [0.3 per cent], For Holy Rus [0.5 per cent] and others'.[215] Union won 1.2 per cent. Even Peace and Unity was still around, scoring 0.25 per cent. The People's Party was indeed crowded out by Rodina, winning only 1.2 per cent. Ziuganov complained that 5-6 per cent of the vote was stolen from the CPRF via administrative resources, and that turnout was boosted by 2.5 per cent for the benefit of others;[216] but the sheer abundance of the vote for the virtual Communist flies explains the party's steep decline from 24.3 per cent in 1999 to an official 12.7 per cent in 2003. (The number of Communists elected in the territorial constituencies was also sharply down from forty-nine in 1999 to twelve in 2003, largely due to administrative resources.)

The moles, moreover, most notably Semigin, remained to continue with their work another day. A Semigin-led breakaway, possibly to join forces with Rodina, still threatened the CPRF. Semigin narrowly failed to become the Communists' candidate for the 2004 presidential election by 105 votes to 123.[217] In the subsequent bitter struggle Ziuganov pulled the CPRF out of the People's Patriotic Union and forced Semigin out of the CPRF, so in May 2004 Semigin set up the rival 'Patriots of Russia' group.[218] In July the two factions held rival communist congresses. Clearly, the Kremlin planned to decide who would win a likely protracted struggle to control the 'real' CPRF.

Conclusions

Who is doing the inventing here? In the Communists' case, it is both the regime inventing rivals and the 'real' Communists inventing themselves, which is not as difficult as it sounds as 'the CPRF is a very broad church' (*ochen shirokii diapazon*), as also are the CPU and CPRM.[219] However, with the Ziuganov era possibly drawing to a close, all the mainstream Communist parties faced difficult challenges. First, they needed to attract the kind of business sponsors that would help them compete under directed democracy without ruining their populist image. Second, the Russian, Ukrainian, Kazakh and even Belarusian Communists undoubtedly had a brighter future as opposition parties than as satellites of the Kremlin or Bankivska, but the latter were equally determined to avoid handing them the role of real opposition. Third, it required a lot of nimble footwork to retain their nostalgic core electorate while evolving into social-democratic-type parties. Other parties could easily be invented by the regimes to compete with them in one or other of those roles.

Regime policy towards Communist successor parties has also vacillated. It has been most successful when it has emphasised cooptation, seeking, as with Ziuganov's party in 1993–96, 'to make the party a minority shareholder in Russia plc'.[220] Isolating such parties has proved much more difficult. Traditionally, moreover, the authorities have avoided the temptation to destroy such parties, in order to keep the 'Red threat' alive. Now that directed democracy has proved so successful, the temptation will be even greater, particularly in Russia after 2004. The consequences of such an action, however, are impossible to predict.

Conclusions

I have chosen to place political technologists, other assorted fixers and their black arts at the centre of this book. This is not because they are the only people who count in post-Soviet politics, but out of a desire to change the perspective from more traditional accounts that take the public performance of politics at face value. Nor because political technologists are omnipotent. The whole point of virtual politics in the post-Soviet world is that it inhabits a middle ground – these are certainly not totalitarian states where everything can be controlled. Even in the Stalin era, it can be argued that certain forms of virtuality were substitutes for more direct methods of control, which could not reach into every social nook and cranny. In the Brezhnev era, elites had to be more realistic about their capacity for social control. That process of retrenchment has since gone further still, but the instinct for control remains.

This book has therefore attempted to explain how practices of control have developed since 1991. In this sense, the Yeltsin and Putin eras can be plotted at different points on the same learning curve. The Kremlin has simply got better at fixing elections. Directed democracy did not arrive *ex nihilo* in the Putin era simply because a few hard men, the so-called *siloviki*, had consolidated their hold on power. The bowdlerisation of politics by reducing it to a series of projects; the creation of virtual brands that disguise a party or politician's real nature; the abuse of administrative resources; the destruction of political opponents with active measures and *kompromat* – all of these processes began in the Yeltsin era. The main differences are, admittedly, that the Kremlin has become more brutally frank about its aims under Putin, and that its capabilities are greater. Directed democracy is now more efficiently directed – but then everything was less efficient in the Yeltsin era. The Kremlin and its equivalents have also become much better at multi-tasking. The most effective projects, such as Unity in 1999 and Rodina in 2003, but also (at least as one-offs) Yeltsin in 1996 and Kuchma in 1999, now seem to be invincible due to their combining all the key elements of virtual politics: state-backed broadcast parties or politicians supported with overwhelming administrative resources, and active measures against potential opponents. However, many questions remain.

Partial Parallels

First, can the political culture that has developed in so many of the post-Soviet states be said to be unique?[1] It is beyond the scope of this study to make a truly comparative enquiry, but several partial parallels could be suggested. Pakistan has a long history of using its intelligence service, the ISI (Inter-Services Intelligence), to manufacture political parties and sabotage the regime's opponents.[2] The Liberal Party regime of the Somoza family in Nicaragua (1937-79) was particularly adept at faking opposition and promoting soft rivals usually from the Conservative Party, or, when that shifted from virtual to real opposition in 1957, from the 'New' Nicaraguan Conservative Party instead. Many other post-Communist states outside the former USSR, of course, share elements of post-Bolshevik culture. The link between national security services and parties of the right, for example, can be noted throughout post-Communist Europe. Former security officials have played prominent roles in the Slovene National Party and Bulgaria's Committee for the Defence of the National Interest. In Croatia under Tudjman, many right radicals (*pravasi*) were similarly manipulated by the ruling HDZ. In Serbia the Milošević regime played with various nationalist parties: Vojislav Šešelj's Serbian Radical Party, Željko Ražnatović's (Arkan) Serbian Unity Party, Vuk Drašković and his Serbian Renewal Movement – all have been accused of 'working in direct collaboration with the regime on the destruction of the opposition'.[3] Romania probably has most parallels with states such as Russia and Ukraine: a redesigned ruling elite entrenched in power, a long list of state-backed nationalist projects such as România Mare (the Greater Romania Party),[4] powerful (former) security services enmeshed in a shadowy parallel state, and carefully staged mass 'provocations' (inter-ethnic violence and the notorious 'dispersal' of student protests in Bucharest in June 1990 by miners bused in from the Jiu valley).

Nevertheless, this book has tried to make it clear that the totality of post-Soviet political culture is *sui generis*. In both Pakistan and Nicaragua party-building techniques remained those of a traditional patrimonial society. TV *dramaturgiia* has never been as important there as in the former USSR; assembling coalitions of local potentates much more so. There was no real election technology industry working alongside the Liberals or ISI. Most other post-Communist states enjoy relative media and political freedom; the expansion of the EU and NATO have proved enormously powerful levers on domestic policies. In Romania, the possibility of EU membership in 2007 offers an antidote to virtual politics. In the former USSR it might be said that the West is by comparison simply not engaged enough. We still defer to Russia's residual international power and its growing role as an energy-supplier. Geopolitics seems to commit the USA to facing down the 'Oriental despotisms', while leaving the 'Slavic autocracies' to the Russian sphere of influence.[5] In Central Asia and Azerbaijan there is geopolitical commitment and lip service to democracy; further to the west nice words about building better standards, but few real sticks and carrots. It is only in small states such as Georgia that the two are properly combined and the West decisively engaged.

Many of the arguments about the hijacking of the political process by televisual virtuality are common to the former USSR (which in terms of TV culture is much closer to first-world standards) and the West. But the sheer cynical trickery practised by post-Soviet technologists is a different matter. The West does not yet have the same corrupted elite, minimal civic society and over-employed former security apparatus as states like Russia and Ukraine.

The Genie of Democracy

It is instructive to compare core post-Soviet examples with other attempts to establish directed democracies in the post-Communist world. East Germany's arch-manipulators, Markus Wolf and Hans Modrow, clearly had something of this type in mind for the GDR in late 1989, but were simply swamped by events. On the eve of the opening of the Berlin Wall, GDR Politburo minutes state that 'the demand for free elections can in principle be supported. . . . nevertheless this should not entail opening the door to bourgeois party pluralism.'[6] The survival strategy, probably planned with the likes of Kriuchkov in Moscow, involved reanimating the 'bloc' parties used to lay formal claim to pluralism in the Communist era (the four satellite parties were the Christian Democrats, National Democrats, Democratic Peasants and yet another Liberal Democratic Party) and manipulating their army of informers, plus the older dissident groups still amenable to the idea of a reformed GDR, and thereby retaining the core element of Communist-Stasi rule. However, the strategy was predicated on the basic sinews of state control remaining intact, which did not happen. Moreover, the influence of the potentially manipulable actors listed above was undermined by the unprecedented flow of information and the appearance of other actors, especially the West German government and its financial promises, and soon enough West German parties.

Countries such as Russia and Ukraine have simply not opened up to the outside world in a similar fashion. The state tottered, but did not collapse, and was able to regenerate itself. In retrospect, the word 'revolution' hardly fits at all. 1991 was not like 1789 (France) or even 1688 (England's elite-led 'Glorious Revolution'). Deep structures were preserved. There was no real social revolution. The post-Soviet states have some new (big-business) elites, but there has been no large-scale displacement, let alone lustration, of the old elites. Some sought to free-ride on the new politics; others have been trying to put the genie back in the bottle ever since. In Russia politics has been moved back off the streets since 1993, and political technologists have become adept at writing virtual dramas instead. 'Since 1993 the Kremlin has tried to maintain a closed political system with a limited number of pieces on a relatively small chessboard – certainly fewer than in a normal chess game.'[7] Until Yushchenko, Ukraine had seen no significant competition since the 1994 election or, arguably, the fight between President Kuchma and Prime Minister Lazarenko in 1997–99. In Kazakhstan the regime has insulated itself from effective challenges since 1994–95, Belarus since 1996. The rare changeovers of power have often been more apparent than real. In Moldova, Communist president Voronin was courted before 2001 to keep things square. Sensibly, he rejected offers to share the power that he hoped to win outright, but his regime has continued to look after the business interests of his predecessor, Lucinschi.

That said, there has undoubtedly been a change of sorts. The Yeltsin era was characterised by 'directed conflict' (*upravliaemyi konflikt*) as much as by 'directed democracy' (*upravliaemaia demokratiia*). The oligarchs' war of all against all needed to be suitably disguised; different dramas had to be invented, but controlled, to distract the public. The Putin era has used political technology to impose the absolute supremacy of the Kremlin and its values. However, the Kremlin and its equivalents have not given up on democracy completely. Though the English word 'direction' barely conveys the sense of *upravlenie*, 'directing' democracy is not the same as eliminating it. Real politics may be marginalised, but it still exists. There are domestic forces and outside influences that can still penetrate and lift the fog. Inevitably, in a book of this sort, I have been unable to give these sufficient attention. I have, for example, mainly written about the 'Stop Yushchenko' project, rather than about where Yushchenko's challenge to the regime came from in the first place.

Political choices are important, both for established elites and oppositions. Russian elites may find themselves with considerably more leeway as their role as European energy-supplier grows. Ukrainian elites are affected differently by the constraints of 'European Choice'. Belarus may decide to go it alone in Lukashenka's twilight years. For different reasons, Russian and Ukrainian oppositions were implicit in the suppression of real pluralism in 1991–92: Russian liberals because they entrusted the economic reform project to the authorities; (one half of) Ukraine's Rukh because it wished to secure the 'national project'. Different choices may be made next time.

It is in their professional interest for political technologists to exaggerate the extent to which public opinion is truly malleable. In fact, it still sets very real limits. I have tried to avoid giving too precise a sociological or psephological account of the effects of their various projects in order to avoid crediting them with too much 'success'. It is enough to give a general idea of how the deed has been done. It is, of course, also possible that, despite the best efforts of the powers-that-be and their hirelings, real challengers to the existing system will eventually emerge.

Will the Powers-That-Be Always Win?

Despite its apparent consolidation in the post-Soviet states, virtual politics may eventually fall victim, either to its own success, or to the concessions it makes to actual democracy. The four key conditions for maintaining virtual politics described in Chapter Two may not be preserved. These are: an effective elite monopoly on politics, a passive electorate, the successful implementation of information control, and the effectiveness or otherwise of external pressure.

Maintaining elite unity is a key precondition for maintaining power. Russian elites were very jumpy in early 1996 and again in 1999. On both occasions, salvation came late. Broadly speaking, since 1993 the elite has felt relatively safe from pressure from below, but continues to fear that it may divide against itself. It is no accident that Verdi's opera *A Masked Ball* (1859) is popular in Russia. Its thinly-disguised portrait of the downfall of Gustav III of Sweden in 1792 – stabbed by his own courtiers in the opera, in a broader historical context undermined when the liberal aristocracy sided against the king and peasantry – has many local parallels. Tsar Paul I suffered a similar fate in 1801. One of the greatest 'triumphs' of post-Soviet political technology was to re-channel and ultimately contain the conflicts that emerged in 1999. The powers-that-be in Ukraine kept a united front at the height of the Gongadze affair in 2000-01 and survived, despite their media counter-campaign not being particularly effective.[8] Georgia's Shevardnadze lost the support of key elites in 2003 and fell; Azerbaijan maintained a united front around the dynastic succession of President (Ilham) Aliyev and therefore got away with the crudest of frauds.

In some post-Soviet states the institutional structure of civil society barely exists. In others, NGOs and civic groups may exist, but so do problems of donor-seeking and 'government organised NGOs'. Gleb Pavlovskii organised a notorious Civic Forum of Kremlin-sponsored Russian NGOs in 2001. The cultural values that permit and support independent action are also weaker than they might be, but are not totally absent. Public opinion in countries such as Russia and Belarus may support a 'firm hand,' but usually values post-Gorbachev freedoms as well. Anti-NGO campaigns are only launched because the authorities fear their influence. The Committee of Voters of Ukraine did sterling work in keeping electoral fraud to a minimum in 2002.

Methodologically, information control is best opposed by media pluralism and general openness, which is why Russia was so clearly headed in the wrong direction in Putin's first term. Significantly, on the other hand, Pavlovskii's grand designs for a Kremlin-sponsored local internet proved too grandiose. In 2004 the Ukrainian authorities tried to silence all independent voices, including *Silski visti* ('Village News'), silenced not by direct censorship, but after an anti-Semitic article was planted in its pages. The elite failed to maintain unified control, however. Poroshenko's Channel 5 and Andrii Derkach's Era gave Yushchenko an outlet.

Flooding election sites with observers helps minimise the use of many types of administrative resource. The events of the hubristic second term of Ukrainian president Leonid Kuchma illustrate the difference this can make. The Melnychenko tapes record his initial overconfident boast to install the 'toughest possible order' (*samyi zhestokii poriadok*) after his re-election in November 1999.[9]

The leading oligarch Oleksandr Volkov organised a Soviet-style 'All-Ukrainian Referendum on Popular Initiative' in April 2000 on increasing presidential power, that seemed purpose-built to demonstrate to voters that their voice didn't matter. International supervision was minimal. Turnout was supposed to be 81.2 per cent, with 'yes' votes (to four questions) of 81.7 per cent to 89.9 per cent.[10] One positive result of the Gongadze affair that erupted in Autumn 2000 was that the results were never implemented (in 2004 the authorities tried to reduce the power of the presidency instead). At the next elections in March 2002 fraud was minimised by a big observer presence and a huge exit poll (see pages 81–2).[11] But the authorities obviously overreached themselves in 2004. The elite was clearly split. Even many 'oligarchs' were lukewarm in their support for Yanukovych, who was forced to over concentrate all too obvious fraud in his home regions of Donetsk and Luhansk. The security apparatus was split. The SBU taped the Zorainy 'team' (see pages 182–3), and a clampdown on protests would have been resisted by many within the apparatus itself. Civil society effectively shadowed the cheats and publicised their efforts; and the crudity of the final fraud meant that the various chinks in the system of information control served to trigger a revolt in other media, which effectively became semi-free by the second week of protests. The protesters were also unexpectedly numerous, their ranks swelling sufficiently to change their character. Suddenly the elite was faced not just with radical students and other usual suspects, but their own wives and daughters on the streets. The protesters had also learnt the lessons of their failure in 2001. They remained entirely peaceful and excluded faux-radical *agent provocateurs* from their ranks. International intervention (from the West) was decisive and unanimous. Whether the same conditions could be recreated elsewhere to challenge the virtual system is another question.

A Dead End?

Russia at least seemed to have completed some sort of cycle by 2003–04. Directed democracy had reached its relative, if not absolute, limits, with the three parties of the Kremlin pie plus the Communists achieving absolute dominance in the December 2003 Duma elections and Putin's ceremonial re-election in March 2004. Stability, however, risked becoming stagnation. Elections no longer conferred mandates or created any kind of political momentum. They were not even proper plebiscites, as no questions of substance were put to the voters, but were instead little more than popularity polls. Such winner-takes-all no-contests could only strengthen zero-sum tendencies in both politics and political economy. As in much of the Third World, political power has become increasingly commodified, valuable not as a means of promoting programmes of social change, but as the gateway for a particular group to seize control of a static or dwindling stock of state assets. Despite much talk of a 'Pinochet scenario' for Russia and its neighbours (authoritarian politics combined with economic liberalisation), political or economic modernisation under virtual politics would be extremely difficult.

The Ukrainian election in 2004 was therefore hugely important, not just for Ukraine, but as a demonstration for the prospects for real politics over directed democracy throughout the region. If there was no real contest in Russia at the elections in December 2003 and March 2004, Ukraine's 'Orange Revolution' showed that local politics need not remain virtual, and that the political technologists could be defeated. The Kremlin remained determined not to import the Ukrainian 'virus', but key contests loomed elsewhere – in Moldova, Armenia and possibly even Belarus.

Popular Cynicism

The longer the established authorities remain in power in an era of virtual competition, the greater the danger of popular disillusion and declining election turnouts. Though disillusion with politics and the media can itself be manipulated (see pages 190–6), voters cannot be repeatedly conned into using the same techniques. This year's tricks may get more inventive, they may get more crude. Either way, there are risks. Russia in particular has suffered from declining turnouts, as there is little to vote for. Even the 55.8 per cent claimed in December 2003 and 64.3 per cent in March 2004 were padded. In Ukraine, where there has been more of a real contest, turnout was 65.2 per cent for the Rada elections in 2002, and 74.9 per cent in 2004.

Local *dramaturgiia*s are not as dramatic as they once were. Manufacturing political interest is problematic – or provocative in unpredictable ways if incidents are invented to spark voters' motivation such as the Tuzla 'crisis' in 2003 or perhaps Lukashenka's 'energy war' with Russia for 2004. The elite wants the public to be sufficiently disengaged to give it a free hand, but sufficiently engaged to give the impression of popular support – a difficult balancing act to maintain. Russia had to resort to cruder administrative methods to raise turnout in 2004.

Lazy Elites

Elite cynicism can be taken for granted, and is a long-term danger. In 1991 many local Communists had what now seem exaggerated fears for their personal and political safely. Famously, Ukrainian Communist leader Stanislav Hurenko declared at a private meting on 24 August 1991, three days after the collapse of the coup he had supported: 'Today we must vote for independence, because, if we don't, we'll find ourselves up to our ears in shit.'[12] A decade and a half later, some elites are becoming complacent. Indeed, why bother with vestigial, and expensive, political parties and projects at all? The developing fashion for administrative technology is driven by the desire to economise on both cost and effort. Used excessively on their own, however, such methods can be brutally crude.

In Russia, Putin undoubtedly enjoyed popular support, but outside of this 'narrow corridor of belief' there was no Plan B.[13] The apostles of virtual politics engineered 'stability', but had no real idea how to deal with the development of new interests that might not feel represented by the system. According to Gelman in 2004, 'if the Kremlin decides it needs an opposition, then it will create one'.[14] His confidence was not borne out, however, by its reactions to earlier unexpected developments such as the Kursk submarine disaster in 2000 or the Dubrovka theatre siege in 2002. Sustained economic growth will lead to the growth of a new middle class, the opposite to a possible upsurge in nationalism (or vice-versa). But if the Kremlin wants to keep motivational politicians off the political chessboard, it may trap itself in a cycle of decline in which anti-system outbursts become more likely – hence more intelligent analysts advocating the cooptation, not isolation, of 'opposition' Communist parties. Even Gleb Pavlovskii is uncertain whether the system of directed democracy is flexible enough to accommodate new groups, ideas and interests – particularly the likely long-term mutations of Russian nationalism.[15] Pavlovskii, *et al.* were, however, well placed for hedging their bets by reinventing the Islamic threat as a 'lesser evil'.

Kremlinology's Comeback?

If so much of the decision-making process is again a matter of secrecy, the study of post-Soviet politics may revert to 'Kremlinology' – the arcane study of the order of precedence at public ceremonies and Aesopian hints in long-winded speeches for some clue as to the real politics within. In Peter Reddaway's apt words, the Russian political system is like 'a big black box in which many of the more important elements are kept deliberately secret'.[16] In such conditions sociology and psephology lose ground to the study of which political technologists are in and which are out, of who is entrusted with which project and why. Analysis of politics becomes more difficult and the quality of that 'analysis' undoubtedly declines.

Of course, a decade and a half is not a particularly long time, but the assumption that post-Soviet politics can be studied within the framework of some kind of 'transition to democracy' was always doubtful and is now untenable. On the other hand, virtual politics is a type of politics, a substitute for a return to totalitarianism. So long as it continues, it will coexist with elements of real politics. Democracy in Russia, Ukraine and the other post-Soviet states is not (yet) dead, it is just distorted. Observers should be realistic about the sheer cynicism that abounds in the former USSR and its capacity to determine power, but they should not be fatalistic about its omnipotence.

Ukraine, 2004. Black PR suggests
Bush (middle) is behind
Yushchenko (top and bottom).
The slogan is 'Yes! For Bushchenko'.

Notes

Introduction

1 Translated into English by Andrew Bromfield as *Babylon* (London: Faber and Faber, 2000), at p. 90.

2 The following list is not exhaustive, but indicates the sheer amount of literature on the subject. Ol'ga Blinova, *Sovetniki: issledovatel'skie i kansultingovye struktury Rossii* (Moscow: GNOM ID, 2002); Ekaterina Egorova-Gantman, *Politicheskaia reklama* (Moscow: Nikkolo-M, 1999); *idem*, *Politicheskii marketing* (Moscow: Nikkolo-M, 1999); *Elektoral'nye tekhnologii i prezydentskie vybory* (Chişinaŭ: CAPTES, 2000); Sergei Faer, *Priemy strategii i taktiki predvybornoi bor'by* (Moscow: Stol'nyi grad, 1998); Farkhad Il'iasov, *Politicheskii marketing: iskusstvo i nauka pobezhdat' na vyborakh* (Moscow: IMA-Press, 2000); Sergei Kara-Muza, *Kratkii kurs manipuliatsii Soznaniem. Vse na vybory* (Moscow: Algoritm, 2003); Aleksei Kurtov and Mikhail Kagan, *Okhota na drakona: Razmyshleniia o vyborakh i politicheskom konsul'tirovanii* (Moscow: State University Higher Economic School, 2002); N.P. Kutyrev, *Tekhnologii pobedy na vyborakh* (Moscow: Priror, 1999); S.F. Lisovskii, *Politicheskaia reklama* (Moscow: Marketing, 2000); S.F. Lisovskii and V.A. Evstaf'ev, *Izbiratel'nye tekhnologii: istoriia, teoriia, praktika* (Moscow: RAU Universitet, 2000); Anatolii Lukashev and Anatolii Ponidelko, *Anatomiia demokratii, ili Chernyi PR kak institut grazhdanskogo obshchestva* (St Petersburg: Biznes-Pressa, 2001); Lukashev and Ponidelko, *Chernyi PR kak sposob ovladeniia vlast'iu, ili Bomba dlia imidzhmeikera* (St Petersburg: Biznes-Pressa, 2002); A.A. Maksimov, *'Chistye' i 'griaznye' tekhnologii vyborov* (Moscow: Delo, 1999); Evgenii Malkin and Evgenii Suchkov, *Osnovy izbiratel'nykh tekhnologii* (2nd edn; Moscow: Russkaia panorama, 2000); Sergei Markov, *PR v Rossii bol'she chem. PR. Tekhnologii i versii* (Moscow: Astrel', 2001); A.A. Mukhin, *Informatsionnaia voina v Rossii: uchastniki, tseli, tekhnologii* (Moscow: Centre for Political Information, 2000); Denis Nezhdanov, *Politicheskii marketing: vchera, segodnia, zavtra* (St Petersburg: Piter, 2004); Georgii Pocheptsov, *Imidzh i vybory* (Kiev: ADEF-Ukraine, 1997); *idem*, *Kak stanoviatsia prezidentami: izbiratel'nye tekhnologii XX veka* (Kiev: Znannia, 1999); *idem*, *Informatsiia & dezinformatsiia* (Kiev: Nika-Tsentr, 2001); *idem*, *Informatsionno-politicheskie tekhnologii* (Moscow: Tsentr, 2003); L.V. Smorgunova (ed.), *Gumanitarnye tekhnologii i politicheskii protsess v Rossii* (St Petersburg: St. Petersburg University Press, 2001); Avtandil Tsuladze, *Bol'shaia manipuliativnaia igra* (Moscow: Algoritm, 2000); Sergei Ustimenko (ed.), *Izbiratel'nye tekhnologii i izbiratel'noe iskusstvo* (Moscow: PR-Intellekt/Russian Political Encyclopedia, 2001).

3 See, for example, M. Steven Fish, 'The Dynamics of Democratic Erosion', in Richard D. Anderson *et al.*, *Postcommunism and the Theory of Democracy* (Princeton: Princeton University

Press, 2001), pp. 54–95; Kataryna Wolczuk, *The Moulding of Ukraine: The Constitutional Politics of State Formation* (Budapest: Central European University Press, 2001).

4 See, for instance, Peter Reddaway and Dmitri Glinski, *The Tragedy of Russia's Reforms: Market Bolshevism versus Democracy* (Washington, DC: United State Institute of Peace, 2001).

5 Jonathan Steele, *Eternal Russia: Gorbachev, Yeltsin and the Mirage of Democracy* (London: Faber and Faber, 1994); Vladimir Brovkin, 'The Emperor's New Clothes: Continuity of Soviet Political Culture in Contemporary Russia', *Problems of Post-Communism*, vol. 43, no. 2, March–April 1996, pp. 21–28.

6 On the notion of 'patrimonial Communism', see Herbert Kitschelt *et al.*, *Post-Communist Party Systems. Competition, Representation and Inter-Party Competition* (Cambridge, UK: Cambridge University Press, 1999).

7 Fareed Zakaria, *The Future of Freedom. Illiberal Democracy at Home and Abroad* (New York: W.W. Norton, 2003).

8 Graeme Gill and Roger D. Markwick, *Russia's Stillborn Democracy? From Gorbachev to Yeltsin* (Oxford: Oxford University Press, 2000). Cf. Ken Jowitt, *New World Disorder: The Leninist Extinction* (Berkeley and Los Angeles: University of California Press, 1992).

9 Stephen Holmes, 'Potemkin Democracy', in Theodore K. Rabb and Ezra N. Suleiman (eds), *The Making and Unmaking of Democracy: Lessons from History and World Politics* (London: Routledge, 2002), pp. 109–33, at pp. 130 and 115–19. Emphasis in original.

10 See the *Journal of Democracy*, vol. 13, no. 2, April 2002. See also M. Steven Fish, 'Authoritarianism despite Elections: Russia in the Light of Democratic Theory and Practice', paper presented at the Annual Meeting of the APSA, San Francisco, 2001.

11 Steven Levitsky and Lucan A. Way, 'The Rise of Competitive Authoritarianism', *Journal of Democracy*, vol. 13, no. 2, April 2002, pp. 51–65, at pp. 52–53. See also http://astro.temple.edu/~lway/levitskyandway, as accessed 22 June 2004.

12 See also Kerstin Zimmer, '*Khozyaistvenniki* and Political Machines in Donetsk: Economic and Political Regionalism in Ukriane', www.essex.ac.uk/ECPR/events/generalconference/marburg/papers/16/4/Zimmer.pdf.

13 William L. Miller, Stephen White and Paul Heywood, *Values and Political Change in Postcommunist Europe* (Basingstoke: Macmillan, 1998).

14 Archie Brown (ed.), 'Introduction', *Political Culture and Communist Studies* (London and Oxford: St Antony's/Macmillan, 1984), pp. 1–12, at p. 2.

15 *RFE/RL Daily Report*, 18 March 2004.

Chapter 1

1 Marat Gel'man, 'Kompromat kak literaturnyi zhanr', *Russkii zhurnal*, 21 Nov. 1997.

2 See the study by Yu.V. Aksiutin *et al.*, *Vlast' i oppozitsiia. Rossiiskii politicheskii protsess XX stoletiia* (Moscow: Russian Political Encyclopaedia, 1995).

3 Christy Campbell, *Fenian Fire: The British Government Plot to Assassinate Queen Victoria* (London: HarperCollins, 2002).

4 Geoffrey Hosking, *Russia and the Russians. A History from Rus to the Russian Federation* (London: Allen Lane/Penguin, 2001), p. 123; citing R.G. Skrynnikov and A.A. Zimin.

5 See Charles A. Ruud and Sergei A. Stepanov, *Fontanka 16: The Tsar's Secret Police* (Montreal: McGill-Queen's University Press, 1999).

6 Fredric S. Zuckerman, *The Tsarist Secret Police Abroad: Policing Europe in a Modernising World* (Houndmills: Palgrave, 2003).

7 S.A. Stepankov, 'Problema dvoinykh agentov v sisteme politicheskogo rozyska nachala XX veka', www.fsb.ru/history/read/1998/stepanov.html. Other estimates have gone as high as thirty or forty thousand.

8 Narit Schleifman, *Undercover Agents in the Russian Revolutionary Movement: The SR Party,*

1902–14 (Houndmills: Macmillan, 1988), pp. 29 and 21. Sudeikin's instructions as quoted at pp. 19–20.

9 Richard Pipes, *The Degaev Affair: Terror and Treason in Tsarist Russia* (New Haven and London: Yale University Press, 2003), pp. 85 and 86. See also Feliks Lure, *Politseiskie i provokatory: politicheskii sysk v Rossii, 1649–1917* (St Petersburg: Chas-pik, 1992).

10 Quoted in Pipes, *The Degaev Affair*, p. 87.

11 Anna Geifman, *Entangled in Terror: The Azef Affair and the Russian Revolution* (Wilmington: Scholarly Resources, 2000), p. 140. See also idem, *Thou Shalt Kill: Revolutionary Terrorism in Russia, 1894–1917* (Princeton: Princeton University Press, 1993), p. 235.

12 Ruud and Stepanov, *Fontanka 16*, pp. 116 and 104.

13 Jacob Langer, *Fighting the Future: The Doomed Anti-Revolutionary Crusade of Vladimir Purishkevich* (Perkins Theses AM, 2003).

14 'Partiiu vlasti zadumali pri imperatore. Retseptam rossiiskoi polittekhnologii uzhe 100 let', www.izvestia.ru/science/article34724, no date, accessed 14 Dec. 2003.

15 Ruud and Stepanov, *Fontanka 16*, p. 150.

16 Pipes, *The Degaev Affair*, p. 83.

17 Robert Service, *Lenin: A Biography* (London: Pan, 2000), pp. 206–7.

18 Ruud and Stepanov, *Fontanka 16*, p. 284.

19 Jonathan Daly, 'The Security Police and Politics in Late Imperial Russia', in Anna Geifman (ed.), *Russia under the Last Tsar: Opposition and Subversion 1894–1917* (London: Blackwell, 1999), pp. 217–40, at pp. 233–34. Daly's *Autocracy under Siege: Security Police and Opposition in Russia, 1866–1905* (DeKalb: Northern Illinois University Press, 1998) takes a more fatalistic approach.

20 Quoted in Stéphane Courtois *et al.*, *The Black Book of Communism: Crimes, Terror, Repression* (Cambridge, Mass. and London: Harvard University Press, 1999), p. 57.

21 Roman Brackman, *The Secret File of Joseph Stalin: A Hidden Life* (London: Frank Cass, 2001). See also Alexander Orlov, *The March of Time. Reminiscences* (London: St Ermin's Press, 2004), pp. 385–404, on Stalin's alleged revenge on all those who could possibly have known of his Okhrana past (something of a circular argument). Robert Service in *Stalin: A Biography* (Houndmills: Macmillan, 2004), p. 72 argues that Stalin spent too long in prison and in exile for an effective double agent.

22 *Lenin: Collected Works* (London: Lawrence and Wishart), vol. 19, pp. 53–54, at p. 53 (translated from the 1963 Moscow edition of *V.I. Lenin: Polnoe sobranie sochinenie*).

23 As translated in Aleksandr Yakovlev, *A Century of Violence in Soviet Russia* (New Haven and London: Yale University Press, 2002), p. 21. Emphasis in original translation.

24 Leonard Schapiro, *The Origins of the Communist Autocracy* (London: Bell/Billing and Sons, 1955), p. 167.

25 Vera Broido, *Lenin and the Mensheviks: The Persecution of Socialists under Bolshevism* (Aldershot: Gower, 1987), pp. 80–85 and 68–70.

26 Aleksandr Solzhenitsyn, *Letter to the Soviet Leaders* (London: Collins and Harvill, 1974), pp. 46–47.

27 Martin Amis, *Koba the Dread: Laughter and the Twenty Million* (London: Jonathan Cape, 2002), pp. 237, 258 and 197.

28 Jeffrey Brooks, *Thank You, Comrade Stalin! Soviet Public Culture from Revolution to Cold War* (Princeton: Princeton University Press, 2000), p. xvii.

29 Ibid., p. xvi.

30 Anne Applebaum, 'Pulling the Rug from Under', *The New York Review of Books*, 12 Jan. 2004, pp. 9–11, at p. 10.

31 Brooks, *Thank You, Comrade Stalin!*, p. xvi.

32 Christoph Neidhart, *Russia's Carnival: The Smells, Sights and Sounds of Transition* (Lanham: Rowman and Littlefield, 2003), p. 65.

33 Sheila Fitzpatrick, 'Making a Self for the Times: Impersonation and Imposture in 20th-Century Russia', *Kritika*, vol. 2, no. 3, summer 2001, pp. 469–87, at p. 482.

34 Sheila Fitzpatrick, *Everyday Stalinism. Ordinary Life in Extraordinary Times. Soviet Russia in the 1930s* (Oxford: Oxford University Press, 1999).

35 Stephen Kotkin, *Magnetic Mountain: Stalinism as a Civilization* (Berkeley: University of California Press, 1995), pp. 198–237.

36 Catherine Wanner, *Burdens of Dreams: History and Identity in Post-Soviet Ukraine* (University Park: Pennsylvania State University Press, 1998), pp. 72–73.

37 Brooks, *Thank You, Comrade Stalin!*, p. 247.

38 Ibid., p. xvi.

39 Ibid., p. xiv.

40 Terhi Rantanen, *The Global and the National: Media and Communications in Post-Communist Russia* (Lanham: Rowman and Littlefield, 2002), pp. 63–64 and 23.

41 See the material smuggled out by Vasilii Mitrokhin in his book written with Christopher Andrew, *The Mitrokhin Archive* (London: Allen Lane, 1999); A.I. Kolpakidi and D.P. Prokhorov, *KGB, Spetsoperatsii sovetskoi razvedki* (Moscow, Izd-vo AST 2000); and the memoir by former agent Pavel Sudoplatov, *Special Tasks: Memoirs of an Unwanted Witness – A Soviet Spymaster* (London: Warner, 1995).

42 Kolpakidi and Prokhorov, *KGB, Spetsoperatsii sovetskoi razvedki*, pp. 492–93.

43 Vasiliy Mitrokhin (ed. and intro.), *KGB Lexicon: The Soviet Intelligence Officer's Handbook* (London: Frank Cass, 2002), p. 261.

44 Ibid., pp. 13 and 251.

45 Ibid., pp. 345–46 and 115.

46 Sudoplatov, *Special Tasks*, p. 31.

47 Kolpakidi and Prokhorov, *KGB, Spetsoperatsii sovetskoi razvedki*, pp. 130–41, at p. 138. Cf. Orlov, *The March of Time*.

48 Sudoplatov, *Special Tasks*, p. 45.

49 Peter Davison (ed.), *George Orwell. Orwell in Spain* (London: Penguin, 2001), p. 208.

50 Ibid., pp. 180, 184 and 201.

51 See also Ronald Radosh, Mary R. Habeck and Grigory Sevostianov, *Spain Betrayed: The Soviet Union in the Spanish Civil War* (New Haven and London: Yale University Press, 2001), pp. 208–33.

52 Kevin O'Brien, 'Interfering with Civil Society: CIA and KGB Covert Political Action during the Cold War', *International Journal of Intelligence and Counter Intelligence*, vol. 8, no. 4, winter 1995, pp. 431–56.

53 Courtois, *et al.*, *The Black Book of Communism*, p. 291.

54 Sean McMeekin, *The Red Millionaire: A Political Biography of Willi Münzenberg* (New Haven and London: Yale University Press, 2004).

55 V. Stanley Vardys, 'The Baltic States under Stalin: The First Experience, 1940–41', in Keith Sword (ed.), *The Soviet Takeover of the Polish Eastern Provinces, 1939–1941* (London: Macmillan, 1991), pp. 268–90, at p. 279.

56 Bohdan R. Bociurkiw, *The Ukrainian Greek Catholic Church and the Soviet State (1939–1950)* (Edmonton: CIUS, 1996), pp. 134 and 144.

57 As quoted in Christopher Andrew and Julie Elkner, 'Stalin and Foreign Intelligence', in Harold Shukman (ed.), *Redefining Stalinism* (London and Portland: Frank Cass, 2003), p. 87.

58 Tomáš Kostelecký, *Political Parties after Communism: Developments in East-Central Europe* (Washington, DC: Woodrow Wilson Center Press, 2002), pp. 18, 28 and 24–25.

59 Jiří Valenta, *Soviet Intervention in Czechoslovakia, 1968: Anatomy of a Decision* (London: John Hopkins University Press, 1991), p. 105; Mark Kramer, 'The Prague Spring and

the Soviet Invasion of Czechoslovakia: New Interpretations', *The Cold War International History Project Electronic Bulletin*, no. 3, fall 1993, p. 14.

60 Andrew and Mitrokhin, *The Mitrokhin Archive*, pp. 333–34.

61 Kieran Williams, *The Prague Spring and its Aftermath: Czechoslovak Politics, 1968–1970* (Cambridge, UK: Cambridge University Press, 1997), p. 113.

62 As quoted in Andrew and Elkner, 'Stalin and Foreign Intelligence', at p. 84.

63 Kolpakidi and Prokhorov, *KGB, Spetsoperatsii sovetskoi razvedki*, pp. 14–112; Roman Kupchinsky, 'The "Trust": A Model Sting Operation', www.rferl.org/ corruptionwatch/2002/10/36-101002.asp, dated 10 Oct. 2002; Lazar Fleishman, *V tiskakh provokatsii: operatsiia 'Trest' i russkaia zarubezhnaia pechat* (Moscow: Novoe literaturnoe obozrenie, 2003).

64 A.I. Kolpakidi and D.P. Prokhorov, *KGB: Prikazano likvidirovat'* – *spetsoperatsii sovetskikh spetssluzhb 1918–1941* (Moscow: Eksmo, 2004), p. 383.

65 Ibid., p. 371.

66 Sudoplatov, *Special Tasks*, pp 11–24 and 249–59; Kolpakidi and Prokhorov, *KGB, Spetsoperatsii sovetskoi razvedki*, pp. 225–83, esp. p. 238 on the 1939–41 split and pp. 273 and 276 on the assassination of Rebet; Boris Chekhonin, *Zhurnalistika i razvedka* (Moscow: Algoritm, 2002), pp. 244–49.

67 Frances Stonor Saunders, *Who Paid the Piper? The CIA and the Cultural Cold War* (London: Granta, 2000).

68 O'Brien, 'Interfering with Civil Society' lists examples from both sides rather more even-handedly.

69 *Le Figaro*, 6 April 1983, as quoted in Mikhail Voslensky, *Nomenklatura: The New Soviet Ruling Class* (Garden City, NY: Doubleday, 1984), p. 380.

70 Anne Applebaum, *The Gulag: A History of the Soviet Concentration Camps* (London: Allen Lane, 2003), p. 442.

71 See the chapters headed 'Security Services Groups of Influence' and 'Participation of Special Services in Information War', in Mukhin, *Informatsionnaia voina v Rossii*, pp. 14–18 and 58–77.

72 Valerii Streletskii, *Mrakobesiye* (Moscow: Detektiv-Press, 1998), p. 15.

73 V. Solov'ev and E. Klepikova, *Zagovorshchiki v Kremle: ot Andropova do Gorbacheva* (Moscow, 1991), p. 73.

74 Heorhii Kas'ianov, *Nezhodni: ukraïns'ka intelihentsiia v rusi oporu 1960–80-kh rokiv* (Kiev: Lybid', 1995), pp. 50, 85 and 163.

75 Ibid., p. 59.

76 Ibid., p. 132.

77 Yurii Danylok and Oleh Bazhan, *Opozytsiia v Ukraïni* (Kiev: Ridnyi krai, 2000), p. 202; Vitalii Vrublevskii, *Vladimir Shcherbitskii: pravda i vymysly* (Kiev: Dovira, 1993), p. 160.

78 Vakhtang Kipiani, '"Ukraïns'kyi visnyk" z pidpillia. P"iatnadtsiat' rokiv tomu V"iacheslav Chornovil vidkryv era nazalezhnoho drukhu', posted at *Ukraïns'ka Pravda* on 21 Aug. 2002; www.pravda.com.ua/archive/?20821-h1-new.

79 Kas'ianov, *Nezhodni*, pp. 106–07. On the affair of the Belgian tourist Yaroslav Dobosh in 1972, see pp. 122–24. On the operation to discredit the World Congress of Free Ukrainians in the 1970s, see p. 141.

80 Kas'ianov, *Nezhodni*, pp. 130–32, quoting from material in the former party archive, now Central State Archive of Civic Organisations of Ukraine, F.1, op. 10, spr. 1494, ark. 60.

81 Aleksandr Yakovlev, *The Fate of Marxism in Russia* (New Haven: Yale University Press, 1993), p. 119.

82 Konstantin Simis, *USSR, The Corrupt Society: The Secret World of Soviet Capitalism* (New York: Simon and Schuster, 1982); Claire Sterling, *Thieves' World: The Threat of the New*

Global Network of Organized Crime (New York: Simon and Schuster, 1994).

83 Stephen Kotkin, *Armageddon Averted: The Soviet Collapse, 1970–2000* (Oxford: Oxford University Press, 2001), p. 145.

84 See Oleg Gordievsky's review of Milt Bearden and James Risen, *The Main Enemy: The Inside Story of the CIA's Final Showdown with the KGB* (New York: Random House, 2003), in *The Literary Review*, July 2003. Gordievsky argues that the KGB was in fact strengthened by its counter-intelligence successes in 1985–86.

85 Reddaway and Glinski, *The Tragedy of Russia's Reforms*, p. 122.

86 Yakovlev, *The Fate of Marxism in Russia*, p. 228; also partially quoted in Reddaway and Glinski, *The Tragedy of Russia's Reforms*, p. 122. See also Aksiutin, *et al.*, *Vlast' i oppozitsiia*, pp. 277 and 295.

87 Reddaway and Glinski, *The Tragedy of Russia's Reforms*, p. 122.

88 Markov, *PR v Rossii bol'she chem PR*, p. 260.

89 Gordon M. Hahn, *Russia's Revolution From Above, 1985–2000: Reform Transition, and Revolution in the Fall of the Soviet Communist Regime* (New Brunswick and London: Transaction Publishers, 2002), p. 98, n. 90.

90 Victor Yasman, 'Elite Think Tank Prepares "Post-*Perestroika*" Strategy', *Report on the USSR*, vol. 3, no. 21, 24 May 1991, pp. 1–6.

91 Hahn, *Russia's Revolution from Above*, pp. 154–55, nn. 49 and 50.

92 As proposed by Gorbachev aide Georgii Shakhnazarov in a memo of December 1989; Hahn, *Russia's Revolution from Above*, pp. 152–53, n. 32.

93 Valerii Solovei, '"Pamiat"': istoriia, idelogiia, politicheskaia praktika', in V.D Solovei and I.A. Erunov (eds), *Russkoe delo segodnia. Kniga 1. "Pamiat'"* (Moscow: Centre for the Study of International Relations, 1991), pp. 12–95, at p. 83.

94 Vladimir Soloukhin, *Posledniaia stupen' (Ispoved' vashego sovremennika)* (Moscow: Delovoi tsentr, 1995).

95 'Aleksandr Yakovlev: Rossiiskikh fashistov porodil KGB', *Izvestiia*, 12 June 1998, as quoted in Dunlop, 'Barkashov', p. 61.

96 Alexander Rahr, 'The KGB's Grey Eminence Retires', *Report on the USSR*, vol. 3, no. 9, 1 March 1991, pp. 10–12, at p. 11. See also the allegations made by Kalugin in *Sovetskaia molodezh'*, 18 July 1990, and Paul Klebnikov, *Godfather of the Kremlin: Boris Berezovsky and the Looting of Russia* (New York: Harcourt, 2000), p. 58.

97 *The New York Times*, 26 July 1987, reported Yeltsin's supposedly favourable endorsement of Pamiat'. See also Reddaway and Glinski, *The Tragedy of Russia's Reforms*, p. 127 and 659, n. 79.

98 Anatoly S. Chernayev, *My Six Years with Gorbachev* (Pennsylvania: Pennsylvania State University Press, 2000), p. 111.

99 John Dunlop, 'Pamiat' as a Social Movement', *Nationalities Papers*, vol. 18, no. 2, fall 1990, pp. 22–27, at p. 23.

100 Solovei, '"Pamiat"', pp. 39 and 45ff.

101 Chernyaev, *My Six Years with Gorbachev*, p. 154; Hahn, *Russia's Revolution from Above*, pp. 419–20.

102 David Remnick, 'The Counterrevolutionary', *The New York Review of Books*, 25 March 1993, pp. 34–38, at pp. 35–36; Vladimir Denisov, '"Krestnyi otets" Niny Andreevoi', *Rodina*, no. 1, 1991.

103 Chernyaev, *My Six Years with Gorbachev*, p. 156.

104 John Dunlop, *The Rise of Russia and the Fall of the Soviet Empire* (Princeton: Princeton University Press, 1995), p. 46 (see also pp. 108–11), citing a document from KGB archives found by the KGB defector Oleg Kalugin.

105 Alexander Rahr, 'New Evidence of the KGB's Political Complexion Published', *Report on the USSR*, vol. 3, no. 3, 18 Jan. 1991, pp. 1–5.

106 See the summary of Sergei Stepashin's report in Bruce Clark, 'Gorbachev Blamed for KGB Network of Telephone Taps', *The Times*, 5 Feb. 1992.

107 Elena Klepikova and Vladimir Solovyov, *Zhirinovsky: The Paradoxes of Russian Fascism* (London: Viking, 1995), p. 5; *Literaturnaia gazeta*, 12 Jan. 1994; *The Washington Post*, 14 Jan. 1994; 'Zhirinovsky Party Has KGB Roots, St. Petersburg Mayor Claims', *Associated Press*, 12 Jan. 1994.

108 Dmitri Volkogonov, *The Rise and Fall of the Soviet Empire: Political Leaders from Lenin to Gorbachev* (London: HarperCollins, 1999), pp. 473–74. His source: TsKhSD (Centre for the Preservation of Contemporary Documentation), Politburo Minutes, no. 87, for 28 May 1990. See also no. 182, for 22 March 1990.

109 Hahn, *Russia's Revolution from Above,* pp. 218–20.

110 For the existing literature on the origins and early years of Zhirinovskii's party, see *Rossiiskiye vesti,* 30 Dec. 1993; Klepikova and Solovyov, *Zhirinovsky,* pp. 23–82; Vladimir Kartsev, *!Zhirinovsky!* (New York: Columbia University Press, 1995), pp. 20–82; S. Plekhanov, *Zhirinovskii: kto on?* (Moscow: Evraziia-Nord, 1994), pp. 56–66; Reddaway and Glinski, *The Tragedy of Russia's Reforms,* pp. 188–94; Dunlop, *The Rise of Russia,* pp. 154–58.

111 Interviewed in Michael McFaul and Sergei Markov, *The Troubled Birth of Russian Democracy: Parties, Personalities, and Programs* (Stanford: Hoover Institution Press, 1993), pp. 32 and 34.

112 Klepikova and Solovyov, *Zhirinovsky,* p. 67.

113 As quoted in Vladimir Pribylovskii, *Dictionary of Political Parties and Organisations in Russia* (Washington, DC: CSIS/Perseus, 1992), p. ix.

114 Reddaway and Glinski, *The Tragedy of Russia's Reforms,* p. 189.

115 Hahn, *Russia's Revolution from Above,* p. 219.

116 Oleksandr Hrynkevych and Anatolii Hutsal, *Oblychchia vlady: rosiis'ka politychna elita. 1998–2000 rr.* (Kiev: Naukova dumka, 2002), p. 356.

117 Michael Urban *et al., The Rebirth of Politics in Russia* (Cambridge, UK: Cambridge University Press, 1997), pp. 385–86, n. 8.

118 Hahn, *Russia's Revolution from Above,* p. 338, reports Gorbachev turning down Lukianov's proposal that he meet with Zhirinovskii in January 1991 as 'there were many parties and Zhirinovskii's had no future'.

119 Hrynkevych and Hutsal, *Oblychchia vlady,* p. 360.

120 Klepikova and Solovyov, *Zhirinovsky,* p. 12.

121 Hrynkevych and Hutsal, *Oblychchia vlady,* pp. 349 and 356; Reddaway and Glinski, *The Tragedy of Russia's Reforms,* p. 193.

122 Hrynkevych and Hutsal, *Oblychchia vlady,* p. 353.

123 Michael McFaul, 'Russian Electoral Trends', in Zoltan Barany and Robert G. Moser (eds), *Russian Politics: Challenges of Democratization* (Cambridge, UK: Cambridge University Press, 2001), pp. 19–63, at pp. 41–42.

124 Dunlop, *The Rise of Russia,* pp. 46–49.

125 Source: official results from ww.fci.ru/WAY/326535.html. (This bizarre internet address, with only two w's, was correct as of November 2004.)

126 Urban, *The Rebirth of Politics in Russia,* p. 235.

127 John B. Dunlop, 'The Leadership of the Centrist Bloc', *Report on the USSR,* vol. 3, no. 6, 8 Feb. 1991, pp. 4–6, at p. 4.

128 Klepikova and Solovyov, *Zhirinovsky,* p. 8.

129 'Coup or Operetta?', *Moscow News,* 18–25 Nov. 1990, p. 6.

130 From his speech to the Russian Congress of People's Deputies, quoted in Hrynkevych and Hutsal, *Oblychchia vlady,* p. 359, n. 16.

131 'Soviet Active Measures in the "Post-Cold War" Era 1988–1991: Internal Front

Groups: Vladimir Zhirinovsky and the "Centrist Bloc"',
http://intellit.muskingum.edu/russia_folder/pcw_era/sect_07.htm, no date.

132 Dunlop, *The Rise of Russia*, p. 209.

133 Ibid., p. 344, n. 62.

134 Yakovlev, *The Fate of Marxism in Russia*, p. 133.

135 Julia Wishnevsky, 'Anatolii Luk'yanov: Gorbachev's Conservative Rival?', *Report on the USSR*, vol. 3, no. 23, 7 June 1991, pp. 8–14.

136 Julia Wishnevsky, 'Multiparty System, Soviet Style', *Report on the USSR*, vol. 2, no. 47, 23 Nov. 1990, pp. 3–6, at p. 4.

137 John Morrison, *Boris Yeltsin: From Bolshevik to Democrat* (London: Penguin, 1991), p. 221.

138 Archie Brown, *The Gorbachev Factor* (Oxford: Oxford University Press, 1996), pp. 279–80.

139 For some sceptical analyses of the events of August 1991, see Reddaway and Glinski, *The Tragedy of Russia's Reforms*, pp. 194–227, and Dunlop, *The Rise of Russia*, pp. 186–225. Archie Brown, on the other hand, in his *The Gorbachev Factor*, pp. 297–98, defends Gorbachev's account. For this see Mikhail Gorbachev, *The August Coup: The Truth and the Lessons* (London: HarperCollins, 1991), which has relatively little of either 'truth' or 'lessons'. See also Hahn, *Russia's Revolution from Above*, pp. 420–30 and p. 433 n. 6, and Jerry F. Hough, *Democratization and Revolution in the USSR, 1985–91* (Washington, DC: The Brookings Institution, 1997), pp. 432–37. For Russian sources, see *Putch. Khronika trevozhnykh dnei*, available online at *The Russia Journal* website, www.russ.ru/antolog/1991/index.htm, as are several others sources at www.russ.ru/antolog/1991/resurs.htm. Nikolai Nepomniashchii, *Tainy sovetskoi epokhi* (Moscow: Veche, 2003), pp. 354–75 provides a fair summary of the main versions of events in Crimea.

140 Yu. M. Baturin et al., *Epokha El'tsina. Ocherki politicheskoi istorii* (Moscow: Vagrius, 2001), p. 145.

141 Ibid., p. 144.

142 Aleksei Volokhov, *Noveishaia istoriia Kommunisticheskoi partii: 1990–2002* (Moscow: Impeto, 2003), p. 18.

143 Baturin et al., *Epokha El'tsina*, p. 145.

144 Reddaway and Glinski, *The Tragedy of Russia's Reforms*, pp. 245–46.

145 Roi (Roy) Medvedev, *Sovetskii Soiuz: poslednii god zhizni* (Moscow: Prava cheloveka, 2003), p. 124.

146 Volodymyr Kovtun, *Istoriia Narodnoho Rukhu Ukraïny* (Kiev: no pub., 1995), pp. 123–24.

147 Leonid Kravchuk, *Maiemo te, shcho maiemo* (Kiev: Lybid', 2002), p. 64.

148 Kovtun, *Istoriia Narodnoho Rukhu Ukraïny*, p. 123.

149 Volodymyr Lytvyn, *Politychna arena Ukraïny: diiovi osobi ta vykonavtsi* (Kiev: Abrys, 1994), pp. 121, 157 and 159. See also Nahaylo, *The Ukrainian Resurgence*, pp. 178, 182, 210–11 and 222.

150 Specific accusations concerning KGB agents within Rukh can be found at www.prima-news.ru/eng/news/news/2002/2/20/7416.html, dated 20 Feb. 2002, and at www.compromat.ru/main/kuchma/yavorivskij.htm, dated 28 Oct. 2003.

151 Oleksandr Boiko, 'Zahostrennia politychnoï konfrontatsiï v Ukraïni: ataka opozytsiï ta kontranastup konservatoriv (serpen'-hruden' 1990 r.)', *Suchasnist'*, no. 2, Feb. 2003, pp. 67–76, at p. 72 quotes archival documents revealing how extensive these plans were. The KGB backed similar 'separatist' groups throughout the USSR, such as Mikola Shaliahovich's Brest movement in Belarus.

152 *Literaturna Ukraïna*, 15 Nov. 1990.

153 Oleksii Haran', *Ubyty drakona. Z istoriï Rukhu ta novykh partii Ukraïny* (Kiev: Lybid', 1993), p. 84.

154 Ibid., p. 76.

155 Hryhorii Honcharuk, *Narodnyi Rukh Ukraïny. Istoriia* (Odesa: Astroprynt, 1997), pp. 88–89.

156 '*Protokol zasidannia Sekretariatu URP vid 20.03.91r*', p. 3.

157 '*Protokol zasidannia Sekretariatu URP vid 5.04.91r*', p. 2; '*Zasidannia Rady URP 16–17.02.1991: Protokol no. 18/ZR*', pp. 10 and 11.

158 From an internal URP document, '*Te, shcho ne uviishlo do protokoly Sekraraiatu vid 27.02.91*' ('That which was not included in the minutes of the Secretariat of 27.02.91').

159 '*Protokol zasidannia Sekretariatu URP vid 25.03.91*', p. 2.

160 Volodymyr Ruban, 'Zakonservovanyi rozkol?', *Moloda Halychyna*, 4 June 1991. See also Haran', *Ubyty drakona*, p. 179.

161 Oleksii Holobuts'kyi (ed.), *S'ohodnishni lidery Ukraïny: prymiriuvannia roli prezydenta* (Kiev: AMS, 2003), pp. 88–89.

162 Mark Beissinger, *Nationalist Mobilization and the Collapse of the Soviet State* (Cambridge, UK: Cambridge University Press, 2002).

163 Lisovskii and Evstaf'ev, *Izbiratel'nye tekhnologii*, p. 75.

Chapter 2

1 Pelevin, *Babylon*, p. 166 and from the mock-disclaimer introduction.

2 From the English translation: Frédéric Beigbeder, *£9.99* (London: Picador, 2002), p. 46.

3 Pelevin, *Babylon*, p. 166.

4 Umberto Eco, *Travels in Hyperreality: Essays* (London: Pan/Secker and Warburg, 1987), pp. 8 and 19.

5 Umberto Eco, *Faith in Fakes: Travels in Hyperreality* (London: Vintage, 1998), pp. 1–58, at p. 6.

6 Umberto Eco, *Baudolino* (London: Secker and Warburg, 2002), pp. 84, 99 and 232.

7 Jorge Luis Borges, *Labyrinths* (London: Penguin, 1970), p. 12.

8 Peter Huber, *Orwell's Revenge: The 1984 Palimpsest* (New York: The Free Press, 1994), p. 91.

9 Manuel Castells, *The Information Age. Volume I. The Rise of the Network Society* (2nd edn; Oxford: Blackwell, 2000), pp. 360–61; also quoting Neil Postman, *Amusing Ourselves to Death* (New York: Penguin, 1985). Final quotation as adapted from Ivan Zassoursky, 'Media and Politics in Russia in the Nineties', at http://www.geocities.com/zassoursky/paper.htm.

10 Manuel Castells, *The Information Age. Volume II. The Power of Identity* (Oxford: Blackwell, 1997), p. 312.

11 Ibid., p. 311.

12 Author's interviews with Andrei Riabov, 8 Nov. 2002 and 21 Feb. 2004.

13 Sheila Fitzpatrick, 'The World of Ostap Bender: Soviet Confidence Men in the Stalin Period', *Slavic Review*, vol. 61, no. 3, fall 2002, pp. 535–57.

14 Ibid., p. 543.

15 Golfo Alexopoulos, 'Portrait of a Con Artist as Soviet Man', *Slavic Review*, vol. 57, no. 4, winter 1998, pp. 774–90.

16 Fitzpatrick, 'The World of Ostap Bender', p. 557.

17 Mikhail Epshtein et al., *After the Future: The Paradoxes of Postmodernism and Contemporary Russian Culture* (Amherst: University of Massachusetts Press, 1995).

18 Mikhail Epshtein et al., *Russian Postmodernism: New Perspectives on Post-Soviet Culture* (New York and Oxford: Berghahn Books, 1999); Nadezhda Man'kovskaia, *Estetika*

postmodernizma (St Petersburg: Aleteiia, 2000); Dmitrii Prigov, *Sovetskie teksty* (Moscow: Iz. Ivana Limbakha, 1997).

19 See Michael M. Naydan's translation of Andrukhovych's novel, *Perverzion (Writings from an Unbound Europe)* (Chicago: Northwestern University Press, 2004).

20 Dmytro Vydrin, 'Sumerki postmodernizma ukrainskoi politiki', *Izvestiia*, 16 March 2001.

21 Martin Wolf in the *Financial Times*, 5 Nov. 2003.

22 Author's interview with Volodymyr Polokhalo, 15 March 2002.

23 Zassoursky, 'Media and Politics in Russia in the Nineties'.

24 Author's interview with Gleb Pavlovskii, 8 Nov. 2002.

25 Ibid.

26 Malkin and Suchkov, *Osnovy izbiratel'nykh tekhnologii*, p. 57.

27 Tsuladze, *Bol'shaia manipiliativnaia igra*, p. 34.

28 Favors'ka, 'Brudni vyborchi tekhnolohii'.

29 A.V. Ermolaev *et al.*, *Ukraine on the Eve of the 'Post-Oligarchic' Period* (Sofia: Social Research Centre, 2000); at http://users.gu.net/postinfo/materials/research_eng/part-_6.htm p. 4.

30 Pelevin, *Babylon*, pp. 170–71.

31 Ihor Koliushko, head of the Centre for Legal and Political Reform in Ukraine, remarks at a round table in Kiev, 11 March 2002.

32 Richard Rose and Neil Munro, *Elections without Order: Russia's Challenge to Vladimir Putin* (Cambridge, UK: Cambridge University Press, 2002), p. 109.

33 Interviewed in *Versty*, 29 July 2003, via *Johnson's Russia List*, no. 7,269, 30 July 2003.

34 Richard D. Anderson, Jr, 'The Discursive Origins of Russian Democratic Politics', in Anderson *et al.*, *Postcommunism and the Theory of Democracy* (Princeton: Princeton University Press, 2001), pp. 96–125, at p. 107.

35 Ukrainian analyst Hryhorii Nemeriia, remarks to the author, 3 Feb. 2003.

36 Borges, 'The Wall and the Books', *Labyrinths*, pp. 221–23, at p. 221.

37 Stephen Holmes, 'Potemkin Democracy', p. 118.

38 Shari J. Cohen, *Politics without a Past: The Absence of History in Postcommunist Nationalism* (North Carolina: Duke University Press, 1999), p. 4.

39 Reddaway and Glinski, *The Tragedy of Russia's Reforms*, *passim*,

40 Aleksei Kara-Murza, 'Rossiiskaia politicheskaia kul'tura i problemy stanovleniia partiinogo pliuralizma', in Michael McFaul, Sergei Markov and Andrei Riabov (eds), *Formirovanie partiino-politicheskoi sistemy v Rossii* (Moscow: Carnegie Centre, 1998), pp. 7–19, at p. 15.

41 Mykola Riabchuk, *Dvi Ukraïny* (Kiev: Krytyka, 2003), pp. 35–36.

42 Anatolii Lukashev and Anatolii Ponidelko, *Anatomiia demokratii, ili Chernyi PR kak institut grazhdanskogo obshchestva* (St Petersburg: Bizness-Press, 2001), p. 107.

43 Ivan Zasoursky, *Media and Power in Post-Soviet Russia* (New York: M.E. Sharpe, 2003).

44 Author's interview with Gleb Pavlovskii, 8 Nov. 2002.

45 See the memoir by the *Pravda Ukrainy* editor Aleksandr Gorobets, *Bosikom po bitomu steklu* (Kiev: Mi, 2003).

46 Interviewed in *Ezhenedel'nyi zhurnal*, no. 107, 16 Feb. 2004.

47 Author's interview with Marat Gel'man, 9 Nov. 2002.

48 Rose and Munro, *Elections without Order*, pp. 131–33.

49 From www.kreml.org, posted and accessed 4 Dec. 2003.

50 Reddaway and Glinksi, *The Tragedy of Russia's Reforms*, p. 492. Emphasis in original.

51 Dominique Arel, 'Kuchmagate and the Demise of Ukraine's "Geopolitical Bluff"', *East European Constitutional Review*, vol. 10, nos 2–3, spring–summer 2001, pp. 54–59.

52 Mykola Riabchuk, 'Ukraïna bez Mugab(e)', *Krytyka*, no. 3, 2002.

53 The term was coined by the French theorist Julia Kristeva. See Kelly Oliver (ed.), *The*

Portable Kristeva (2nd edn; New York: Columbia University Press, 2002).

54 Author's interview with Aleksei Sitnikov, 4 Nov. 2002.

55 'Eurasianism', a theory mainly developed by Russian émigrés in the 1920s, extols a unique Russian mission in bridging the geographies and cultures of Europe and Asia.

56 Author's interview with Valerii Solovei, 5 Nov. 2002.

57 Ronald Inglehart, *Culture Shift in Advanced Industrial Society* (Princeton: Princeton University Press, 1990); Kay Lawson and Peter Merkl, *When Parties Fail: Emerging Alternative Organizations* (Princeton: Princeton University Press, 1988); Paul Webb *et al.*, *Political Parties in Democratic Societies. Emergence, Adaptation and Decline* (Oxford: Oxford University Press, 2001).

58 Giovanni Sartori, *Homo videns: la sociedad teledirigide*, trans. Ana Díaz Soles (Madrid: Taurus, 1998).

59 Norman Ornstein and Thomas E. Mann (eds), *The Permanent Campaign and its Future* (Washington DC: The AEI Press, 2000); Dick Morris, *Behind the Oval Office: Getting Reelected against All Odds* (Los Angeles: Renaissance Books, 1998).

60 Mark Lawson, 'Some Mistake?', *Guardian*, 9 Oct. 2003.

61 See the original article by Carey McWilliams, 'Politics of Personality: California', http://www.thenation.com/doc.mhtml%3Fi=19621027&s=mcwilliams, (re-)posted 14 Aug. 2003.

62 Georgii Pocheptsov, *Imidzh i vybory* (Kiev: ADEF-Ukraine, 1997), p. 20.

63 Jean Baudrillard, *Simulacra and Simulation*, trans. Sheila Faria Glaser (Ann Arbor: University of Michigan Press, 1994), p. 80. Emphasis in original.

64 Juan J. Linz and Alfred Stepan, *Problems of Democratic Transition and Consolidation: Southern Europe, South America, and Post-Communist Europe* (Baltimore and London: John Hopkins, 1996), p. 8.

65 Jean Baudrillard, *In the Shadow of the Silent Majority* (New York: Semiotext(e), 1983). On the difficulties of constructing civil society in Ukraine from below, see Mykola Riabchuk, *Dylemy ukraïns'koho Fausta: hromadians'ko suspil'stvo i 'rozbudova derzhavy'* (Kiev: Krytyka, 2000), especially section one; and Paul Kubicek, *Unbroken Ties: The State, Interest Associations, and Corporatism in Post-Soviet Ukraine* (Ann Arbor: University of Michigan Press, 2000) on social control from above. On Russia, see M. Steven Fish, *Democracy from Scratch. Opposition and Regime in the New Russian Revolution* (Princeton: Princeton University Press, 1995).

66 Pocheptsov, *Imidzh i vybory*, p. 72.

Chapter 3

1 From his introduction to Lisovskii and Evstaf'ev, *Izbiratel'nye tekhnologii*, pp. 8–12, at p. 10.

2 Michael McFaul, *Russia's 1996 Presidential Election: The End of Polarized Politics* (Stanford: Hoover Institution Press, 1997).

3 Avtandil Tsuladze, *Bol'shaia manipuliativnaia igra* (Moscow: Algoritm, 2000); Timothy J. Colton and Michael McFaul, *Popular Choice and Managed Democracy: The Russian Elections of 1999 and 2000* (Stanford: Hoover Institution Press, 2003).

4 See the *mea culpa* by Clinton's tormentor, David Brock, *Blinded by the Right: The Conscience of an Ex-Conservative* (New York: Crown, 2002).

5 See, for example, James Ellroy, *American Tabloid* (London: Century, 1995).

6 James Moore and Wayne Slater, *Bush's Brain. How Karl Rove Made George W. Bush President* (Hoboken: John Wiley and Sons, 2003), p. 15.

7 Author's interview with Gleb Pavlovskii, 8 Nov. 2002. Emphasis in original.

8 Markov, *PR v Rossii bol'she chem PR.*

9 The following website addresses for Russian political technology firms were correct as of December 2003: for Pavlovskii www.fep.ru, for Sitnikov www.sitnikov.com and www.image-contact.ru, for Shchedrovitskii www.shkp.ru, for Koshmar'ov www.novokom.ru, and for Mintusov's Nikkolo-M www.nikkolom.ru and www.publicity.ru, Ostrovskii's peripatetic website was then at http://eostrovsky. region56.ru/new/p_eo.html. The political PR magazine *So-obshchenie* has a site at www.soob.ru

10 Olesia Favors'ka, 'Brudni vyborchi tekhnolohiï', www.spa.org.ua/ShowAnalysisArticle.php?ID=БруАНi%20Виборчi%20Технологiï.

11 *Profil*, 20 Jan. 2003, via *Johnson's Russia List*, no. 7,035, 27 Jan. 2003.

12 Julie A. Corwin, 'Campaign Finance: Voodoo Arithmetic', *RFE/RL Russia Votes.* www.rferl.org/specials/russianelections/stories/story-46.asp, accessed 21 Oct. 2003.

13 Author's interview with Andrei Riabov, 8 Nov. 2002.

14 Lola Kuchina, 'Vybory-2003: osobennosti PR-tekhnologii', at www.politcom.ru/2003/bigpr12.php, written 29 Oct. 2003, accessed 4 Nov. 2003.

15 For a profile of Surkov, see the *RFE/RL Russian Political Weekly,* vol. 1, no. 13, 1 May 2001.

16 In the Ukrainian version of his book, *Beheaded,* J.V. Koshiw asserts that two agents of the Interior Ministry unit Sokil ('Hawk') and an associate of the Kiev gangster Kysel killed Gongadze, and that the former boss of the Ukrainian Security Service (SBU) Yevhen Marchuk and his men were behind the moving and finding of the body – and possibly the taping operation, too: Jaroslav Koshiv, *Obezholovlenyi* (Kiev: Sobor, 2004), pp. 254–55 and 260–62.

17 'Oligarchs' is the local term so I have used it, even though there is no oligarchy in the sense of the collective rule of a few (businessmen) – as such. 'Tycoons' or 'magnates' would serve just as well.

18 Boris Kagarlitsky, 'Pavlovsky's Tricky Situation', *Moscow Times,* 21 Oct. 2003.

19 Author's interview with Pavlovskii, 8 Nov. 2002.

20 Author's interview with Ekaterina Egorova, 21 March 2001.

21 Marcus Warren, 'E-mail from Russia', *Electronic Telegraph,* filed 30 Jan. 2001; *Zerkalo tyzhnia,* no. 39, 6–12 Oct. 2001.

22 Mukhin, *Informatsionnaia voina v Rossii,* p. 30; *Versiia,* no. 43, 1999. See also the profile at www.russ.ru/journal/dosie/pavlovsk.htm.

23 From the profile at www.rferl.org/businesswatch/2001/11/17–061101.asp.

24 Gleb Pavlovskii, 'Slipa pliama (deshcho pro Bilovez'kykh liudei)', *Ï,* no. 18, 2000, pp. 141–59, at p. 157. (In Ukrainian translation.)

25 Author's interview with Pavlovskii, 8 Nov. 2002.

26 *Rossiiskaia gazeta,* 19 Nov. 1994.

27 For his black PR, see Julia Wishnevsky, *Russia's Communists,* p. 239.

28 Interested readers could compare these with sites such as 'Gore-Lieberman 2000. Unofficial', at http://crm114.com/algore/scandals/html.

29 *Profil,* 27 Dec. 1999.

30 *Ot pervogo litsa. Razgovory s Vladimirom Putinym* (Moscow, 2000), p. 105.

31 Gleb Pavlovskii, 'Proshchai, belovezhe! Kreml' vziat silami bol'shinstva. Grazhdanskaia voina zakonchena', *Nezavisimaia gazeta,* 9 Dec. 2000. See also the attack on Pavlovskii by Aleksandr Minkin, 'Tak i zhivem. Oshibka prezidenta', in *Moskovskii komsomolets',* 2 March 2001.

32 *Moskovskii komsomolets',* 15 Feb. 2002.

33 On Gel'man's career, see Grigorii Nekhoroshev, 'Gel'man iz galerei. Na postupakh k pereustroistvu Rossii', *Nezavisimaia gazeta,* 26 April 2001.

34   Ilia Musorgskii, 'Galereia intellektual'nykh provokatsii', www.compromat.ru/main/gelman/provokator.htm.
35   Laura Belin, 'Lebed's Presidential Campaign: His Most Enduring Legacy', *RFE/RL Russian Political Weekly*, vol. 2, no. 14, 29 April 2002.
36   For a profile of Koshmar'ov, see *RFR/RL Russian Political Weekly*, vol. 2, no. 8, 14 March 2002.
37   Brian Whitmore, 'St Petersburg Reformers Battle a Russian Tammany Hall', *Prism*, vol. 4, no. 22, 13 Nov. 1998.
38   *Moscow Times*, 30 May 1996; Castells, *The Information Age*. Volume II, p. 326.
39   *The Times*, 11 Feb. 2000.
40   Timothy J. Colton and Michael McFaul, *Popular Choice and Managed Democracy: The Russian Elections of 1999 and 2000* (Washington, DC: Brookings Institute Press, 2003), p. 35.
41   Corwin, 'Campaign Finance: Voodoo Arithmetic'.
42   Yurii Lypa, *Rozpodil' Rossiï* (L'viv: Academy of Sciences, 1995; reprint of the edition published in New York by Hoverlia in 1954), p. 65.
43   Author's interview with Pikhovshek, 25 July 2001.
44   Other reports linked www.provokator.com to the Donets'k group: Holobuts'kyi *et al.*, *S'ohodnishni lideri Ukraïny. IV*, p. 91.
45   Author's interview with Volodymyr Polokhalo, 15 March 2002.
46   From the long interview with Gel'man by Serhii Leshchenko for *Ukraïns'ka pravda*, 'Marat Hel'man: Omel'chenko – orhanizator "Kasetnoho skandalu-2". Tse naibil'sh pravdopodibnyi variant', www.pravda.com.ua/?2024-2-new, posted 4 Feb. 2002.
47   'FEPu Pavlovs'koho zamalo odniieï SDPU(o)', *Ukraïns'ka pravda*, 8 Nov. 2001.
48   *Nezavisimaia gazeta*, 29 Dec. 2001.
49   Holobuts'kyi *et al.*, *S'ohodnishni lideri Ukraïny. IV*, p. 73.
50   Author's interview with Olesia Favor'ska, 6 Dec. 2003.
51   Maliarenko, 'Ostrov sokrovishch, ili Kto piarit "Donchan"'. See the websites www.diac.dn.ua and www.finfort.com.
52   Author's interview with Ekaterina Egorova of Nikkolo-M, Moscow, 21 March 2001.
53   Efim Ostrovskii, 'Zakonchiv polnyi tsikl: 1989–2001 gody – ot zmei do zmei', *Soobshchenie*, no. 9, Sept. 2002, pp. 6–9, at p. 7.
54   Author's interview with Efim Ostrovskii, 4 Nov. 2002.
55   Author's interview with Marat Gel'man, 9 Nov. 2002. Gel'man accompanied his remarks by lifting the table.
56   Speaking at a round table organised by *Nezavisimaia gazeta*, 23 March 2000, as quoted in James H. Billington, *Russia in Search of Itself* (Baltimore: John Hopkins University Press, 2004), p. 92.
57   Author's interview with Gleb Pavlovskii, 8 Nov. 2002.
58   Guy Debord, *Society of the Spectacle* (Paris: Buchet Chastel, 1967 – for a recent edition, see the 1995 version by Zone).
59   Author's interview with Piotr Shchedrovitskii, 3 Nov. 2002.
60   Author's interview with Marat Gel'man, 9 Nov. 2002.
61   Mukhin, *Informatsionnaia voina v Rossii*, p. 24.
62   Author's interview with Efim Ostrovskii, 4 Nov. 2002.
63   Ibid.
64   Author's interview with Yurchyshyn, 5 Dec. 2003.
65   'Why Does Russia Need So Many Parties?', *The Russia Journal*, 15 March 1999.
66   Lytvyn, *Politychna arena Ukraïny*, pp. 287–88.
67   Halyna Korotka, 'In the Epicentre of a Scandal – O. Tkachenko, the Deputy Speaker of Ukraine's Parliament', *Demoz*, vol. 1, no. 1, Oct. 1994, pp. 13–14.

68 Terhi Rantanen, *The Global and the National: Media and Communications in Post-Communist Russia* (Lanham: Rowman and Littlefield, 2002).

69 Author's interview with Sergei Mikhailov, managing partner of Mikhailov and Partners, 5 Nov. 2002.

70 Jacques Séguéla, *Natsional'nye osobennososti okhoty za golosami: Tak delaiut prezidentov* (Moscow: Vagrius, 1999).

71 Author's interview with Efim Ostrovskii, 4 Nov. 2002.

72 For a summary, see Alan Davis and Mark Grigorian (eds), *Polls Apart: Media Coverage of the Parliamentary Elections, Belarus, October 2000* (London: Institute for War and Peace Reporting, 2001), pp. 82–86.

73 Author's interview with Aleksei Sitnikov, 4 Nov. 2002.

74 Author's interview with Andrei Riabov, 8 Nov. 2002.

75 Ibid.

76 Author's interview with Marat Gel'man, 9 Nov. 2002. See also A. Zolotov, 'ORT Gets a New Pre-Election Strategist', *Moscow Times*, 18 June 2002.

77 Mukhin, *Informatsionnaia voina v Rossii*, pp. 8–9.

78 See the section entitled 'Media-killers' in Mukhin, *Informatsionnaia voina v Rossii*, pp. 43–52.

79 Lukashev and Ponidelko, *Anatomiia demokratii*, p. 112.

80 Tatiana Strepkova, 'Imidzh "po-chernomu", a po-belomu – pablisiti', *Sovetnik*, no. 7, 1997.

81 Viktor Bondarev, 'Klonirovanie kandidatov', in Sergei Ustimenko (ed.), *Izbiratel'nye tekhnologii i izbiratel'noe iskusstvo* (Moscow: PR-Intellekt/Russian Political Encyclopaedia, 2001), pp. 48–53, at p. 48.

82 Markov, *PR v Rossii bol'she chem PR*, p. 251.

83 Georgii [Heorhii] Pocheptsov, *Informatsionno-politicheskie tekhnologii* (Moscow: Tsentr, 2003), p. 43.

84 Ekaterina Larina, 'Strategists Develop the Art of Dirty Campaign', *The Russia Journal*, 21 Dec. 1999.

85 Vladimir Shlapentokh, *The Politics of Sociology in the Soviet Union* (Boulder and London: Westview, 1987), pp. 126–27; Jeffrey W. Hahn, 'Public Opinion Research in the Soviet Union: Problems and Possibilities', in Arthur H. Miller, William M. Reissinger and Vicki Hesli (eds), *Public Opinion and Regime Change: The New Politics of Post-Soviet Societies* (Boulder: Westview, 1993), pp. 37–47.

86 Quoted in Yuliia Mostova, 'Sotsopytuvannia i adminresurs – ne odne i te same', *Zerkalo tyzhnia*, no. 6, 16–22 Feb. 2002.

87 V"iacheslav Yakubenko, 'Yak ya pratsiuvav imidzhmeikerom Kuchmy', *Den'*, 14 Oct. 1999.

88 *Zerkalo nedeli*, 2 Oct. 1999.

89 Anatolii Zhanik, 'Kuchmisty nastupatymut' na Verkhovnu Rady z chotyr'okh flanhiv', *Ukraïns'ka pravda*, 23 Dec. 2001.

90 Heorhii Pocheptsov, *Informatsiia i dezinformatsiia* (Kiev: Nika-Tsentr, 2001), p. 196.

91 Favors'ka, 'Brudni vyborchi tekhnolohii'.

92 Kutyrev, *Tekhnologii pobedy na vyborakh*, pp. 70–71.

93 A.Yu. Koshmarov and G.S. Kuznetsov, 'Novye podkhody v izbiratel'nykh tekhnologiiakh', *Materialy Vserossiiskogo seminara-konferentsii 'Obshchestvo-vybory-SMI-1999-god: Mezhdu "chistymi" i "griaznymi" politicheskimi tekhnologiiami'*; at www.foris.ru/vibori/koshmarov.htm.

94 Favors'ka, 'Brudni vyborchi tekhnolohii'.

95 Pocheptsov, *Informatsionno-politicheskie tekhnologii*, p. 44.

96 Keith Darden, 'Blackmail as a Tool of State Domination: Ukraine under Kuchma', *East European Constitutional Review*, vol. 10, nos 2–3 spring–summer 2001, pp. 67–71.

97 Tsuladze, *Bol'shaia manipuliativnaia igra*, p. 61.
98 Koshiw, *Beheaded*, pp. 172–73.
99 Author's interview with Efim Ostrovskii, 4 Nov. 2002.
100 Castells, *The Information Age*. Volume II, p. 341.

Chapter 4

1 Artem Storozhenko, 'From Old to New Administrative Resources. Only with Peculiarities of 2002', part.org.ua, Jan. 2002.

2 Dmytro Vydrin, 'Pentahrama-2002 formula osoblyvostei parlaments'koï vyborchoï kampanii', *Dzerkalo tyzhnia*, no. 39, 6–12 Oct. 2001.

3 Viktor Nebozhenko, speaking at a round table organised by *Ukraïns'ka pravda*, www.pravda.com.ua/?2024-4-new.

4 Ihor Popov, head of the Committee of Voters of Ukraine, speaking at the same round table.

5 Vydrin, 'Pentahrama-2002'.

6 '28 + 13 + 13 + 10 + 3 = 67 per cent. I tse bez Lytvyna! *TUNDRA* – monopolist adminresursu', *Ukraïns'ka pravda*, 7 Dec. 2001.

7 Oleksandr Bulavin, 'Ne "adminresurs" keruie suspil'stvom, a yakraz navpaky', *Den'*, 15 Aug. 2001.

8 Mykola Riabchuk, '"Bezlad" zarady "zlahody"', *Krytyka*, no. 4, April 2002, pp. 6–13. For the CVU analysis, see www.cvu.kiev.ua/eng/.

9 Volodymyr Polokhalo, 'Ukraïns'ki dity leitenanta Shmidta (Natsional'ni osoblyvosti parlaments'kykh vyboriv)', www.politdumka.kiev.ua/s0201-1.html.

10 According to the account by Viacheslav Kostikov, Yeltsin's presidential spokesman from 1992 to 1995, in his *Roman s prezidentom* (Moscow: Vagrius, 1997), pp. 266–67, Nikolai Riabov, head of the Central Election Commission, presented Yeltsin with a document the day after the voting, on which turnout was described as 'more than 50 per cent'. Someone had made a crude adjustment by hand to '60 per cent'. As quoted in Alexander N. Domin, 'President Yeltsin vs. the First Russian Parliament: Forgotten Lessons?', www.uiowa.edu/~cyberlaw/domrin/andart02.html, as accessed 28 June 2004.

11 Vera Tolz and Julia Wishnevsky, 'Election Queries Make Russians Doubt Democratic Process', *RFE/RL Research Report*, vol. 3, no. 13, 1 April 1994.

12 The phrase 'dead souls', which is the title of a novel by Gogol (1842), refers to voting by the already dead. In Gogol's story, the hero, Chichikov, collects dead peasants in order to be able to pose as a gentleman of substance.

13 See A. Sobianin and V. Sukhovol'skii, *Demokratiia, organichennaia falsifikatsiiami: Vybory i referendumy v Rossii v 1991–93* (Moscow: Project Group on Human Rights, 1995).

14 Michael McFaul and Nikolai Petrov (eds), *Politicheskii al'manakh Rossii 1997* (Moscow: Carnegie Centre, 1998), vol. 1, section on 'Falsification', pp. 319–24, at p. 320.

15 Kronid Liubarskii and Aleksandr Sobianin, 'Fal'sifikatsiia-3', *Novoe vremia*, no. 15, 1995, p. 10; as quoted in John B. Dunlop, 'Sifting through the Rubble of the Yeltsin Years', in *Problems of Post-Communism*, vol. 47, no. 1, Jan.–Feb. 2000, pp. 3–15, at pp. 7–8. Sobianin's estimates were also published in *Izvestiia*, 4 May 1994.

16 Valentin Mikhailov *et al.*, *Osobaia zona: Vybory v Tatarstane* (Ul'ianovsk: Kazan Section of the International Human Rights Assembly, 2000).

17 Sobianin's figures are summarised in McFaul and Petrov (eds), *Politicheskii al'manakh Rossii 1997*, p. 321.

18 Author's interview with Aleksei Sitnikov, 4 Nov. 2002.

19 Baturin *et al.*, *Epokha El'tsina*, p. 572.

20 Author's interview with Aleksei Sitnikov, 4 Nov. 2002. See also the *Financial Times*, 1 Oct. 1996 on the 'talony'.

21 Author's interview with Sitnikov, 4 Nov. 2002.

22 The main parallel, observers', count had united Russia on 33.3 per cent (−4.3), the CPRF and LDPR unchanged, Rodina on 10.75 per cent (+1.6) Yabloko at 6 per cent (+1.7) and URF on 5.1 (+1.1); www.russiajournal.com/news/cnews-article.shtml?nd =41696, 'Alternative Results of Duma Elections Appear', 8 Dec. 2003.

23 E-mail from Andrei Riabov, 4 March 2004.

24 See www.eng.yabloko.ru/Publ/2004/PAPERS/02/040130_mose_koms.html.

25 See Ziuganov's declaration in *Sovetskaia Rossiia*, 4 April 2000.

26 See the Special Report/Electoral Fraud in *Moscow Times*, 9 Sept. 2000; and at www.themoscowtimes.com/indexes/90.html.

27 Author's interview with Vital' Silitski, 16 Sept. 2003.

28 See the OSCE-ODIHR report at www.osce.org/documents/odihr/2003/04/1203_en.pdf.

29 *Belta*, 19 Oct. 2000; *BBC SWB*, 20 Oct.; *Belaplan*, 24 Oct.

30 Alexander Nemets, 'Russia's Latest Census Reports Population Gains − or Losses', *Eurasia Daily Monitor*, vol. 1, no. 42, 30 June 2004.

31 *Tovarysh*, no. 5, Jan. 1999.

32 See the detailed figures in *Vybory 98. Dokumenty, statystychni dani, analiz* (Kiev: Centre of Social-Psychological Research and Political Management, 1998), pp. 98, 134, 282–84 and the end-maps (nos 10 and 28).

33 Koshiw, *Beheaded*, pp. 42–43. A slightly different translation can be found in 'New Tape Translation of Kuchma Allegedly Ordering Falsification of Presidential Election Returns', *Kyiv Post*, Feb. 14, 2001.

34 *UNIAN*, 9 March 2002.

35 See Serhii Rakhmanin *et al.*, 'P"iat' dzherel, p"iat' skladovykh chastyn blok "Za edynu Ukraïnu"', *Zerkalo tyzhnia*, no. 11, 23–29 March 2002, on Mykhalchenko's role for the FUU.

36 Riabchuk, '"Bezlad" zarady "zlahody"'.

37 Volodymyr Bioko, 'Vybory po-donets'komu: rozhul zakonnosty ta pravoporiadku', *Ukraïns'ka pravda*, 10 April 2002.

38 Oleksii Holobuts'kyi *et al.*, *Segodniashnie lidery Ukrainy: primerka roli prezidenta: VIII Kandidaty v prezidenty Ukrainy: osnovnye svedeniia i analiz rasstanovki sil* (Kiev: AMS, 2004), pp. 11 and 13; Mykola Velychko, '"Yanukovych? Kozak?" − "Yaka vam riznytsia?"', http://www.ukrpravda.com/archive/2004/august/27/1.shtml, dated 27 Aug. 2004.

39 See the protest letter by Serhii Taran, Director of the Institute of Mass Information, 'Sotsiolohichni doslidzhennia staiut' na pokaznykom ob"iektyvnosti vyboriv, a zvychainoiu politychnoiu tekhnolohiieiu', http://imi.org.ua/?read=251:2, dated 8 Oct. 2004.

40 Vladimir Pribylovsky, 'The Use and Abuse of "Administrative Resources"', *Moscow Times*, 1 Dec. 2003.

41 Anatolii Lukashev and Anatolii Ponidelko, *Chernyi PR kak sposob ovladeniia vlast'iu, ili Bomba dlia imidzhmeikera* (St Petersburg: Biznes-Pressa, 2002), p. 22.

42 Volodymyr Polokhalo, '"Politychna sim"ia L. Kuchmy na vyborakh-2002', www.politdumka.kiev.ua/index.php?old_site=1&aid=69.

43 Radio Svoboda, 'Fragmenti rozmov Leonida Kuchmi [*sic*] iz zapisiv, zroblenikh ofitserom Mikoloiu Melnichenkom', episode 20. Quoted in Keith A. Darden, 'Blackmail as a Tool of State Domination', pp. 67–71, at p. 69.

44 Koshiw, *Beheaded*, p. 172.

45 Mykola Riabchuk, 'From "Dysfunctional" State to "Blackmail" State: Paradoxes of the

Post-Soviet Transition', 38th Annual Shevchenko Lecture, University of Alberta, 12 March 2004, available online at http://www.ualberta.ca/~cius/announce/media/Media%202004/2004–03-14_Text%20of%20Ryabchuk%20Lecture.pdf. Emphasis in original.

46 See www.opensecrets.org/2000elect/index/AllCands.htm, as accessed 2 July 2004.

47 Nick Paton Walsh, 'Russia Foils Conman's Fledgling Ministry', *Guardian*, 6 Dec. 2002.

48 Yulia Latynina, 'The Cost of the Kremlin's Slush Fund', *Moscow Times*, 9 Oct. 2002.

49 Author's interview with Andrei Riabov, 8 Nov. 2002.

50 Ibid.

51 Author's interview with Ekaterina Egorova, 6 Nov. 2002.

52 Interview with Gel'man, *Ezhenedel'nyi zhurnal*, no. 107, 16 Feb. 2004.

53 Official results at www.cec.gov.az/en/main_az.htm, See also the *Christian Science Monitor*, 15 Oct. 2003.

54 *Le Monde Diplomatique*, 10 June 2003.

55 *Kyiv Post*, 14 March 2002, p. 2.

Chapter 5

1 Edith Wharton, *The Age of Innocence* (London: Penguin, 1974), p. 67.

2 In this category, the Baltic States are not so squeaky-clean for once. Latvia's Way (Latvijas Ceļš), the leading party through three elections in 1993, 1995 and 1998, advertised itself as a neo-liberal 'small'-business party and the key to Latvia's 'European Way'. On closer inspection, however, it turned out not to be the party of manifest destiny that it seemed. Its roots lay in the influx of former nomenclatura and careerists through Club 21 – a kind of Latvian version of the Freemasons – into the *perestroika*-era Popular Front. Latvia's Way eventually became mainly a front for the Ventspils Oil transit and terminal company and for the Russian energy interests that used it, much as the rival People's Party was backed by the Ave Lat food-processing company. Latvian society has relatively free media and is more than relatively open to the West. Eventual exposure of its business links led to Latvia's Way crashing to 4.9 per cent in the 2002 elections. See Mel Huang, 'Is This Really Latvia's Way?', www.ce-review.org, 8 Feb. 1999.

3 On the other hand, when patronage relations are relatively open, it can be rational in the short term for politicians to boast about their ability 'to put a team together', or casually to mention their links with energy companies in one paragraph and the need for 'urgent gasification' of local villages in the next. For a selection of Ukrainian manifestos, see Mykola Tomenko, 'Suchasna Ukraïna: politychni oliharkhy, kholdynhy, syndykaty: metodolohiia analizu diial'nosti real'nykh politychnykh aktoriv v Ukraïni', *Politichnyi kalendar*, no. 2, 1999; and oligarchs' own websites such as www.bakai.zhitomir.ua.

4 V. Matviienko, 'There Will Be a Fight For Sure', *Den'*, 11 July 2000.

5 From the introduction to Borges, *Labyrinths*, p. 18.

6 N.P. Kutyrev, *Tekhnologii pobedy na vyborakh* (Moscow: Prior, 1999), p. 70.

7 Ibid.

8 Michael Urban, 'December 1993 as a Replication of Late-Soviet Electoral Practice', *Post-Soviet Affairs*, vol. 10, no. 2, April–June 1994, pp. 127–58.

9 Reddaway and Glinski, *The Tragedy of Russia's Reforms*, pp. 680–81, n. 33.

10 Ellen Mickiewicz, *Changing Channels: Television and the Struggle for Power in Russia* (rev. edn; Durham: Duke University Press, 1999), p. 158.

11 Oleh Protsyk and Andrew Wilson, 'Center Party Politics in Russia and Ukraine: Power, Patronage and Virtuality', *Party Politics*, vol. 9, no. 6, Nov. 2003, pp. 703–27.

12 McFaul, *Russia's Unfinished Revolution*, p. 281. Satarov was then Yeltsin's political adviser; Urban headed the typically named Analytical Administration.

13 The key Kremlin memo was reported in *Nezavisimaia gazeta*, 20 May 1995.

14 Quoted in Lilia Shevtsova, *Yeltsin's Russia: Myths and Reality* (Washington, DC: Carnegie Endowment for International Peace, 1999), p. 137.

15 *Interfax*, 26 April 1995.

16 Lisovskii and Evstaf'ev, *Izbiratel'nye tekhnologii*, p. 224. Only Our Home Is Russia and the Liberal Democrats spent more.

17 Lisovskii and Evstaf'ev, *Izbiratel'nye tekhnologii*, pp. 254–55.

18 Leonid Krutakov, 'Nash Dom – "Gazprom"', *Moskovskii komsomolets*, 3 June 1999; Streletskii, *Mrakobesiye*, p. 15.

19 *Versiia*, 13–19 April 1999; Mukhin, *Informatsionnaia voina v Rossii*, pp. 234–35.

20 Mukhin, *Informatsionnaia voina v Rossii*, p. 116.

21 McFaul, *Russia's Unfinished Revolution*, pp. 292–93.

22 Michael McFaul, 'Russia's 1996 Presidential Elections', *Post-Soviet Affairs*, vol. 12, no. 4, Oct.–Dec. 1996, pp. 318–50, at p. 325, n. 8.

23 Lisovskii and Evstaf'ev, *Izbiratel'nye tekhnologii*, pp. 250–52.

24 Ibid., p. 252.

25 Klebnikov, *Godfather of the Kremlin*, pp. 221 and 224.

26 Markov, *PR v Rossii bol'she chem PR*, pp. 74–75; Lisovskii and Evstaf'ev, *Izbiratel'nye tekhnologii*, p. 276.

27 Author's interview with Gleb Pavlovskii, 8 Nov. 2002.

28 Reddaway and Glinski, *The Tragedy of Russia's Reforms*, p. 521, quoting Korzhakov.

29 Talbott, *The Russia Hand*, p. 208, specifically discussing the 'loans-for-shares' deal but also musing on whether, given more time for reflection, the West should have been more generally conditional in its support.

30 Foundation for Effective Politics, *Strategicheskie doklady*, no. 1, March 1996, *Prezident v 1996 godu: stsenarii i tekhnologii pobedy*.

31 Author's interview with Gleb Pavlovskii, 8 Nov. 2002.

32 See Kathleen E. Smith, *Mythmaking in the New Russia: Politics and Meaning During the Yeltsin Era* (Ithaca: Cornell University Press, 2002), ch. 7, 'Campaigning on the Past in the 1996 Presidential Race'.

33 Quoted in David E. Hoffman, *The Oligarchs: Wealth and Power in the New Russia* (New York: Public Affairs, 2002), p. 344.

34 Colton and McFaul, *Popular Choice and Managed Democracy*, p. 56.

35 Quoted in Pinsker, 'Medvezhii ugol zreniia'.

36 Timothy J. Colton and Michael McFaul, 'Reinventing Russia's Party of Power: "Unity" and the 1999 Duma Elections', *Post-Soviet Affairs*, vol. 16, no. 3, July–Sept. 2000, pp. 201–24,

37 Markov, *PR v Rossii bol'she chem PR*, p. 120.

38 Ibid., p. 121.

39 Lisovskii and Evstaf'ev, *Izbiratel'nye tekhnologii*, p. 283.

40 Rose and Munro, *Elections without Order*, p. 130.

41 Author's interview with Aleksei Sitnikov, 4 Nov. 2002.

42 Ibid.

43 Lisovskii and Evstaf'ev, *Izbiratel'nye tekhnologii*, pp. 284 and 289.

44 Colton and McFaul, *Popular Choice and Managed Democracy*, p. 274, n. 24.

45 Lola Kuchina, 'Vybory-2003: osobennosti PR-tekhnologii', www.politcom.ru/2003/bigpr12.php, dated 29 Oct. 2003, accessed 4 Nov. 2003.

46 Author's interview with Piotr Shchedrovitskii, 3 Nov. 2002; Shchedrovitskii, 'SPS spasli sil'nye menedzhery', *Soobshchenie*, no. 1, 2000.

47 Kosktikov, 'Ferzi i peshki kremlevskikh shakhmat'.

48 Author's interview with Shchedrovitskii, 3 Nov. 2002.

49 Author's interview with Gleb Pavlovskii, 8 Nov. 2002.

50 Laura Belin, 'The SPS's Television Ads: A Case Study of Poor Image Construction', *RFE/RL The Russian Federation Votes: 2003–04*, 9 Dec. 2003.

51 Quoted in Roi (Roy) Medvedev, *Vladimir Putin – deistvuiushchii prezident* (Moscow: Vremia, 2002), p. 43.

52 Elena Tregubova, *Baiki kremlevskogo diggera* (Moscow: Ad Marginem, 2003), p. 85.

53 Andrei Piontkovsky, 'The Putin Regime's Birth Defect', *The Russia Journal*, 23 March 2001.

54 Aleksei Zudin, 'Kreml' kak sub"ekt izbiratel'noi kampanii', in Michael McFaul *et al.*, *Rossiia v izbiratel'nom tsikle 1999–2000 godov* (Moscow: Carnegie Centre, 2000), pp. 99–111, at p. 107.

55 Author's interview with Sitnikov, 4 Nov. 2002. Yumashev worked for Berezovskii in the early 1990s and, in turn, hired Aleksandr Voloshin.

56 Tregubova, *Baiki kremlevskogo diggera*, p. 200. See also p. 201 and Belianinov, *Gospoda s geksogenom*, pp. 4–5.

57 On his early life, see Richard Sakwa, *Putin: Russia's Choice* (London: Routledge, 2004), ch. 1; and Andrew Jack, *Inside Putin's Russia* (London: Granta, 2004), ch. 3, 'The Man from Nowhere'.

58 Talbott, *The Russia Hand*, p. 355.

59 A Quentin Tarantino trademark: the stalemate that results if all the protagonists pull their guns simultaneously.

60 Dmitrii Pinsker, 'Medvezhii ugol zreniia', *Itogi*, no. 42, 30 Oct. 2000.

61 Talbott, *The Russia Hand*, p. 356.

62 Interested readers can check the material assembled on the website http://terror99.ru and in English at http://eng.terror99.ru/publications/035.htm. For the main conspiracy theories, see Yuri Felshtinsky and Alexander Litvinenko, *Blowing Up Russia: Terror from Within* (New York: Liberty Press, 2001). Extracts from this book were published by *Novaia gazeta* on 27 Aug. 2001, available online at http://2001.novayagazeta.ru/nomer/2001/61n/n61n-s00.shtml.

63 Tregubova, *Baiki kremlevskogo diggera*, p. 203.

64 Ibid., p. 72.

65 Sergei Sharapov, 'Diktator. Politicheskaia fantaziia', in *Zavtra. Fantasticheskii al'manakh*, no. 3 (Moscow, 1991); Taras Batenko, *Preliudiia Putina: 'Perebudova' v Kremli* (L'viv: Dzyha, Meta, 2001), pp. 86–87.

66 Author's interview with Sitnikov, 4 Nov. 2002.

67 'Pobeda rossiiskikh kuchmeikorov', *Kommersant'-vlast'*, no. 45, 16 Nov. 1999.

68 V''iacheslav Yakubenko, 'Yak ya pratsiuvav imidzhmeikerom Kuchmy', *Den'*, 14 Oct. 1999.

69 As quoted in *Zerkalo tyzhnia*, no. 47, 1–7 Dec. 2001.

70 'Skil'ky koshtuie brend "ZaYedu"?', *Ukraïns'ka pravda*, www.pravda.com.ua/?20322-4-new, posted 22 March 2002. See also the popular Russian translation of Séguéla's book, *Natsional'nye osobennosti okhoty za golosami: Tak delaiut prezidentov* (Moscow: Vagrius, 1999).

71 Data kindly supplied by Valerii Khmel'ko of KIIS.

72 Kimitaka Matsuzato, 'All Kuchma's Men: The Reshuffling of Ukrainian Governors and the Presidential Election of 1999', *Post-Soviet Geography and Economics*, vol. 42, no. 6, Sept. 2001, pp. 416–39.

73 'Moroz: Prichina raspada "Edu" – nasil'stvennost' ee sozdaniia', www.part.org.ua/index.php?news=47319172, dated 12 June 2002.

74 Martha Brill Olcott, *Kazakhstan: Unfulfilled Promise* (Washington, DC: Carnegie Endowment for International Peace, 2002), p. 93.

75 Olcott, *Kazakhstan*, p. 251.

76 For a summary of election results in Kazakhstan, see ibid., pp. 251–52.

77 Ibid., p. 95.

78 Remarks made at a press conference, 6 Feb. 2002, www.fednews.ru.

79 Dmitrii Orlov, 'Korporativnye vybory', www.politcom.ru/2003/pvz62.php, posted 19 Feb. 2003.

80 Alexander Nudelman, 'Unified Russia: A Firmer Hand Sought – But Not Necessarily Found', *RFE/RL Russian Political Weekly*, vol. 3, no. 3, 17 Jan. 2003.

81 *Moskovskii komsomolets*, 16 Nov. 2002.

82 *Nezavisimaia gazeta*, 23 Sept. 2003.

83 Information supplied by sources in Nikkolo-M.

84 The lower figure was given by Anders Åslund in a talk at St Antony's, Oxford, 9 Feb. 2004, the higher in an interview with Podberezkin in www.stringer.ru, no. 7, May 2003, via *Johnson's Russia List*, no. 7,159, 29 April 2003.

85 Artyom (Artiom) Borovik, *The Hidden War: A Russian Journalist's Account of the Soviet War in Afghanistan* (New York: Grove Press, 1990).

86 Oksana Yablokova, 'Posters Failed to Unite Voters', *Moscow Times*, 31 Oct. 2003.

87 Vitalii Tsepliaev, 'Levaia ugroza', *Argumenty i fakty*, 30 July 2003.

88 Anna Dolgov, 'Yudin: Yukos Paid United Russia', *Moscow Times*, 4 Dec. 2003. Deputy Vladimir Yudin was threatened with expulsion for making the allegation that fourteen oilmen were on the United Russia list, including two from Yukos; but the truth of his assertion was widely attested.

89 Francesca Mereu, 'Yukos Takes a Bite out of Yabloko's Party List', *Moscow Times*, 3 Dec. 2003.

90 Author's interview with Andrei Riabov, 21 Feb. 2004.

91 See the discussion of and quotation from Pavlovskii's commentary 'On the Negative Consequences of the Summer Attacks' in *Novaia gazeta*, no. 66, 8 Sept. 2003.

92 Stanislav Belkovskii, 'Odinochestvo Putina', *Zavtra*, no. 19, 6 May 2003.

93 Author's interview with Andrei Riabov, 21 Feb. 2004.

94 Author's interview with Valerii Solovei, 5 Nov. 2002.

95 *Rodnaia gazeta*, 16 May 2003.

96 On 2 February 2004 Rybkin published an advert in *Kommersant-Daily* accusing Putin of having links with three businessmen, the Kovalchuk brothers, Mikhail and Yurii, and Gennadii Timchenko, who together controlled a secret network of share holdings and media interests that was taking over former Yukos assets.

97 Author's interview with Andrei Riabov, 21 Feb. 2004.

98 'Kandidat Putin prosil podderzhki bez reklami. Nachalo vystupleniia Vladimira Putina pered doverennymi litsami 12 fevralia', *Kommersant'*, no. 32, 21 Feb. 2004, p. 3.

99 Aleksandr Vybornii, 'Ukhodia, gasite svet. Surkov na proshchanie khlopnul Khakamadoi', *Versiia*, no. 4, 2004.

100 Leonid Radzhikhovskii, 'Vybor Khakamady, ili novye russkie samurai', www.politcom. ru/2004/pvz332.php, 8 Jan. 2004; 'Khakamada otkazalas' byt' "kremlevskim proektom"?', *Novaia gazeta*, no. 3, 19–21 Jan. 2004.

101 Vybornii, 'Ukhodia, gasite svet'.

102 As quoted in the *Washington Post*, 13 Feb. 2004.

103 See the comments by leading experts, 'Glaz'ev i Putin – bliznetsy-brat'ia', *Nezavisimaia gazeta*, 2 Feb. 2004.

104 Tat'iana Stanovaia, 'Kak sglazili Glaz'eva', www.politcom.ru/2004/analit109.php, dated 9 March 2004.

105 Author's interview with Valerii Solovei, 18 Feb. 2004. Solovei was then working as one of Glaz'ev's top advisers.

106 Author's interview with Riabov, 21 Feb. 2004.

107 Anatolii Kostiukov, 'Esli Kharitonova snimut, Vid'manova posadiat. Kommunisty reshili ne riskovat' den'gami i tovarishchami', *Nezavisimaia gazeta*, 5 March 2004.

108 Author's interviews with Solovei, 18 Feb., and Riabov, 21 Feb. 2004.

109 Natal'ia Arkhangel'skaia, 'Oppozitsiia ego prevoskhoditel'stva', *Ekspert*, no. 8, 1–7 March 2004.

110 Aleksandra Samarina *et al.*, 'Strana vziala pod kozyrek', *Nezavisimaia gazeta*, 15 March 2004.

111 Following the circuitous official web site of the Russian Electoral Commission, these figures can be found at http://gd2003.cikrf.ru/etc/prot_fed_2003.doc, and http://www.izbirkom.ru/izbirkom_protokols/sx/page/protokol.

112 Maksim Glikin, Sergei Kez and Andrei Riskin, 'Yavka v obmen na transferty. Izbranie Putina raskololo regional'nye elity', *Nezavisimaia gazeta,* 16 March 2004.

113 Author's interview with Ekaterina Egorova, 6 Nov. 2002.

114 'Kremlin Tightening Reins ahead of Polls', *Moscow Times*, 14 Feb. 2003.

115 BBC Monitoring, 'Russia's Big Business Starts Funding Putin's Election Campaign', TVS Moscow, 29 May 2003, via *Johnson's Russia List*, no. 7,202, 31 May 2003.

116 Author's interview with Aleksei Sitnikov, 4 Nov. 2002.

117 See his review of Yeltsin's memoir at www.exile.ru/shite/103/marathon.htm, dated 9–23 Nov. 2000.

118 Mukhin, *Informatsionnaia voina v Rossii*, pp. 132 and 143.

119 Author's interview with Sitnikov, 4 Nov. 2002.

120 Reddaway and Glinski, *The Tragedy of Russia's Reforms*, pp. 501–03.

121 Author's interview with Sitnikov, 4 Nov. 2002; Reddaway and Glinski, *The Tragedy of Russia's Reforms*, p. 693, n. 20.

122 Klebnikov, *Godfather of the Kremlin*, pp. 220 and 240.

123 Reddaway and Glinski, *The Tragedy of Russia's Reforms*, pp. 502–03.

124 Hoffman, *The Oligarchs*, p. 349.

125 'V prezidentskoi gonke vyigryvaiut oligarkhi-"vyborshchiki". Kak i kem finansirovalas' kampaniia El'tsina . . . i po kakim skhemam finansiruetsia kampaniia Putina', *Novaia gazeta*, 20 March 2000.

126 Ibid.

127 Remarks made at a press conference given by Vladimir Bukovskii, Mykola Mel'nychenko and Oleksandr Yeliashkevich in London, 17 Feb. 2003.

128 *Ezhenedel'nyi zhurnal*, no. 2, Jan. 2003; Kosihkina, 'Facing the Elections'.

129 *Vedomosti*, 12 Oct. 1999; Irina Dubrova, 'Kharizmatiki i ortodoksy', *Novoe vremia*, no. 26, July 1999; Bohdan Sikora, *Rosiis'ka ekonomichna ekspansiia v Ukraïni* (Kiev: Ekonomika i pravo, 2003), pp. 134 and 153.

130 'Leonid Kuchma vydal Vladimira Putina: Plenki Mel'nichenko – o finansirovanii vyborov v Rossii', *Kommersant*, 18 Oct. 2002.

131 Balhakaw, *The Political System of Belarus*, p. 98.

132 Pavel Sheremet and Svetlana Kalinkina, *Sluchainyi prezident* (Yaroslavl': Niuans, 2003), pp. 50–58.

133 Sheremet and Kalinkina, *Sluchainyi prezident*, pp. 52–53.

134 'O politicheskoi prostitutsii i imperatore Bokasse', www.5element.net, posted and accessed 9 Jan. 2003.

135 'Was the Prosecutor-General Bribed?', *RFE/RL Organised Crime and Terrorism Watch*, vol. 2, no. 15, 19 April 2002.

136 There are several slightly different translations of this passage. The one used is from

Koshiw, *Beheaded*, pp. 45–46, quoting from the recordings held by the Vienna International Press Institute.

137 Roman Kupchnisky, 'Naftohaz Ukrayiny – A Study in State-Sponsored Corruption', *RFE/RL Organised Crime and Terrorism Watch*, vol. 3, nos 25, 26 and 28, 18 July, 5 and 15 Aug. 2003.

138 *RFE/RL Newsline*, 6 April 2004.

139 *RFE/RL Russian Political Weekly*, vol. 4, no. 3, 29 Jan. 2004.

Chapter 6

1 Iryna Havrylova and Oleh Pechenih, 'Satelity oliharkhichnykh frakstii', *Tochka zoru* 9, 2000, www.tz.cvu.kiev.ua/?lang=ukr&num_gl=57&page=article&num_art=5.

2 Author's interview with Andrei Riabov, 8 Nov. 2002.

3 Mukhin, *Informatsionnaia voina v Rossii* p. 132.

4 See Keith Forrest, 'Gender and the Transition to Democracy: The Case of Women in Russia', www.isanet.org/noarchive/forrest.html, accessed 15 March 2004.

5 Mukhin, *Informatsionnaia voina v Rossii*, p. 153.

6 See the analysis of voting patterns in Protsyk and Wilson, 'Center Party Politics in Russia and Ukraine'.

7 Yu.M. Baturin *et al.*, *Epokha El'tsina. Ocherki politicheskoi istorii* (Moscow: Vagrius, 2001), p. 542.

8 Author's interview with Gleb Pavlovskii, 8 Nov. 2002.

9 Solovei, 'Kommunisticheskaia i natsionalisticheskaia oppozitsiia', p. 233.

10 Reddaway and Glinski, *The Tragedy of Russia's Reforms*, p. 586.

11 Author's interview with Andrei Riabov, 8 Nov. 2002.

12 Ibid.

13 Foundation for Effective Politics, *Strategicheskie doklady*, no. 1, March 1996, 'Prezident v 1996 godu: stsenarii i tekhnologii pobedy'.

14 Viktor Bondarev, 'Klonirovanie kandidatov', in Sergei Ustimenko (ed.), *Izbiratel'nye tekhnologii i izbiratel'noe iskusstvo* (Moscow: PR-Intellekt/Russian Political Encyclopaedia, 2001), pp. 48–53.

15 *Argumenty i fakty*, no. 27, 1996; Faer, *Priemy strategii i takttiki*, p. 129.

16 Quotation from McFaul, *Russia's 1996 Presidential Election* p. 119, n. 6; Reddaway and Glinski, *The Tragedy of Russia's Reforms*, pp. 516–20 and 705, nn. 258 and 262.

17 Benjamin S. Lambeth, *The Warrior Who Would Rule Russia* (Santa Monica: RAND Corporation, 1996), pp. 26–27. Another source claims that Lebed had been working for the Yel'tsin team 'since April 1996'; (Kutyrev, *Tekhnologii pobedy na vyborakh*, quoting S. S. Sulakshin, *Izbiratel', ostorozhno!* (Moscow, 1997), p. 6; although the uplift in Lebed's campaign clearly came earlier.

18 McFaul, *Russia's 1996 Presidential Election*, p. 109, n. 47.

19 Korzhakov, *Boris El'tsin: ot rassveta do zakata*, pp. 374 and 375.

20 Klebnikov, *Godfather of the Kremlin*, pp. 236–37; Howard Elletson, *The General against the Kremlin. Aleksandr Lebed: Power and Illusion* (London: Little, Brown & Co, 1998), p. 253.

21 Hoffman, *The Oligarchs*, p. 348.

22 Author's interviews with Aleksei Sitnikov and Andrei Riabov, 4 and 8 Nov. 2002.

23 E-mail from Valerii Solovei, 21 Feb. 2003; Mukhin, *Informatsionnaia voina v Rossii*, p. 118.

24 Author's interview with Aliaksandr Feduta, 12 Sept. 2003.

25 Mukhin, *Informatsionnaia voina v Rossii*, p. 216.

26 Ibid., p. 223.

27 Ibid., p. 6.

28 Author's interview with Ekaterina Egorova, 6 Nov. 2002.

29 'Katya's Kitchen Table', *The Russia Journal*, 4 Oct. 1999.

30 Gleb Cherkasov, '"Ekzoticheskie" partii', in Michael McFaul, *et al.* (eds), *Rossiia nakanune dumskikh vyborov 1999 goda* (Moscow: Carnegie Centre, 1999), pp. 174–77, at p. 175.

31 See the comments by Andranik Migranian in *Nezavisimaia gazeta*, 23 Oct. 1999.

32 Cherkasov, '"Ekzoticheskie" partii', p. 177.

33 Author's interview with Aleksei Sitnikov, 4 Nov. 2002.

34 Author's interview with Valerii Solovei, 5 Nov. 2002.

35 Regina Smyth, 'What Does Winning Mean in 2003? A Candidate Centred Analysis of Upcoming Parliamentary Elections', PONARS Policy Memo No. 258, www.csis.org/ruseura/ponars/policymemos/pm_0258.prf.

36 As quoted in Julie Corwin, 'Two Parties Are Better than One', *RFE/RL Russia Political Weekly*, vol. 2, no. 31, 26 Sept. 2002.

37 Author's interview with Ekaterina Egorova, 6 Nov. 2002.

38 Francesca Mereu, 'Summer's Campaign Ads Tug at Heart', *Moscow Times*, 19 Aug. 2003.

39 *Vremia-MN*, 8 Aug. 2003.

40 Mikhail Vinogradov and Natalya Ratiani, 'Political Ads Start Early, Some Innovation, Quality Disappointing', *Izvestiia*, 8 Aug. 2003, via *Johnson's Russia List*, no. 7,285, 8 Aug. 2003.

41 *Argumenty i fakty*, 16 Sept. 2003.

42 *Gazeta*, 15 Dec. 2003.

43 Viacheslav Kostikov, 'Ferzi i peshki kremlevskikh shakhmat', *Argumenty i fakty*, no. 37, 10 Sept. 2003.

44 'Pro novitnu politychnu stratehiiu Rosiïshchodo Ukraïny: spetsoperatsiia "Tuzla"', www.politdumka.kiev.ua/index.php?arch_num=3&cat2=1, dated and accessed 12 Nov. 2003.

45 Vitalii Silitskii (Vital' Silitski), 'Kreml' meniaet vassalov, ili skromnoe obaianie putinskogo avtoritarizma', www.belarusfree.org, 8 Dec. 2003.

46 Serhii Rakhmanin, 'Pidrakhunok i kontrol'', *Zerkalo tyzhnia*, no. 35, 8-14 Sept. 2001.

47 Holobuts'kyi *et al.*, *S'ohodnishni lideri Ukraïny: prymiriuvannia roli prezydenta. IV. Osnovni pretendenty: osoblyvosti informatsiinykh ta piar-kampanii*, pp. 39–40.

48 *Nezavisimaia gazeta*, 24 Dec. 1997, citing Ukrainian sources.

49 Tat'iana Maliarenko, 'Ostrov sokrovishch, ili Kto piarit "Donchan"', http://www.ostro.org/shownews_tema.php?id=273, 18 March 2004.

50 Chornovil, *Pul's ukraïns'koï nezalezhnosti*, p. 507. See also the accusations he makes against the National Front at pp. 506 (concerning its suspiciously successful 16 per cent in Ivano-Frankivs'k) and 518-19. He also hints (at p. 519) that the *Vechernii Kyïv* editor Vitalii Karpenko was encouraged by the president's supporters to back the far right.

51 Vadym Halynovs'kyi, '"Novi kholdyngy" vkliuchylysia v borot'bu za vladu', www.tz.cvu.ua/2000tz16u/2.shtml.

52 See the analysis by Serhii Rakhmanin, 'Stysla istorychna dovidka. "Zelenbud"', part 1 of the special series 'Ukraïna partiina', in *Zerkalo tyzhnia*, no. 6, 16-22 Feb. 2002.

53 Bondarenko, *Atlanty i kariatydy*, pp. 145–46.

54 Serhii Leshchenko, 'Ukraïna postachala zbroiu "Talibanu"? U Moskvi vkazuiut' na Rabinovycha', *Ukraïns'ka pravda*, 10 Dec. 2001. See also the allegations repeated in *Der Spiegel*, 7 Jan. 2002.

55 *Kyiv Post*, 5 July 2001; Jürgen Roth, *Der Oligarch. Vadim Rabinovich bricht das Schweigen* (Hamburg and Vienna: Europa verlag, 2000).

56 Oleksii Haran', Oleksandr Maiboroda *et al.*, *Ukraïns'ki livi: mizh leninizmom i sotsial-demokratiieiu* (Kiev: UKMA, 2000), pp. 136-37.

57 For some lurid allegations about Volkov's past, see 'Vse pro Oleksandra Volkova', *Ukraïns'ka pravda*, 5 Sept. 2000. The Volkov quotation is from this source. See also the various open letters and parliamentary speeches of Ukrainian MP Hryhorii Omel'chenko, head of the Anti-Mafia group, in Viktor Honta, *Ukraïns'kyi polkovnyk i ukraïns'ka mafiia: kompromisu buty ne mozhe* (Kiev: Bumerang, 1999), pp. 82-89 and 99-127.

58 Belianinov, *Gospoda s geksogenom*, p. 30.

59 Dmytro Chobit, *Nartsys. Shtrykhy do politychnoho portreta Viktora Medvedchuka* (Kiev: Prosvita, 2001), pp. 108, 123 and 111.

60 Quoted in Kost Bondarenko, 'Owners of the Country' (itself a useful guide to the country's various clans), at http://blackseahall.ca/timages/clans.doc, accessed 1 Oct. 2003.

61 Ferents Fridmanchuk, 'Totalitaryzm u sotsiial-demokratychnii shkiri', *Krytyka*, no. 11, Nov. 2003.

62 Mel'nichenko, *Khto ye khto. Na dyvani prezydenta Kuchmy*, pp. 80-83.

63 Dynamo Kiev was secured by a reverse takeover, via the holding company Dynamo-Atlantic that Medvedchuk and Surkis had first attached to the business.

64 '"Dinamo" v zakone', *Versiia*, 6 June 2000.

65 Mel'nichenko, *Khto ye khto. Na dyvani prezydenta Kuchmy*, pp. 83-84. Also available at www.pravda.com.ua/archive/2002/december/29/1.shtml.

66 Interviewed in *Zerkalo tyzhnia*, no. 11, 22-28 March 2003.

67 Viktor Medvedchuk, *Suchasna ukraïns'ka natsional'na ideiia i pytannia derzhavotvorennia* (Kiev: Ukraïna, 1997); and *idem*, *Dukh i pryntsypy sotsial-demokratii: ukraïns'ka perspektyva* (Kiev: Osnovni tsinnosti, 2000).

68 Remarks by Anders Åslund in a talk at St Antony's, Oxford, 9 Feb. 2004.

69 Yehor Sobolev and Serhii Rakhmanin, 'SDPU (otaborena)', *Zerkalo tyzhnia*, no. 10, 15-21 March 2003.

70 Yevhenii Bulavka, '"Boikie" rukhovtsy vystupili v roli predvybornogo rupora?', http://part.org.tua/index.php?art=34206533, dated and accessed 10 Jan. 2002.

71 Leonid Amchuk, 'Znaiomtesia: Viktor Medvedchuk, tretii prezydent Ukraïny. (Tekhnolohiia zakhvatu)', *Ukraïns'ka pravda*, www.pravda.com.ua/?20325-7-new, posted 25 March 2002.

72 Yevhenii Bulavka, 'SDPU(o)-UNCYO: Secrets Do Come Out', http://part.org.ua/eng/index/php?art=34548743 15 Jan. 2002.

73 Iryna Havrylova and Oleh Pechenih, 'Satelity oliharkhichnykh fraktsii', www.tz.cvu.ua/2000tz09u/5.shtml.

74 Mel'nichenko, *Kto est' kto. Na dyvane prezydenta Kuchmy*, p. 83. See also 'Viktor Medvedchuk. Chastyna druha', www.pravda.com.ua/archive/2002/december/29/1.shtml.

75 Andrii Duda, 'Marhinalitet. U Verkhovnii Radi z"iavylasia fraktsiia z nainyzhchoiu politychnoiu kul'turoiu', www.tz.cvu.ua/2000tz07u/5.shtml.

76 Luk"ianenko, *Neznyshchennist'*, p. 62.

77 Observation made to the author by Yaroslav Koshiw.

78 Artyom Storozhenko 'Which Ally Is Grach Going to Dupe?', http:// part.org.ua/eng/index.php?art=35184412 22 Jan. 2002.

79 Koshiw, *Beheaded*, pp. 75-76.

80 Ibid. p. 92.

81 See the analysis by Serhei Datsiuk, 'Politychna ta sotsial'na telereklama na vyborakh 2002 roku v Ukraïni', www.telegrafua.com/article.php?pid=524, posted 8 July 2002.

82 Danylo Pobut, 'FEPu Pavlovs'koho zamalo odniieï SDPU(u)', *Ukraïns'ka pravda*, www.pravda.com.ua/?1118-3-new, posted 8 Nov. 2001.

83 Sobolev and Rakhmanin, 'SDPU (otaborena)'.

84 Oleksandr Zinchenko interviewed in *Zerkalo tyzhnia*, no. 11, 22-28 March 2003.

85 Data kindly supplied by Valerii Khmel'ko of KIIS. See also Kiev International Institute of Sociology, 'Before and After Parliamentary Elections 2002 in Ukraine', www.kiis.com.ua.

86 See the allegations made in the article by Leonid Amchuk, 'Znaiomtesia: Viktor Medvedchuk, tretii prezydent Ukraïny. (Tekhnolohiia zakhvatu)', *Ukraïns'ka pravda*, www.pravda.com.ua/?20325-7-new, posted 25 March 2002.

87 Sobolev and Rakhmanin, 'SDPU (otaborena)'.

88 Ibid.

89 Nora Dudwick, 'Postcommunist Armenia: Images and Realities', in Karen Dawisha and Bruce Parrott (eds), *Conflict, Cleavage and Change in Central Asia and the Caucasus* (Cambridge, UK: Cambridge University Press, 1997), pp. 69-109, at p. 96.

90 Dudwick, 'Postcomunist Armenia', p. 89.

91 Atom Markarian, 'Big Business Representation in Armenian Parliament Grows', *RFE/RL Caucasus Report*, vol. 6, no. 20, 2 June 2003.

92 Gasan Kuliev, 'Trudnaia istoriia Milli Medzhlisa (Natsional' nogo Sobraniia) Azerbaidzhana', in Dkmitrii Furman (ed.), *Azerbaidzhan i Rossiia: obshchestva i gosudarstva* (Moscow: Prava cheloveka, 2001), pp. 234-55, at p. 240.

93 See Vladimir Socor, 'Where Is Moldova's Democratic Opposition?', *Jamestown Monitor*, vol. 7 no 60, 27 March 2001.

94 Olcott, *Kazakhstan,* p. 95.

95 Annette Bohr, *Uzbekistan: Politics and Foreign Policy* (London: Royal Institute of International Affairs, 1998), p. 6.

96 Ill'ia Arnol'dovich Il'f and Evgenii Petrovich Petrov, *The Twelve Chairs* (Evanston, Illinois: Northwestern University Press, 2000, 2nd printing, p. 176.

Chapter 7

1 Slobodan Milošević used similar tactics in Serbia's first 'free' elections in 1990. He was accused by the Croats of stealing $1.8 billion of federal (i.e., Yugoslav) funds to disable his key moderate opponent Dragoljub Mičunović's Democratic Party, and support 'so-called mosquito parties run by his [Milošević's] agents to discredit and weaken the opposition' instead; Dusko Doder and Louise Branson, *Milosevic: Portrait of a Tyrant* (New York: The Free Press, 1999), p. 76.

2 Reddaway and Glinski, *The Tragedy of Russia's Reforms*, pp. 323-29.

3 Supposedly, in the contest between the two absent candidates, Pazniak won 2.4 million votes and Chyhir 1.6 million. See the Belarus country report in the *East European Constitutional Review*, vol. 8, no. 3, summer 1999.

4 For Pazniak's version of events, see the 'Political Report' to his party's 2001 congress, www.bpfs.boom.ru/0201.htm, dated 18 Feb 2001, accessed 22 March 2004.

5 Remarks by the political scientist Volodymyr Polokhalo, *LIGA Online*, 7 May 2001.

6 Author's interview with Polokhalo, 7 Dec 2003.

7 V"iacheslav Chornovil, *Pul's ukraïns'koï nezalezhnosti* (Kiev: Lybid', 2000), p. 461.

8 The author was present. All the main delegations had declared for Chornovil on Saturday 1 March, forcing Drach to make his threat to hold a rival assembly the following morning.

9 Chornovil, *Pul's ukraïns'koï nezalezhnosti*, p. 606.

10 Volodymyr Lytvyn, *Politychna arena Ukraïny: diiovi osobi ta vykonavtsi* (Kiev: Abrys, 1994), pp. 387-8.

11 Bohdan Harasymiv, *Post-Communist Ukraine* (Edmonton: Canadian Institute of Ukrainian Studies Press, 2002), p. 120.

12 Kost' Bondarenko, 'Kryza Rukhu', *L'vivs'ka hazeta* 8 May 2003.

13 Ibid.

14 Ivan Lozowy, 'There Will Be Only One', *Ukrainian Insider*, vol. 3, no. 2, 8 Oct. 2003, via *The Ukraine List*, no. 215.

15 Koshiw, *Beheaded* p. 19.

16 Kost' Bondarenko, *Atlanty i kariatydy z-pid 'dakhu' Prezydenta* (L'viv: Kal'variia, 2000), pp. 45-46.

17 See the article on Ishchenko in *Holos Ukraïny* 25 Nov. 1995.

18 See V"iacheslav Chornovil, 'Sproba rozkolu Rukhu. Prychyny. Vykonavtsi. Zamovnyky', in Chornovil, *Pul's ukraïns'koï nezalezhnosti* pp. 603-15; quotation at pp. 608 and 614.

19 Jaroslav Koshiw, 'Chornovil is the Cause of Rukh's Split', *Kyiv Post* 25 Feb. 1999. Koshiw makes the same allegations against Ishchenko.

20 *Den'*, 13 Dec. 1997; Yurii Khomych, 'Ukusit' drakona', *Zerkalo nedeli*, 20 Feb. 1999.

21 According to Iryna Chemerys, 'Legacy of the Sentinel', *Den'*, 4 April 2000, 'both the Communists and Rukh were fed from Lazarenko's hand'.

22 See the latter two's comments in *Den'*, 26 Jan. 1999.

23 'O politicheskoi prostitutsii i imperatore Bokasse', www.5element.net, posted 9 Jan. 2003.

24 Evgenii Bulavka, '"Boikie" rukhovtsy vystupili v roli predvybornogo rupora?', www.part.org.ua/index.php?art=34206533, dated 10 Jan. 2002.

25 'Mykola Mel'nychenko proty pokhoronnoï komandy', www2.pravda.com.ua/archive/?2031-1-new, posted 2 Feb. 2002.

26 Bulavka, '"Boikie" rukhovtsy vystupili v roli predvybornogo rupora?'

27 Natalia Ligacheva, 'Wars with Known Endings', www.telekritika.kiev.ua/tv_week/?id=2390, 14 Feb. 2002, English slightly adapted.

28 The title of an excellent book by Kiev academic Oleksii Haran', *Ubyty drakona: Z istorii Rukhu ta novykh partii Ukraïny* (Kiev: Lybid', 1993).

29 Koshiw, *Beheaded*, p. 74.

30 Ibid., pp. 140 and 165.

31 Ibid., p. 181-82.

32 Ibid., p. 181.

33 Author's conversation with Mykola Riabchuk, 6 Dec. 2003.

34 Nikolai Vavilov, 'Na Ukraine gotoviatsia k vyboram', *Nezavisimaia gazeta*, 24 Dec. 1997. The document was printed in full on pp. 1 and 3.

35 On Lazarenko, see Roman Kupchinsky, 'The Tractor Driver of the State – The Case of Pavlo Lazarenko', parts 1-6, www.rferl.org/corruptionwatch, vol. 1, nos. 6-9 and vol. 2, no. 3, dated 6 Dec. 2001 to 24 Jan. 2002.

36 Tetiana Korobova, '"Kanivs'ka chetvirka" – za Marchuka', *Den'*, 26 Oct. 1999; Haran' and Maiboroda (eds), *Ukraïns'ki livi*, pp. 180-81.

37 Koshiv, *Obezholovlenyi*, p. 261; and Oleksandr Nezdolia, with Sergei and Elena Nesterenko, *Dos'e generala gosbezopastnosti Aleksandra Nezdoli* (Bila Tserkva': Chervona ruta, 2003). See also http://www.agentura.ru/library/nezdolya/, accessed 22 June 2004.

38 Holobuts'kyi *et al.*, *S'ohodnishni lideri Ukraïny: prymiriuvannia roli prezydenta*, IV, p. 16.

39 See Volodymyr Zolotor'ov, 'Petro Symonenko i zupynynyi chas', *Den'*, 15 July 1999, reporting on the Russian technologists' 'scenario' for the Communists.

40 'Mykola Mel'nychenko proty pokhoronnoï komandy'.
41 Remarks by Kazhegeldin at a 2000 press conference in Russia; http://kazhegeldin. addr.com/english/congr.htm.
42 See the story at www.eurasianet.org/resource/Kazakhstan/hypermail/200202/0074/ shtml, accessed 30 June 2003. Original in *Respublika*, 7 Feb. 2002.
43 'US Engagement in Central Asia: Successes', www.state.gov/p/eur/rls/fs/15561.htm dated 27 Nov. 2002, accessed 30 June 2003; *The Economist*, 18 Oct. 2002.
44 'End Note', *RFE/RL Daily News*, 24 Sept. 2002 and 14 May 2003. The covert link goes back to Kocharian's supposed promise of an eventual premiership to Geghamian in 1998.
45 See the report at www.prima-news.ru, 24 Jan. 2003.
46 Official results from the website of the Central Election Commission of Armenia, http://pre03.elections.am/?&lan=eng&go=results.
47 Author's interview with Marat Gel'man, 9 Nov. 2002.
48 'Kremlin Tightening Reins ahead of Polls', *Moscow Times*, 14 Feb. 2003.
49 'Mask, I Know You . . . Some Details of the "Twins Show" in the 2002 Election Race', *UCIPR Research Update*, no. 6, 11 Feb. 2002.
50 *Ukraïna moloda*, 31 Jan. 2002.
51 Volodymyr Alekseiev, 'Human Rights and Ukrainian Electoral Practices', *Kyiv Post*, 3 April 2003, p. 7.
52 Author's interview with Ihor Ostash, 3 Feb. 2003.
53 Elena Rotkevich and Aleksandr Badanov, 'Korabl' dvoinikov', *Izvestiia*, 30 Oct. 2003.
54 Lukashev and Ponidelko, *Chernyi PR kak sposob ovladeniia vlast'iu*, pp. 79–80.
55 Bondarev, 'Klonirovanie kandidatov', p. 53.
56 Markov, *PR v Rossii bol'she chem PR*, p. 239.
57 Il'f and Petrov, *The Golden Calf* [1931] with preface and annotation by Richard D. Schupbach (Berkeley Russian Readers, 1994), p. 27.
58 Volodymyr Polokhalo, 'Ukraïns'ki dity leitenanta Shmidta (Natsional'ni osoblyvosti parlaments'kykh vyboriv)', www.politdumka.kiev.ua/s0201-1.html.
59 Kutyrev, *Tekhnologii pobedy na vyborakh*, p. 71.
60 Favors'ka, 'Brudni vyborchi tekhnolohiï'.
61 *Tovarysh*, no. 5 Jan. 2002.
62 Asia Riazanova, 'Piar Protiv "Yabloka": zachem SPS nuzhen raskol v demokraticheskom lagere?', www.politcom.ru/2003/analit84.php. On 6 Nov. 2003 stringer-news.ru published what it claimed were copies of internal URF memoranda to this effect. See 'Plan bor'by SPS protiv "Yabloka". Plan izbiratel'noi kampanii SPS protiv "Yabloka", www.stringer-news.ru/loadedimages/IMG_2003-11-06-Yablo.01.gif, and further, up to Yablo07.gif, accessed 21 Nov. 2003. Other sites published internal SPS conversations. See 'Proslushki shtaba SPS', www.compromat.ru/main/ sps/prosl.htm, posted 31 Oct. 2003, accessed 21 Nov. 2003.
63 See the examples posted at www.eng.yabloko.ru/Press/2003/6/290503.html.
64 In the 2002 Slovak elections many Western observers bought the idea that the HZD (Movement for Democracy) that split from strongman Vladimír Mečiar's HZDS (Movement for a Democratic Slovakia) was now the 'main source of Mečiar's current woes'. See Kathleen Knox, 'Slovaks Gear Up for Key Elections on Road to EU, NATO', *RFE/RL Weekday Magazine – Slovakia*, 6 Sept. 2002. Others saw it as a simple smuggler's ruse. See Tom Nicholson, 'Who Is the HZD? A Mečiar-free HZDS, Says Analyst', *Slovak Spectator*, 9–15 Sept. 2002. HZDS won 19.5 per cent and HZD 3.5 per cent; Mečiar stayed in opposition.
65 Leonid Zaiko (ed.), *Natsional'no-gosudarstvennye interesy Respubliki Belarus'* (Minsk, Makaturov Fund/Strategiia, 1999), p. 107.

66 Despite two rounds of elections in May and November–December 1995, sixty-two out of 260 seats remained empty because of turnout provisions. The CPB won twenty-seven out of 119 seats in the first round and fifteen out of seventy-nine in the second.

67 Author's interview with Aliaksandr Feduta, 12 Sept. 2003.

68 The Communist Party of Belarus (CPB) was first suspended in August 1991. Revivalists therefore chose the name Party of Communists of Belarus (PCB) in December 1991. After the legality of the original ban was questioned in 1993, the CPB was briefly revived, but formally merged with the PCB at a special 'unity' congress in April 1993. When the *third* version of the CPB was established to support Lukashenka in October–November 1996, the April 1993 merger decision was simply ignored.

69 Author's interviews with PCB leader Siarhei Kaliakhin, 15 Sept. 2003, and Aliaksandr Fiaduta, 12 Sept. 2003; Joan Barth Urban, 'Kommunisticheskie partii Rossii, Ukrainy i Belorussii (bezuspeshnyi poisk edinstva v raznobrazii)', in Furman (ed.), *Belorussiia i Rossiia*, pp. 393–415, at p. 409. Posakhaw, who wrote his doctorate on 'Electoral Technology and the Formation of the Higher Organs of Power in the Republic of Belarus', was also the 'practical initiator' of the 1996 referendum; V.F. Holubev *et al.*, *Khto est' khto v Belarusi* (Minsk: Asoba i hramadstva, 1999), p. 114.

70 Galina and Yurii Drakokhrust and Dmitrii Furman, 'Transformatsiia partiinoi sistemy Belarusi', in Dmitrii Furman (ed.), *Belorussiia i Rossiia: obshchestva i gosudartsva* (Moscow: Prava cheloveka, 1998), pp. 106–52, at p. 139.

71 Author's interview with Kaliakhin, 15 Sept. 2003.

72 Ibid.

73 *Country Profile 2001. Belarus, Moldova* (London: Economist Intelligence Unit, 2001), p. 9. See also the European Forum for Democracy and Solidarity making the same mistake at www.europeanforum.net/country_update/belarus_update, accessed 26 Sept. 2003.

74 Elena A. Korosteleva, Colin W. Lawson and Rosalind J. Marsh (eds), *Contemporary Belarus: Between Democracy and Dictatorship* (London: RoutledgeCurzon, 2003), pp. 83–84.

75 Davis and Grigorian (eds), *Polls Apart*, pp. 48–49; from a transcript of the BT show *Panorama* broadcast on 5 Oct. 2000.

76 Valer Bulhakaw (ed.), *Miastsovyia vybary w nainowshai paliitychnai historyi Belarusi* (Minsk: Analytical Group, The East European Democratic Centre, IDEE, 2003), p. 241.

77 Drakokhrust, Drakokhrust and Furman, 'Transformatsiia partiinoi sistemy Belarusi', p. 120.

78 Valer Bulhakaw (ed.), *The Political System of Belarus and the 2001 Presidential Election* (Minsk: Analytical Group, The East European Democratic Centre, IDEE, 2001) p. 216.

79 The conversation can be found in Nikolai Mel'nichneko (Mykola Mel'nychenko), *Kto est' kto na divane prezidenta Kuchmy* (Kiev: no pub. 2002), pp. 48–49.

80 McFaul, 'Russia's 1996 Presidential Elections', p. 325, n. 8.

81 Yuliia Mostova and Serhii Rakhmanin, '"Nasha Ukraïna". Spohady i mirkuvannia', part 2 of the special supplement 'Ukraïna partiina', in *Zerkalo tyzhnia*, no. 6, 16–22 Feb. 2002.

82 See the analysis of the party lists by Mykhailo Zlochevskyi, 'Business + Deputy Mandate' www.part.org.ua/eng/index.php?art=36549849, dated 7 Feb. 2002.

83 Volodymyr Polokhalo, first interviewed in www.part.org.ua.

84 Interviewed in *Ukraïns'ka pravda* www2.pravda.com.ua/archive/?2024-2-new. See also Leonid Amchuk, 'Lytvyn z usmishkoiu sotsial-demokrata', www2.pravda.com.ua/archive/?202529-1.

85 Kiev International Institute of Sociology, 'Before and After Parliamentary Elections 2002 in Ukraine', also available on www.kiis.com.ua.

86 The Vitrenko Bloc won 3.22 per cent, KOP 2.01, New Generation 0.77, Women for

the Future 2.11, the Greens 1.3, Yabluko 1.15 and the block of the People's Movement of Ukraine 0.16.

87 'Z Bankovoï vykradeno konfidentsiinyi tsenarii vyboriv-2002', www2.pravda.com.ua/archive/?20315-3-new, posted 15 March 2002.

88 'The Price of Lytvyn', www.unian.net/eng/news/news-14684.html, dated 20 May 2002.

89 Sharon Lafraniere, 'Scare Tactics on the Rise in Ukraine', *Washington Post*, 18 Dec. 2002.

90 'Pivmil'iona dolariv SShA za vykhid z "Nashoï Ukraïny" – Orobets'', www.pravda.com.ua, 20 Dec. 2002.

91 Author's interview with Marat Gel'man, 9 Nov. 2002; 'Moskva nachinaet smotr preemnikov Kuchmy', *Nezavisimaia gazeta*, 27 January 2003. Gel'man claimed to be working as a 'gallerist'; Pavlovski to be running Kiev's new 'Russian club'.

92 Kost' Bondarenko, 'Faktor tumannogo Al'biona', www.for-ua.com/critic/2003/04/14/175206.html, posted 14 April 2003.

93 Holobuts'kyi *et al.*, *S'ohodnishni lideri Ukraïny*. IV, pp. 57-58.

94 *Nezavisimaia gazeta*, 20 Jan. 2003.

95 Holobuts'kyi *et al.*, *S'ohodnishni lideri Ukraïny*. IV, p. 59.

96 Ibid., p. 81.

97 Mykhailo Brods'kyi, '"Kinder-siupryz" Khoroshkovs'kyi – tse peredvyborna tekhnolohiia "sim'ï"', www2.pravda.com.ua/archive/2004/january/5/1.shtml, posted and accessed 5 January 2004.

98 'Tretii termin Kuchmy. Yak tse povynno bulo buti. Chastyna 2'. See note 109, below.

99 Andrei Okara, 'V Moskve startovala aktsiia "Ukraina bez Yushchenko" ... ', www.glavred.info/print.php?art=68597165, posted 13 Feb. 2003.

100 'Authority May Play Tymoshenko Against Yushchenko', *Ukraïns'ka pravda*, www.pravda.com.ua/en/archive/2003/January/24/news/2.shtml.

101 'Tretii termin Kuchmy. Yak tse povynno bulo buti. Chastyna 3, zakliuchna', *Ukraïns'ka pravda*, 1 July 2004.

102 Leonid Amchuk, 'Prezydents'ki vybory-2004: start "chornoho PR"', *Ukraïns'ka pravda*, www.pravda.com.ua/archive/2003/Feb./14/3.shtml.

103 'Tretii termin Kuchmy. Yak tse povynno bulo buti. Chastyna 2'.

104 'Tretii termin Kuchmy. Yak tse povynno bulo buti. Chastyna 3, zakliuchna'.

105 This particular document 'Ne upustit' shans!' published at www.provokator.com.ua/p/2004/02/26/090819.html indicates an intent to exploit a coincidence of interests, and only hints at wider plots. On Gel'man's role, see Holobuts'kyi *et al.*, *S'ohodnishni lideri Ukraïny*. IV, p. 71.

106 'Tretii termin Kuchmy. Yak tse povynno bulo buti', *Ukraïns'ka pravda*, 25 June 2004.

107 Stanislav Shumlians'kyi, 'Rozkol Ukraïny yak virtual'na realnist'', *Krytyka*, no. 11 (Nov.) 2002, pp. 2-5. Pavlovskii quote at p. 4.

108 See also Lilia Buzhurova, '18 travnia v Krymu chekaiut' na provokatsiï', www2.pravda.com.ua/archive/?40517-4-new, 17 May 2004, on more leaked documents with 'provocation' plans.

109 The document was published in three parts on the *Ukraïns'ka pravda* website. The first part, 'Tretii termin Kuchmy. Yak tse povynno bulo buti' on 25 June 2004, www2.pravda.com.ua/archive/?40625-4-new; the second, 'Tretii termin Kuchmy. Yak tse povynno bulo buti. Chastyna 2' on 30 June, www2.pravda.com.ua/archive/?40630-1-new; and the third, 'Tretii termin Kuchmy. Yak tse povynno bulo buti. Chastyna 3, zakliuchna' on 1 July, www2.pravda.com.ua/archive/2004/july/1/2.shtml.

110 'Tretii termin Kuchmy. Yak tse povynno bulo buti. Chastyna 3, zakliuchna'.

111 Alexandra Prymachenko, 'Pin-Point Blasting', *Zerkalo tyzhnia*, no. 35, 4-10 Sept. 2004, http://www.mirror-weekly.com/ie/show/510/47682/.

112 Tetiana Nikolaienko, 'Troieshchyna – kashyrs'ke shose Yanukovycha?', at http://www. ukrpravda.com/archive/?40828-1-new dated 29 Aug. 2004.

113 Holobuts'kyi *et al.*, *Segodniashnie lidery Ukrainy: primerka roli prezidenta*, pp. 235-36 and 14.

114 Andrii Duda, '"Natsyky" z Bankovoi', www.tribuna.com.ua/politics/2004/05/17/9843.html, dated 17 May 2004.

115 See the declaration at http://www.scnm.gov.ua/ua/a?news_ofic_105.

116 Holobuts'kyi *et al.*, *Segodniashnie lidery Ukrainy: primerka roli prezidenta*, p. 237.

117 Although Kinakh had a personal website at www.kinah.com.ua, as did the Union at www.uspp.org.ua and party at http://pppu.com.ua, Sergei Gaidar was employed to do Kinakh's PR.

118 Volodymyr Boiko, 'Taiemnytsi "tainoï vecheri"', at http://www.pravda.com.ua/archive/2004/october/7/2.shtml, dated 1 Oct. 2004.

119 AdReport, 'Zhak Sehela skomprometuvav Yushchenka za zamovlennia Pinchuka?', http://www2.pravda.com.ua/archive/october/7/2.shtml, dated 7 Oct. 2004.

120 The video could be viewed at the *Ukraïns'ka pravda* website, as of the date of access on 4 Oct. 2004, at http://www.pravda.com.ua/archive/2004/september/24/video.shtml.

121 Koshiw, *Beheaded*, p. 41; quoting from Mel'nychenko's video statement to the Ukrainian parliament on 14 Dec. 2000.

122 Koshiw, *Beheaded*, p. 41.

123 Mel'nichenko, *Kto est' kto. Na divane prezidenta Kuchmy*, p. 90.

124 Ibid., p. 89.

125 Tyshchenko, *Vybory-99: yak i koho my obyraly*, p. 180, quoting *Den'*, 5 Oct. 1999.

126 Bulhakaw, *The Political System*, p. 156. See also the assertion that Haidukevich's LDPB's 'only objective was to paralyse the [opposition] Council'; ibid., p. 202.

127 'SPS i Yabloko stali zhertvoi igry spetssluzhb', www.stringer-news.ru/Publication. mhtml?PubID=2486&Part=37, posted and accessed 13 Nov. 2003; Orkhan Dzemal, 'Who Devised the SPS "Military Doctrine"?' www.eng.yabloko.ru/Publ/2003/ PAPERS/11/031117_nov_gzt.html, from *Novaia gazeta*, 17 Nov. 2003.

128 Peter Dailey, 'Haiti's Betrayal', *New York Review of Books*, 27 March 2003.

129 *Libération*, 23 Dec. 2002.

130 Sergei Blagov, 'Russia Plays Down Turkmenistan Taunt', *Asia Times*, 12 Dec. 2002.

131 Hrynkevych and Hutsal (eds.), *Oblychchia vlady*, p. 204, n. 1; Reddaway and Glinski, *The Tragedy of Russia's Reforms*, p. 611. The alleged 'scenario' was published in *Moskovskaia pravda*, 22 July 1999.

132 Author's interview with Andrei Riabov, 8 Nov. 2002.

133 Klebnikov, *The Godfather of the Kremlin*, pp. 303 and 301. See also the collected articles at www.tjetjenien.dk/baggrund/bombs.html. This is the site of the Danish Support Committee for Chechnia. See also the counter-argument by Robert Bruce Ware and Ralph David, 'Was Aslan Mashkadov Involved in the Moscow Hostage Crisis?', *The Journal of Slavic Military Studies*, vol. 16, no. 3, Sept. 2003, pp. 66-71.

134 John Dunlop, 'The October 2002 Moscow Hostage-Taking Incident', *RFE/RL Corruption Watch*, 18 Dec. 2003, 8 and 15 Jan. 2003; and Dunlop, 'The Moscow Hostage Crisis: One Year Later', *RFE/RL Russian Political Weekly*, vol. 3, no. 43, 29 Oct. 2003. See also the material posted at http://zolozhniki.ru and at the victims' families' site, www.nordostjustice.org.

135 The criticism can be found verbatim on line at http://revolutionarydemocracy.org/rdv3n2/ivant.htm.

Chapter 8

1 Aleksandr Dudberg, 'Griaznaia osen' 2003 goda', *Moskovskii komsomolets*, 12 Sept. 2003; *Versiia*, 2 Sept. 2003; *Argumenty i fakty*, 16 Sept. 2003.

2 Anfisa Voronina, 'Party Election Ads Take a Break', *Moscow Times*, 8 Sep. 2003.

3 'Tainye sponsory. Partii skryvaiut, na ch'i sredstva oni zhivut', *Vedomosti*, 16 Oct. 2003.

4 Tat'iana Stanovaia '"Narodnaia Partiia": mezhdu vlast'iu i levymi', www.politcom.ru/2003/partii23.php, from the section 'Ne sovsem levye', posted 27 Aug. 2003, accessed 4 Nov. 2003.

5 Remarks by Mikhail Saakashvili at the Nixon Center, www.nixoncenter.org/publications/Program%20Briefs/Pbrief%202003/041403saakashvili.htm.

6 Aleksei Makarkin, 'Shevardnadze: konets epokhi lisa', www.politcom.ru/2003/pvz301.php, posted and downloaded 25 Nov. 2003.

7 Andrey Lyakhovich, 'The Introduction of the Presidency: Preconditions and Results', in Valer Bulhakaw (ed.), *The Political System of Belarus and the 2001 Presidential Election*, pp. 57-65, at p. 61. At p. 64 Lyakhovich refers to 'blatant betrayal by his [Kebich's] closest entourage'. See also Vasilii Leonov, *Rabota nad oshibkami* (Smolensk: Skif, 2003).

8 See the book on Lukashenka, supposedly compiled from materials collected by the Belarusian KGB, by Vladimir Matikevich (a pseudonym), *Nashestvie* (Moscow: Yauza, 2003), which can be found on the web at www.batke.net/download/nashestvie.doc; downloaded 19 Sept. 2003. The account was confirmed as broadly accurate by Vital' Silitski.

9 E-mail from Vital' Silitski, 18 Feb. 2004; Sheremet and Kalinkina, *Sluchainyi prezident*, pp. 32-33.

10 Lyakhovich, 'The Introduction of the Presidency', p. 63; Sheremet and Kalinkina, *Sluchainyi prezident*, pp. 35-36.

11 Lech Wałeşa, *The Struggle and the Triumph* (New York: Arena, 1992), p. 284.

12 Levko Luk'"ianenko, *Neznyshchennist'* (Kiev: Diokop, 2003), p. 77.

13 Analysis by the Freedom of Choice coalition of Ukrainian NGOs, 'Public Monitoring of Election Campaign 2002 Financing', www.vybory.org.ua/indexe.shtml.

14 According to KIIS's regular polls, 5.5 per cent on 30 December 2001 and a peak of 7.5 per cent on 27 January 2002; data kindly supplied by Professor Valerii Khmel'ko of KIIS.

15 Ol'ha Dmytrycheva, 'Yakby vybory vidbulysia 8 bereznia . . .', *Zerkalo tyzhnia*, no. 3, 26 Jan.–1 Feb. 2002.

16 The author watched the programme.

17 Confidential interview.

18 For a detailed analysis of Khoroshkovs'kyi's career, see Oleg Sinel'nikov, 'Sverkhnovyi komsomolets', www.context-ua.com/politperson/19967.html, posted 1 March 2003. See also www.pravda.com.ua/archive/2003/july/17/2.shtml.

19 *Delovaia nedelia*, 5-11 June 2003, p. 3. Ostrovskii, on the other hand, claimed to the author that the campaign was short of money; interview, 4 Nov. 2002. Both sources could be correct, if the money was diverted for other purposes.

20 For some Western reports buying the myth of a 'new generation . . . not just politicians . . . those who are interested in moving beyond the politics of the old generation', see David R. Sands, 'New Crop Grows in Ukraine', *The Washington Times*, 10 Feb. 2002, and Douglas Burton, 'Gen-Xers Give Ukraine New Hope', www.insightmag.com, posted 4 Feb. 2002.

21 *Zerkalo nedeli*, 13 April 2002.

22 Favors'ka, 'Brudni vyborchi tekhnolohiï'.

23 Anatolii Khanik, 'Rozshyriuiut'sia media-kholdyngy Derkacha i Khoroshkovs'koho', *Ukraïns'ka pravda*, posted 14 Aug. 2002, www.pravda.com.ua/?20814-2-new.

24 Luk"ianenko, *Neznyshchennist'*, p. 60.

25 KOP won an estimated 5-6 per cent of the under-thirties vote, not a big improvement. See 'Zhertvy polittekhnolohii', *Ukraïns'ka pravda*, posted 20 May 2002, www.pravda.com.ua/?20520-5-new.

26 Author's interview with Shchedrovitskii, 3 Nov. 2002.

27 Author's interview with Vasyl' Yurchyshyn, economics spokesman for the KOP, 5 Dec. 2003.

28 Author's interview with Rostyslav Pavlenko, 15 April 2003.

29 See the report in *Den'*, 28 March 2000.

30 See the report at www.pravda.com.ua/archive/?2129-3-printnews, posted 9 December 2002.

31 Dmitrii Vereshchagin and Sergei Lozhkin, 'Rabota nad oshibkami', *Belorusskaia delovaia gazeta*, 13 Nov. 2001; also available at http://bdg.press.net.by/2001/11/2001/_11_13.1064/index.htm.

32 Bulhakaw, *The Political System*, p. 217.

33 Ibid., p. 216.

34 *RFE/RL Newsline*, 5 Feb. 2004.

35 Bulhakaw, *The Political System*, p. 288.

36 See, *inter alia*, *Zviazda*, 31 Aug. 2001.

37 Davis and Grigorian (eds), *Polls Apart: Media Coverage of the Parliamentary Elections*, Belarus, October 2000, pp. 49-50.

38 Bulhakaw, *The Political System*, p. 215.

39 Ibid., p. 216.

40 Author's interview with Vital' Silitski, 16 Sept. 2003.

41 Zianon Pazniak alleges that Domash was yet another pseudo-candidate to divide the opposition, but the author has found no evidence in support of this claim. See www.bpfs.boom.ru/zVyhad.htm, dated 25 Aug. 2001, accessed 13 Sept. 2003.

42 Vadim Dovnar, 'Akela promokhnulsia!', *Belorusskaia gazeta*, 15 Sept. 2003. Also available at www.belgazeta.by.

43 Author's interview with Vital' Silitski, 11 Sept. 2003.

44 See the analysis by Oleh Manaev, head of IISEPS, 'Pobediteli ne poluchaiut nichego', *Belorusskii Rynok*, no. 46, 19-26 Nov. 2001, also available at www.br.minsk.by/index.php?article=8247&year=2001; www.isseps.by; Bulhakaw, *The Political System*, p. 224.

45 Bulhakaw, *The Political System*, p. 250.

46 Ibid., pp. 226-27.

47 Manaev, 'Pobediteli ne poluchaiut nichego'.

48 Korosteleva *et al.*, *Contemporary Belarus: Between Democracy and Dictatorship*, pp. 52 and 30.

49 Vital' Silitski, 'Hrantavy skandal', in Bulhakaw (ed.), *Miastsovyia vybary w nainowshai paliitychnai historyi Belarusi*, pp. 109 and 114; *The Christian Science Monitor*, 10 Sept. 2001; Ian Traynor, 'Belarussian [sic] Foils Dictator-buster . . . For Now', *Guardian*, 14 Sept. 2001.

50 William Fierman, 'Political Development in Uzbekistan: Democratization?', in Dawisha and Parrott, *Conflict, Cleavage and Change in Central Asia and the Caucasus*, pp. 360-408, at pp. 372-73. At p. 403, n. 39, Fierman quotes Karimov as boasting 'that it was I who helped him [Salih] in the creation of this party, and he cannot deny it'. Erk was originally the name of the party of the 'Turkestani' intelligentsia, active across Central Asia in the 1920s.

51 George O. Liber, *Alexander Dovzhenko: A Life in Soviet Film* (London: British Film Institute, 2002), p. 89.

52 Mykola Riabchuk, *Dvi Ukraïny: real'ni mezhi, virtual'ni viiny* (Kiev: Krytyka, 2003), p. 307.

53 Remarks via e-mail to the author by Zaal Anjaparidze, Georgian contributor to the *Jamestown Monitor*, 14 Nov. 2003. See also Zurab Tchiabirashvili, 'Shevardnadze Waltzes with a Scarecrow in Presidential Elections', www.cacianalyst.org/April%2012/SHEVARDNADZE.htm, posted 12 April 2000.

54 Bill Clinton. *My Life* (London: Hutchinson, 2004), pp. 504 and 549.

55 Talbott, *The Russia Hand* p. 103.

56 Valerii Solovei, 'Kommunisticheskaia i natsionalisticheskaia oppozitsiia v kontekste postkommunisticheskoi transformatsii Rossii', in Lilia Shevtsova (ed.), *Rossiia Politicheskaia* (Moscow: Carnegie Centre, 1998), pp. 195-272, at p. 215.

57 On the events of October 1993, see Reddaway and Glinski, *The Tragedy of Russia's Reforms*, pp. 423-24 and 427; Alexander Buzgalin and Andrei Kolganov (eds), *Bloody October in Moscow: Political Repression in the Name of Reform*, trans. Renfrey Clark (New York: Monthly Review Press, 1994); Artiom Tarasov, *Provokatsiia* (Moscow: Feniks, 1993); A.P. Surkov (ed.), *Moskva. Osen'-93: Khronika protivostoianiia* (Moscow: Respublika, 1994); Postfactum Information Agency, *Politicheskii krizis v Rossii, sentiabr'-oktiabr' 1993* (Moscow: Postfactum, 1993); and Gleb Pavlovskii (ed.), *Oktiabr' 1993. Khronika perevorota*, available online at www.russ.ru/antolog/1993/index.htm. These and other materials are also available at the comprehensive website http://1993.sovnarkom.ru.

58 Viacheslav Likhachev, *Natsizm v Rossii* (Moscow: Tsentr 'Panorama', 2002), p. 41. The subsection on pp. 40-43 provides a general discussion of the 'RNU [Russian National Union, Barkashov's party] in October 1993'.

59 The author was coincidently in Moscow at the time (to research a piece on the Crimean Tatars). My own necessarily cautious observations were that Anpilov's marchers were given a free ride, and that provocateur sniping continued through the Monday night, long after the ragtag White House militia had supposedly been defeated.

60 Oleg Fochkin and Dmitrii Bolgarov, 'Belye piatna chernogo oktiabria', *Moskovskii komsomolets*, 3 Oct. 2003; Aleksandr Melenberg, 'Chernyi oktiabr' v belom dome', *Novaia gazeta*, nos. 71 and 72, 25-28 Sept. and 29 Sept.–1 Oct. 2003. Both anniversary reports contain material from Leonid Proshkin, who led the Prosecutor's Office's attempts to investigate the affair in 1993-95. See also the anniversary interviews with Proshkin, Rutskoi and others in *Gazeta*, no. 183, 3 Oct. 2003.

61 *Nezavisimaia gazeta*, 9 Oct. 1993; *Moscow News*, no. 42, 15 Oct. 1993.

62 Aleksei Kurtov and Mikhail Kagan, *Okhota na drakona: Razmyshleniia o vyborakh i politicheskom konsul'tirovanii* (Moscow: State University Higher Economic School, 2002), p. 60.

63 E-mail from Valerii Solovei, 21 Feb. 2003.

64 See also McFaul and Petrov, *Political Almanac of Russia, 1989-1997*, vol. 1, pp. 178-79 and 320-24.

65 Talbott, *The Russia Hand*, pp. 209, 199 and 105.

66 Author's interview with Gleb Pavlovskii, 8 Nov. 2002.

67 Solovyov and Klepikova, *Zhirinovsky*, pp. 164-65.

68 Bruce Clark, *An Empire's New Clothes: The End of Russia's Liberal Dream* (London: Vintage, 1995), p. 272. Clark argues that Yeltsin's 'ear-splitting silence during the final days of the campaign' was indicative: 'one word from Yeltsin could have shaved five percentage points off its [the LDPR's] score'. Deferential voters, used to reading signals from the Kremlin, were therefore encouraged to back Zhirinovskii. Ibid., pp. 277 and 273.

69 Lisovskii and Evstaf'ev, *Izbiratel'nye tekhnologii*, p. 252.

70 Sergei Kibalnik, *Zhirinovsky as a Nationalist 'Kitsch Artist'* (Washington, DC: Kennan Institute Occasional Paper #264, 1996), p. 1.

71 Solovyov and Klepikova, *Zhirinovsky*, pp. 176–77.

72 Hrynkevych and Hutsal *Oblychchia vlady*, p. 360, n. 17.

73 Mukhin, *Informatsionnaia voina v Rossii*, p. 131; referring also to *Moskovskii komsomolets*, 19 Dec. 1996.

74 Stephen D. Shenfield, *Russian Fascism: Traditions, Tendencies, Movements* (Armonk, NY: M.E. Sharpe, 2001), p. 97.

75 Solovei, 'Kommunisticheskaia i natsionalisticheskaia oppozitsiia', p. 235.

76 E-mail from Valerii Solovei, 21 Feb. 2003.

77 McFaul, *Russia's Unfinished Revolution*, p. 284.

78 Author's interview with Andrei Riabov, 8 Nov. 2002.

79 Hrynkevych and Hutsal, *Oblychchia vlady*, pp. 365–66.

80 John B. Dunlop, 'Zhirinovsky's World', *Journal of Democracy*, vol. 5, no. 2, April 1994 pp. 27–32, at p. 30.

81 See Stephen Blank, 'Russia: Proliferation Personified', *Asia Times*, 7 Jan. 2003; although Blank also makes unsubstantiated allegations that Russia stood behind other controversial deals made by Belarus and Ukraine.

82 Roman Kupchinsky, 'Iraqi Paper Lists Companies and Organizations Hussein Allegedly Bribed with Oil', *RFE/RL*, 29 Jan. 2004; Francesca Mereu, 'Political Parties Saw Fortunes Rise and Fall', *Moscow Times*, 8 Oct. 2004.

83 Aleksandr Zhilin, 'Vladimir Zhirinovsky: A Scarecrow in Yeltsin's Garden?', *Prism. The Jamestown Foundation*, 4 Nov. 1995.

84 McFaul, 'Russia's 1996 Presidential Elections', p. 56.

85 Oleg Davydov, 'Pribyl'nyi biznes LDPR', *Nezavisimaia gazeta*, 24 Sept. 1999.

86 Author's interview with Andrei Riabov, 8 Nov. 2002.

87 E-mail from Valerii Solovei, 21 Feb. 2003.

88 Sergei Pravosudov, 'Biznes na politike. LDPR ne izmeniaet sebe, vkliuchaia v spisok vsekh, kto mozhet za eta zaplatit'', *Russkii fokus*, 24 Nov. 2003.

89 *Expert*, Feb. 2004, p. 21.

90 Valerii Solovei, 'Rossiia ne obrechena na fashizm', *Nezavisimaia gazeta*, 29 March 1995.

91 E-mail from Valerii Solovei, 4 March 2003.

92 Yitzhak M. Brudny, *Reinventing Russia: Russian Nationalism and the Soviet State, 1953–1991* (Cambridge, Mass: Harvard University Press, 1998), p. 132.

93 E-mail from Valerii Solovei, 21 Feb. 2003.

94 'Versiia nomer tri: Barkashov preduprezhdaet o gotoviashchemsia putche', www.stringer-news.ru/Publication.mhtml?PubID=1192&Part=37, dated 19 June 2002, accessed 1 Aug. 2003.

95 Likhachev, *Natsizm v Rossii*, p. 49.

96 Mark Ames, 'Free Edward Limonov', www.exile.ru/114/babylon.php.

97 Shenfield, *Russian Fascism*, p. 117.

98 Author's interview with Andrei Riabov, 8 Nov. 2002.

99 E-mail from Valerii Solovei, 4 March 2003; Shenfield, *Russian Fascism*, pp. 141 and 142.

100 Likhachev, *Natsizm v Rossii*, p. 46.

101 Shenfield, *Russian Fascism*, p. 175. See also the interview with the Russian anarchist and eyewitness Vadim Demin dated December 1994 at http://lgp.social-ecology.org/issues/lgp32.html.

102 E-mail from Valerii Solovei, 4 March 2003.

103 Likhachev, 'RNE i spetssluzhby', *Natsizm v Rossii*, pp. 43–50.

104 From the biography of Barkashov in Likhachev, *Natsizm v Rossii*, p. 54.

105 John B. Dunlop, 'Barkashov and the Russian Power Ministries, 1994-2000', *Demokratizatsiya*, vol. 9, no. 1 winter 2001, pp. 60-74; Dunlop, 'Alexander Barkashov and the Rise of National Socialism in Russia', *Demokkratizatsiya*, vol. 4, fall 1996, pp. 519-30.

106 Shenfield, *Russian Fascism*, pp. 174-76.

107 Andrei Arkhilov, 'Raspad "Russkogo edinstva". Chast' I', www.stringer-news.ru/Publication.mhtml?PubID=1924&Part=39, posted 2 April 2003. According to Valerii Solovei, these 'articles were written with the words of former participants of this organisation' and can be taken as accurate. The RNU was clearly 'an object of manipulation . . . for certain political interests'. I have omitted materials from this source which in his judgement 'retrospectively exaggerate the importance [of the RNU] in the eyes of the Russian elite'; e-mail from Valerii Solovei, 3 July 2003.

108 Arkhilov, 'Raspad "Russkogo edinstva". Chast' I'.

109 'Barkashov prodal za bol'shie den'gi spiski chlenov RNE', www.stringer-news.ru/Publication.mhtml?PubID=1797&Part=37, dated and accessed 17 Feb. 2003.

110 Arkhilov, 'Raspad "Russkogo edinstva". Chast' I'.

111 E-mail from Valerii Solovei, 4 March 2003. See also the suitably cynical analysis by Valerii Soloviov in *Vremia MN*, 26 June 2002.

112 Arkhilov, 'Raspad "Russkogo edinstva". Chast' I'.

113 See the analysis at www.panorama.ru/works/patr/bp/4.eng.html.

114 E-mail from Valerii Solovei, 4 March 2003.

115 Andrei Arkhilov, 'Raspad "Russkogo edinstva". Chast' II', at www.stringer-news.ru/Publication.mhtml?PubID=1923&Part=39, posted 2 April 2003.

116 E-mail from Valerii Solovei, 4 March 2003.

117 E-mail from Valerii Solovei, 21 Feb. 2003.

118 Ibid.

119 See *Versiia*, no. 19, 29 May-4 June 2001 on the party's roots and Kremlin links, and the allegations and denials in *Nezavisimaia gazeta*, 31 July 2001.

120 See www.dugin.ru, www.arctogaia.com, www.evrazia.org and www.eurasia.com.ru.

121 Grigorii Osterman, 'Esli vakhkhabizm ne sdaetsia, ego ispravliaiut', www.smi.ru/01/06/28/112857.html, which also details Dugin's and Suslov's connections.

122 'Tainye sponsory. Partii skryvaiut, na ch'i sredstva oni zhivut'.

123 Author's interview with Valerii Solovei, 18 Feb. 2004.

124 Aleksandr Gorianin, *Mify o Rossii i dukh natsii* (Moscow: Pentagraphic Ltd, 2002). Part of Gorianin's work was used for the official programme of United Russia.

125 Aleksei Makarkin, 'Partiia "Rus'": Patrioty ot piara', www.politcom.ru/2003/pvz226.php, posted 29 Aug. 2003, accessed 21 Nov. 2003.

126 Author's interview with Valerii Solovei, 18 Feb. 2004.

127 It is possible to read between the lines in Viktor Mel'nyk's polemic, 'OUN: sproba povernennia', *Ukraïns'ki obriï*, no. 6, 1992.

128 See the argument of Ola Hnatiuk, *Pożegnanie z imperium: Ukraińskie dyskusje o tożsamości* (Lublin: Wydawnictwo Uniwersytetu Marii Curie-Skłodowskiej, 2003), part 6.

129 Author's interviews with UNA-UNSO leaders Viktor Mel'nyk and Dmytro Korchins'kyi, 7 and 12 May 1992.

130 See the series of articles by Vasilii Anisimov in *Nezavisimost'*; dated, *inter alia*, 13 Oct. 1993, 18 Nov. 1997 and 15 May 1998.

131 Author's interview with Mykola Riabchuk, 6 Dec. 2003.

132 'Yevhen Marchuk i Oleksandr Skipal'skyi: razom i okremo', *Ukraïna moloda*, 23 Feb. 2001.

133 See Korchyns'kyi's unconvincing denials in *Segodnia* (Ukraine), 11 April 2002.

134 Serhii Rakhmanin, 'Peredchuttia nemozhlyvoho', *Zerkalo tyzhnia*, no. 11, 17-23 March 2001.

135 Myroslava Dovhal', 'Sud nad unsovtsiamy – u hlukhomu kuti', *Postup*, no. 7, 22-23 Jan. 2002.

136 See the attack on Kovalenko by Andrii Shkil', leader of the UNA-UNSO, 'Tranzyt "Heniches'k-Bankova" z zupynkoiu "UNA"', 2 July 2004, www2.pravda.com.ua/archive/2004/july/2/1.shtml.

137 Dmytro Lykhovii, 'Zvychainyi fashyzm – zbroia Bankovoï. Vlada pustyla v khid vazhku artyleriiu peredvyborchykh provokatsii', *Ukraïna moloda*, 30 June 2004, http://www. umoloda.kiev.ua/number/210/115/7453/. The four hundred UNA members who took part in the demonstration in Kiev on 26 June were allegedly paid 40 hrivnia (about $7 each).

138 Peter Huber, *Orwell's Revenge: The 1984 Palimpsest* (New York: The Free Press, 1994), pp. 96ff.

139 Allegations made by former National Intelligence chief Irakli Batiashvili; see www. eurasianet.org/resource/georgia/hypermail/200102/0011.html and www.prima-news.ru/ eng/news/news/2001/2/8/19209.html, both accessed 24 June 2003.

140 Author's interview with Sitnikov, 4 Nov. 2002.

141 *Daily Georgian Times*, 9 Oct. 2003; *Svobodnaia Gruziia*, 24 Oct. 2003. Zaal Anjaparidze talks of 'covert consultation ... with those who seceded from the CUG in 2001', e-mail to author, 14 Nov. 2003.

142 Tetiana Korobova, 'Another Yuryk for Poor Yoricks. Or a Ukrainian Version of Lebed?', *Den'*, no. 32, 31 Aug. 1999.

143 An obvious nickname – the fiery Vitrenko represented the constituency of Konotop and 'The Konotop Witch' was a short story by Hryhorii Kvitka-Osnov"ianenko, written in 1837.

144 'Pryntsyp Vitrenko', www.grani.kiev.ua/2002/texts/10/Matyushenko29L_ukr.htm. See also Vitrenko's implausible replies when confronted on this question in *Zerkalo tyzhnia* 3 July 1999.

145 Source: author's calculations from information on deputy movements in *Parlament*, no. 5, 2001, pp. 58-65. Zadorozhna, Malolitko and Savenko remained with Labour Ukraine; Tykhonov joined first Labour Ukraine and then Oleksandr Volkov's Regions of Ukraine; Kviat joined the SDPU(o) in February 2000.

146 Sergei Rudenko, 'Nataliia Vitrenko: vid "A" do "Ya"', www.glavred.info/ukr/?art=70827149, dated 11 March 2003.

147 Ibid.

148 'Nataliia Vitrenko: nezakinchena istoriia populizmy', in Volodymyr Ruban (ed.), *Naperedodni. Vybory 99* (Kiev: Ukraïns'kyi vymir, 1999), pp. 30-33, at p. 32.

149 Dmytro Chobit, *Svystun, abo Chy mozhna politychnoho bankruta obyraty kerivnykom derzhavy?* (Kiev: no pub., 1999), p. 53; Korobova, 'Another Yuryk for Poor Yoricks'.

150 Rudenko, 'Nataliia Vitrenko: vid "A" do "Ya"'.

151 Author's interview with Olesia Favor'ska, 6 Dec. 2003.

152 For the original by I. Toidze, see among others N. Baburina (ed.), *Russia 20th Century: History of the Country in Posters* (Moscow: Panorama, 2000), p. 130.

153 'Mykola Mel'nychenko proty pokhoronnoï komandy', www.pravda.com.ua/?2031-1-new, posted 2? Feb. 2002.

154 'Yak Vitrenko na pobachennia z Kuchmoiu khodyla. . . . Nove z plivok Mel'nychenka', www.pravda.com.ua/?2034-5-new, posted and accessed 4 March 2002.

155 *Den'*, 21 Aug. 1999.

156 Yuliia Mostova and Serhii Rakhmanin, 'Ukraïna partiina. Chastyna V. Sotsialistychna partiia Ukraïny', *Zerkalo tyzhnia*, no. 9, 8-15 March 2002, p. 4; Ol'ha Dmytrycheva, '. . . A iz nashego okna ploshchad' krasnaia vidna', *Zerkalo tyzhnia*, no. 10, 16-22 March 2002, p.1.

Chapter 9

1 'Zolota KPSS – desiat' let spustia', *Moskovskie novosti*, 8 May 2001.

2 Luke March, 'The Pragmatic Radicalism of Russia's Communists', in Joan Barth Urban and Jane Leftwich Curry (eds), *The Left Transformed in Post-Communist Societies: The Cases of East-Central Europe, Russia and Ukraine* (Lanham: Rowman and Littlefield, 2003), pp. 163-208, at p. 198.

3 Korzhakov, *Boris El'tsin: ot rassveta do zakata*, p. 369.

4 March, 'The Pragmatic Radicalism of Russia's Communists', p. 174.

5 Klebnikov, *Godfather of the Kremlin*, p. 65.

6 'Old Square', home to the headquarters of the Central Committee of the CPSU.

7 March, *The Communist Party in Post-Soviet Russia*, p. 45, n. 89.

8 Aleks Makhravskii, 'Zolotaia kletka dlia krasnogo Geny', www.stringer-news.ru, 5 Oct. 2002, also at www.compromat.ru/main/zuganov/kletka.htm, accessed 24 Nov. 2003.

9 Aleksei Volokhov, *Noveishaia istoriia Kommunisticheskoi partii: 1990-2002* (Moscow: Impeto, 2003), pp. 18, 20 and 34.

10 Vladimir Sverdlov, 'Plemennoi byk Berezovskogo', *Kompromat.ru*, no. 11 (from the issue on Gennadii Ziuganov entitled 'Krasnyi GENAtsid' ['Red GEN(A)cide'], a bad pun on his name), www.kompromat.ru/material.phtml?id=3561, written 11 Nov. 2002, accessed 9 July 2003.

11 Reddaway and Glinski, *The Tragedy of Russia's Reforms*, pp. 329-31 and 344-46.

12 Igor' Korotchenko, '"Dukhovnoe nasledie" podderzhivaet Ziuganova. S"ezd dvizheniia posetili predstaviteli neskol'kikh samykh vliiatel'nykh bankov', *Nezavisimaia gazeta*, 5 June 1996, p. 2.

13 March, *The Communist Party in Post-Soviet Russia*, p. 150.

14 March, 'The Pragmatic Radicalism of Russia's Communists', p. 186.

15 Reddaway and Glinski, *The Tragedy of Russia's Reforms*, p. 578. According to Luke March, 'Many of the [CPRF] radicals saw him [Podberezkin] as an obvious *éminence grise* acting in the interests of the Yeltsin regime': *The Communist Party in Post-Soviet Russia*, p. 70; citing *Pravda-5*, 20-27 Dec. 1997 and *Segodnia*, 19 Dec. 1996.

16 March, *The Communist Party in Post-Soviet Russia*, p. 244; citing *Obshchaia gazeta*, 7-13 Dec. 2000.

17 Vitalii Trubetskoi, 'Berezovskii zovet na barrikady', *Vesti nedeli*, 2 Nov. 2003.

18 March, *The Communist Party in Post-Soviet Russia*, p. 167, n. 150.

19 Korzhakov, *Boris El'tsin: ot rassveta do zakata*, pp. 368-69. Zorkaltsev was also close to Seleznev.

20 March, *The Communist Party in Post-Soviet Russia*, p. 35.

21 Ibid., p. 124.

22 Volokhov, *Noveishaia istoriia Kommunisticheskoi partii: 1990-2002*, pp. 20 and 39.

23 Sergei Cherniakhovskii, *Protivorechivost' kommunisticheskoi oppozitsii v sovremennoi Rossii* (Moscow: International Ecological-Political University, 2003), p. 39 argues that until December 1993 the CPRF was just one Communist group among others, with an 'amorphous structure' and 'weak identity'.

24 From *Argumenti i fakti*, 2 Feb. 1999, as quoted in Otto, 'Gennadii Ziuganov', p. 44.

25 Author's interview with Valerii Solovei, 5 Nov. 2002.

26 *Komsomol'skaia pravda*, 31 Oct. 1991, as quoted by Elizabeth Teague and Vera Tolz, 'CPSU R.I.P', *Report on the USSR*, vol. 3, no. 47, 22 Nov. 1991, pp. 1-8, at p. 5. On capital flight, see *Moscow News*, no. 38, 1991; and *Komsomol'skaia pravda*, 1 Oct. 1991. For a detailed analysis, see the Congressional testimony of the CIA's Richard Palmer, http://financialservices.house.gov/banking/92199pal.htm.

27 Klebnikov, *Godfather of the Kremlin*, pp. 58-59.

28 Allegations against Kravchuk centre on his role in the fate of Blasco, the Ukrainian

Black Sea Shipping Company, i.e. merchant marines, which more or less completely disappeared in the early 1990s. Also accused were Kravchuk's son, Oleksandr, his father's close confidant, Pavlo Kudiukyn, who headed the company, and Yukhym Zviahil's'kyi, Kravchuk's prime minister 1993-94. After leaving office, Kravchuk was involved in the tax-free import of alcohol and tobacco via his 'arts foundation', See Honta/Omel'chenko, *Ukraïns'kyi polkovnyk i ukraïns'ka mafia*, pp. 81, 143, 154-55 and 164.

29 Hahn, *Russia's Revolution from Above*, p. 253, n. 26. See also Klebnikov, *Godfather of the Kremlin*, pp. 56-62; and Volokhov, *Noveishaia istoriia Kommunisticheskoi partii: 1990-2002*, p. 67.

30 'Prizraki vokrug zolota Kompartii', www.kompromat.ru/material1.phtml?id=824, original in *Le Temps*, 9 June 2001; 'Zolota KPRS – desiat' let spustia'.

31 Aleksei Zverev and Aiter Muzhdibaev, 'Gidra iz Nizhnego', *Moskovskii komsomolets*, 30 July 1998.

32 From the analysis of the CPRF's finances circa 1995-96 posted on the National News Service website www.nns.ru/elects/izbobyed/finansy.html. See also March, *The Communist Party in Post-Soviet Russia*, pp. 154-55; and *Segodnia*, 28 June 1995.

33 Robert C. Otto, 'Gennadii Ziuganov: The Reluctant Candidate', *Problems of Post-Communism*, vol. 46, no. 5 (Sept.-Oct. 1999), pp. 37-47, at p. 43. See also 'Vladimir Semago: "Ya znaiu, otkuda den'gi u partii"', www.kompromat.ru/material.phtml?id=3565.

34 Klebnikov, *Godfather of the Kremlin*, p. 225.

35 March, 'The Pragmatic Radicalism of Russia's Communists', p. 173.

36 *Nezavisimaia gazeta*, 2 Dec. 1998.

37 Reddaway and Glinski, *The Tragedy of Russia's Reforms*, pp. 598 and 713-14, n. 234.

38 Both Berezovskii and Voloshin were also allegedly involved in Chara's collapse.

39 On Vidmanov, see Aleksei Makarkin, 'Kassir Kompartii', *Ezhenedel'nyi zhurnal*, 2-8 June 2003.

40 'KPRF finasirovalas' "chechenskimi" den'gami', www.kompromat.ru/material.phtml?id=3564, posted 25 March 2000; Volokhov, *Noveishaia istoriia Kommunisticheskoi partii: 1990-2002*, pp. 71-2.

41 'Kto finansiruet KPRF?', *Nezavisimaia gazeta*, 11 April 1999; and the different version of 'KPRF finansirovalas' "chechenskimi" den'gami', at www.flb.ru, via www.kompromat.ru/material1.phtml?id=831, posted 24 March 2000; *Moskovskii komsomolets'*, 25 June 1999.

42 *Moskovskii komsomolets*, 25 June 1999; March, *The Communist Party in Post-Soviet Russia*, p. 159; 'Le Club Lobbystov', *The Russia Journal*, 22 Feb. 1999.

43 Author's interview with Andrei Riabov, 8 Nov. 2002.

44 *Kommersant'*, 23 March 1999.

45 Francesca Mereu, 'Political Parties Saw their Fortunes Rise and Fall'.

46 Gennadii Ziuganov, *Drama vlasti* (Moscow: Paleia, 1993), p. 64.

47 Volokhov, *Noveishaia istoriia Kommunisticheskoi partii: 1990-2002*, p. 72.

48 'Prizraki vokrug zolota Kompartii'; 'Zolota KPSS – desiat' let spustia'.

49 Author's interview with Sitnikov, 4 Nov. 2002.

50 As quoted in 'Zolota KPSS – desiat' let spustia'. Dmitri Volkogonov, *Lenin: Life and Legacy* (London: HarperCollins, 1994), p. 58, accepts that Morozov may have given 100,000 roubles to the Bolsheviks. Morozov's nephew, Nikolai, was also a major donor.

51 See *Ekspert*, no. 27, 21 July 1997, pp. 38-41.

52 'Zolota KPSS – desiat' let spustia'.

53 As quoted in Guy Chazan, 'Votes for Sale in the Duma, Says Russian Banker', www.telegraph.co.uk, 10 Sept. 2000.

54 Author's interview with Ekaterina Egorova, Moscow, 21 March 2001.

55 March, *The Communist Party in Post-Soviet Russia*, p. 159. Volokhov, *Noveishaia istoriia Kommunisticheskoi partii: 1990-2002*, p. 74, describes the following price scale: the top five seats were not for sale; a place between the fifth and twelfth spots cost $1.5 million, between the thirteenth and twenty-fifth only $1 million.

56 Vitalii Tsepliaev and Liudmila Pivovarova, 'Gennaia terapiia KPRF', *Argumenty i fakty*, 19 Feb. 2003.

57 Mikhail Rostovskii, 'Pokupka krasnogo konia. Kak razlagalas' KPRF', *Moskovskii komsomolets*, 12 Feb. 2003.

58 Andrei Zolotov, 'The Art of the Deal', *Moscow Times*, 19 Aug. 2000.

59 Volokhov, *Noveishaia istoriia Kommunisticheskoi partii: 1990-2002*, pp. 67-68.

60 Most of the material in this section is from Sverdlov, 'Plemennoi byk Berezovskogo'.

61 Kirill Belianinov, *Gospoda s geksogenom* (Moscow: Moskovskaia Pravda, 2003), pp. 32-34.

62 Trubetskoi, 'Berezovskii zovet na barrikady'.

63 Belianinov, *Gospoda s geksogenom*, p. 63. By 2003 so much black PR was being directed against the Communists that I decided to ignore the wilder allegations and include only information confirmed by respectable sources. Transcripts of supposed conversations between Berezovskii and Ziuganov can be found on the internet at http://ord4.i8.com.

64 Tat'iana Stanovaia, 'KPRF riskuet lishit'sia sponsora', www.politcom.ru/2003/partii9.php, accessed 25 June 2003. The web site politcom.ru is run by Igor Bunin's Centre of Political Technologies. Both have a good reputation for objective analysis.

65 Aleksei Makarkin, 'KPRF nakanune vyborov', www.politcom.ru/2003/partii27php, posted 29 October 2003, accessed 4 Nov. 2003.

66 Ivan Preobrazhenskii, 'KPRF lishaiut kreditovaniia', www.politcom.ru/2003/zloba3276.php, posted and accessed 14 Nov. 2003.

67 Dmitrii Orlov, 'Korporativnye vybory', www.politcom.ru/2003/pvz62.php, posted 19 Feb. 2003; Boris Kagarlitsky, 'Better Well-Fed Than Red', *Moscow Times*, 22 Jan. 2003.

68 Rostovskii, 'Pokupka krasnogo konia. Kak razlagalas' KPRF'.

69 Belianinov, *Gospoda s geksogenom*, pp. 60-61.

70 Author's interview with Valerii Solovei, 18 Feb. 2004.

71 Belianinov, *Gospoda s geksogenom*, p. 63. See also Rostovskii, 'Pokupka krasnogo konia', on Abramovich and the Communists.

72 Sergei Mikhailov, 'Politicheskaia sreda. Ch'i den'gi zin?', *Rossiiskie vesti*, 19 Feb. 2003; Mavra Kosihkina, 'Facing the Elections: Whom are Party Finances Serenading?', *Politruk*, no. 3, 28 Jan. 2003, http://felist.com/archive/media.politics/200301/29111319.text, accessed 7 Aug. 2003. Kompromat.ru was forced to withdraw its issue no. 15 in 2003, when Khodorkovskii took offence at the idea that he was funding the Communists. Cf. Sergei Permiakov, 'Dvoinoe samoubiistvo?', *Russkii zhurnal*, 20 Jan. 2003.

73 See the information supposedly from presidential and FSB sources at www.compromat.ru/main/kprf/zapiska.htm, dated 4 Nov. 2003, accessed 21 Nov. 2003. The author could not verify this source independently.

74 Ekaterina Larina, 'Communists at the Crossroads', *The Russia Journal*, 9 April 2003.

75 Kosihkina, 'Facing the Elections'.

76 Author's interview with Valerii Solovei, 18 Feb. 2004.

77 Francesca Mereu, 'Power Struggle Splits Communists', *Moscow Times*, 20-22 Feb. 2004.

78 Quoted in Makhrovskii, 'Zolotaia kletka dlia krasnogo Geny'.

79 Ibid.

80 Volokhov, *Noveishaia istoriia Kommunisticheskoi partii: 1990-2002*, p. 53.

81 Korzhakov, *Boris El'tsin: ot rassveta do zakata*, pp. 367-68.

82 Belianinov, *Gospoda s geksogenom*, pp. 44-46.

83 Ibid., pp. 32, 53 and 57.

84 March, *The Communist Party in Post-Soviet Russia*, p. 238.

85 Makhrovskii, 'Zolotaia kletka dlia krasnogo Geny'.

86 March, *The Communist Party in Post-Soviet Russia*, p. 217; citing *Segodnia*, 22 Dec. 1999.

87 Author's interview with Volodymyr Polokhalo, editor of the journal *Political Thought*, Kiev, 15 March 2002.

88 Author's interviews with Polokhalo, 8 Dec. 2003, and Volodymyr Kyzyma, author of the first Socialist Party programme, 6 Feb. 1996.

89 Speech given 6 April 1992, reprinted in a brochure put out by the Rukh-based opposition, *Ye taka partiia* (Kiev: no pub, 1992, pp. 2-3.

90 Kravchuk alleges the strikes were orchestrated by the same 'red directors' who backed his opponent Kuchma and the CPU; Leonid Kravchuk, *Maiemo te, shcho maiemo* (Kiev: Lybid', 2002), pp. 214 and 216.

91 Volodymyr Lytvyn, *Politychna arena Ukraïny: diiovi osobi ta vykonavtsi* (Kiev: Abrys, 1994), p. 276.

92 Author's interview with Polokhalo, 8 Dec. 2003.

93 Kravchuk, *Maiemo te, shcho maiemo*, p. 42.

94 Ibid., pp. 253 and 252. Yurii Lukanov, *Tretii prezydent*, p. 82, also describes the informal agreement.

95 Author's interview with Vladimir Malinkovich, Kuchma's chief of information strategy in 1994, 5 Dec. 2003.

96 Lytvyn's book, *Politychna arena Ukraïny*, pp. 273-80, attacks the 1991 ban and describes how 'those manipulating the law, made lightning career[s]' in terms clearly sympathetic to the Communists (quotation at p. 274).

97 Author's interview with Polokhalo, 8 Dec. 2003.

98 Author's interview with Polokhalo, 15 March 2002.

99 Koshiw, *Beheaded*, p. 141, quoting Mel'nychenko's interview with Tom Warner of the *Financial Times*, 15 Sept. 2001.

100 Mel'nichneko (Melnychenko), *Kto est' kto. Na divane prezidenta Kuchmy*, p. 49.

101 Author's interview with Marat Gel'man, 9 Nov. 2002.

102 Serhii Rakhmanin and Ol'ha Dmytrycheva, 'Ukraïna partiina. Chastyna IV. Komunistychna Partiia', *Zerkalo tyzhnia*, no. 8, 2-8 March 2002, p. 3.

103 *Den'*, 17 and 18 Feb. 1999.

104 Bondarenko, *Atlanty i kariatydy*, p. 63.

105 *UNIAN*, 20 Feb. 2000. See also the report at www.wz.lviv.ua/wz162/policy.html.

106 'Lyst Mel'nychenka', at *Ukraïns 'ka pravda*, www.ukrpravda.com/archive/?41021-3-new, dated and accessed 21 October 2004.

107 Rakhmanin and Dmytrycheva, 'Komunistychna Partiia', p. 4.

108 Kupchinsky, 'Iraqi Paper Lists Companies and Organizations Hussein Allegedly Bribed with Oil'; Rostyslav Khotyn, Sotsialisty, Komunisty i khusein: shcho Spil'noho?', BBC Ukranian Service, 7 Oct. 2004.

109 Rakhmanin and Dmytrycheva, 'Komunistychna Partiia', p. 4.

110 Author's interview with Rostyslav Pavlenko, Kiev, 24 July 2001.

111 Author's interview with Polokhalo, Kiev, 15 March 2002; Rakhmanin and Dmytrycheva, 'Komunistychna Partiia', p. 4.

112 Yurii Butusov's interview with Symonenko, *Ukraïns'ka pravda*, 1 Feb. 2002.

113 Rakhmanin and Dmytrycheva, 'Komunistychna Partiia', p. 4.

114 Author's interview with Volodymyr Polokhalo, 8 Dec. 2003.

115 According to the analysis in Haran', Maiboroda *et al.*, *Ukraïns'ki livi*, pp. 138-39, n. 5,

Tkachenko tried to transform Ukraïna into a Peasant Mortgage Bank. Instead part of the stock was transferred to Ukrros, under the control of a close colleague from the Village Party, Volodymyr Satsiuk. 'Ukrenerhokompleks, headed by his son-in-law Anatolii Peshkov, received a range of important orders.' His niece, the deputy Liudmyla Suprun, was the former head of Interahro; and her husband Mykola became first deputy in the Rada administration.

116 See, for example, the attack by Symonenko and Kriuchkov in *Holos Ukraïny*, 26 Dec. 1995.

117 Rakhmanin and Dmytrycheva, 'Komunistychna Partiia', p. 3.

118 Ibid.,

119 Vladimir (Volodymyr) Marchenko, 'KPU – levaia podporka rezhima Prezidenta Kuchmy', *Dosvitni ohni*, no. 35, 2000.

120 'Komunisty domovylysia z Poteben'kom?' and 'Poteben'ko ide do komunistiv. Poteben'ko ide z prokuratury?', *Ukraïns'ka pravda*, 9 Jan. 2001 and 5 Jan. 2002.

121 Ivan Lozowy, 'Kinakh Appointment Overshadowed by State Secretaries', *The Ukraine Insider*, vol. 1, no. 3, 1 June 2001, via *The Ukraine List*, no. 140, reports allegations by the outgoing Yushchenko government that the money was paid to ensure that the Communists did not block the appointment of his successor, Anatolii Kinakh (by abstaining in the key vote).

122 Aleksandr Mikhel'son, 'Kommunisty ne rvutsia k vlasti. Oni s nei rabotaiut', www.part. org.ua/print.php?art=47514363, posted 14 June 2002.

123 Ekaterina Marchenko, 'Ot KPU popakhivaet donetskimi resursami', www.part.org.ua/ index.php?art=46045467, dated, 28 May 2002.

124 Vasilii Andreev, 'Vodka zapakhnet kommunizmom. A Iliukhin – vodkoi', *Russkii kur'er*, 9 July 2003.

125 March, *The Communist Party in Post-Soviet Russia*, ch. 3, especially pp. 66–67, quotation at p. 84.

126 Author's interviews with leading Crimean journalists, Sept. 1993; Nikolai Grigoriev, 'Roots and Principles of Crimean Communism', *Tavricheskie vedomosti*, 6 Aug. 1993.

127 When interviewed by the author in the middle of the White House events, on 30 Sept. 1993 (in Crimea), Grach boasted of his recent appearance on the barricades and close relationship with Rutskoi. Strangely, he was wearing socks marked 'USA'.

128 Most of the material on Grach comes from the article by Mykola Semena, Crimean correspondent of the most respectable Kiev paper, *Dzerkalo tyzhnia*, 'Leonid Hrach: dos'e ochyma opozytsiinoho zhurnalista', which can be found at www.glavred.info/ mission/?man=1054724489&art=1054897155, accessed 4 Feb. 2004.

129 Author's conversation with Kiev political scientist ValentinYakushik, 17 March 2002.

130 See Lilia Budzhurova, 'Riatuisia, khto mozhe – v Krymu novyi prem"ier', *Ukraïns'ka pravda*, 24 July 2001; and her article in *Grani*, 31 July 2001.

131 See Novokom's own post-election analysis, blaming its failure on the 'harsh adminis-trative pressing' of Kiev and Kunitsyn and their manipulation of the Crimean Tatars against the 'Russian-speakers': 'Rossiiskii faktor v krymskikh vybornykh bitvakh', www.novocom.org/comments/c010520020.htm.

132 'Krym. Rosiis'kyi hambit', *Zerkalo tyzhnia*, no. 10, 16–22 March 2002.

133 See the analysis by Petru Bogatu in *Tsara*, 13 March 2001.

134 See www.ifes.md/elections/electionresults/2001parliamentary/listofdeputies for a list of Communist deputies' formal affiliations.

135 *Flux*, 16 Oct. 2002; 'Vasile Tarlev Is Involved in Corruption Mega-Scandal', www.transparency.md/News/a147.htm.

136 For an attack on CPRF's moves against the UCP, see the translation, 'In the Communist Movements in Russia There Is a Smell of a Fifth Column', www.northstarcompass.org/nsc0106/shenin.htm, accessed 25 June 2003.

137 Lisovskii and Evstaf'ev, *Izbiratel'nye tekhnologii*, pp. 270–72.

138 Volokhov, *Noveishaia istoriia Kommunisticheskoi partii: 1990-2002*, p. 20.

139 Hahn, *Russia's Revolution from Above*, pp. 412–13. See also p. 411.

140 Dunlop, *The Rise of Russia*, p. 368, n. 65; citing Yeltsin, *The Struggle for Russia*, pp. 177–78. The same accusations are reported in Reddaway and Glinski, *The Tragedy of Russia's Reforms*, pp. 423-24.

141 Author's interview with Andrei Riabov, 8 Nov. 2002.

142 Lisovskii and Evstaf'ev, *Izbiratel'nye tekhnologii*, p. 286, assert that 'at these elections everybody practically forgot about the Communists', which is true of the main election drama (Unity versus FAR), but not of the 'backroom' insurance measures.

143 Aleksei Zverev, 'Piatigolovyi tianitolkai', *Moskovskii komsomolets*, 14 Dec. 1999.

144 Prokhanov quoted in Sergei Cherniakhivskii, 'Kommunisticheskoe dvizhenie', in *Rossiia na dumskikh i prezidentskikh vyborakh* (Moscow: Carnegie Centre, 2000), available online at www.carnegie.ru/ru/pubs/books/volume/58362.htm.

145 Ibid. Cherniakhivskii's own comments.

146 Kremlin support for all the left-wing flies was confirmed by Andrei Riabov, interview with the author, 8 Nov. 2002.

147 Aleksandr Prokhanov, '"Chernyi poias" Putina, "Krasnyi poias" Ziuganova', *Zavtra*, no. 51, 21 Dec. 1999.

148 Belianinov, *Gospoda s geksogenom*, pp. 39–43.

149 Tsuladze, *Bol'shaia manipuliativnaia igra*, pp. 271–72.

150 Colton and McFaul, *Popular Choice and Managed Democracy*, p. 132.

151 Data from http://elections.ru/duma/kprf and www.duma.gov.ru.

152 Roman Solchanyk, *Ukraine and Russia: The Post-Soviet Transition* (Lanham: Rowman and Littlefield, 2001), p. 125; *Parlament*, no. 5, 2001.

153 Martha Brill Olcott, *Kazakhstan: Unfulfilled Promise* (Washington, DC: Carnegie Endowment for International Peace, 2002), p. 93

154 Ibid., p. 94.

155 See Abdildin's complaint that the Communist People's Party was 'linked with the authorities and . . . fulfilling their orders' at www.eurasia.net.org, 9 March 2004.

156 Pavel Ivanov, 'Red Tide Rising in Former Soviet States', www.atimes.com, 18 May 2001.

157 *RFE/RL News Report*, 17 July 2002.

158 In Slovakia, covert support from Vladimír Mečiar's right-wing HZDS helped the ZRS (Workers' Association of Slovakia) to a handy 7.3 per cent in the 1994 elections (collapsing to 1.3 per cent when no longer useful in 1998), as Mečiar needed the ZRS to compete with the post-Communist Party of the Democratic Left (SDL, 14.7 per cent), and act as a coalition partner for the HZDS.

159 Oleksandr Yurchuk, '"Tsifrovoi format" bol'shinstva. Koalitsiia s kommunistami vpolne veroiatna', *Kiievskii telegraf*, 12-18 Feb. 2001.

160 Petro Serov, of the CPU Secretariat, interviewed by Sarah Whitmore of the University of Birmingham, May 2000, as quoted in her *Fragmentation or Consolidation? Parties in Ukraine's Parliament* (Birmingham: Research Papers in Russian and East European Studies, no. REES02/2, 2002), p. 21 n. 44. Emphasis in original.

161 All quotations are from TV broadcasts watched by the author in March 2002.

162 When Communist leader Petro Symonenko attacked his likely new rival as an artificial force that would be 'pseudo-Communist, nationalist and pro-presidential', he was largely correct, but he got its name wrong, assuming it would be called the UKP. Symonenko, 'Vyklyk chasu i Kompartiia Ukraïny', *Komunist*, no. 26, June 2000, p. 4; *Komunist*, no. 10, March 2000; *Komunist Ukraïny*, no. 1, 2000.

163 *RFE/RL Poland, Belarus and Ukraine Report*, vol. 1, no. 3, 8 June 2000.

164 Savenko had originally been elected in 1998 as a member of the equally notorious Progressive Socialist Party, whose story is told on pages 218–20.

165 Information confirmed by two separate sources (Pavlenko, Polokhalo).

166 'Bol'she vsego deneg na reklamu potratila SDPU(o)', www.ukraine.ru/news/127360.html, posted 5 April 2002.

167 Vasyl' Stoiakin, 'Vybir "tovaru": Chomu v Ukraïni ne vdalysia "krasyvi" kampaniï', *Den'*, 8 May 2002, p. 4.

168 A running average of polls by VTsIOM, FOM and ROMIR in 2001-03 had both rising and falling between a low of 17 per cent and a high of 25 per cent: Igor' Zadorin, 'Malye partii kak zerkalo rossiiskogo politicheskogo protsessa', www.politcom.ru/2003/analit56.php, dated and accessed 16 July 2003. Another poll had the CPRF at 35 per cent and United Russia dipping below 20 per cent: 'Seleznev sdal kommunistov', *Moskovskii komsomolets*, 6 April 2002.

169 Gleb Pavlovskii, 'Kak nam reorganizovat' KPRF? Kommunisty – vsego lish' mif, sozdannyi antikommunistami', *Nezavisimaia gazeta*, 27 May 1999. See also his plan for the year 2000 in Reddaway and Glinski, *The Tragedy of Russia's Reforms*, p. 621.

170 Putin press conference, *Johnson's Russia List*, no. 5,353, 19 July 2001.

171 Author's interview with Valerii Solovei, 5 Nov. 2002.

172 Kosktikov, 'Ferzi i peshki kremlevskikh shakhmat'.

173 Kosikhina, 'Facing the Elections'.

174 Author's interview with Andrei Riabov, 8 Nov. 2002.

175 Kosihkina, 'Facing the Elections'.

176 Mikhailov, 'Politicheskaia sreda. Ch'i den'gi zin?'. Typically, Kondaurov, another former major-general in the KGB, was head of the 'analytical department' at Yukos.

177 Vitalii Ivanov *et al.*, 'Krasnye millionery', *Vedomosti*, 15 Oct. 2003, also at www.compromat.ru/main/zuganov/declkprf.htm; 'Chem bogaty kommunisty?', *Kommersant'*, 15 Oct. 2003.

178 Franseca Mereu, 'Business Will Have Big Voice in Duma', *Moscow Times*, 13 Nov. 2003.

179 'Peizazh posle bitvy. Spisok KPRF kak otrazhenia vnutripartiinoi bor'by', *Russkii fokus*, 4 Nov. 2003.

180 Volokhov, *Noveishaia istoriia Kommunisticheskoi partii: 1990-2002*, p. 115.

181 For Ziuganov's distrust of Semigin, see 'Ziuganov rasskazal o den'gakh Berezovskogo', www.gazeta.ru/2003/01/30/zuganovrassk.shtml, accessed 17 June 2003.

182 Valentin Chikin and Aleksandr Prokhanov, 'Operatsiia "Krot"', *Zavtra*, no. 2, 5 Jan. 2003.

183 Author's interview with Andrei Riabov, 8 Nov. 2002.

184 Author's interview with Marat Gel'man, 9 Nov. 2002.

185 Viktor Bondarev, 'Klonirovanie kandidatov', in Sergei Ustimenko (ed.), *Izbiratel'nye tekhnologii i izbiratel'noe iskusstvo* (Moscow: PR-Intellekt/Russian Political Encyclopaedia, 2001), pp. 48-53, at p. 50.

186 Author's interview with Marat Gel'man, 9 Nov. 2002.

187 *RIA Novosti*, 6 March 2003.

188 Tat'iana Stanovaia, 'Kak sglazili Glaz'eva', www.politcom.ru/2004/analit109.php, dated 9 March 2004; 'Taina Glaz'eva', www.stringer-news.ru/Publication.mhtml?PubID =2901&Part=37, dated 4 March 2004; Natal'ia Arkhangel'skaia, 'Oppozitsiia ego prevoskhoditel'stva', *Ekspert*, no. 8, 1-7 March 2004.

189 Leonid Sergienko, 'Ziuganov and the Void', *Vremia MN*, 23 May 2003, via *Johnson's Russia List*, no. 7194, 23 May 2003.

190 Aleksandr Dudberg, 'Griaznaia osen' 2003 goda', *Moskovskii komsomolets*, 12 Sept. 2003.

191 Rostovskii, 'Pokupka krasnogo konia. Kak razlagalas' KPRF'.

192 For a critique of Shein's collaboration with the Kremlin, see
http://www.left.ru/inter/october/shein.html.

193 Tat'iana Stanovaia, 'KPRF bez Glaz'eva: patrioti i prokurory',
www.politcom.ru/2003/partii24.php, posted 1 Sept. 2003, accessed 4 Nov. 2003.

194 Rogozin had helped set up KRO in the early 1990s (see page 122). At the time Rodina
was created, he was head of the Duma committee on international affairs and
presidential representative on the Kaliningrad problem.

195 Aleksei Makarkin, 'Blok Glaz'eva: "Medved'" nomer dva',
www.politcom.ru/pvz222.php, posted and accessed 25 Aug. 2003.

196 Her key book is *Rossiia i russkie v mirovoi istorii* (Moscow: Izdatel A.V. Solevov, 2003).
See also her website at www.narotchnitskaia.ru.

197 Aleksei Makarkin, 'Blok Glaz'eva: "Rodina" protiv "Tovarishcha"',
www.politcom.ru/2003/partii25.php, posted 24 Sept. 2003, accessed 4 Nov. 2003;
Sergei Glaz'ev, *Genotsid. Rossiia i novyi mirovoi poriadok. Strategiia ekonomicheskogo rosta na
poroge XXI veka* (Moscow: Astra Sem, 1997).

198 Although Gel'man 'claimed the role of chief constructor of the election campaign'
and was responsible for Rodina's adverts on ORT, Valerii Solovei (who worked for
Glaz'ev) insists that Kremlin resources and financial backing were more important.
The Rodina rank and file eventually forced him out. E-mail from Solovei, 1 March
2004.

199 Dugin interviewed by Ol'ga Redichkina, 'SLON pokinul "Rodiny". Blok Sergeia
Glaz'eva neset poteri', *Gazeta*, 23 Sept. 2003,
www.gzt.ru/rubricator.gzt?rubric=novosti&id=37050000000008077, accessed 4 Nov.
2003.

200 Author's interview with Pavlovskii, 8 Nov. 2002.

201 *Argumenty i fakty*, 16 Sept. 2003, via *Johnson's Russia List*, no. 7378, 18 Sept. 2003.

202 See the discussion on what to do with the CPRF at www.kreml.org/decisions/
25222479, accessed 16 June 2003. The debate is framed in terms of political 'technology'; various possible 'projects' are discussed, but little sociology.

203 Author's interview with Marat Gel'man, 9 Nov. 2002.

204 Anna Dolgov, 'Lesin Warns Rodina May Act on Promises' (a truly wonderful headline),
Moscow Times, 16 Dec. 2003.

205 Valery Stroyev, 'The Tortuous Tale of the Genesis of Rodina', *Moscow Times*, 17 Dec.
2003. Stroyev had worked on the 'Tovarishch' stage of the project.

206 Quoted in Kyrill Dissanayake and Mike Rose, 'Media Fails to Stir Debate', *BBC
Monitoring*, 5 Dec. 2003, also found at
http://news.bbc.co.uk/1/hi/world/europe/3294263.stm.

207 'Operatsii podavleniia', *Sovetskaia Rossiia*, 9 Dec. 2003.

208 Svetlana Ofitova and Aleksandr Maksimov, 'Telekillerov nikto ne otmenial', *Nezavisimaia
gazeta*, 8 Dec. 2003; 'Operatsii podavleniia'.

209 Author's interview with Valerii Solovei, 18 Feb. 2004.

210 Vitalii Silitskii (Vital' Silitski), 'Kreml' meniaet vassalov, ili skromnoe obaianie
putinskogo avtoritarizma', www.belarusfree.org, 8 Dec. 2003.

211 Susan B. Glasser and Peter Baker, 'How Nationalist Party Became a Powerhouse', *The
Washington Post*, 16 Dec. 2003.

212 'Alternative Results of Duma Elections Appear.'

213 Ofitova and Maksimov, 'Telekillerov nikto ne otmenial'.

214 'Oligarkhi zasevaiut elektorat', www.flb.ru/material.phtml?id=17182. See also *Sobesednik*,
23 April 2003.

215 'Operatsii podavleniia'.

216 Sergei Martynov, 'Vybory: otsenka fal'sifikatsii',

www.polit.ru/publicism/country/2003/12/10/vbros.html, posted and accessed 10 Dec. 2003.

217 *RFE/RL Newsline,* 29 Dec. 2004.

218 Tat'iana Stanovaia, 'KPRF: problemy ostaiutsia', www.politcom.ru/2004/analit137.php, 8 June 2004.

219 Author's interviews with Valerii Solovei, 22 March 2001 and 5 Nov. 2002.

220 Author's interview with Andrei Riabov, 8 Nov. 2002.

Conclusions

1 See Andreas Schedler, 'The Menu of Manipulation', *Journal of Democracy,* vol. 13, no. 2, April 2002, pp. 36–50.

2 Bidanda M. Chengappa, 'The ISI's Role in Pakistan's Politics', *Strategic Analysis,* vol. 23, no. 2, Feb. 2000, pp. 1,857–78, also at www.idsa-india.org/an-feb00-2.html. See also General Mirza Aslam Beg's confession that he set up 'fake competition' for the Pakistan People's Party; Ifran Husain, 'The Deepening Contradiction', *The Dawn,* 11 Nov. 2000, available on the PPP website www.ppp.org.pk/ppp_govt.html; and the series of articles by Ardeshir Cowasjee, 'We Never Learn from History', *The Dawn,* 31 July, 4 and 11 Aug. 2002.

3 Leonard J. Cohen, *Serpent in the Bosom: The Rise and Fall of Slobodan Milošević* (Boulder: Westview, 2002), p. 413.

4 See V.G. Baleanu, *The Dark Side of Politics in Post-Communist Romania* (Camberley: Conflict Studies Research Centre, 2001).

5 *Expert,* Feb. 2004, p. 23.

6 As quoted in Mary Fulbrook, *Anatomy of a Dictatorship: Inside the GDR 1949–1989* (Oxford: Oxford University Press, 1995), p. 261.

7 Author's interview with Andrei Riabov, 8 Nov. 2002.

8 On that campaign, see Georgii [Hryhorii] Pocheptsov, *Informatsiia i dezinformatsiia* (Kiev: Nika-Tsentr, 2001), pp. 195-208.

9 Mel'nichenko, *Kto est' kto. Na divana prezidenta Kuchmy,* p. 7; also at www.pravda.com.ua/?10211-3-01, dated 11 Feb. 2001.

10 The respective questions asked voters to support expanded presidential dissolution powers, the abolition of deputy immunity, a reduction in the number of deputies from 450 to three hundred, and the creation of an upper house 'to represent the interests of the regions of Ukraine', which it was presumed would be made up of the local 'prefects', appointed by the president.

11 *RFE/RL Newsline,* 16 April 2002.

12 Vasyl' Kremen, Dmytro Tabachnyk and Vasyl' Tkachenko, *Ukraïna: al'ternatyvy postupu. Krytyka istorychnoho dosvidu* (Kiev: ARC-Ukraine, 1996), p. 465.

13 Author's interview with Gleb Pavlovskii, 8 Nov. 2002.

14 Interviewed in *Ezhenedel'nyi zhurnal,* no. 107, 16 Feb. 2004.

15 Author's interview with Gleb Pavlovskii, 8 Nov. 2002.

16 Remarks made in a talk given at the London School of Economics, 14 Jan. 2003.

Index

ANDREW WILSON

VIRTUAL POLITICS

Faking Democracy in the Post-Soviet World

States such as Russia and Ukraine may not have gone back to totalitarianism or the traditional authoritarian formula of stuffing the ballot box, cowing the population and imprisoning the opposition – or not obviously. But a whole industry of 'political technology' has developed instead, with shadowy private firms and government 'fixers' on lucrative contracts dedicated to the black arts of organising electoral success.

This book uncovers the sophisticated techniques of the 'virtual' political system used to legitimise post-Soviet regimes: entire fake parties, phantom political rivals and 'scarecrow' opponents. And it exposes the paramount role of the mass media in projecting these creations and in falsifying the entire political process.

Wilson argues that it is not primarily economic problems that have made it so difficult to develop meaningful democracy in the former Soviet world. Although the West also has its 'spin doctors', dirty tricks and aggressive ad campaigns, it is the unique post-Bolshevik culture of 'political technology' that is the main obstacle to better governance in the region, to real popular participation in public affairs and to the modernisation of the political economy in the longer term.

7705